Drafting Employment Contracts

THIRD EDITION

Other titles available from Law Society Publishing:

Disability Discrimination
Karen Jackson and Lydia Banerjee

Employment Law Handbook (7th edn)
Daniel Barnett, Gus Baker and Stephen Butler

Employment Tribunals (2nd edn)
Isabel Manley and Elaine Heslop

Remedies in Employment Law
Susan Belgrave and Philip Jones

Titles from Law Society Publishing can be ordered from all good bookshops or direct (telephone 0370 850 1422, email **lawsociety@prolog.uk.com** or visit our online shop at **bookshop.lawsociety.org.uk**).

Drafting Employment Contracts

THIRD EDITION

Gillian Howard

The Law Society

All rights reserved. The purchaser may reproduce and/or store the contents of the disk that accompanies this publication for the firm's internal legal practice purposes only. The contents of this disk may not be reproduced in whole or in part for resale or commercial use, or for distribution otherwise to any third parties. No other part of this publication may be reproduced in any material form, whether by photocopying, scanning, downloading onto computer or otherwise without the written permission of the Law Society except in accordance with the provisions of the Copyright, Designs and Patents Act 1988. Applications should be addressed in the first instance, in writing, to Law Society Publishing. Any unauthorised or restricted act in relation to this publication may result in civil proceedings and/or criminal prosecution.

The author has asserted the right under the Copyright, Designs and Patents Act 1988 to be identified as author of this work.

Whilst all reasonable care has been taken in the preparation of this publication, neither the publisher nor the author can accept any responsibility for any loss occasioned to any person acting or refraining from action as a result of relying upon its contents.

The views expressed in this publication should be taken as those of the author only unless it is specifically indicated that the Law Society has given its endorsement.

© Gillian Howard 2017

Crown copyright material is reproduced with the permission of the Controller of Her Majesty's Stationery Office

ISBN-13: 978-1-78446-011-2

First published in 2004
2nd edition 2010
This third edition published in 2017 by the Law Society
113 Chancery Lane, London WC2A 1PL

Typeset by Columns Design XML Ltd, Reading
Printed by TJ International Ltd, Padstow, Cornwall

The paper used for the text pages of this book is FSC® certified. FSC (the Forest Stewardship Council®) is an international network to promote responsible management of the world's forests.

There have been several people who have inspired me in my life and to whom I dedicate this third edition.

First of all my father, Alexander Howard, who believed in me, taught me so much and loved me and who in turn I loved and adored.

Secondly my wonderful and loving husband Barry, without whom I could never have pursued my career.

I do not forget my two sons Daniel and Ben, who have been the most supportive and loving boys of whom I am immensely proud.

I owe another huge debt to the late Professor Paul O'Higgins who inspired my love of labour law and who taught me so much. He was indeed an inspirational teacher and one of the kindest men I have had the honour to meet and know.

And finally to my editors at the Law Society, especially Paul Milner; I would like to thank them and him for their patience and loyalty in waiting for me to produce this text. It is a great honour and privilege to be asked again to write an updated edition of Drafting Employment Contracts.

Contents

Preface   xxi
Table of cases   xxiii
Table of statutes   xxxi
Table of statutory instruments   xxxv
Table of international legislation   xxxix
Abbreviations   xli

1	The start of the employment relationship and making the offer	1
1.1	Drafting contracts	1
1.2	In the beginning...	5
1.3	Collateral contract: to employ	5
1.4	Express and implied terms	6
1.5	Conditional offers/pre-offers	9
1.6	Importance of careful drafting	14
1.7	References	14
1.8	The advertisement	16
1.9	The application form	17
1.10	The interview	17
1.11	Data protection	17
1.12	Making promises and representations	18
1.13	Probationary periods	19
1.14	Asking the right medical questions	20
PRECEDENT 1A:	Expression of interest/invitation to treat	21
PRECEDENT 1B:	Conditional offer of employment	22
PRECEDENT 1C:	Background check permission (comprehensive) for prospective employee	23
PRECEDENT 1D:	Conditional offer of employment (professional partnership)	24
PRECEDENT 1E:	Offer conditional on references, etc.	24
PRECEDENT 1F:	Application form (care staff)	24
PRECEDENT 1G:	Probationary or trial periods	27
PRECEDENT 1H:	Pre-employment health questionnaire	28
2	The offer and written particulars: the principal statement	35
2.1	Making the offer	35

2.2	Reneging on the offer	36
2.3	References	40
2.4	Acceptance with signature of employee	42
2.5	Principal statement	42
2.6	Holidays	44
2.7	Incorporation of terms	46
2.8	Ensuring that employee is not breaching covenants	47
2.9	Probationary period	47
2.10	Changes to contracts	48
2.11	Induction	48
2.12	Employment of close relatives	48

PRECEDENT 2A:	Unconditional offer with continuing obligation to remain registered	49
PRECEDENT 2B:	Unconditional offer with continuing conditions: examinations	49
PRECEDENT 2C:	Offer letter	49
PRECEDENT 2D:	Policy on prevention of illegal working	53
PRECEDENT 2E:	Confirmation of offer to secretary/PA	54
PRECEDENT 2F:	Offer letter for transfer of managing director from Paris to London office	55
PRECEDENT 2G:	Authority to obtain references and credit checks	55
PRECEDENT 2H:	Incorporation of terms	56
PRECEDENT 2I:	Probationary period/trial period	56
PRECEDENT 2J:	Principal statement	60
PRECEDENT 2K:	Employment of close relatives	65

3	**Different types of contracts**	**67**
3.1	Determining who is an 'employee'	67
3.2	Agency workers	67
3.3	Different types of workers/contracts	68
3.4	Self-employed	68
3.5	Individuals who work through intermediaries	73
3.6	Ministers of religion are not 'employees'	73
3.7	Casual workers	74
3.8	Seasonal workers	74
3.9	'Bank' staff	75
3.10	Surveillance staff	76
3.11	Hospitality staff/banqueting staff	76
3.12	Interns	76
3.13	Part-time workers: flexible hours, job-sharing, term-time working and career breaks	77
3.14	Zero-hours contracts	79
3.15	The 'gig' economy	81
3.16	Voluntary workers	82
3.17	Specialist consultants	83

3.18	Nanny's contract		83
PRECEDENT 3A:		Model term-time agreement	84
PRECEDENT 3B:		Sub-contractor's terms and conditions	85
PRECEDENT 3C:		Consultancy agreement	91
PRECEDENT 3D:		Indemnity clause for contract for services	102
PRECEDENT 3E:		Casual workers: terms of engagement	102
PRECEDENT 3F:		Casual workers: appointment form	105
PRECEDENT 3G:		Casual workers: weekly timesheet/payment form	105
PRECEDENT 3H:		Contract of employment for surveillance staff	106
PRECEDENT 3I:		Job description for hospitality/stewards/banqueting manager/director	111
PRECEDENT 3J:		Contract of employment for security guard	113
PRECEDENT 3K:		Consultancy agreement	115
PRECEDENT 3L:		Contract of employment for nanny	120
4	**The 'Martini contract': 'any time, any place, anywhere'**		**123**
4.1	The job description		123
4.2	The start date		124
4.3	Defining the duties		125
4.4	Requirement to travel		125
4.5	Relocation		126
4.6	Travel during times of adverse weather, strikes or volcanoes and other Acts of God		128
4.7	Requirement to drive		128
4.8	Requirement to be trained and to keep up to date		129
4.9	Work permits		130
4.10	Requirement to work fast and accurately		131
4.11	Hours of work		131
4.12	Clean desk policy		138
4.13	Travelling abroad		138
4.14	Working alone		140
PRECEDENT 4A:		Variation clause	140
PRECEDENT 4B:		Clauses relating to duties	141
PRECEDENT 4C:		Clauses relating to requirement to travel	142
PRECEDENT 4D:		Mobility clauses	142
PRECEDENT 4E:		Clauses related to unforeseen circumstances, e.g. adverse weather, strikes, etc.	142
PRECEDENT 4F:		Clause relating to training	143
PRECEDENT 4G:		Work permit letter	144
PRECEDENT 4H:		Work permit contract term	144
PRECEDENT 4I:		Clauses relating to fast and accurate work	144
PRECEDENT 4J:		Clause relating to overtime	145
PRECEDENT 4K:		Clause where there are no set working hours	145

PRECEDENT 4L:	Flexible time: annualised hours	146
PRECEDENT 4M:	On-call arrangements	149
PRECEDENT 4N:	Working Time Regulations: disapplication letter	149
PRECEDENT 4O:	Working Time Regulations: security guards, surveillance workers, messengers, chauffeurs	150
PRECEDENT 4P:	Working Time Regulations: dealers, traders, senior staff	151
PRECEDENT 4Q:	Working Time Regulations: computer operators who work at night	152
PRECEDENT 4R:	Working Time Regulations: secondary employment	153
PRECEDENT 4S:	Clear desk and screen policy	153
PRECEDENT 4T:	Working or travelling abroad guidelines	154
PRECEDENT 4U:	Lavatory breaks	163
PRECEDENT 4V:	Sample risk assessment for domiciliary visits	163
PRECEDENT 4W:	Sample risk assessment for working alone in buildings	164
PRECEDENT 4X:	Guidance for outdoor and peripatetic workers	165

5 Salary package and other financial terms and benefits 169

5.1	Basic salary terms	169
5.2	Salary reviews	169
5.3	Bonus schemes and bonus payments	170
5.4	Maternity and bonuses	180
5.5	Commission payments	180
5.6	Share options/stock options	182
5.7	Car or car allowance	182
5.8	Pension and life assurance	183
5.9	Private health cover	183
5.10	Other allowances	184
5.11	Expenses	184
5.12	Loans and deductions	185
5.13	Repayments for training expenses, overpayments and advance payments	189
5.14	Relocation expenses	191
5.15	Policy for world or sporting events	192

PRECEDENT 5A:	Salary terms	192
PRECEDENT 5B:	Salary terms: senior director	193
PRECEDENT 5C:	Review of salaries	193
PRECEDENT 5D:	Guaranteed bonus	194
PRECEDENT 5E:	Discretionary bonus	194
PRECEDENT 5F(i):	Clauses relating to conditional bonus	194
PRECEDENT 5F(ii):	Repayable bonus	195
PRECEDENT 5G:	Shares and options	195
PRECEDENT 5H:	Share dealings	196

PRECEDENT 5I:	Change of control	196
PRECEDENT 5J:	Car or car allowance	197
PRECEDENT 5K:	Car and company vehicle	201
PRECEDENT 5L:	Pension terms	209
PRECEDENT 5M:	Private medical insurance	209
PRECEDENT 5N:	Deputising conditions	210
PRECEDENT 5O:	Shoe and stocking allowance	210
PRECEDENT 5P:	Expenses clause	210
PRECEDENT 5Q:	Expenses policy	211
PRECEDENT 5R:	Travel expenses policy	212
PRECEDENT 5S:	(1) Deductions clause and (2) loan form	213
PRECEDENT 5T:	Repayment clause due to negligence, carelessness, etc.	214
PRECEDENT 5U:	Loan agreement for training expenses	214
PRECEDENT 5V:	Degree funding	216
PRECEDENT 5W:	Relocation policy	216
PRECEDENT 5X:	Olympic Games and other events	218

6	**Absence and sick pay**	**221**
6.1	Absence	221
6.2	Time-keeping	222
6.3	Sick pay	223
6.4	Medical evidence and Fit Notes	225
6.5	Medical examinations	226
6.6	Need to inform doctor of the purpose of examination and report	228
6.7	Instructions to doctors	229
6.8	Where the employer receives an incomprehensible medical report	232
6.9	Home visits	232
6.10	Occupational health advice	233
6.11	Conflicting medical opinions	233
6.12	Dangers of not seeking a medical opinion	234
6.13	How long is it reasonable for an illness or injury to last?	235
6.14	Stress	237
6.15	Conduct during sickness absence	240
6.16	Holidays	241
6.17	Holidays during sick leave	241
6.18	Alcohol and drugs	243
6.19	Light duties/alternative duties	243
6.20	Smoking	244
6.21	Absence through negligence of third parties	244
6.22	Permanent health insurance or long-term disability	244
6.23	Tension between dismissal and length of sick pay	245
6.24	Equality Act 2010	246
6.25	Time off for IVF treatment	247

6.26	Requirement to report medication	248
6.27	Malingering and moonlighting	248
6.28	Dealing with short-term absences	252
PRECEDENT 6A:	Requirement to report for work (full policy)	253
PRECEDENT 6B:	Severe weather and other unforeseen circumstances policy	255
PRECEDENT 6C:	Time-keeping for a private dental practice	258
PRECEDENT 6D:	Fit Note	258
PRECEDENT 6E:	Clause relating to medical examination	258
PRECEDENT 6F:	Consent form for the disclosure of medical information	259
PRECEDENT 6G:	BMA model letter for long-term or acute sickness absence	261
PRECEDENT 6H:	Letter of instruction to consultant	262
PRECEDENT 6I:	Expert witness's declaration	264
PRECEDENT 6J:	Occupational health advice letter	265
PRECEDENT 6K:	Stress management: risk assessment	266
PRECEDENT 6L:	Letter to GP relating to 'stress'	267
PRECEDENT 6M:	Clause relating to stress before or during disciplinary hearings or triggered by an event at work	267
PRECEDENT 6N:	Conduct during sickness absence	268
PRECEDENT 6O:	Exceptions to occupational sick pay	270
PRECEDENT 6P:	Holiday clauses	270
PRECEDENT 6Q:	Sickness during holidays and public holidays	271
PRECEDENT 6R:	Sickness and holidays in home country abroad	272
PRECEDENT 6S:	Terms relating to fitness for work	273
PRECEDENT 6T:	Light duties policy	274
PRECEDENT 6U:	No smoking policy	275
PRECEDENT 6V:	Absence through negligence of third party	276
PRECEDENT 6W:	Permanent health insurance/long-term disability scheme	276
PRECEDENT 6X:	Sick pay and termination of employment	277
PRECEDENT 6Y:	Disability	277
PRECEDENT 6Z:	Clause relating to IVF treatment	278
PRECEDENT 6AA:	Clause relating to requirement to report medication	278
PRECEDENT 6AB:	Management procedure for malingerers	278
PRECEDENT 6AC:	External business activities or interests and 'moonlighting'	280
PRECEDENT 6AD:	Note to all staff about use of private detectives	281
PRECEDENT 6AE:	Instructions to private detectives	281
PRECEDENT 6AF:	Absence control for managers	282
PRECEDENT 6AG:	Letters relating to absence	287

7	Maternity, paternity, adoptive and parental leave		291
7.1	The law		291
7.2	Statutory maternity pay, statutory adoption pay and maternity allowance		292
7.3	Pay and benefits during maternity leave		292
7.4	Career breaks		298
7.5	Paternity leave		299
7.6	Shared parental leave		300
7.7	Nanny's contract		300
PRECEDENT 7A:	Maternity leave and accrual of holiday		300
PRECEDENT 7B:	Maternity leave and pay policy		301
PRECEDENT 7C:	Maternity/adoption/shared maternity leave cover		304
PRECEDENT 7D:	Job-share contract		307
PRECEDENT 7E:	Career breaks		309
PRECEDENT 7F:	Paternity and adoptive paternity pay and leave policy		311
PRECEDENT 7G:	Shared Parental Leave Policy		314
PRECEDENT 7H:	Flexible working requests		315
8	Rules and standards of conduct		319
8.1	Introduction		319
8.2	The Anti-Slavery provisions		319
8.3	The Bribery Act 2010		320
8.4	Codes of conduct		320
8.5	Rules for the staff of doctors and dentists in private practice/repute clauses		322
8.6	Bringing the employer into disrepute ('repute clauses')		322
8.7	Other disciplinary rules		323
8.8	Christmas/office parties, business lunches and dinners		324
8.9	Lecturing, writing and appearing on TV, etc.		326
8.10	Alcohol and drugs		327
8.11	Gambling or taking part in betting syndicates at work		328
8.12	Children on company premises		328
8.13	Money collections		328
8.14	Insider dealing, compliance rules and taking secret profits, etc.		328
8.15	Personal searches		330
8.16	Dress and appearance		330
8.17	Moonlighting		334
8.18	Consensual relationships at work		334
8.19	Harassment		336
8.20	Duty to report the misconduct of others		337
8.21	Requirement to work at weekends		338
8.22	Stealing company intellectual property		338

PRECEDENT 8A:	Anti-slavery policy statement	340
PRECEDENT 8B:	Hospitality and gifts policy	342
PRECEDENT 8C:	Anti-corruption, bribery and fraud policy	344
PRECEDENT 8D:	Code of conduct and common responsibilities	348
PRECEDENT 8E:	Conduct for professional practices	353
PRECEDENT 8F:	Rules for company functions/parties/dinners and lunches	353
PRECEDENT 8G:	Drinking, drugs and driving policy	355
PRECEDENT 8H:	Alcohol and drug control policy	356
PRECEDENT 8I:	Rules on gambling	370
PRECEDENT 8J:	Prohibition on children and young persons on company premises	370
PRECEDENT 8K:	Clause relating to money collections	371
PRECEDENT 8L:	Compliance rules	371
PRECEDENT 8M:	Clause relating to personal searches	383
PRECEDENT 8N:	Dress and appearance	384
PRECEDENT 8O:	Dress code (museum)	386
PRECEDENT 8P:	Guidelines on professional relations between student and academic staff	387
PRECEDENT 8Q:	Harassment	388
PRECEDENT 8R:	Duty to report wrongdoing	389
PRECEDENT 8S:	Requirement to work on Saturdays	390
PRECEDENT 8T:	Checklist for Christmas parties	391

9 Disciplinary and performance procedures — 395

9.1	Disciplinary procedures: Code and Guidance	395
9.2	Conduct issues	395
9.3	Interviews of concern/alternative less serious procedure	396
9.4	Suspension	397
9.5	Confidentiality	399
9.6	Investigations	399
9.7	Whistleblowing	404
9.8	Investigating dishonesty	404
9.9	Legal representation	405
9.10	Ordinary right to be accompanied	406
9.11	Distinction between 'formal' and 'informal' warnings	406
9.12	Other representative allowed?	407
9.13	Performance as well as conduct issues: cumulative procedure	407
9.14	Warnings	408
9.15	Extending the lifetime of a warning	410
9.16	Not fair to hold a hearing	410
9.17	'Undertaking to behave'	411
9.18	Warnings and discipline where staff are abroad	411
9.19	Recording the hearing	412
9.20	If the employee refuses to attend or cannot attend the hearing	413
9.21	Appeals	415

9.22	Admissions of guilt	416
9.23	Resigning before a gross misconduct hearing	416
9.24	Raising a grievance during a disciplinary process	417
9.25	Criminal convictions or charges	418
9.26	Performance	418
9.27	Termination checklist	419
9.28	Duty of disclosure	420
9.29	Sex in the office	421
9.30	Prohibition on discussing salary or bonus	421
PRECEDENT 9A:	Clauses excluding disciplinary procedure	422
PRECEDENT 9B:	Suspension	423
PRECEDENT 9C:	Letter reminding suspended employee of obligations	423
PRECEDENT 9D:	Undertaking of confidentiality clause	424
PRECEDENT 9E:	Letter responding to allegation of breach of confidentiality	425
PRECEDENT 9F:	Complaints handling policy	426
PRECEDENT 9G:	Investigating dishonesty	432
PRECEDENT 9H:	Combined procedure	432
PRECEDENT 9I:	Lapsed warnings	433
PRECEDENT 9J:	Dismissal letter following a lapsed final warning	433
PRECEDENT 9K:	Final written warning	434
PRECEDENT 9L:	Consolidated disciplinary warning letters	435
PRECEDENT 9M:	Undertaking to behave	441
PRECEDENT 9N:	Recording the hearing	442
PRECEDENT 9O:	Letter regarding secret recording	442
PRECEDENT 9P:	Admissions of guilt	443
PRECEDENT 9Q:	Improved performance review (IPR) or performance improvement procedure (PIP)	444
PRECEDENT 9R:	Disciplinary and dismissal procedures	447

10	**Redundancy**	**455**
10.1	Redundancy dismissals	455
10.2	Procedure	457
10.3	Bumping	457
10.4	Redundancy checklist	459
10.5	Failure to consider suitable alternative employment	468
10.6	Redundancy during maternity leave	469
10.7	Warning and consultation	470
10.8	Selection criteria	471
10.9	Questions and answers	474
10.10	Redundancy procedure	474
10.11	Redundancy letters	474
PRECEDENT 10A:	Script for consultation meeting	474
PRECEDENT 10B:	Model selection criteria	475

PRECEDENT 10C:	Consultation on redundancy: questions and answers	478
PRECEDENT 10D:	Model redundancy policy	483
PRECEDENT 10E:	Model redundancy letters	489

11 Grievances, harassment, bullying and 'whistleblowing' — 493
11.1 Company grievance procedures — 493
11.2 Stages of the procedure — 494
11.3 Grievance procedures — 495
11.4 Special complaints procedures for harassment or bullying — 496
11.5 Making sure the decision in the grievance letter is correct — 499
11.6 Personal liability, indemnifying individual respondents and conflict of interest — 500
11.7 Monitoring recruitment and gender pay reporting — 501
11.8 Harassment and/or bullying — 501
11.9 Whistleblowing: what it is and policies — 505

PRECEDENT 11A:	Clause defining when grievance procedure may be initiated	507
PRECEDENT 11B:	Undertaking of confidentiality	507
PRECEDENT 11C:	Letter confirming terms of suspension	508
PRECEDENT 11D:	Personal liability	509
PRECEDENT 11E:	Ethnic and gender monitoring in recruitment and training	510
PRECEDENT 11F:	Model harassment/bullying policy	513
PRECEDENT 11G:	Whistleblowing policy	522

12 Notice and notice clauses — 527
12.1 Notice term: statutory and contractual — 527
12.2 When notice is deemed to be given — 527
12.3 Withdrawing notice or not accepting notice — 529
12.4 When does notice expire? — 530
12.5 Short notice agreed or not agreed — 530
12.6 Payment in lieu of notice clauses — 532
12.7 Where there is no PILON clause — 532
12.8 No notice provision: common law/reasonable notice — 533
12.9 Duty to mitigate — 533
12.10 Notice during absence — 534
12.11 Notice during probationary periods — 534
12.12 Garden leave — 534
12.13 References — 535

PRECEDENT 12A:	Letter refusing to accept short notice	537
PRECEDENT 12B:	Letter accepting short notice	539
PRECEDENT 12C:	Clause relating to notice during probation	539
PRECEDENT 12D:	Garden leave	539

PRECEDENT 12E:	Reference policy and waiver		540
PRECEDENT 12F:	Clauses related to notice		542

13 Emails, the internet, social media and data protection 543
13.1 The issues 543
13.2 Defamation on social media 544
13.3 Summary of legislation concerning emails 544
13.4 Gateways 545
13.5 Duty to inform staff/third parties 546
13.6 Email misuse 546
13.7 Disciplinary action for email and internet misuse 547
13.8 Checklist 548
13.9 Covert surveillance 550
13.10 'Cyber-liability' 550
13.11 Prosecutions 551
13.12 Human rights 551
13.13 Social networking 553
13.14 Data protection 556

PRECEDENT 13A:	Email monitoring	562
PRECEDENT 13B:	Log on banner	563
PRECEDENT 13C:	Clause relating to email and internet monitoring	564
PRECEDENT 13D(1):	Internet and email policy	564
PRECEDENT 13D(2):	Social media policy	567
PRECEDENT 13E:	IT and computer equipment policy	572
PRECEDENT 13F:	Social networking policy	573
PRECEDENT 13G:	Letter relating to transfer of occupational health records	574
PRECEDENT 13H:	Clause relating to TUPE	575
PRECEDENT 13I:	Data protection policy 2017	575
PRECEDENT 13J:	Email footer	581

14 Restrictive covenants and confidentiality 583
14.1 Status of post-termination restrictions 583
14.2 General issues 584
14.3 Enforcing the notice period/garden leave 585
14.4 Are damages an appropriate remedy? 586
14.5 Types of clauses 587
14.6 Implied terms 587
14.7 Preamble 588
14.8 Confidentiality clauses 589
14.9 What is a 'trade secret'? 590
14.10 Misusing company facilities 592
14.11 Not to bring materials into or take them out of work 593
14.12 Non-compete clauses 593

14.13	Area covenants	593
14.14	Scope of clause	594
14.15	Injunctions/damages against third parties	595
14.16	Non-solicitation/non-dealing	596
14.17	Non-poaching	597
14.18	Breach of contract: accounting for profits	598
14.19	Outside employment: 'whole time and attention' clauses	598
14.20	Representing the employer	599
14.21	Return of company property	599
14.22	Whistleblowing duty to report misconduct of self as well as others	599
14.23	Inventions and patents	599
PRECEDENT 14A:	Clause relating to confidential information	600
PRECEDENT 14B:	Confidentiality clause (senior executive)	600
PRECEDENT 14C:	Confidentiality clause (software)	601
PRECEDENT 14D:	Confidentiality agreement for temporary staff	601
PRECEDENT 14E:	Confidentiality clause (occupational health)	602
PRECEDENT 14F:	Confidentiality agreement for non-medical staff	603
PRECEDENT 14G:	Confidentiality agreement for reception staff	603
PRECEDENT 14H:	Contact with, participation in or disclosure to the media	604
PRECEDENT 14I:	Conflict of interest clauses	605
PRECEDENT 14J:	Clause relating to misuse of company facilities	606
PRECEDENT 14K:	Using own tools and equipment; and borrowing company property	606
PRECEDENT 14L:	Non-compete clause	607
PRECEDENT 14M:	Area covenant	607
PRECEDENT 14N:	Clause warranting not in breach of former restrictive covenants	608
PRECEDENT 14O:	Clause relating to notification of restriction	608
PRECEDENT 14P:	Non-solicitation/non-dealing clause	608
PRECEDENT 14Q:	Non-poaching clause	609
PRECEDENT 14R:	Whole time and attention clause	609
PRECEDENT 14S:	Clause relating to return of company property	610
PRECEDENT 14T:	'Whistleblowing' clause	610
PRECEDENT 14U:	Inventions and patents	611
PRECEDENT 14V:	Set of restrictive covenants	611
15	**Settlement agreements**	**619**
15.1	General rule	619
15.2	Statutory rules for settlement agreements	619
15.3	What if there is no complaint or no proceedings?	620
15.4	Breach of contract claims	621
15.5	Categories of claims that can be compromised	622
15.6	Settlement agreements which are *ultra vires*	622

15.7	Consideration	624
15.8	Relevant independent adviser	625
15.9	Terms agreed	625
15.10	Special terms	626
15.11	TUPE and use of settlement agreements	627
15.12	Specific terms	627
15.13	Private medical insurance	630
15.14	Staged payments: duty to mitigate	630
15.15	Taxation	630
15.16	Indemnity from employee	631
15.17	'Protected conversations' and 'without prejudice' discussions	632
15.18	Mediation	634

PRECEDENT 15A:	Clauses relating to private medical insurance	635
PRECEDENT 15B:	Clause relating to duty to mitigate	636
PRECEDENT 15C:	Without prejudice letter	636
PRECEDENT 15D:	Model settlement agreement	637

Index 655

Preface

The contents of this edition have been updated to take account of new legislation (e.g. the General Data Protection Regulation) as well as very important developments on matters such as holiday pay and how it should be calculated; the meaning of a 'worker' in the 'gig' economy; the status of travelling time for peripatetic workers; the payment of bonuses and commission payments; notice clauses; anti-slavery policies; whistleblowing, etc.

It includes new precedents, forms, clauses and agreements, policies and procedures on sickness absence; stress-related absence; withholding of notice pay; loans and deductions from wages; restrictive covenants; enforcing conditions during garden leave; the misuse of trade secrets; non-solicitation clauses; settlement agreements, etc.

Chapter 12 (*Notice and notice clauses*) has additional discussion on protected conversations and without prejudice discussions, and a new grievance investigation protocol has been added to Chapter 11 (*Grievances, harassment, bullying and 'whistleblowing'*). Of course Chapter 13 (*Emails, the internet, social media and data protection*) has been updated to include sections on internet abuse; use of blogs, Twitter, etc.; and the new Defamation Act 2013 and its implications for employers.

I hope as ever that my precedents, forms, letters and policies will prove useful in drafting employment contracts and policies for your clients, and for your company if you are an HR specialist. I have gathered ideas from my clients over these past years, drafting policies, letters and contracts for them. Thank you all for giving me the opportunity to draft such documents for you.

I would like to thank Paul Milner at the Law Society, for asking me to undertake this third edition and for the great patience he has shown in waiting for it, and Josephine Gibbons and her team for so painstakingly and patiently going through the manuscript and pointing out so many better ways of writing some of the text, and for correcting errors that had crept in. Any errors remaining in the book are my responsibility entirely.

Most of all, I could not have done any of this without the everlasting love of Barry, Dan, Ben and Aliza, my new grandson Max Monty, my twin brother Charles, and all my wonderful nieces and nephews and great-nieces and -nephews in Israel. You are all my inspiration.

The law is accurate as at July 2017.

Gillian Howard

Table of cases

Achbita v. G4S (Case C-157/15) 8.16
Airbus UK Ltd v. Webb [2008] ICR 561, CA 9.14
Alex Lawrie Factors Ltd v. Morgan, Morgan and Turner, *The Times*, 18 August 1999, CA 9.6
Alexander v. Home Office [1988] 1 WLR 968; [1988] IRLR 190, CA 11.8
Alexander v. Standard Telephones & Cables Ltd (No.2) [1991] IRLR 286 .... 2.7
Allma Construction Ltd v. Bonner UKEATS/0060/09/BI 15.9
Amwell View School Governors v. Dogherty [2007] ICR 125 .... 9.19
Andreou v. Lord Chancellor's Department [2002] IRLR 728 .... 9.20
Aslam and Farrar v. Uber BV, Uber London Ltd and Uber Britannia Ltd (Case No.2202550/2015) 3.15
Aspden v. Webbs Poultry and Meat Group (Holdings) Ltd [1996] IRLR 521, QBD 6.21
Aspin v. Metric Group Ltd [2004] EWHC 1265, QB 2.3
Atrill v. Dresdner Kleinwort 5.2
Attorney-General v. Blake [1998] Ch 439; [1998] 1 All ER 833, CA 14.6, 14.18
Attorney-General v. Blake [2001] IRLR 36 .... 8.14, 14.18
Auguste Noel Ltd v. Curtis [1990] IRLR 326, EAT 9.13
Autoclenz v. Belcher [2010] IRLR 70, CA; [2011] UKSC 41; [2011] ICR 1157 .... 5.2
Aylward v. Glamorgan Holiday Hoe Ltd UKEAT/0167/02 (unreported) 10.1
Aziz v. Crown Prosecution Service [2007] ICR 1523 .... 9.4

B v. A [2010] IRLR 400 .... 11.4
Baldwins (Ashby) Ltd v. Andrew Maidstone [2011] EWHC B12 (Mercantile) 14.15
Balston Ltd v. Headline Fitters Ltd [1993] FSR 385 .... 14.12
Barbulescu v. Romania (App.No.61496/08) 6.27
Bartholomew v. Hackney LBC [1999] IRLR 246, CA 2.3, 9.23
Bartholomews Agri Food v. Thornton [2016] EWHC 648 (QB) 14.14
Bass Leisure v. Thomas [1994] IRLR 104, EAT 4.5
Bateman v. Asda Stores Ltd [2010] IRLR 370 .... 2.10, 4.1
Bellman v. Northampton Recruitment [2016] EWHC 3104 (QB) 8.8
Bland (Mr Hamilton Edwin) v. Mr David Sparkes [1999] EWCA Civ J120-35, *The Times*, 17 December 1999 .... 8.6
Bliss v. South East Thames Regional HA [1985] IRLR 308, CA 6.5
BNP Paribas v. Mezzotero [2004] IRLR 508 .... 15.17
Bonsor v. RJB Mining (UK) Ltd [2004] IRLR 164 .... 4.1
Bougnaoui v. Micropole Univers (Case C-188/15) 8.16
Braid Group (Holdings) Ltd, *Re* [2016] CSIH 68 .... 12.13
Brand v. Compro Computer Services Ltd [2004] EWCA Civ 204 .... 5.5
Brigden v. American Express Bank [2000] IRLR 94 .... 1.1, 5.3
Briscoe v. Lubrizol Ltd [2002] IRLR 607 .... 6.5, 6.22
British Aerospace plc v. Green [1995] ICR 1006, CA 10.8
British Gas v. Breeze, EAT 503/87 .... 6.11

British Gas Trading Ltd v. Lock and Secretary of State for Business, Innovation
 and Skills [2016] EWCA Civ 983 .... 2.6, 5.3
British Home Stores v. Burchell [1978] IRLR 379, EAT 6.27, 9.6
British Telecommunications plc v. Reid [2004] IRLR 327 .... 11.8
Brooks v. Olyslager OMS (UK) Ltd [1998] IRLR 590, CA 14.8
Broome v. Cassell [1972] AC 1027, HL 11.8
Buckley v. Waters Edge Ceramics 13.7
Burton and Rhule v. De Vere Hotels Ltd [1996] IRLR 596, EAT 8.8
Byrne v. Arvin Meritor LVS (UK) Ltd EAT/239/02/MAA 10.3

Calvin v. Carr [1980] AC 574, PC 9.21
Cassley v. GMP Securities Europe LLP [2015] EWHC 722 (QB) 4.13
Cavendish Square Holding BV v. Talal El Makdessi 15.10
Celestina Mba v. Mayor and Burgesses of Merton LBC [2013] EWCA Civ
 1562 .... 4.11
Cerberus Software Co Ltd v. Rowley [2001] IRLR 160 .... 12.9
Cheltenham BC v. Laird [2009] IRLR 621 .... 1.14
Chesterton Global Ltd v. Nurmohamed EAT/U335/14 .... 11.9
Chief Adjudication Officer v. Banks and Stafford [2001] ICR 877 .... 3.13
Chief Constable of West Yorkshire Police v. Khan [2001] IRLR 830 .... 2.3
Clark v. BET plc [1997] IRLR 348, QBD 5.3
Clark v. Nomura International plc [2000] IRLR 766 .... 5.2, 5.3
Clark v. Oxfordshire HA [1998] IRLR 125, CA 3.9
Clark v. TDG Ltd (t/a Novacold) [1999] 2 All ER 977; [1999] IRLR 318,
 CA 6.23
Cleeve Link Ltd v. E Bryla [2014] IRLR 86 .... 5.12
Clifford v. Union of Democratic Mineworkers [1991] IRLR 518, CA 1.1
Clyde & Co LLP v. Bates Van Winkelhof [2014] 1 WLR 2047 .... 3.4
CMC Group plc v. Zhang [2006] EWCA Civ 408 .... 15.10
Coleman v. Attridge Law [2008] IRLR 722 .... 8.19
Colley v. Corkindale [1995] ICR 965, EAT 3.14
Commerzbank AG v. Keen [2006] EWCA Civ 1536 .... 1.1, 5.2, 5.3
Commissioner of Police for the Metropolis v. Shaw UKEAT/01125/11/ZY 11.8
Commissioners for HMRC v. Julian Martin [2014] UKUT 429 (TCC) 5.3
Copsey v. WWB Devon Clays Ltd [2005] EWCA Civ 932 .... 4.11
Cornelius v. Swansea University [1987] IRLR 141 CA 2.3
Coulson v. Felixstowe Dock & Railway Co Ltd [1975] IRLR 11, IT 6.23
Courtaulds Northern Spinning Ltd v. Sibson and TGWU [1988] IRLR 305,
 CA 4.5
Courtaulds Northern Textiles Ltd v. Andrew [1979] IRLR 84, EAT 1.4
Craig v. Transocean [2009] IRLR 519 .... 2.6
Crampton v. Decorum Motors [1975] IRLR 168, IT 6.12
Cresswell v. Board of Inland Revenue [1984] 2 All ER 713; [1984] IRLR
 190 .... 4.8
Crossley v. Faithful & Gould Holdings Ltd [2004] EWCA Civ 293 .... 1.1, 6.22
CRS Computers Ltd v. Mackenzie [2002] Emp LR 1048 .... 5.12
Curr v. Marks & Spencer plc [2003] IRLR 74 .... 7.4

Dabson v. David Cover & Sons Ltd UKEAT/0374/10/SM 10.8
Dacas v. Brook Street Bureau Ltd [2004] IRLR 358 .... 1.2
Dawnay, Day & Co Ltd v. De Brachonier D'Alphen [1997] IRLR 285, ChD 14.17
De Keyser Ltd v. Wilson [2001] IRLR 324 .... 6.7
Deadman v. Bristol City Council [2007] IRLR 888 .... 11.4
Department of Work and Pensions v. Brindley UKEAT/0123/16/JOJ 15.7
Dewhurst v. CitySprint UK Ltd ET/2202512/2016 .... 3.15

Diosynth Ltd v. Thomson, Court of Session 9.14
Durant (John) v. Financial Services Authority [2003] EWCA Civ 1746 .... 13.14
Dusek v. Stormharbour Securities LLP [2016] EWCA Civ 604 .... 4.13

East Lindsay DC v. Daubney [1977] IRLR 181, EAT 6.7
Eastbourne BC v. Foster [2001] EWCA Civ 1091 .... 15.6
Eaton Ltd v. King [1995] IRLR 75, EAT 10.8
Edinburgh City Council v. Dickson UKEATS/0038/09 .... 13.7
Edwards v. Bramble Foods Ltd, EET/20601556/2015 .... 8T
Elsevier Ltd v. Munro [2014] EWHC 2648 (QB) 14.3
Equality & Human Rights Commission v. Earle UKEAT/0011/14/MC 5.2
Essop v. Home Office (UK Border Agency); Naeem v. Secretary of State for
  Justice [2017] UKSC 27 .... 6.25
Evening Standard Co Ltd v. Henderson [1987] IRLR 64, CA 12.5
Eweida v. United Kingdom [2013] ECHR 37; [2013] IRLR 231 .... 4.11, 8.16

Faccenda Chicken Co Ltd v. Fowler [1987] Ch 117; [1986] IRLR 69, CA 14.6, 14.8,
                                                                                        14.9
Faithorn Farrell Timms plc v. Bailey UKEAT/0025/16/RN 15.17
FC Gardner Ltd v. Beresford [1978] IRLR 63, EAT 5.2
Federacion de Servicios Privados del Sindicato Comisiones obreras v. Tyco
  Integrated Security SL (Case C-266/14) 4.4, 4.11
Ferguson v. John Dawson & Partners (Contractors) Ltd [1976] 1 WLR 346;
  [1976] IRLR 345, CA 1.2
Financial Techniques (Planning Services) Ltd v. Hughes [1981] IRLR 32,
  CA 1.8
Fish v. Dresdner Kleinwort Ltd; Hatzistefanis v. Dresdner Kleinwort Ltd
  [2009] IRLR 1035 .... 5.3
Framlington Group v. Barnetson [2007] IRLR 598 .... 15.17

General Billposting Ltd v. Atkinson [1909] AC 118 .... 12.6
Gibb v. Maidstone and Tunbridge Wells NHS Trust [2010] EWCA Civ 678 .... 15.5
Gill v. Cape Contracts Ltd [1985] IRLR 499 .... 1.3, 1.12
Gill v. SAS Ground Services UK Ltd ET/2705021/09 .... 6.27
Gimson v. Display By Design Ltd, ET/1900336/2012 .... 8T
Gisda Cyf v. Barratt [2010] UKSC 41 .... 12.2
Glitz v. Watford Electric Co Ltd [1979] IRLR 89, EAT 4.1
Gloystarne & Co Ltd v. Martin [2001] IRLR 15 .... 15.8, 15.9
GM Packaging (UK) Ltd v. Haslem UKEAT/0259/13/LA 9.29
Godfrey v. Demon Internet [2003] 3 WLR 1020 .... 13.10
Gogay v. Hertfordshire CC [2000] IRLR 703 .... 9.4
Grampian Joint Police Board v. Sighe EAT/951/00 (unreported) 11.8
Green v. DB Group Services (UK)Ltd [2006] IRLR 764 .... 11.8
Greenwich LBC v. Robinson, EAT 745/94 .... 6.25
Griffiths and Moore v. Salisbury DC [2004] EWCA Civ 162 .... 2.7
Gus Home Shopping Ltd v. Green [2001] IRLR 75 .... 7.3
GX Networks Ltd v. Greenland [2010] EWCA Civ 784 .... 5.3

Halford v. United Kingdom (1997) 24 EHRR 253; [1997] IRLR 471, ECHR 13.12
Hall v. Lorimer 66 TC 349 .... 3.4
Hanover Insurance Brokers Ltd v. Shapiro [1994] IRLR 82, CA 14.17
Hardwick v. Leeds Area HA [1975] IRLR 319, IT 6.23
Harmer v. Cornelius (1858) 5 CBNS 236 .... 4.1
Harper v. Virgin Net Ltd [2004] IRLR 390, CA 12.7
Hawker Siddeley Power Engineering Ltd v. Rump [1979] IRLR 425, EAT 1.12

Hayward v. Zurich Insurance Co plc [2016] UKSC 48 .... 15.3
Hendy Banks City Print Ltd v. Fairbrother 10.8
Herry v Dudley MBC UKEAT/0100/16/LA 6.14
Hershaw v. Sheffield City Council UKEAT/0033/14/BA 11.5
High Table Ltd v. Horst [1997] IRLR 513, CA 4.5
Hill v. General Accident Fire & Life Assurance Corp plc [1998] IRLR 641,
  OH 6.23
Hinton & Higgs (UK) Ltd v. Murphy and Valentine [1989] IRLR 519 .... 14.1, 14.7
Hivac v. Park Royal Scientific Instruments Ltd [1946] Ch 169, CA 14.19
HM Land Registry v. McGlue EAT/0435/11 .... 11.8
HM Prison Service v. Salmon [2001] IRLR 425 .... 11.8
HM Revenue & Customs v. Stringer [2009] IRLR 677 .... 2.6
Holmes v. Whittington & Porter Ltd (unreported) 6.12
Horkulak v. Cantor Fitzgerald [2004] IRLR 942 .... 5.3
Howman & Son v. Blyth [1983] ICR 416, EAT 1.4
Hoyland v. Asda Stores Ltd [2006] IRLR 468 .... 7.3
Hutchinson v. Enfield Rolling Mills Ltd [1981] IRLR 318, EAT 6.4

Interfoto Picture Library Ltd v. Stiletto Visual Programmers Ltd [1989] 1 QB
  433, CA 4.4
International Sports Co Ltd v. Thomson [1980] IRLR 340, EAT 6.28
Item Software (UK) Ltd v. Fassihi [2004] IRLR 928 .... 8.20

J v. DLA Piper UKEAT/0263/09/RN 6.14
JA Mont Ltd v. Mills [1993] IRLR 172, CA 14.1
Jessemey v. Rowstock Ltd [2014] EWCA Civ 185 .... 2.3
Jones v. The Post Office [2001] IRLR 384 .... 6.11
Jones v. Warwick University [2003] 3 All ER 760 .... 6.27, 13.12
Joyce v. Northern Microwave Distributors Ltd (ET/5564/93) 6.25

Kapadia v. Lambeth LBC [2000] IRLR 669 .... 6.5
Kara v. Hackney LBC, EAT 25/95 .... 8.16
Kennedy v. Dresdner Kleinwort Wasserstein [2004] EWHC 1103 (Comm) 5.3
Khatri v. Cooperatieve Centrale Raiffeisen-Boerenleenbank BA [2010] IRLR
  715 .... 5.3
Kulkarni v. Milton Keynes Hospital NHS Trust [2009] IRLR 829 .... 9.9

Ladbroke Racing Ltd v. Arnott [1983] IRLR 154, Court of Session 9.22
Ladbroke Racing Ltd v. King, EAT/202/88 .... 8.20, 14.22
Lansing Linde v. Kerr [1991] 1 WLR 251; [1991] IRLR 80, CA 14.9
Laughton and Hawley v. Bapp Industrial Supplies Ltd [1986] IRLR 245,
  EAT 14.12
Leach v. Office of Communications (OFCOM) [2012] IRLR 839, CA 1.4
Leisure Leagues UK Ltd v. Maconnachie [2002] IRLR 600 .... 2.6
Lennon v. Commissioner of Police of the Metropolis [2004] IRLR 385 .... 6.22
Lewen v. Denda [2000] IRLR 67 .... 7.3
Lewisham LBC v. Malcolm [2008] IRLR 700 .... 6.24
Linfood Cash and Carry Ltd v. Thomson, Greenwell and Bell [1989] IRLR
  235 .... 6.27, 9.6
Littlewoods Organisation Ltd v. Harris [1978] 1 All ER 1026, CA 14.7
Locke v. Candy and Candy Ltd [2011] IRLR 163 .... 5.3, 5.5
London Underground v. Edwards (No.2) [1988] IRLR 364 .... 4.5
Lynock v. Cereal Packaging Ltd [1988] IRLR 510, EAT 6.28

MvAdie v. Royal Bank of Scotland [2007] IRLR 895 .... 6.23

McAndrew v. Prestwick Circuits Ltd [1990] IRLR 514, EAT 4.5
MacCartney v. Oversley House Management [2006] IRLR 514 .... 4.11
McClory v. Post Office [1993] IRLR 159 .... 9.4
McGivney v. Portman Mansions Management Ltd UKEAT/0308/09 .... 6.14, 9.12
McMillan Williams v. Range [2004] 1 WLR 1858 .... 5.13
McNally v. Welltrade International Ltd [1978] IRLR 497 .... 1.12
Majrowski v. Guy's and St Thomas's NHS Trust [2006] UKHL 34 .... 11.8
Marshall v. Alexander Sloan & Co Ltd [1981] IRLR 264, EAT 6.3
Mashi v. Awaz FM (Case No.S/116403/08) 3.16
Mason v. CXC Advantage Ltd ET/2203930/2013 .... 13.7
Mayr v. Backerei und Konditorei Gerhard Flockner OHG [2008] IRLR 387 .... 6.25
MCI Worldcom International Inc v. Primus Telecommunications Inc [2004]
    EWCA Civ 957 .... 5.13
Meadows v. East Riding of Yorkshire Council ET/1805363/2012 .... 13.7
Mears v. Safecar Security Ltd [1982] 3 WLR 366; [1982] IRLR 183, CA 1.4
Mezey v. South West London and St George's Mental Health NHS Trust
    [2007] EWCA Civ 106; [2010] IRLR 512 .... 9.4, 9.16
Migrant Advisory Service v. Chaudri UKEAT/1400/97 .... 3.16
Miller Bros and FP Butler Ltd v. Johnston [2002] IRLR 386 .... 15.4
Morgan v. Staffordshire University [2002] IRLR 190 .... 6.12, 6.14
Morgan v. Welsh Rugby Union [2011] IRLR 376 .... 10.8
Murco Petroleum Ltd v. Forge [1987] IRLR 50, EAT 5.2
Murphy v. Stakis Leisure Ltd ET Case Nos.S/0534/89 & S/0590/89 .... 8.16
Murray v. Foyle Meats Ltd [1999] 3 WLR 356; [1999] IRLR 562, HL 10.1
Murray v. Newham Citizens Advice Bureau [2001] ICR 708, EAT 3.16
Muschett v. HM Prison Service [2010] IRLR 451 .... 3.2

Nagarajan v. London Regional Transport [1999] 3 WLR 425; [1999] IRLR
    572, HL 13.7
Nahhas v. Pier House (Cheyne Walk) Management Ltd (1984) 270 EG 328 .... 1.7
Nawaz v. Ford Motor Co Ltd [1987] IRLR 163 .... 6.11
Neary v. Dean of Westminster [1999] IRLR 288 .... 14.19
Newcastle Upon Tyne NHS Foundation Trust v. Haywood [2017] EWCA Civ
    153 .... 12.2
NHS Leeds v. Larner [2012] EWCA Civ 1034 .... 6.17
North v. Lionel Leventhal Ltd UKEAT/0265/04/MAA 10.3
Nottingham University v. Fishel [2000] IRLR 471 .... 14.19
Nova Plastics Ltd v. Froggatt [1982] IRLR 146, EAT 14.19

O'Brien v. Prudential Assurance Co Ltd [1979] IRLR 140, EAT 1.5
Office Angels Ltd v. Rainer Thomas and O'Connor [1991] IRLR 214, CA 14.1
Ottoman Bank v. Chakarian [1930] AC 277 .... 4.5

P v. S and Cornwall CC (Case C-13/94) [1996] All ER (EC) 397; [1996] IRLR
    347 .... 8.16
Packman (Mr Ron) (t/a Packman Lucas Associates) v. Ms P Fauchon
    UKEAT/0017/12/LA 10.3
Padden v. Arbuthnot Pensions & Investments Ltd [2004] EWCA Civ 582 .... 15.16
ParkingEye Ltd v. Beavis 15.10
Parkins v. Sodexho Ltd 11.9
Peninsula Business Services Ltd v. Sweeney [2004] IRLR 49, EAT 1.1, 5.5
Pennwell Publishing (UK) Ltd v. Ornstein [2007] IRLR 700 .... 13.10
Pereda v. Madrid Movilidad SA [2009] IRLR 959 .... 2.6, 6.17
Pimlico Plumbers Ltd v. Smith [2017] EWCA Civ 51 .... 3.4

Pinewood Repro Ltd (t/a County Print) v. Page [2010]
  UKEAT/0028/10/1310 .... 10.7
Pinkerton v. Hollis Brothers & ESA plc (21 July 1988, Court of Session) 1.12
Plumb v. Duncan Print Group Ltd UKEAT/2015/0071 .... 6.17
PMC Holdings Ltd v. Smith [2002] All ER (D) 186 .... 8.14
Post Office v. Foley [2000] IRLR 827 .... 8.10
Post Office v. Mughal [1977] IRLR 178, EAT 1.13
President of the Methodist Conference v. Preston [2013] UKSC 29 SC 3.6
Profit plc v. Huggett [2014] EWCA Civ 1013 .... 14.2
Provident Financial Group and Whitegates Estate Agency Ltd v Hayward
  [1989] 3 All ER 298; [1989] IRLR 84; [1989] ICR 160, CA 14.4, 14.15
PSM International plc v. Whitehouse and Willenhall Automation Ltd [1992]
  IRLR 279, CA 14.16
Punjab National Bank v. Gosain UKEAT/0003/14/SM 9.19

Quinton Hazell Ltd v. Earl [1976] IRLR 296, EAT 10.5

R (on the application of G) v. X School Governors & Y City Council
  (Interested Party) [2010] IRLR 222 .... 9.9
R v. Maxwell-King [2001] 2 Cr App R (S) 28 .... 13.11
Racal Services (Communications) Ltd v. Flockhart, Appeal No.EAT/701/00 .... 8.10
Ralph Martindale & Co Ltd v. Harris [2008] UKEAT/166/07 .... 10.5
RDF Media Group plc v. Clements [2008] IRLR 207 .... 2.2
Read v. Tiverton DC and Bull [1997] IRLR 202 .... 11.6
Richards v. IP Solutions Group Ltd [2016] EWHC 1835 (QB) 12.13
Roberts v. West Coast Trains Ltd [2004] IRLR 788 .... 9.21, 12.3
Robinson v. Crompton Parkinson Ltd [1978] IRLR 61, EAT 5.2
Robinson-Steele v. RD Retail Services Ltd [2006] IRLR 386 .... 2.6
Rock Refrigeration v. Jones [1997] 1 All ER 1; [1996] IRLR 675, CA 5.12, 12.6
Rock-It Cargo Ltd v. Green [1997] IRLR 581, EAT 15.4
Roger Bullivant Ltd v. Ellis [1987] IRLR 491, CA 14.9
Rolls Royce Ltd v. Walpole [1980] IRLR 343, EAT 6.28
Royal Mail Group Ltd v. Aldous UKEAT/0593/12/BA 5.13
RS Dhillon and GP Dhillon Partnership v. HMRC [2017] UKFTT 17 (TC) 3.4
Russell v. Transocean International Resources Ltd [2011] UKSC 57 .... 2.6
Rutherford v. Seymour Pierce Ltd [2010] EWHC 375 (QB) 5.3

Safeway Stores Ltd v. Burrell [1997] IRLR 200, EAT 10.1
Sahota v. Home Office UKEAT/0342/09/LA 6.25
Salvation Army v. Dewsbury [1984] IRLR 222, EAT 4.2
Samuel Smith Ltd v. Marshall UKEAT/0488/09 .... 9.24
Sarkar v. West London Mental Health NHS Trust [2010] IRLR 508 .... 9.3
Sartor v. P & O European Ferries [1992] IRLR 271, CA 9.6
Savings & Investment Bank Ltd (in liquidation) v. Finken [2003] EWCA Civ
  1630 .... 15.17
SCA Packaging Ltd v. Boyle [2009] IRLR 746, HL 1.14
Scally v. Southern Health and Social Services Board [1992] 1 AC 294; [1991]
  IRLR 522, HL 1.1, 4.1
Schmidt v. Austicks Bookshops Ltd [1977] IRLR 360, EAT 8.16
Scotts Co (UK) Ltd v. Budd [2003] IRLR 256 .... 12.10
Sefton BC v. Wainwright UKEAT/0168/14/LA 10.6
Shah v. First West Yorkshire Ltd (Case No.1809311/2009) 6.17
Sindicato de Médicos de Asistencia Publica (SIMAP) v. Conselleria de Sanidad
  y Consumo de la Generalidad Valenciana (Case C-303/98) [2000] IRLR
  845 .... 4.11

Singh-Deu v. Chloride Metals Ltd [1976] IRLR 56, IT 6.11
Slater v. Leicestershire HA [1989] IRLR 16, CA 9.6
Smith v. Safeway plc [1996] IRLR 456, CA 8.16
Smiths Industries Aerospace & Defence Systems Ltd v. Brookes [1986] IRLR 434, EAT 6.23
Solectron Scotland Ltd v. Roper [2004] IRLR 4 .... 15.11
South East Sheffield Citizens Advice Bureau v. Grayson [2004] IRLR 353 .... 3.16
South West Trains Ltd v. Ireland, EAT/873/01 (unreported) 8.10
Southern Cross Healthcare Co Ltd v. Perkins [2010] EWCA Civ 1442 .... 1.4
Spring v. Guardian Assurance plc [1993] 2 All ER 273, CA; [1994] IRLR 460, HL 2.3, 12.13
State Trading Corp of India Ltd v. M Golodetz & Co Inc Ltd [1989] 2 Lloyd's Rep 277, CA 2.2
Stevenson v. Teesside Bridge and Engineering Ltd [1971] 1 All ER 296 .... 4.5
Stott v. Next Retail Ltd, ET/2100960/11 .... 8T
Stratford v. Auto Trail VR Ltd UKEAT/0116/16 .... 9.14
Stringer v. HM Revenue and Customs; Schultz-Hoff v. Deutsche Rentenversicherung Bund (Joined Cases C-520/06 and C-350/06) [2009] IRLR 214 .... 6.17
Stubbes v. Trower, Still & Keeling [1987] IRLR 321, CA 1.5
Sunrise Brokers LLP v. Michael William Rodgers [2014] EWHC 2633 (QB) 12.5
Surrey Police v. Marshall [2002] IRLR 843 .... 6.11
Sutherland v. Network Appliance Ltd [2001] IRLR 23 .... 15.2
Sybron Corp v. Rochem Ltd [1985] Ch 299; [1983] IRLR 253, CA 8.20

Talbot v. Elsbury (2011) HC (CDR) LR 2012, 19(5), 220 Law Review (CTLR 142) 13.2
Taylor v. OCS Group Ltd [2006] EWCA Civ 702 .... 13.7
Taymech v. Ryan 10.8
Teinaz v. Wandsworth LBC [2002] IRLR 721 .... 9.20
Thomas v. Farr plc [2007] EWCA Civ 118 .... 14.13
TNS UK Ltd v. Swainston UKEAT/0603/12 (unreported) 10.1
Toll v. GB Oils Ltd UKEAT/0569/12/LA 9.8
Tower Hamlets HA v. Anthony [1988] IRLR 331, EAT 9.24
Tullett Prebon Group Ltd v. Ghaleb El-Hajjali [2008] EWHC 1924, QB 2.2
Tullett Prebon plc v. BGC Brokers and 13 Defendants [2010] EWHC 484, QB 2.2

Underwood v. Wincanton plc UK EAT/0163/15 .... 11.9
United Bank v. Akhtar [1989] IRLR 507, EAT 4.5

Vaughan v. Lewisham LBC [2013] UKEAT/0534/12 .... 9.19
Victoria & Albert Museum v. Durrant [2011] IRLR 290 .... 7.3

Walls v. Sinet 60 TC 150 .... 3.4
Walton v. TAC Construction Materials Ltd [1981] IRLR 357, EAT 1.5
Warren v. Mendy [1989] 1 WLR 853; [1989] IRLR 210, CA 14.15
Watkins v. Crouch (t/a Temple Bird Solicitors) [2011] IRLR 382 .... 10.8
Weight Watchers (UK) Ltd v. Revenue & Customs Commissioners [2010] UKFTT 54 (TC) 3.4
West v. Kneels Ltd [1986] IRLR 430, EAT 12.2
Westlake v. ZSL London Zoo, ET/2201118/2015 .... 8T
Whitbread plc v. Mills [1988] IRLR 501 .... 6.6, 9.21
Wigan BC v. Davies [1979] IRLR 127, EAT 4.1
William Hill Organisation Ltd v. Tucker [1998] IRLR 313, CA 1.4, 4.1, 12.12

Williams v. Compair Maxam Ltd [1982] IRLR 83, EAT 10.2, 10.7, 10.8
Williamson v. Chief Constable of Greater Manchester Police
    UKEAT/0346/09 .... 9.19
Wilson v. St Helen's BC [1998] IRLR 706 .... 15.11
Wise (Dennis) v. Leicester City Football Club [2004] All ER (D) 134 .... 9.21
Wishart v. NACAB [1990] IRLR 393, CA 1.7
Witley & District Men's Club v. Mackay [2001] IRLR 595 .... 2.6
WM Computer Services Ltd v. Passmore (1988) EAT 721/86 .... 6.8
Woodroffe v. British Gas (1985), unreported, CA) 4.8
Wrexham Golf Club v. Ingham UKEAT/0190/12/RN 10.8

X v. European Commission (Case C-404/92P) [1995] IRLR 320, ECJ 1.5

Yizhen Li v. (1) First Marine Solutions Ltd (2) Dan Moutrey
    UKEATS/0045/13/BI 5.12, 12.5

Zaiwalla & Co v. Walia [2002] IRLR 697 .... 11.8

Table of statutes

Access to Medical Reports Act
1988 .... 6F, 6G, 6T
    s.2 .... 6.5

Anti-terrorism, Crime and
Security Act 2001 .... 13.14

Banking and Financial Dealings
Act 1971 .... 2.6

Bribery Act 2010 ...... 8.3, 8B, 8C, 8D, 8L
    s.9 .... 8.3

Care Standards Act 2000 .... 1F

Children and Families Act
2014 .... 7.6

Companies Act 1985 .... 5.6
    s.736 .... 3C

Companies Act 2006
    s.256 .... 3B

Computer Misuse Act 1990 .... 13I
    ss.1, 2 .... 13.11

Consumer Credit Act 1974
    s.8 .... 5.13

Contracts of Employment Act
1963 .... 2.5

Contracts of Employment Act
1972
    s.4 .... 1.12

Contracts (Rights of Third
Parties) Act 1999 .... 3K, 15D

Copyright, Designs and Patents
Act 1988 .... 13D(2)
    Part I, Chapter IV 3C, 15D

Criminal Justice Act 1967
    s.9 .... 9.6

Criminal Justice Act 1988 .... 8D

Criminal Justice Act 1993 .... 5.6
    Part V 8L

Data Protection Act 1998 ..... 1E, 1F, 2C,
3C, 3K, 6AE, 13.14,
13D(2), 13H, 13I,
15D
    s.1 .... 13.14
    s.2 .... 1.5, 1.11
    s.7 .... 13H
    Sched.1, Principle 2 .... 13.14
        Principles 3–5 .... 1.11, 13.14
    Scheds.11, 12 .... 13.14

Defamation Act 2013 .... 13.2
    s.1(1)(b), (c) 13.10
    s.5 .... 13.2, 13.10

Disability Discrimination Act
1995 .... 1.5, 6.12
    s.17A 15D

Employers' Liability
(Compulsory Insurance) Act
1969 .... 3.1

Employment Act 2002 .... 2J
    s.38(6) 2.5

Employment Relations Act
1999 .... 2J
    s.10 .... 9.8
    ss.11, 12 .... 15D
    s.13 .... 9.8
        (4) 9.10
            (a) 9.11

Employment Rights Act 1996 ..... 2J, 3.15
    Part I
        ss.1–13 .... 2.5
        s.1 .... 4.11
            (4)(f) 4.1
        s.3 .... 11.1
        s.4(3) 4.1
        s.11 .... 15D
            (1) 1.4
    Part II 15D
        ss.13–27 .... 3H, 5.12
        s.13 .... 11.5
            (1) 5.12
        ss.23 .... 15D

Employment Rights Act 1996 (contd)
  Part III
    s.34 .... 15D
  Part IVA 11.9
    s.43A 11.9, 14V
    s.43B 11.9
    s.47B 3.4
  Part V 15D
    s.48 .... 15D
  Part VI
    s.51 .... 15D
    s.54 .... 15D
    s.57 .... 15D
      B 15D
    s.60 .... 15D
    s.63 .... 15D
      C, 70, 80 .... 15D
  Part VII
    s.70 .... 15D
  Part VIII
    s.80 .... 15D
  Part VIII A
    s.80F 3.13
    s.80H 15D
  Part IX
    s.86 .... 1.4, 12.1
      (2) 12.1
      (3) 12.7, 12.11
      (4) 12.1
      (5) 3.8
      (6) 12.1
    s.87(4) 12.10
    ss.88–91 .... 12.10
    s.88(1)(b) 12.10
    s.92 .... 15D
      (4) 7.1
      (7) 1.13
    s.93 .... 15D
  Part X 15D
    s.95 .... 9.27
      (1)(c) 1.4
    s.97(1)(a) 12.4
      (2) 1.13
      (b) 12.6
    s.98 .... 4.11
      (1) 9.29
      (b) 7.3
      (2)(c) 10.1
      (4) 7.3, 9.14
    s.106(1) 7.3
      (2)(a) 7.3
    s.108 .... 12.2
    s.111 .... 15D
      (2)(a) 12.2
    s.111A 15.1, 15.17

      (4) 15.17
  Part XI
    s.135 .... 15D
    s.139 .... 10.1, 10.7
    s.163 .... 15D
  Part XIII
    s.203 .... 15.1, 15.5
      (2)(f) 15.5
      (3) 15.2, 15D
  Part XIV
    s.211 .... 4.2
    s.212(3)(c) 7.4
    s.224 .... 3.14
    s.230(3) 3.4

Employment Rights (Dispute
  Resolution) Act 1998
    Sched.1, Para.24(3) 15.8

Employment Tribunals Act
  1996
    s.3(2) 15.4
    s.18 .... 15.5, 15.9
      (1)(d) 15.5

Enterprise and Regulatory
  Reform Act 2013 .... 8.8, 11.9
    s.23 .... 15.1

Equal Pay Act 1970
    s.2 .... 15D

Equality Act 2010 .... 1.5, 1.8, 2.1, 2I, 5D,
                        6.11, 6.12, 6.23,
                        6.25, 6H, 6T, 6X,
                        6AF, 8.16, 11D,
                        15.5, 15D
    s.13 .... 8.19
    s.18 .... 10.5, 10.6
    s.19 .... 3.13
    s.27 .... 2.3, 9.30
    s.40 .... 8.8
    s.60 .... 1.5, 1.14, 6.24
      (3) 1.5
    s.77 .... 5.2, 9.30
    s.109(4) 11.6
    ss.120, 127 .... 15D
    s.147(3)(c), (d) 15D
    Sched.1 .... 6.24
    Sched.9, para.1 .... 1.5

Financial Services Act 1986 .... 2.3

Foreign Corrupt Practices Act
  1977 (USA) 8.3, 8L

Fraud Act 2006 .... 8.22
    s.2 .... 6.27

TABLE OF STATUTES

Health and Safety at Work etc
  Act 1974 .... 9.6, 11D

Human Rights Act 1998 .... 3.10, 3H, 6.9,
                  6AE, 13D(2), 15D
  Sched.1 .... 13.12

Immigration, Asylum and
  Nationality Act 2006 .... 2D, 4.9
    ss.15–25 .... 2.1

Income Tax (Earnings and
  Pensions) Act 2003
    ss.225, 226 .... 15.15
    s.271 .... 5.14
    s.272(1)(a), (c) 5.14
    ss.310, 311 .... 15.15
    ss.393–399, 401 .... 15.12

Legal Aid, Sentencing and
  Punishment of Offenders Act
  2012 .... 1.5

Limited Liabilities Partnerships
  Act 2000
    s.4(4) 3.4

Misrepresentation Act 1967
    s.2(1) 1.12

Misuse of Drugs Act 1971
    s.28 .... 8H

Modern Slavery Act 2015 .... 8.2
    s.54 .... 8A

National Minimum Wage Act
  1998 .... 15D
    ss.11, 18, 19D, 24 .... 15D
    s.49 .... 15.5
      (4) 15D

Offences against the Person Act
  1861 .... 11.8

Official Secrets Act 1989 .... 4S, 8D

Patents Act 1977 .... 14.23
    ss.39–42 .... 14U
    s.39(1)(b) 14U
    s.40 .... 5U

Pension Schemes Act 1993 .... 2J

Pensions Act 2008
    Part 1 .... 2J
    s.56 .... 15D

Pensions Act 2014 .... 15D

Police and Criminal Evidence
  Act 1984 .... 9.6, 9.22

Private Security Industry Act
  200 .... 6.27

Protection from Harassment Act
  1997 .... 11.8, 15D
    s.2 .... 11.8
    s.4 .... 11F

Public Order Act 1986 .... 11F

Public Interest Disclosure Act
  1998 .... 11.9, 11G, 15D

Race Relations Act 1976
    s.54 .... 15D

Regulation of Investigatory
  Powers Act 2000 .... 13.3, 13D(2)
    Part I
      s.1(3) 13.3
    Part II 13.12
      s.29(5) 13.9
    Part IV
      s.71 .... 13.12

Rehabilitation of Offenders Act
  1974 .... 1.5, 1B, 1F, 3E

Sex Discrimination Act 1975 ...... 7.3, 8.8
    s.1(1)(b)(i) 4.5
    s.3A(3)(a)(i)–(iii) 6.25
    s.41(1), (2) 11.6
    s.63 .... 15D

Sexual Offences (Amendment)
  Act 2002 .... 8P

Sunday Trading Act 1994 .... 4.11
    Sched.4 .... 4.11

Theft Act 1968
    s.16 .... 8.22

Trade Union and Labour
  Relations (Consolidation) Act
  1992
    ss.68A, 87, 137, 145A, 145B, 146,
      168, 168A, 169, 170, 174 .....
                                      15D
    s.188 .... 10.7, 10B, 15D
    ss.190, 192 .... 15D
    s.195(1) 10.7
    s.236 .... 14.3
    s.288(2A) 15.5
      (2B) 15D

Unfair Contract Terms Act
  1977 .... 1.1
    s.2(1) 15.12
    s.3 .... 1.1, 5.3
    (2)(b) 5.5
Work and Families Act 2006
    s.2 .... 7.2

Table of statutory instruments

Additional Paternity Leave Regulations 2010, SI 2010/1055 .... 7F
Additional Statutory Paternity Pay (General) Regulations 2010, SI
   2010/1056 .... 7F
Agency Workers Regulations 2010, SI 2010/93 .... 3.2
      regs.5, 12, 13 .... 15D
      reg.17(2) 15D
Companies (Cross-Border Mergers) Regulations 2007, SI 2007/2974
      regs.45, 51 .... 15D
Employment Equality (Age) Regulations 2006, SI 2006/1031
      reg.36 .... 15D
      Sched.5, Part 1, para.2(2) 15D
      Sched.6, paras.11, 12 .... 15D
Employment Equality (Religion or Belief) Regulations 2003, SI 2003/1660 .... 4.11, 15D
      reg.3(1)(b)(i) 4.11
      reg.28 .... 15D
      Sched.4, Part 1, para.2(2) 15D
Employment Equality (Sexual Orientation) Regulations 2003, SI 2003/1661 .... 8.16
      reg.28 .... 15D
      Sched.4, Part 1, para.2(2) 15D
Employment Protection (Part-time Employees) Regulations 1995, SI
   1995/31 .... 3.13
Employment Relations Act 1999 (Blacklists) Regulations 2010, SI 2010/493
      regs.5, 6, 9 .... 15D
Enterprise Act 2016 (Commencement No.2) Regulations 2017, SI 2017/70 .... 15.6
Equality Act 2010 (Gender Pay Gap Information) Regulations 2017, SI
   2017/172 .... 11.7
Exclusivity Terms in Zero Hours Contracts (Redress) Regulations 2015, SI
   2015/2021 .... 3.14
Fixed-term Employees (Prevention of Less Favourable Treatment) Regulations
   2002, SI 2002/2034 .... 15D
      regs.7, 10 .... 15D
      Sched.2, para.2(a) 15.5
          3(17) 15.5
Flexible Working (Procedural Requirements) Regulations 2002, SI
   2002/3207 .... 3.13, 7.1
Health and Safety (Display Screen Equipment) Regulations 1992, SI
   1992/2792 .... 4.12
Immigration (Restrictions on Employment) Order 2007, SI 2007/3290 .... 4.9

Income Tax (Pay As You Earn) (Amendment No.2) Regulations 2015, SI
2015/171 .... 3.5

Industrial Tribunals Extension of Jurisdiction (England and Wales) Order
1994, SI 1994/1623
    art.3 .... 15.4

Information and Consultation of Employees Regulations 2004, SI
2004/3426 .... 10.4
    regs.27, 29, 32, 33 .... 15D
    reg.40(4) 15D

Maternity and Parental Leave etc (Amendment) Regulations 2014, SI
2014/3221 .... 7.1, 7.5

Maternity and Parental Leave etc Regulations 1999, SI 1999/3312 .... 15D
    reg.10 .... 10.4, 10.5, 10.6
    reg.15 .... 7.5

Occupational and Personal Pension Schemes (Consultation by Employers and
Miscellaneous Amendment) Regulations 2006, SI 2006/349 .... 15D
    Sched., paras.4, 8, 13 .... 15D

Part-time Workers (Prevention of Less Favourable Treatment) Regulations
2000, SI 2000/1551 .... 3.13, 15D
    reg.7 .... 15.5
    regs.8, 9 .... 15D

Regulation of Investigatory Powers (Covert Surveillance: Code of Practice)
Order 2002, SI 2002/1933 .... 13.9

Regulation of Investigatory Powers (Source Records) Regulations 2000, SI
2000/2725 .... 13.9

Rehabilitation of Offenders Act 1974 (Exceptions) Order 1975, SI
1975/1023 .... 1F

Shared Parental Leave Regulations 2014, SI 2014/3050 .... 7.1, 15D

Smoke-free (Premises and Enforcement) Regulations 2006, SI 2006/3368 .... 6.20

Statutory Maternity Pay, Social Security (Maternity Allowance) and Social
Security (Overlapping Benefits) (Amendment) Regulations 2006, SI
2006/2379
    reg.3 .... 7.2

Statutory Paternity Pay and Statutory Adoption Pay (General) and the
Statutory Paternity Pay and Statutory Adoption Pay (Weekly Rates)
(Amendment) Regulations 2006, SI 2006/2236
    reg.4 .... 7.2

Statutory Sick Pay (General) Regulations 1982, SI 1982/894
    reg.2 .... 6.3

Telecommunications (Lawful Business Practice) (Interception of
Communications) Regulations 2000, SI 2000/2699 .... 13.3, 13.12, 13D(2)
    reg.3(1)(a)(i)(aa), (bb), (cc) 13.4
        (iv), (v) 13.4
        (2)(c) 13.5

Transfer of Undertakings (Protection of Employment) Regulations 1981, SI
1981/1794 .... 3.15, 5F(ii), 15.11

reg.12	15.11
Transfer of Undertakings (Protection of Employment) Regulations 2006, SI 2006/246	13.14, 13H, 14V, 15D
reg.4	15.11
regs.13–15, 18	15D
Transnational Information and Consultation of Employees Regulations 1999, SI 1999/3323	15D
reg.41(4)	15D
regs.27, 32	15D
Working Time Regulations 1998, SI 1998/1833	2.4, 2.6, 2J, 3.9, 3.13, 3B, 3H, 3I, 4.4, 4N–R, 6.16, 6S, 15D
reg.4(1)	4.11, 4N
reg.13	2.6
(9)	6.17
reg.14	2.6
reg.16	5.5
reg.18	4.11
reg.20	4.11, 4P
reg.21	4.11
reg.30	15D
reg.35(2)	15.5
(3)	15D

Table of international legislation

Directive 76/207/EEC of 9 February 1976 on the implementation of the principle of equal treatment for men and women as regards access to employment, vocational training and promotion, and working conditions
Arts.3–5 .... 8.19
Directive 93/104/EC of 4 November 2003 concerning certain aspects of the organisation of working time ('Working Time Directive') 4L, 6.17, 6S
Art.2(1) 4.11
Art.7 .... 2.6, 5.3
(1) 5
Directive 2000/78/EC of 27 November 2000 establishing a general framework for equal treatment in employment and occupation ('Equal Treatment Framework Directive') 3.16
Directive 2016/943 of 8 June 2016 on the protection of undisclosed know-how and business information (trade secrets) against their unlawful acquisition, use and disclosure ('Trade Secrets Directive') 14.9
Art.2 .... 14.9
European Convention on Human Rights (Convention for the Protection of Human Rights and Fundamental Freedoms 1950 (ECHR)) 8.16, 13.12
Art.6 .... 9.9
Art.8 .... 3.10, 3H, 4.14, 6.9, 6.27, 8.18, 13.12
Art.9 .... 4.11
Regulation (EU) 2016/678 of 27 April 2016 on the protection of natural persons with regard to the processing of personal data and on the free movement of such data, and repealing Directive 95/46/EC ('General Data Protection Regulation') 2C, 13.14

Abbreviations

ABPI	Association of the British Pharmaceutical Industry
ACAS	Advisory, Conciliation and Arbitration Service
ADR	alternative dispute resolution
AML	additional maternity leave
AMRA	Access to Medical Reports Act 1988
APL	additional paternity leave
ASPP	additional statutory paternity pay
ATCSA	Anti-terrorism, Crime and Security Act 2001
BEIS	Department for Business, Energy & Industrial Strategy
BIS	Department for Business, Innovation and Skills (now BEIS)
CAB	Citizens' Advice Bureau
CIPD	Chartered Institute of Personnel and Development
CJA	Criminal Justice Act 1988
CPR	Civil Procedure Rules
CSP	Communications Service Providers
DBS	Disclosure and Barring Service
DPA	Data Protection Act 1998
DRIPA	Data Retention and Investigatory Powers Act 2014
DWP	Department for Work and Pensions
EAT	Employment Appeal Tribunal
ECHR	European Court of Human Rights
ECJ	Court of Justice of the European Union
EEA	European Economic Area
EHRC	Equality and Human Rights Commission
ERA	Employment Rights Act 1996
ERRA	Enterprise and Regulatory Reform Act 2013
EWC	expected week of childbirth

FBP	Fair Blame Policy
FCA	Financial Conduct Authority
GDPR	General Data Protection Regulation
GMC	General Medical Council
HCA	Housing and Communities Agency
HMRC	Her Majesty's Revenue and Customs
HR	human resources
HSE	Health and Safety Executive
IANA	Immigration, Asylum and Nationality Act 1996
IPR	improved performance review
IRD	intended retirement date
ISP	Internet Service Provider
IVF	in vitro fertilisation
KIT	keeping in touch
LIFO	last in, first out
MA	maternity allowance
MPL	Maternity and Parental Leave etc. Regulations 1999, SI 1999/3312
NHS	National Health Service
NICs	National Insurance Contributions
OHP	occupational health physician
OML	ordinary maternity leave
OTC	over the counter
P&L	profit & loss
PACE	Police and Criminal Evidence Act 1984
PAYE	Pay As You Earn
PCP	provision, criterion or practice
PHI	permanent health insurance
PILON	payment in lieu of notice
PIP	performance improvement plan
PSV	passenger service vehicle
RIPA	Regulation of Investigatory Powers Act 2000
ROA	Rehabilitation of Offenders Act 1974

RoSPA	The Royal Society for the Prevention of Accidents
SAL	statutory adoption leave/standard acknowledgement letter
SML	statutory maternity leave
SMP	statutory maternity pay
SOSR	some other substantial reason for dismissal
SPP	statutory paternity pay
SRA	Solicitors Regulation Authority
SRN	State Registered Nurse
SSP	statutory sick pay
TOIL	time off in lieu
TULR(C)A	Trade Union and Labour Relations (Consolidation) Act 1992
TUPE	Transfer of Undertakings (Protection of Employment) Regulations 1981, SI 1981/1994
UCTA	Unfair Contract Terms Act 1977

1

The start of the employment relationship and making the offer

1.1 Drafting contracts

Often the most junior of HR staff are tasked with drafting and sending out offer letters and contracts. I have often wondered why. The words of the offer letter and contract are vital. They must be accurate and clear and say what they mean.

Drafting offer letters and contracts is not an art but a science. It is knowing what you want to say, knowing what you need to say, and then saying it.

It is most important in drafting contractual documents to use clear, intelligible and unambiguous language, reflecting what the terms are in plain language and anticipating the scope and extent of a particular term and how it might be interpreted by the other party.

The *contra proferentem* rule operates where there is doubt about the meaning of the contract. The words will be construed against the party who drafted them, i.e. the employer.

So, for example, if business has to be placed and revenues earned by a particular date to trigger a commission payment and if, for a reason through no fault of the employee, they do not reach the target by that date, there will be no entitlement to that commission. This will be the case even where the product or service was not physically available to sell and therefore the business cannot be done by the date specified. It will be vital for an additional clause to be added to the commission payments clause, to allow for a future date to be fixed by which the business must be placed. If there is no such caveat, the commission will be lost no matter whose fault it was.

The identity of the employer

Whilst this may seem an obvious point, there are some cases where the identity of the employer is unclear, disputed or simply wrong on the face of the contract (or, more commonly, the pleadings in an Employment Tribunal claim).

The identity of the employer is essentially an issue of fact.

The question of whether an employee is employed by A or B is a question of law but the resolution of that issue depends upon the construction of all the relevant contractual documents and the finding and evaluation of the relevant facts, and this is the task of the Employment Tribunal (*Clifford* v. *Union of Democratic Mineworkers* [1991] IRLR 518).

In *Clifford*, the Court of Appeal held that the tribunal was entitled to find that the appellant was originally employed by the Nottingham Area of the National Union of Mineworkers (NUM) rather than by the NUM itself. The tribunal had treated the factor of control as the dominant one in this case. In circumstances which lack clarity, 'control' is an important factor because it demonstrates the reality of a relationship.

Informing employee of onerous or other terms

A traditional view was that however onerous a term is for an employee, once they have signed the contract, that term will apply and the employee has no right to have that term explained.

In *Peninsula Business Services Ltd* v. *Sweeney* [2004] IRLR 49, the Employment Appeal Tribunal (EAT) held that as a matter of law, once an employee signs a contract, that contract becomes legally binding and the principle that the onerous term must have been brought to the employee's notice does not apply.

The EAT held that (para 23):

> It would make for wholly unacceptable commercial uncertainty if it were open to B, who has signed a written agreement, to say that he was not bound by one of the terms expressly contained in it because A had not first drawn his attention expressly to it. By signing, B is treated as having agreed to that term (and all the others), however onerous it may be and whether he has read it or not.

This is however a very traditional, legal analysis, and another division of the EAT could have taken a different view as to whether an employee is bound by any term in an agreement, however unreasonable, so long as the employee has signed the contract.

A term in a contract of employment which is unduly onerous is also potentially challengeable under the Unfair Contract Terms Act (UCTA) 1977. In the *Sweeney* case (above) the term was found by the Employment Tribunal to offend UCTA because of its 'penal and confiscatory nature'. However, on appeal, the EAT decided that the clause did not fall within UCTA because it was not a term claiming to entitle the employers to render a contractual performance substantially different from that which was reasonably expected of them. Once the job applicant had signed the commission document, according to the EAT, he could have had no expectation of being paid post-termination commission. There was therefore no question of reasonableness.

No duty to advise staff of the consequences of the terms

The courts have drawn a clear line between drawing a term to the employee's attention and advising the employee of its meaning and consequences.

In *Crossley* v. *Faithful & Gould Holdings Ltd* [2004] EWCA Civ 293 the Court of Appeal confirmed the High Court's approach that there was no implied term in a contract of employment imposing an obligation on the employers which required them to alert an employee to the effect that resigning would have on his entitlement to benefits under a long-term disability insurance scheme.

The court held that there is no standardised implied term in all contracts of employment that the employer will take reasonable care of employees' economic well-being. Lord Justice Dyson held (para.43):

> [The implied term proposed] would impose an unfair and unreasonable burden on employers. It is one thing to say that, if an employer assumes the responsibility for giving financial advice to his employee, he is under a duty to take reasonable care in the giving of that advice ... It is quite a different matter to impose on an employer the duty to give his employee financial advice in relation to benefits accruing from his employment, or generally to safeguard the employee's economic well-being.

Limited duty and specific duty to advise employees

Contrast a different approach in *Scally* v. *Southern Health and Social Services Board* [1991] IRLR 522. Here the House of Lords held that there is a contractual obligation on the employers to take reasonable steps to bring the existence of the term to the employee's attention where three specific conditions pertain:

(a) where the terms of the contract have not been negotiated with the individual employee, e.g. they have been negotiated under a collective agreement;
(b) a particular term of the contract provides a valuable benefit to the employee contingent upon action being taken by them to avail themselves of its benefit; and
(c) the employee cannot reasonably be expected to be aware of the term unless it is drawn to their attention.

In this case the term involved the right of the plaintiff doctors to enhance their pension entitlement by the purchase of added years.

In such circumstances there is a clear duty on employers to inform employees of changes to their terms and conditions, not just in relation to pension rights.

Employers should inform employees of any changes to their contractual rights or obligations resulting from relevant collective agreements and should do so in such a manner that there can be no doubt that the term was drawn to the employee's attention, i.e. not just by way of advising the employee to read about it on the company intranet. A favoured approach is to hand to each employee a copy of the changes with an explanation, and to ask employees to sign and date a receipt stating that their manager has explained the terms and changes to them.

Although the obligation set out by the House of Lords in *Scally* refers only to a 'benefit' to the employee, the same principle is likely to impose an obligation on employers to draw an employee's attention to any contractual terms which might operate as a 'detriment', such as changes to disciplinary rules or qualifying periods to become eligible for sick pay, etc.

Unfair Contract Terms Act 1977

UCTA 1977 has featured in several important employment cases involving contracts of employment. However, in England and Wales, the Court of Appeal has put a nail in the coffin in respect of any applicability of UCTA as a potential remedy for an unreasonable term in a contract of employment.

It was *Commerzbank AG v. Keen* [2006] EWCA Civ 1536 which tolled the death knell for employees seeking to use UCTA (see *Brigden v. American Express Bank* [2000] IRLR 94). The bonus clause in Mr Keen's contract read (para.7):

> You are eligible to participate in the [Bank's] discretionary bonus scheme. The decision as to whether or not to award a bonus, the amount of any award and the timing and form of the award are at the discretion of the [Bank]. Factors which may be taken into account by the [Bank] in deciding whether or not to award a bonus and the amount of any bonus include
>
> - The performance of the [Bank]
> - The performance of your business area
> - Your individual performance and your contribution to the [Bank's] performance and the performance of your business area
> - The strategic objectives of the [Bank]
> - Whether you will be remaining in the employment of the [Bank]
>
> No bonus will be paid to you if on the date of payment of the bonus you are not employed by the [Bank] or if you are under notice to leave the [Bank's] employment whether such notice was given or received by you.
>
> Bonus may be reduced for any period of absence in excess of one month whether through illness, maternity leave or any other reason other than absence on holiday.

Mr Keen was awarded bonuses of almost €3 million for the years 2003 and 2004. This was less than the recommendation of his line manager. In June 2005, the particular desk where he worked was closed down and Mr Keen was made redundant. Accordingly, he was not awarded any bonus for the year 2005, as he was not employed by the bank at the payment date of the bonus for that year in March 2006.

Mr Keen brought proceedings for damages for breach of contract in respect of under-payment of the discretionary bonuses for 2003 and 2004, and in respect of non-payment of a discretionary bonus for 2005.

In respect of the bonuses for 2003 and 2004, he claimed that no reasonable employer would have exercised its discretion under the bonus scheme in the way the bank did as regards the size of the bonus pool for those years and that this was a breach of the implied term that the bank would not exercise any discretion it had in relation to his bonus award irrationally or perversely.

In respect of the bonus for 2005, Mr Keen contended that the contractual provision on which the employers relied was caught by UCTA, s.3, as a result of which the employers were not entitled to treat him as ineligible. Section 3 'applies as between contracting parties where one of them deals as consumer or on the other's written standard terms of business'.

The Court of Appeal rejected his arguments. It held that an employee is not dealing with their employer 'as consumer' in contracting with it in respect of pay for work. Nor does an employee deal with their employer on its 'written standard terms of business', the business in this case being banking. Mr Keen unsuccessfully challenged the calculation of his bonus.

1.2 In the beginning...

It is still the case, even though nowadays uncommon, for some employers to either fail to put terms and conditions in writing at all or fail to update them (so that the only written statement is one that was issued many years ago when the individual first started work).

Mummery LJ in *Dacas* v. *Brook Street Bureau Ltd* [2004] IRLR 358 said:

> In the field of employment it is not uncommon to find that a contract of employment has come into being through the conduct of the parties without a word being put in writing or even, on occasion, spoken. In particular, conduct which might not have manifested such a mutual intention had it lasted only a brief time may become unequivocal if it is maintained over weeks or months. Once the intention to enter into an employment relationship is so expressed, the common law will imply a variety of terms into it and simultaneously will spell vicarious liability out of it; and statute will add a series of other rights and obligations.

A contract can be as simple as you like. In the early days of employment, they were very simple (and according to Mummery LJ, some still are).

In an early reported decision, when Mr Ferguson came with four other Irishmen, already working for the defendants, and one of his friends asked if he could 'come along', the employer said 'he could start on Monday and that was it. But I did inform him there were no cards; we were purely working as a lump labour force' (*Ferguson* v. *John Dawson & Partners (Contractors) Ltd* [1976] IRLR 346). This was held to be a legally binding contract of employment (of service) as opposed to a contract for services (working on a self-employed basis).

In such a case it is left to the court to determine the nature of the employment relationship and it will look at the reality of the relationship. The intention of the parties is only one relevant factor (p.346):

> Whilst the expression of the parties' intention may be a relevant factor, it is not a conclusive factor in deciding what is the true nature of the contract. Where there is no written contract, the Court is entitled to find contractual terms by implication. On the facts of the present case, the judge below had correctly found that, according to the established tests, in reality the relationship of employer and employee existed and the concept of 'the lump' was no more than a device which each side regarded as being capable of being put to his own advantage.

1.3 Collateral contract: to employ

A contract must consist of an offer, acceptance, consideration, an intention to be legally bound and the terms must be certain. The contract need not be in writing to be legally binding and fully enforceable. The evidential burden is much greater if there is no documentary evidence of what has been agreed.

Similarly the consideration does not have to be wages. It can be a 'promise for a promise' – a promise of employment in consideration for the promise of supplying the job applicant's services (this amounts to a contract to employ).

In *Gill* v. *Cape Contracts Ltd* [1985] IRLR 499, an unconditional offer of employment was made to Mr Gill and his colleagues who had been working at Harland & Woolf in Northern Ireland, to come to work at Sullum Voe on a six-month fixed-term contract. The offer was accepted and Mr Gill and his colleagues resigned from their jobs in Northern Ireland. The offer was subsequently withdrawn when industrial action was threatened by workers in Scotland.

The withdrawal of the offer was deemed by the court to be a breach of contract – the contract to employ, a collateral contract. This collateral contract was supported by consideration: the plaintiffs agreed to terminate their employment in Northern Ireland upon the representation that they would be employed for a six-month period on considerably higher wages than they were earning in Northern Ireland.

The High Court (Northern Ireland) held that:

> In the present case representations were made by the defendants which they intended the plaintiffs to act upon and which the plaintiffs did act upon. Those representations formed a collateral contract to the contract of employment that in consideration of their terminating their existing contracts of employment, the Defendants would provide the plaintiffs with employment for a period of six months... The argument on behalf of the Defendants that there was never a binding contract ignored the realities of the situation.

In giving such assurances (the plaintiffs were assured of six months' employment) the defendants were intending the plaintiffs to act upon them. Those assurances constituted a warranty and the failure to honour them gave rise to a claim.

Damages were awarded not on the basis of the notice period provided for under the contract of employment (which was two hours' notice in the first four weeks) but for the entire contract, subject to the duty to mitigate and on the basis of a wage discounted from the wage offered of £358.75 per week (which had taken into account having to work in harsh conditions, which now did not apply). The sum of £2,500 damages was awarded to each of the plaintiffs.

1.4 Express and implied terms

There are terms of a contract which are not put in writing yet which apply with equal force. These are implied terms, which 'the law gives away for free'. They are unspoken and unwritten yet they dominate the employment relationship.

The most common implied term is that of mutual trust and confidence, i.e. that neither the employer nor the employee will do anything that is likely to or which does break the mutual trust and confidence which is so essential to the employment relationship.

This implied term is the most common term relied upon by employees when claiming constructive dismissal pursuant to s.95(1)(c) of the Employment Rights Act 1996. It is the employer's unreasonable 'conduct' under this heading that many employees rely upon to demonstrate that their employer no longer intends to be bound by the terms of the contract. As the EAT held in *Courtaulds Northern Textiles Ltd* v. *Andrew* [1979] IRLR 84, the employer must not conduct itself 'in a manner calculated or likely to damage the relationship of trust and confidence between the parties'.

When employers assert they have dismissed for breach of the term of trust and confidence, Employment Tribunals are naturally suspicious since it is a catch-all allowing an employer to dismiss for practically anything.

In *Leach* v. *Office of Communications (OFCOM)* [2012] IRLR 839 the Court of Appeal approved the comments made by the EAT regarding the use of 'loss of trust and confidence' as an 'automatic solvent of obligations' in employment litigation.

The Court of Appeal held that it is not a 'convenient label to stick on any situation', i.e. it is not a panacea for any occasion where there is no conduct reason for dismissal. The Employment Tribunal has to examine 'all the relevant circumstances in the particular case' to decide if there is in fact any reason for dismissal and, if so, whether it is a substantial enough reason to justify dismissal.

Examples of other implied terms are the implied term that the employer will generally pay wages (but not necessarily provide work) and that the employee will serve the employer faithfully, i.e. the implied term of fidelity.

There are exceptions to the rule that the employer has no obligation to provide the work, only the pay. For example, where doing the work is absolutely necessary to the exercise of the skill required, such as an airline pilot, or where the work is essential in order to earn commission, such as sales representatives (see *William Hill Organisation Ltd* v. *Tucker* [1998] IRLR 313 where, in the absence of an express garden leave clause, the employer was found to be in breach of the duty to provide work by placing a senior dealer working in spread betting on garden leave, even though he suffered no financial loss as a result), or where the work is essential to the reputation of the individual, such as in the performing arts.

The legal tests for implied terms

A term will only be implied into an employment contract if a court decides that the aim of the parties at the time the contract was entered into must have been that the clause be included. One of the below tests must be satisfied in order to fulfil this criterion.

- *Business efficacy*: where a term is necessary to give a contract business

efficacy (e.g. a term requiring a sales manager supplied with a company car to hold a current driver's licence).
- *Custom and practice*: where it is the normal custom and practice to include a particular term in such contracts such that it is 'reasonable, notorious and certain' that it will be followed and there is a sense of legal obligation to do so (e.g. a term entitling employees to payment of a bonus which has been paid every year for many years and which is well known to employees).
- *Officious bystander*: the proposed term is so obvious that it would go without saying that, had an officious bystander suggested to the parties that it be included in the contract, it would have been readily agreed without contention. If the parties would instantly retort that such a term is 'of course' already mutually part of the agreement then it is apt for implication (e.g. a term that an employer will not, without good reason, dismiss an employee if this would prevent him or her from benefiting from a permanent health insurance scheme).
- *Conduct after the contract is made*: the way in which the contract has been carried out demonstrates an intention to include the term (e.g. a term allowing an employer to demote an employee, where that employee has been demoted in similar circumstances previously and has not suggested that the employer had no right to do so).
- *Characteristic terms*: these are implied by law because they are a necessary part of a particular type of contract (e.g. a term that an employee will service their employer with good faith and fidelity).
- *Terms implied by statute* (e.g. a term setting out a minimum notice period on termination of employment).

The relationship between express and implied terms

In general, an implied term cannot override an express contractual term. In some cases, however, the courts have implied a term which does so, for example:

- an implied term that restricts or qualifies an express term giving an employer a particular discretion (e.g. a discretion to award a bonus based on individual performance must not be exercised perversely or irrationally);
- an implied term that relates to something that the parties must have overlooked when drafting the contract (e.g. the implied clause mentioned above which prevents dismissal without cause of an employee benefiting under a permanent health insurance scheme).

An express 'entire agreement' clause (stating that the express contract sets out all the terms agreed between the parties) may stop other terms being implied into the contract. This will only apply to terms that would otherwise be implied by custom and practice.

Where a term is implied by statute, the statute will usually state explicitly that the prescribed term will override any conflicting express term. For example, even if an employment contract states that an employee will be entitled to one month's notice regardless of his or her length of employment, s.86 of the Employment Rights Act 1996 provides that this contract will be varied once he or she has five years' service, to give him or her a week's notice per year of service (capped at 12 weeks).

Where there are no terms in the contract

In some cases the Employment Tribunals will construct a term into the contract where the contract is silent – but they are very cautious about doing so. It is very rare nowadays that employers will omit essential terms of the contract such as sick pay, but if they do the Employment Tribunals may imply a term.

In relation to the payment of sick pay the Employment Tribunals may be prepared to imply a term that full pay will be paid where this has been paid in the past, i.e. the Employment Tribunal will look at the employer's past practice (*Mears* v. *Safecar Security Ltd* [1982] IRLR 183 (CA)).

In such cases they have held that full sick pay should be paid for a 'reasonable period of time' (*Howman & Son* v. *Blyth* [1983] ICR 416).

In *Southern Cross Healthcare Co Ltd* v. *Perkin* [2010] EWCA Civ 1442, the Court of Appeal said that although tribunals had jurisdiction in relation to some issues concerning written statements of particulars, they could not construe (interpret) contractual terms if the disputed term was not clear.

Maurice Kay LJ held that s.11(1) provides that the tribunal may determine 'what particulars ought to have been included' but this was not 'an invitation to judicial creativity, even under the rubric of "construction"'.

He held that the alternative would 'open the door to a multitude of cases advanced on a contractual basis in a manner totally at variance with the consistent reluctance to enlarge the breach of contract jurisdiction of Employment Tribunals to embrace workplace disputes during the currency of employment'.

1.5   Conditional offers/pre-offers

In order to avoid making an offer of employment that the job candidate can accept unconditionally, the employer can choose to:

- make an invitation to treat, i.e. make a pre-offer to the job applicant (see **Precedent 1A**); or
- make a conditional offer which cannot be accepted until the conditions have been met (see **Precedents 1B, 1D** and **1E**).

Pre-conditions for offer of employment or continued employment

These pre-conditions that must be satisfied can range from:

(a) references which satisfy the prospective employer, including a reference from a number of previous employers, one being the current employer;
(b) creditworthiness;
(c) meeting the medical standards of fitness;
(d) proof of academic and professional qualifications and experience;
(e) proof of eligibility to work in the UK, e.g. a work permit (see **Chapter 4** for further discussion of work permits);
(f) the passing of certain professional examinations;
(g) criminal records check (Disclosure and Barring Service (DBS) check);
(h) proof of full valid UK driving licence.

In this way the employer can ensure that all the preconditions of employment are met and that the second candidate on the list can be approached if the first candidate decides that they are not interested in the job.

Background checks

For some employers it is essential that they conduct background checks on prospective employees. See **Precedent 1C** for a typical permission form.

Medical examinations

If a medical examination is to be conducted prior to the offer of employment or as a condition of acceptance of the offer, it is essential that informed consent is obtained from the job candidate to any tests that are to be undertaken and for the disclosure of the report to the potential employer or their medical representative. In other words, the individual must not be misled or kept in the dark about the nature of the tests to be performed. If blood tests are to be undertaken then the purpose for which the blood has been taken must be spelt out (*X* v. *European Commission* [1995] IRLR 320). In this case a blood test was taken for the purposes of testing for the AIDS virus but that was unknown by the job applicant.

The Information Commissioner has provided clear and unambiguous guidance in Part 4 of the Data Protection Code of Practice about informed consent, especially in light of the requirement to obtain 'express consent', i.e. written informed consent of an individual, before obtaining medical information, i.e. sensitive data under the Data Protection Act 1998, s.2.

Dealing with medical conditions at interview

Several cases prior to the former Disability Discrimination Act 1995 (now the Equality Act 2010) held that if a prospective employee lied about a material health condition, then this would give the employer 'some other substantial reason' for dismissal when this lie was discovered (*O'Brien* v. *Prudential Assurance Co. Ltd* [1979] IRLR 140 and *Walton* v. *TAC Construction Materials*

Ltd [1981] IRLR 357). In *Walton* it was held that, in the normal case, not volunteering medical information was not lying, other than in response to a direct question.

Under the Equality Act 2010 employers could be guilty of disability discrimination if they dismissed an employee for failing to disclose a material medical condition unless this was a material non-disclosure.

There is a distinction between dismissing because the employee had the medical condition and dismissing for lying about a material matter such as a relevant and material medical condition. In the latter case this could constitute some other substantial reason for dismissal but in such a case the employer would have to be able to argue that this deception by itself was so material and significant that it destroyed the trust and confidence between the employer and employee. Any suggestion that had the employer known about the disability they would not have employed the individual could raise the spectre of disability discrimination.

Under the Equality Act 2010, employers must of course be aware of their obligations not to discriminate. This means being even more careful not to ask candidates about their health record.

Section 60 of the Equality Act 2010, under the heading 'Recruitment' and by-line 'Enquiries about disability and health', prohibits employers from asking about a job applicant's health (including any disability) before offering them work or, where the employer is not in a position to offer work immediately, before including the applicant in a pool of persons to whom the employer intends to offer work in the future.

Section 60 'Recruitment' states:

Enquiries about disability and health

(1) A person (A) to whom an application for work is made must not ask about the health of the applicant (B) –

    (a) before offering work to B, or
    (b) where A is not in a position to offer work to B, before including B in a pool of applicants from whom A intends (when in a position to do so) to select a person to whom to offer work.

Once a job offer has been made, questions about health may be asked in order to make reasonable adjustments if necessary and to assess whether the health condition would render that person unsuitable for that position where there are no reasonable adjustments that can be made.

Section 60(3) makes it clear that the mere asking of questions about health and disabilities at interview is not itself unlawful but the use to which that information may be put may be unlawful.

Section 60(3) states:

A does not contravene a relevant disability provision merely by asking about B's health; but A's conduct in reliance on information given in response may be a contravention of a relevant disability provision.

Health questions in general should be removed from application forms and all recruiting managers should be made aware of this change.

So, it is *not* discriminatory to ask about a job applicant's health at the interview, but if that person is rejected for the job any reliance on information given in response may lead a tribunal to conclude that the employer has committed a discriminatory act. In these circumstances, the burden of proof will shift to the employer to show that no discrimination took place.

This is not quite a blanket ban on pre-employment health enquiries.

Note: s.60 does not apply to questions that are necessary to establish whether the job applicant will be able to comply with a requirement to undergo an assessment (such as an interview or selection test); whether a duty to make reasonable adjustments will arise in connection with any such assessment; or whether the applicant will be able to carry out a function that is *essential* to the work concerned, e.g. working at heights or in confined spaces.

This provision, despite being headed 'Recruitment', would also include internal recruitment, promotion, transfer, etc.

Employers are also entitled to ask questions necessary to monitor diversity in the range of job applicants; to enable the company to take positive action; or to establish whether the job applicant has a particular disability, where having that disability is an occupational requirement.

An occupational requirement arises where having a protected characteristic is a genuine and determining requirement for the job in question. Under the Equality Act 2010, Sched.9, para.1, disability is included within this exception.

Under these provisions an employer can require a particular protected characteristic if the employer shows that, having regard to the nature or context of the work:

(a) it is an occupational requirement;
(b) the application of the requirement is a proportionate means of achieving a legitimate aim; and
(c) the person to whom the employer applies the requirement does not meet it (or the employer has reasonable grounds for not being satisfied that the person meets it).

The Explanatory Notes state that 'An organisation for deaf people might legitimately employ a deaf person who uses British Sign Language to work as a counsellor to other deaf people whose first or preferred language is BSL'. This suggests a fairly low standard for 'occupational requirement', at least where disability is concerned – there is no need for a particular disability to be indispensable to a person's ability to perform a particular role.

It also means that employers must make reasonable adjustments for disabled candidates so that they are not disadvantaged because of a provision, criterion or policy that indirectly discriminates against them.

So, for example, a candidate with learning difficulties or mental health problems will need reasonable adjustments in order to have a fair interview. Information on good practice on employing people with learning difficulties is available from MENCAP.

The Equality and Human Rights Commission (EHRC) has published some useful guidance, titled 'Pre-employment health questions – Guidance for job applications on Section 60 of the Equality Act 2010', May 2014.

Asking questions about past criminal convictions

Guidance on the Rehabilitation of Offenders Act (ROA) 1974 by the Ministry of Justice, published on 4 March 2014, includes background information on the ROA 1974, explains who benefits from it, and sets out rehabilitation periods for offences covered by the Act – **www.gov.uk/government/publications/new-guidance-on-the-rehabilitation-of-offenders-act-1974**. It has been revised following the implementation of changes to the ROA 1974 included in the Legal Aid, Sentencing and Punishment of Offenders Act 2012.

It explains the difference between spent and unspent convictions, and which convictions have to be declared when applying for jobs or insurance.

It also explains where exceptions to ROA 1974 exist, when certain spent cautions or convictions must be disclosed.

Conditional offer subject to final examination results

It is important for employers to draft clear and unambiguous offer letters where they are offering jobs to graduates who have taken final examinations (but not yet received the results) from a vocational course such as the Legal Practice Course (LPC), banking, accountancy or occupational health qualification. If the offer of employment or continued employment is subject to the passing of these examinations, the offer letter must be crystal clear. Similarly, if continued employment is conditional upon passing certain examinations, this must be spelt out in the offer letter or any subsequent letter issued during employment. There is no room to argue that there is an implied term that the job applicant will pass these examinations as a condition precedent to employment.

The Solicitors Regulation Authority (SRA) Training Regulations 2014 came into force on 1 July 2014. The SRA regulates the training of trainee solicitors. Its requirements guide, 'Authorised Training Provider Information', updated on 12 December 2016, can be found on its website (**www.sra.org.uk**).

It is critically important for employers to stipulate whether the passing of an examination is a condition for the continuation of employment or for confirmation of the job offer (*Stubbes* v. *Trower, Still & Keeling* [1987] IRLR 321).

Some firms of accountants used to take the view that when accepting a trainee for employment and investing in that individual, there was a normal progression and career plan for that individual. It was expected that the trainee would 'repay' the firm by loyalty and commitment. As long as it is made clear in the contract what the individual is expected to commit to, if that individual fails to comply with those commitments, it will be lawful to terminate the contract.

See **Precedent 1D** for a term including such a commitment.

1.6 Importance of careful drafting

The drafting of the offer letter must be careful. Sloppy wording in clauses in a contract which convey ambiguous meanings can be declared void for uncertainty. For example, if an employer tried to enforce a term that stated, 'Your hours of work are those to which you are directed to work from time to time by your employer', this may be declared void for uncertainty as neither party at the time when the clause was agreed would have known what the hours of work were.

1.7 References

Careful recruiters will always check references before permitting the applicant to start work. This is because an employer owes a duty of care to various target populations including its own staff and clients, customers or other third parties, and failing to carry out a careful recruitment procedure may be regarded as a breach of such a duty.

The test as to whether an employer is satisfied with a reference is subjective – does it satisfy the employer in question? – rather than objective, i.e. would it satisfy a reasonable employer? (*Wishart* v. *NACAB* [1990] IRLR 393 (CA)).

The wording of an offer letter should be:

> This offer of employment and any continued employment is conditional upon us receiving written references which satisfy us. It will ultimately be a matter for us alone to decide whether we are entirely satisfied with any reference and we reserve the right to terminate the employment without notice or refuse to confirm employment in any case where we are not satisfied with any reference or part of a reference.

The Data Protection Code of Practice Parts 1 and 2 both contain important guidance to employers and prospective employers who wish to check references and matters disclosed by a job applicant (available from the Information Commissioner's website: **www.ico.org.uk**).

In Part 1, the advice is:

> Applicants may not always give complete and accurate answers to the questions they are asked. Employers are justified in making reasonable efforts to check the truthfulness of the information they are given. The verification process should be open; applicants should be informed of what information will be verified and how this will be done. Where external sources are to be used to check the responses to questions, this should be explained to the applicant.
>
> Access to certain records needed for the verification process may only be available to the individual concerned. You should not force applicants to use their subject access right to obtain records from a third party by making it a condition of their appointment. This is known as 'enforced subject access'. Requiring the supply of certain records in this way, including certain criminal and social security records, will become a criminal offence under the [Data Protection Act 1998] when the Criminal Records Bureau starts to issue 'disclosures'.

The benchmarks that employers are recommended to use when checking references and other issues are:

1. Explain to applicants as early as is reasonably practicable in the recruitment process the nature of the verification process and the methods used to carry it out.
2. If it is necessary to secure the release of documents or information from a third party, obtain a signed consent form from the applicant unless consent to their release has been indicated in some other way.
3. Give the applicant an opportunity to make representations should any of the checks produce discrepancies.

If an employer makes an offer conditional upon receiving satisfactory references but permits the individual to start work before all such references are received, the employer has waived that condition.

The wording of the offer will therefore have to be amended to read as in **Precedent 1E**.

Nahhas v. *Pier House (Cheyne Walk) Management Ltd* (1984) 270 E.G. 328 is a rare example of an employer being held liable for the criminal acts of one of its employees (a porter) who was negligently employed. The porter did not have any reference checks done before he was recruited and he turned out to be a 'professional thief'. The employer (Managing Agent) was held to have breached its duty to the residents.

Many employers now offer only standard, factual references such as the following:

> Mr/s X was employed in the capacity of Y from [*date*] to [*date*] and left by reason of redundancy.
>
> It is not the policy of the Firm to provide any further information for references. This does not imply any comment, positive or negative about the employee or the course of employment with the Firm.
>
> In accordance with the policy of the Firm this information is given in the strictest of confidence and is given by the Firm and is received by you without financial or other liabilities on behalf of the Firm or any of its officers.
>
> Any use of the term Director is purely to reflect titular status. This does not imply any shareholding or legal interest in the Firm on behalf of the above named employee.
>
> Please be advised that no additional information concerning the above named employee will be given over the telephone.

Regulatory references: new rules from 7 March 2017

From March 2017, new rules on regulatory references (for people in senior and key roles in regulated professions) were introduced which apply to the following organisations:

- banks;
- building societies;
- credit unions;
- PRA-designated investment firms;
- insurance and re-insurance firms within the scope of Solvency II; and
- other large non-directive firms.

However, the new rules will be relevant to all organisations in the financial services sector, as 'regulated firms' have to be ready to comply with the requirement to provide an 'enhanced' level of information about former employees if they receive a request for a regulatory reference.

Very useful guidance can be found on the following website: **www.burges-salmon.com/news-and-insight/legal-updates/regulatory-references-making-informed-decisions-on-recruitment**.

1.8 The advertisement

The start of the employment relationship is normally when an advertisement is placed describing the organisation, the job and person specification. This will not form part of the contract unless in a very rare case it is necessary for the court to look at the advertisement to help determine what terms have been agreed.

In *Financial Techniques (Planning Services) Ltd* v. *Hughes* [1981] IRLR 32, Mr Hughes was induced to apply for the job of consultant on the wording of the advertisement, which promised 'exciting career prospects', a 'sophisticated remuneration package, which through a profit-sharing scheme offers a substantial earnings potential'. Nothing was said at the interview about the profit-sharing scheme nor was there any reference to it in his offer letter. Several months later, when Mr Hughes asked about it, the company argued that it was a discretionary bonus based on reaching and then exceeding set financial targets each quarter. In Mr Hughes' final quarter he failed to achieve the minimum target, so his employers offset the deficit in that quarter against the surplus earned in the preceding quarter.

Mr Hughes viewed this as a repudiatory breach of contract and resigned, claiming constructive dismissal. The Court of Appeal upheld the EAT's decision that the profit-sharing scheme was part of the contract, and the purported breach by the employers was a fundamental breach of contract by them justifying Mr Hughes' resignation and claim for constructive dismissal. The Court of Appeal held that (p.32):

> The evidence pointing to the profit sharing scheme being part of the contract was all one way. The respondent had said that he was never told, at the material time for the purpose of deciding what were the terms of his employment, that the scheme was not to create any sort of legal arrangement. Secondly, the advertisement on the face of which he had started negotiations with the appellants had referred to 'a sophisticated remuneration package, which, through a profit-sharing scheme, offers very substantial earnings potential'. That kind of language was wholly inconsistent with the kind of situation which arises when employers offer discretionary bonuses.... The commonsense of the situation pointed to that fact that [Mr Hughes] was negotiating with his employers on the basis that he was paid a salary, plus the advantages of the scheme, if he qualified under it.

Note: Ensure that a job advertisement does not make promises in relation to essential terms of the contract that do not in fact apply.

Issues such as discrimination may arise if the wording refers to or implies that the employer seeks one sex rather than the other, younger workers, heterosexuals, no pregnant women, etc.

The wording of advertisements can be called into evidence in an Employment Tribunal in a discrimination claim, as discriminatory advertisements are unlawful under the Equality Act 2010. Suffice it to say that most employers are now careful to ensure that they or the recruitment agencies who place advertisements on their behalf do not use sexist, racist or ageist language such as 'men', 'young, dynamic' or 'experienced and senior' in their advertisements.

1.9 The application form

The recruitment process normally begins with job applicants completing an application form or sending in their curriculum vitae. Only relevant questions should be asked of job candidates in order to long-list or short-list candidates for interview. Employers must be careful to avoid questions that could discriminate against disabled candidates, such as days of sickness absence, etc. Questions must be geared to offering reasonable adjustments either at interview and/or during employment.

1.10 The interview

Employers should ensure that standard, validated and relevant questions are asked of all candidates so that fairness can be achieved among candidates as far as possible. Reasonable adjustments to interviews for those with special needs must be made, e.g. using an interview room without strip lighting for people with photosensitive epilepsy; using an interview room on a ground floor for someone with impaired mobility; allowing longer time for an interview and asking factual questions concentrating on their experience for those with a learning disability, etc.

Interview notes are critical in order to ensure fairness, to be able to validate the successful candidate and to defend at any later stage any allegations of unfairness, bias or discrimination or any allegations of promises made at interview but not kept. Interview notes for unsuccessful candidates should always be kept for one year.

1.11 Data protection

Under the Data Protection Act 1998, recruitment information must be relevant and must not be kept for longer than is necessary, be excessive or out of date (Sched.1, Principles 3–5). Any health data or data on ethnic origin, religious beliefs or political opinions, information on trade union membership, information on sexual life or any criminal convictions obtained is regarded as 'sensitive' data under s.2 and special rules and safeguards apply in relation to this information.

The Chartered Institute of Personnel and Development (CIPD) recommends that application forms and interview notes be kept for a maximum of one year in order to be Data Protection Act compliant (see CIPD website at **www.cipd.co.uk**).

1.12   Making promises and representations

Inconsistencies: which term prevails?

In theory, there should not be any inconsistencies in the terms described at interview and those which appear in the offer letter or written terms, but it happens. What is critical is that any inconsistencies or changes to the terms first described are drawn to the job applicant's attention and, in particular, that any offers made at interview are now overtaken and superseded by the written terms of the contract. This is called an 'entire agreement clause'. Wording such as the following should be used:

> Any earlier agreement or offer made in respect of any term of this contract which contradicts or conflicts with any of the written terms of this Agreement shall be regarded by the parties as null and void and inapplicable to this employment and any such agreement(s) shall be regarded as having been superseded by this Agreement.

Making promises

In *Hawker Siddeley Power Engineering Ltd* v. *Rump* [1979] IRLR 425, Mr Rump was promised that he would never have to relocate outside South East England, yet his contract failed to reflect that promise and he was asked to sign a contract of employment form which indicated that he would be liable to travel all over the country. In 1976, he was issued with a further document pursuant to the Contracts of Employment Act 1972, s.4 which expressly stated that: 'You may be required to transfer from one workplace to another on the instruction of the Employer in accordance with the provisions of the appropriate Working Rule Agreement'.

In March 1978, Mr Rump was told to go home on stand-by, as work had ceased in South East England. He was then instructed to drive to Scotland and he refused. He was told that he was deemed to have dismissed himself as a result of his conduct. The Employment Tribunal and the EAT found that he had been unfairly dismissed because (p.426):

> The arrangement between the employee and the employers under which he was not to be required to work outside southern England was an oral contractual term ... in the present case there was a direct promise by the employers which must have become part of the contract of employment because it was following upon the promise that the employee signed the contract.
>
>   That several years later the employee had signed a contract of employment, the terms of which required him to be mobile throughout the British Isles, could not justify the conclusion that there had been a variation by agreement so as to exclude the oral term previously agreed ... In the present case, however, the employee had no notice that the oral term he had secured was going to form no part of his new contract. The mere putting in front of him of a document and invitation to him to sign it could not be held to be a variation by agreement so as to exclude the important oral term which he had previously secured. Rather, if there was a variation at all to the contract, it was a unilateral variation which was not binding upon the employee.

Misrepresentations

We have already seen how a representation about offering employment can amount to a warranty and a collateral contract (*Gill's* case, above).

If an employer makes a misrepresentation of fact to a job candidate that they will be competent to do the job being offered and in fact that job candidate is not, that employee could have a successful claim under the Misrepresentation Act 1967, s.2(1) (not applicable in Scotland). Such a misrepresentation, even though innocent, may result in a breach of the Act and this being a statutory tort, damages at large can be awarded (*McNally* v. *Welltrade International Ltd* [1978] IRLR 497). In another case a person who applied for a job advertised in the media was held to hold themselves out as being competent for the job. In *Pinkerton* v. *Hollis Brothers & ESA plc* (21 July 1988, Court of Session), a managing director who was summarily dismissed for incompetence shortly after his appointment lost his claim for wrongful dismissal. He argued that because there was no express term in the contract, there was no implied term that he had to demonstrate any particular level of competence. The Court of Session thought otherwise. It held that the implied term to serve his employer faithfully and loyally meant that he had impliedly promised to have the standard of skill that a reasonably competent managing director would possess.

1.13 Probationary periods

It is common for employers to offer employment subject to a trial or probationary period. The tribunals have made clear statements about what a probationary period is supposed to offer employees.

A probationary period implies that the employer, before dismissing a probationer:

(a) will take reasonable steps to maintain appraisal of the probationer throughout the period of probation;
(b) will give guidance by advice or warning when such is likely to be useful or fair; and
(c) will ensure that an appropriate officer made an honest effort to determine whether the probationer came up to the required standard, having informed themselves of the appraisals made by supervising officers and any other facts recorded about the probationer.

In *The Post Office* v. *Mughal* [1977] IRLR 178, the EAT held that (p.178):

> In considering the fairness of the dismissal of an employee during a probationary or trial period, the question for the Industrial Tribunal is: Has the employer shown that he took reasonable steps to maintain appraisal of the probationer throughout the period of probation, giving guidance by advice or warning when such is likely to be useful or fair; and that an appropriate officer made an honest effort to determine whether the probationer came up to the required standard, having informed himself of the appraisals made by supervising officers and any other facts recorded about the probationer? If this procedure is followed, it is only if the officer responsible for deciding upon selection of probationers then arrives at a decision which no

reasonable assessment could dictate that an Industrial Tribunal should hold the dismissal to be unfair.

Some employers seek to exclude the operation of the disciplinary procedure during the continuation of a probationary period. There may be other benefits or terms that do not apply during the probationary period and if this is the case these must be clearly spelt out.

A typical probationary period clause can be found at **Precedent 1G**.

Employers should note that if an employee has achieved one year's continuous service at the effective date of termination (in practical terms this is 11 months and three weeks), then the employee will be entitled to claim unfair dismissal. This is because the Employment Rights Act 1996 allows for the addition of the statutory notice that the employer would have had to provide in order to determine whether the employee has one year's continuous service at the effective date of termination (ss.92(7) and 97(2)). Employers must therefore take care to consider and if necessary terminate the employment of an employee on probation before 11 months and three weeks have elapsed from the commencement date of employment.

Thus, if an employee commenced employment on 5 January 2017, the employee would need to have an effective date of termination on or after 4 January 2018 to qualify for unfair dismissal protection. If the employer dismissed that person on 31 December 2017 without notice, the employee would qualify as having one year's continuous service.

1.14 Asking the right medical questions

The case of *Cheltenham Borough Council* v. *Laird* [2009] IRLR 621 is a timely lesson in asking the right question.

Mrs Laird was employed as chief executive. She completed a medical questionnaire after she had been offered the post, subject to medical clearance. After an acrimonious dispute between her and the council leader and a significant amount of time off due to stress-related illness, she was retired on an ill health pension. The essence of the High Court claim brought by the Council for recovery of the sick pay (the claim was for fraudulent misrepresentation) was that the medical questionnaire which Mrs Laird had completed in January 2002 after she was offered the post did not mention any history of depression, stress-related illness or any anti-depression medication.

The medical questionnaire, by which Mrs Laird declared that the statements 'are true and given to the fullest of my ability and knowledge', imposed on her a duty to take reasonable care in making the statement.

The High Court held that the medical questionnaire was to be construed objectively, as a reasonable person in the position of Mrs Laird would have done, taking into account that she was a lay rather than a medical person. On that basis, the judge found that the representations made by Mrs Laird in answer to the medical questionnaire were not false, nor, given the terms of the questions asked, were they misleading.

In the period from May 1997 to January 2002, when she was appointed, Mrs Laird had three episodes of depression with associated anxiety. These were all associated with periods of stress and were work-related. Her answer 'Yes' in response to the question 'Do you normally enjoy good health' was a correct answer because although when she was depressed she did not enjoy good health, that was not her 'normal' state of health. For the great majority of the time, she was not depressed and therefore a reasonable person in her position would regard herself as normally enjoying good health. She also correctly answered 'No' in response to the question 'Do you have either a physical and/or mental impairment?'

This case highlights the importance of careful drafting of medical questionnaires. The judge agreed that the Council's questionnaire 'was poorly drafted'.

A better question would be to ask about an ongoing condition that 'would' affect her employment – 'i.e. a condition that is going to do so, not one that might do so or even is likely to do so.'

There should always be a 'sweeping up' question calling for disclosure outside the questions asked, such as:

> Is there anything else in your history or circumstances which might affect our decision to offer you employment or affect your ability to perform your duties or affect your ability to render regular and efficient service?

However, when considering an employee with a history of mental illness, employers should be aware that such an illness will almost certainly fall under the Equality Act 2010. Illness which is 'likely to recur', i.e. 'could well happen' (*SCA Packaging Ltd* v. *Boyle* [2009] IRLR 746 (HL)), or where the employee may suffer a relapse or which, if not controlled by medication or treatment would have an adverse effect upon a normal day-to-day activity, would fall under the 2010 Act and count as a 'disability'.

From a statistical point of view, over 50 per cent of patients with a depressive illness will suffer a relapse and will have a second or further episode of depression. Since the Equality Act 2010, s.60 makes it unlawful for the employer generally to ask about health questions at the recruitment stage, health questionnaires should now only be completed at the pre-placement stage, i.e. when a conditional job offer is made.

PRECEDENT 1A: Expression of interest/invitation to treat

We are delighted to have met you at the interview on [*date*]. We are very interested in pursuing the possibility of making an offer to you and of you taking up the job of [*specify*].

If you would be interested in progressing this matter, please would you write to us within the next 14 days, confirming your interest in the job and we will then commence the pre-offer stages of seeking references and asking you to submit to a medical assessment/credit check/checking your qualifications. Once these have been completed to our entire satisfaction, we will be in a position to make you a formal offer of employment.

Please note that this is NOT an offer of employment and that you should on no account resign your current employment on receiving this letter. We look forward to hearing from you within the next 14 days.

PRECEDENT 1B: Conditional offer of employment

We are delighted to inform you that we have decided to make you an offer of employment subject to the following conditions being satisfied:

1. that we receive at least two former employment references, one being from your current or last employer (or school or educational institution if you do not have two previous employers) which entirely satisfy us. If you are not willing to allow us to approach your current employer until we confirm our offer of employment, we will do this but please be advised that we will retain the right to revoke this offer if your current employer's reference does not satisfy us;
2. [that we receive a full and satisfactory credit check on you;]
3. [that we receive a satisfactory response from the Financial Conduct Authority as to your registration;]
4. that we receive a medical assessment[1] with which we are satisfied OR a satisfactory report from our occupational health physician about your fitness for this job;
5. that we receive satisfactory evidence of the qualifications, etc. that you have declared at interview;
6. that we receive satisfactory checks from the Disclosure and Barring Service (DBS) (**www.gov.uk/disclosure-barring-service-check/overview**) concerning any former criminal convictions. [Please note that this employment is not subject to the Rehabilitation of Offenders Act 1974[2] and that you are required to declare all criminal convictions to us];
7. [that you pass to the satisfactory level your [Law Society/Accountancy, etc.] final examinations;]
8. that you produce a full valid UK driving licence.

Please do not resign from your current employment until we have confirmed that we are satisfied with all these matters. Please note we reserve the right to withdraw this conditional offer in the light of any responses to the above conditions about which we are not satisfied.

[*Notes:*

1. *A model pre-employment health questionnaire is reproduced as* **Precedent 1H**. *It is an example only and any employer wishing to use a pre-employment health questionnaire should modify this one to suit its own requirements and needs. Any such employer should take the advice of an Occupational Health practitioner as to what questions to ask on such a questionnaire.*
2. *This includes posts that involve particular risks, such as work with children or vulnerable adults, national security, the administration of justice or financial services. For all these posts applicants will always be required to disclose all their previous convictions, whether they are 'spent' or not.*]

PRECEDENT 1C: Background check permission (comprehensive) for prospective employee

In connection with my application for employment with [*company name*] ('the Company'), I hereby agree as follows:

1. **General consent to background investigation**

As a condition of the Company's consideration of my employment application, I give permission to the Company to investigate my personal and employment history. I understand that this background investigation will include, but not be limited to, verification of all information on my employment application.

2. **Consent to contact past employers**

I specifically give permission to the Company to contact my previous employers listed on my application form/given at interview, for references.

I further give permission to my current or previous employers and/or managers or supervisors to discuss my relevant personal and employment history with the Company, consent to the release of such information orally or in writing and hereby release them from all liability and agree not to sue them for defamation or other claims based upon any statements they make to any representative of the Company save that they must ensure that they are given factually accurate statements and opinions based on fact.

I further waive all rights I may have under law to receive a copy of any written statement(s) provided by any of my former employers to the Company. I further agree to indemnify all past employers for any liability they may incur because of their reliance upon this Agreement.

3. **Consent to contact government agencies**

I further give permission to the Company to receive a copy of any information obtained in the file of any court, or government agency or regulatory body concerning or relating to me.

I further consent to the release of such information and waive any right under law concerning notification of the request for a release of such information.

4. **Cooperation with investigation**

I agree to fully cooperate in the Company's background investigation and to sign any waivers that may be required of me.

I understand that this offer and your continued employment of me is conditional upon me participating in the Company's pre-employment screening processes and the outcome of such being satisfactory to the Company.

X company checks:

- Proof of right to work in the UK/proof of identity;
- Two years' previous work history (if possible);
- DVLA driving licence check (where applicable);
- Proof of residence check;
- Credit reference check (covering financial sanctions and proof of residence);
- Basic level criminal record check;
- An employment reference covering two years' previous work and/or education history/activity (whichever is applicable), with gap analysis over a three-month period.

These are essential checks with which the Company must be entirely satisfied in its entire discretion. If for any reason any of these checks are deemed to be unsatisfactory this will render either your offer of employment to be withdrawn without any compensation becoming due or if you have commenced employment, your contract being terminated with immediate effect, i.e. without notice or payment in lieu of notice and without recourse to the disciplinary procedure.

Signed . ... Date ....

PRECEDENT 1D: Conditional offer of employment (professional partnership)

1. The offer of the post of [specify] [and your continued employment] is conditional upon you passing the [specify] examination on the [first/second/third] occasion.

2. Should you fail this examination on the [first/second/third] occasion, this offer of employment will be revoked on the basis of your failure to perform an essential and material term of this offer [or your employment will be terminated without notice or pay in lieu/with statutory notice or pay in lieu].

3. It is the Firm's policy that a salaried partnership is a normal preliminary to full equity partnership. The normal progression to equity partnership would be two to two-and-a-half years from appointment to salaried partner. It would be our expectation in your case that you would, in the normal case, be offered an equity partnership on or after [date]. Any such offers either to salaried or equity partnership are made at the entire discretion of the Firm and do not form part of any contractual entitlement on your part or obligation on the part of the Firm.

4. It is a condition of your engagement that if you are offered an equity partnership, you will accept such offer subject to the terms being agreed. Because of the investment the Firm will have made in you, should you unreasonably decline any such offer of equity partnership, the Firm will deem this to be a breach of these terms and conditions and will terminate your contract of employment with immediate effect.

PRECEDENT 1E: Offer conditional on references, etc.

1. Your employment and continued employment is subject to our receiving [references/a medical assessment/credit checks, etc.] that satisfy the Company.

2. In the event that you start employment before we have completed all the checks on your [reference/medical fitness/credit check, etc.], we reserve the right to terminate your employment without notice or pay in lieu on the basis that an essential/material condition of your employment has not been satisfied.

3. You will have the right under the Data Protection Act 1998 to see any reference that we receive on you. We will discuss any aspect of a reference received if you request us to do so.

PRECEDENT 1F: Application form (care staff)

Please complete this application form in full. If you wish, you may also attach your Curriculum Vitae as additional information.

1. **Position**

Post at:

Job title:

Closing date for completed applications:

How did you hear about this vacancy?

Please return completed form to:

2. **Personal information**

Title (e.g. Mr, Ms, Mrs, Miss):

Surname:

Forename(s):

Address:

Postcode:

Home tel.:

Mobile:

Work tel. (only complete if it is acceptable for us to contact you at work):

Email address:

3. **Are you eligible to work in the UK?**

Yes   No

(Evidence will be required)

4. **Employment history**

Present employment:

Job title:

Name and address of employer:

Date employment commenced:

Present salary:

Please describe your current duties:

Reason for wishing to leave:

Previous employment (last 10 years):

Please list in order the organisations you have worked for, full-time and part-time, paid and unpaid, including relevant voluntary work and include any periods of non-employment (continue on additional paper if there is insufficient space):

Name and address of previous employer	Job title	Dates employed (from and to)	Reason for leaving

5. **Summary of qualifications**

Schools attended from age 11	From	To	Examinations passed/grades

Further education College/University	From	To	Qualifications gained/grades

5.1   Please state any relevant professional qualifications/training/membership of professional bodies with dates and levels attained. Please indicate where these are currently being continued:

5.2   Please list any training you have received or courses which did not lead to a qualification but which you feel are relevant to the post for which you are applying:

6. **Professional registration details: nurses only**

Registration number:

Date of registration:

Registration body:

Date of next renewal (if applicable):

Registration: Limited/Full/Provisional (delete as appropriate)

7. **Additional relevant information**

Please give details of relevant experience and any other information which you consider may be helpful in assessing your suitability for the post for which you are applying (please continue on an additional sheet if necessary):

8. **Equal opportunities**

8.1   [Name of employer] is an equal opportunities employer. The sole criterion for selection is the suitability of an applicant for the job for which they are applying. We do not discriminate on any grounds.

8.2   We are required by law to monitor the effectiveness of our Equal Opportunities Policy and would therefore ask you to complete the enclosed confidential form. Thank you.

9. **Health**

9.1   Do you have an existing medical condition which may affect your ability to work in the role/environment for which you have applied?   Yes   No

9.2   If your answer is yes, you may be required to supply a certificate of good health from your doctor.

9.3   Please complete the enclosed Medical Screening Questionnaire and return this in the sealed envelope provided. This information is confidential and will be reviewed by the organisation's appointed Occupational Health Adviser.

10. **Convictions**

10.1   Rehabilitation of Offenders Act 1974: Please state any convictions/offences, information of which you are not entitled to withhold, under the Rehabilitation of Offenders Act 1974 (Exceptions) Order 1975, in view of the nature of the work for which you are applying:

10.2 Care Standards Act 2000: Please state any police cautions and incidents with the police, in view of the nature of the work for which you are applying:

10.3 If your application is successful you will be required to provide a satisfactory check with the Disclosure and Barring Service (DBS). We will offer our full support throughout this process.

11. **References**

11.1 Please give details of three referees (who should not be relatives or friends), at least one of whom should be your current or last employer relating to a period of not less than three months' employment. If you have not worked for some time or have never worked, please give the name of someone who can comment on your ability to do the job for which you are applying. Please note that all offers of employment are conditional upon receipt of at least two satisfactory references, i.e. that fully satisfy us.

Referee

Name:

Organisation:

Address:

Period of employment (From/To):

Telephone number:

Email address:

11.2 References will only be taken after an offer of employment has been made.

12. **Other interests**

Please give details of your personal interests and hobbies:

13. **Declaration**

I understand that the data I have given will be processed and used in accordance with the Data Protection Act 1998 and hereby give permission for my details to be retained.

I confirm that to the best of my knowledge and belief, the information I have given is correct. I hereby give [*employer*] permission to contact my referees and understand that any contract given to me is based on the information provided.

Signed.. Date..

[*job applicant*]

To help us reduce costs we do not acknowledge receipt of application forms. We regret that we may not be able to advise applicants who have not been shortlisted for interview. If you have not heard from us within four weeks, please assume that you have been unsuccessful.

PRECEDENT 1G: Probationary or trial periods

1. Your initial employment will be subject to a trial/probationary period of up to [three/six/nine/twelve] months. During that time management will review and monitor

your work, performance and progress. Your [line manager/supervisor] will have regular one-to-one discussions with you and these will be recorded on your file and you will be given copies.

2. If at any time during your [trial/probationary] period, your work, [performance/progress/attitude] or other matter is not deemed to be satisfactory by your [line manager/supervisor], then the Company reserves the right to terminate your employment giving you one week's notice or pay in lieu.

3. Please note that during your [trial/probationary] period, the Company's disciplinary procedure will not apply to you. This means that your employment can be terminated at any time without any formal or informal warnings, a disciplinary hearing or a right of appeal. Please note all the rules apply.

4. Your rate of pay during your trial period will be £... [which is 10 per cent lower than the normal rate for the job]. Your pay will be uprated to the normal rate of pay once it has been confirmed in writing that you have satisfied your [probationary/trial] period.

5. You will receive written confirmation that you have satisfied your [trial/probationary] period normally at least one week before it is due to finish. If however you have not received written confirmation that you have passed your [probationary/trial] period, you will continue in a [probationary/trial] period until or unless you receive written confirmation that you have satisfied the conditions of your [probation/trial] period.

6. Management reserves the right to extend your [trial/probationary] period if in its opinion you still have not reached the standards required and need some additional time to do so.

PRECEDENT 1H: Pre-employment health questionnaire

MEDICAL IN CONFIDENCE: The information contained on this form will not be disclosed to anyone within the Company other than a medically qualified occupational health physician or nurse unless you give your express, informed, written consent.

Section 1: To be completed by the Human Resources department

Dr/Mr/Mrs/Miss/Ms Delete as appropriate	Position applied for
Surname	
....	
	Proposed start date
First name	....
....	
	Site
Home address	....
....	
....	Department
....	....
....	

....	Yes / No
....	Day work?
....	
Telephone (work)	Shift work?
....	
	Night work?
(home)	
....	Part-time?
(mobile)	If part-time, hours worked
....	....
Currently working on site? Yes / No	Duration of contract?

Circle the activities/conditions that apply to the role applied for:

Heavy manual work: lifting / bending / standing

Driving work: chauffeur / HGV / fork-lift / crane / off-loader / own car / other

Working at heights / ladder / below ground

Exposure to: sewage / clinical waste / blood / body fluids

Exposure to: hazardous chemicals / skin-respiratory sensitisers

Exposure to: wood dusts / grain dusts / fumes / extremes of temperatures

Working with: moving machinery / vibrating tools / grinding

Working in a designated noisy area / need for hearing protection

Working in a confined space / outside / isolation

Required to wear breathing apparatus

Food handling

VDU / DSE user

Working with the public / children and parents / students / pupils

Requires normal colour vision

Requires other duties: walking / standing / using hands / working with electrical equipment / other

Section 2: To be completed by the applicant

Medical information is retained confidentially in the Occupational Health Department, but you should be aware that your contract of employment is issued on the basis of the information contained in this document being a true statement. If any medical information or any answer that you have provided is found to be misleading or untrue, then the Company may decide to terminate your employment with or without notice or pay in lieu.

Date of birth	Name, address and telephone number of doctor
Height Weight	

Please circle the relevant response for each question. If a 'yes' response is given, provide further details below (attach additional sheet if necessary):

1. Have you had any days off work due to illness in the last two years? Yes / No
   State the reason and duration of absence for each incidence.
2. Have you ever been off work continuously for a period of four weeks or more? Yes / No
   State the reason and duration of this absence.
3. Have you ever attended hospital as an in-patient or out-patient? Yes / No
   State the reason and dates.
4. Do you wear spectacles/contact lenses? Yes / No
5. Are you colour blind? Yes / No
6. Are you taking any prescribed medication at present? Yes / No
   Provide details.
7. Are you undergoing any medical treatment at present? Yes / No
   Provide details.

Do you have or have you had any of the following:

8. sinus trouble? Yes / No
9. neck swelling/glands? Yes / No
10. difficulty in breathing? Yes / No
11. ear discharge? Yes / No
12. asthma/bronchitis? Yes / No
13. hay fever/other allergy? Yes / No
14. skin trouble? Yes / No
15. tuberculosis? Yes / No
16. shortness of breath? Yes / No
17. coughing or vomiting blood? Yes / No
18. severe abdominal pain? Yes / No
19. a stomach ulcer? Yes / No
20. recurrent indigestion? Yes / No
21. jaundice or hepatitis? Yes / No
22. gall bladder disease? Yes / No
23. marked changes in bowel movement? Yes / No
24. blood in stools? Yes / No
25. blood in urine? Yes / No
26. painful passage of urine? Yes / No
27. marked changes in weight? Yes / No
28. varicose veins? Yes / No
29. a lump in breast/armpit? Yes / No
30. cancer? Yes / No
31. an abnormal heart beat? Yes / No
32. high blood pressure? Yes / No
33. serious chest pain? Yes / No
34. heart disease? Yes / No
35. a stroke? Yes / No
36. rheumatic fever? Yes / No
37. blood disease? Yes / No
38. kidney disease? Yes / No

39. diabetes? Yes / No
40. headaches/migraines? Yes / No
41. dizziness/fainting? Yes / No
42. epilepsy? Yes / No
43. joints/spinal trouble? Yes / No
44. neck, shoulder, arm or hand trouble (incl. repetitive strain injury (RSI), otherwise referred to as work-related upper limb disorder (WRULD))? Yes / No
45. x-rays or other medical investigations, such as electrocardiograph (ECG)? Yes / No
46. a surgical operation? Yes / No
47. gynaecological treatment? Yes / No
48. a serious accident/fracture? Yes / No
49. a fear of heights? Yes / No
50. mental condition, e.g. depression/anxiety? Yes / No
51. alcohol or drug abuse or dependency? Yes / No
52. exposure to toxic substances or excessive noise? Yes / No
53. an illness not listed above? Yes / No

If a 'yes' response has been given to any of the questions 8–53, please provide further details below (attach additional sheet if necessary):

54. Have you ever suffered illness or injury as a result of your work? Yes / No
    Provide details:
55. Have you ever had to leave a job for health reasons or been medically retired? Yes / No
    Provide details:
56. Do you currently suffer from or have you ever in the past 10 years suffered from any physical or mental, psychiatric, psychological or emotional condition that has made it necessary for you to have had any time off work or that needed any form of treatment or referral for medical treatment or which could or did affect your ability to provide regular and efficient service to your then employer? Yes / No
    If so please give details and relevant dates.
57. Have you, during the last six months, taken any prescribed medication/treatment? Yes / No
    Provide details:

Food hygiene

Have you ever suffered from any of the following:

58. dysentery? Yes / No
59. typhoid or paratyphoid? Yes / No
60. tuberculosis? Yes / No
61. parasitic infections? Yes / No
62. has anyone living in your household suffered from any of the above? Yes / No

If a 'yes' response has been given to any of the questions 58–62, please provide details of dates and any treatment below (attach additional sheet if necessary):

Have you suffered from any of the following in the last six months:

63. food poisoning? Yes / No
64. diarrhoea or vomiting? Yes / No
65. skin rash? Yes / No
66. recurring boils? Yes / No
67. discharge from ear/eye or nose? Yes / No

68. any other medical problems which may affect employment for food handling? Yes / No

If a 'yes' response has been given to any of the questions 63–68, please give details of dates and any treatment below (attach additional sheet if necessary):

69. Which countries have you travelled to in the last six months?

Immunisations

If you have ever had any of the following immunisations, please indicate which year in the relevant box:

Polio	Tetanus	Hepatitis A	Hepatitis B	Rubella

Lifestyle

State approximate quantities of cigarettes/tobacco smoked per day	
State approximate units of alcohol consumed per week (1 unit = 1 small glass of wine, or 1 measure of spirits, or 1/2 pint of ordinary strength beer)	
Give details of any regular weekly exercise undertaken	
What are your hobbies/interests?	

Disability

Do you feel that you have any disability that may affect your ability to do this job? i.e. speech, co-ordination, disfigurement, learning abilities, physical strength, stamina, mobility, mental illness, etc?

Please describe:

The information will help us comply with the provisions of the Equality Act 2010 and is consistent with our Diversity Policy. This information will be used only to assist us in accommodating any special needs that you may have. Depending upon any answer given, you may be asked to attend an occupational health assessment so that we can be properly advised as to any reasonable adjustments which may be required.

Previous employment

Please provide details of occupations in the last 10 years (the Occupational Health Department does not have access to your application form).

Name of employer	Type of employment	Start date	End date	Specific hazards

Declaration

I declare these statements to be true to the best of my knowledge and belief. I am willing to undergo a medical examination, and provide specimens if appropriate, in order that the Company may receive a report on my fitness for the position applied for.

I am aware that the results of this medical questionnaire in general terms, i.e. whether I am fit for the post, fit with adjustments or modifications or unfit for the post, may be revealed to the Company if required, and the details to my own doctor if this is considered necessary by the occupational health adviser. However, the medical information on this form will not be disclosed to anyone without my express, informed, written consent.

I understand that any false or untrue answers or statements or material omissions may lead to my summary dismissal and if relevant repayment of any or all sick pay received if there has been any misrepresentation made or omissions by me.

Signature .... Date ....

Print name ....

The completed form should be returned in the envelope provided, direct to:

Occupational Health Department

[address]

2

The offer and written particulars: the principal statement

2.1 Making the offer

Once all the conditions of an offer have been met, an unconditional offer can be made. However, there may be continuing conditions or obligations for the employee to satisfy (such as continuing reference checks, checking registration with the Financial Conduct Authority (FCA) or the obligation to pass a medical examination or professional examination, entitlement to work in the UK), and if this is the case then this must be clearly set out in the offer letter.

A typical term in the offer letter and the principal statement is shown in **Precedent 2A**.

Similarly, if the employee fails or continues to fail a professional examination which is material and relevant to their employment, this can be grounds for summary dismissal: see **Precedent 2B**.

It is common for a brief offer letter to be sent to the prospective employee along with a document entitled 'Written particulars' and either a copy of a staff handbook or reference to a staff handbook, containing details of the terms and conditions offered.

In the final section there will be other documents forming part of the contract of employment, including a Compliance Manual, Confidentiality Agreement, Personal Account Dealing Rules, etc.

A typical offer letter is shown in **Precedent 2C**.

Applicants with no automatic right to work in the UK

Where job candidates have no automatic right to work in the UK, i.e. are non-European Economic Area (EEA) nationals, ss.15–25 of the Immigration, Asylum and Nationality Act (IANA) 2006 make it a requirement that the employer complies with the prescribed requirements. So, for example, the employer must require evidence of the right to work and remain in the UK. The Home Office has produced a helpful guide, 'An Employer's Guide to Acceptable Right to Work Documents' (2015): www.gov.uk/government/uploads/system/uploads/attachment_data/file/441957/employers_guide_to_acceptable_right_to_work_documents_v5.pdf.

Precedent 2D highlights the employer's duties to check and keep copies of certain documents evidencing the right to work.

Employers must of course be careful not to discriminate under the race, nationality, colour or ethnic origin provisions of the Equality Act 2010. The Secretary of State is required to issue Codes of Practice to assist employers to avoid racial discrimination in the context of complying with their obligations under IANA 2006.

These Codes are available on the UK government's website (**www.gov.uk**), e.g. 'Code of practice for employers – Avoiding unlawful discrimination while preventing illegal working' (May 2014) and 'Frequently asked questions about the illegal working civil penalty scheme' (May 2015).

2.2 Reneging on the offer

If an offer of employment is made and accepted by the job candidate, then a contract to employ has been formed and if revoked by either party, then there will be a breach of contract – not of the contract of employment, but of the contract to employ.

The potential employer is technically able to sue for breach of contract, as is the prospective employee, depending on which party breached the contract.

If the prospective employee reneged on their acceptance of the job but there is another good candidate who could be offered the job and could perform substantially the same contract, then it is probable that no financial loss would be suffered by the employer.

If, however, an entirely fresh recruitment process has to be initiated by the employer, e.g. organising assessment centres, psychometric testing, etc. then the employer may be able to sue the prospective employee for such losses incurred.

One employer, the money broker Tullett Prebon, has developed an intriguing and apparently enforceable set of terms of offer, which have allowed it to sue successfully for damages where individuals are offered and accept a job offer and then renege upon that offer. See below:

> You agree (a) to take all such steps and do all such acts and things within your power and to execute all documents and papers as may reasonably be required by the Company to give full force and effect to this Employment Agreement and (b) to take up your employment with the Company as provided by this Employment Agreement and should you fail to do so, to pay to the Company, by way of agreed liquidated and ascertained damages, a sum equal to 50% of the net basic salary and (if any) 50% of your signing payment (if any) that the Company has contracted to pay to you during the Term of this Employment Agreement. You agree that this is a genuine pre-estimate of the Company's loss, given the loss of profit it will suffer as a direct consequence of the loss of your anticipated revenue generation under this Employment Agreement.

The contractual letter contained the following:

> NOTE: Once signed by you, this Employment Agreement forms an irrevocable legal commitment by you to join the Company, which you agree to fulfil if you are already employed elsewhere, by promptly giving notice of your resignation (if you have not done so already) of such other employment and starting work for the Company as

soon as that notice has expired. ... You should also refer to Clause 19.4 of the attached Schedule of Standard Terms in this regard.

The essence of these terms is that there is an accepted ratio of salary to income generation and that therefore, subject to any duty to mitigate in any damages claim, Tullett Prebon can genuinely pre-estimate its losses if the individual fails to honour the agreement to take up the employment. This approach is particularly ideal in the City environment where many jobs are money-making by their very nature.

In *Tullett Prebon Group Ltd v. Ghaleb El-Hajjali* [2008] EWHC 1924 (QB), the first case in the UK to examine penalty clauses in employment contracts, the High Court held that a sum that was to be paid pursuant to a clause in an employment contract after a prospective employee, in breach of contract, failed to start work for the employer was 'not extravagant or unconscionable' compared to the greatest loss or range of losses that could conceivably be proven to follow the breach of contract and, therefore, the clause was a liquidated damages clause rather than an unlawful penalty clause.

The prospective employer, Tullett Prebon Group ('Tullett') claimed damages for alleged breach of an employment contract by the defendant broker, Mr El-Hajjali. Tullett decided to hire a specialist broker and had entered into negotiations with Mr El-Hajjali. Both parties had legal advice. Tullett sought to include a liquidated damages clause in the contract and had allegedly received advice that it should avoid the clause being seen as an unlawful penalty clause. The clause (set out above) provided that if Mr El-Hajjali failed to take up employment he would have to pay a sum equal to 50 per cent of his net basic salary and 50 per cent of the signing payment that Tullett had contracted to pay.

Mr El-Hajjali's solicitors drew this repayment clause to his attention before he signed the contract and he was advised that if he failed to take up employment after signing it Tullett would be likely to sue. Nevertheless, he signed the agreement but subsequently changed his mind. Tullett searched for a replacement employee but failed to find a suitable candidate. Tullett argued that Mr El-Hajjali had failed to discharge the burden upon him to show that the clause was an unlawful penalty clause rather than a liquidated damages clause.

The High Court held that where an employee was to be hired for a particular project or particular function and their presence was critical to that project or function and as a result of their failure to honour the bargain loss was sustained by the prospective employer, there was no reason why a liquidated damages clause should not operate to compensate the employer, provided it was not on its proper construction a penalty clause.

In this case, the clause in question was a liquidated damages clause and not a penalty clause. Mr El-Hajjali had entered into the employment contract, which included the clause, with the benefit of expert legal advice. He had been fully aware of its terms and had agreed to them when he signed the contract.

The court held that (para.74):

> Where a bargain has been struck by two parties of equal bargaining power, with each party legally represented, a court should consider long and hard before permitting

one of them to resile from the agreement. In such circumstances it was only where a stipulated sum was extravagant or unconscionable in amount compared with the greatest loss or range of losses that could conceivably prove to follow a breach that the clause should be held to be a penalty.

Tullett would probably be able to establish a loss from Mr El-Hajjali's failure to work for it and establish that such a loss was probably considerably in excess of the sum calculated on the basis of the clause.

Furthermore, there had been specific discussion about the need to avoid the clause being regarded as a penalty clause. That was sufficient consideration of the matter, in circumstances where the loss was difficult to assess, to render the clause a liquidated damages clause. The failure of the parties to discuss or agree what the loss might be was not fatal to Tullett's case. It was only necessary that Tullett should have considered the stipulated sum and sought to ensure it was not pitched at such a level as to be greater than any damages it might recover. The fact that any liquidated damages clause would also deter a potential payee from breach of contract did not in itself make the clause a penalty.

Deterrence had to be the predominant purpose of the clause, and in the instant case that was not so. Mr El-Hajjali could not succeed in his attempt to escape the consequences of his clear unfettered agreement to the clause. Tullett had done its best to find a replacement employee but had failed to do so. It was, therefore, not in breach of any duty to mitigate. The correct measure of damages where a substitute could not be found was consequential loss rather than the cost of a replacement, depending on Tullett's choice. Mr El-Hajjali's argument on causation failed and he was liable for the breach of contract.

Third party conspiracy

Employers who conspire with prospective employees to lure them away from their employer, knowing that they would be in breach of their employment contracts with the former employer, can be successfully sued for conspiracy, aiding and abetting and/or inducing a breach of contract, for which an injunction may be granted and damages may be awarded.

Prospective employers are also warned not to assist in contriving constructive dismissals in order to argue that the former employer has breached the contract thereby seeking to argue that the post-termination restrictions are unenforceable.

In another case, *Tullett Prebon plc v. BGC Brokers and 13 Defendants* [2010] EWHC 484 (QB), the High Court held that BGC Brokers, a broker company which brokers from a rival company (Tullett Prebon) had agreed to join after their existing contracts ended, had conspired to enable the brokers to leave early by contriving constructive dismissal situations.

Tullett Prebon ('Tullett') sued BGC Brokers ('BGC') for conspiracy and inducing breach of contract in respect of the defendant brokers/former employees. BGC had counterclaimed for damages against Tullett for inducing breach of contract by three further brokers. BGC had attempted to recruit brokers from Tullett. Two former Tullet brokers had signed 'forward contracts' to join BGC when their contracts with Tullett permitted, and received signing-on payments. The brokers' contracts included garden leave provisions and post-termination restrictions. BGC wanted the brokers to join earlier than their contracts allowed and indemnified them against any claim made by Tullett. Managers at Tullett held meetings with these brokers. One broker complained about Tullett's treatment of him. The other broker decided not to join BGC as he considered that BGC was unlawfully conspiring to induce them to leave their contracts early. He returned the signing-on payment to BGC.

The second broker gave evidence that Tullett had indicated that it would indemnify him against claims from BGC and would cover the repayment to BGC. Tullett applied for an injunction preventing BGC from inducing Tullett's employees to breach their contracts. The first broker then resigned. Tullett alleged that BGC had with its employees and with this first broker conspired to enable him to leave early by contriving constructive dismissal situations. In their defence, the first broker claimed that he had been constructively dismissed as Tullett had breached the implied term of trust and confidence. BGC claimed that Tullett had induced the second broker to renege on his forward contracts.

The High Court held:

1. The first broker's constructive dismissal allegations failed. He could rely on any conduct by Tullett which, objectively considered, constituted a breach of its duty not seriously to damage the degree of trust and confidence which the first broker was entitled to have. It did not matter whether that conduct in fact caused them to leave because they were not seeking damages. Although it had been tentatively suggested that an employee who was himself in repudiatory breach of contract could not accept a breach by his employer to end the contract, the ordinary position in that situation was that the contract remained in being and could be terminated by one party if the other committed a repudiatory breach: *RDF Media Group plc* v. *Clements* [2008] IRLR 207 and *State Trading Corp of India Ltd* v. *M. Golodetz & Co. Inc. Ltd* [1989] 2 Lloyd's Rep 277 CA (Civ Div) were considered. Whether the employer's conduct had sufficiently damaged the trust and confidence which the employee had in the company was to be judged in all the circumstances, including the employee's own conduct to the extent that that was relevant. The arguments of employees who had already secured alternative employment before resigning would be scrutinised closely. On the facts, Tullett's conduct did not breach the implied term.
2. The alleged conspiracy was approached as one to injure Tullett by unlawful means. It was not necessary to establish that BGC's dominant intention was to injure Tullett's business. It was sufficient that it intended to injure Tullett's business as a means to an end: BGC had intended to advance its business by recruiting Tullett's employees. That would necessarily injure Tullett's business and was sufficient intention if unlawful means were shown. On the facts, there had been a plan to call out the

first broker regardless of whether they had grounds to leave Tullett. The first broker had not been constructively dismissed. It was his decision to leave, but it was essential to his leaving that BGC had indemnified him and they had all known that BGC wanted them to go. The claim in conspiracy was made out against BGC and its employees. However, it could not be shown that the first broker had been party to the conspiracy. He had followed his own course when he was called out by BGC.

3. Tullett had induced the second broker to repudiate the forward contract. It had been Tullett's intention in its meetings to induce the brokers to change their minds about going to BGC, and the meetings were a factor in the second broker's decision to stay. Further, the second broker would not have decided to renege on the forward contracts without the indemnity and the repayment money from Tullett. However, BGC had by its conduct repudiated the contracts and so had suffered no loss from Tullett's inducement to the second broker. It had showed a cynical disregard for the law and employees' duties. Its conduct was such that the second broker could have no trust and confidence in it as his future employer: a person could have no trust in an employer who had recruited him in such a manner and should not be obliged to serve the employer. The second broker was entitled to treat his obligation to join BGC as ended.

4. Injunctions would be granted to enforce the garden leave and post-termination provisions against some of the other defendants for 12 months in most cases. The interim injunction prohibiting BGC from recruiting from Tullett would end after 14 days: the exposure of BGC's conduct would curb future unlawful recruitment. Tullett was also entitled to recover signing-on payments and loyalty bonuses paid to the first broker in respect of contract periods he had not completed.

2.3 References

There are a number of significant points concerning the giving and receiving of references from external sources:

1. There is no legal duty to give a reference other than under the Financial Services Act 1986 as amended and new Regulations which came into force on 7 March 2017 (see **Chapter 1**). However, if a reference is given it must be 'honest and accurate' (*Spring* v. *Guardian Assurance plc* [1994] IRLR 460 (HL)).

2. This extends to ensuring that, by omission, the picture painted in the reference is not erroneously glowing. For example, where an employee resigns during or at the end of an investigation or during a hearing for gross misconduct it could be misleading or inaccurate not to refer to the fact of those investigations or disciplinary matters and the fact that the employee resigned during them (*Bartholomew* v. *London Borough of Hackney* [1999] IRLR 246 (CA)).

3. This duty does not extend to making the prospective employer aware of the actual reasons for dismissal (*Aspin* v. *Metric Group Ltd* [2004] EWHC 1265 (QB)).
4. The subject of the reference may have a right to see the reference under the subject access rights of the Data Protection Act 1998. There is no general exemption from the right of subject access to a reference other than in respect to one special exemption from the right of access to a confidential reference, when in the hands of the organisation which gave it. This exemption does not apply once the reference is in the hands of the person or organisation to whom the reference has been given. The recipient is, however, entitled to take steps to withhold information that reveals the identity of other individuals such as the author of the reference.

   Clear guidance is given in the Data Protection Code of Practice, Part 2 Employment Records, in section 10:

   > Some employers have concerns about defamation and being sued for libel. Libel is only actionable if the information is untrue and prompted by malice and it has been published.

   An obvious way to show malice is for the claimant to show that the employer knew that what had been written was untrue. However, there is a defence to libel – that of qualified privilege. This defence has been traditionally applied to circumstances such as the provision of a reference to a prospective employer, when it can be shown that an individual is exercising a legal or moral duty to communicate information to someone who has an interest in receiving it.
5. Any refusal to give a reference or giving a bad or unfavourable reference in response to a complaint or claim of discrimination has been held to be an act of victimisation which is unlawful under s.27 of the Equality Act 2010. In *Jessemey* v. *Rowstock Ltd* [2014] EWCA Civ 185 the Court of Appeal held that the Equality Act 2010 did cover post-termination victimisation such as the refusal to provide a reference or providing an unfavourable reference (despite a drafting error omitting this kind of claim from the wording of the Act).
6. However, merely refusing to give a reference pending litigation, even if it is a discrimination claim, has been held not to be victimisation and a perfectly legitimate decision for an employer to take.

In *Chief Constable of West Yorkshire Police* v. *Khan* [2001] IRLR 830, an employee alleged that he had been victimised for bringing a race discrimination claim. The employer argued that he had been treated no less favourably than someone who had commenced other litigation of an 'unprotected' nature against the employer. The House of Lords held that:

(1) The decision in *Cornelius* v. *University of Swansea* showed that once proceedings had been commenced a new relationship was created between employer and employee: that of adversaries in litigation.

(2) Employers ought to be able to protect themselves in pending proceedings, by preserving their position, without laying themselves open to a charge of victimisation. That conclusion accorded with the spirit and purpose of the Act. Furthermore, an employer who so acted did so because of the pending proceedings (or the determination of them) rather than because of the discrimination complained of.

(3) Mr Khan's case proffered the unacceptable prospect that his ex-employer would have had to give a reference that would later be rejected by a judicial body or else simply mention, without further explanation, that proceedings were pending.

2.4 Acceptance with signature of employee

It may sound trite but it is very important that job applicants or employees sign to confirm that they have 'read, understood and accept the terms of the employment contract'. There are often disputes taken to Employment Tribunals years after the contract commenced where the terms and conditions have not been signed and there is a dispute over exactly what terms and conditions were accepted and prevailed at the material time, i.e. at the time of the dispute or at the date of termination.

It is particularly important to obtain the signature of the employee where there is an agreement for the employee to opt out of the Working Time Regulations 1998, SI 1998/1833, 48-hour week. Without a written and signed agreement, there can be no valid 'opt out'.

2.5 Principal statement

Since the original Contracts of Employment Act 1963, employers have been required to put certain basic terms in writing. This requirement can now be found in ss.1–13 of the Employment Rights Act 1996, as amended. Such terms must be put in writing no later than two months from the start of the employee's employment.

There is a penalty for failure to provide written particulars (Employment Act 2002, s.38(6)). Employers who fail to provide the required statutory particulars or fail to do so on time (i.e. within two months of an employee starting employment) can be financially penalised. Employment Tribunals have been given powers to make an award of either two or four 'weeks' pay' for failure to provide written particulars or failing to do so on time, capped at the statutory weekly maximum. For 2016 the maximum 'week's pay' was £479. However, the right to sue for failing to provide written particulars is not a free-standing right. The employee must be bringing another claim, for unfair dismissal or discrimination.

These basic particulars are required to be given to 'employees' and not to independent contractors or freelance staff.

The following are the basic statutory particulars which the employer must put in writing, either in full or by reference to a document where the written particulars may be found. Unless otherwise stated below, the terms must be set out in full in the written statement:

1. Name of the parties to the contract, i.e. employee and employer.
2. The date when the employment began and the commencement date of any continuous service.
3. The scale or rate of remuneration and the intervals at which it is to be paid (i.e. weekly, monthly or other intervals).
4. Any terms relating to hours of work including whether there are any normal working hours.
5. Any terms relating to holiday entitlement, including public holidays and terms relating to holiday pay (in particular how holiday pay is calculated for the payment of accrued holiday entitlement upon termination of employment).
6. Any terms relating to sickness absence for illness or injury and for sick pay.
7. Any terms relating to pensions and pension schemes or a note specifying the document where these can be found, including a note specifying whether a contracting-out certificate is in force for that particular employment.
8. Notice period to terminate the contract for employer and employee (subject to statutory minimum period).
9. Job title or brief job description.
10. Where the employment is not intended to be permanent, the period for which it is expected to continue or if it is fixed term, the date when it is to end.
11. The place of work or if there is a requirement for the employee to work at different locations, the fact of this and of the address of the employer (e.g. sales representatives who often travel from home to their territory every day).
12. Any collective agreements which provide for all or some of the terms and conditions.
13. Details if the employee is required to work outside the UK for more than one month.
14. Details of the disciplinary rules and the disciplinary procedure or a note referring to a document specifying such rules and procedure.
15. Details of the procedure (including the person) through which an employee may appeal a disciplinary decision or a note referring to a document setting this out.
16. Details of the person to whom a grievance may be addressed.

The following terms can be referred to by way of reference to another document:

(a) absence due to sickness or injury;
(b) pensions;
(c) notice;

(d) disciplinary procedures.

A typical principal statement can be found at **Precedent 2J**.

2.6 Holidays

Under the Working Time Regulations 1998, SI 1998/1833, all employees are entitled to 28 days' paid holiday every year. However, whether they are entitled to bank, public or statutory or proclaimed holidays in addition is a matter for each employer, save for those staff covered by the Banking and Financial Dealings Act 1971 which provides an entitlement to those staff for bank holidays. Bank holidays are days on which banks in the whole or part of the UK may close for business.

What is included in holiday pay?

There has been a flurry of litigation up to and back from the Court of Justice of the European Union (CJEU) concerning what holiday pay should and should not include.

In *British Gas Trading Ltd* v. *Lock and Secretary of State for Business, Innovation and Skills* [2016] EWCA Civ 983 the Court of Appeal held that holiday pay should include all commission in contractual results-based commission schemes paid to workers, and the reference period for that calculation should be the 12 weeks that is designated in our national legislation.

The Court of Appeal refused to rule on the wider aspects of whether any other form of variable pay, voluntary overtime or bonuses should be included in the calculation for holiday pay, LJ Rimer saying that 'it is no part of this court's function to do more than deal with the instant appeal'.

How do you calculate holiday pay?

The calculation of 'holiday pay' is made by dividing 'normal earnings' or 'normal pay' by the number of working days, e.g. 260 or 262 rather than the number of calendar days (see *Leisure Leagues UK Ltd* v. *Maconnachie* [2002] IRLR 600).

In some contracts employers 'roll up' holiday pay in the hourly or weekly rate and thus there is no additional entitlement to holiday pay when holidays are taken or upon termination of employment. The CJEU ruled in *Robinson-Steele* v. *RD Retail Services Ltd* [2006] IRLR 386 that this practice is unlawful. In other words, holiday pay cannot be entirely rolled up into remuneration. It must be identifiable as a separate additional sum on every payslip so that the holiday pay is clearly set out as an identifiable sum.

It is therefore essential to state:

> Your hourly rate of pay is [£ . . .] gross. This is made up of a basic hourly rate of [£...] and a further [£...] as the rate attributable to holiday pay.

Forfeiture of accrued holiday pay

It used to be a fairly common rule that employees dismissed for gross misconduct would be liable to forfeit any accrued but untaken holiday pay at the effective date of termination. However, this rule became unlawful upon the introduction of the Working Time Regulations 1998. Where such a rule is in place, whether the employer is required to pay all the accrued holiday pay is a moot point.

In *Witley & District Men's Club* v. *Mackay* [2001] IRLR 595, the applicant received no accrued holiday pay when he was dismissed for gross misconduct, in line with the industry-wide rule in the collective agreement. The EAT held that this contravened reg.14 of the Working Time Regulations 1998 which specifies that the payment due (as pay in lieu of leave) is 'such sum'. 'Such sum' does not include 'no sum'. Accordingly, that part of the agreement which provided for no sum to be paid in respect of outstanding leave entitlement was rendered void by the no contracting-out provisions of the Working Time Regulations. However, in such circumstances, there would appear to be nothing in the EAT's decision to preclude an agreement providing for payment of a nominal sum in respect of leave entitlement outstanding on termination.

Holidays for offshore workers

In *Craig* v. *Transocean* [2009] IRLR 519, a case involving offshore workers, the Court of Session held that the definition of 'rest period' in the Working Time Regulations 1998 (WTR) meant that field breaks were capable of constituting 'annual leave'.

The Court of Session held that:

> The time conceded to be available in the field breaks is not working time nor is it compensatory rest. Further, during that available time, the claimants are free of all and any actual work obligations and not subject to the possibility of being called on to work. It is a rest period and is a rest period during which none of the three criteria involved in the definition of working time in the WTD [Working Time Directive 2003] and WTR apply either actually or potentially. It is time that is available for annual leave; it is available to afford to the claimants the rest from work which the WTD and WTR seek to achieve. It does not matter that, because of the working patterns in the industry, the claimants would not otherwise be working during those periods.

In another case on holiday entitlement for offshore workers, the Supreme Court decided in *Russell* v. *Transocean International Resources Ltd* [2011] UKSC 57 that the statutory holiday entitlement for offshore workers is provided for by regular onshore 'field breaks'.

The Supreme Court held that as long as workers had a time when they were not at work, the requirements were met. The employer was therefore entitled to insist that their offshore workers had to take their paid annual leave during periods other than their 26 working weeks, when they are onshore on field break. This is permitted by Regulation 13 of the WTR in conformity with Article 7 of the WTD.

The court held that:

> The contract in question is a contract for the whole of the year, in which the employees were required to work for 26 weeks.
>
> The purpose of the entitlement to annual leave is to enable the worker to rest and enjoy a period of relaxation and leisure.
>
> The ECJ has not said that a pre-ordained rest period, when the worker is free from all obligations to the employer, can never constitute 'annual leave'.
>
> On the contrary, the term 'rest period' simply means any period which is not working time, and 'any period' means every such period irrespective of where the worker is at that time and what he is doing, so long as it is a period when he is not working.
>
> It is plain that any period when the Appellants are on field break onshore will fall into that category.
>
> The Respondents are therefore entitled to insist that the Appellants must take their paid annual leave during periods other than their 26 working weeks when they are onshore on field break. This is permitted by Regulation 13 of the WTR, read in conformity with Article 7 of the WTD.

The Supreme Court also commented that employers could not require employees to take their annual leave in single or two or three days at a time, otherwise an employer could argue that as Saturdays or Sundays are rest days, they had to be taken as annual leave days. Entitlement to annual leave is measured in **weeks**, and not days, so that whilst workers could choose to take their leave in single or additional days, employers could not **require** employees to do this.

Points to consider

The decision is not only of relevance to the oil and gas industry, where shift patterns involving field breaks are common. It also applies to other sectors where employees are required to take leave during periods when they are not required to work, such as teachers, professional footballers or those who work in the tourist industry.

Holidays during sickness absence

We refer to holidays which accrue during sickness absence in **Chapter 6**, in light of the House of Lords' ruling in *HM Revenue & Customs* v. *Stringer* [2009] IRLR 677. The House of Lords ruled that staff accrue paid holiday for their entire sick leave and must be allowed to take it on their return or be paid in lieu if their employment ends.

The case of *Pereda* v. *Madrid Movilidad SA* [2009] IRLR 959 (the Spanish wheel clamper) will also be discussed later (see **6.17**). This case confirms the employee's right to take their accrued leave after they have returned from sick leave, even if this occurs in a new holiday year.

2.7   Incorporation of terms

In some cases, terms can be incorporated into the contract by way of express or implied incorporation. The most commonly incorporated terms are those agreed under a collective agreement, from staff handbooks, rules and regulations compliance manuals and the like. It is wise to refer expressly to those terms in the individual contract of employment: see **Precedent 2H**.

In some cases the courts will deem terms to be incorporated by way of a collective agreement and in other cases they will not. In the case of *Griffiths and Moore* v. *Salisbury District Council* [2004] EWCA Civ 162 the Court of Appeal held that an implementation agreement agreed with the local trade unions relating to a new pay and grading structure was 'apt for incorporation' into the contracts of employment. This was because the Green Book (the nationally agreed terms) contemplated that there would be a regrading exercise. The clauses in the implementation agreement (para.13):

> make clear that, if there is a regrading, and if it is done in consultation with the recognised unions and if the unions agree to terms for the protection from loss of remuneration (if any), then the regrading is to take effect. Clauses 11 and 12 of the Implementation Agreement use the natural language of obligation ... and in my judgment are entirely apt for incorporation as legally binding commitments into the claimants' contracts of employment.

See further *Alexander* v. *Standard Telephones & Cables Ltd* (*No. 2*) [1991] IRLR 286 where the selection procedure (last in, first out – LIFO) agreed in a collective agreement was not deemed to be incorporated into the written particulars because there was nothing in the written particulars governing redundancy, and none of the other clauses in the collective agreement were apt for incorporation or intended to be incorporated by implication.

2.8   Ensuring that employee is not breaching covenants

It is particularly important when recruiting senior staff, sales representatives and traders in the City to ensure that the candidate will not be breaching any restrictive covenants if they commence employment with a new employer (e.g. that there are no non-competition, non-solicitation or non-poaching clauses in their former contracts).

Apart from asking for a copy of their current or former contract at interview, it may be wise to include the following clause in the contract:

> The Executive warrants that by virtue of entering into this Agreement (or the other agreements or arrangements made or to be made between the Company or any Associated Company and them) they will not be in breach of any express or implied terms of any contract with or of any other obligation to any third party binding upon them.
> The Executive warrants that they have disclosed to the Company all relevant employment documents relating to their former employment in which their restrictive covenants may be found.

2.9   Probationary period

A probationary period was discussed briefly in **Chapter 1**. If the employer wishes to place new employees on a probationary period or trial period, it would be wise to consider the following points:

(a) definition of the probationary or trial period;
(b) its purpose;
(c) duration of the period;
(d) extension of the period and reasons for extension;
(e) training provided;
(f) aspects of performance to be monitored;
(g) objectives and target-setting;
(h) requirement to follow rules of the organisation;
(i) exclusion of warning and hearing and appeals procedure during the period;
(j) standards of attendance and time-keeping;
(k) expectation of team-working;
(l) standards of reliability;
(m) standards of health;
(n) pregnancy and maternity during the probationary period;
(o) regular reviews;
(p) decisions as to continued employment;
(q) whether there will be any right of appeal against a decision to dismiss.

2.10 Changes to contracts

If an employer wishes to reserve the right unilaterally to change terms and conditions of employment then there must be a clear and unambiguous right in the contract to do so. See *Bateman* v. *Asda Stores Ltd* [2010] IRLR 370.

A typical clause would be:

> The Company reserves the right to review, revise, amend or replace the content of this handbook, and introduce new policies from time to time to reflect the changing needs of the business and to comply with new legislation. A copy of the handbook is displayed on the colleague communication board in your store and on the Company intranet and replacement copies are available from your HR Manager. You should keep yourself up to date with any changes by attending meetings and by keeping your eye on the colleague communication board for any updates, etc.

2.11 Induction

Many employers have well-defined induction procedures to ensure that new employees are properly introduced into the organisation, instructed on procedures and trained in emergency procedures, etc.

2.12 Employment of close relatives

Some employers place restrictions on the employment of close relatives to avoid allegations of nepotism, racial or sex discrimination, possible collusion or dishonest behaviour or personnel problems if a relative is disciplined or dismissed in the future. Examples of these rules can be found at **Precedent 2K**.

PRECEDENT 2A: Unconditional offer with continuing obligation to remain registered

1. It is a continuing obligation on your part to remain registered with your registering body [e.g. *for a doctor* the General Medical Council (GMC); *for a nurse* the Nursing and Midwives Council (NMC); *for the financial services industry* the Financial Conduct Authority (FCA); *for in-house/employed lawyers* the Law Society or Bar Council; *for chartered accountants* the Royal Institute of Chartered Accountants].

2. If you are or become subject to any disciplinary matter or charged with any criminal offence then you are required to report this matter to your line manager immediately.

3. If you are struck off the [register/Roll, etc.] and are therefore debarred from practising in your professional capacity, this will be regarded as gross misconduct and a fundamental breach of your contract and the Company reserves the right to dismiss you summarily following a disciplinary hearing and your right of appeal.

PRECEDENT 2B: Unconditional offer with continuing conditions: examinations

1. You will be required to sit and pass your [final/preliminary] examinations set by the [Law Society/Royal Institute of Chartered Accountants/banking/regulatory authorities]. You are permitted to sit these examinations no more than [three times in three years]. However, should you fail such examinations more than once, the Company reserves the right to regard such conduct as a fundamental and repudiatory breach of contract giving it the right to terminate your employment summarily, i.e. without notice or payment in lieu.

2. You are required to notify the Company in writing as soon as you know the results of such examinations.

3. In the happy circumstances of you passing such examinations on the first occasion, the Company will pay you a bonus at its entire discretion not exceeding 10 per cent of your current annual basic salary.

PRECEDENT 2C: Offer letter

[*To be printed on company letterhead*]

Our ref: [*reference number*]

[*name*]

[*address*]

[*date*]

Dear [*name*]

RE: Offer of employment – [*job title*]

I refer to our recent meeting and am now pleased to write formally making you a conditional offer of employment with [*company name*] ('the Company') as a [*job title*].

I would ask you to forgive the formality of this letter but trust you will appreciate it is intended to form the basis of the contractual agreement between us. Subject to your conditional acceptance of our offer, you will be provided with a formal contract of employment when you start work with us. Please note that this provisional offer can be withdrawn if any of the conditions listed below in this letter are not met. It is advisable not to resign from your existing position until we have confirmed that you have satisfied these conditions.

This offer will be confirmed in writing, once we have received:

1. three satisfactory employment references (one from your current or last employer or your school or college if you do not have three previous employers);
2. a satisfactory medical questionnaire and/or satisfactory medical examination;
3. satisfactory evidence of your right to work in the UK;
4. evidence of your school, post school and professional qualifications – the original certificates;
5. evidence of your FCA/GMC/NMC registration;
6. a satisfactory credit rating check.

('Satisfactory' means satisfactory to the Company.)

We may require you to give your consent for the disclosure of GP and hospital records to our occupational health physician or physician whom we have appointed. Failure to give your consent will mean that our conditional offer will be withdrawn.

Turning now to the terms of the employment initially offered, I list these below as follows:

1. **Role**

Your role will be as [*job title*]. You will report directly to the [*job title of senior manager*]. A summary of your duties will be given to you by way of a job description when you join but please note that you are required to be flexible and undertake any duties that it would be reasonable to expect you to undertake either in your own department, another department or at another location. Given the nature of our business it is essential that you are willing to be co-operative, flexible, willing, committed, courteous and customer-focused at all times.

2. **Location**

Your principal place of work will be the [*location*] office. However, on occasion it may be necessary to work from one of our other offices. You also agree to be mobile and work from any office within the UK on either a temporary or permanent basis. If it is the latter you will be given reasonable notice and relocation expenses.

3. **Salary**

We can offer you a commencing salary of [£*amount*] per annum, subject to tax, which is paid monthly in arrears direct to your bank.

Salaries are reviewed annually, with the date of any revision being effective on 1 May each year. Your salary will next be eligible for review on 1 May [*year*], although a review does not guarantee an increase in your salary.

4. **Expenses**

The Company shall reimburse to you all expenses reasonably and properly incurred by you in the performance of your duties subject to the production of such receipts or other evidence of expenditure as the Company may reasonably require.

5. [Bonus

The Company is in the process of introducing a new bonus scheme. The terms of the scheme are yet to be agreed, but it is likely to be based on the Company's overall performance against annual budget and your achievement of personal objectives for the year.

The potential bonus payable is likely to be expressed as a percentage of your salary. Whether any bonus is paid in any year will remain entirely at the discretion of the Company.

You will be granted access into the bonus scheme from the commencement of the new financial year which runs from 1 April 2018 to 31 March 2019.]

6. Pension scheme

We operate our own group personal pension plan which personnel are invited to join on completion of their probationary period. The rate of contribution to this scheme by employees, elected by the employee, is between three and five per cent with the Company contributing a matched percentage within that range. The policy will be arranged in your name as this gives you maximum control over your benefits.

Full details of the scheme shall be provided to you at the appropriate time. There is no requirement upon you to join the Company's pension plan if you prefer not to do so. Should you choose not to join the Company's pension plan, however, the Company will not be prepared to contribute to any other plan or private pension arrangements you may have.

7. [Private health insurance and life assurance

You will be invited to join the Company's private health insurance scheme, at our expense. You will be eligible to join the scheme from the date your employment commences subject to completion of the appropriate formalities and the normal terms and conditions of the scheme. The cost of your subscriptions will of course rank as a benefit in kind and will be subject to tax in the usual way.

Should you be interested in taking part in the scheme please let me know and I shall arrange for details to be sent to you.

From the time you join us, you will also be enrolled in the Company's life assurance scheme subject to normal terms and conditions.]

8. Office hours

Normal office hours are from [time] to [time] with the usual [unpaid/paid] one hour's break for lunch, Monday to Friday inclusive. However, owing to the nature of your role you may be required to work additional hours (i.e. outside normal office hours) and in some cases where absolutely necessary at weekends or on bank, statutory or public holidays, for which you shall not be entitled to receive any additional remuneration. You may be granted time off in lieu at the entire discretion of your line manager.

9. Holidays

You will be entitled to a total of [number] days paid holiday per calendar year of employment or a pro rata proportion thereof inclusive of all bank, statutory and public Holidays. We ask that, unless there are very special circumstances, no more than two consecutive weeks' holiday be taken at any one time and that at least one month's notice is given of any intended holiday. The Company reserves the right to refuse holiday where the needs of the business dictate or where other employees are also on leave at that time and the office would be deemed to be understaffed. The Company operates on a 'first come first served' basis.

We shall honour any existing holiday arrangements you may have made, provided that you notify us of these prior to joining the Company. Any period of absence over your pro rata entitlement, however, shall have to be regarded as unpaid leave.

10. **Probationary period**

There is a standard probationary period of at least three months, during which time either party can terminate the employment with one week's written notice or payment in lieu. The probationary period may be extended if this is necessary in the opinion of management. Following satisfactory completion of your probationary period, which will be confirmed to you in writing, the period of notice for termination of employment is three months' written notice from either party or payment in lieu.

11. **Conditions**

This offer is subject to the following conditions:

- all information supplied by you to the Company being completely true and complete;
- receipt by us of two employment references one of which must be from your last employer, which are entirely satisfactory to the Company;
- the Company obtaining satisfactory declaration of your medical fitness and your state of health remaining satisfactory prior to you joining;
- you producing to the Company your passport or such other documentation as we may require evidencing your right to remain and work in the UK.

This offer will automatically lapse and be of no effect if any of the above conditions are not satisfied or it becomes clear to the Company that the condition will not be satisfied prior to the commencement of your employment.

12. **Data protection**

Under the EU's General Data Protection Regulation and the UK's amended Data Protection Act 1998, you have a right to choose whether or not to give your consent to us holding, processing and disclosing your personal data.

You understand that we need to keep and maintain records in respect of all employees and that it is necessary to record, keep and process your personal data. This data may be kept and maintained in computer and/or manual format.

It may be necessary, in the course of the Company's duties and obligations as an employer, to disclose such data to third parties, including other employees, potential purchasers of the Company, potential investors, the Company's professional advisers, clients and potential clients, HMRC, etc.

We obtain, process and disclose your personal data for the following purposes:

1. performing this contract of employment,
2. making decisions regarding your employment,
3. as referred to in the disciplinary procedure,
4. obtaining business,
5. complying with legal requirements,
[6. *additional purposes*].

You also acknowledge and agree to us disclosing your personal data after the termination of your employment. This does not affect your rights as a data subject or the Company's obligations and responsibilities under the Data Protection Act 1998 as amended. Your consent will be obtained if we need to do this.

From time to time, you will have access to and will deal with personal data relating to other persons, including other employees and customers. You shall not record, remove, keep, process or disclose personal data relating to other persons, other than in accordance with the Company's specific instructions.

You have the right not to give your consent to any form of processing of your personal data and if you give your consent to withdraw it at any time without any penalty or detriment or disadvantage to you.

Please sign below that you agree to the processing, holding and disclosing of your personal data or indicate that you do not agree.

If you choose not to accept this offer, however, we will destroy the information which we currently hold about you within six months from the date of this letter.

13. Commencement date

Subject to obtaining satisfactory references, we invite you join us from [date].

If you choose to accept our offer, I should be grateful if you would telephone me in the first instance and then follow this up with a letter, confirming both your proposed commencement date and that you are able to agree the terms and conditions of employment as set out in this letter.

I look forward to hearing from you but please feel free to give me a call should you have any queries whatsoever.

Yours sincerely

[Manager's name and job title]

PRECEDENT 2D: Policy on prevention of illegal working

Policy on Immigration, Asylum and Nationality Act 2006

IMPORTANT NOTE – PLEASE READ CAREFULLY

PREVENTION OF ILLEGAL WORKING

The Immigration, Asylum and Nationality Act 2006 states it will be an offence to employ a person who is not entitled under the Immigration Rules to work in the UK.

All candidates/employees will be required to provide one or more of the original documents listed below.

- A document issued by previous employer, HM Revenue and Customs, the Benefits Agency, the Contributions Agency or the Employment Service (or their Northern Ireland equivalents) which states the National Insurance number of the person named.
- This could include a P45, a payslip, a P60, a National Insurance (NINO) card (the newer plastic cards or the older style cards) or a letter issued by one of the government bodies concerned.
- A Passport describing the holder as a British Citizen or as having the right of abode in – or an entitlement to re-admission to – the UK.
- A Passport containing a Certificate of Entitlement issued by or on behalf of the government of the UK certifying that the holder has the right of abode in the UK.
- A Certificate of Registration or Naturalisation as a British Citizen.
- A Birth Certificate issued in the UK or in the Republic of Ireland.

- For these purposes the UK includes England, Wales, Scotland, Northern Ireland, the Channel Islands and the Isle of Man.
- A Passport or National Identity Card issued by a State which is party to the European Economic Area Agreement and which describes the holder as a national of that State.
- A Passport or other travel document endorsed to show that the person named is exempt from immigration control, has indefinite leave to enter, or remain in, the UK or has no time limit on his or her stay or a letter issued by the Home Office confirming that the person named has such status.
- A Passport or other travel document endorsed to show that the person named has current leave to enter or remain in the UK and is not precluded from taking the employment in question; or a letter issued by the Home Office confirming that this is the case.
- A UK Residence Permit issued to a national of a State which is party to the European Economic Area Agreement.
- A Passport or other travel document endorsed to show that the holder has a current right of residence in the UK as the family member of a named national of the State which is a party to the European Economic Agreement and who is resident in the UK.
- A letter issued by the Immigration and Nationality Directorate of the Home Office indicating that the person named in the letter is a British Citizen or has permission to take employment.
- A Work Permit or other approval to take employment issued by the Department of Education and Employment or, in Northern Ireland, by the Training and Employment Agency.
- A Passport describing the holder as a British Department Territories citizen and which indicates that the status derives from a connection with Gibraltar.

If you are uncertain about which documents to provide, please contact the address where the application form is to be returned.

Please note it is a requirement that we keep a photocopy of the document if you are successful in your application.

PRECEDENT 2E: Confirmation of offer to secretary/PA

Private and confidential

[Name]

[Address]

[Date]

Dear [name]

Offer of employment

I am delighted to confirm our offer of a position as a Secretary/PA with [name of employer]. Your starting salary will be £... per annum. Your start date is [date].

I am pleased to confirm that both your references and your medical report were satisfactory.

I enclose a written statement of the terms and conditions on which you will be employed by us and which I should be grateful if you would read carefully. If you are happy with the terms, please would you sign and return the copy to me as soon as possible, together with the signed Confidentiality Agreement.

THE OFFER AND WRITTEN PARTICULARS: THE PRINCIPAL STATEMENT 55

We are delighted you will be joining us and feel sure that you will enjoy your work here.

Yours sincerely

PRECEDENT 2F: Offer letter for transfer of managing director from Paris to London office

Strictly private and confidential

[Name]

[Address]

[Date]

Dear [name]

I am pleased to confirm our earlier conversation, when we discussed your transfer from the Paris to the London office to head the Media and Telecoms team.

We recognise that the transition from Paris to London will be disruptive. Your overall development and performance will be reviewed as usual at the end of each year, but we will not expect you to meet our typical standards for a Managing Director until year-ended [specify], when we will review you against our normal standards.

Please find enclosed two copies of your contract of employment for the London office employment, which you should sign and return one copy to me.

Yours sincerely

PRECEDENT 2G: Authority to obtain references and credit checks

Authorisation form for credit checks and employment references

[Name of employee]

1. I hereby authorise you to take up references from my two previous employers including my present employer (once the offer of employment has been confirmed in writing) from the two named people whom I have submitted as referees. In addition, I hereby authorise you to take up other reference checks as deemed appropriate.

2. I authorise the Company to request that all corporations, companies, educational institutions, persons and former employers release information that they may have about me and release them from any liability and responsibility arising from so doing.

3. I authorise credit agencies to release information that they may have about me to any authorised officer of this Company; this may include but is not limited to any information about any debts, arrears on credit cards, mortgage payments and any county court judgments made against me.

Signed . ...   Date ....

Employee

PRECEDENT 2H: Incorporation of terms

1. Any collective agreements agreed with the relevant trade unions from time to time will form part of your terms and conditions of employment.

2. A Staff Handbook exists governing your terms and conditions of employment, giving more detail than can be covered in this Written Statement. The Staff Handbook is divided into three sections: the first section gives you information about the Company, its personnel, its offices worldwide and its business ethics and philosophy; the second section contains your terms and conditions and is of contractual status and is thus very important for you to read; the third section contains policies and procedures some of which are contractual and some of which do not form part of your contract but provide useful information and guidance. Those sections of the Handbook that contain contractual terms are coloured red and those that are intended merely as a guide are coloured blue.

3. Any Rules and/or Regulations that are published by our Regulatory Body will automatically be incorporated into your contract of employment and you will be sent a copy of such Rules making their status clear within four weeks of any such new Rules or Regulations being sent to the Company.

PRECEDENT 2I: Probationary period/trial period

1. **Definition of Probation/Trial Period**

1.1 All new recruits must undertake a period on Probation/Trial Period.

1.2 Confirmation of appointment is dependent on satisfactory completion of the Probation/Trial Period.

1.3 The minimum requirement for successful completion of your Probation/Trial is that the post-holder achieves the normal requirements of the post, including the key objectives to the standards of performance set and shows a willingness, co-operation and collegiate behaviour.

1.4 If any aspect of performance or conduct or attitude is not satisfactory and it is considered that the post-holder will not be able to reach the necessary standard by the end of the Probation/Trial Period, a defined extension to the Probation/Trial Period may be appropriate. However, the appointment can be terminated within or at the end of the original Probation/Trial Period where it is considered that an extension would not bring about a sustained improvement. During the Probation/Trial Period, the Disciplinary and Grievance Procedures do not apply and dismissal may take place without any warnings or hearing or right of appeal.

2. **Training needs**

Objectives set for the Probation/Trial Period will reflect that the post-holder is 'new in job'. The line manager will set, organise and evaluate appropriate training and developmental objectives for the post-holder.

3. **Length of probation**

As stated in the Summary Statement of Terms and Conditions of Employment:

- For indefinite appointments/period appointments of over one year – normal Probation Period is one year.
- For period appointments of one year or less – a shorter Probation Period may apply. The minimum Probation Period is six months, or the length of the appointment, whichever is the shorter.

4. Qualifications

If an appointment is conditional on the post-holder obtaining a specific qualification within the Probation Period, this will be specified in the Offer Letter. Failure to obtain the qualification within the timescale specified may result in termination of employment.

5. Aspects of performance

5.1 Probation is assessed on the following:

(a) Capability and achievement of specified objectives: the post-holder will be assessed on his/her ability to achieve the specified objectives, agreed upon appointment.
(b) Conduct: the post-holder must be made aware of the employer's rules as part of the induction process. Any breaches will be taken into account when probation is being assessed.
(c) Attendance: hours of attendance must be in accord with the Company's rules and as per the post-holder's Statement of Terms and Conditions. Poor time-keeping and unauthorised absence will be noted and addressed. Line management must consider difficulties over attendance in the context of the Company's family friendly policies. Poor attendance on grounds of ill health is dealt with below.
(d) Team-working (if applicable): this will be assessed where effective team work is required in order to perform the role satisfactorily.
(e) Reliability: where reliability is not already covered, i.e. under performance, attendance and team work, it should be considered and assessed separately. An objective assessment will be made of factors such as decision-making, recommending, problem-solving and use of initiative. Similarly, the post-holder's reliability in terms of his/her ability to: follow instructions, manage his/her own time, prioritise, use his/her initiative and use other resources in a cost-effective and appropriate manner will be assessed, if they are relevant to the job.
(f) Attendance record and health: if the post-holder accumulates more than five working days' intermittent sickness absence or more than 10 working days' medically certified sickness absence during the Probation Period, the reasons and circumstances will be carefully considered. The assessment will also consider any effects of poor health on the work of the individual and the department in which he/she works. Serious problems will be dealt with under our medical referral procedure and consideration will be given to a medical assessment by our Occupational Health Physician.
(g) The employer will comply with the requirements of the disability discrimination provisions of the Equality Act 2010. If the post-holder has a medical condition which comes within the terms of the Equality Act, necessary and reasonable adjustments will be made to enable the post-holder to perform effectively within the limitations of the disability or condition. Objectives will be adjusted accordingly and the post-holder's performance during the Probation/Trial Period and beyond will be monitored on this basis. Where necessary, the Occupational Health Department (OHD) or an external professional body will be consulted.
(h) Sick absences linked to a medical condition which is covered by the Equality Act 2010 will be assessed during the Probation/Trial Period and further reasonable adjustments will be made, where appropriate. The OHD or equivalent will normally be consulted. Similar arrangements will apply if the post-holder's health appears to be adversely affected by the nature of the work or working environment.
(i) Further advice on the applicability and operation of the Equality Act can be obtained from the HR Manager.
(j) Sick absences for minor reasons will be taken into account when assessing overall

performance during the Probation/Trial Period. Frequent short-term absences will be investigated, in consultation with the OHD or equivalent where appropriate.

(k) Where an employee has been injured in an accident or has suffered a relatively serious, but non-recurring illness, probation may be extended.

6. Maternity and pregnancy

Under no circumstances will changes in performance caused by pregnancy or absence on maternity leave form any part of a probation assessment.

7. Assessment and reporting

7.1 Probation assessments will be undertaken by the post-holder's immediate line manager and the co-signatory.

7.2 The form 'Forward Job Plan and Probation Assessment' will be used. This stipulates:

(a) First Performance Review.
(b) Second Performance Review.
(c) Final Performance Review.

7.3 The post-holder will be kept fully informed of his/her progress and will see the Probation/Trial Form, may add written comments if desired, and will be required to sign off the form before it is submitted to the Director.

7.4 Assessment of performance is continuous and any deficiencies or problems will be brought to the post-holder's attention immediately they are identified, rather than at the next formal Probation/Trial Review. The line manager, co-signatory and post-holder will together agree how the post-holder can be enabled to attain the necessary standard.

8. Decisions

8.1 At any stage of the decision process, the employee may invite a trade union representative or a fellow employee to make representations on his/her behalf.

8.2 To merit confirmation of appointment, the post-holder's performance over the Probation/Trial Period as a whole must indicate that there will be sustained successful performance.

8.3 A decision on confirmation of appointment or on dismissal will be made by the Director/nominee, based on the recommendation of the line manager and/or co-signatory, as per the Probation/Trial Form.

8.4 The post-holder will be notified, in writing, of the outcome of probation, at or shortly before the end of the Probation Period.

9. Warnings/termination of employment

9.1 Other than in the circumstances where the Company considers that summary dismissal of the employee is appropriate, where the line manager and/or co-signatory considers that there are serious or significant problems with an aspect of the post-holder's performance, s/he will be given a written statement of the basis of the alleged misconduct or incapability which have led to the problems. Once the employee has been given this statement and the employee has had a reasonable opportunity to consider his/her response, the employee will be invited to attend a meeting to discuss the matter. The employee must take all reasonable steps to attend the meeting. At this meeting the employee may invite a trade union representative or a fellow employee to make representations on his/her behalf. After the meeting, the Company will inform the employee of its decision (which may be a written warning or dismissal, if justified) and notify the employee of his/her right to appeal against that decision if s/he is not satisfied with it. If a written warning is issued, it will state the problem and the consequences of failure to rectify the problem: namely, dismissal on grounds of failed probation.

9.2 Pay in lieu of notice will be given where management considers this is appropriate.

10. Appeals

10.1 If an employee wishes to appeal against a warning issued, s/he must inform his/her line manager. If s/he does so, the Company will invite the employee to attend a further meeting, which the employee must take all reasonable steps to attend. At this meeting the employee may invite a trade union representative or a fellow employee to make representations on his/her behalf. (This meeting may take place after the dismissal or disciplinary action takes effect.) A post-holder who is dismissed for not successfully completing his/her probation has the right of appeal to the Director of Human Resources within two months of receiving the letter of termination.

10.2 After an appeal meeting, the Company will inform the employee of its final decision.

11. Extension of Probation/Trial for defined period

11.1 Extension of Probation/Trial for a defined period may be made if there is a reasonable prospect that, given further time, confirmation of appointment will follow. Extensions on grounds of performance will normally be for three months in the first instance, with a maximum of 18 months.

11.2 If a longer period of Probation/Trial is required on medical grounds (see above) or because of absence on maternity leave, the Probation/Trial Period will not last longer than two years.

11.3 Where an extension is given, the post-holder will be fully informed of the reasons for the extension; the standard s/he is required to achieve and maintain; the time limits required; and that dismissal will result if the required objectives/standards are not achieved and maintained throughout the remaining period of extended probation.

11.4 Formal reporting is likely to be more frequent than during normal probation.

11.5 The whole Probation/Trial Period must be reviewed when considering whether to confirm appointment during or at the end of an extension.

12. Probationary pay

12.1 During Probation/Trial, a post-holder's pay may be adjusted at each Probation Review. Any adjustment must be based on the person specification for the particular job and the post-holder's performance during Probation.

12.2 Upon satisfactory completion of Probation, s/he may also receive a final adjustment as appropriate for the level of competence and contribution to the Company. This final adjustment cannot take the salary above the Standard Pay Point.

13. Transfer to an associated company

If, before the completion of Probation, the post-holder is transferred to an associated company, the period of Probation/Trial already served will be taken into account in assessing the Probation/Trial Period to be served at the new location.

14. Pension scheme benefits

An employee who fails Probation for any reason is not regarded as having been retired in the public interest or on grounds of inefficiency and is not, therefore, entitled to any benefits under the Company's Pension Scheme.

PRECEDENT 2J: Principal statement

Statement of written employment particulars

This Statement comprises the Principal Statement of Terms and Conditions of your employment with [name of employer]. It is issued in accordance with the Employment Rights Act 1996, the Employment Relations Act 1999, the Employment Act 2002 and other related legislation. Terms and Conditions are negotiated with reference to the [GMB], the recognised trade union at [employer].

1. Parties

This is the Contract of Employment between [employer] and [employee].

1.1 Your full name and address is [employee's full name and address].

1.2 The Company's name and address is [employer's name and address].

2. Commencement of service

Your employment will begin on [date].

3. Continuous employment

Your employment with any previous employer does not count as part of your continuous period of employment.

4. Job details

4.1 Your job title is [specify].

4.2 The section you will work in is [specify].

4.3 You will initially work at head office at [address] but you may be required to work at any of the Company's locations in the [specify] area (i.e. within reasonable daily commuting distance of your home) on either a temporary or permanent basis following reasonable notice and where the needs of the business require it.

4.4 You will be responsible to [specify].

4.5 Your duties are as set out in the job description accompanying your letter of appointment. Because of the nature of our business (a 24-hour continuous shift), on occasion the Company may have to make reasonable amendments to your job description where necessary for the good of the organisation; any such changes will be made in consultation with the employee(s), and staff have the right to take advice from their trade union if they have any concerns about this process.

5. Salary

5.1 You will be paid £ ... Your starting salary is: £ ...

5.2 Salaries are paid monthly by bank transfer by the [20th] of each month. [Increments based upon incremental points on this scale will be paid after 12 complete months' service and annually thereafter, until the maximum of the scale is reached, subject to satisfactory review. Increments will also be paid after 12 months' complete service and annually thereafter following any interim regrading or promotion.] Overtime payments are not made.

6. Reviews and appraisals

6.1 Your appointment is subject to the satisfactory completion of a probationary period of up to 12 weeks. During this period you will be reviewed and supervised. You will have two weekly one-to-one supervisions and notes will be made and placed in your file (copies of which will be given to you). Your probationary period shall be completed with a formal written probationary review, the purpose of which is to determine whether there are any insuperable problems with your employment, either from the Company's point of view or from yours. The probationary period may be extended for up to a further 12 weeks as deemed appropriate by your managers, as laid out in the Review and Appraisal Policy. During your probationary period you will not be subject to the formal disciplinary procedure although you will be subject to all the Company's rules and regulations. This means that if at any time during your probationary period, the Company deems it appropriate to terminate your employment, you will not receive any prior formal warnings nor will you have the right to a hearing or an appeal.

6.2 There will be an annual appraisal at the end of each completed year of service. Details are given in the separate document Review and Appraisal Policy in the Staff Handbook.

7. Hours of work

7.1 Your contracted hours of work each week will be 37. The Company offers an optional flexi-time system, by application to your line manager; details of this are given in the Flexi-time Guidelines document in the Staff Handbook. Staff who choose not to work flexi-time or to whom flexi-time is not available will agree a normal pattern of working hours with their line manager.

7.2 Time worked outside of the defined hours on the Flexi-time Guidelines/agreed normal hours (i.e. unpaid overtime) must be agreed with your line manager. This time may be redeemed by taking time off in lieu (TOIL), as laid out in the Lieu Time Policy in the Staff Handbook, and this must normally be taken within two months of the entitlement arising. Your total working week, including any overtime, must not exceed an average of 48 hours, in line with the Working Time Regulations 1998.

7.3 You are required to fill in a monthly timesheet as attached to the Flexi-time Guidelines and to keep records of any overtime worked. You are allowed to take a 15-minute break away from your desk each morning and afternoon, which is paid time. Lunch breaks, which are unpaid, are as detailed in the Flexi-time Guidelines.

8. Holidays

8.1 Full-time staff are entitled to the following days' public holidays with pay: these are New Year's Day, two days at Easter, one day for early May Bank and one day at Spring Bank, one day at Summer Bank, two days at Christmas. (Part-time staff: see clause 8.5.)

8.2 The annual leave year runs from 1 April to 31 March. In your first full leave year full-time staff are entitled to 20 working days' paid holiday. Up to 31 March in the leave year in which you are appointed, you are entitled to 1.3 days for each completed month of service (to be calculated on a pro rata basis for part months worked). Your entitlement to paid annual leave calculated as above starts from the first day of your employment by the Company.

8.3 Holidays may only be taken at times agreed with your line manager. At least one month's prior written notice must be given for any holidays taken.

In the case of any issues over holiday, the Company will use the 'first come first served' principle. It is therefore advisable to put in your holiday leave forms as early as possible. The Company reserves the right to decline any holiday request for legitimate business or other reasons.

The Company also reserves the right to require the taking of annual leave at particular times during a holiday year, e.g. during any period of Garden Leave during a notice period; during a non-busy time; over Christmas and New Year, etc.

8.4 Holiday entitlement may only be carried over from one year to the next and for one year only, with the agreement of your line manager and up to a maximum of five days. Holidays are meant to be taken in the relevant year for the purposes of rest and relaxation. This provision does not apply to women on maternity leave, fathers on extended paternity leave or those who are or have been on sick leave where holidays have accrued.

8.5 All holiday entitlement for part-time staff (public and annual holidays) shall be on a pro rata basis. This means that if you work half-time (i.e. 18.5 hours per week), you will be entitled to half the annual allowance (i.e. 10 days). Part-time workers may make up any time owed for public holidays by working on other days of the week or by using lieu time or annual leave. If this is not possible, pay will be adjusted in public holiday weeks.

8.6 On termination of employment, any outstanding holiday entitlement should be taken during the notice period. If this is not possible, you will be paid for any accrued leave outstanding at the effective date of termination. A day's pay for this purpose will be calculated by dividing your annual salary by the number of working days, e.g. 260.

9. **Sickness payments**

9.1 Provided that the procedure laid out in section 10 is followed, you will be entitled to sickness payments on the following scale:

(a) During the first six months of service: two weeks' full pay.
(b) Thereafter and up to 12 months' service: four weeks' full pay, four weeks' half pay.
(c) After one year of service: six weeks' full pay, six weeks' half pay.
(d) After two years' service: two months' full pay, two months' half pay.
(e) After three years' service: three months' full pay, three months' half pay.
(f) After four years' service: four months' full pay, four months' half pay.
(g) After five years' service: five months' full pay, five months' half pay.
(h) After six or more years' service: six months' full pay, six months' half pay.

(The maximum amount will remain at six months' full pay, six months' half pay for any subsequent number of years worked subject always to review in special cases.)

Sickness payments will be calculated on a cumulative basis within a rolling 12-month period, e.g. a person with one year's completed service returning to work in April after six weeks' sickness who has a further period of sickness in August will receive half pay for this second period. The probationary period counts as full service when calculating sickness entitlement.

9.2 The Company reserves the right to refer staff to a doctor appointed by the Company at any time during employment and to request that the employee gives their consent to any relevant GP or other health records being disclosed to the Company-appointed doctor and for that doctor to give to the Company a report stating fitness for work.

9.3 Payments on full pay include statutory sick pay. On half pay, statutory sick pay will be paid in addition to half pay, but in no case will sickness payments be greater than your normal full pay. Sickness payments will be paid to any member of staff owing to illness; illness is deemed to include injury or other disability or impairment.

10. **Sickness procedure**

10.1 If you are unfit and unable to work you must ensure that your line manager or another manager is notified in person on the first day of your absence as soon as possible, and in normal circumstances no later than 10 am; if sickness extends to three days, you are required to contact your line manager on the third day to discuss your situation. You are required to provide a completed self-certification form, provided by the Company for any absence due to sickness up to seven calendar days in length.

10.2 If the period of sickness exceeds seven calendar days you must submit a doctor's Fit Note (formerly referred to as a Sick Note or MED 3). This and subsequent doctor's certificates must be submitted without delay to cover your continued period of sickness. A Fit Note does not provide conclusive evidence of incapacity for work and the Company reserves the right to determine by other means whether an employee in any given circumstances could attend work albeit doing reduced or other light duties.

10.3 The Company defines all seven days of the week as qualifying days, regardless of the number of contracted working hours.

10.4 In the event of your falling sick during your annual leave, you should notify your line manager. Depending upon the medical evidence received, this may be regarded as sick leave from the date of notification. Staff on long-term sick leave continue to accrue entitlement to paid holiday, even if they have used up all their SSP or contractual sick pay.

10.5 Any absence not covered by sickness procedure as outlined above or any other reason allowed within these Terms and Conditions (e.g. holidays) will not be paid, and the Company reserves the right to make salary deductions for any unauthorised absences.

11. Sickness or injury caused by a third party

If sickness or injury is caused by the act of negligence or omission of a third party, you must include in any claim for damages against such a third party, a claim in respect of monies paid by the Company as detailed above, and must refund to the Company any damages so recovered.

12. Pensions

A very useful guidance note and template from DLA Piper (**unltd.org.uk/wp-content/uploads/2015/03/DLA-Piper-Contract-of-Employment-Guidance-Note-and-Template.pdf**), sets out the following:

OPTION 1

Employer has reached its staging date and will only do what is needed to comply with the minimum requirements of the Act (using the processes under the Act and NOT contractual enrolment):

12.1 The Company will comply with any duties it may have in respect of you under Part 1 of the Pensions Act 2008.

12.2 The Company is currently using the pension scheme in respect of its duties under Part 1 of the Pensions Act 2008. Membership of the scheme is strictly subject to the rules of the scheme as amended from time to time. The Company reserves the right to vary or discontinue any scheme in place from time to time.

12.3 The Company shall be entitled to deduct from your salary any amounts payable by you as member contributions to such pension scheme as the Company is using from time to time.

12.4 There is [no] [a] contracting-out certificate in force under the Pension Schemes Act 1993 as amended.

OPTION 2

Employer has reached its staging date and will only automatically enrol or enrol those eligible under the Act (using the processes under the Act and NOT contractual enrolment) but will exceed the minimum contribution requirements of the Act:

12.1 The Company will comply with any duties it may have in respect of you under Part 1 of the Pensions Act 2008.

12.2 The Company is currently using the [name] pension scheme in respect of its duties under Part 1 of the Pensions Act 2008. Membership of the scheme is strictly subject to the rules of the scheme as amended from time to time. The Company reserves the right to vary or discontinue any scheme in place from time to time.

12.3 The Company shall be entitled to deduct from your salary any amounts payable by you as member contributions to such pension scheme as the Company is using from time to time.

12.4 There is [no] [a] contracting-out certificate in force under the Pension Schemes Act 1993 as amended.

13. Retirement

There is no normal or compulsory retirement age. Prior to your retirement, full-time workers may be able to transfer to part-time work after consultation, and at no detriment to their pension entitlements. At least six months' and no longer than 12 months' notice should be given by you when you decide to retire from the Company.

14. Notice of termination

14.1 The minimum period of notice to which you are entitled during your probationary period is one week in writing. The minimum notice period you are required to give is also one week in writing during this period. The Company reserves the right to terminate your employment with no notice and make a payment in lieu of notice at its entire discretion.

14.2 After the probationary period, the minimum period of notice to which you are entitled is four weeks in writing. The minimum notice you are required to give the Company is four weeks in writing. The Company reserves the right to terminate your employment with no notice and make a payment in lieu of notice at its entire discretion.

14.3 After four years of service, the period of notice from the Company will be increased by one additional week for each year of service, up to a maximum of 12 weeks' notice or pay in lieu.

14.4 All managers on Grade A and above will receive three months' notice or pay in lieu following the satisfactory completion of the probationary period. They will also be required to give three months' written notice to terminate their employment.

14.5 During any period of notice the Company reserves the right to ask the employee to remain away from work on 'Garden Leave' and not to attend the office or in any other respect undertake any duties on behalf of the Company.

14.6 The Company reserves the right to terminate the employee's employment with no notice and make a payment in lieu of notice at its entire discretion.

14.7 It may be possible for an employee to negotiate to give a shorter period of notice or to be released early from their notice, with the Chief Executive, in special circumstances if this is mutually satisfactory.

14.8 The Company has a Redundancy Policy which applies to termination of this contract on the grounds of redundancy.

15. Disciplinary procedure

The Disciplinary Procedure is set out in the separate document Disciplinary Procedure in the Staff Handbook. This document includes the General Rules. The Disciplinary

Procedure forms part of the Terms and Conditions of Employment. Please note that the Procedure does not apply to any employee during their probationary period.

16. Grievance procedure

The Grievance Procedure is set out in the separate document Grievance Procedure in the Staff Handbook. The Grievance Procedure forms part of the Terms and Conditions of Employment.

17. Collective agreements

The Company negotiates with the [Union] in respect of all staff below Grade A (i.e. non-managers) for all terms and conditions governing your employment save for pensions. Any agreed changes to any existing collective agreements or any new terms agreed with the union will automatically form part of your contract of employment whether you are a trade union member or not.

18. Staff Handbook

The Company has a Staff Handbook which contains further details of your Terms and Conditions of Employment, parts of which are incorporated into this contract of employment. You are encouraged to read this very carefully. Regular updates are sent to all members of staff either through the intranet or by internal mail. The Staff Handbook is on the Company's intranet and is available to download via your email.

19. Changes to your terms of employment

OPTION 1

These Terms and Conditions of Employment may be varied (changed) or withdrawn or new terms added, at the entire discretion of the Company. Any such proposed changes will be discussed with staff or union representatives in advance where possible and will be notified to staff within four weeks of any change. The Company reserves the right at the end of the period of consultation to vary the contract of employment if the changes are deemed reasonable and necessary for a business or any other substantial reason.

OPTION 2

The Company reserves the right to make reasonable changes to any of your terms and conditions of employment and you will be notified of minor changes of detail by way of a general notice to all employees and any such changes will take effect from the date of the notice. You will be given not less than one month's written notice of any significant changes which may be given by way of an individual notice or a general notice to all employees.

Signed .... Date ....

[employer]

I have read, understood and accept the terms and conditions of employment

Signed .... Date ....

[employee]

PRECEDENT 2K: Employment of close relatives

Overview

The following guidelines relate to appointment, promotion, transfer and supervision for members of staff who have close relationships and/or financially connected relationships with other members of staff outside work.

Any decisions about recruitment, promotion, etc. will be based on merit only and the needs of the Company.

However, the employment of close relatives may compromise either themselves or others, particularly where one supervises the other or one makes decisions about pay, appraisals, promotion, etc. about the other. Bias and lack of objectivity may creep in.

A useful policy may be found on the website: **www.acu.edu.au/policies/hr/recruitment_ and_selection/employment_of_close_relatives**.

Its main principles include:

1. a member of staff (A) reporting to their line manager any relationship with another member of staff (B) where A may be able to influence B's appointment, promotion, appraisal, etc;
2. the appointment of another supervisor or line manager for B;
3. B's appointment or pay rise or promotion, etc. must be signed off by a Director or the Chief Executive Officer.

3

Different types of contracts

3.1 Determining who is an 'employee'

For a number of important reasons, employers need to determine the correct status of a 'worker', i.e. whether they are an 'employee' or another class of worker.

Only 'employees' have unfair dismissal protection and a right to a redundancy payment, although other classes of workers are protected and have rights under anti-discrimination legislation.

The requirement of employers to insure against negligent acts committed by their employees (under the Employers' Liability (Compulsory Insurance) Act 1969) applies only to 'employees'. If an employee becomes ill or is injured as a result of their work, since 1971 employers have had to insure against the risk of any claims for compensation made by such an employee.

As far as tax liabilities are concerned, Her Majesty's Revenue and Customs (HMRC) requires employers to deduct Pay As You Earn (PAYE) income tax (called withholding tax) and Class 1 employer and employee national insurance contributions (NICs) from the wages of 'employees' at source, i.e. from the payroll.

Other classes of workers, e.g. consultants and freelancers, may be Schedule D taxpayers and therefore their fees may be paid to them gross without withholding tax and NICs.

3.2 Agency workers

The Agency Workers Regulations 2010, SI 2010/93 came into force on 1 October 2011. The equal treatment provisions of the Agency Workers Regulations apply only to those workers taking up work through an employment business (as opposed to an employment agency). An 'employment business' is a business that arranges temporary work with a 'hiring company'. An 'employment agency' is a business that introduces job-seekers to employers (e.g. a recruitment consultant). Agency workers contracted to an umbrella company are covered, but the genuinely self-employed, personal service company and managed service company workers are outside the scope of the regulations.

Agency workers need to have accrued 12 weeks' service with a hirer to benefit from equal treatment in terms of pay, holidays and other terms as well as equal access to on-site facilities such as childcare.

The 12-week qualifying period is calculated on the basis of 12 calendar weeks, regardless of an individual's working pattern during that period (e.g. part-time hours).

In relation to anti-avoidance measures, any breaks between assignments need to be of a minimum length (as yet unspecified) before breaking the period, and to prevent hirers changing the agency worker's role before the end of the 12-week period (and thus claiming that this represents a new engagement resetting the clock), a rule should be included stating that a new qualifying period will only begin if the new assignment with the same hirer is substantially different.

The legal status and rights of an agency worker were clarified in the Court of Appeal in *Muschett* v. *HM Prison Service* [2010] IRLR 451. The court held that a temporary agency worker was unable to bring a claim for discrimination and unfair dismissal against either the end user client for whom he performed work or the agency that supplied him.

3.3 Different types of workers/contracts

There are 'employees' who may work on a permanent or temporary basis, full-time or part-time, casual, seasonal and homeworkers; 'agency temps'; fixed-term contract or project-only staff; freelancers or self-employed workers; consultants and independent contractors; relief or bank staff and staff on zero hours contracts; workers in the 'gig' economy such as Uber drivers; workers on 'the lump'; salaried and equity partners; job-sharers and volunteers, for example those working for charities in different roles, and interns.

3.4 Self-employed

The following factors will be pertinent when considering whether the person is genuinely self-employed for employment protection purposes:

(a) *mutuality of obligation*: whether the individual is free to decline the work and the employer has the ability not to offer any work;

(b) *the right to delegate the duties to someone else*: a person who has the freedom to choose whether to do the job themselves or sub-contract to someone else is probably self-employed;

(c) *provision of equipment*: a self-employed contractor will generally provide the equipment required for the job (although in some trades workers will have their own personal hand tools whether employed or self-employed);

(d) *financial risk*: an individual who quotes a fixed price for a job or who buys equipment or materials is more likely to be self-employed;

(e) *basis of payment*: employees tend to be paid a fixed wage or salary at regular weekly or monthly intervals;

(f) *part of the organisation*: if someone has been engaged to work for one client for long periods they will often be treated by the client as if they

were one of its own employees; to determine whether this is the case, one must look at the whole relationship between the worker and the client;
(g) *right of dismissal*: where there is provision in the contract for dismissal by giving a period of notice or dismissal for misconduct these are features of employment rather than self-employment; the contract for services can usually be terminated by either party without giving any notice or once the job or task has been completed;
(h) *intention*: it is the reality of the relationship that matters and this may or may not be clear from the wording of the contract; however, a court or tribunal will normally look at the contract wording to try to determine the intention of the parties.

In *Weight Watchers (UK) Ltd* v. *Revenue & Customs Commissioners* [2010] UKFTT 54 (TC) the tribunal held that the workers (B and others) who ran meetings for the company were 'employees' rather than self-employed workers because there was a mutuality of obligations: those workers were not free to delegate their duties to anyone of their choice and Weight Watchers had a considerable degree of control over B and her colleagues to ensure that they delivered their programme at every meeting. B and her colleagues did not have an unfettered discretion about the time, date and place of the meetings or how to run them. They could also be prevented from going to work for any rival weight control meetings and could not undertake any work for other personal weight management businesses.

The Court of Appeal upheld the EAT's decision that one of Pimlico Plumbers' operatives was a worker rather than self-employed – *Pimlico Plumbers Ltd* v. *Smith* [2017] EWCA Civ 51.

Mr Smith and his co-workers wore company uniforms, drove Pimlico Plumbers' (PP) distinctive vans, could only be contacted and booked through PP's offices and all the paperwork was done on PP's notepapers, estimates and bills, etc. To the public they looked in all respects as if they were employees of PP.

However, the Employment Tribunal found as fact that these workers were:

1. described in the paperwork as self-employed independent contractors, being in business on their own account. The paperwork stated that 'Nothing in this Agreement shall render you an employee, agent or partner of the Company' and they were liable to pay their own income tax, NICs and VAT;
2. required to provide all their own tools, equipment, materials and other necessary items;
3. personally liable for work undertaken by them;
4. required to provide their own insurance;
5. working normally five days per week and a minimum of 40 hours;
6. not permitted to provide a substitute person if they were unable to attend a job or to attend work for any day. They could swap one day or one job with another PP plumber like many unionised shift workers may do.

The Court of Appeal upheld the EAT's decision. Dismissing Pimlico Plumbers Ltd's appeal, the Court accepted that:

> Having considered all those factors, the ET rightly stood back and asked and answered (in paragraphs 52 and 53 of the decision) the over-arching question whether the better conclusion was that PP was a client or customer of Mr Smith's business or rather PP should be 'regarded as a principal and Mr Smith was an integral part of PP's operations and subordinate to [PP]'.

According to the Court, the Employment Tribunal had been right to regard Mr Smith as 'an integral part of [Pimlico Plumbers'] operations and subordinate to [Pimlico Plumbers]'.

The Employment Tribunal was entitled to regard Pimlico Plumbers as more than just a 'client or customer of Mr Smith's business'.

Unlike recent high-profile judgments involving Uber drivers and CitySprint couriers, this ruling is binding on other courts and tribunals.

This means that the Court of Appeal decision in this case is likely to be an important authority in any cases on employment status in the 'gig' economy.

Equity partner of a law firm is a 'worker' for whistleblowing purposes

In *Clyde & Co LLP* v. *Bates Van Winkelhof* [2014] 1 WLR 2047 the Supreme Court held that an equity partner in Clyde & Co who brought claims of whistleblowing was a 'worker' within the meaning of s.230(3) of the Employment Rights Act 1996. She was therefore entitled to the protection of s.47B of the Act for having suffered a detriment by reason of 'whistleblowing'.

The majority of the Supreme Court decided that Ms Bates Van Winkelhof was a 'worker' under s.230(3) as she could not market her services as a solicitor to anyone other than the respondent and was an integral part of its business. The respondent could also not be seen to be the appellant's client or customer.

See **ukscblog.com/case-comment-clyde-co-llp-and-anor-v-bates-van-winklehof-2014-uksc-32** for an excellent review of this case.

The Supreme Court found that s.4(4) of the Limited Liabilities Partnerships Act 2000 was not wide enough to include 'workers'. However, the questions: 'can a partner never be an employee of a partnership?'; and, therefore, 'can a partner never be a "worker" of a partnership?' were not considered.

LLPs need to ensure that their whistleblower protections extend to all equity partners, to ensure that any allegation is properly investigated and to avoid situations in which the whistleblower is dismissed from the partnership as a result of reporting the incident.

The decision also means that members of LLPs are entitled to rights under the Working Time Regulations, to paid annual leave and to not suffer unauthorised deductions from wages. LLPs should also seek advice regarding compliance under the auto-enrolment pension legislation in respect of their members.

A recent First Tier Tax Tribunal in *RS Dhillon and GP Dhillon Partnership* v. *HMRC* [2017] UKFTT 17 (TC) had to decide whether drivers engaged by the appellant to make deliveries using the appellant's lorries were employees or independent contractors. The Tribunal decided that they were employees for tax purposes. Please see **www.accountingweb.co.uk/tax/personal-tax/ employment-status-testing-casual-drivers** for an excellent explanation of this case.

Determining whether a worker carries on a business on their own account was considered in *Hall* v. *Lorimer* 66 TC 349. Mummery J said (at 366G):

> To decide whether a person carries on business on his own account, it is necessary to consider many different aspects of that person's work activity. This is not a mechanical exercise of running through items on the checklist to see whether they are present in, or absent from, a given situation. The object of the exercise is to paint a picture from the accumulation of detail. The overall effect can only be appreciated by standing back from the detailed picture which has been painted, by viewing it from a distance and by making an informed, considered, qualitative appreciation of the whole. It is a matter of evaluation of the overall effect of the detail, which is not necessarily the same as the sum of the individual details. Not all details are of equal weight or importance in any given situation. The details may also vary in importance from one situation to another.

Mummery J's comments were approved on appeal by Nolan LJ, with whom Dillon LJ and Roch LJ concurred. Nolan LJ continued (at 375I) by expressing approval of the comments of Vinelott J in *Walls* v. *Sinett* 60 TC 150 at 164 where the Judge said:

> It is in my judgement quite impossible in the field where a very large number of factors have to be weighed to gain any real assistance by looking at the facts of another case and comparing them one by one to see what facts are in common, what are different and what particular weight is given by another tribunal to the common facts. The facts as a whole must be looked at, and what may be compelling in one case in the light of all the facts may not be compelling in the context of another case.

Drafting points in a sub-contractor's/consultant's contract for services

For examples of contracts for services see **Precedents 3B** and **3C**. The first is a contract for services with a contractor who has formed a limited company and the second is for a consultant who is self-employed.

Issues such as the following need to be addressed:

(a) name the consultant and set out the fact of that person's skill, knowledge and experience upon which the client will rely;
(b) if the contract is with a limited company, confirm that the contract is for the supply of services as set out in the contract;
(c) set out the length of the assignment/consultancy, whether any notice needs to be given and the return of company property;
(d) set out the payment of fees and any commission;
(e) set out the duties, the fact that care and skill in relation to the work done is essential, the standards of the work to be done and other obligations of the contractor, the days of work for the client, whether any travel is required and if so where and when the consultant must provide written

reports to the board or to others and the keeping of statutory records; there may also be a restriction on working for a competitor during the currency of the agreement, etc;

(f) set out the consultant's obligations concerning professional indemnity insurance (and, where relevant, public liability insurance and employers' liability insurance at a minimum level of cover);

(g) set out the consultant's obligations concerning intellectual property, including trade secrets, inventions and confidentiality during and following the expiry of the agreement, etc;

(h) set out what could result in termination of the agreement by default;

(i) set out the warranties, undertakings, etc;

(j) set out what will happen in the case of a dispute between the parties.

Checklist for a contract for services

1. What does the contract say? How does it describe the relationship? Does it cover the points below?

2. Is the contract signed by both parties?

3. Are there any obvious separate reasons for avoiding employment status (wages below minimum level, etc.)?

4. Is this an industry where HMRC has traditionally accepted or refused to accept self-employment?

5. Is this an industry where it is common for people to work both as self-employed and as independent contractors?

6. Must the worker follow company instructions as to how (particularly) and when and where to work?

7. Does the company provide training? Is there any provision for repayment or loan arrangements in respect of any training fees?

8. How closely are the services integrated within the company?

9. Must the services be provided personally? Can the worker sub-contract?

10. Does the worker provide alternative cover for holidays and sickness?

11. Where the work requires further assistance, who provides this?

12. Is there a continuing relationship between the company and the worker where work is performed at intervals?

13. Does the company set the work hours and schedule?

14. Must the worker devote substantially their full time to the business of the company?

15. Does the worker perform services on the company's premises?

16. Must the worker submit oral or written reports to the company?
17. Is the worker paid by the hour, week or month?
18. Is the worker paid on invoice?
19. Does the company pay the business or travelling expenses of the worker?
20. Does the company furnish significant tools, materials and equipment?
21. Does the company have the right to fire the worker?
22. Can the worker quit without incurring a liability to the company?
23. Does the worker have a significant investment in tools or facilities?
24. Does the worker keep a profit or loss account?
25. Does the worker provide services to several companies at the same time?
26. Does the worker regularly advertise or make their services available to the general public?

3.5 Individuals who work through intermediaries

IR 35 entitled 'Countering Avoidance in the Provision of Personal Services' was issued to remove opportunities for the avoidance of tax and Class 1 NICs by the use of intermediaries, such as service companies or partnerships, in circumstances where an individual worker would otherwise be an employee of the client or the income would be income from an office held by the worker. Those unlucky enough to be caught by these rules are effectively deemed to be employees and taxed accordingly.

Updated guidance on 'Employment Intermediaries – Reporting Requirements' was published by HMRC on 1 November 2016, following the Income Tax (Pay As You Earn) (Amendment No. 2) Regulations 2015. These Regulations gave HMRC information that enabled it to decrease false self-employment and abuse of offshore working.

Employers should be extremely wary of employing individuals through intermediaries and should always seek clearance from their tax office/inspector before entering into any contractual relationship.

3.6 Ministers of religion are not 'employees'

In *President of the Methodist Conference* v. *Preston* [2013] UKSC 29 SC the Supreme Court ruled that a minister of religion was not an employee and could not therefore claim unfair dismissal. See **www.xperthr.co.uk/editors-choice/employment-status-supreme-court-decides-church-minister-was-not-an-employee/116167**.

Whether an employment arrangement is in fact and law an employment relationship may be determined in part by the intentions of the parties, but several other more important factors are determinative of this question including mutuality of obligation, exclusivity of employment and ability or not to delegate work to another.

3.7 Casual workers

Casual workers are normally engaged on short-term contracts. As such, there are breaks in their continuity of service, which means that they rarely, if at all, qualify for any of the employment protection rights that require a one-year qualifying period of service. In some cases, however, tribunals have held that such workers are not employees because of lack of mutual obligation, i.e. the fact that the casual worker does not have to accept the next assignment and the employer does not have to provide the next assignment.

Following this line of reasoning, in some organisations the human resources (HR) department has set up a central organisation called a 'Job Shop' from which any casual worker is assigned to a department or division. The contract that is provided is a contract for services in an attempt to ensure that no employment relationship is created. For a model casual workers contract see **Precedent 3E**. It can be modified to a short-term contract of employment ending at the end of each assignment.

3.8 Seasonal workers

Some seasonal workers who are taken on an indefinite or periodic contract – say, a weekly contract during hop-picking, or during the January sales – may be entitled to minimum periods of notice or pay in lieu. This will depend, however, on whether they are excluded by the operation of the Employment Rights Act 1996, s.86(5) which excludes those who are employed on a contract made in contemplation of the performance of a specific task which is not expected to last for more than three months. If, however, the employee has in fact been continuously employed for more than three months, then the employee will become entitled to minimum statutory notice or pay in lieu.

Careful wording of 'the season'

Employers need to be careful in the way in which they word their seasonal contract arrangements. During a university vacation, the author was offered a contract in a factory 'during the summer holidays'. The personnel manager was ready to thank her for her services at the end of August, arguing that he had meant 'summer holidays' to mean 'the school holidays'. The author had meant the 'university summer holidays', which were not due to end until the end of September. She successfully argued that he therefore owed her another month's wages – the *contra proferentum* rule would have applied had not the personnel manager graciously paid up!

3.9 'Bank' staff

'Bank' staff agree to have their names and addresses kept in a 'bank' and agree to be called upon when needed. If they are free, they agree to work for the employer. The advantage to the employer is that the bank employee is normally trained and familiar with the procedures of that employer and, during the periods when the individual is not working, there is no contract and therefore no obligation to pay wages. However, when the employer wishes to end that particular period of employment, there is an issue as to whether or not the individual has continuity of employment and is therefore eligible for employment protection rights that require a minimum period of continuous service.

It is always important to understand whether:

1. Bank staff are employees or workers/independent contractors. They are most probably 'employees' working on zero-hours contracts, thus working under separate contracts as and when they are called to come to work.
2. Even if they are deemed to be workers, would they be entitled to holiday pay? Yes, as statutory holiday pay (four weeks' holiday) applies to workers under the Working Time Regulations 1998.

In a case involving a 'bank nurse' – *Clark* v. *Oxfordshire Health Authority* [1998] IRLR 125 – a staff nurse who worked for the health authority in its 'nurse bank' was offered and accepted employment, when it was available, at any of the authority's hospitals and was paid hourly on the applicable scales (with deduction of PAYE and NICs).

However, she received no payment during periods when she was not supplying her services and had no entitlement to sick pay or holiday pay. Her terms of employment stipulated that she had no entitlement to guaranteed or continuous work. Apart from gaps totalling about four and a half months she worked some three years before being 'dismissed'. The question for the Industrial Tribunal was whether or not she was an 'employee' within the statutory definition.

The Court of Appeal held that the EAT had erred in holding that the nurse's relationship with the health authority was governed by a global contract of employment, notwithstanding a lack of mutuality of obligation during the periods between engagements. In the court's view, 'a contract of employment within the statutory definition could not exist in the absence of mutual obligations subsisting over the entire duration of the relevant period'. This the court considered 'was absent during the periods between engagements and the Authority was under no obligation to offer the applicant work, nor was she under any obligation to accept it during these periods'.

However, this case, like some others, concentrates on whether or not a global contract of employment existed rather than whether a contract of employment existed at the time the employee provided their services. Perhaps the more relevant question is not whether the casual worker is obliged to turn up for, or do, the work, but rather, if the worker turns up for and does the work, whether they do so under a contract of service or for services.

3.10 Surveillance staff

Contracts for surveillance staff must be carefully drafted providing for:

1. Checks for honesty.
2. Requirement to work long hours and opting out of the 48-hour per week limit stated by the Working Time Regulations 1998.
3. Checks for physical and mental stamina.
4. Notice that surveillance work involves waiting for many hours where nothing happens.
5. Reminders of the Human Rights Act 1998 and the European Convention on Human Rights, Article 8 right to respect for privacy and the need to take care not to intrude on an individual's privacy.
6. Prohibition of tricking their way into someone's home.
7. Need to take careful video and recording evidence and careful notes, etc.
8. Availability and willingness to give evidence in court.
9. Requirement of utmost probity and integrity.
10. Reliability and punctuality.
11. Ability and willingness to get up early and work late when required.
12. Compensatory rest breaks.
13. No alcohol/drugs/etc. rules.
14. Rules about company cars.
15. Rules about preferred contractors.
16. Rules about dress and appearance.

An example of a surveillance staff contract appears at **Precedent 3H**.
An example of a contract for a security guard can be found at **Precedent 3J**.

3.11 Hospitality staff/banqueting staff

Hospitality and banqueting staff should have a job description that sets out their main duties and skill-sets required, etc. A model job description is set out at **Precedent 3I**.

3.12 Interns

An intern's rights depend on their employment status – see **www.gov.uk/employment-rights-for-interns** and an extract from this website below:

> If an intern is classed as a worker, then they're normally due the National Minimum Wage.
>
> Internships are sometimes called work placements or work experience. These terms have no legal status on their own. The rights they have depend on their employment status and whether they're classed as:
>
> - a worker
> - a volunteer
> - an employee

If an intern does regular paid work for an employer, they may qualify as an employee and be eligible for employment rights.

Rights to the National Minimum Wage

An intern is entitled to the National Minimum Wage if they count as a worker. Employers can't avoid paying the National Minimum Wage if it's due by:

- saying or stating that it doesn't apply
- making a written agreement saying someone isn't a worker or that they're a volunteer

Promise of future work

An intern is classed as a worker and is due the National Minimum Wage if they're promised a contract of future work.

When interns aren't due the National Minimum Wage

Student internships

Students required to do an internship for less than one year as part of a UK-based further or higher education course aren't entitled to the National Minimum Wage.

School work experience placements

Work experience students of compulsory school age, i.e. under 16, aren't entitled to the minimum wage.

Voluntary workers

Workers aren't entitled to the minimum wage if both of the following apply:

- they're working for a charity, voluntary organisation, associated fund raising body or a statutory body
- they don't get paid, except for limited benefits (e.g. reasonable travel or lunch expenses)

Work shadowing

The employer doesn't have to pay the minimum wage if an internship only involves shadowing an employee, i.e. no work is carried out by the intern and they are only observing.

3.13 Part-time workers: flexible hours, job-sharing, term-time working and career breaks

'Part-time' work is no longer defined since the abolition in 1995 of the hours' qualification for bringing a complaint to an Employment Tribunal (Employment Protection (Part-time Employees) Regulations 1995, SI 1995/31).

A significant proportion of part-time workers are women (approximately 41 per cent of women work part-time as compared to 11 per cent of men).

Since the Part-time Workers (Prevention of Less Favourable Treatment) Regulations 2000, SI 2000/1551 (as amended in 2002), part-time workers are protected from less favourable treatment as compared with full-time workers doing the same work and have pro rata statutory rights to matters such as holidays under the Working Time Regulations 1998 and access to pensions.

Most employers define 'part-time hours' as those which are less than full-time (37.5 hours per week). However, there is still no right to work on a part-time basis, merely the right to request to work on a flexible basis (Employment Rights Act 1996, s.80F). Women returning to work following maternity leave have a right not to be discriminated against by an employer refusing without justification to agree to a request to work on reduced or part-time hours (s.19 of the Equality Act 2010).

Some employers recognise the disadvantages that part-time workers may still face and have introduced policies and terms of the contract to assist such workers.

Precedents for job-sharers and employees taking career breaks can be found in **Chapter 7**.

Maternity cover

Where a fixed-term or temporary employee is engaged as maternity cover, the terms of that engagement should be clearly spelt out. A contract for an employee engaged to provide maternity cover appears in **Chapter 7**.

Flexible working

It is now common to see agreements setting out the procedure for seeking flexible working. The Flexible Working (Procedural Requirements) Regulations 2002, SI 2002/3207, provide the procedural steps.

Term-time working

For some working parents with school-age children, a term-time only contract provides the necessary flexibility to work and to care for their children during the school holidays. In some cases employees are able to arrange for cover from the end of the school day until they arrive home from work but it may be impossible for them to arrange cost-effective cover during several weeks of school holidays.

If an employer is prepared to offer term-time only contracts, these are the matters to bear in mind:

1. What posts can be offered on this basis? If a manager deems a particular job unsuitable for such a contract, the manager must be required to put a sound business case.
2. Which staff should have the right to request term-time only contracts ahead of others?
3. Will pay be spread evenly throughout the year and, if so, what arrangements will be made if the individual leaves part way through the year?
4. Specify the maximum length of the contract.

5. Specify what annual leave requirements there will be.
6. Specify what sick leave arrangements there will be.

Staff on term-time only contracts should note that even if their salary is not paid during the holidays, they are not entitled to claim Jobseeker's Allowance during this period. The House of Lords ruled on this in *Chief Adjudication Officer* v. *Banks and Stafford* [2001] ICR 877 and held that ancillary workers who did not work and were not paid during the school holidays were not entitled to claim Jobseeker's Allowance because they were regarded as 'being engaged in remunerative work'. A model term-time only agreement can be found at **Precedent 3A**.

3.14 Zero-hours contracts

The ACAS website (see **www.acas.org.uk/index.aspx?articleid=4468**) states that the expression 'zero hours' (or 'nil hours') contract is not legally defined. It is commonly used to describe a contract under which the employer does not guarantee to provide work and pays only for work actually done. The ACAS guidance states:

> A zero hours contract is generally understood to be a contract between an employer and a worker where:
>
> - the employer is not obliged to provide any minimum working hours
> - the worker is not obliged to accept any work offered.
>
> [The Exclusivity Terms in Zero Hours Contracts (Redress) Regulations 2015 were enacted, in force on 1 January 2016.] The [Regulations] prevent employers from enforcing 'exclusivity clauses' in a zero hours contract. An exclusivity clause would be where an employer restricts workers from working for other employers.
>
> . . .

Key points:

- Zero hours contracts normally mean there is no obligation for employers to offer work, or for workers to accept it.
- Most zero hours contracts will give staff 'worker' employment status.
- Zero hours workers have the same employment rights as regular workers, although they may have breaks in their contracts, which affect rights that accrue over time.
- Zero hours workers are entitled to annual leave, the National Minimum Wage and National Living Wage and pay for work-related travel in the same way as regular workers.
- Protection is given for those on zero hours contracts from an exclusivity clause.

When are zero hours contracts used?

Zero hours contracts can be used to provide a flexible workforce to meet a temporary or changeable need for staff. Examples may include a need for workers to cover:

- unexpected or last-minute events (e.g. a restaurant needs extra staff to cater for a wedding party that just had their original venue cancel on them)
- temporary staff shortages (e.g. an office loses an essential specialist worker for a few weeks due to bereavement)

- on-call/bank work (e.g. one of the clients of a care-worker company requires extra care for a short period of time).

It is important for employers to actively monitor their need for zero hours contracts. In many cases, it may be more effective or appropriate to make use of agency workers, or recruit staff on fixed-term contracts – or it may turn out that the need is permanent and therefore a permanent member of staff can be recruited.

Consideration for the employer	Consideration for the worker
• Easily accessed pool of staff to assist when demand arises	• Provides flexible employment on same basic terms as most workers
• No ongoing requirement to provide guaranteed levels of work for staff	• No ongoing requirement to accept offers of work and no consequences
• Can be cheaper alternative to agency fees	• Gives employment experience and skills

Breaks between employment

Depending on the specific agreements in the contract, a zero hours contract might mean that the contract only exists when the work is provided.

Where a zero hours contract does mean that the contract only exists when the work is provided, a full calendar week without work from Sunday to Saturday is required to bring about a break in employment.

When employment is continuous certain employment rights accumulate over time. For example, after their first year, workers don't need to accrue their annual leave before taking it.

Equally, when employment is broken, an employer has certain responsibilities too. This includes a need to pay the worker for any accrued and untaken holiday pay.

Employment status

In most cases zero hours contracts mean that an employer recruits a 'worker'. However, the way the relationship with that worker develops may enhance the employment status to that of an 'employee', who has additional employment rights. For example, employee status provides statutory notice rights. Developments that contribute to such a change could include subjecting the worker to disciplinary procedures or punishing them in some way if they do not accept all the hours they are offered.

Zero hours status should also be clear in a contractual form.

In some cases zero hours employees who work regularly can build up continuity of employment and then gain employment protection rights.

In *Colley* v. *Corkindale* [1995] ICR 965, EAT, an employee worked only every other Friday but was still held to have continuity of employment for the purposes of the qualification period of continuous employment required to claim unfair dismissal.

Statutory redundancy pay for a zero-hours employee who qualifies will be based on the employee's average wages over the previous 12 weeks (Employment Rights Act 1996, s.224).

A typical zero-hours clause would be:

> Your hours of work will vary according to the workload of our business. It is a condition of your employment that you work flexibly in accordance with the working arrangements we operate. Accordingly, you acknowledge that there

may be periods when no work is available and that we have no obligation to provide you with any work or to provide any minimum number of hours in any day or week. However, we will endeavour to allocate suitable work to you when it is available. We will give you as much advance notice as is reasonably practicable (normally not less than 24 hours) of the hours you are required to work.

3.15 The 'gig' economy

Workers such as food delivery drivers, Uber drivers, bike couriers, video producers and so on, work in what is called the 'gig' economy. This is a way of working that is based on people having temporary jobs or doing separate pieces of work, each paid separately, rather than working for an employer. It is estimated that there are five million of these workers in the UK.

There are three ongoing government and independent reviews of the changing nature of the workforce.

The Commons Select Committee on Business, Energy & Industrial Strategy (BEIS) (previously BIS) launched an inquiry into the future world of work, focusing on the rapidly-changing nature of work and the status and rights of agency workers, the self-employed and those working in the 'gig' economy. Consultation ended on 16 December 2016.

The inquiry also looks at issues such as low pay and poor working conditions for people working in these non-traditional employee roles.

The full terms of reference on www.parliament.uk/business/committees/committees-a-z/commons-select/business-energy-industrial-strategy/news-parliament-2015/the-future-world-of-work-and-rights-of-workers-launch-16-17 are:

1. Is the term 'worker' defined sufficiently clearly in law at present? If not, how should it be defined?

    • What should be the status and rights of agency workers, casual workers, and the self-employed (including those working in the 'gig' economy), for the purposes of tax, benefits and employment law?

2. For those casual and agency workers working in the 'gig' economy, is the balance of benefits between worker and employer appropriate?
3. What specific provision should there be for the protection and support of agency workers and those who are not employees? Who should be responsible for such provision – the government, the beneficiary of the work, a mutual, the individual themselves?
4. What differences should there be between levels of government support for the self-employed and for employees, for example over statutory sick pay, holiday pay, employee pensions, maternity pay?

    • How should those rights be changed, to ensure fair protection for workers at work?
    • What help should be offered in preparing those people who become self-employed (with, for example, financial, educational and legal advice), and who should be offering such help?

5. Is there evidence that businesses are treating agency workers unfairly, compared with employees?

6. Should there be steps taken to constrain the use by businesses of agency workers?
7. What are the issues surrounding terms and conditions of employees, including the use of zero-hour contracts, definitions of flexible contracts, the role of the Low Pay Commission, and minimum wage enforcement?
8. What is the role of trade unions in representing the self-employed and those not working in traditional employee roles?

In two recent Employment Tribunal cases the Employment Judges have had to grapple with the employment status of such workers.

In both cases – *Aslam and Farrar* v. *Uber BV, Uber London Ltd and Uber Britannia Ltd* Case No: 2202550/2015 and *Dewhurst* v. *CitySprint UK Ltd* ET/2202512/2016 – the drivers in the first case and the bike courier in the latter were held to be workers and therefore gained certain employment rights, e.g. the National Minimum Wage (NMW) and right to paid holiday.

In the *Uber* case, the Uber drivers were held to be 'workers' within the meaning of the Employment Rights Act 1996 and for the purposes of NMW, paid holiday and whistleblowing.

This means they will only have limited employment rights to holiday pay, the 48-hour week, the National Minimum Wage and National Living Wage, protection from unlawful discrimination and protection to the 'whistleblowing' provisions of the Employment Rights Act 1996.

They will not have any rights to claim unfair dismissal, statutory redundancy payments or protection under TUPE if the business or part of it is transferred to a new owner.

In the *CitySprint* case the courier was also found to be a 'worker' for the purposes of the Employment Rights Act 1996, despite the contractual documents describing her as a self-employed contractor.

3.16 Voluntary workers

It has been clarified that the employment status of voluntary workers, such as those who work in charity shops and Citizens Advice Bureaux (CAB), turns on the presence, or rather absence, of a mutuality of obligations.

In *South East Sheffield Citizens Advice Bureau* v. *Grayson* [2004] IRLR 353 the EAT held that this arrangement did not impose a contractual obligation on the volunteer to do work, 'such that, were the volunteer to give notice immediately terminating his relationship with the Bureau, the latter would have a remedy for breach of contract against him'.

The agreement did not say that the volunteer must work the usual minimum hours, let alone that there was a legal obligation for them to do so. 'Like many similar charitable organisations, similarly dependent on the services of volunteers, the Bureau provides training for its volunteers and expects of them in return a commitment to work for it, but the work expected of them is expressed to be voluntary.'

The fact that the CAB was legally bound to reimburse the volunteers for expenses incurred and indemnified them against negligence claims did not impose any obligation on the volunteer actually to do any work.

A previous case suggests that it is at least possible that someone who is rejected as a volunteer may have a right to complain under discrimination law (*Murray* v. *Newham Citizens Advice Bureau* [2001] ICR 708, EAT). The general question of whether or not volunteers fall within the protection of the Equal Treatment Framework Directive has been referred to the Court of Justice of the European Union by a Scottish Employment Tribunal (see *Mashi* v. *Awaz FM*, Case No. S/116403/08).

The status of a person as to whether or not they are an employee or a true volunteer will depend on their legal relationship.

In one case, *Migrant Advisory Service* v. *Chaudri* UKEAT/1400/97, Mrs Chaudri was considered to be a volunteer by the Migrant Advisory Service.

Her work was admin for four mornings a week for two years and she was paid £40 per week, referred to as 'volunteer's expenses' (she had no expenses). Mrs Chaudri was also paid while on holiday or off sick.

The Employment Tribunal (and Employment Appeal Tribunal) held that Mrs Chaudri was an employee, as she was paid for her work and the word expenses was a sham.

3.17 Specialist consultants

Specialist consultants are often engaged on a self-employed basis or through their own limited companies.

Examples of such contracts appear at **Precedent 3C**.

3.18 Nanny's contract

It is often very difficult to make a formal arrangement with the carer of one's children but it is essential that this is done. A contract used by the author successfully when she employed nannies is given at **Precedent 3L**.

The matters to be included are provisions:

(a) regarding the nature of the job, which is one of the provision of personal services and as such is not a 'nine-to-five' office job;
(b) as to whether the position is live-in or live-out;
(c) as to whether the nanny is expected to go away on weekends when they are not working;
(d) setting out the trust and honesty required, responsibility with money and credit cards, etc;
(e) setting out that the nanny is required to use their common sense and intelligence;
(f) providing a guide to their duties and the standards expected;
(g) setting out the expected standards of driving (if required to drive);
(h) as to baby-sitting duties and any weekend working;
(i) on pay (in the nanny's hands) and pay reviews, holidays including

whether the nanny is required to accompany the family on holiday, time off, whether there is a car for personal use and the terms, sick pay, pensions, etc;
(j) requiring the nanny to have a valid current passport;
(k) as to whether any boyfriends/girlfriends are permitted to stay overnight or retire to their room and whether they can entertain their friends in the house;
(l) regarding dress and appearance, alcohol consumption and smoking;
(m) concerning security matters; and
(n) concerning when the child is ill or suspected to be ill.

PRECEDENT 3A: Model term-time agreement

1. Duration

A Term-Time Contract will not exceed 39 weeks per annum in duration.

2. Salary payments

You will receive salary payments distributed equally in 12 monthly payments. Should you leave part way through the year, any adjustments to salary for money owed either way will be made in your final salary.

3. Annual leave

You will not be allowed to take annual leave in normal circumstances outside the school holiday periods. Your line manager does have the right exceptionally to approve unpaid leave. Any periods of unpaid leave will need to be taken into account in calculating annual leave.

You will receive payment for your annual leave in your 12 equal salary payments. The salary and annual leave allowances are based on the number of weeks worked by you compared to the number of weeks worked by a full-time employee.

Example

The exercise below shows how to calculate the annual leave and salary for a person working 39 weeks on a term-time contract. A comparison is made with a full-time employee who has 5.4 weeks (27 days) of annual leave and who therefore works 46.7 weeks per annum (52.143 − 5.4 = 46.7).

(a) Annual leave entitlement:
Number of weeks worked on term-time contract × Leave entitlement for full-time employee
i.e. 39/46.7 × 5.4 = 4.5
(b) Total salary:
Pay for number of weeks on term-time contract + Pay for annual leave entitlement
i.e. 39 + 4.5 = 43.50 weeks' pay

4. Sick leave

Staff are entitled to sick leave in accordance with the provisions in the Staff Handbook. If you are ill or injured during the school holidays, when you are not at work, you are required to report it for recording and sick pay purposes and you may be entitled to SSP only.

PRECEDENT 3B: Sub-contractor's terms and conditions

Terms and Conditions for the supply of services to [name of company] (performed by a limited company sub-contractor)

1. **The contract**

1.1 These Conditions apply to all contracts entered into by the Company with other companies for the supply by them of services to the Company's Clients and are deemed to be accepted by the Sub-Contractor by virtue of the Sub-Contractor offering to perform the Work Scope. The Sub-Contractor agrees to deal with the Company on these Conditions to the exclusion of all other terms, conditions, warranties and (except when made fraudulently) all representations.

1.2 No variation or alteration to these Conditions shall be valid unless approved in writing and signed by a director of the Company and the Sub-Contractor.

2. **Definitions**

In all contracts to which these terms and conditions apply:

2.1 'Associated Company' means any company which controls, is controlled by or is under common control with the company in question within the meaning of s.256 of the Companies Act 2006;

2.2 'Client' means the person for whom the Work Scope is executed;

2.3 'Commencement Date' means the date on which the Work Scope is to commence;

2.4 'Company' means [*name of company*];

2.5 'these Conditions' means these terms and conditions of business;

2.6 'the Contract' means the agreement between the Company and the Sub-Contractor for the execution of the Work Scope by the Sub-Contractor, subject to these Conditions;

2.7 'Estimated Completion Date' means the date by which the Work Scope is intended to be completed as specified in the contract offer letter;

2.8 'Notice Period' means seven days expiring at the end of any working day unless specified to the contrary;

2.9 'Personnel' means the personnel of the Sub-Contractor who are engaged, at the discretion of the Sub-Contractor, in the execution of the Work Scope on behalf of the Sub-Contractor from time to time (including any personnel who may be identified in the contract offer letter);

2.10 'Fee' means the fee specified in the contract offer letter (being either a fixed total sum or a fee payable in respect of a particular period of time) which is payable by the Company to the Sub-Contractor in respect of the execution of the Work Scope;

2.11 'Work Scope' means the work or project identified in the contract offer letter and/or notified to the Sub-Contractor by the Client;

2.12 'Sub-Contractor' means the company undertaking the Work Scope;

2.13 'Regulations' means the Working Time Regulations 1998.

3. **Work Scope**

3.1 The Sub-Contractor shall carry out the Work Scope with effect from the Commencement Date until properly completed using reasonable care and skill and in accordance with the requirements and to the standards reasonably required by the Company.

3.2 The Sub-Contractor shall ensure that all the facts upon which the Company makes its decision to accept the Sub-Contractor or the Client makes its decision to engage the Sub-Contractor shall be materially correct. Without prejudice to the foregoing, the Sub-Contractor shall ensure that all Personnel have the necessary skill, qualifications and experience required to execute the Work Scope on behalf of the Sub-Contractor and that all such skills, qualifications and experience claimed by Personnel have been checked out thoroughly and found to be correct by the Sub-Contractor. The Sub-Contractor shall, if required by the Company or the Client, provide satisfactory proof of the skills, qualifications and experience of any or all of the Personnel. In the event that the Sub-Contractor does not provide any such proof, the Company shall be entitled (but not obliged) to terminate the Contract immediately by notice in writing.

3.3 The Sub-Contractor shall undertake the Work Scope to the reasonable satisfaction of the Client. The Sub-Contractor will determine the method of work appropriate to the most effective execution of the Work Scope. The Company shall not be entitled (and will not seek) to supervise, direct or control the Sub-Contractor in the manner of execution of the Work Scope. The Sub-Contractor will, therefore, be exclusively liable (including, for the avoidance of doubt, vicarious liability for the Personnel) to the Client for any claim, loss, damage, cost or expense incurred by the Client or otherwise arising in connection with any act, omission or neglect on the part of the Sub-Contractor in or in connection with the execution of the Work Scope. The Sub-Contractor shall indemnify and save harmless the Company against any claims, loss, damage, cost, expense, demand or proceeding whatsoever incurred by the Company arising out of or in connection with the execution of, or any failure to execute, the Work Scope.

4. Sub-Contractor's obligations

The Sub-Contractor agrees on its own part that it shall:

4.1 not engage in any conduct detrimental to the interests of the Company or the Client;

4.2 if agreed with the Company or the Client (and subject to any rights which the Personnel may have under the Regulations), execute the Work Scope at such times and/or complete the execution of the Work Scope within any period as may be so agreed;

4.3 take such steps as may be reasonably practicable to safeguard the health and safety of the Personnel and the health and safety of any other person who may be affected by the execution of the Work Scope;

4.4 comply with any rules or obligations in force at the premises where the Work Scope is being executed, only to the extent that they are reasonably applicable to independent contractors or visitors, to include security and health and safety procedures;

4.5 furnish the Company with any progress reports as may be reasonably requested from time to time;

4.6 where work permits are required, ensure that all Personnel have the appropriate and valid work permits required for them to work at the location, or locations, agreed with the Company;

4.7 where any part of the Work Scope requires the driving of a motor vehicle on the public highway or the premises of the Client, ensure that any Personnel carrying out such driving on behalf of the Sub-Contractor shall have full and valid driving licences and shall be fully insured whilst driving such a vehicle against damage caused to third parties and their property;

4.8 at its own expense provide all necessary tools, communications equipment and safety equipment, computer hardware and software that may be necessary to execute the Work Scope or as may be reasonably required in any agreement between the Company and the Client and which have been notified to the Sub-Contractor; and

4.9 be responsible for effecting and maintaining (at its own cost) all relevant insurance including (for the avoidance of doubt but without limitation):

(a) employers' liability insurance in an amount not less than the statutory minimum;
(b) public liability insurance in an amount not less than £500,000 per occurrence or in the aggregate;
(c) professional indemnity insurance.

The Sub-Contractor shall at the request of the Company produce such evidence of insurance as the Company requires.

5. Payment of fees

5.1 The Company shall be solely responsible for the payment of all fees due to the Sub-Contractor in respect of the execution of the Work Scope.

5.2 The Sub-Contractor shall submit to the Company on a weekly basis or on another basis agreed with the Company:

(a) tax invoices for fees calculated by reference to the time spent executing the Work Scope (as evidenced by Authorised Records of Work Scope signed by the Client), the Fee and any expenses which the Company has agreed with the Client to pay on behalf of the Client in respect of the Work Scope. In the event that the cost to the Company of undertaking the Work Scope for the Client shall be increased at any time during the term of the Contract by reason of the introduction, variation or imposition of any tax or similar imposition which becomes payable by the Company the Fee shall be reduced by the extent to which such increase is not recoverable from the Client; and
(b) such written information as the Company may from time to time request in support of such invoices including but not limited to copies of certificates of incorporation of the Sub-Contractor and VAT registration documents; and
(c) a written record of the Work Scope actually executed by the Sub-Contractor ('Authorised Record of Work Scope') in a form approved by the Company and signed by an authorised representative of the Client. The Company shall not be obliged to pay for any Work Scope executed by the Sub-Contractor unless an Authorised Record of Work Scope is submitted to the Company.

5.3 The Company shall make payment of amounts properly invoiced to the Company by the Sub-Contractor. Payment will generally be made by BACS transfer on Wednesday in respect of all invoices received by second post on Tuesday in any week so that monies should be in the Sub-Contractor's bank account by the following Friday. If such payment is not made, whether due to public holidays or for any other reason, the Company will make payment to the Sub-Contractor as soon as reasonably possible by a method agreed with the Sub-Contractor.

5.4 The Fee and all other fees and expenses payable by the Company are quoted exclusive of VAT which shall if applicable additionally be payable by the Company.

5.5 The Company shall be entitled to deduct from any amount due to the Sub-Contractor any amount it is required by law to deduct and shall account for such amounts to the appropriate authorities.

6. Expenses

In the event of the Company agreeing with the Client that the Company is to make payment of expenses to the Sub-Contractor, then the Company shall be responsible for all reimbursement of such expenses but only to the extent that tax invoices have been received by the Company, the expenses have previously been approved in writing by the Client and the Company has received payment in respect of such expenses from the Client. The Company shall use its reasonable efforts to obtain such payment including any applicable VAT but for the avoidance of doubt shall not be obliged to commence legal proceedings or terminate or suspend any contract with or the execution of Work Scope to the Client in order to obtain such payment.

7. National insurance, income tax, statutory sick pay and incapacity benefit

The Sub-Contractor shall be responsible for any PAYE, income tax, national insurance contributions and any other taxes and deductions payable in respect of the Personnel arising from the execution of the Work Scope which the Company does not deduct under clause 5.5 above. The Sub-Contractor shall indemnify the Company against any such taxes, contributions or deductions as shall from time to time be due from or assessed on the Company.

8. Liability

The Company accepts liability for personal injury or death to the Personnel caused by the Company's negligence. The Company accepts no other responsibility for or to the Sub-Contractor or the Personnel except as specifically set out in the Contract, whether in respect of earnings, pension rights, health, safety or protection from injury or loss of or damage to property while engaged in the execution of the Work Scope or otherwise and the Sub-Contractor shall indemnify the Company against any claim, loss, damage, cost, expense, demand or proceeding whatsoever incurred or brought by the Personnel other than in respect of such personal injury or death.

9. Use of motor vehicles

Any motor vehicle used by the Sub-Contractor or any of the Personnel in connection with the execution of the Work Scope is the responsibility of the Sub-Contractor and the Company shall have no liability in respect of any such vehicle. For the avoidance of doubt, any motor vehicle used by the Sub-Contractor or any of the Personnel shall be provided by the Sub-Contractor at its own expense.

10. Trade secrets and inventions

10.1   The Sub-Contractor agrees:

(a) that all information furnished to or obtained by the Sub-Contractor or the Personnel in the course or as a result of executing the Work Scope shall be kept confidential by the Sub-Contractor and the Personnel and shall not be used for any purpose other than the execution of the Work Scope;
(b) that all copyright, trademarks, patents and other intellectual property rights arising from the Work Scope shall belong to the Client;
(c) to deliver up to the Client or the Company at the end of the execution of the Work Scope all documents and other materials belonging to the Client (and all copies thereof) which are in the possession of the Sub-Contractor or the Personnel including documents and other materials created during the course of the execution of the Work Scope; and
(d) not at any time to make any copy, abstract, summary or précis of the whole or any part of any document or other material belonging to the Client except when required to do so in the course of its duties in the execution of the Work Scope in which event any such item shall belong to the Client.

10.2 The provisions of this clause shall not apply to any information which comes into the public domain otherwise than as a result of any unauthorised disclosure by the Sub-Contractor or the Personnel.

10.3 The Sub-Contractor shall draw the provisions of this clause to the attention of the Personnel and procure that the Personnel comply with them.

11. Termination

This contract shall automatically terminate upon the earlier of the Estimated Completion Date as agreed between the parties or the actual and satisfactory completion of the Work Scope in the reasonable opinion of the Client.

11.1 Either the Company or the Sub-Contractor may terminate the Contract by giving the other written notice of not less than the Notice Period.

11.2 The Sub-Contractor acknowledges that the continuation of the execution of the Work Scope is subject to and conditional upon the continuation of the Contract entered into between the Company and the Client. In the event that the Contract between the Company and the Client is terminated for any reason then the requirement of the Sub-Contractor to execute the Work Scope shall cease and the Contract shall automatically terminate at the same time, provided that the Company shall give the Sub-Contractor as much notice as possible (if any) of such termination.

11.3 The Company may terminate the Contract immediately by written notice to the Sub-Contractor in the event that the Work Scope is not being executed to the reasonable satisfaction of the Company or the Client, or if the Sub-Contractor is or any relevant Personnel are found guilty by a court of competent jurisdiction of a criminal act that is inconsistent with the continuation of this Agreement, unprofessional conduct (as defined by [*give details*]) or any material breach of or non-observance of their obligations under the Contract which is not remedied within 30 days of formal notification thereof or are guilty of conduct tending to bring itself, themselves, the Client or the Company into disrepute.

11.4 The Company shall be entitled to terminate the Contract with immediate effect by writing to the Sub-Contractor if the Sub-Contractor becomes insolvent or is unable to pay its debts or convenes a meeting of its creditors or if a proposal shall be made for a voluntary arrangement or for any other composition, scheme or arrangement with (or assignment for the benefit of) its creditors or a receiver, administrative receiver, administrator or similar officer is appointed over all or a substantial part of its undertaking or assets or if steps are taken for the winding-up of the Sub-Contractor or for the making of an administration order.

12. Restriction

Whilst the Sub-Contractor shall be fully entitled to service other contracts during and after the currency of this Contract, where they do not conflict with its obligations hereunder, it shall not supply its services or those of the Personnel (and shall procure that the Personnel do not supply their own services) directly or indirectly, whether under a contract of service or for services or in partnership or under a licence or franchise arrangement (including reintroduction by or through another company, partnership, agency or any other organisation) to the Client or any Associated Companies of the Client or any person, firm or company for which it has or relevant Personnel have carried out services via the Company during the previous six months or to any other person, firm or company to whom it or they have been introduced by the Company during the previous six months.

13. Relationship between the parties

13.1 The parties agree and acknowledge that nothing in these Conditions shall constitute the relationship of master and servant or employer and employee or any partnership between the Company and the Sub-Contractor or any Personnel or the Client and the Sub-Contractor or any Personnel.

13.2 Neither the Company, the Client nor the Sub-Contractor is obliged to provide future work following completion of the Work Scope, and if any such offer is made, the Sub-Contractor is not obliged to accept it.

14. General

14.1 The remedies available to the Company under the Contract shall be without prejudice to any other rights, either at common law or under statute, which it may have against the Sub-Contractor.

14.2 The failure or delay of the Company to enforce or to exercise, at any time or for any period of time, any term of or any right, power or privilege arising pursuant to the Contract does not constitute and shall not be construed as a waiver of such term or right and shall in no way affect its right later to enforce or exercise it.

14.3 Each provision of the Contract is severable and distinct from the others. If any such provision is or at any time becomes to any extent invalid, illegal or unenforceable under any enactment or rule of law, it shall to that extent be deemed not to form part of the Contract but (except to that extent in the case of that provision) it and all other provisions of the Contract shall continue in full force and effect and their validity, legality and enforceability shall not be thereby affected or impaired.

14.4 The Sub-Contractor shall be entitled to substitute alternatives for the Personnel, with the prior written consent of the Company – such consent not to be withheld if the proposed replacement has the appropriate skills, qualifications and abilities in the reasonable opinion of the Client.

14.5 Clause headings are purely for ease of reference and do not form part of or affect the interpretation of the Contract.

14.6 The construction, validity and performance of the Contract are governed by the law of England and the parties accept the jurisdiction of the English courts.

14.7 Any dispute between the parties relating to these Conditions shall be referred with the agreement of the parties to an arbitrator appointed by the President of the Law Society ('the Arbitrator') and the decision of the Arbitrator in relation to the dispute shall be binding on the parties.

Signed   ....   Date   ....

[*employer*]

Signed   ....   Date   ....

[*contractor*]

PRECEDENT 3C: Consultancy agreement

Example 1

Agreement made on [date]

Between

(1) [name of company] [company number] whose registered office is at [address] ('the Company'); and
(2) [name] of [address] ('the Consultant').

Whereas:

1. The Consultant is engaged in business offering consultancy services in relation to [give details] and has considerable skill, knowledge and experience in that field.
2. In reliance on that skill, knowledge and experience the Company wishes to engage the Consultant to provide services in relation to [give details].

1. Definitions

1.1 In this agreement:

(a) 'Board' means the board of directors for the time being and from time to time of the Company;
(b) 'Commission' means the commission payable to the Consultant in accordance with Clause 4;
(c) 'Confidential Information' includes all and any patents, trademarks and service marks, rights in designs, trade, business or domain names, database rights, topography rights, copyrights (including rights in computer software) (whether or not registered and including applications for (and the right to apply for) registration of any such thing) and all rights and forms of protection of a similar nature or having equivalent or similar effect to any of these which may subsist anywhere in the world for the full period of them and all extensions or renewals of them;
(d) 'Effective Date' means the date of this agreement;
(e) 'Fee' means the basic fee of £... per annum;
(f) 'Group Company' means the Company or any other company which is for the time being its subsidiary or its holding company or a subsidiary of such holding company and the terms 'subsidiary' and 'holding company' have the meanings ascribed to them in section 736 of the Companies Act 1985;
(g) 'Intellectual Property Rights' include all or any patents, trademarks and service marks, rights in designs, trade, business or domain names, database rights, topography rights, copyrights (including rights in computer software) (whether or not registered and including applications for (and the right to apply for) registration of any such thing) and all rights or forms of protection of a similar nature or having equivalent or similar effect to any of these which may subsist anywhere in the world for the full period of them and all extensions or renewals of them;
(h) 'Working Day' means any day (other than a Saturday or Sunday) on which the banks in London are open for business.

1.2 A reference in this agreement to the Company includes any Group Company.

1.3 A reference in this agreement to a Clause, Sub-Clause or Schedule is a reference to a Clause, Sub-Clause or Schedule in this agreement.

1.4 A reference to a statutory provision includes references to any statutory modification, consolidation or re-enactment happening after the date of this agreement along with any statutory instruments or orders made under it.

1.5 The clause headings in this agreement are for ease of reference only and have no interpretative value.

1.6 Where appropriate words denoting a singular member only shall include the plural and vice versa.

1.7 The words 'including' or 'includes' are not used by way of limitation.

2. Term of engagement

2.1 The Consultant shall provide his services to the Company on the terms of this agreement (the 'Engagement'). The Engagement shall continue until terminated:

(a) as provided for elsewhere in this agreement; or
(b) [no earlier than the [1st] anniversary of the date of this agreement] by either party giving the other not less than [six] months' prior written notice.

2.2 The Company will pay the Consultant the Fee and the Commission during the applicable notice period. This shall apply unless both parties agree otherwise.

2.3 Upon termination of the Engagement, at the request of the Company, the Consultant shall deliver up all documents (including correspondence, list of clients or customers, plans, drawings, accounts and other documents of whatsoever nature and all copies of them, whether on paper, computer memory disc or otherwise made) made, compiled or acquired by him during the Engagement and concerning the business, finances or affairs of the Company or its clients together with any other property of the Company in the Consultant's possession.

3. Duties

3.1 The Consultant performs the duties of [*give details*] in accordance with the terms of this agreement. [The Consultant's duties are more specifically set out in Schedule 1.]

3.2 The Consultant shall:

(a) spend [. . .] Working Days per annum working for the Company;
(b) faithfully and diligently perform his duties and use his best endeavours to promote and protect the interests of the Company;
(c) work at any of the Company's places of work within the UK or such other places of business in the world as his position requires;
(d) make such reports to the Board on any matters concerning the affairs of the Company as the Board may reasonably require and comply with all codes of practice of the Company applicable to [*give details*] and all rules and regulations (as amended from time to time) of all regulatory authorities relevant to the Company with which the Consultant is concerned;
(e) obey all reasonable directions given to him by the Board.

3.3 The Consultant shall not be engaged or concerned in or become an employee, agent, partner, consultant or director of or assist or have any financial interest in any business or profession which is similar to or in competition with the business carried on by the Company or which may interfere, conflict or compete with the proper performance of the Consultant's duties.

3.4 The Consultant shall work such reasonable hours during each Working Day as are necessary for the proper performance of his duties. The work will involve overtime, travel time and time abroad which it is agreed that the Fee and Commission compensate for.

3.5 The Company may transfer the Engagement to any other Group Company.

4. **Fee**

4.1 The Company shall pay the Consultant the Fee. The Fee shall be payable by bank credit transfer in equal monthly instalments in arrears on the last Working Day of each calendar month.

4.2 The Board will award the Consultant Commission in accordance with Schedule 2.

4.3 The Company may deduct from any sums owed to the Consultant all sums which he from time to time owes the Company.

5. **Expenses**

The Company shall reimburse the Consultant for all reasonable travel, accommodation and other expenses properly authorised by the Board and incurred in or about the performance of the Consultant's duties under this agreement, which expenses shall be evidenced in such manner as the Board may reasonably require from time to time.

6. **Data protection**

6.1 The Consultant consents to the Company holding, disclosing to third parties, or otherwise processing (in particular processing any 'sensitive personal data' as defined in the Data Protection Act 1998) any data relating to him, including data relating to ethnic or racial origins, political opinions, religious beliefs or beliefs of a similar nature, trade union membership, health and criminal records and to the transfer of all or any part of such data outside the European Economic Area.

6.2 Subject to their having complied with the Data Protection Act 1998, the Company may make any such data available to Group Companies, professional advisers, those who provide products or services to the Company, regulatory authorities, potential or future employers, governmental or quasi-governmental organisations.

7. **Confidential information**

7.1 Without prejudice to his common law duties, the Consultant shall not (except in the proper course of his duties, as required by law or as authorised by the Company) use or communicate to any person (and shall use his best endeavours to prevent the use or communication of) any Confidential Information relating to the Company which he creates, develops, receives or obtains during the Engagement. This restriction shall continue to apply after the termination of the Engagement except to the extent that such information comes into the public domain other than as a result of a breach of this Clause 7.1.

7.2 During the Engagement the Consultant shall not make (other than for the benefit of the Company) any record (whether on paper, computer memory, disk or otherwise) relating to any matter within the scope of the business of the Company or their customers and suppliers or concerning its or their dealings or affairs or (either during the Engagement or afterwards) use such records (or allow them to be used) other than for the benefit of the Company.

8. **Inventions and creative works**

8.1 The Consultant shall promptly disclose to the Company any idea, invention or work which is relevant to (or capable of use in) the business of the Company made by him in the course of the Engagement (whether or not in the course of his duties). The Consultant acknowledges that all Intellectual Property Rights subsisting (or which may in the future subsist) in any such ideas, inventions or works will, on creation, vest in and be the exclusive property of the Company and if they do not do so he shall assign them to the Company (upon its request and at its cost). The Consultant hereby irrevocably waives any moral rights which he may have in any such ideas, inventions or works under Chapter IV of Part I of the Copyright, Designs and Patents Act 1988.

8.2 The Consultant hereby irrevocably appoints the Company to be his attorney in his name and on his behalf to execute and do any such instrument or thing and generally to use his name for the purpose of giving to the Company or its nominee the full benefit of this clause and acknowledges in favour of any third party that a certificate in writing signed by any director or secretary of the Company that any instrument or act falls within the authority hereby conferred will be conclusive evidence that such is the case.

9. Termination by events of default

9.1 The Company may terminate the Engagement by notice but with immediate effect if the Consultant:

(a) is guilty of gross misconduct or commits any serious or (after written warning) repeated or continued material breach of his obligations to the Company;

(b) becomes bankrupt or makes any arrangement or composition with or for the benefit of his creditors;

(c) is convicted of any criminal offence (other than an offence under any road traffic legislation in the UK or elsewhere for which a fine or non-custodial penalty is imposed) which involves dishonesty or which the Company reasonably considers is incompatible with the Engagement;

(d) becomes of unsound mind or a patient under any statute relating to mental health;

(e) fails in the reasonable opinion of the Board (but only where such failure can be reasonably established) to perform his duties to a satisfactory standard;

(f) does anything which brings the Company into serious disrepute;

(g) acts in a way which is materially adverse to the interests of the Company;

(h) is guilty of a serious breach of the rules and regulations as amended from time to time of any regulatory authority relevant to the business of the Company or any compliance manual of the Company implementing such rules and regulations; or

(i) is unable to perform his duties for a period of 20 working days in aggregate in any period of 12 months.

9.2 Any reasonable delay by the Company in exercising such right to terminate after the matter in question comes to the attention of the Board will not constitute a waiver of it.

10. Restrictions after termination of the Engagement

10.1 The Consultant acknowledges that he has obtained and will obtain during the course of the Engagement knowledge of the trade connections and secrets and other confidential information of the Company and therefore the Consultant agrees to be bound by the following restrictions:

(a) He shall not for a period of [six] months after the termination of the Engagement, whether on his own behalf or on behalf of any other person, firm or Company, directly or indirectly solicit or canvass the custom or business of or deal with any person, firm or company who within a period of [12] months prior to the termination of the Engagement was a customer or client of the Company having contact with the Consultant in the course of the business in which the Consultant will have been concerned during the said [12] month period; and

(b) He shall not for a period of [six] months after the termination of the Engagement, whether on his own behalf or on behalf of any other person, firm or company, directly or indirectly, employ or endeavour to entice away from the Company any senior employee or consultant of the Company employed at the date of termination and with whom the Consultant has had regular dealings during the [12] months immediately preceding the termination of the Engagement; and

(c) He shall not for a period of [six] months after the termination of the Engagement interfere or seek to interfere with the continuance of supplies to the Company or the terms of such supplies from any suppliers with whom he shall have dealt in the period of [12] months prior to the termination of his Engagement.

10.2 The restrictions in each sub-clause above are enforceable independently of each other and their validity shall not be affected if any of the others are invalid. If any such restrictions are found to be void, but would be valid if some part of them were deleted or the period of application were reduced, such restrictions shall apply with such deletions or modifications as may be necessary to make them valid or effective.

10.3 The Consultant acknowledges that the provisions of this clause (in respect of which he has had the opportunity to take independent advice) are no more extensive than is reasonable to protect the legitimate interests of the Company.

10.4 The Consultant shall (at the request and cost of the Company) enter into a direct agreement with any Group Company under which he shall accept restrictions corresponding to the restrictions contained in this clause (or such as will be reasonably appropriate in the circumstances) in relation to such Group Company.

10.5 If the Consultant at any time during the operative period of any of the restrictive covenants referred to in Clause 10.1 (the 'Covenants') considers that any of the Covenants are unreasonable or unfair in all the circumstances he may request the Board to relax them in such a way as to provide reasonable protection of the Company's legitimate business while, if possible, permitting the Consultant to pursue his chosen business activity. If the Board refuses to do so it must provide full written reasons to the Consultant for doing so and shall, if requested, offer him an opportunity to discuss the Board's objection with a view to seeking agreement if possible. The Consultant shall make full and frank disclosure to the Board of his planned activities as a condition of it considering his request.

10.6 If the Consultant is offered employment or a consultancy arrangement with a third party at any time during the Engagement or in the 12 months following termination of this agreement (howsoever arising), he must supply that third party with a full copy of this clause.

11. Consultant's warranties, undertakings and obligations

11.1 The Consultant warrants and represents to the Company:

(a) that he has the necessary skill and knowledge to carry out his duties under this agreement; and
(b) that he will not, in entering this agreement or carrying out his duties under this agreement be in breach of any terms of the Engagement, whether express or implied or any other obligation binding upon him;
(c) that he is an independent contractor.

11.2 Nothing in this agreement shall render the Consultant an employee, agent or partner of the Company and the Consultant shall not hold himself out as such.

11.3 The Consultant undertakes to the Company that he will duly pay the tax and National Insurance Contributions which are due from him whether in the UK or elsewhere in relation to the payments to be made to him by the Company pursuant to this agreement and further agrees to fully indemnify the Company in respect of all and any income tax and National Insurance Contributions which may be found due from the Company on any payments made to him under this agreement together with any interest, penalties or gross-up on it.

11.4 The Consultant will take out and maintain professional indemnity insurance with a reputable insurance company providing a minimum cover of £ . . . and will supply the Company with copies of current certificates of insurance for the duration of this agreement.

12. Notices

Any notice to be given under this agreement shall be in writing. Notices may be given by either party by personal delivery or post or by fax addressed to the other party at (in the case of the Company) its registered office for the time being and (in the case of the Consultant) his last known address. Any such notice given by letter or fax shall be deemed to have been served at the time at which the notice was delivered personally or successfully transmitted or (if sent by post) would be delivered in the ordinary course of post.

13. Proper law

This agreement shall be governed by and construed in accordance with English law and the parties submit to the exclusive jurisdiction of the courts of England.

14. Previous contracts

This agreement contains the entire understanding between the parties and is in substitution for any previous agreement or arrangement between the parties, which are deemed to have been terminated by mutual consent as from the Effective Date.

15. Amendment

No modification, variation or amendment to this agreement shall be effective unless such modification, variation or amendment is in writing and has been signed by or on behalf of both parties.

16. Assignment

Neither party shall assign, transfer, sub-contract or in any other manner make over to any third party the benefit or burden of this agreement without the prior written consent of the other.

17. Third party rights

Nothing in this agreement confers any third party rights which they would not have had but for the Contract (Rights of Third Parties) Act 1999.

This agreement has been executed and delivered as a Deed on the date first above written.

Executed and delivered as a Deed by [company] acting by

Director:

Director/Secretary:

Executed and delivered as a Deed by [consultant] in the presence of

Name

Address

Occupation

SCHEDULE 1 – CONSULTANT'S DUTIES

[give details]

SCHEDULE 2 – COMMISSION

[give details]

Example 2

[Letterhead of company]

This Agreement confirms that we will retain you to act as, and you will act as, a consultant to *[insert name of Company]* beginning on *[insert date]* on the terms set out in this Agreement.

1. Your Services

1.1 You will provide the services listed in the Schedule (the Services), provided you will be required to devote a minimum of [X] days performing the Services during the period of your appointment.

1.2 You will put at our disposal your knowledge and experience relating to those activities in the field in which we are engaged in order to provide the Services.

1.3 You warrant that you are under no obligation which is inconsistent with your duties to us, and that you will not enter into any agreement with a third party, the terms of which may be inconsistent with those duties.

1.4 You agree and accept that following the completion of the said minimum [X] days there will be no obligation on the part of the Company to provide you with any further work under this Agreement.

1.5 This Agreement will terminate if not earlier on your 65th birthday without further notice.

2. Fees

2.1 We will pay you:

2.1.1 A per diem rate of £[X] per day subject to any statutory deductions; and

2.1.2 reasonable expenses necessarily incurred by you in the proper performance of your duties.

2.2 You should address all invoices to *[insert address]*, for the attention of *[insert details]*. We will pay each invoice within [30] days after we receive your invoice.

2.3 The payments made by us under paragraph 2.1 above are full and complete compensation for all obligations assumed by you under this Agreement and for all Intellectual Property you assign to us under or pursuant to paragraph 4.2 below. For the avoidance of doubt no benefits, pension contributions or bonus will fall due under this Agreement.

2.4 All amounts payable to you under this Agreement are inclusive of any VAT (or any similar tax).

3. Confidentiality

3.1 You will during the period of your consultancy and for 12 months after its end keep confidential, and not use for any purpose except acting as our consultant and providing services to us, any information that we or our Group Companies (that is any undertaking which is, on or after the date of this Agreement from time to time, our subsidiary undertaking, our parent undertaking or a subsidiary undertaking of our parent undertaking, as those terms are defined in section 258 of the Companies Act 1985) make known to you or about the work you do for us, and you agree that you will not disclose the same to any third party without first obtaining our written consent.

3.2 At the end of your consultancy, you will immediately deliver to us all materials, records, databases, documents and other papers that are in your possession, custody or control and that are our property, or that otherwise relate to our business, and you will not retain any copies.

3.3 The above obligations of confidentiality do not apply to any information that:

3.3.1 was already known to you, and not already subject to any obligation of confidentiality to us, before we made it available to you;

3.3.2 is or becomes publicly known through no fault of yours;

3.3.3 is given to you by a third party who has the right to do so.

4. Intellectual Property

4.1 You will disclose to us promptly the results of the Services, including any inventions and improvements that you make or conceive, either alone or jointly with others, in the course of, or as a direct result of, the work done for us, or as a consequence of information we or our Group Companies have supplied to you for the purposes of this Agreement.

4.2 To the extent that any Intellectual Property in the work you do for us is capable of prospective assignment, you now assign that Intellectual Property to us; and to the extent any Intellectual Property in that work cannot prospectively be assigned, you will assign that Intellectual Property to us as and when it is created, at our request.

4.3 You warrant to us that in relation to any assignment made under or pursuant to paragraph 4.2:

4.3.1 you have the right to dispose of the Intellectual Property assigned to us and that you will, at your own cost, do all that you reasonably can to give the title that you purport to give; and

4.3.2 the Intellectual Property assigned to us is free from all charges and encumbrances and rights of any third party (except those that you are unaware or could not reasonably be aware of).

4.4 You will take any action and execute any document we reasonably require to give effect to our rights under paragraph 4.2, or to enable their registration in any relevant territory provided we pay your reasonable expenses.

4.5 The expression 'Intellectual Property' means patents, trademarks, service marks, registered designs, copyrights, database rights, design rights, confidential information, applications for any of the above, and any similar right recognised from time to time in any jurisdiction, together with all rights of action in relation to the infringement of any of the above.

5. Independent Contractor Relationship

5.1 You agree that you will be working for us as an independent contractor and that nothing in this Agreement creates, implies or evidences the relationship of employer and employee, or principal and agent. You have no authority to make any representation or commitment or to incur any liability on our behalf.

5.2 You agree to effect professional indemnity insurance and to keep insured throughout the period of this Consultancy with respect to any negligence, act or omission or accident or injury occasioned by or caused by you in the course of performing your duties under this Agreement capped at a maximum liability of [£X MILLION]. You agree to show to [name of person] a copy of your duly executed insurance policy and to keep the said insurance up to date and fully effective.

6. Termination

6.1 Either you or we may terminate this Agreement with immediate effect by giving notice to the other if:

6.1.1 the other is in breach of any provision of this Agreement and (if it is capable of remedy) the breach has not been remedied within 30 days after receipt of written notice specifying the breach and requiring its remedy; or

6.1.2 the other becomes insolvent, or if an order is made or a resolution is passed for its winding up (except voluntarily for the purpose of solvent amalgamation or reconstruction), or if an administrator, administrative receiver or receiver is appointed over the whole or any part of the other's assets, or if the other makes any arrangement with its creditors.

6.2 Paragraphs 3, 4, 5, 6.2, 7, 8, 10, 11 and 12 will survive the termination or expiry of this Agreement for any reason and continue indefinitely.

7. Data Protection

You consent to our holding and processing any personal data we collect about you for the purpose of administering and managing our business.

8. Tax

You will be responsible for paying all income tax and national insurance contributions in relation to the fees paid to you under this Agreement.

9. Conflict of Interest

You agree that while you are providing the Services to us you will not be directly engaged in, or concerned with any other business or profession which either competes with us or that might otherwise cause a conflict of interest without first obtaining our written consent. If in any doubt as to whether a conflict of interest might exist you should immediately discuss the matter with us before accepting any position or appointment.

10. Force Majeure

If the performance by either you or us of any obligation under this Agreement (except a payment obligation) is delayed or prevented by circumstances beyond your or our reasonable control, you or we (as the case may be) will not be in breach of this Agreement because of that delay in performance. However, if the delay in performance lasts for more than three months, the other party may terminate this Agreement with immediate effect by giving written notice.

11. Liability

11.1 You warrant to us that, to the best of your knowledge and belief (having made reasonable enquiry of those likely to have relevant knowledge, but not having made any search of any public register) any advice or information given by you, or the content or use of any materials, works or information you provide to us in connection with this Agreement, will not constitute or result in any infringement of third-party rights.

OR

11.1 You make no representation nor give any warranty to us that any advice or information given by you, or the content or use of any materials, works or information you provide to us in connection with this Agreement, will not constitute or result in any infringement of third-party rights.

11.2 [Except under the limited warranty in paragraph 11.1, and] subject to paragraph 11.6, you accept no responsibility for any use which may be made by us of any materials, works or information that you provide to us nor for any reliance which we may place on any advice or information you give to us.

11.3 We will indemnify you, and keep you fully and effectively indemnified, against each and every claim made against you as a result of our use of any materials, works or information received from you pursuant to the terms of this Agreement, provided that you must:

11.3.1 promptly notify us of the details of the claim;

11.3.2 not make any admission in relation to the claim;

11.3.3 allow us to have conduct of the defence or settlement of the claim; and

11.3.4 give us all reasonable assistance (at our expense) in dealing with the claim.

The indemnity in this paragraph will not apply to the extent that the claim arises as a result of your negligence, breach of paragraph 3 or the deliberate breach of this Agreement.

11.4 Subject to paragraph 11.6, your liability for any breach of this Agreement, any negligence or arising in any other way out of the subject matter of this Agreement, will not extend to any indirect damages or losses, or any loss of profits, loss of revenue, loss of data, loss of contracts or opportunity, whether direct or indirect, even if we have advised you of the possibility of those losses or if they were within your contemplation.

11.5 Subject to paragraph 11.6, your aggregate liability to us for all and any breaches of this Agreement, any negligence or arising in any other way out of the subject matter of this Agreement, will not exceed in total [the amount paid to you under this Agreement].

11.6 Nothing in this Agreement limits or excludes either party's liability for:

11.6.1 death or personal injury;

11.6.2 any fraud or for any sort of liability that, by law, cannot be limited or excluded; or

11.6.3 any loss or damage caused by a deliberate breach of this Agreement or a breach of paragraph 3.

11.7 The express undertakings and warranties given by you and us in this Agreement are in lieu of all other warranties, conditions, terms, undertakings and obligations, whether express or implied by statute, common law, custom, trade usage, course of dealing or in any other way. All of these are excluded to the fullest extent permitted by law.

12. General

12.1 **Notices:** Any notice to be given under this Agreement must be in writing, may be delivered to the other party by any of the methods set out in the left hand column below, and will be deemed to be received on the corresponding day set out in the right hand column:

Method of service	Deemed day of receipt
By hand or courier	the day of delivery
By pre-paid first class post	the second Business Day after posting (a Business Day is Monday to Friday (inclusive) except bank or public holidays in [England])
By recorded delivery post	the next Business Day after posting

Method of service	Deemed day of receipt
By fax (provided the sender's fax machine confirms complete and error-free transmission of that notice to the correct fax number)	the next Business Day after sending or, if sent before 16.00 (sender's local time) on the Business Day it was sent

The parties' respective representatives for the receipt of notices are, until changed by notice given in accordance with this paragraph, as follows:

For the Consultant:	For the Company:
Name:	Name:
Address:	Address:
Fax number:	Fax number:

12.2　**Headings**: The headings in this Agreement are for ease of reference only; they do not affect its construction or interpretation.

12.3　**Assignment**: Neither you nor we may assign or transfer this Agreement as a whole, or any of our rights or obligations under it, without first obtaining the written consent of the other party. That consent may not be unreasonably withheld or delayed.

12.4　**Illegal/unenforceable provisions**: If the whole or any part of any provision of this Agreement is void or unenforceable in any jurisdiction, the other provisions of this Agreement, and the rest of the void or unenforceable provision, will continue in force in that jurisdiction, and the validity and enforceability of that provision in any other jurisdiction will not be affected.

12.5　**Waiver of rights**: If either you or we fail to enforce, or delay in enforcing, an obligation of the other party, or fail to exercise, or delay in exercising, a right under this Agreement, that failure or delay will not affect your or our right to enforce that obligation or constitute a waiver of that right. Any waiver of any provision of this Agreement will not, unless expressly stated to the contrary, constitute a waiver of that provision on a future occasion.

12.6　**No agency**: Nothing in this Agreement creates, implies or evidences any partnership or joint venture between the parties, or the relationship between them of principal and agent. Neither party has any authority to make any representation or commitment, or to incur any liability, on behalf of the other.

12.7　**Entire Agreement**: This Agreement constitutes the entire agreement between you and us relating to its subject matter. You and we each acknowledge that we have not entered into this Agreement on the basis of any warranty, representation, statement, agreement or undertaking except those expressly set out in this Agreement. You and we waive any claim for breach of this Agreement, or any right to rescind this Agreement in respect of any representation which is not an express provision of this Agreement. However, this paragraph does not exclude any liability which you or we may have to the other (or any right which either of us may have to rescind this Agreement) in respect of any fraudulent misrepresentation or fraudulent concealment prior to the execution of this Agreement.

12.8　**Formalities**: Each party will take any action and execute any document reasonably required by the other party to give effect to any of its rights under this Agreement, or to enable their registration in any relevant territory provided the requesting party pays the other party's reasonable expenses.

12.9 **Amendments:** No variation or amendment of this Agreement will be effective unless it is made in writing and signed by you and on our behalf.

12.10 **Third parties:** No one except you or us has any right to prevent the amendment of this Agreement or its termination, and no one except you or us may enforce any benefit conferred by this Agreement, unless this Agreement expressly provides otherwise.

12.11 **Governing law:** This Agreement is governed by, and is to be construed in accordance with, English law. The English Courts will have exclusive jurisdiction to deal with any dispute which has arisen or may arise out of, or in connection with, this Agreement, except that either party may bring proceedings for an injunction in any jurisdiction.

THE SCHEDULE

[insert details of the Services]

If the above terms and conditions are acceptable to you, please sign and return the enclosed copy of this letter to me.

Yours sincerely

[Signed on behalf of the Company]

[ON COPY]

I agree to the terms and conditions set out in this letter.

Signed: .... Date: ....

Position: ....

PRECEDENT 3D: Indemnity clause for contract for services

If in any doubt, employers should include the following indemnity in the contractor's/consultant's/freelancer's agreement:

1. The parties hereto believe that the Consultant is a Schedule D taxpayer and Class 2 and 4 national insurance contributions payer and is exempt from deduction at source of PAYE tax and Class I national insurance liability by virtue of his status.

2. Save for any tax and national insurance contributions deducted by the Company, the Consultant hereby undertakes to indemnify and hold the Company harmless against all other taxes and national insurance contributions in respect of any payments and benefits provided or to be provided pursuant to this agreement, and all costs, claims, expenses or proceedings, penalties and interest incurred by the Company which arise out of or in connection with any liability to pay (or deduct) tax or national insurance contributions in respect of any payments and benefits provided pursuant to this agreement (save for any such costs, claims, expenses or proceedings, penalties and interest incurred as a result of the Company's default).

PRECEDENT 3E: Casual workers: terms of engagement

Agreement made on [date]

Between:

(1)   The Job Shop of [name of company] ('the Job Shop'); and
(2)   [name and address] ('the Casual Worker').

1. Definitions

In these terms of engagement the following definitions apply:

The 'Client' means the Department/Division/Associated or subsidiary Company or corporate body requiring the services of the Casual Worker.

The 'Assignment' shall mean any period during which the Casual Worker performs services for a Client under this Contract.

2. The contract

2.1 These terms constitute a contract for services and shall continue to apply until the earliest of the following events, on the happening of which this contract and all contractual relations between the Casual Worker and the Job Shop shall end with immediate effect.

(a) The Casual Worker not attending work as part of an Assignment for any reason and for any period during the currency of this Contract without notifying the Job Shop in advance.
(b) With or without notice the Casual Worker not performing any services in respect of an Assignment for the duration of any period of four whole weeks (which for these purposes shall start on a Sunday and end on a Saturday).
(c) The Casual Worker or the Job Shop for any reason terminating this Contract, which need not be of any minimum duration.

2.2 If following the ending of this Contract as a result of any of the events referred to in 2.1 above the Casual Worker performs services at the behest of the Job Shop then it is agreed that such services shall be governed by a new contract.

2.3 For the avoidance of doubt, these terms do not give rise to a contract of employment between the Job Shop and the Casual Worker.

2.4 No variation or alteration to these terms shall be valid unless approved by the Company in writing.

2.5 For the avoidance of doubt, nothing in this Contract requires the Job Shop to offer or provide the Casual Worker with any Assignments or work of a particular kind or at all or creates any obligation on the Casual Worker to perform any work or accept any Assignments.

2.6 If the Job Shop requires services to be performed, the services, rates of pay and hours will be notified as and when necessary. However, the Job Shop shall pay the Casual Worker remuneration calculated at a minimum rate of at least the National Minimum Wage or above for each hour worked during an Assignment. The rates of pay will be in accordance with appropriate (market rate) pay scales, taking into account age or other factors which may be relevant. This will be paid weekly in arrears subject to any deductions which the Job Shop may be bound by law to make.

3. Pension

3.1 The occupational pension scheme applicable to this post is the Company Scheme. An explanatory booklet is available for reference from the Human Resources Department.

3.2 A contracting-out certificate under the Social Security Pensions Act 1975 is in force in respect of the Company Pension Scheme. It follows that if you choose to join the Company Scheme a contracting-out certificate under the Social Security Pensions Act 1975 will be in force in respect of your employment. Should you choose not to join the Company Scheme you must join the State Pension Scheme or take out a personal pension.

3.3 The compulsory retirement age is 65.

4. **Sickness and maternity pay**

4.1   There may be an entitlement to Statutory Sick Pay (SSP) and Statutory Maternity Pay (SMP), providing that the criteria for earnings and service are met, in accordance with legal requirements. There is no entitlement to contractual maternity or sick pay.

4.2   The Casual Worker is not entitled to payment from the Job Shop or its Clients for time not spent on Assignments in respect of other absences.

5. **Holiday pay**

5.1   The Casual Worker is entitled to 20 days' paid holiday per year, including statutory and customary holidays. Holiday pay will be paid on a weekly basis at an hourly rate which is additional to the rate of pay for the Assignment.

5.2   The Casual Worker is not obliged to accept any Assignment offered by the Job Shop but if he does so, during every Assignment afterwards, as appropriate, he will cooperate with the Client's staff and accept the directions, supervision and instruction of any responsible person in the Client's organisation; observe any rules and regulations of the Client's establishment to which attention has been drawn or which the Casual Worker might reasonably be expected to ascertain; unless arrangements have been made to the contrary conform to the normal hours of work in force at the Client's establishment at the time of Assignment; take all responsible steps to safeguard his own safety and the safety of any other person who may be present or affected by his actions on the Assignment and comply with the Client's Health and Safety Policy; not engage in any conduct detrimental to the interest of the Client.

5.3   At the end of each week of an Assignment (or at the end of the Assignment where an Assignment is for a period of less than one week or is completed before the end of the week), the Casual Worker shall deliver to the Job Shop his timesheet duly completed to indicate the number of hours worked by the Casual Worker during the preceding week and signed by an authorised representative of the Client. The Job Shop shall not be obliged to make any payment to the Casual Worker unless a properly authenticated timesheet has been submitted.

6. **Ending an Assignment**

6.1   The Job Shop may without notice and without liability instruct the Casual Worker to end an Assignment at any time.

6.2   If the Casual Worker is unable for any reason to work on an Assignment he should inform the Company by no later than the first day of absence to enable alternative arrangements to be made.

7. **Confidentiality**

The Casual Worker accepts that during Assignments, he will be exposed to the Client's (and the Company's) confidential information and accordingly agrees to treat as secret and confidential and not during the Assignment, nor at any time after the Assignment, for any reason to disclose or permit to be disclosed to any person or otherwise make use or permit to be made use of any confidential information of the Client or Company which shall include but shall not be limited to information relating to the Client's or Company's technology, technical processes, research activities, inventions, designs, business affairs, finances, employees or officers or any such information relating to a subsidiary, supplier, customer or client of the Client or Company where knowledge or details of the information was received during the Assignment. The Casual Worker further agrees that upon termination of this Contract for whatever reason, he shall, without retaining any copies, deliver up to the Client or Company or the Job Shop all working papers or other material and copies provided to him pursuant to this Contract or prepared by him during the Assignment.

I have already declared any criminal convictions (subject to the Rehabilitation of Offenders Act 1974).

Declaration

I declare that I have read and understood the above contract and I am prepared to abide by its terms and conditions.

Signed .... Date ....

[*casual worker*]

Signed .... Date ....

[*employer*]

PRECEDENT 3F: Casual workers: appointment form

DEADLINE FOR APPOINTMENT INFORMATION IS 12.00 WEDNESDAY OF EACH WEEK. DETAILS SENT AFTER THIS DEADLINE WILL RESULT IN LATE PAYMENT.

NAME: .... DOB:...

PAY NO: .... NI NUMBER: ....

SECTION 1: APPOINTMENT DETAILS TO BE COMPLETED BY JOB SHOP

APPOINTMENT START DATE: REVIEW DATE:
....

TITLE OF POST:
....

MOC/SBC CODE: HOURLY RATE:
....

SECTION 2: APPOINTMENT EXTENSION

START DATE:................................. END DATE:...............................

SECTION 3: APPOINTMENT DETAILS

REASON FOR CASUAL APPOINTMENT: ....

SIGNED ON BEHALF OF JOB SHOP: ....

DATE: ....

SECTION 4: PAYROLL USE ONLY

PAYROLL NUMBER: ....

APPOINTMENT NUMBER: ....

Input to PMS (Signature) DATE : ....
....

PRECEDENT 3G: Casual workers: weekly timesheet/payment form

ALL SECTIONS MUST BE COMPLETED TO ENSURE PAYMENT

PAYROLL LOCATION
....

FACULTY/SCHOOL/DIVISION	HOURS AUTHORISED BY
....	....
AUTHORISED SIGNATURE FOR TIMESHEET	
....	
WEEK ENDING WEEK NO.	AUTHORISED SIGNATURE FOR PAYMENT
....	....
BY JOB SHOP:	
....	

HOURS WORKED

PAY NUMBER	FULL NAME	RATE		PAYROLL USE	
....	....	....		....	
MON	TUE	WED	THU	FRI	SAT	SUN	WEEKLY TOTAL
......	......	......	......	......	......	......	......

PRECEDENT 3H: Contract of employment for surveillance staff

1. **Conditional employment**

1.1 Your continued employment is conditional upon the satisfactory completion of an initial probationary period during which the Company will assess and review your work performance and only if the Company deems your performance to be satisfactory will you be confirmed in post.

1.2 The Company normally operates a probationary period of up to [six] months. However the Company reserves the right to extend the trial period if it deems it appropriate.

1.3 You will be notified of the satisfactory completion of your probationary period by receiving confirmation in writing from our Employee Information System. Should your performance not be deemed satisfactory either during or at the end of your probationary period, the Company reserves the right to terminate your employment without following the disciplinary procedure, i.e. without giving any formal warnings, a disciplinary hearing or a right of appeal. In such a case either notice or pay in lieu of notice will be given save in any case of gross misconduct where you may be summarily dismissed, i.e. without notice or payment in lieu of notice.

1.4 Your role requires you to demonstrate utmost integrity, honesty and probity. We rely upon you to detect the crimes and dishonesty of others. You must be above reproach. This includes retaining our utmost trust in your conduct and reporting.

1.5 Any suspicion of dishonesty, the taking or giving of bribes, false reporting or any conduct on your part which is dishonest or improper or unethical in any way will lead us to deem you inappropriate for this role and you will be the subject of disciplinary proceedings which could result in your summary dismissal.

1.6 You must at all times follow your instructions and advice given to you regarding any particular surveillance operation. You must be aware of and follow the protocols for any particular surveillance exercise. You must also be aware of the Human Rights Act 1998 and the European Convention on Human Rights, Article 8 which give every individual the right to respect for their privacy. This means that it is unlawful to use long camera lenses to film inside someone's home or to trick your way into someone's home and secretly video them or their activities. If you are in any doubt about any activities, then please ask your line manager or HR Director.

2. Job title, flexibility and mobility

2.1 Your job title initially is Surveillance Operative but this may be amended at the Company's entire discretion from time to time.

2.2 Your job entails working long hours often setting off from home very early in the morning and returning late at night or staying overnight. It also involves many hours of monotony and waiting when nothing happens. You are required to be vigilant and diligent in your duties. You will be required to carry out all reasonable, different and/or additional duties that are within your capabilities and which are deemed reasonable by your line management for you to undertake. Where reasonably possible you will be consulted before being asked to carry out any additional or different duties.

2.3 In addition or as an alternative to your normal duties you may from time to time be required to undertake, on a temporary or permanent basis, other reasonable duties within any department or section of the Company or within a different division or at different locations within the UK, i.e. that it is reasonable for someone in your position to carry out and that fall within your capabilities, as the needs of the Company's business may require from time to time.

2.4 In your capacity of Surveillance Operative for the Company you agree to be transferred and/or to accept any surveillance assignment to any location within the UK as may be deemed necessary if and when so requested by the Company as may be dictated by the needs of our business. Reasonable notice and reasonable relocation costs will be given to you if your change in location requires a move of residence. Whether relocating your home is reasonable will remain at the entire discretion of the Company.

3. Hours of work

3.1 The Company operates a surveillance service on the basis of 24 hours per day, 365 days a year.

3.2 Your contracted working hours will be based on a minimum number of variable hours per week between Sunday and Saturday.

3.3 For the purposes of these terms and conditions you are contracted to work [*enter hours*] hours per week which will consist of working variable hour shifts. The times you commence/finish work will vary (and may be longer on occasion than those that you normally work) due to the nature of the surveillance assignments and will take account of operational requirements.

3.4 This may involve you working during nights as well as during the days. There are no set or core hours for your employment. You may be required to work up to [10] additional hours per week over [four] weeks per annum as the Company considers necessary to meet the needs of the business, customer and client demands.

3.5 These additional hours will be paid at basic rate. However, you should be prepared at all times to be flexible and available to work additional hours at the Company's request.

3.6 Advance notice of 72 hours will normally be given if you are asked to work additional hours. However, you may in exceptional circumstances be required to work additional hours at the end of your shift, e.g. to cover shortfalls in daily customer and/or client demands, when it may only be possible to give notice of such requirement to you during that shift. Clearly if you have domestic or other arrangements that dictate that you cannot remain at work any later than your contracted hours, then you should discuss this with your line manager as soon as possible.

3.7 Should you work in excess of the agreed flexi-hours you will be eligible to receive payment in accordance with the Company's standard overtime policy. Please note overtime must be authorised in advance of working additional hours. The overtime policy is on the intranet and you are strongly advised to access and read it carefully.

3.8 Due to the nature of our business and the need to provide services to our customers and clients you may be required to work on a Public or Bank Holiday. In such circumstances advance notice of 72 hours will normally be given if you are asked to work.

3.9 For work undertaken on a Public or Bank Holiday you will be reimbursed at your normal salary and you will then be entitled to a day off in lieu. If you have any constraints such as childcare or the care of dependants, your manager will as far as possible accommodate your needs.

3.10 You will be required to complete timesheets for the hours that you work. These must be completed accurately and in a timely fashion.

3.11 Lunch breaks and other breaks provided to you will not constitute 'working time' and therefore do not count towards your shift nor do they count as 'working time' for the purposes of the Working Time Regulations 1998 as amended nor for the purposes of accruing annual leave. Breaks are provided to ensure the welfare of our employees and to ensure compliance with Health and Safety Legislation.

3.12 Due to the nature of your role it will not always be possible to take a structured break during your shift. In these circumstances you will receive 'compensatory' rest. An equivalent period of rest is considered to be a period of rest as long as that you were entitled to but unable to take, e.g. if you only had 10 hours' rather than 11 hours' rest between shifts then one hour compensatory rest must be given.

3.13 Compensatory rest must be provided within a reasonable time from when the entitlement to rest was due. Compensatory rest does not necessarily have to be during paid time. In the example above, where one hour compensatory rest was owed, if the member of staff had a 13 hour break between their next two shifts then one hour of this would be deemed 'compensatory'. This example is for illustrative purposes only. For any further information you should go to the Directgov website: **www.gov.uk/browse/working/time-off**.

3.14 The Company reserves the right to introduce further flexible working hours and/or temporary short time working through a reduction in the minimum number of hours you are required to work in any calendar month should economic, operational or other circumstances prevent the Company from providing you with work for these basic hours.

3.15 If it is necessary to introduce short time working, the Company will make an adjustment to your minimum working hours and to your remuneration, i.e. you agree your wages/salary may decrease as well as increase during the course of your employment. By signing this contract you give the Company your express consent to reduce your wages/salary if it is necessary to reduce your working hours due to a downturn in business (as required under ss.13–27 of the Employment Rights Act 1996). You will be notified in writing if this occurs and your payslip will itemise your reduced salary.

3.16 By your signature to this statement (pursuant to the Working Time Regulations 1998 as amended), you confirm that you do not undertake any other work for any employer (whether in competition with this Company or otherwise and whether paid or unpaid), unless you have obtained the prior written consent of the Company; such consent will not unreasonably be withheld.

3.17 By virtue of the role you perform on behalf of the Company you will be deemed a remote employee and a peripatetic worker and will not have a fixed or definite area of assignment or place of work. You will be required to undertake and accept surveillance assignments in any location, if and when so requested by the Company as may be dictated by the needs of our business. Any travel and other expenses will be explained to you upon joining and the expenses policy will apply to you which is amended from time to time. You will find this on the Company intranet and it is strongly recommended that you read it.

4. Provision of a vehicle

4.1 If you are eligible, the provision of a company vehicle or participation in an alternative car scheme will be discussed with you by your line manager. Please note that details of the car scheme(s) you may be eligible to participate in are subject to the terms of the Company's car policy, which the Company reserves the right to amend and update as and when business needs and/or legal requirements dictate.

4.2 However, if at any time the Company considers that you no longer need a car for the purpose of carrying out your duties or you are absent other than for the reason of annual leave you may be required to return the car.

4.3 If you are provided with a company vehicle you will be entitled to use the car privately subject to adhering to the provisions of the Company's car policy. The Company will pay for all maintenance costs, including regular servicing and changing of tyres but this does not include the provision of private fuel.

4.4 Should you be required to drive in any capacity in order to fulfil your duties and are provided with a Company vehicle then it is a condition of your employment that you hold a full current driving licence and continue to do so. If at any time you cease to hold such a licence the Company will be entitled to terminate your employment.

4.5 On the occasions where you may wish to use your own car on company business all relevant documentation must be approved by Car Fleet prior to any journey taking place.

4.6 The Company operates a mandatory driver training and licence checking scheme which all drivers are required to comply with as directed by Car Fleet. Where driving standards or licence checking do not meet legal requirements the Company reserves the right to address this formally in accordance with the Company's disciplinary procedures.

4.7 Should you be required to drive in any capacity on company business you are required to take an eye test prior to doing so and again at least every two years thereafter whether you require corrective lenses or not. Confirmation should be provided to Car Fleet.

4.8 Should the Company suspect drug and/or alcohol abuse the company vehicle will be removed pending further investigation.

4.9 You are required to adhere to the Company's car policy at all times which you can find on the intranet. There are important rules about not leaving property in the car when the car is unattended and not allowing unauthorised users to drive the vehicle as well as who is liable to pay parking and other fines. Please make sure you have read and regularly read the Company's car policy.

4.10 It is necessary to ensure that your company vehicle is fully maintained in accordance with the Company's car policy including ensuring it has a current MOT and is serviced at the correct times. Any cost or damage incurred as a result of any breach will be deducted by the Company directly from salary. Such breaches may also result in disciplinary action.

5. **Activities outside working hours**

You are required to devote your full time and attention during normal working hours to the performance of your duties and to act in the best interests of the Company at all times. You must not, at any time during your employment, except with the Company's prior written permission, undertake any work or be in any way concerned or interested in any business or activity which may in the Company's opinion adversely affect the proper performance of your duties.

6. **Confidentiality and probity**

6.1 You must not at any time during your employment (except so far as may be necessary for the proper performance of your duties) or after the termination of your employment use for any purpose other than the Company's business or disclose to any person or body any Confidential Information obtained during your employment. For the purposes of this clause 'Confidential Information' means any information of a confidential nature relating to the Company its customers or their business finances transactions or affairs which belongs to and is of value to the Company or in respect of which the Company owes an obligation of confidence to any third party. Such information includes but is not limited to:

(a) lists and particulars of the clients and potential clients of the Company;
(b) the facts and handling of claims;
(c) company manuals, software and practice notes; and
(d) any financial information relating to or business plans of the Company.

6.2 You understand that your engagement as a Surveillance Operative depends upon the continued trust and confidence of the Company and our clients in your trustworthiness and integrity. Any breach of such trust may render you liable to disciplinary action that could result in your summary dismissal.

6.3 It is recognised that we risk placing ourselves in a difficult position if we recommend a contractor to a policyholder. To prevent accusations of fraud and to avoid unnecessary burden with issues that may arise it is necessary to restrict the use of contractors to:

(a) The insurance companies' preferred contractor(s).
   (i) X
   (ii) Y

(b) The policyholder's own contractors who must be instructed and authorised by the policyholder.
(c) Specialist suppliers under established arrangements.

Note: In the event a supplier within the terms of the directive is not available within the timescales required and to delay implementing work would prejudice insurers' position or potentially increase the loss, a suitable alternative supplier can be utilised but the reason for the selection must be clearly justified and recorded on file. These will be exceptional cases and likely to involve major losses.

6.4 You must return to the Company immediately on termination of your employment or at any time during your employment upon request by the Company any Confidential Information which is in your possession or under your control in any format (whether prepared by you or any other person and whether stored electronically on paper on audio or audio visual tape or otherwise). You must not retain any copy or extract of such information in any format.

7. Standards of conduct and performance

7.1 Rules and procedures governing the highest standards of dress, appearance, attitude, language, etc. towards third parties and colleagues, conduct and performance are necessary in order to promote fairness and consistency in the treatment of all employees. Your attention is drawn to the Company's disciplinary rules and performance standards together with the mutual respect and fair treatment policy as published on the intranet.

7.2 You are strictly forbidden from drinking alcohol either before you come on duty or during your shift and any such conduct would constitute gross misconduct which could lead to your summary dismissal. The taking of illicit substances either before or during your shift is also regarded as gross misconduct which could lead to your summary dismissal.

7.3 If you take prescribed medication which could affect your ability to drive or undertake your duties then you are required to report this immediately to HR and your line manager who will take a view as to whether or not you are fit for your duties.

7.4 Additional rules and standards with which you are expected to comply may be set out in the Company policy or procedure documents issued from time to time as posted on the intranet, staff notice boards or otherwise made known to you by your manager.

PRECEDENT 3I: Job description for hospitality/stewards/banqueting manager/director

Name
Appointment   Banqueting/Hospitality manager/director
Department
Location
Responsible to   The Chairman and Hon Secretary and nominated Deputy
Commence Employment
Job Description Agreed

1. Main purpose of job

To lead, direct and command a well-organised client-focused team which supports the work of the Banqueting Rooms and to ensure that the strategy for and the marketing of its facilities to outside organisations are at the highest standards of excellence and vision. To enable and ensure and support the team that will ensure that the Banqueting Rooms can be open and busy throughout a seven day working week. To present the facilities to potential clients as a vibrant and welcoming centre of excellence.

2. Person specification: required qualifications, skills and experience

2.1 The main qualifications for this position are a combined background of knowledge of catering and hospitality and marketing and strategic thinking.

2.2 The Banqueting Director/Hospitality Director must be someone who is used to working to a high degree of self-management and initiative. In addition this person must be an excellent motivator of staff and an excellent team-player – used to influencing others as well as working in a team. Skills of diplomacy and tact are essential with a willingness to work long hours when necessary.

2.3 To guide and direct an assistant and other staff members in an enthusiastic, disciplined and encouraging manner.

2.4 The jobholder must display a high level of diplomacy, but will need an assertive manner in dealing with colleagues and clients. Tact and resilience are essential qualities.

2.5 An effective communicator, both orally and in writing with a good command of written and spoken English.

2.6 Personally professional-looking, being efficient and very well organised, with excellent time-management skills, with good control of diary systems and competent with email, computer and other IT facilities.

3. Main responsibilities

3.1 To lead, drive and manage the day to day operation of the Banqueting Rooms in accordance with laid down procedures and quality standards.

3.2 To ensure that all rooms are laid out for meetings in accordance with the client's requests.

3.3 To deal wherever possible with routine client enquiries for all the Organisation's functions and private functions.

3.4 To be proactive in marketing and obtaining bookings for the centre with external visits to clients.

3.5 At all times to exercise the highest standards of client care in a professional and pleasant manner.

3.6 To ensure the confidentiality and security of all the Organisation's and client's documentation and information.

3.7 To maintain clear and precise communications with other staff and communicate clearly and regularly with the office and the Hon Secretary.

3.8 To ensure good working relationships with external institutions and organisations.

3.9 To comply with the policies and procedures set out in the Organisation's Handbook as amended by the management committee from time to time.

3.10 To carry out any specific training of staff when required to do so and overall to have a responsibility towards self-development.

3.11 To be responsible for health and safety.

4. Specific responsibilities and objectives

4.1 To operate the Banqueting Rooms in conjunction with an assistant from the hours of 8.30 am to 1130 pm. daily Monday to Saturday and Sundays as required. To provide bar facilities as required during those times (the Director and staff may be asked to agree to opt out of the 48-hour week under the Working Time Regulations 1998).

4.2 To provide function rooms and bar facilities on a Sunday and on bank, public and statutory holidays in accordance with any function bookings which may be made from time to time.

4.3 Both the Director and the assistant must work a system of shifts to ensure that the facilities of the Banqueting Rooms are available as and when required.

4.4 In particular, to ensure that the rooms (including anterooms) are properly furnished and laid out for meetings and other functions which may take place from time to time.

4.5 To open and close the bar and to be responsible for its conduct strictly in accordance with the club licence, the licensing laws and the instructions from the council.

4.6 To be responsible after consultation with the Chair or Hon Secretary for the employment of casual bar staff and cleaners, ensuring that they meet the current employment regulations.

4.7 Receive in conjunction with the caterers, dining requests and ensure that the function rooms reflect the requirements.

4.8 To order all wines, spirits, beers, mineral waters, and keep proper accounts of all such purchases for submission to the accounts department for payment as required.

4.9 To ensure that all cash is deposited in the safe overnight and banking is undertaken within three days of receipt of money.

4.10 To be responsible for the security of the premises and in particular to ensure that all windows and doors are closed when the premises are vacated at night.

4.11 To make a daily inspection of the premises and report any damage or discrepancies to the Chairman or Hon Secretary.

4.12 To assist in dealing with queries raised by the client and any of their third party providers for customers.

4.13 To carry out from time to time any further tasks reasonably requested by the Organisation and which are within the capabilities of the post-holder, after consultation (whenever possible) with the employee.

PRECEDENT 3J: Contract of employment for security guard

Employment contract

[Date]

[Name of employee]

[Address]

Dear [name]

[Name of Security Agency], hereinafter referred to as the 'Agency' hereby engages your services as a SECURITY GUARD to serve and to perform such duties at such times and places and in such manner as the Agency may from time to time direct. For your services, you shall receive a compensation which shall be computed based on the contract rate with the client to which you will be assigned.

You are hereby hired for a period of […] months starting on [date] renewable at the instance of the Agency depending on your performance. However, the Agency does not warrant that you will have an assignment during the whole period of this contract as the continuity of your assignments shall be subject to the availability of clients that would engage our services. During the period that you are without an assignment, you will be considered temporarily laid off without pay, but you shall remain on call to take up new assignments that the Agency may get from time to time.

You will not have a fixed or definite area of assignment or place of work and you agree to be transferred and/or to accept any assignment to any location, if and when so requested by the Agency as may be dictated by business exigencies.

You are required to strictly comply with all the rules, regulations and policies of the Agency and its client where you will be assigned, including but not limited to those governing order and discipline, honesty, safety and security, working hours, work assignments and standard operating procedures, uniform, use of Agency properties and access to matters of confidentiality, and such other rules deemed necessary in the conduct of the Agency business.

You agree that all records, documents or information pertaining to the business or affairs of the Agency or its clients where you will be assigned are absolutely confidential and the unauthorised disclosure or reproduction of the same will not be made by you at any time during or after your employment. You agree that any breach of confidentiality will constitute sufficient ground for immediate termination of your employment for cause and/or civil and criminal liability.

You likewise agree that any problem that you will encounter during your assignment with a particular client should first be taken up with the Agency and must not in any way be discussed with the client where you are assigned or decided or acted upon on your own.

You understand that your engagement as a Security Guard depends upon the continued trust and confidence of the Agency and its clients in your person, integrity and trustworthiness. As such, the Agency may terminate your services at any time, even prior to the expiration of this Contract, for any of the just or authorised causes provided by existing law, breach of trust, for unsatisfactory performance, or for any violation of the rules, regulations or policies of the Agency or the client where you are assigned. The Agency likewise reserves the right to terminate your employment in case of termination or expiration of the contract of the Agency with the client where you are assigned.

In case you intend to resign from the Agency, you are required to submit a thirty (30) day written notice prior to the taking effect of such resignation, otherwise, failure on your part to do so will render you liable for damages. However, it is within the sole discretion of the Agency whether or not to accept such resignation earlier than the expiration of said period.

If you agree with the above terms and conditions of your employment with the Agency, please indicate your conformity by signing on the space provided below for this purpose and this shall constitute the Document of our Agreement.

Yours sincerely

[name of security agency]

By: ………..

General Manager

I HEREBY CERTIFY that I have read and have fully understood the foregoing terms and conditions of my employment with the Agency and that I accept the same completely.

Signed ……………………….. Date ………..

PRECEDENT 3K: Consultancy agreement

CONSULTANCY AGREEMENT
Between
X United Kingdom – Specialist Adjusting Network
and
QQ Cost Consultants
(External Loss Adjusters)

This Agreement is dated [date]

between:

X, registered as:

X UK LTD

[address]

And

Z External Loss Adjuster registered as:

QQ COST CONSULTANTS

[address]

WHEREAS

(A) In reliance on the External Loss Adjuster's skill, expertise and knowledge, X Specialist Adjusting Network, herein referred to as X, wishes to engage the External Loss Adjuster to provide the 'Services'.
(B) The External Loss Adjuster agrees to provide the 'Services' to X on and subject to the terms and conditions set out in this agreement and its schedules (the 'Agreement').

IT IS AGREED as follows:

1. **Provision of services**

1.1 X engages the External Loss Adjuster to provide services including but not limited to loss adjusting and surveying services (the 'Services') and the External Loss Adjuster agrees to provide the Services on and subject to the terms and conditions contained in this Agreement.

1.2 X engages the Services of the External Loss Adjuster effective from [date] and shall continue in effect for [six] calendar months; subject to clause 11.

1.3 The supplier shall be available to provide their services for 46 weeks per year (pro rata); however the work of X is subject to fluctuation therefore the hours of work provided to the External Loss Adjuster may vary on a weekly basis and cannot be guaranteed.

2. **X operating standards**

2.1 All work under this Agreement must be undertaken by an accredited X External Chartered Loss Adjuster who must undertake the work branded as X in a diligent fashion in accordance with X Operating Standards, current at the time of inspection.

2.2 X may require the External Loss Adjuster to attend occasional product and operational training as a part of its accreditation process.

2.3   X may amend its accreditation process and X Operating Standards from time to time and may request further evidence from the External Loss Adjuster of appropriate skills.

2.4   X will require the External Loss Adjuster to produce all documentation, all correspondence, reports, letters, etc. using X standard formats.

2.5   Should a dispute or conflict of interest arise X will be the sole arbiters.

3.   **Service agreements**

Where X has a Service Agreement with a third party and is subcontracting part of that work to the External Loss Adjuster, then any Service Agreement conditions that apply to the work shall also apply to this contract.

4.   **Communication**

Regular and prompt communication with X, Loss Adjuster clients and its customers is required at all times, including the notification of any delays and problems. The standards and timing of such communication will be notified to the External Loss Adjuster from time to time.

5.   **Quality assurance and audit**

Work undertaken under this contract is subject to X Quality Assurance processes, which shall, from time to time, require internal or third party auditing.

6.   **Complaints**

Work undertaken under this contract is subject to the X Customer Complaints Handling policy. All complaints or claims should be notified to X immediately in writing and will be handled as agreed between X and the External Loss Adjuster.

7.   **Professional indemnity**

The External Loss Adjuster shall operate at all times under his own Professional Indemnity Insurance cover whilst working for X. The original current Certificate of Insurance showing the level of cover will be shown to [nominated person] X before commencing any work under this Agreement.

8.   **Confidential company information**

The External Loss Adjuster will have access to confidential information and intellectual property belonging to X and/or X customers. The External Loss Adjuster agrees to keep this absolutely confidential and not to use or disclose any part of it for his own use or for the use of any other third party without written authority from X. Upon completion of any work, or upon written request from X, the External Loss Adjuster will return to X all documents including any and all copies that may be in the External Loss Adjuster's possession and agrees to delete all data kept in electronic form.

9.   **Exclusivity of engagement**

The External Loss Adjuster shall be free to be employed by, perform work for and/or accept any engagements with any third party during the continuance of this Agreement with the exception of third parties where providing services would cause a conflict of interest for X. Such third parties include competitors of X. However, direct instructions to provide loss adjusting or surveying services from any product line within X UK Ltd will be deemed to operate under this Agreement (including fee arrangements).

10.   **Declining instructions**

The External Loss Adjuster has the right to decline instructions from X, and X would expect this in those cases where the External Loss Adjuster considers the scope of work required to be outside the External Loss Adjuster's experience or level of ability.

11. Termination

11.1 This Agreement may be terminated by either party giving to the other not less than six months' notice in writing.

11.2 Without prejudice to any other rights or remedies to which X may be entitled whether under this Agreement or at law, X shall be entitled to terminate this Agreement immediately by notice in writing if:

- the External Loss Adjuster is in breach of any obligations under this Agreement and such breach (if capable of remedy) is not remedied by the External Loss Adjuster within 14 days of receipt of a notice from X specifying the breach and requiring its remedy;
- the External Loss Adjuster for whatever reason is unable to provide the Services for a continuous period of eight weeks or for 10 weeks in aggregate;
- the External Loss Adjuster's performance or conduct falls below the standard required or brings or is in the opinion of X likely to bring X into disrepute; or
- the External Loss Adjuster causes loss or damage to X by negligent or wilful act or omission.

11.3 In the event of termination in accordance with sub-clause 11.2 X shall be entitled to withhold any or all of the fees and expenses whether or not they may have accrued and without prejudice to any other rights X may have in respect of the External Loss Adjuster's breach, performance or conduct.

11.4 The External Loss Adjuster shall not be required to fulfil an obligation under this Agreement and the provisions of sub-clause 11.2 shall not apply, if the External Loss Adjuster is prevented from fulfilling the obligation by any acts or omissions of X. The External Loss Adjuster shall only be entitled to rely on the provisions of this clause if the External Loss Adjuster gives written notice to X of any act or omission which prevents the External Loss Adjuster from fulfilling the obligation within 72 hours of the occurrence of the X act or omission.

12. Fees

12.1 X shall agree and pay to the External Loss Adjuster a fee each time the External Loss Adjuster's Services are utilised under this Agreement. The fee will be based upon the standard agreed rate of £... per hour between X and the External Loss Adjuster, without deduction of tax or NICs. The timing and proportion of the fee raised to X will be in accordance with the existing X fee arrangements at the time the External Loss Adjuster is appointed. This arrangement is subject to alteration to meet internal requirements. Invoices for fees submitted outside this criterion will not be accepted for payment at that time and no payment of interest or other charges will become due on these unauthorised invoices whilst they remain outstanding.

12.2 The External Loss Adjuster is not entitled to be paid for any services which the External Loss Adjuster does not provide, including where the reason for the External Loss Adjuster's non-provision of the services is at the request of X.

12.3 The fees shall be payable by X on submission by the External Loss Adjuster of an invoice in respect of Services performed to the satisfaction of X.

13. Relationship

13.1 For the avoidance of doubt, it is stated that the parties intend and agree that this Agreement shall be treated for all purposes as a contract for services with the relationship between X and the External Loss Adjuster being one of independent contractors.

13.2 Nothing contained in this Agreement shall be construed as having or will have the effect of constituting any relationship of employer and employee between the contracting parties and the External Loss Adjuster shall not be entitled to receive any benefits available to employees of X including, without limitation, any salary, overtime payments, payment of sick pay, and pension contributions.

14. Tax liabilities

14.1 The External Loss Adjuster shall have the status of a self-employed person, sole proprietor, partnership or incorporated company and shall be responsible for all tax liabilities arising in connection with the provision of the Services including but not limited to liability for the payment of income tax and national insurance in respect of the fees. The External Loss Adjuster must provide evidence of self-employed tax status before commencing this contract.

14.2 The External Loss Adjuster agrees to fully indemnify and keep X fully indemnified against and from all claims, demands, awards, damages, actions, losses, costs (including legal costs) and other expenses arising as a result of or in connection with any claims that may be made by the relevant authorities against X in respect of tax and/or national insurance or similar contributions owed by the External Services in connection with the Services.

15. Substitution and provision of service

15.1 If the External Loss Adjuster is self-employed and is unable to personally provide all or part of the Services to X, the External Loss Adjuster shall be entitled to nominate a substitute to provide all or part of the Services on the External Loss Adjuster's behalf. Any substitute must be considered by X to be suitably qualified and experienced and must be approved in advance in writing.

15.2 If the External Loss Adjuster is a sole proprietor, partnership or incorporated company, the External Loss Adjuster shall be entitled to provide all or part of the Services using any person that is considered by X to be suitably qualified and experienced and approved in advance in writing by X.

16. Property

16.1 For the purposes of this Agreement, the expression 'Property' shall mean all or any property belonging to X which is provided to or prepared by the External Loss Adjuster in connection with the Services (including but not limited to site notes and photographs) and includes without limitation any confidential information belonging to X whether stored as part of a document or in any other medium (including electronic and digital media).

16.2 The External Loss Adjuster agrees, whenever requested by X and in any event on the termination of this Agreement to surrender to X promptly any Property in the External Loss Adjuster's possession, custody or control. The External Loss Adjuster acknowledges and agrees that, on the expiry or termination of this Agreement, the External Loss Adjuster shall not be entitled to retain and shall not retain any Property.

17. Confidential information

17.1 Save in the proper performance of the provision of the Services and subject to clause [x] the External Loss Adjuster shall not, at any time, use, copy, disclose, communicate and/or publish or enable or cause any person(s) to become aware of and/or use, copy, disclose, communicate and/or publish any confidential information belonging to X.

17.2 The obligation contained in clause [x] shall not apply to any information which:

(a) the External Loss Adjuster is ordered to disclose by a court or tribunal of competent jurisdiction or which he is otherwise required or permitted to disclose by law; and
(b) otherwise than through the External Loss Adjuster's breach of clause [x], is available to the public generally.

17.3 The obligations contained in this clause are capable of surviving the termination of this Agreement and shall continue to apply following the termination of this Agreement.

18. Data Protection Act

18.1 X believes that in connection with the provision of the Services, the External Loss Adjuster may be required to process personal data (as such term is defined in the Data Protection Act 1998 (the 'Act')) on behalf of X. The parties acknowledge that for the purposes of the Act, the External Loss Adjuster is a data processor in respect of any personal data which the External Loss Adjuster may process and accordingly the External Loss Adjuster agrees:

(a) not to process any personal data other than in accordance with the prior instructions of X;
(b) not to do or omit to do anything which may result in X being in breach of its obligations under the Act; and
(c) if, under the Act, X is required to provide any personal data which is in the possession or under the control of the External Loss Adjuster to any individual, to provide all necessary co-operation to X to enable X to meet its obligations under the Act.

18.2 The obligations contained in this clause are capable of surviving the termination of this Agreement and shall continue to apply following the termination of this Agreement.

19. General

19.1 Neither party intends that any term of this Agreement shall be enforceable by virtue of the Contracts (Rights of Third Parties) Act 1999 by any person who is not a party.

19.2 This Agreement shall be governed by and interpreted in accordance with the law of England and Wales and each of the parties submits to the exclusive jurisdiction of the English and Welsh Courts as regards any claim or matter arising under this Agreement.

19.3 The failure or delay by X to enforce at any time any one or more of the provisions of this Agreement shall not be a waiver of them or of the right at any time subsequently to enforce all provisions of this Agreement.

19.4 The External Loss Adjuster will notify X of any change of name or address or circumstances that may affect the operation of this Agreement.

19.5 In the event that any provision in this Agreement is declared by any judicial or other competent authority to be void, voidable, illegal or otherwise unenforceable, the parties hereto shall amend that provision in such reasonable manner as achieves the intention of the parties without illegality or at the discretion of X it may be severed from this Agreement. The remaining provisions of this Agreement shall remain in full force and effect.

(Name) ....

For X

(Name) ....

For QQ

PRECEDENT 3L: Contract of employment for nanny

Employers: [*Name and address*]

Employee: [*Name and address*]

Date of commencement of employment: [*Date*]

1. Job title

Your job title is 'Nanny'.

2. Salary

Your salary will be £ . . . (after deduction of tax and NICs) per week. Your salary will be reviewed at least twice a year.

3. Working hours

3.1 Your working week will be five calendar days with two days off, those days being Saturday and Sunday unless there is any other prior arrangement with you to work at a weekend. You will be a live-in nanny.

3.2 In addition, there may be some baby-sitting in any week. Baby-sitting will be minimal and in some weeks you will be free on every evening. Prior notice where possible will be given, should you be required to baby-sit. In any event you will not normally be required to baby-sit on more than two out of the five days in the week, Monday to Friday.

3.3 There will be a few occasional weekends in the year when we will need you to work whilst we are away or when we all go away. For these we will pay you £ . . . per day, after deduction of tax and NICs. Advance notice will be given to you on any such occasion when this occurs.

3.4 On weekends when you are not required to work we have agreed that you will go away for the weekend to stay with friends or family. We have said that we may at our entire discretion make you payments for your additional travel costs.

4. Duties

4.1 Your duties are primarily to care for [*give details*] and to undertake all duties associated thereto. These will include but are not limited to teaching our children basic language and numeracy, training, guiding, playing and encouraging general development in skills such as music, reading, dressing, telling the time, etc. Nursery duties include, but are not limited to, keeping the nursery and the children's bathroom and toilet clean and tidy every day, laundry and ironing of the children's clothes, polishing the children's shoes regularly, ensuring that their clothes are kept in good repair and doing any repairs necessary or having them done, keeping the kitchen and morning room clean and tidy after use by you and the children.

4.2 In addition, we would ask you to undertake shopping for food and other items for the household. There will be other reasonable duties that we will discuss with you from time to time. No housework or ironing for the family is required.

4.3 This position is one essentially of trust. It is a position providing personal services and as such is not a 9 am to 5 pm job. We are entrusting you with our most precious possessions, our children. We will expect from you the highest standards of care, honesty, integrity and probity. You will also need a great deal of patience and a great sense of humour and to use your common sense and intelligence. For example, if another mother asks you to look after her child or asks you to go to her house to look after her child, we would expect you politely to refuse to do so without that mother first speaking to one of us and gaining our permission.

4.4 Furthermore, if a stranger comes to the door, you are not permitted to let in anyone whom you are not expecting and you should put the chain on the door and not open the door but merely ask politely who is there. We will advise you if anyone is expected on any given day. You are also expected to keep the back door locked when you are in the house unless you are in the garden and you are responsible for the security of the house during your working day.

4.5 If either of the children is ill or you are not happy about anything, please ring one of us but in the event that you cannot speak to us, you are expected to use your discretion and to take them to our doctor if in any doubt whatsoever.

4.6 Since you will be required to drive a car, we also rely upon your assurances that you are an experienced and careful but confident driver [and have experience of driving in London].

4.7 We are sure that you will fulfil our expectations that we have of you [particularly as you are Norland trained].

4.8 You will also have access to our money, valuables, credit cards, etc. We will be giving you money to buy food for the children and their clothes and for their entertainment and clubs, etc. You will also be given a credit card/credit cards for use for your duties. Money and the credit cards will be solely for you in order to perform your duties. You will be trusted on this account and will be expected to be careful not to lose any cards, money or keys to the house, etc.

4.9 You will be living in our home which will be your home. We trust that we shall have mutual respect for each other. We are providing you with [the top floor of the house which consists of a bedroom and ensuite bathroom, sitting room (with colour TV and stereo)]. We expect you to keep these rooms clean and tidy and in good repair.

4.10 Whilst nanny friends may of course accompany the children in their care during the day, we do not expect you to offer to put up any of your friends overnight. Otherwise, if you wish to invite any friends into the house and into your room, we would ask you to seek our prior permission to do so. You are required to provide a model of excellent conduct and are a role model for our children.

4.11 We do not expect that you will drink alcohol on any evening off so that you are not fully competent and fit for duty first thing the next morning. It goes without saying that you will not be permitted to drink any alcohol whilst on duty.

4.12 We have a 'no smoking' policy in our home and would ask you to ask any friends or visitors to respect this. [We note that you have confirmed that you do not smoke even occasionally.]

5. **Start time and dress**

You will be expected to be ready for work, i.e. up and dressed by no later than [time]. We expect suitable dress, which could include sweatshirts and trousers as long as they are clean and smart. We will provide you with aprons/other clothing that you should wear during the working day.

6. **Holiday**

6.1 You will be entitled to four weeks' paid annual holiday for a complete year's service and a pro rata amount should you leave at any earlier date. In addition you will be entitled to the nine public and bank holidays or days off in lieu.

6.2 Any accrued and untaken holiday when you leave will either be paid on a daily basis of £... per day or be taken at a mutually agreed time. Any holiday taken in excess of any entitlement must be repaid on any basis acceptable to us which may include deducting an amount calculated on a daily basis of £... per day in respect of such excess holiday from your final salary.

6.3 Your paid leave may be taken during the course of the year commencing [specify], subject to the provisions concerning your initial three months' service below, the dates of which are to be notified and agreed with us in advance so that a temporary nanny may be found in good time.

6.4 No holiday (annual or other) accrues or may be taken until the first three calendar months' service have elapsed, but if you have made any prior arrangements, these will be honoured but taken on an unpaid basis.

6.5 In addition, you will accompany us on all or some of our holidays that we will be taking with the children both in the UK and abroad. This will not count towards your holiday entitlement. Please ensure that you have a valid, current passport.

7. **Use of car**

7.1 A car is available for all on-duty working during the week and during weekends, if you are working. You may also use the car provided for any evenings that you are free in the week. You are therefore required to have a full, clean driving licence with no penalty points or convictions of any sort. We will ask to see your driving licence before you start work with us.

7.2 We undertake to ensure that you are fully insured to drive the car and will pay all expenses connected thereto except [out of London petrol expenses], parking fines or fines for clamps/towing away and all expenses connected thereto.

8. **Sick pay**

Should you fall sick during your employment we will pay full pay for a maximum of two weeks, inclusive of statutory sick pay (SSP) in any 12-month period and thereafter SSP. Any additional pay will be made at our discretion.

At our discretion we may arrange for private health treatment for you.

9. **Term and notice**

It is expected that this post will last for a minimum of one year. Both parties agree to give at least four weeks' written notice to terminate this contract. Longer notice will normally be given in order for both parties to make alternative arrangements. Shorter notice may only be given with the mutual agreement of both parties.

10. **Pension**

There is no pension scheme associated with this position but, should you wish to take out a policy, we would be happy to refer you for professional advice.

Signed .... Date ....

[employers]

Signed .... Date ....

[employee]

4

The 'Martini contract': 'any time, any place, anywhere'

4.1 The job description

There are express and implied terms concerning the job and the duties that an individual is expected or required to do. Implied terms include the implied terms of fidelity and loyalty; the duty to exercise reasonable skill and care of themselves and others; to obey lawful and reasonable instructions; to act with probity and honesty; not to take secret profits or commissions; etc.

There is an implied warranty when an employer takes on a skilled worker that the worker will carry out their duties with the degree of skill expected of a skilled worker (*Harmer* v. *Cornelius* (1858) 5 CBNS 236).

The obligation of trust and confidence is a mutual obligation. On the part of the employer it includes the duty to pay the agreed wages or provide the work (but there are exceptions where employees have a right to be provided with work: *William Hill* v. *Tucker* [1998] IRLR 313); to render reasonable support to their staff (*Wigan Borough Council* v. *Davies* [1979] IRLR 127); to provide a safe system of work and safe place of work (*Bonsor* v. *RJB Mining (UK) Ltd* [2004] IRLR 164); and to inform their staff of some of their contractual rights (*Scally* v. *Southern Health and Social Services Board* [1991] IRLR 522). Examples of express clauses covering most of these areas can be found in later chapters of this book.

The best way of ensuring that the main duties are clear is to set them out in writing. In the written particulars, either a job title or a brief description of the work for which the employee is employed is required to be put in writing (Employment Rights Act 1996, s.1(4)(f)).

It is best in less senior jobs to make them as generic as possible in order to give maximum flexibility for requiring staff to undertake other duties within the same generic job title or job description.

So, in a small office with a small clerical staff, the ambit of 'general clerical duties' was wide enough to include the operation of a duplicating machine, according to the EAT in *Glitz* v. *Watford Electric Co Ltd* [1979] IRLR 89. In the absence of a more detailed job description, a 'clerk/typist' was held to have been contractually obliged to operate a duplicator, even though at the time she was engaged it was contemplated that the duplicator would be operated by someone else and she did not operate the duplicator during the first three years of her employment.

Change to terms

Whether the employer has the right unilaterally to vary the terms of a contract will depend entirely on whether there is an express right to do so in the contract (*Bateman* v. *Asda Stores Ltd* [2010] IRLR 370).

In this case, the provisions of the staff handbook stated that the employers 'reserved the right to review, revise, amend or replace the contents of this handbook, and introduce new policies from time to time reflecting the changing needs of the business'. The handbook was incorporated into the contract of employment and allowed the employer to make changes to pay and conditions without obtaining the further consent of the employees. This was the case even though at least one employee suffered financial loss as a result of the changes. Although the variation was not a breach of contract, because the changes caused a substantial detriment it might well be held to be in breach of the implied duty of trust and confidence in any constructive dismissal claim.

When terms change, it is a requirement that 'at the earliest opportunity' and in any event no later than four weeks after the change, the employer notifies the employee in writing of the change (Employment Rights Act 1996, s.4(3)). See **Precedent 4A**.

No express term/no confirmation of change

Employment Tribunals will look at the conduct of the parties to find the correct terms. So if, for example, a day shift worker has moved permanently to night shift but there is no written record of that change, the tribunals will deem the term about their hours to be that under which both parties have been working over a period of time and not the old written term which has clearly been superseded.

4.2 The start date

It is essential to agree the date when the employment began. This is important not only for the start of contractual benefits but also for the determination of continuous employment.

The date expressed on written particulars is the starting point for determining this question. In *Salvation Army* v. *Dewsbury* [1984] IRLR 222, the start date of employment was written as 1 May 1982 but as that date was a Saturday and it was a bank holiday the following Monday, the employee actually started work on Tuesday 4 May. She was dismissed on 30 April 1983 and her employers argued that she did not have one year's continuous service. The EAT held that the correct 'start date of employment' was 1 May 1982.

> The phrase 'starts work' [now in s.211 of the Employment Rights Act 1996] was not intended to refer to the undertaking of the full duties of the employment but to the beginning of the employee's employment under the relevant contract of employment.

4.3 Defining the duties

It is important to leave some flexibility within a job description – so it is proper to give examples only of the kind of duties that the employee may be required to undertake. Directors are often subject to a 'whole time and attention clause' such as the one set out in **Precedent 4B**, which sets out two forms of clauses relating to duties.

4.4 Requirement to travel

Working time for peripatetic workers such as sales staff, where they are required to travel on company business, starts when they leave home for their first appointment.

If someone is travelling within the UK or abroad as part of the job, then it is essential to spell this out and make clear that this constitutes working time under the Working Time Regulations 1998.

This may mean that in order to start a business meeting on a Monday morning, the employee will have to travel on a Sunday. Whilst this may count as 'working time' for the purposes of the Working Time Regulations 1998 if the business meeting is not at the office, the individual may opt out of the 48-hour week requirement or the employer may offer to make up the time by way of time off in lieu (see section on Working Time Regulations 1998 below). It will be absolutely essential that employers can prove that this particular clause has been drawn to the attention of the employee before it can be relied upon. It will therefore be sensible to ask employees to sign that they have read, understood and accept this particular clause in the contract (see *Interfoto Picture Library Ltd v. Stiletto Visual Programmers Ltd* [1989] 1 QB 433 (CA)).

Employers will need to establish at the interview that the job candidate does not suffer from claustrophobia or agoraphobia and cannot therefore fly or travel by other modes of public transport, and that the job candidate has a valid passport and if necessary will be eligible for any visas required.

Those employers whose staff work offshore also need to establish that the job candidate does not suffer from hydrophobia or a fear of heights. A trip offshore before offering the post would seem sensible.

Travelling time is working time for peripatetic workers

The time taken by a peripatetic worker to travel from home to their first customer or client and the time taken from their last customer to home at the end of the working day is now deemed to be 'working time' for the purposes of the Working Time Regulations 1998 – *Federacion de Servicios Privados* v. *Tyco Integrated Security SL* Case C-266/14 – but does not fall within the minimum wage regulations so does not have to be paid.

An excellent article on this case, written by the employment team at 11 KBW, can be found at **employment11kbw.com/2015/09/14/when-is-travelling-time-working-time-and-when-does-working-time-not-earn-the-minimum-wage/#more-586**.

4.5 Relocation

If the employer envisages moving an employee's place of work during their employment, it is essential to spell this out unless it can be implied that the worker will relocate where the work is once a project is complete, such as in the construction industry (*Stevenson* v. *Teesside Bridge and Engineering Ltd* [1971] 1 All ER 296).

Whilst there is an implied obligation on the employee to be 'reasonably mobile', this is normally limited for manual workers to 'within reasonable daily commuting distance' (*Courtaulds Northern Spinning Ltd* v. *Sibson and TGWU* [1988] IRLR 305).

Further, if it would put the individual's life in danger if they were to move to the country where so directed, then any such instruction to relocate would be deemed unlawful whether there was an express mobility clause or not. An old authority which still holds good is *Ottoman Bank* v. *Chakarian* [1930] AC 277, where an Armenian sentenced to death in Turkey who had then escaped was held not to be under any implied obligation to return to Istanbul when ordered to do so.

More difficult questions arise after major disasters such as the '9/11' terrorist attack where some individuals refused to fly to the USA. Most employers dealt sensibly and reasonably with these circumstances and made use of facilities such as video-conferencing.

Even where there is an express mobility clause, there are implied terms that the employer will give 'reasonable notice and reasonable relocation expenses' and in some cases that relocation will be 'within a reasonable distance' (*United Bank* v. *Akhtar* [1989] IRLR 507 and *McAndrew* v. *Prestwick Circuits Ltd* [1990] IRLR 191).

A further example of whether a request to travel or work abroad could be unreasonable would be instructing staff to travel to, or work in, countries where human rights abuses take place or where the treatment of women or gay people is abusive or unacceptable, e.g. China, Pakistan, etc.

In such circumstances a refusal to travel or work in such countries could be deemed to be reasonable and the instruction to do so should be withdrawn.

A typical mobility clause is given at **Precedent 4D**.

There are important considerations of possible indirect sex discrimination in applying these mobility clauses but this is outside the scope of this book, save to say that a mobility clause would have to be justified if a woman with childcare issues could not agree to be mobile.

These would be similar considerations as those in *London Underground* v. *Edwards (No 2)* [1988] IRLR 364. Here a single mother argued she could not agree to work flexible shifts as she could only work during the day on weekdays. The Court of Appeal upheld the Employment Tribunal and Employment Appeal Tribunal decisions that the new rostering indirectly discriminated against female train operators and could not be justified.

The Court focused on the question of whether the new rostering arrangements imposed a condition that 'a considerably smaller proportion of female train operators than of male operators could comply'.

The Court ruled that:

> The industrial tribunal did not err in law in concluding that the proportion of female train operators who could comply with new rostering arrangements was 'considerably smaller' than the proportion of male train operators within the meaning of s.1(1)(b)(i) of the Sex Discrimination Act, where 100% of 2,023 male train operators could comply compared with 95.2% (20 out of 21) women. The tribunal, therefore, was entitled to conclude that the requirement to work the new roster indirectly discriminated against the applicant, who was the woman unable to comply with the arrangements.

Careful wording of mobility clauses is essential. The courts and tribunals have generally reviewed mobility clauses in claims for a redundancy payment where the employer is denying any redundancy because the work 'in the place where the employee is so employed' may not have ceased or diminished. The 'place of employment' matters when an employer's work ceases in that place of work and the employer is seeking to rely upon a mobility clause to argue that there is a much wider place of work than one location.

This is a different question from whether the employer has a right to give a lawful instruction to the employee to move to a different location, which may constitute a valid reason for dismissal if disobeyed.

In *High Table Ltd* v. *Horst* [1997] IRLR 513, three silver-service waitresses worked for one particular client, Hill Samuel. Their contracts provided that:

> Your normal place of work is as stated in your letter of appointment which acts as part of your terms and conditions. However, given the nature of our business, it is sometimes necessary to transfer staff on a temporary or permanent basis to another location. Whenever possible this will be within reasonable daily travelling distance of your existing place of work.

The letters of appointment clearly stated that the waitresses were appointed to work at Hill Samuel. The work reduced at Hill Samuel and, following a reorganisation, the waitresses were dismissed as redundant. The employees challenged the fairness of the dismissal and then the employer challenged the issue of whether they were redundant.

The Court of Appeal eventually held that for statutory redundancy purposes the 'place where the employee is so employed' had to mean at the particular client's premises, i.e. the client for whom they worked, and that therefore there was a redundancy. Giving an explanation for this decision based on sound policy reasons, the Court of Appeal added: 'It would be unfortunate if the law were to encourage the inclusion of mobility clauses in contracts of employment to defeat genuine redundancy claims.'

In *Bass Leisure* v. *Thomas* [1994] IRLR 104, the employees were employed under a mobility clause but based in the depot in Coventry. The clause stated that 'The Company reserves the right to transfer any employee either temporarily or permanently to a suitable alternative place of work ... domestic circumstances will be taken into account in reaching a decision if relocation is involved'.

The EAT held that in order to determine what is the place of employment, the issue to consider is the extent or area of a single place; it does not involve the question of whether the employer has the right to transfer the employee to another place of work. The mobility clause allowed the company, provided the conditions were met, to transfer the employee from one place to another. The place of employment was the Coventry depot. The issue of whether or not the employer has the right to transfer the employee was a separate question and not relevant for redundancy payment purposes.

4.6 Travel during times of adverse weather, strikes or volcanoes and other Acts of God

In 2010 the whole of Europe's airways temporarily shut down due to volcanic ash from a volcano in Iceland which had spread over European airspace. Many employees who had enjoyed an Easter break abroad were unable to return to work as planned and those on business trips were stranded abroad and unable to return.

There have been other occasions where either severe weather conditions or transport strikes have also meant that employees have found it impossible to travel to work.

The legal position is that employees are in breach of contract and are therefore entitled to no pay for any day when they fail to make themselves 'ready, willing and available for work' (implied term).

Nevertheless some employers provide contingency plans where either an employee is expected to try to travel (usually by foot, car or bicycle) to a nearby office, or is allowed to work from home. In such cases normal pay will be paid.

In the case of employees being stranded abroad without any transport to get them home, employers may choose to treat this as either unpaid leave, additional paid leave or, in some cases, staff may be asked to make up the time during the following year.

See **Precedent 4E** for clauses related to unforeseen circumstances.

4.7 Requirement to drive

Certain members of staff are required to drive as an essential element of their employment: chauffeurs, bus drivers and passenger service vehicle (PSV) drivers are typical examples. Salespeople may also be required to drive in order to carry out their jobs and many managers and head office specialists, such as health and safety managers, often have to travel to different locations.

If driving is an essential or integral part of the job, then this must be spelt out in the job description and the contract.

A requirement to produce the original, clean (i.e. no points, etc.) full UK driving licence should be a pre-requisite at interview.

It is also essential to require any drivers, whether driving their own private cars or company cars, to report any driving charges or convictions and any loss of a licence immediately. Precedents regarding car drivers are provided in **Chapter 5**.

4.8 Requirement to be trained and to keep up to date

New technology and advanced procedures in many areas of business and professional life may mean that original job descriptions become out of date. There are constant requirements to be trained and retrained in learning new skills or updating old skills. How does an employer cater for such eventualities?

The courts have recognised for a long time that there is a duty on all staff to update their skills, acquire new skills and adapt to new techniques and technology introduced during the course of their employment. The introduction of computerisation of manual tasks was a classic case.

In *Cresswell* v. *Board of Inland Revenue* [1984] IRLR 190, the High Court held that being required to learn new computer skills in order to undertake the former manual PAYE duties was not a breach of contract nor did it fall outside the scope of the employees' original job description (p.191):

> the degree of such alteration was nothing like sufficient to fall outside the original description of the proper functions of the grade concerned.
>
> An employee is expected to adapt himself to new methods and techniques introduced in the course of his employment. On his side, the employer must provide any necessary training or retraining. . . .
>
> In the present case, after computerisation of the PAYE scheme, each of the jobs in question was the same as it was before, though in part done in a different way. Computerisation merely introduced up-to-date methods for dealing with bulk problems. Though there may have been some loss of job satisfaction on the part of the employees concerned, that was regrettable but by itself provided no cause for action. . . .
>
> The defendants had not committed any act in breach of contract in refusing to allow the plaintiffs to continue working manually and in refusing to pay them as long as they refused to work the new computerised system.

The acquisition of marketing skills and marketing duties, e.g. developing new customer lists or marketing the company facilities and services, may not in many roles nowadays be held to fall outside the original job description.

However, where the skills are additional or new, there may be a different argument deployed. In *Woodroffe* v. *British Gas* (1985, unreported, CA), Ms Woodroffe was a state registered nurse (SRN), employed from 1980 as an occupational health nurse. Her job description did not refer to any requirement for her to take blood samples or to give talks on health matters. When a new occupational health physician (OHP) was appointed, he decided that she should do so (he was under the false impression that an SRN's training included taking blood samples). Ms Woodroffe explained that she saw these duties as extending her role and that she had not been trained to undertake such tasks. The OHP offered her training but she refused. She reluctantly then took on those additional duties. When the OHP became dissatisfied with her performance, including the keeping of medical records, he recommended her dismissal. She was dismissed.

Her claim for unfair dismissal (eventually taken to the Court of Appeal) failed. The EAT noted that had she refused to take on those additional duties she could not have been criticised and if she had been persuaded to take specialist training in occupational health, then the difficulties might have been resolved!

This decision is now over 30 years old. There is now a requirement for all doctors and nurses to have training and continuing education. From 2005, revalidation is required for all doctors wishing to practise medicine. They must demonstrate that they remain fit to practise. If employers employ professional staff such as OHPs and SRNs, this requirement for continuous training and revalidation should be expressly stated in their terms and conditions. Revalidation will be required over a five-year cycle and this will require the OHP/doctor to collect and submit information on all matters that have a bearing on fitness to practise.

4.9   Work permits

Work permits allow employers based in the UK to employ people who are not nationals of a European Economic Area country and who are not entitled to work in the UK.

It is necessary for an employer to ask whether an employee needs permission to work in the UK in view of the obligations under the Immigration, Asylum and Nationality Act 2006. However, asking for an applicant's nationality, passport or national insurance number can involve a risk of this being regarded as evidence of potential discrimination on racial grounds. This risk can be reduced by adhering to the Home Office's *Code of Practice on Preventing Illegal Working* (May 2014) and *Employer's Guide to Right to Work Checks* (12 July 2016).

Under the latest regime certain 'secure' documents are sufficient on their own and the employer will only need to see one such document. These include UK passports, EEA passports and national identity cards and UK residence permits (Code of Practice, Table 4, List A).

Where no secure document can be produced, the employer must check two documents from another list, Table 5 List B:

(a)   an official document bearing a national insurance number, along with a birth certificate, or a letter from the Home Office, or an Immigration Status Document;

(b)   a work permit, along with either a passport or a letter from the Home Office, which in either case must confirm that the holder has permission to enter or remain in the UK and take the work permit employment in question.

See **Precedents 4G** and **4H**.

The employer must in all cases see the original of any document, take a photocopy, and be satisfied (having regard to any photographs or dates of birth on the document) that it relates to the individual in question. It should be noted that a standard acknowledgement letter issued to an asylum seeker by the Home Office can no longer be relied upon as proof of entitlement to work and has been removed from the list. Similarly, a Construction Industry Scheme Card or a short UK birth certificate is no longer acceptable.

A comprehensive list of acceptable documents is contained in the Immigration (Restrictions on Employment) Order 2007, SI 2007/3290.

This is a specialist and complex area for which specialist advice from an immigration lawyer should be taken. Work Permits (UK) working on behalf of the government has adopted a stricter approach to the requirement for employers to notify Work Permits (UK) if a prospective new work permit holder fails to take up their position in the UK, or if a work permit holder leaves their position prior to the expiry of the work permit. Despite the Home Office's attempts to argue that a termination of employment would have the effect of automatically curtailing a work permit holder's leave to remain in the UK, there is no legal basis for this argument and the notification requirements, although strongly recommended, have yet to be made compulsory.

Employers are advised to complete a Notification of End of Employment form and return this to Work Permits (UK) to inform them that the work permit employment for which the work permit was issued either never came into effect or was terminated prematurely.

4.10 Requirement to work fast and accurately

It may be a requirement for some jobs for the incumbent to work fast and accurately. If this is the case, it is essential that this is made a material term of the contract. For example, some IT staff are required to work with great speed because they provide technical support to other staff. In other cases the work involves the rapid transfer of data. Instructions often come from the electronic display unit and not from an individual. In call centres, staff are required to answer calls within a minimum number of rings and to answer a minimum number of calls per hour.

In this regard, see **Precedent 4I**.

4.11 Hours of work

Any terms and conditions relating to hours of work (including any terms and conditions relating to normal working hours) must be included in the statement of written particulars of employment which must be given to each employee under the Employment Rights Act 1996.

Section 1 of the Employment Rights Act 1996 requires the employer to set out the 'normal working hours'. 'Normal working hours' are the number of hours in a week, or other period, after which the employee is entitled to overtime pay or, if greater, the number or minimum number of working hours fixed by the contract of employment.

Overtime

Apart from setting out the normal working hours, it is common for employers to make provision for requiring employees to work additional hours and stating whether they will be paid. The contract should also make it clear whether overtime is compulsory or voluntary or if it is a guaranteed contractual entitlement.

This is important for several reasons. If the overtime is not compulsory it will not be a breach of contract if the employee refuses to do it. If it is guaranteed it may form part of the employee's normal pay and withdrawal of guaranteed overtime may constitute a breach of contract by the employer. Rates of pay for overtime working are normally also spelt out as well as the fact that permission must be obtained from a line manager before overtime can be sanctioned. **Precedents 4J** and **4K** are examples.

Some employees, who are either senior or who are 'task-orientated' such as sales representatives, may be given the details of office hours but advised that there are no normal working hours for their position.

Please note that under recent case law relating to holiday pay, all overtime paid in the 12 weeks prior to the taking of holiday must be aggregated with basic pay and averaged for the purposes of calculating holiday pay as holiday pay has to be 'normal pay' (see **Chapter 5**).

Shift or unsocial hours

Any rules on shifts and shift working should be set out in the contract or another document, with details of any shift premiums or other payment for working unsocial hours.

Annualised hours

As a way of trying to give themselves greater flexibility some employers have opted for the idea of 'annual (or annualised) hours'. This is an alternative to the standard working week in which the number of hours to be worked is averaged over the year. The actual number of hours worked in any week can be varied to meet changing, perhaps seasonal, production and demand. The aim is to maximise the efficiency and productivity of the workforce and minimise the need for overtime working at premium rates. See **Precedent 4L** for an annualised hours contract and terms in a contract.

Sunday working

If the contract of employment or written statement of terms and conditions requires an employee to work on Sundays then this will be lawful. There are special rules for shop and betting workers.

In England and Wales the Sunday Trading Act 1994 (the provisions of which have been consolidated into the Employment Rights Act 1996) was designed to ensure that shop work on a Sunday remains voluntary.

The Sunday Trading Act 1994 introduced the concept of a 'protected shop worker' and an 'opted-out shop worker'. A protected shop worker is an employee who was in employment before the Act came into force and who is not required under their contract to work on a Sunday. An opted-out shop worker is an employee who may be required under their contract to work on a Sunday but who gives three months' written notice to opt out.

An employer must give an employee who has to work on Sundays (but not one only employed on Sundays) a written statement explaining their rights under the Act. This statement must be given within two months of starting work and the required contents can be found in Sched.4 to the Act.

If an employee is a Christian whose religious beliefs would prevent them from working on a Sunday, it could be unlawful under the Employment Equality (Religion or Belief) Regulations 2003, SI 2003/1660 to require that employee to work on a Sunday or to apply any detriment.

In *Copsey* v. *WWB Devon Clays Ltd* [2005] EWCA Civ 932 the Court of Appeal dismissed the appellant's appeal against the dismissal of his discrimination complaint, holding that an employee's freedom to manifest his religious beliefs, under Article 9 of the European Convention on Human Rights, was not infringed by his (fair) dismissal for refusal to work on Sunday.

The tribunal and the EAT were mistaken in finding that Article 9 was outside the concept of unfair dismissal under section 98 of ERA. However, on the facts of this case, the tribunal was correct to find that the employer had not failed to make reasonable accommodation for the employee's religious beliefs.

In a later case, *Celestina Mba* v. *Mayor and Burgesses of the London Borough of Merton* [2013] EWCA Civ 1562, the Court of Appeal also dismissed a complaint of religious discrimination, this time against Merton Council. The claimant, a Christian, resigned as she did not wish to work on a Sunday following a change in work patterns.

The Employment Tribunal identified the relevant provision, criterion or practice (PCP) as the 'requirement that staff worked Sunday shifts as rostered' and after balancing the evidence concluded that the imposition of the PCP was proportionate and dismissed the indirect discrimination claim.

The EAT upheld that decision but expressed misgivings about the wording of one paragraph in its judgment, where the Employment Tribunal gave weight to the view that the belief in not working on a Sunday was 'not a core component of the Christian faith': that concern led to this appeal.

In the lead judgment Maurice Kay LJ identified one of the primary issues as whether the Employment Tribunal was entitled to give weight to that view.

He found that it did err in law as 'it is not necessary to establish that all or most Christians, or all or most non-conformist Christians, are or would be put at a particular disadvantage' and therefore the Employment Tribunal should have found that the application of the Sunday working PCP satisfied Regulation 3(1)(b)(i).

However, after discussion of the relevance of Article 9 and *Eweida* v. *United Kingdom* [2013] IRLR 231 (which he distinguished as in that case the claimant's rights did not impinge on others) he concluded that the legal error would have made no difference as the change to the rosters was in accordance with the claimant's contract and so inexorably the requirement was proportionate.

Ms Mba had been employed as a care assistant at a children's home run by the London Borough of Merton (the Council). The job description included the following provision:

> ... to undertake duties outside normal working hours as required by the shift rota including weekends, Bank holidays and sleeping duties.

Such a provision was necessary to give 24/7 coverage. The children in question had serious disabilities and complex care needs arising from challenging behaviour, medical needs, feeding difficulties and similar problems.

She argued that her religious belief attached great significance to the Fourth Commandment:

> Remember the Sabbath day to keep it holy. Six days shalt thou labour, and do all thy work: But the seventh day is the Sabbath of the Lord thy God: in it thou shalt not do any work ...

When the Council began to roster her for Sunday working, a dispute arose. She raised a grievance. It was rejected. She was scheduled to work certain weekends, including Sundays. She declined to do so. Disciplinary proceedings ensued, leading to a final warning. An appeal against that was rejected on 25 May 2010. Five days later Mrs Mba resigned 'with regret'. Her claim for constructive dismissal was rejected on contractual grounds. Her complaint of religious discrimination was also rejected.

The Court of Appeal held that there was no need to show a group disadvantage.

> The right to religious freedom under Article 9 is engaged, as it directly is in this case given that the Council is a public body. The protection of freedom of religion conferred by that Article does not require a claimant to establish any group disadvantage; the question is whether the interference of that individual right by the employer is proportionate given the legitimate aims of the employer: see the analysis of the Strasbourg court in *Eweida* v. *United Kingdom* [2013] IRLR 231 paras 79–84. In substance the justification is likely to relate to the difficulty or otherwise of accommodating the religious practices of the particular individual claimant.

Useful guidance on working hours and time off is available on the government website (**www.gov.uk**). ACAS has also published a guide, *Religion or Belief and the Workplace* (March 2014), giving advice about holy days and working on the Sabbath for a number of common religions.

Flexi-time

Some employers introduce a flexible working time arrangement to allow employees to modify their working hours to suit their own personal preferences. These arrangements are known as flexi-time. It is important when drafting such provisions that the scheme ensures that employees are available during 'core times' in the working day, i.e. from 10 am to 4 pm, that they are not allowed to adopt working practices which are inefficient, and that they are not allowed to store up large amounts of 'time off in lieu' (TOIL) which result in them being away from work for extended periods of leave.

For example, under a flexi-time scheme, employees might agree to:

- arrive at work between 7.30 am and 9.30 am (flexi-time) and guarantee to be there from 10 am until noon (core time);
- take their lunch break between noon and 2 pm (flexible lunch hour);
- guarantee to be there from 2 pm to 4 pm (core time);
- leave between 4 pm and 7.30 pm (flexi-time).

The hours the employees work between these times are credited to them. In effect, they set up a time bank with their employer. Most schemes allow a credit or debit margin, often of about 10 hours. Say the employee works a 35-hour week, then, over four weeks, they will 'owe' their employer 140 hours. These four weeks are the 'accounting period': if they work more than 140 hours in four weeks then they will be in credit, and if they work fewer hours then they will owe time to their employer. If they go beyond the credit margin, into surplus, they may lose those extra hours; if they go beyond the debit margin, into debt, they might be disciplined or lose pay.

One of the best-liked features of flexi-time is flexi-leave. The employees can turn their credit hours into time off. Depending on the scheme, this might be two half days a month or one full day, or employees may be able to add days to their holiday entitlement.

Time-keeping

Where the employer requires employees to record their start and stop times by using a computer or other form of time-recording system, it is important to ensure employees are told that the employer will treat any attempt to distort or interfere with the proper operation of the system as a serious breach of discipline.

Recording workers' hours is a requirement under the Working Time Regulations 1998. This may be difficult where the employee works from home or is peripatetic and rarely comes into the office. However, there are means of recording remote workers' hours: by logging their hours when they log on to their PCs or laptops; recording devices in cars such as part of a global positioning system (similar to a tachograph in a PSV); asking them to ring someone or a recorded voicemail logging on to work remotely, leaving a message as to the time they have started work; or asking them to record their hours in a diary (the latter not recommended).

Working Time Regulations

Hours of work are regulated by the Working Time Regulations 1998, SI 1998/1833, as amended. Regulation 4 sets a limit of an average of 48 hours per week. The standard period over which the average will be calculated is 17 weeks, but this can be extended to 26 weeks if the workers are covered by 'derogations' of up to 12 months by agreement between employers and employees.

Regulation 4(1) confers a freestanding legal right for workers not to work more than 48 hours. However, individuals can voluntarily agree to work in excess of the minimum weekly working hours limit, but the employee can terminate this by giving written notice. Records must be kept of those who have opted out, and those who do not agree to 'opt out' of the limit must not suffer detriment as a result.

There are a number of excluded sectors where this 48 hour week rule does not apply (reg.18) and other special cases (reg.21):

- (a) Where the worker's activities are such that his place of work and place of residence are distant from one another or his different places of work are distant from one another;
- (b) where the worker is engaged in security and surveillance activities requiring a permanent presence in order to protect property and persons, as may be the case for security guards and caretakers or security firms;
- (c) where the worker's activities involve the need for continuity of service or production, as may be the case in relation to –

    - (i) services relating to the reception, treatment or care provided by hospitals or similar establishments, residential institutions and prisons;
    - (ii) work at docks or airports;
    - (iii) press, radio, television, cinematographic production, postal and telecommunications services and civil protection services;
    - (iv) gas, water and electricity production, transmission and distribution, household refuse collection and incineration;
    - (v) industries in which work cannot be interrupted on technical grounds;
    - (vi) research and development activities;
    - (vii) agriculture;

- (d) where there is a foreseeable surge of activity, as may be the case in relation to –

    - (i) agriculture;
    - (ii) tourism; and
    - (iii) postal services;

- (e) where the worker's activities are affected by –

    - (i) an occurrence due to unusual and unforeseeable circumstances, beyond the control of the worker's employer;
    - (ii) exceptional events, the consequences of which could not have been avoided despite the exercise of all due care by the employer; or
    - (iii) an accident or the imminent risk of an accident.

Unmeasured time

Regulation 20 provides an exception to the 48-hour maximum working rule for workers whose time is unmeasured because of the specific characteristics of the activity in which they are engaged, or the duration of whose working time is not measured or predetermined or can be determined by the workers themselves, e.g. managing directors or other persons with autonomous decision-taking powers.

On-call time

In C-303/98 *Sindicato de Médicos de Asistencia Publica (SIMAP)* v. *Conselleria de Sanidad y Consumo de la Generalidad Valenciana* [2000] IRLR 845, the ECJ considered the time spent on call by doctors in primary healthcare teams. Article 2(1) of the Working Time Directive 93/104/EC of 23 November 1993 appears to require three elements in the definition of 'working time': (a) working, (b) at the employer's disposal, (c) carrying out the activity or duty. The ECJ adopted a fairly liberal interpretation of what constituted (c).

In *MacCartney* v. *Oversley House Management* [2006] IRLR 514, all the on-call hours that the manager of a housing estate for the over 60s was expected to 'work' (on call for 24 hours on four days a week) were held to count towards working time.

Lunch breaks

The government also suggests that a lunch break will not be working time unless it is designated a working lunch.

Travelling time

Travelling may also give rise to difficulties as to what constitutes working time. The time taken to travel from a first appointment from home for peripatetic (mobile) workers who have no normal workplace is now deemed to be 'working time' (*Federacion de Servicios Privados del sindicato Comisiones obreras* v. *Tyco Integrated Security SL, Tyco Integrated Fire & Security Corporation Servicios SA* C-266/14).

Time spent travelling to and from the home to the place of work is not deemed to be working time for other workers with a normal workplace. But the worker who, for example, spends the journey on their mobile phone contracting business (aside from the commission of any offence under road traffic legislation) will probably be working to the extent of satisfying the definition of 'working time', particularly if the job, to the employer's knowledge, necessarily involves this.

'Business travel' is also likely to be 'working time' and time spent working abroad counts as working time for the purposes of the Working Time Regulations 1998.

Taking work home will not count as working time unless the work is performed on a basis previously agreed with the employer.

For model letters for staff to opt out or explaining why the 48-hour week does not apply to their employment see **Precedents 4N** to **4R. Precedent 4R** requires staff to report to their main/primary employer any additional hours worked each week outside their main employment, whether paid or unpaid, as these hours must be added together to determine the 48-hour limit.

4.12 Clean desk policy

Have you heard of 'irritable desk syndrome'? NEC-Mitsubishi Electronics Display European commissioned a survey in March 2004, which revealed that because office workers were spending more time at their desks in front of their computer screens (two-thirds said that they spent longer at their office desk than they did two years previously), they report that they have suffered from increased irritability, general apathy and disorganisation, and bad necks or backs. They ate lunch at their desks, cluttered their desks with paperwork and had fewer breaks from the screen. This has led, according to the survey, to an increase in the reporting of illness.

In order to combat this phenomenon, employers should consider one or more of these measures:

1. Insist that workers whose main tasks require visual display unit (VDU) work take compulsory breaks from the screen/keyboard every hour for at least 10 minutes (in accordance with guidance to the Health and Safety (Display Screen Equipment) Regulations 1992, SI 1992/2792 published by the Health and Safety Executive: this guidance has no legal status but may well be used by the courts to assess whether the employer complied with both the terms and the spirit of the Regulations).
2. Have a facility for the screen to cut out at the end of each hour with a message on screen 'Log out and take a break'.
3. Have a facility for the keyboard to lock at the end of each hour.
4. Have an immediate mandatory reporting procedure for anyone who starts to feel ill or aching during the working day.
5. Have a 'clear desk' policy for the end of each day – the Civil Service has such a policy. (See **Precedent 4S**.)

4.13 Travelling abroad

An employer could be held to be negligent and therefore liable for any injuries or illness suffered as a consequence unless the employee is fully briefed, advised and inoculated and vaccinated against any diseases known to be a risk in the countries where the employee will be visiting or working. This is particularly important in the context of diseases such as malaria where preventative medication can be taken. There are also vaccines available for other diseases such as yellow fever, and in a number of countries it is a requirement that a vaccination has been given and a certificate shown at Customs.

Similarly, advice should be given and measures taken concerning driving abroad, particularly in countries where insurance may not be compulsory or is limited.

For more information on travelling abroad see the NHS and MASTA websites (**www.nhs.uk** and **www.masta-travel-health.com**).

There is a duty on employers to inform, instruct and in some cases supervise their staff who will be working abroad. In this context employers who send their staff abroad should have detailed written policies about working abroad and these policies should be signed by such employees as an acknowledgement that they have read and have agreed to abide by them.

Employer negligence

Two recent negligence cases highlight employers' health and safety duties to their employees travelling for work abroad.

In *Dusek v. Stormharbour Securities LLP* [2016] EWCA Civ 604, the Court of Appeal dismissed the employer's appeal after the High Court found the employer (Stormharbour) liable for the injuries sustained after a chartered helicopter ride, abroad.

For an excellent article on this case please see **www.withersworldwide.com/news-publications/employers-duties-to-employees-travelling-overseas**.

In *Cassley v. GMP Securities Europe LLP* [2015] EWHC 722 (QB), the High Court held that:

- The employer had breached its duty to take reasonable care to ensure that its employee was reasonably safe when travelling in the course of his employment.
- Although entitled to rely on the charterer to a large extent, the employer should have satisfied itself that the trip was reasonably safe by checking the Foreign and Commonwealth Office website for information about the two countries, and by asking the charterer about:
    – the carrier;
    – the route;
    – how the charterer had satisfied itself that the proposed flight was safe;
    – whether the carrier had an air operator's certificate;
    – the carrier's insurance position;
    – whether the carrier had been recommended;
    – whether the charterer had used the carrier before to its satisfaction.

Employers should have known for many years now that they owe their staff who travel or work abroad duties of health and safety.

Employers should ensure that employees are insured when driving or being driven abroad against being injured or causing injuries to others.

They should ensure that someone in that country abroad has carried out a risk assessment of known or hidden risks to health and safety, e.g. risk of kidnapping, terrorism, disease, bribery and corruption, the laws around drinking alcohol, etc. This should also include ensuring the safety of all travel arrangements and the safety of bus, coach, taxi or chauffeur services abroad. Lastly, employers must ensure that the employee has proper insurance cover against accident, loss of life, theft and kidnapping (where this is a risk).

See **Precedent 4T** for model travel and working abroad guidelines.

4.14 Working alone

There are serious health and safety issues for staff who work either alone or in remote places. For this reason many employers have laid down clear rules and safety standards for staff who work alone.

The Health and Safety Executive (HSE) has issued updated guidance, *Working Alone: Health and Safety Guidance on the Risks of Lone Working* (May 2013).

Staff whose work takes them out on the streets, such as parking attendants, or whose job it is to call on home owners, such as meter readers, are often required to report in either via their 'walkie-talkie' or mobile telephone regarding any comfort break that they wish to take. See **Precedent 4U**. There may well be an issue as to whether or not this is a legitimate instruction or whether it contravenes the individual's right to respect for their privacy under Article 8 of the European Convention on Human Rights.

Precedents 4V and **4W** set out typical risk assessments.

Identifying lone workers

The following are categories of lone workers at risk:

1. *Staff working alone in fixed establishments*: e.g. reception staff; boiler-house staff; facilities and maintenance staff; radiographers.
2. *Staff working outside normal work hours*: e.g. domestic staff; transport staff; nursing and medical staff.
3. *Mobile workers working away from their fixed base*: e.g. community nursing and midwifery staff; chiropody and podiatry staff; speech and language therapy staff.

Useful reading

The following are useful reference works on this issue:

- Royal College of Nursing, *Violence in the Workplace*, RCN, London.
- Suzy Lamplugh Trust, *Personal Safety at Work: A Guide for Everyone*, (2009) Suzy Lamplugh Trust, London.
- UNISON, *Working Alone: A Health and Safety Guide on Lone Working for Safety Representatives* (2013) UNISON, London (also available at **www.unison.org.uk**).

PRECEDENT 4A: Variation clause

The Company reserves the right to review, revise, amend or replace the content of the contract and the Staff Handbook and introduce new Terms and Conditions and new policies from time to time or to vary existing policies, etc. to reflect the changing needs of the business and to comply with new legislation. A copy of the handbook is displayed on the notice board and on the intranet and replacement copies can be obtained from your HR Manager. You should keep yourself up to date with any changes by attending meetings and by keeping your eye on the notice board for any updates, etc.

PRECEDENT 4B: Clauses relating to duties

Listed below are examples of your main job duties as at the start of your employment. Please note that because of the evolving nature of our business and over the passage of time, your job duties will inevitably change. You will be notified of any changes when they occur. You are required to be flexible in the duties that you undertake and co-operate with all lawful and reasonable instructions and to carry out any reasonable duties that you are requested to do, that fall within your capabilities, even if these fall outside the scope of your current job description and are to be carried out in a different department/division/location/for different clients, etc.

1. The Executive shall at all times during the period of this Agreement:
(a) devote the whole of his time, attention and ability to the duties of his appointment;
(b) faithfully and diligently perform those duties and exercise such powers consistent with them, which are from time to time assigned to or vested in him;
(c) obey all lawful and reasonable directions of the Board;
(d) use his best endeavours to promote the interests of the Company and its Associated Companies;

2. The Executive shall (without further remuneration) if and for so long as the Company requires:
(a) carry out the duties of his appointment on behalf of any Associated Company;
(b) act as an officer of any Associated Company or hold any other appointment or office as nominee or representative of the Company or any Associated Company;
(c) carry out such duties and the duties attendant on any such appointment as if they were duties to be performed by him on behalf of the Company.

3. The Executive shall at all times keep the Board promptly and fully informed in writing if so requested of his conduct of the business or affairs of the Company and its Associated Companies and provide such explanations as the Board may require.

OR

1. You will perform all acts, duties and obligations, and comply with such rules, instructions and other directions and policies and procedures, as may from time to time relate to your employment and be required or be made by the Company. During your employment you shall:
(a) unless prevented by ill health or other unavoidable cause devote the whole of your working time, attention and abilities to carrying out your duties hereunder and will work such hours as may reasonably be required for the proper performance of your duties;
(b) well and faithfully serve the Company and its subsidiary or associated companies (as appropriate) to the best of your ability and carry out your duties in a proper and efficient manner and use your utmost endeavours to promote and maintain the interests and reputation of the Company;
(c) provide such explanations, information and assistance as to your activities relating to the business of the Company as may from time to time be required from you by the Company;
(d) refrain from doing or permitting any matter which causes any regulatory authority in the UK or elsewhere to withdraw permission or in any way prevent the

Company from employing or otherwise using your services and refrain from doing or permitting any matter which is contrary to the interests of the Company.

2. Your contract is with the Company, not with your individual unit. Therefore, the impact of your work performance in the Group must always take priority over the needs of your individual unit. Continuation of your employment will depend upon your role modelling and championing of the values and behaviours of the Company of which you are fully aware.

PRECEDENT 4C: Clauses relating to requirement to travel

Your duties will involve you travelling away from the office both within the UK and abroad. You will be expected to travel outside normal working hours with no additional pay. In some cases this may mean travelling in the evenings or early mornings or catching planes or trains or driving at weekends, if this is required, so that you can attend meetings first thing on Monday morning. These duties form part of your job description and your overall remuneration package takes account of these duties. If you exceed the 48-hour week requirement and you have not signed the 'opt-out' agreement, you will need to speak to your line manager. However, we are hopeful that averaged over 17 weeks, your hours should not exceed the maximum permitted hours of work. You are required to hold a valid and current passport as part of your employment.

For a salesforce:

The territory in which you are required to work initially is that which is specified in your offer letter. Territories are made up of sales bricks and those will be notified to you when you start work. Management reserves the right to alter the sales bricks and the territorial boundaries and where necessary require you to cover an entirely different territory. If this is the case and you are required to relocate, the Company will provide you with its relocation package as set out in its relocation policy and as much advance notice as possible.

PRECEDENT 4D: Mobility clauses

Your initial place of work is [*give details*]. However you are required to move from this location to any location in [UK/Europe/worldwide] to any of our offices whether current or future. We will give you reasonable notice and relocation and other expenses as set out in our Relocation Policy from time to time.

For area manager of sales team:

You may be moved from one Sales Area/Territory to another upon being given four weeks' notice by your line manager. This may mean a move to either a larger sales territory or a smaller sales area. Our salary scales are determined by the area and gross profitability in which you work and any such move could mean a decrease in your basic salary as well as an increase. You agree to any such changes to your salary in this way when you move to a different sales area/territory.

PRECEDENT 4E: Clauses related to unforeseen circumstances, e.g. adverse weather, strikes, etc.

In the event of unexpected problems getting to work – e.g. where there is a rail or tube strike or severe weather problems which prevent you from travelling to work – we would look sympathetically at paying you for any day that you are unable to attend work provided that:

(a) You make all reasonable efforts to get to work using other means of transport, e.g. if it is possible to walk, then we would expect you to do so, arranging car shares with other people if possible, or travelling by bus, bicycle, etc.
(b) If there is a branch office which is nearer to your home, then we would expect you to attend there for duty.
(c) If it is possible for us to have work couriered, faxed or emailed to your home, then we would try to arrange for this to happen.

If the difficulties are prolonged, i.e. last for more than one calendar week, then the Company reserves the right where you are unable to make any other alternative arrangements to get to work, to require you to take days of holiday if you wish to be paid for any or all of those days (i.e. all the days for which you are unable or prevented from attending work).

We will be sympathetic to all staff who we know will or have made an effort to attend work despite the problems with weather, transport, etc. and in any such case, we may be willing to agree not to deduct pay for those days not in the office/workplace, but may ask employees to make up their hours once the disruption is over.

Airspace closed

In the event that the UK and Europe's airspace has been closed due to adverse conditions, e.g. the volcanic eruptions and ensuing ash clouds from Iceland, the following terms will apply.

We are most sympathetic to those members of staff who have been unable to return to the UK by air and who have not been able to arrange alternative means of transport, e.g. train, car, coach or ferry.

We appreciate that this difficulty is not of your own making and that you will have been trying your best to return by alternative means of transport.

We can offer you the following options as to how you would wish us to treat this additional unplanned leave:

(a) unpaid leave;
(b) additional paid leave from either this year's leave or next year's (you can borrow some leave from next year); or
(c) you will make up the time as overtime or working during weekends for no additional pay or time off in lieu.

PRECEDENT 4F: Clause relating to training

1. Your employment requires you to be and continue to be appropriately qualified in Occupational Health with a minimum requirement to have and continue to have either the Associate Membership of the Faculty of Occupational Medicine (for an Occupational Health Physician) or the Diploma in Occupational Health Nursing (for an Occupational Health Nurse). You must bring the originals of such qualifications to your interview and on your first day of work.

2. You are required to update yourself continuously in relation to any advances or new knowledge including legal developments in Occupational Health and to undergo regular training that either you and/or the Company deem necessary or reasonable within the agreed budget limits.

3. This includes ensuring the provision of the relevant and appropriate books, publications and online services whether one-off purchases or subscription services. The library and training budgets will be agreed annually.

4. Your job description and/or contract will be revised from time to time, after consultation with you, to reflect additional or new responsibilities that it is reasonable to expect you to undertake. If you disagree with any of these new duties or responsibilities, then you may take out a formal grievance, the final stage of which will be to appoint an agreed external professional to make a final decision.

5. In the event that you are subject to any disciplinary proceedings from either your registering body [GMC or NMC] or any other professional body [such as the Faculty of Occupational Medicine] you are required to report this immediately you are put on notice. If you are suspended or struck off the register this will render your employment terminable by us without notice or pay in lieu.

PRECEDENT 4G: Work permit letter

1. It is a requirement for obtaining employment with us that you are a national of an EEA country.[1] If not, you must have a valid work permit or other authority to work here. As a result we will ask you to bring with you to the interview one of the following documents which must be an original:

(a) A document showing your National Insurance number and name, e.g. a P45, a National Insurance card, or a letter from a government agency or previous employer.
(b) A document showing that you can stay indefinitely in the UK, or that you have no restriction preventing you from taking employment, e.g. an endorsement in a passport or a Home Office letter.
(c) A work permit or other approval to take employment.
(d) A document showing that you are a UK citizen, or have the right of abode in the UK, e.g. a passport, an endorsement in a passport, a birth certificate, a registration or naturalisation document or a letter from the Home Office.
(e) A document showing you are a national of a European Economic Area country, e.g. a passport or national identity card.

2. Should you fail to provide us with any of the above documents, we reserve the right not to conduct the interview but to curtail and end the recruitment process.

Note:

1. Austria, Belgium, Cyprus, Czech Republic, Denmark, Estonia, Finland, France, Germany, Greece, Hungary, Iceland, Ireland, Italy, Latvia, Liechtenstein, Lithuania, Luxembourg, Malta, Netherlands, Norway, Poland, Portugal, Slovakia, Slovenia, Spain, Sweden and UK. From 1 June 2002, nationals of Switzerland have also had the same rights as EEA citizens to obtain employment without any immigration restrictions.

PRECEDENT 4H: Work permit contract term

The appointment shall be conditional upon you obtaining an entry visa to the UK and a UK work permit as well as fulfilling any other requirements of UK law.

PRECEDENT 4I: Clauses relating to fast and accurate work

1. All employees are required to carry out promptly all instructions given by the Unit's management or on electronic display.

2. In particular, you are employed as an input clerk and as such you are required to work at a fast and accurate pace. The speed with which you input data will be agreed with you and will be reviewed regularly. This means that the speeds could increase or decrease. You are reminded that the Company operates a VDU procedure, which it takes very seriously. You are required to take breaks from your keyboard at least once an hour, for at least 10 to 15 minutes. To ensure that this happens, we have arranged that your screen logs off at the end of each hour, and that your keyboard locks at the same time and will not release itself for a minimum of 10 minutes. This is to ensure your health and safety.

OR

Working in this call centre, you are required to answer a call within three rings and complete 240 calls an hour. Your performance will be carefully monitored. Should you fall below this standard we reserve the right to investigate your performance and start the Performance Improvement Procedure (PIP) which could ultimately lead to your dismissal. This is a job where you are required to work under considerable stress and deadlines and where you might encounter rude or aggressive customers. If you find that you cannot cope with either the standards of performance or the content of the calls, you should alert your supervisor immediately.

PRECEDENT 4J: Clause relating to overtime

1. Your normal working hours are 35 per week, Monday to Friday with a start time of 9 am and finish time of 5 pm. You have a one-hour unpaid lunch break each day taken at a time agreed between you and your manager and other designated breaks during the day about which you will be notified by your manager from time to time.

2. However, you are required to work any such additional hours as may be necessary for the proper performance of your duties. You will normally be rostered to work overtime and the roster will be put up on the notice board by no later than Wednesday (5 pm) of each week. If you have any personal difficulties in doing any particular overtime rostered in any week, then you are requested to see your line manager immediately and they will do their best to rearrange the roster. You may if you wish arrange your own swap (arrange a 'mutual') and in such a case please let your line manager know the name of the person who has agreed to take over your overtime. There may be rare occasions where overtime is required at short notice. In such a case it is part of your terms and conditions that you will agree to work overtime at short notice or no notice. Only in exceptional cases, e.g. where you have an important prior appointment or have domestic difficulties, will you be permitted on any occasion to refuse to do the overtime.

3. [Any hours worked over and above these hours, duly authorised in writing by your line manager, will be paid at time and a half as set out in the Union agreement, determined from time to time. If weekend or bank holiday working is required, overtime is paid on the basis of time and a half for all hours worked on a Saturday and double time for Sunday and bank holiday working.] *or* [Overtime will not be paid nor time off in lieu granted as your remuneration package takes account of any additional hours that may be worked.]

PRECEDENT 4K: Clause where there are no set working hours

Normal office hours are 9 am to 5.30 pm. You have a one-hour unpaid lunch break each day taken at a time agreed between you and your manager. However, due to the nature of your role, there are no set or standard working hours for you. You are required to work such hours as the nature of the job and demands of the business require or dictate. You may be required to start work before 9 am and finish work past 5.30 pm for the proper performance of your duties. No additional remuneration will be paid for this work or time off in lieu.

PRECEDENT 4L: Flexible time: annualised hours

(*This example is reproduced by kind permission of Angela Parratt and Jackie Vowles of Bath & North East Somerset Council.*)

Annualised hours is a flexible working option where the employee is paid for the total number of hours worked over the whole year, and the actual weekly contractual hours vary to account for busy and quiet periods. Employees with an annualised hours working arrangement work a longer day when the service is busy and work shorter hours when there is less demand, but are paid the same amount each month.

As with most other time flexibilities, annualised hours can be combined with any of the location flexibility options.

When is annualised hours appropriate?

Annualised hours should be introduced on a team rather than an individual basis, to provide greater flexibility in accommodating peaks and troughs in demand. Where individuals make requests to work in this way, then they should be considered in the context of the team (whether there are sufficient resources to provide cover during periods of reduced working, etc.).

This flexible working arrangement is appropriate when the benefits of introducing annualised hours (see below) will be realised and the disadvantages can be managed.

Benefits of annualised hours

- Improve customer satisfaction by providing the necessary level of cover at the required times and match resources to demand across the working day or week or more concentrated cover at core times of the day.
- Benefits for employees include having a more flexible working pattern (work-life balance), enabling them to work shorter hours at particular times of the year.
- Benefits for the employer include an improved use of resources, enabling them to cover fluctuations in workloads more flexibly, match resources to seasonal work demands and provide better customer service.
- The scheme contributes to the recruitment and retention of staff with other commitments who may wish to work reduced hours at certain times of the year. This can help to reduce the need for temporary/agency staff to cover busy periods.

Disadvantages of annualised hours

- Managers will need to carefully manage such schemes, agreeing with employees the pattern of hours to be worked across the year.
- More employees may request annualised hours than can be accommodated without causing problems for colleagues, team members or customers.
- An arrangement on overtime will need to be agreed because the hours have been calculated on an annual basis. Working regular additional hours over and above this will require a recalculation of the annualised hours rather than regular payment of overtime for additional hours. If this becomes the norm, then managers should review resourcing arrangements for the work to be done.
- Annualised hours require careful planning and communication and periods of intense working (longer hours) require careful health and safety management.

Who can work in this way?

Potentially all employees could work some form of annualised hours particularly if they are employed within services with identifiable peaks and troughs in customer demand and service delivery. Examples of services where this scheme has worked include [X Department] and staff in finance departments, to enable them to manage additional workloads at year end.

Annualised hours will not be suitable for staff who work in services with defined service delivery hours (based on customer requirements) all year round.

How does it work?

Employees work an agreed number of hours per year but work longer hours when the service is busy and shorter hours when there is less demand. Payment is in 12 equal instalments. Other conditions of the scheme:

1. *Rate of pay and pay-related benefits*

The rate of pay and pay-related benefits are affected by annualised hours. Annual salary is based on the average hours over the whole year and would be calculated as follows:

Full year: 52.143 weeks

The employee works 37 hours per week for 40 weeks = 1480 hours

15 hours per week × 12.143 (the remaining weeks) = 182.145

Total hours for the year: 1662.145

1662.145 / 52.143 = 31.88 hours per week

The rate of pay is then worked out as normal: 31.88 hours per week @ their hourly rate, × 52.143 weeks for total annual salary (and divided into 12 equal monthly amounts).

2. *Overtime*

The need for overtime payments will be reduced (but may not disappear completely). Normal overtime rules apply, and under single status these are:

- The premium for night workers (time and a third) (for work undertaken between 22.00 and 06.00 hours). Christmas Day will be an additional payment of single time for all hours worked.
- Overtime at plain time will be paid if you work on a Bank Holiday which you were not rostered to work.
- Staff working in services which need to operate outside traditional office hours will be required to work within whatever rota pattern the service might reasonably require subject to a maximum working week of 37 hours (unless varied by local or individual arrangements). Staff will be required to work at weekends or on Bank Holidays or in the evenings (NOT nights) if this is necessary to deliver the services in your area of work. All overtime must be approved by your line manager before it is worked.

3. *Work outside normal hours*

Managers are responsible for identifying and agreeing the length of the service day (through customer and employee consultation) and for ensuring that the necessary resources are available to provide adequate cover.

Staff who work in services which need to operate outside traditional office hours will be required to work within whatever rota pattern the service might reasonably require, subject to a maximum working week of 37 hours (unless varied by local or individual arrangements).

Employees will be required to work at weekends, or on Bank Holidays or in the evenings (not nights) if this is necessary to deliver the services in your area of work.

4. *Details: how the scheme works and examples of Annualised Hours calculations*

Example 1

If an employee wanted to work longer hours during term time and shorter hours during school holidays then the calculation would be as follows:

Full year: 52.143 weeks

Term time: 38.4 weeks @ 37 hours per week = 1420.8 hours

Holidays (52.143 − 38.4) = 13.743 weeks @ 10 hours per week = 137.43

Total annual hours: 1558.23 hours (1420.8 + 137.43)

Total weekly hours (for pay and annual leave calculations: 29.88 hours (29 hours and 53 minutes)

Annual leave

5 weeks × 29 hours and 53 minutes (29.88) = 149.40 hours

6 weeks × 29 hours and 53 minutes (29.88) = 179.28 hours

Bank Holidays

1.6 weeks × 29 hours and 53 minutes (29.88) = 48 hours

Example 2

The service has identifiable peaks and troughs in service delivery. They are particularly busy in December, January, February, March and April (five months) and during this period would like full-time staff to work 42 hours per week (an additional hour a day).

Total hours @ 37 hours per week (52.143 weeks) = 1929.29 hours per year

Increased period

52.143 (full year) / 12 = 4.35 weeks per month (average)

4.35 × 5 months = 21.75 weeks @ 42 hours per week

21.75 × 42 hours = 913.5 hours

Decreased period

Total normal hours (1929.29) − 913.5 = 1015.791 hours to be worked over remaining weeks (30.39) = 33.43 hours per week.

So the employee will work:

42 hours per week from 1 December to 31 April and

33.43 hours per week from 1 May to 30 November

But be paid for 37 hours per week

Annual leave and Bank Holidays are not affected.

5. *Variations*

Annualised Hours can be used over a three or six month period rather than a full year, particularly where there is a short-term need for additional cover or longer hours.

Examples of variations include:

- Working more than 37 hours per week during busy periods (perhaps 40) and reverting to normal full-time hours during quieter periods (provided that the requirements of the Working Time Directive are met).
- Full-time hours during busy periods and part-time hours during quieter periods.
- Part-time hours during busy periods and reduced part-time hours during quieter periods (perhaps varying from 25 hours per week for part of the year to 13 hours per week during quieter times).

All Annualised Hours arrangements depend on the service's ability to predict peaks and troughs in service delivery and customer demand.

To discuss local variations, Managers should contact HR in the first instance.

PRECEDENT 4M: On-call arrangements

1. Hours of work: core hours

The normal working day consists of a seven-hour 'working' shift (core hours) but this may change to an eight-hour shift in the near future. It is a requirement that, in order for you to reach your earnings potential, you are available to take additional jobs after the core hours have been worked, during the 12-hour 'on-call' period. Please note that you will begin to accrue your core hours when you receive your first job. The journey to the scene of the job and completion/repair of the job will be included in this accrual. However, once the job is completed and unless you have another job to go to, the return journey to your home will not count as part of your core hours.

2. On call

2.1 In your designated location of work you will be required to be 'on call' from 7 am to 7 pm, Monday to Friday and 8 am to 6 pm Saturday and Sunday and bank holidays.

2.2 'On call' means that your mobile phone/pager should be switched on during these times and your datatrack system activated and you should be ready to accept call outs as passed to you by the Operations Centre.

2.3 Your working day will begin when you receive your first job. Once that job is completed, i.e. at the scene of the repair, you will be on call until you receive the next job.

3. Out of on-call hours

Jobs attended outside your 'on-call' hours will attract premium rate payments.

Please note that on rostered weekends off you will not be offered work unless you specifically request it.

PRECEDENT 4N: Working Time Regulations: disapplication letter

[Name of employee]

[Address]

[Date]

Dear [name]

RE: Agreement to dis-apply the 48-hour limit under the Working Time Regulations 1998 as amended

Your normal hours of work are [specify hours] Monday to Friday, excluding one hour for lunch, or such hours as may be necessary to ensure the proper performance of your duties.

Your agreement is requested to dis-apply regulation 4(1) in order that the Company may comply with its obligations under the Working Time Regulations 1998 as amended.

You acknowledge that you may be required to work in excess of 48 hours per week from time to time and that the limit specified in regulation 4(1) should not apply in your case.

However, you understand that if you wish to terminate this agreement to dis-apply the 48-hour limit, you can do so by giving three months' notice in writing.

You also agree that, in order to enable the Company to maintain accurate records of your time spent working, you will comply in a comprehensive and timely manner with the Company's time-recording procedures as advised to you.

Please would you sign both copies of this letter and return one copy duly signed and dated to [specify] as soon as possible.

Yours sincerely

I, [name], understand that I may agree to work in excess of 48 hours in any seven-day period averaged over a 17-week period and willingly agree to such working arrangement where it becomes necessary for me to do so.

Signed .... Date ....

[employee]

PRECEDENT 40: Working Time Regulations: security guards, surveillance workers, messengers, chauffeurs

[Name of employee]

[Address]

[Date]

[2 copies]

Dear [name]

RE: Working Time Regulations and you

You may have read about the Working Time Regulations have been in force since 1 October 2003.

They provide that the average working time including overtime should not exceed 48 hours in any seven-day period, averaged over a 17-week period.

However, there are many exceptions to this rule including a very important exclusion under regulation 21, for all those who work in security or surveillance, where for obvious reasons, it is absolutely essential that such staff may have to work more than the 48-hour week.

[For messengers, chauffeurs: Your job description and job title include security and surveillance duties so that we have ensured that you are of the highest integrity and can be trusted to ensure the safety of our very senior executives based both in the UK and in the USA. It is for this reason that we employ you, and one of your tasks is to drive our senior executives on business and to keep them safe from any possible physical dangers.]

In practice this does not alter your current working conditions as you currently agree to work any additional hours as and when requested and when needed.

If you have questions concerning this letter then please contact your HR Adviser.

We would ask you to sign both copies of this letter and to return one copy to us for our files and keep one safely for yourself.

Yours sincerely

I, [name], have read and understood this letter.

Signed .... Date ....

[employee]

PRECEDENT 4P: Working Time Regulations: dealers, traders, senior staff

[Name of employee]

[Address]

[Date]

[2 copies]

Dear [name]

RE: Working Time Regulations and you

You may have read about the Working Time Regulations have been in force since 1 October 2003.

They provide that the average working time including overtime should not exceed 48 hours in any seven-day period, averaged over a 17-week period.

However, there are many exceptions to this rule including a very important exclusion under regulation 20, where the maximum working hours rule does not apply to any member of staff whose working time is unmeasured including those who make and take decisions on their own.

This means that you fall within this exception. [The Bank] wishes to advise you further that the Regulations concerning daily and weekly rest breaks also do not apply to your employment.

In practice this does not alter your current working conditions as you currently agree to work any additional hours as and when requested and when needed.

We will of course continue to ensure that you work safely and do not put yourself or others in any physical or mental danger.

If you have questions concerning this letter then please contact your HR Adviser.

We would ask you to sign both copies of this letter and to return one copy to us for our files and keep one safely for yourself.

Yours sincerely

I, [name], have read and understood this letter.

Signed .... Date ....

[employee]

PRECEDENT 4Q: Working Time Regulations: computer operators who work at night

[Name of employee]

[Address]

[Date]

[2 copies]

Dear [name]

RE: Working Time Regulations and you

You may have read about the Working Time Regulations which have been in force since 1 October 2003.

They provide that the average working time including overtime should not exceed 48 hours in any seven-day period, averaged over a 17-week period.

There are, however, many exceptions to this rule including a very important exclusion under regulation 21, where the maximum working hours rule does not apply to any member of staff whose work cannot be interrupted for technical reasons.

This means that you fall within this exception. [The Bank] wishes to advise you further that the Regulations concerning daily and weekly rest breaks also do not apply to your employment.

There are, however, other special rules concerning night shift workers. One of these rules affects anyone working at night, i.e. between the hours of midnight and 5 am. In such cases the Regulations provide that unless the worker has agreed in writing, the night shift worker cannot work more than an average of eight hours in any 24-hour period.

Obviously [at the Bank], you have worked more than these prescribed hours when necessary. Sometimes you have stayed on after your shift has finished to complete some work and have been entitled to overtime. Sometimes you have stayed to cover the next shift because someone has not come to work due to sickness or other reasons.

These Regulations allow you to continue to do these additional hours provided that you agree to do so.

We are therefore providing you with an agreement, attached, which we would ask you to consider and then if agreeable, sign both copies and return one signed copy to [specify].

In practice this will not alter your current working conditions as you have agreed in your current contract of employment to work any additional hours as and when requested and when needed.

We will, of course, continue to ensure that you work safely and do not put yourself or others in any physical or mental danger. The other rules about night shift workers, concerning free health assessments, ensuring your health and safety during the night shift and transferring you to day work if night work proves dangerous to your health, all still apply to your employment.

[The Bank] will ensure that all its obligations in relation to night shift workers such as you and all its other staff are strictly adhered to.

If you have any questions concerning this letter then please contact your HR Adviser.

We would ask you to sign both copies of this letter and the agreement attached and to return one copy of both the letter and the agreement to us for our files and keep one safely for yourself.

Yours sincerely

I, [name], have read and understood this letter.

Signed .... Date ....

[employee]

PRECEDENT 4R: Working Time Regulations: secondary employment

1. Under your contract of employment, we are your main/primary employer. You are free however to take part-time or secondary employment in your time off. You are required to report any additional hours of work other than those which you work for us so that we can include any such hours in our determination of your normal working week for the purposes of the Working Time Regulations 1998.

2. Please would you ensure that you put this information in writing and hand it either to your line manager or to the Human Resources Department within 7 days of receipt of this letter.

3. If you do not have any other paid or unpaid employment, please will you confirm this in writing. Should we fail to receive anything in writing from you, you will be deemed to have no other employment outside this employment.

4. Thank you for your co-operation in this matter.

PRECEDENT 4S: Clear desk and screen policy

Because of the nature of our business [you have been asked to sign the Official Secrets Act], it is Company policy that you keep a clear desk as far as you can during the working day. Files or papers that have been used or are not being used at that particular time should be locked away securely.

Similarly, if you are looking at or typing any confidential information on your screen, you must ensure that your screen is angled in such a way that no one could watch what you are typing or read what is on your computer screen. If you leave your desk for any reason, even momentarily, you must log off, with your secure password. Breach of this policy is a disciplinary offence.

At the end of the working day or at any time after you have finished work, you must ensure that all files and paperwork are securely locked away in their appropriate place and that you have logged off securely and in line with our PC procedures. Security is authorised to use your home/mobile telephone number to require you to return to the office if this Policy has been breached by you and to report such a breach of security to the Head of Department. If this occurs more than once, you may be subject to serious disciplinary action which could result in dismissal. We thank you for your co-operation. Regular reminders of this Policy will be sent via email and placed on notice boards.

PRECEDENT 4T: Working or travelling abroad guidelines

Wherever we are in the world there are always risks to health. Careful planning and preparation is vital to ensuring you and your colleagues are safe and healthy on overseas business trips or work placements.

These Guidelines have been developed for all employees to use in preparation for an overseas trip or placement. They include useful information and clarification on main risks associated with overseas travel.

This Guide is to be used in association with guidance from Occupational Health, your travel provider and your own GP.

In addition, where drugs are suggested, employees must investigate whether these substances are permitted in the destination country before travelling and must investigate what the side effects are and whether they can tolerate these drugs.

Deep vein thrombosis (DVT)

DVT happens when a blood clot forms in a deep vein. DVT is most common in the deep veins of your lower leg (calf), and can spread up to the veins in your thigh. DVT can also first develop in the deep veins in your thigh and, more rarely, in other deep veins, such as the ones in your arm.

Deep veins pass through the centre of your leg and are surrounded by a layer of muscle.

When blood clots form in the superficial veins, which lie just under your skin, the condition is known as superficial thrombophlebitis. These superficial blood clots are different to DVT and are much less serious.

Symptoms of DVT

Many blood clots that cause DVT are small and do not produce any symptoms. Your body will usually be able to gradually break them down with no long-term effects.

Larger clots can partly or completely block the blood flow in your vein and cause symptoms such as:

- swelling of the affected leg;
- pain and tenderness in the affected leg – you may also find it difficult to stand properly with your full weight on the affected leg;
- a change in the colour of your skin, for example, redness;
- skin that feels warm or hot to the touch.

Although not necessarily a result of DVT, if you have these symptoms you should visit your GP.

Complications of DVT

DVT may not cause you any further problems, but possible complications can include the following.

Pulmonary embolism

This is the most serious complication of DVT. A pulmonary embolism happens when a piece of the blood clot from a DVT breaks off and travels through your bloodstream to your lungs, where it blocks one of the blood vessels in your lungs. This is serious and in severe cases, can be fatal.

Post thrombotic syndrome

This is something that happens if DVT damages the valves in your deep veins, so that instead of flowing upwards, the blood pools in your lower leg. This can eventually lead to long-term pain, swelling and, in severe cases, ulcers on your leg.

Limb ischaemia

This is a rare complication that only happens in a very extensive DVT. Because of the blood clot, the pressure in your vein can become very high. This can block the flow of blood through your arteries, so less oxygen is carried to the affected leg. This can be painful and lead to skin ulcers, infection and even gangrene.

Causes of DVT

You are more likely to get DVT if you:

- are over 40;
- are immobile, for example, if you have had an operation (especially on a hip or knee) or are travelling for long distances, and so are not able to move your legs;
- have had a blood clot in a vein before;
- have a family history of blood clots in veins;
- have a condition causing your blood to clot more easily (this is called thrombophilia);
- are very overweight (obese);
- have cancer or have had cancer treatment;
- have heart disease or circulation problems;
- are a woman taking a contraception pill that contains oestrogen, or hormone replacement therapy (HRT);
- are pregnant or have recently had a baby.

Travel risks

There is evidence that long-haul flights (lasting over four hours) can increase your risk of developing DVT. The risk is mainly the result of sitting down for long periods of time, which can happen during any form of long-distance travel, whether by car, bus, train or air.

It is difficult to say whether the travelling itself directly causes DVT, or whether people who develop DVT after travelling are at risk for other reasons. Generally, your risk of developing DVT when travelling is very small unless you have at least one of the other risk factors mentioned above (such as a history of DVT or cancer). If this is the case, you should talk to your GP before you travel on a flight of more than four hours.

Diagnosis of DVT

Your GP will ask about your symptoms and examine you. If your GP thinks that you might have a DVT, you may be referred to a specialist. You may have the following tests in hospital.

- A blood test called a D-Dimer. This measures a substance which develops when a blood clot breaks down. If this is negative it is unlikely that you have a DVT.

- A Doppler ultrasound. This is a test that uses sound waves to look at your blood as it flows through your blood vessels. It is the best test to detect blood clots above your knee.
- A venogram. In this test, a special dye is injected into your vein, which shows up the vein on X-ray. This is the best way of showing clots below your knee.

Treatment of DVT

Medicines

Anticoagulant medicines are the standard treatment for DVT. They change chemicals in your blood to stop clots forming so easily. Anticoagulants include heparin and warfarin. Anticoagulants can stop new blood clots from forming and old ones from getting any bigger. They cannot dissolve clots that you already have – your body will do that itself over time.

Thrombolytic medicines are medicines that work by dissolving blood clots; but they can cause bleeding and so are rarely used to treat DVT.

Compression stockings

These are also called graduated compression stockings. Your doctor may ask you to wear these to ease your pain and reduce swelling, and to prevent post-thrombotic syndrome. You may need to wear them for two years or more after having a DVT.

Prevention of DVT

Ask your GP for advice if you think you are at risk of developing a DVT.

There are a number of things you may be able to do to reduce your risk, such as stopping smoking if you smoke, or losing weight if you're overweight. Regular walking can help to improve the blood circulation in your legs and help to prevent another DVT from developing.

There is no good evidence that taking aspirin reduces your risk of developing DVT.

If you're having surgery

Surgery and some medical treatments can increase your risk of developing DVT. So, if you're going to hospital for an operation, you will usually have an assessment to check your risk of developing DVT before you have your operation. There are many things that can be done to keep your risk of developing DVT during surgery as low as possible. You may be given anticoagulant medicines before and after surgery, or be asked to wear compression stockings. You may also be given a mechanical pump to use on your feet and legs in the first few days after the operation. This is called an intermittent compression device. The pump automatically squeezes your feet and lower legs to help your blood circulate.

If you're travelling

Although it is unlikely that you will develop DVT when you are travelling, there are some steps you can take to reduce your chances of developing a blood clot. These include:

- take short walks – if you are a passenger, walk up and down the aisle of the coach, train or plane;
- exercise the muscles of your lower legs, which act as a pump for the blood in your veins – regularly bend and straighten your toes, ankles and legs;
- wear loose-fitting clothes;
- keep hydrated by making sure you drink enough water;
- don't drink too much alcohol or too many drinks that contain caffeine, such as coffee;

- don't take sleeping tablets, as these will stop you keeping your legs active; and
- wear compression stockings if you have other risk factors for DVT.

If your GP has told you that you are at high risk for DVT (for example, if you have a previous history of DVT or a blood clotting disorder), you may need heparin injections as well for flights longer than four hours. Talk to your GP or haematologist for more information.

If you develop swelling or pain in your calf or thigh, or if you have breathing problems or chest pain after travelling, you should seek urgent medical attention.

Jet lag

If your flight crosses more than three time zones then you might experience jet lag symptoms.

This can mean disturbed sleep patterns, weakness and disorientation caused by travelling. It happens when our normal body clock is disrupted by travelling through several time zones. It's worse when we are moving from west to east because the body finds it harder to adapt to a shorter day than a longer one.

Ten tips to combat jet lag

1. Top up your sleep before you travel
   Make sure you're fully rested before you travel. If you're flying overnight and you can get a bit of sleep on the flight, it will help you to stay up all day once you arrive at your destination.
2. Have a stopover on the way
   Including a stopover in your flight will make it easier to adjust to the time change, and you'll be less tired when you arrive. Take advantage of a stopover to have a refreshing shower or swim at the airport hotel.
3. Plan when to take medication
   People who have to take medication at certain times of the day should seek medical advice before travelling. Your GP will be able to tell you what times you should take your medicine when you're crossing time zones.
4. Adjust to your destination as soon as possible
   A few days before you travel, start getting up and going to bed earlier (if travelling east) or later (if travelling west). During the flight, try to eat and sleep according to your destination's local time.
5. Keep hydrated
   Dehydration can intensify the effects of jet lag, especially after sitting in a dry aeroplane cabin for many hours. Avoid alcoholic drinks and keep your fluid levels topped up with a cup of juice or water every hour during the journey.
6. Be active
   Try to do a little exercise and light stretching during your flight and your trip. Stretch your legs with a few walks around the cabin, and take advantage of long airport queues to move up and down on tiptoes, exercising your calf muscles.
7. Allow recovery time
   It takes around one day to recover for each time zone you cross and can take up to a week to adjust fully to the time zone of your destination, so take things easy when you arrive.
8. Natural light
   By controlling your exposure to daylight you can trick your brain into beating jet lag more quickly. As soon as you arrive, spend some time outdoors in the daylight if you can. This will help regulate your body clock.
9. Stay up till 11 pm

When you arrive, don't go straight to bed for a nap, however quick it is. You'll feel better temporarily, but you'll only confuse your body clock and delay making the time change. Stay up until 11 pm if you can.

10. Use remedies with caution
Many airline staff take melatonin, a hormone formed by the body at night or in darkness, to try to fight jet lag. Sleeping medication is not recommended as it doesn't help your body to adjust naturally to a new sleeping pattern.

Safe sun exposure

Ultraviolet (UV) rays are an invisible form of radiation. They can penetrate your skin and damage your skin cells. Sunburns are a sign of skin damage. Suntans are not healthy, either. They appear after the sun's rays have already killed some cells and damaged others. UV rays can cause skin damage during any season or at any temperature. They can also cause eye problems, wrinkles, skin spots and skin cancer.

To protect yourself:

- Stay out of the sun when it is strongest (between 10 am and 4 pm);
- Use sunscreen with an SPF of 15 or higher;
- Wear protective clothing;
- Wear wraparound sunglasses that provide 100 per cent UV ray protection;
- Avoid sunlamps and tanning beds;
- Avoid strenuous exercise during the hottest hours;
- Drink plenty of non-alcoholic fluids to replace the fluids lost through perspiration;
- Ensure you are wearing appropriate clothing;
- Check your skin regularly for changes in the size, shape, colour or feel of birthmarks, moles and spots. Such changes are a sign of skin cancer.

Avoid contaminated foods

The most common problem that is likely for a traveller is travellers' diarrhoea but other more serious diseases such as polio, typhoid fever, hepatitis A and cholera are also transmitted via contaminated food or water. Try to avoid eating re-heated or stored food. Food that has been left at room temperature for a few hours is likely to pose a risk, so buffets are best avoided. Avoid undercooked meat and fish. Shellfish pose a particular risk because they filter large quantities of water and concentrate micro-organisms within their tissues.

Raw vegetables and salads are best avoided unless you know they have been thoroughly washed in uncontaminated water. If you are preparing your own salads you should wash them well and leave them to soak in water containing chlorine from sterilising tablets or alternatively you can use household bleach. If you do use household bleach, use approximately four drops per litre. Washing salads in water at a temperature of at least 60°C will reduce the risk. It is good practice to peel all fruit and vegetables that are to be eaten raw.

It is best not to drink unpasteurised cow, sheep or goats' milk. Dairy products such as ice-cream, butter and cheese if from an uncertain source are best avoided.

Don't forget to wash your hands before eating and to dry them thoroughly on a clean cloth.

Avoiding contaminated water

Water is a frequent source of infection. Even in areas where the tap water is safe to drink the level of chemical treatment may be sufficient to render it unpalatable to the

UK traveller. Bottled water is widely available nowadays and is generally safe as long as the seal is intact when it is purchased. Tea, coffee and other bottled drinks especially fizzy drinks are normally safe. Remember to use safe water for brushing your teeth and for washing any vegetables or salad to be eaten raw.

If you do not have access to safe water the following alternative means of treatment are available. The most effective method of treating water is to bring it up to a rolling boil and to allow it to cool. Prolonged boiling is unnecessary but if you will be storing the water make sure it is transferred to a clean vessel and covered.

The next best way of treating water is to use an iodine resin water purifier. These light modern systems both filter and purify freshwater from any source. They're convenient and very effective and do not leave a strong taste of iodine. Disinfectants can be used but these are often ineffective if the water is visibly cloudy in which case it would first need to be filtered. Iodine is probably the most effective; you can use four drops of a two per cent tincture of iodine added to each one litre of water and leave for 15–20 minutes. This will taste of iodine and will be protective against most viruses and bacteria, although you should be aware that certain organisms like giardia can form cysts which are more resistant to iodine and chlorine.

The next best alternative to iodine is to use chlorine based sterilisation treatments. These are widely available as tablets and can be purchased from chemists. They are less effective than iodine against cysts.

Guidelines

- Remember ice may be made from contaminated water and is probably not safe to drink.
- Bottled water and drinks are normally safe, especially fizzy drinks.
- Use safe water for brushing your teeth and for washing vegetables or salad that is to be eaten raw.
- The water from the hot tap in the hotel is likely to be safer than that in the cold tap. Run the water for a minute or so and it can be used for brushing teeth in an emergency.

Malaria

The most common and potentially fatal disease affecting travellers to tropical destinations is malaria. This disease is transmitted by a bite from an infected female mosquito. The malaria-carrying mosquitoes are most active from dusk to dawn.

Malaria can be fatal if not treated immediately.

Other diseases carried by mosquitoes are yellow fever, dengue fever, Japanese encephalitis. Most mosquitoes, but not all, bite after dusk and before dawn.

Avoiding mosquito bites

1. Apply protection to your skin before dressing, preferably using a natural compound such as incognito.
2. Apply a protective solution to your clothing, again a natural product is recommended to avoid staining. Remember that DEET dissolves synthetic fabrics and is likely to stain natural ones.
3. Use ambient safeguards such as incognito citronella incense sticks, smoke rings (never sleep in the same room as burning smoke rings as this can cause serious respiratory problems), citronella or oil burners as these can halve the number of insects around you.

In fact it is a good idea to always cover up with suitable clothing and wear protection at night – preferably chemical free.

Always sleep under a good quality impregnated net and have it ready before you go out for the evening. Avoid emitting carbon dioxide, for example by burning a candle, as this invites insects in.

Tips:

- Spray on and around your door before entering, as mosquitoes often lie in wait on the outside of doors and windows and this simple procedure helps to keep them out of your dwelling.
- Wrap laundry up in plastic bags or other airtight containers and keep all luggage closed. Stay in screened accommodation or other safe refuges, where possible.
- Avoid all fragrances. Some, such as lavender actually attract insects – just look closely at a lavender plant! Be aware that many toiletries and sunscreens along with most fabric softeners contain scent.
- Exfoliate every two or three days to remove the impurities within skin pores that skin bacteria feed off emitting a powerful kairomone in the process.
- Use special soaps to be fully camouflaged. Most ordinary soaps contain insect attractants.
- Pick a breezy spot when sitting or standing around. In the tropics this is usually a relief from the heat. Mosquitoes don't fly well in windy conditions or in air-conditioned rooms.
- Reapply natural products more frequently than toxic chemical ones.
- Mosquitoes are also drawn to water as this is where they breed. Stay away from stagnant water if possible.
- Perspiration is a common kairomone. Reapply protection after swimming and washing. Any exposed non-protected skin is an open invitation.
- A lot of mosquitoes go in on the ears, wrists and ankles because this is where the skin is thinner and blood vessels are nearer the surface. So, it is a good idea to wash with special soaps or a spray.
- Machines and plug-ins can be useful.
- DEET is a powerful anti-mosquito spray but you should put on special cream between your skin and the DEET to minimise absorption into your skin.

Medicines to prevent malaria

It is essential that you start taking anti-malarial medicines before you go abroad, during your stay and after leaving a malarial area. Unless there are clear medical reasons to the contrary, all employees travelling abroad to malarial areas are required to take the appropriate anti-malaria tablets.

The main signs and symptoms of malaria are:

- flu-like symptoms
- fever
- chills with sweating
- headache
- general aches and pains
- diarrhoea
- nausea
- jaundice

If you have any of these symptoms you must seek urgent medical help and undergo a blood test and examination.

Returning traveller

Malaria can take three months to develop so be vigilant. If you feel unwell with a temperature of over 38°C attend your local A&E department immediately.

If you have been to a malarial zone in the last 12 months you must inform your doctor and what anti-malarial tablets you are taking and whether the course was completed.

Please take your vaccination card from any independent travel clinic to your doctor.

Avoiding tick bites

When in tick habitat (grassy, brushy or woodland areas), several precautions can minimise your chances of being bitten by a tick.

- Tuck your trousers legs into your socks. Tuck your shirt into your trousers. Ticks grab on to feet and legs and then climb up. This precaution will keep them on the outside of your clothes, where they can be spotted and picked off.
- Wear light coloured clothing. Dark ticks can most easily be spotted against a light background.
- Inspect your clothes for ticks often while in tick habitat. Ask a companion to inspect your back.
- Wear repellents such as DEET, applied according to label instructions. Application to shoes, socks, cuffs and trouser legs are most effective against ticks.
- Inspect your head and body thoroughly when you get in from the field. Ask a companion to check your back, or use a mirror.
- When working in tick habitat on a regular basis, do not wear work clothing home. This will reduce the chances of bringing ticks home and exposing family members.

What to do if bitten by a tick

Remove the tick as soon as possible. The easiest method is to grasp the tick with fine tweezers, as near to the skin as you can, and to gently pull it out. You may want to save the tick in a small jar for later identification. Check to see whether the mouthparts broke off in the wound. If they did, seek medical attention to get them removed. If you develop any symptoms of Lyme disease in the following week to several months, see a physician immediately. Be sure to tell the doctor that you were bitten by a tick. A blood test can help determine if you have been exposed to Lyme disease.

Accidents

More travellers die from accidents than from any other cause and most accidents are avoidable. Abroad, emergency treatment may not be available and communication difficulties may arise.

You should find out how to summon emergency help if needed and to travel with first aid kits including needles and syringes.

The same accident reporting procedures for within the UK are applicable abroad.

Take care on the road

- Always check local traffic regulations and stick to the speed limit.
- Wear a seatbelt when travelling on the road and ensure children are restrained.

- If you have to travel by motorcycle or moped always wear a helmet and protective clothing.
- Check the condition of the car or motorbike for hire and ensure adequate insurance cover is provided.
- Never drink alcohol and drive.
- Try to avoid driving at night.

Take care in water

Take great care when swimming or diving into a swimming pool as many injuries occur when diving into shallow water.

Sports and leisure pursuits

These carry a degree of risk. Check equipment, be fit enough, ensure you have had adequate training with properly qualified personnel, build up your fitness gradually and do not overdo things. Not all insurance policies will cover mountaineering, scuba diving or motorcycling.

Women's health and pregnancy

[Insert details.]

Chronic disease and other health problems

Chronic disease is not an absolute bar to travel abroad but you must take expert advice before going abroad.

Some vaccines are live and cannot be administered to people with certain auto-immune diseases.

MedicAlert bracelets should be worn and advice sought from the MedicAlert Foundation about taking medication through Customs.

Drugs and medicines should be kept close at hand. Take a list with you of your medicines with their generic names so that in the event of loss or damage to drugs you should be able to replace them. Take a good supply of your drugs, together with syringes and needles. It may be wise to obtain a doctor's letter and to declare these and explain why they are needed at the Security gates if they are carried as hand luggage, or to place them in the luggage in the hold and again declare their existence when checking in the bags.

Special rules for diabetic patients

[Insert details.]

Rules for flying long distances

Avoid alcohol and wear comfortable loose-fitting clothes. See also the sections on DVT and jet lag.

The returning traveller

On your return if you experience any unusual symptoms see your doctor immediately.

Diarrhoea is frequent among returning travellers. Sometimes this is caused by parasites. If the diarrhoea lasts for 48 hours and you have a high fever then you must seek urgent medical help and ask for tests to be carried out.

A skin rash may be caused by sunburn but it could also indicate a more serious condition such as adverse drug reaction or typhoid, dengue fever, etc.

PRECEDENT 4U: Lavatory breaks

When you take lavatory breaks during the course of your working day, you are required to report to Central Office at the time of starting and finishing the break. This is required for safety reasons so that management knows where you can be located in the case of any emergency or safety issue.

PRECEDENT 4V: Sample risk assessment for domiciliary visits

Description of work activity or danger: *Potential violence when carrying out community or home visits.*	People exposed to risk:	
Department:	Location:	
Risk assessment carried out by:	Date completed:	Review date:
Main risks and issues of concern	Tick if this applies	Assess whether the degree of risk is high, medium or low
Do staff carry out visits in high-risk locations (for example, areas with high crime rates)? Do staff carry out visits in isolated rural areas? Do staff visit unfamiliar clients or relatives? Do staff visit a high-risk or unstable or unpredictable client group? Do staff carry out visits during unsocial hours? Do you use staff who are new or inexperienced in community work? Do you use staff easily identifiable as healthcare workers (for example, those who wear uniforms)? Do staff carry valuables or drugs? Others (please give details):		

Existing control measures – Tick if these are in place	
Do you assess new clients in a health centre or clinic? Do you provide accompanied visits when there are concerns about safety? Do you include potential or known risk factors in referral documents and care plans? Do you share risk information with other professionals and agencies? Are there systems for monitoring staff whereabouts and movements and for regularly reporting to base? Others (please give details):	Have you issued personal attack alarms? Do staff use mobile phones? Do staff have information and training on basic personal safety? Are staff trained in strategies for preventing and managing violence? Do staff carry forms for reporting incidents or near misses and appreciate the need for this procedure? Others (please give details):
Are the existing control measures adequate?	Yes/No
If 'no', what modifications or additional actions are necessary? 1 2 3 4	

PRECEDENT 4W: Sample risk assessment for working alone in buildings

Description of work activity or danger: *Working alone in buildings.*	People exposed to risk:	
Department:	Location:	
Risk assessment carried out by:	Date completed:	Review date:
Main risks and issues of concern	Tick if this applies	Assess whether the degree of risk is high, medium or low
Do staff work alone? Do staff work outside normal office hours? Do staff meet with clients or patients in isolated locations? Is there enough security provision? Is there poor access to the building? Is there first aid available if staff become ill or injured? Do staff activities involve working in confined spaces? Do staff activities involve handling dangerous substances? Others (please give details):		

Existing control measures – Tick if these are in place	
Do you provide joint working for high-risk activities (in other works, in confined spaces and with dangerous substances)? Do you use closed-circuit television within or around the building? Do you use entrance security systems (for example, digilocks or swipe cards)? Is there security lighting around access points and parking areas? Have you installed panic buttons linked to manned locations? Do you use reporting checking-in systems? Others (please give details):	Do you carry out regular supervisor or colleague checks during activities? Do you use two-way radios or other communication systems? Do staff have information and training on basic personal safety? Are staff trained in strategies for preventing and managing violence? Do staff have access to forms for reporting incidents or near misses and appreciate the need for this procedure? Others (please give details):
Are the existing control measures adequate?	Yes/No
If 'no', what modifications or additional actions are necessary? 1 2 3 4	

PRECEDENT 4X: Guidance for outdoor and peripatetic workers

General statement

Where employees are required to work outdoors or at locations away from their normal base, the Company will ensure that, so far as is reasonably practicable, all steps are taken to ensure their safety and health.

It will be the duty of the employee to carry out the activities in the way which the risk assessment has shown to be best, to control the risk and to comply with any safe systems of work and standard operating procedures. Where there is any doubt about the employee's ability to work to these agreed methods, owing to the nature of the particular location of the activity, work should not commence until the situation has been reported to and reviewed by [insert details] and a specific system of work has been prepared.

Arrangements for securing the health and safety of workers

Planning

Prior to commencement of any outdoor activity, the site will be visited and inspected to identify any particular hazards to which the employee(s) may be exposed and any conditions which may necessitate modification of any standard operating procedures or specific risk assessment.

Where the site is under the control of another party, this party's relevant risk assessments will be reviewed and an agreed method statement will be prepared.

Assessment

All risks associated with work activities will be assessed, appropriate control measures will be developed and safe systems of work will be prepared.

Training

Any employee required to work outdoors or at the premises of a third party will not only be instructed in the appropriate safe systems of work and risk assessments associated with the activity, but will also be informed of any specific requirements for procedures and precautions relevant to the conditions in which the work will be carried out, e.g. hazards in a third party's workplace, climatic conditions, site accessibility, etc.

Control

On arrival at any site under the control of a third party, the employee must report to a responsible person, e.g. a safety adviser, to ensure familiarisation with safety precautions relating to that site and the activities being carried on there. Should there be no person in a position to provide such a briefing the employee should contact their supervisor for further instructions. Work should not commence until an appropriate briefing has taken place. If, during the period of the work, the conditions change or any aspect of the task alters in such a way as to affect the degree of risk, work should stop, unless doing so presents a greater risk, and the supervisor should be contacted to agree any additional control measures which may be necessary.

Personal protective equipment (PPE)

Where the need for PPE has been identified by the risk assessment for the activities being carried out or can be reasonably foreseen prior to arrival at site, this will be provided. Where there is a requirement for specialised equipment related to a third party's activities, this should be identified at the planning stage and be supplied by the party in control of the site.

First aid

Where employees regularly work away from their base, portable first aid kits will be provided by the Company. Where work is being carried out at the premises of a third party, employees should ensure that they are made familiar with the first aid arrangements applicable there and should follow these.

Accidents

Any accidents to employees working away from their base must be reported directly to their manager or supervisor. In addition, accidents occurring on a third party's site should be reported in accordance with the local arrangements applying at that site.

Transport

Outdoor and peripatetic workers driving either a Company vehicle or their own vehicle on Company business must have a valid driving licence which will be inspected annually by their supervisor. Any changes which may affect the employee's ability to drive, e.g. certain health conditions or conviction or prosecution for driving offences, must be reported to a responsible person.

Children

Under no circumstances are employees working outdoors or at other locations to be accompanied by any children or other unauthorised persons.

Reporting procedures

Where an employee experiences problems in relation to outdoor and peripatetic work, they should inform a responsible person immediately, so that the Company can investigate and rectify the situation.

Safe system of work

The risks to the outdoor worker and others who may be present can be eliminated or reduced by careful preparation and planning of the activity. In particular, the following precautions should be taken.

1. Devote sufficient time at the planning stage to ensure that all potential problems have been anticipated.
2. Ensure that all parties with control over the activities and the place of work are involved in the planning. Outside, expert advice may be required in certain instances.
3. If a risk assessment has not already been carried out, ensure that this is completed.
4. Provide the employee(s) with appropriate training.
5. Take all necessary precautions to prevent injury.
6. Employees must report to the responsible person when the site is under another party's control.
7. When working alone ensure that the employee's whereabouts are known and arrange for contact to be made at intervals.
8. When others may be present, ensure that they are informed of the activities.
9. Ensure that first aid facilities are available.
10. Children and other unauthorised persons must not be allowed to accompany the employee on site.

Summary policy statement

Outdoor work and work at changing locations pose special problems with regard to identification of hazards and control of workplace risks. To ensure that such employees are not exposed to unnecessary or excessive risk, the standards which the Company would apply to activities in locations under its direct control must be reviewed, where appropriate in association with any other parties involved, to ensure that allowance is made for any additional hazards which arise due to the location itself or any changes in degree of risk resulting from essential changes to the way of working.

APPENDIX I – Cell (mobile) phone usage

The Company policy is that you should:

1. Keep calls short.
2. Use landlines where possible.
3. Limit the number of calls using cell phones.
4. Where possible, keep the phone as far away from the body/ear/head as possible.

The Company will monitor research developments concerning cell phones.

Distractions

There is some evidence that where high levels of concentration are required, the use of cell phones can cause accidents. Driving is a prime example. The Royal Society of

Accidents believes that there have only been a handful of cases involving road deaths in which cell phones were involved.

- You must exercise proper control of your vehicle at all times.
- Switch off the cell phone before starting the engine.
- Never make or receive calls whilst driving. It is a criminal offence to use a hand-held device or mobile telephone while driving, and even if you use Bluetooth and an earpiece or a hands-free kit, it is still distracting to conduct a conversation by telephone.
- Check messages and deal with calls when you are parked.
- You must not stop on the hard shoulder of a motorway to answer or make a call, except in an emergency.
- The Highway Code carries specific advice and guidance for drivers about the use of cell phones. Ensure you know what it is.
- Do not make or receive calls during other activities of high concentration when you might be a danger to yourself or others, such as climbing scaffolding.
- Do not use machinery when using a cell phone.
- When walking, do not try to cross roads during calls. Stop on the pavement.

Interference

There are instances when the use of a cell phone interferes with other sensitive electronic equipment, e.g. monitors in hospital, pacemakers and aircraft systems. You should switch phones off before entering an area where the use of the phone might interfere with sensitive electronic equipment and remove the battery on board aircraft.

Explosions

The electrical energy within mobile phones is sufficient to ignite chemical and petrol fumes and the frequency to ignite explosives.

- Observe 'Turn off two-way radio' signs, such as those near stores of fuel, chemicals or explosives.
- Switch off mobile phones at refuelling points, e.g. petrol stations even if you are not refuelling your car.
- Do not carry or store flammable or explosive materials in the same compartment as a cell phone.

APPENDIX II – *Prevention of deep vein thrombosis*

Deep vein thrombosis (DVT) is a condition that can occur when individuals are sitting in confined positions for extended periods, e.g. long-haul flights. DVT can result in death. It is caused by the formation of a blood clot within a deep vein, usually the thigh or calf. It can be caused by poor blood circulation due to problems such as heart disease, a recent stroke, heart attack, varicose veins or from prolonged inactivity.

Those most at risk include the elderly, the very overweight, pregnant women, heavy smokers, coronary disease sufferers and those whose feet do not touch the floor when sitting in aircraft seats. Passengers travelling economy class are more susceptible to DVT because leg movement is restricted due to lack of space between seats.

The symptoms include pain and swelling in the areas drained by the vein where the blood clot is located, rapid heartbeat, sudden and unexplained coughing, pain in the joints and a high temperature.

Prevention is simple:

- Keep lower limbs moving.
- Avoid long static positions.

5

Salary package and other financial terms and benefits

5.1 Basic salary terms

Since to most employees the terms concerning their salary package are the most important to them, it is vital to ensure that the wording of the salary and remuneration terms are absolutely accurate and clear.

The statutory particulars which are required must set out the scale or rate of remuneration or the method of calculating it and the pay intervals. Any additional allowances also need to be spelt out, including whether they count as pensionable pay or not.

Whilst it is common to quote the salary in the offer letter, there have been occasions where the wrong figure has been stated. It may therefore be safer to cite the salary in the main principal statement/service agreement with the overriding clause that any earlier agreements concerning terms and conditions are superseded by the agreement.

5.2 Salary reviews

It is normal to review salaries annually, but it is important to make it clear that reviews do not necessarily mean increases and that in some cases it could mean that the salary decreases. However, it may be safer to say nothing in the contract about salary increases because of the trend now to argue that any discretion reserved to the employer cannot be exercised in an 'arbitrary, capricious or irrational manner' (see *Clark* v. *Nomura International plc* [2000] IRLR 766).

Some employees may believe that if their employer awards them a salary increase year after year and then in one year awards them nothing, this will be a breach of an implied term that they will receive a pay increase each year. This is not the case where the employer has made no reference to any pay increase in the contract. Such conduct by an employer will not create an implied term in such a case. In *Murco Petroleum Ltd* v. *Forge* [1987] IRLR 50, the EAT held:

> Where a contract of employment makes no reference whatsoever to pay increases it is impossible to say that there is an implied term in the contract that there will always be a pay rise. An implied contractual obligation to increase pay is not part of the industrial structure and neither employers nor unions would wish it to be so. Whilst

for the last 25 years annual pay increases have been a pattern of life in the industrial field, that is not the same as saying that they are built into the contract.

However, it may be the case that even where there is no reference to a pay increase in the contract, the courts may consider an argument that the employer's conduct in a particular case was 'arbitrary, capricious and irrational'. The *Murco* case suggested such an approach. The EAT went on to hold:

> The Industrial Tribunal had also misdirected themselves in failing to consider whether, in not awarding the respondent a pay increase, the employers had acted arbitrarily or capriciously so as to be in breach of the implied duty of mutual trust and confidence as set out by the EAT in *Robinson* v. *Crompton Parkinson Ltd* [1978] IRLR 61 and *FC Gardner Ltd* v. *Beresford* [1978] IRLR 63. Had they done so they would have found it impossible to find that the employers' action was entirely arbitrary or capricious.

If the contract is clear that salary increases are entirely discretionary, then that is how the contract must be construed and it cannot be construed as giving a right to a pay increase subject to satisfactory performance.

In *The Equality & Human Rights Commission* v. *Earle* UKEAT/0011/14/MC the EAT overturned the Employment Tribunal's decision (applying *Autoclenz* v. *Belcher* and *Commerzbank* v. *Keen*), holding that the parties could not overrule a discretion contractually agreed.

Daniel Barnett's Employment Bulletin sets out the case brilliantly (see **www.danielbarnett.co.uk/site/blog/employment-blog/construction-of-salary-increase-clause-in-contract.html**):

> The Claimant was employed by the Respondent as a senior legal policy adviser. The parties' written contract gave a base starting salary and a higher figure representing the top salary for the position with a chart including five points showing an incremental rise from base to top salary.
>
> Clause 5.3 provided for annual salary review with the possibility of increase on assessment of the previous year's performance but providing no obligation on the Respondent to increase salary.
> [It read that:
> 'Progression through the salary range will be reviewed annually on or around 1 October in each year until the maximum of the range for your role has been reached. Any progression review will include an assessment of your performance during the preceding 12 months. There is no obligation on the EHRC to increase the level of your basic salary at a review. Any increase awarded in one year will not create any right or entitlement or set any precedent in relation to subsequent years.']
>
> The employment tribunal found one of the Respondent's staff authorised to discuss salaries assured the Claimant her salary would increase yearly subject to satisfactory performance. The employment tribunal found this to be a contractual arrangement relying on *Atrill* v. *Dresdner Kleinwort* rather than 'puff'.

The respondent (employer) appealed against the finding that it had broken the terms of the contract by not reviewing the claimant's performance and as a result not giving her incremental pay rises. Appeal was allowed and the decision was set aside.

5.3   Bonus schemes and bonus payments

Many employers in the financial sector offer bonuses – guaranteed for new employees in their first year as they may have resigned from their previous employment in advance of a bonus payment date and therefore would lose their bonus from that employment. If this is the case, then a carefully drafted term in the offer letter or contract is essential.

In other cases employers may wish to reserve to themselves the discretion as to whether or not to pay a bonus and, if so, the amount.

The rules of most discretionary bonus schemes require the employee not to be under notice of termination (save for redundancy) or under any live disciplinary warning on the bonus payment date to become eligible for the annual bonus. If the wording is clear the courts will uphold those terms and will not make any finding in favour of the employee/claimant.

Some employers require employees to keep their bonus number and the fact that they have been awarded a bonus strictly confidential. Such a clause can be found at **Precedent 5D**.

Equality Act and 'gagging' clauses

The Equality Act 2010 did not ban pay secrecy or 'gagging' clauses.

Section 77 of the Equality Act 2010 makes void any clauses in contracts that seek to penalise the employee who makes or solicits a 'relevant pay disclosure' when seeking information as to whether, and if so to what extent, they have been discriminated against because of any of the protected characteristics, e.g. sex, race, pregnancy or maternity, etc.

These clauses have been referred to as secrecy clauses seeking to 'gag' staff from discussing their salary or bonus payment when, for example, a woman is seeking pay information in an equal pay dispute.

Discretionary bonus

The wording of a discretionary bonus has to be extremely careful. Any reference to 'entitlement', payments becoming 'due', or words such as 'will' be paid, etc. may render void any attempt to make the bonus discretionary. Suitable wording for a discretionary bonus is shown in **Precedent 5E** and in the following extract from an executive's contract:

> The Executive may receive a bonus as the Board may in its absolute discretion determine from time to time. Payment of any bonus for any year will not confer on the Executive any right to be paid a Bonus in the following year or years. Any payments are conditional upon the Board being satisfied with the Executive's performance and conduct up to the date of payment. [Initial bonus arrangements for the Executive are set out in Schedule 2 to this Service Agreement.] Unless expressly agreed in writing with the Executive, no payment will be made if, on the payment date, the Executive has given or been given notice of termination of employment or is no longer employed by the Company. Any bonus payments made to the Executive are non-pensionable and are subject to PAYE deductions.

However, an employer does not have unfettered discretion when considering to award a discretionary bonus. Mr Justice Burton, in *Clark* v. *Nomura International plc* [2000] IRLR 766, held that:

An employer exercising a discretion which on the face of the contract of employment is unfettered or absolute, will be in breach of contract if no reasonable employer would have exercised the discretion in that way. This test of irrationality or perversity is simpler to understand and apply than the test of capriciousness, which can carry with it aspects of arbitrariness or domineeringness, or whimsicality and abstractedness.

On the other hand, the concept of an obligation on an employer to act reasonably in the exercise of its discretion is too low a test and suggests that the court could simply substitute its own view for that of the employer. In applying a test of perversity or irrationality, the court does not substitute its own view but asks the question whether any reasonable employer could have come to such a conclusion.

The courts appear reluctant to favour the banks when they seek to avoid paying a bonus despite calling it discretionary.

In *Khatri* v. *Cooperatieve Centrale Raiffeisen-Boerenleenbank BA* [2010] IRLR 715, the Court construed a bonus clause in a contract in its ordinary and natural meaning and refused to allow the words of entitlement to be nullified by a short phrase at the end of the bonus clause which stated that the bonus scheme could be withdrawn 'at any time'. (My thanks to Alex Kleanthous of Gannons Solicitors, who acted for Mr Khatri and who sent me details of this decision.) The Court held that the words giving entire discretion to the bank had to be clear and unambiguous and not, as the Court found, giving with one hand and taking away with another.

The bank in this case sought to vary unilaterally the terms of the bonus agreed by the parties (see below) by re-drafting the bonus term thus:

> any future applicable bonuses are made entirely at the discretion of the bank on the basis of your financial and managerial performance viewed across Rabobank International.

Further, under the heading 'Discretionary Bonus' (following a guaranteed bonus) the unilaterally varied terms stated:

> For future calendar years you will also be eligible to participate in the Bank's annual discretionary performance related bonus scheme. This scheme will vary from year to year. Bonuses are made entirely at the discretion of the Bank, on the basis of a number of factors including your individual performance, the performance of the business area in which you work and the performance of the Bank.
>
> For clarification please note that following the closure of the London Desk, the formula driven bonus relating to this desk will cease with immediate effect and you will be eligible to participate in the discretionary bonus for 2008.

The revised terms also stated that 'Any payment due will be made at the time the Bank makes its annual performance bonus payment but in any event no later than 31 March in the year following the performance year for which you are being awarded'.

The employee concerned refused to accept these revised terms and continued to work under the former terms. He made large profits for the Bank.

The bonus terms found to have been agreed between the parties were these:

> You will also be eligible to receive a performance related bonus from the Bank, subject to your individual revenue generation. Any payment due will be made at the time the Bank makes its annual performance bonus payment but in any event no later

than 31 March in the year following the performance year for which you are being awarded (i.e. 31 March 2009 in respect of 2008). The formula used to calculate the bonus due to you will be as follows and will be calculated for 2008:

%	Threshold	Total Revenues (net of brokerage fees)
0%		€550,000
12%	€550,000	€551,000

12% will be linked to your individual performance providing the individual total revenue threshold of €550,000 has been reached.

The above table is applicable to your 2008 bonus. The Bank maintains the right to review or remove this formula linked bonus arrangement at any time.

Mr Khatri's book had made severe losses in July but was very profitable in September and October, wiping out the losses, and by the end of the year was about €16 million in profit.

He was then dismissed by reason of redundancy and was not paid any bonus. He sued for this bonus.

The Court of Appeal held that the guaranteed bonus was for a fixed sum and the other bonus depended upon 'performance'.

The court held that the words 'in the year following the performance year for which you are being awarded' were clearly speaking of a performance-related bonus being applicable on a yearly basis. The language was one of 'entitlement', i.e. 'you will also be eligible'; 'the formula used to calculate the bonus due'; 'all payments due to you'.

The court rejected the view that these entitlements could be taken away by the words 'at any time' at the end of the clause.

The court interpreted the bonus clause as 'this bonus formula applies for this year; but it may all be different next year'.

It held that:

> If the bank was really intending to say that the 2008 bonus remained discretionary with only an initial expectation of calculation according to the formula, three little words at the end was not the way to convey that to the employee or to the reasonable reader...
>
> Accordingly I conclude that the contract did confer on the claimant a right to a bonus according to the formula.

The Court of Appeal stated that it had 'no regret' in making this finding because if the bank wanted to reward its employees with 'purely discretionary bonuses then they should say so openly and not seek to dress up such a bonus with the language of entitlement qualified by a slight phrase which does not make it absolutely clear that there is in fact no entitlement at all. If you are to give with one hand and take away with the other, you must make that clear' (para.39).

Furthermore, the courts will not imply a term that in order to become eligible for a bonus the employee must be employed and not under notice on bonus payment date. This has to be expressly stated.

In *Rutherford* v. *Seymour Pierce Ltd* [2010] EWHC 375 (QB) the High Court refused to imply such a term so as to disentitle Mr Seymour from the bonuses that he had earned before he was (unlawfully) summarily dismissed.

Mr Seymour's contract only referred to a bonus in this way:

> On satisfactory completion of your probationary period you will be eligible to participate in the Company's discretionary bonus scheme. Any bonus payments or amendments made to the scheme are at the discretion of the Company.

The High Court cited *Clark* v. *Nomura International plc*, saying that (para.74):

> The fact that Mr Rutherford had been summarily dismissed was not of itself a reason to conclude that he was not eligible for a bonus. Otherwise, as I have said (and Burton J said in *Nomura*), unscrupulous employers could sack an employee the day before the bonus was due to be distributed and then say that, as a matter of principle, the employee was not entitled to be considered for a bonus. Of course, whether or not Mr Rutherford was entitled actually to be paid a bonus was a different question . . .

If the employer wanted such a term then this must be expressly stated in the bonus term of the contract such as:

> Any bonus payment is entirely at the discretion of the employer and payment or an award of a bonus one year does not create any right or entitlement to a bonus in any other year.
>
> Furthermore no bonus will become payable if the employee is under notice (whomsoever gave notice) or has left the employment on bonus payment day, i.e. the day that the bonus is actually paid.

Where dismissals have been effected without notice in circumstances where this is a breach of contract, thereby depriving the employee of the bonus as they are not in employment on the bonus payment date, the Courts will award the bonus on the basis of a breach of contract.

In *Locke* v. *Candy and Candy Ltd* [2011] IRLR 163 the Court of Appeal again held that to imply such a term would have been manifestly unreasonable because it would allow an employer to dismiss summarily an employee the day before bonus payment day in order solely to avoid paying the bonus.

No pro rata bonuses

Further High Court litigation has confirmed that no pro rata bonuses become due if the employee leaves employment, for whatever reason, during the course of the bonus year.

There is also no entitlement to a pro rata bonus. If the terms of the bonus scheme require employment on bonus payment day, the Courts will not determine that a pro rata bonus falls due if the employee leaves partway through the year.

UCTA?

It might have been thought that such draconian rules depriving an employee of the whole of their bonus were unreasonable and contrary to UCTA but this is not the case. The Court of Appeal ruled unequivocally in *Commerzbank AG* v. *Keen* [2006] EWCA Civ 1536 that UCTA does not render a term unreasonable in a contract of employment.

Section 3 of UCTA 'applies as between contracting parties where one of them deals as consumer or on the other's written standard terms of business'. In *Brigden* v. *American Express Bank* [2000] IRLR 94, it was suggested that UCTA could apply where the contractual term allows the employer to render performance substantially different from that expected.

In *Commerzbank AG* v. *Keen*, the Court of Appeal held that an employee is not dealing with their employers 'as consumer' in contracting with it in respect of pay for work. Nor does an employee deal with their employers on its 'written standard terms of business', the business, in this case, being banking.

Mr Keen alleged that the bank had breached his contract in relation to the calculation of a bonus. The contract provided that no bonus would be awarded if the employee was no longer in employment. That related to 2005.

The employee was awarded bonuses of almost €3m for the years 2003 and 2004, but as this was less than the recommendation of his line manager, he also claimed that he was entitled to more.

The Court of Appeal struck out the claim, making it clear that the courts are unwilling to get involved in adjudicating on the size of City bonuses.

Although cases such as *Clark* v. *Nomura International plc* [2000] IRLR 766 and *Horkulak* v. *Cantor Fitzgerald* [2004] IRLR 942 have established that it is a breach of contract for an employer to exercise its discretion to award a bonus payment in an 'arbitrary, capricious or irrational' manner, Lord Justice Mummery in *Keen* held that (para.59):

> The burden of establishing that no rational bank in the City would have paid him a bonus of less than his line manager recommended is a very high one. It would require an overwhelming case to persuade the court to find that the level of a discretionary bonus payment was irrational or perverse in an area where so much must depend on the discretionary judgment of the Bank in fluctuating market and labour conditions.

Discretionary bonuses are therefore what they say, with the courts only being prepared to adjudicate on them when little or no bonus is paid (where the other conditions for eligibility are met such as being in employment and not under notice on bonus payment day) and the decision is plainly 'irrational', i.e. having no rational basis (not unreasonable), 'capricious or arbitrary'.

Some contracts merely provide for the payment of a bonus 'at the entire discretion of the employer'. Others define in some way what factors will count for the determination of bonus such as individual performance in terms of profit & loss (P&L); effective management duties; overall performance of the team/department/bank, seat value, replacement value, etc.

The written criteria are essential in order to justify a difference in bonus pay or other payments where an equal pay claim is made (paras.30–32 of the Equality and Human Rights Commission's 'Equal pay – Statutory Code of Practice' (8 March 2016)).

Challenging the size of the bonus

Challenging the size of the bonus will not be a matter with which the courts will normally interfere. In the case of *Kennedy* v. *Dresdner Kleinwort Wasserstein*

[2004] EWHC 1103 (Comm) the court refused to interfere with the employer's decision on the size of the bonus once the court was satisfied that the employer had applied the correct formula to determine the bonus.

Contrast that case with that of *Fish v. Dresdner Kleinwort Ltd; Hatzistefanis v. Dresdner Kleinwort Ltd* [2009] IRLR 1035 where the employees had complied with the term of the contract and the employer had irrationally and arbitrarily refused to apply the contractual term and pay the bonus that had become due. Here the court made a bold decision.

In the case of *Fish*, five senior banking executives claimed substantial bonuses and severance payments, each in excess of €1 million. Their employment was terminated after the investment bank incurred massive losses during the banking crisis. Their contracts provided that they 'shall at all times act in the best interests of' their employer.

It was contended that in accordance with this term, and with the implied duty of good faith owed by the claimants, they were required to waive their contractual entitlement to payment of the sums in question. Since it was not contended that the claimants had acted in breach of their contracts in the way in which they fulfilled their management functions, this was certainly one of the bolder submissions of 2009.

It was given short shrift by Mr Justice Jack in the Queen's Bench Division. He stated that there is no authority to support the view that either the trust and confidence duty or the employee's duty to act in the best interests of the employer could be deployed to defeat a claim such as in this case.

So far as the latter term was concerned (p.1041):

> That is not a provision that can be used to cut down the express provisions of the agreement for payment of bonus and severance pay. Its effect is that provided the employee continues to act in the best interests of the company he will get those moneys. It is not that if it ceases to be in the best interests of the company to pay those moneys he will not get them.

Nor were the claimants in breach of a fiduciary duty. According to the judge, if an employee in the position of a fiduciary agrees a contractual term with the employer (p.1035):

> there is no principle that provides that if subsequent events make the bargain one which the employer would not have made had he foreseen those events, he may require the fiduciary employee to release him.

If there is any evidence that the employer has dismissed the employee prior to bonus payment date for the primary or sole reason of depriving them of that bonus, the courts have been prepared to award damages for breach of contract on the basis that the employer had acted in 'bad faith' or 'capriciously' (*Clark v. BET plc* [1997] IRLR 348).

The decision in *GX Networks Ltd v. Greenland* [2010] EWCA Civ 784 shows how important it is for employers to draft bonus schemes carefully to place a cap on any bonus or commission payments.

If an employer seeks to depart from the formula for paying a bonus or commission because of 'exceptional' circumstances then there must be exceptional circumstances before departing from that formula.

In *GX Networks Ltd* v. *Greenland* the terms of the employer's bonus scheme allowed the employer to make changes to the scheme during the bonus year by either adjusting the targets until the final quarter to ensure that they remained 'challenging but achievable' or adjusting the 'capping' provision of 100 per cent of salary but 'by exception only [requiring] HR and Finance agreement'.

In this case the employer increased the cap to 130 per cent of Ms Greenland's salary in circumstances which she argued (successfully) were not exceptional. She was not prepared to accept the bonus offered (130 per cent of her salary) because she had exceeded her targets by 205 per cent or by a factor of 2.05 and, therefore, according to her, her bonus should have been £163,503 – a difference of £125,523.

The Court of Appeal agreed with Ms Greenland and held that the wording of the capping provision was not clear, and that the proposed cap could only be applied in 'exceptional circumstances' and, even then, an employer must apply its discretion 'fairly' when undertaking such a decision.

Exceptional circumstances might be a very serious financial position or an employee's serious misconduct – which could explain why the reference to the HR and Finance departments was made in the provision.

Points for drafting for a bonus scheme:

- Ensure there is a cap relating to a formula for a bonus, e.g. it cannot exceed a percentage of salary or achievement of targets.
- Any cap must be drafted clearly and appropriately. Clear drafting would be:

    A bonus cannot exceed 150 per cent of your base salary unless this is expressly agreed by the Board.

- The scheme should expressly provide for the employer to be able to adjust targets to deal with changing circumstances.
- An employer should operate a formal review of targets during the year and ensure that if targets need to be changed, i.e. increased (weighing up the disproportionate impact on morale this can have), this is effectively communicated.
- 'Exceptional' circumstances are exceptional, i.e. rare or uncommon, so give some examples, e.g. where profits in one year are significantly less than forecasted.

Holiday pay and bonus payments

Whether one-off bonuses form part of the definition of 'normal pay' for the determination of holiday pay is not clear.

The Court of Appeal in *British Gas Trading Ltd* v. *Lock* [2016] EWCA Civ 983 refused to consider whether, for example, a one-off single results-based bonus payment for a senior executive also fell within the definition of 'normal remuneration' in Article 7 of the Working Time Directive, to be included in that executive's holiday pay. Sir Colin Rimer stated:

In the course of the argument, there was some discussion about how a conforming interpretation of the WTR might apply to different types of case.

The court was, for example, exercised by the case of the salaried banker who receives a single, large results-based annual bonus in, say, March. Is he entitled on his summer holiday to leave pay including an element referable to his bonus? And how does or ought the WTR deal with the type of worker who is employed on terms like Mr Lock but who only becomes entitled to commission at the point in the year when a particular level of turnover, profit or other threshold is reached, which may mean that he receives no commission for some months of each year? Other types of case will raise other questions.

My response to questions such as these – and to others covering other situations – is that nothing in this judgment is intended to answer them. It is no part of this court's function to do more than to deal with the instant appeal. In the case of the banker example, there may indeed be a question as to what his 'normal remuneration' is, and whether its calculation ought to reflect the fact of his annual bonus and, if so, how. There may also be questions as to what, in any particular case, is the appropriate reference period for the calculation of the pay. I say nothing about any of that.

Repayable bonus

In some cases employers provide for a repayable bonus, either if the employee leaves within a fixed period (e.g. one to five years) or if they are dismissed for gross misconduct.

An interesting question that has arisen is, what tax can the employee claim back, if any, and what should the employer claw back – the gross or net amount?

The answer appears to be that the employer should draft the repayment clause and reclaim or be repaid the gross amount and not just the net amount.

A typical clause can be found in **Precedent 5F(ii)**.

Income tax issues

The income tax paid on a bonus payment which is later clawed back by an employer can be reclaimed by the taxpayer, i.e. the employee, but only in certain circumstances.

In *The Commissioners for HMRC v. Julian Martin* [2014] UKUT 429 (TCC),[1] Mr Martin entered into an employment contract with JLT Risk Solutions which included a £250,000 'signing bonus' in return for Mr Martin's commitment to remain employed for five years. The bonus was repayable on a time-apportioned basis if the employment relationship ended before the five years.

Mr Martin received the bonus together with his first salary payment, both of which were treated as 'emoluments' subject to income tax and NICs. This resulted in Mr Martin receiving a net bonus of £147,500. One year later, Mr Martin gave JLT formal notice of his intention to resign and, as a result, he

---

[1] My thanks to Nigel Popplewell of Burges Salmon for kindly giving me permission to reproduce this summary and discussion of this case.

became liable to repay £162,500 of the bonus. Mr Martin then brought a claim against HMRC for tax relief on the basis that he was entitled to a repayment of tax.

The dispute centred on whether the signing bonus ceased to be 'earnings' when repaid or whether it became 'negative taxable earnings'. HMRC tried to argue that the repayment was liquidated damages for breach of an implied provision that the employee would not leave before the fifth anniversary of the contract, and therefore not earnings at all.

The First Tier Tribunal accepted that the clawed-back proportion of the bonus should be treated as negative taxable earnings, but disagreed with Mr Martin's argument that this could be offset against the tax liability in the year that the bonus was paid (2005/06). Instead, it must be recognised in the tax year in which repayment was made.

The Upper Tribunal upheld the First Tier Tribunal's decision, agreeing that:

- the full amount of the bonus was taxable when Mr Martin received it on 25 November 2005;
- Mr Martin's earnings in 2005/06 could not be reduced by the payments made to JLT in a subsequent tax year;
- negative earnings should be deductible from any positive earnings in the tax year in which repayment is made. If this results in a negative figure for taxable earnings, relief may be available under s.128 Income Tax Act 2007.

The Upper Tribunal ruled that a payment from an employee to their employer or certain third parties would fall within the category of negative taxable earnings if the payment had 'attributes of positive taxable earning' with suitable adjustments to reflect the fact that payment is flowing in the opposite direction. Very broadly, if a payment would be considered taxable earnings, its repayment would be considered negative taxable earnings.

The UT's decision relied heavily on the contractual arrangement between Mr Martin and JLT:

- The initial payment of £250,000 had been made as consideration for Mr Martin agreeing to enter into the new contract of employment – it was fully taxable in the year that it was originally paid to him and could not be seen as a contingent payment on account.
- The terms of the contract were clear – if Mr Martin left before the fifth anniversary of the entry into the new contract, then he would be liable to repay a proportion of the bonus; the repayment could not be seen as compensation for a repudiatory breach of contract because it was being made in accordance with the explicit terms of the contract.

The tribunal emphasised that the decision was based on the particular contractual terms at issue and a different set of facts could produce a radically different conclusion.

If there had been proper planning when the contract was first put in place, Mr Martin would not have had this argument at all. It is worth employers thinking at the outset about situations in which employees might be asked to make repayments. If the drafting is correct when the contract is first signed there will be no need to rely on a highly fact-specific situation when the repayment actually happens.

5.4   Maternity and bonuses

This is covered in **Chapter 7** on maternity, paternity, adoptive and parental leave.

5.5   Commission payments

Commission payments make up a large part of a sales representative's earnings. Often there is only a very small basic salary and in some cases no basic salary at all. It is therefore very important to draft clearly the terms of the commission payments, how they are earned and when they are earned, and when they become payable.

Holiday pay and commission payments

In the *Lock* decision cited above, the Court of Appeal held that holiday pay must include 'all contractual results-based commission payments' in order to make the words 'payment in respect of periods of leave' in Regulation 16 of the Working Time Regulations 1998 conform with the meaning of Article 7 of the Directive.

The Court of Justice of the European Communities (CJEU) in that case had held that:

> Although the wording of Article 7 of Directive 2003/88 does not give any express indication as regards the remuneration to which a worker is entitled during his annual leave, the Court has already stated that the term 'paid annual leave' in Article 7(1) means that, for the duration of 'annual leave' within the meaning of that directive, remuneration must be maintained and that, in other words, workers must receive their *normal remuneration* for that period of rest.

Commission payments

The difference between a contract that specifically provides for no payment of commission after termination of employment and one that does not, has led to diametrically opposed decisions and results for the salespeople concerned in the case. If the contract sets out in writing, clearly and unambiguously, that 'the employee has no claim for any commission payments whatsoever that would otherwise have been generated and paid, if he or she is not in employment on the date when such payments would normally have been paid', then once the employment has terminated, the employee will not be eligible to receive any further payments.

In *Peninsula Business Services Ltd* v. *Sweeney* [2004] IRLR 49, Mr Sweeney was offered just such an agreement, as a sales executive. He signed a contract which made reference to a staff handbook. In Section A, it provided for 'commission payments at the end of the calendar month following payment by the customer of 25 per cent of the fee'. Section B of the handbook contained the commission scheme rules which included the rule that an employee was excluded from receiving any commission once they had left employment.

Mr Sweeney resigned and was owed a considerable amount of commission. Many of the respondents' clients agreed to a three-year contract but paid in 36 monthly instalments. He therefore argued that he was owed the outstanding commission on those contracts either as a debt under the contract or as damages for breach of contract. The Employment Tribunal agreed with Mr Sweeney, holding that the clause in Section B of the handbook either was not incorporated into his contract or was unlawful under UCTA, s.3(2).

The EAT disagreed and overturned the Employment Tribunal's decision. It held that where a clause was written fairly and clearly in unambiguous language which needed no interpretation or explanation from a lawyer and the employee signed those terms, those terms became binding upon that employee even where the employee had not read them carefully at the time of signing nor fully comprehended their effect or impact.

As regards the argument that the commission term was void under UCTA, the EAT rejected this. It said that the commission clause was not of a 'penal and confiscatory nature', and therefore was not a clause to which UCTA, s.3(2)(b) applied. The clause in question was one that set out the applicant's entitlement and the limits of his rights. From the moment the applicant signed the commission document, he could have had no expectation of being paid post-termination commission. Since that was the case, there was no question of reasonableness otherwise arising. Section 3(2)(b) only arose where the clause purported to entitle the employers to render a contractual performance substantially different from that which was reasonably expected of them, or to render no performance at all in respect of any part of their contractual obligations.

Finally, Mr Sweeney's argument that the clause providing for no payment of commission after termination amounted to an unlawful restraint of trade, also failed. The fact that the clause was in part designed to provide an economic disincentive or discouragement to established salespeople from leaving their employment and working elsewhere did not turn the clause into a contract in restraint of trade.

His contract did not impose any restraint on Mr Sweeney as to whom he might work for or what he might do after leaving his employment. It could not seriously be argued, therefore, that the commission penalty which he suffered on resignation arose under a contractual term involving an unlawful restraint of trade.

The EAT held that:

(a) Mr Sweeney was not entitled to commission payments after his employment had ended;

(b) the clause in question was incorporated into his contract;
(c) the clause was not unduly onerous and therefore the *Interfoto* principle (which requires employers who seek to rely upon a clause which is unduly onerous to show that they have first reasonably and fairly brought the clause to the attention of the employee) played no part in this case.

In contrast, in *Brand v. Compro Computer Services Ltd* [2004] EWCA Civ 204, the Court of Appeal upheld the claimant's claim for commission payments payable after his termination of employment. It upheld his claim on the grounds that it was clear from the language of the contract and the commission scheme that the applicant was entitled to commission after the date of termination relating to commission earned before that date. One of the relevant conditions was the completion of timesheets and this the applicant had done.

5.6   Share options/stock options

Offering share and stock options is another form of benefit granted to senior staff and those in the financial sector. There are strict HMRC rules about how long the employee must be employed before shares are permitted to vest, etc. In some companies, part of the bonus is granted by way of share options as a way of tying the employee in to that employer. See **Precedent 5G**.

Share dealings

Directors are required to comply with complex rules preventing the use of insider information. Insider dealing is a criminal offence, prohibited under the Companies Act 1985 and Criminal Justice Act 1993. It happens when individuals use, or encourage others to use, information about a company which is not generally available (which they have obtained through inside knowledge or contacts), to deal for their own profit. The law applies to transactions on the Stock Exchange and to off-market trading. The Stock Exchange has its own rules reinforcing the law on insider dealing.

A typical clause concerning dealing with shares can be found at **Precedent 5H**.

Change of control

In the event of a change of control of the company, it is common to see in the contract a clause in the form shown in **Precedent 5I**.

5.7   Car or car allowance

A car or car allowance may be given to an employee either as a work car or as a 'perk' car. It is important to make it clear into which category the car falls. Those given company vehicles (e.g. a van) will also be under strict rules as to how to handle and maintain the vehicle. See **Precedent 5J**.

Alcohol, fatigue, bad weather and parking offences

There is a need to spell out what rules are in force regarding company car (and personal car) users and the drinking of alcohol. The safest rule is to ban employees from drinking any alcohol when driving the company car/vehicle. Employees also need to be warned about the dangers of driving in bad weather or dangerous road conditions and what alternatives they have. Model policies can be found in **Precedent 5K**.

Driving whilst fatigued is also something that needs to be addressed in the rules of the car policy. The Royal Society for the Prevention of Accidents (RoSPA) has produced a factsheet, *Driver Fatigue and Road Accidents* (June 2011), and a useful checklist appears in it under the heading 'Employers' (see **www.rospa.com**).

Maternity and company cars

This is covered in **Chapter 7**.

5.8 Pension and life assurance

Legislation that came into effect on 30 June 2012 requires all employers in the UK automatically to enrol eligible workers in a pension scheme and pay mandatory minimum contributions. A jobholder who has been auto-enrolled has the right to opt out of scheme membership, but if they remain an active member their employer is required to make minimum pension contributions on their behalf.

Implementation of the new employer duties was staged month by month over a five-and-a-half year period that started on 1 October 2012, with employers separated into bands according to their payroll size.

With certain exceptions, a worker cannot bring a claim in an Employment Tribunal if their employer does not comply with these duties. Instead, the Pensions Regulator was given the role of overseeing the introduction of auto-enrolment.

It is now less common for employers to offer occupational pension schemes on a defined final salary basis. If there is a pension scheme as part of the contractual package, then it is often common to offer a death-in-service benefit of up to four times the annual salary.

5.9 Private health cover

Private health cover is a valuable benefit provided as a group scheme. The terms of a contract are normally in the form shown in **Precedent 5M**.

It may be wise to advise an employee who is leaving, but before they leave, to contact the person at the insurance provider dealing with the group cover, to ask for private cover (if they do not join another employer with private health insurance). The cover would be on the basis of continuous cover (not being regarded as a new member). In that way, all pre-existing medical conditions of the employee and their family will continue to be covered.

5.10 Other allowances

Some employees in certain occupations are required to wear uniforms or protective clothing and equipment and are given an allowance for such items. In other cases when employees are asked to deputise for a more senior manager, they are paid an additional allowance.

Deputising

Deputising may be defined as 'temporary employment in a higher grade or pay band other than through normal promotion'. It normally occurs where a more senior manager is long-term sick or absent for reasons not relating to their normal duties. Rather than sharing the manager's duties among other members of staff or merely waiting for the manager to return to work, one person is given the manager's duties until they return. See **Precedent 5N**.

Shoe and stocking allowance

For a clause providing a shoe and stocking allowance see **Precedent 5O**.

5.11 Expenses

Where expenses are incurred as wholly necessary for the purposes of employment, then they may be reimbursed. Generally, business expenses include travel, overnight and subsistence allowances as well as for entertaining clients. There may be occasions where it would be sensible for the employee to sit down with a manager to agree the categories of expenses allowable and the expenses limit, and to go through the itinerary in some detail.

In some cases where less senior staff are sent abroad on behalf of the employer, it may be necessary to spell out in some detail what expenses would be legitimate. There have been cases where individuals have been sent abroad to obtain new business for the company and it has been discovered that the individual has 'tacked on' skiing trips and the like, or has taken days out of the trip to go skiing. Skiing equipment, lost watches, upgrades of air tickets and entertaining skiing friends have either appeared on the company expenses claims form or have been 'covered up' as legitimate business expenses. The individuals involved often feign ignorance!

For example, company expenses that will not normally be paid for include:

(a) consumption of alcohol or consumption at a bar (either personal or for others) other than reasonable wine bills accompanying a meal;

(b)   items of clothing, jewellery, shoes or gifts;
(c)   trips taken whilst abroad (and all associated expenses) that have no direct connection with business or are not authorised in advance in writing by a senior manager;
(d)   any replacement items if items are lost, damaged or stolen whilst abroad (employees are expected to be insured for loss, damage or theft of their own personal belongings and luggage);
(e)   entertaining anyone other than someone who is an authorised agent, client, customer or potential client or customer and this has been cleared in advance with the line manager; this is restricted to reasonable drinks and a meal only;
(f)   upgrading (unless a free upgrade) of air or other travel tickets unless authorised in advance by the company;
(g)   taxis, unless there is no alternative or safe alternative means of transport;
(h)   any points or cards or offers of gifts or free travel as a result of 'Air-miles'; these are credited because of business mileage and are the property of the company. A line manager may decide what if any part of such concessions or free gifts the employee can take.

Often the employer requires expenses to be claimed within a specified period of time.

In some cases a corporate credit card is provided solely for use for business purposes.

In one case, staff were using the corporate AMEX card for personal spending and then repaying those expenses to their employer – before the employer paid AMEX but some time after making the purchases. They were, in effect, obtaining an interest-free loan. That employer stopped such a practice.

For typical expenses clauses see **Precedents 5P and 5Q**.

5.12   Loans and deductions

An employer can only make deductions from wages if they are required or authorised by a statutory provision or provided for in the contract or the individual has given their prior written consent (Employment Rights Act 1996, s.13(1)).

Deductions such as union dues, private health insurance contributions, share-save payments, subscriptions to journals, etc. are sometimes made at source by the employer but the legitimacy of such deductions is always subject either to the prior written consent of the individual or provision in the contract or collective agreement which is incorporated into the contract.

Where an employer makes a loan or an advance to an employee, such as a season ticket loan, advance of salary, etc, it is essential that this arrangement is put in writing in accordance with the strict rules of s.13.

Where a company policy, e.g. car policy, was incorporated into the contract and this required the settlement of charges made under the terms of that policy at the termination date of employment, the EAT upheld the employer's right to deduct those monies from the final salary (*CRS Computers Ltd* v. *MacKenzie* [2002] Emp LR 1048). Here the employee was allowed to have a company car in excess of the permitted value (£350 per month). The standard car allowance was £4,200 per annum and therefore the employee had to contribute £2,160 per annum for the car and extras that he wanted. The policy was worded in this way: 'Acceptance of this offer will constitute commitment to pay any settlement charges on the lease of the vehicle should you leave for any reason within the first year of employment. You also agree that any sums due under this clause may be deducted from salary and any other payments due to you. For your information this has been estimated at £5,000 if lease termination occurs at 6 months'. Mr MacKenzie was dismissed and given two weeks' pay in lieu of notice (even though his contract only stipulated notice and there was no option for the employer to make a payment in lieu of notice).

However, the EAT applied the ruling as in *Rock Refrigeration* v. *Jones* [1996] IRLR 675, CA, that not every breach of contract makes the terms favourable to the wrongdoer unenforceable. The breach has to be 'material going to the root of the contract' and the EAT found that in this case the breach did not go to the root of the contract. The term was enforceable and therefore the employer's counterclaim for £1,991.30 would be restored.

Deduction from final salary for employee's failure to give due notice

It is the bane of employers that in some cases employees leave without giving any notice, or insufficient notice, after they have been paid for the entire month and it is rare that an employer can recoup any wages paid or sue for any losses suffered. In the latter case this is because it is extremely difficult, and in most cases impossible, to show a direct loss as a result of the breach by the employee.

Furthermore, any repayment or clawing back of monies if proper notice is not given or served may be viewed as a penalty clause and not a genuine pre-estimate of loss.

Even where, in the case *Yizhen Li* v. *(1) First Marine Solutions Ltd (2) Dan Moutrey* (2014) UKEATS/0045/13/BI below, such a recoupment clause was upheld, the EAT warned that:

> Tribunals which consider such clauses in future might wish to think carefully, in the light of the evidence before them in the particular case, whether the parties actually intended such a clause to operate as a penalty clause, liquidated damages clause, or simply as a provision that entitled the employer to withhold pay for a period of time not worked during a notice period.

In *Yizhen Li* there was a clause in an employment contract allowing the employer to deduct one month's salary which, when the employee resigned and refused to work her one month notice period, was enforceable.

The relevant clause (12(1)) stated: 'If an employee leaves, without working the appropriate notice, the company will deduct a sum equal in value to the salary payable for the shortfall in the period of notice.'

The Employment Tribunal and EAT held that the clause represented a genuine pre-estimate of loss rather than a penalty.

However, that decision was not authority that in every similar case there would necessarily be a clause which operated as a genuine pre-estimate of damage.

The first respondent provided services to the oil trade. The second respondent had headhunted Ms Li, a project engineer, to work for the first respondent. Ms Li worked for the first respondent for three years until a dispute arose and she resigned. She was required to give one month's notice but asserted that she had outstanding holiday entitlement in excess of one month and therefore did not need to work her notice period.

The respondents maintained that Ms Li had already used up her holiday leave and deducted one month's salary from her final salary payment in accordance with clause 12(1) of the employment contract.

Ms Li offered to return to work her notice but the first respondent had already engaged a replacement at considerable extra cost.

The tribunal found that Ms Li was not entitled to accrued holiday pay which would cover her notice period and that she fell within clause 12(1) as someone who had left without working the appropriate notice.

It stated that the first respondent had placed a high value on retaining Ms Li's services and loyalty, and to that end included in her remunerative package 'a generous reassurance against the eventuality of her employment coming to an end at short notice'.

It decided that clause 12(1) was a genuine pre-estimate of loss that might be incurred as a consequence of breach of contract, rather than a penalty clause, and was thus enforceable. It held that the clause did not operate as a penalty but was, rather, a genuine pre-estimate of the losses that might be incurred if at short notice a senior professional such as a project engineer had to be recruited to fill an important gap.

The EAT held that:

(1) The facts of the instant case were distinct from those in another case (*Giraud*) where the employee was a driver and fairly easily replaceable.

   By contrast, Ms Li was a project engineer on a relatively high salary. To obtain a replacement at short notice was always likely to be particularly difficult and significant expense might be incurred.

   On examination of the contract as a whole in the context of what the parties had intended at the time it was made, the fact that Ms Li was headhunted meant that the first respondent had placed a particular value on her services.

   ... It seemed implicit that if cl.12 was to be construed as providing for a sum to be paid because an employee left early, it would be only that sum and no other which would be paid in the event of the breach ...

   The tribunal's language was concerning because to place a high value on retaining services and loyalty and, to that end, to include a generous reassurance against the employment coming to an end looked very much as if the employer was contending that there should be a marked disincentive within the contract for the employee to go. That would be something which sought to penalise the employee for leaving rather than to compensate the employer for the loss that would be incurred if the employee did go.

... In all the circumstances, the tribunal had been entitled to conclude that cl.12(1) was not a penalty clause: it was an agreement between the parties that should be performed (see paras 35–37, 40–41 of judgment).

(2) (Obiter)

...There was nothing in the language of cl.12(1) which suggested that the First Respondent had in mind the additional expenses of recruitment and replacement such as might result from early termination. It was not drafted as if to indicate that the parties had in mind 'penalty' or 'genuine pre-estimate of loss' at all.

Tribunals which considered such clauses in future might wish to think carefully, in the light of the evidence before them in the particular case, whether the parties actually intended such a clause to operate as a penalty clause, liquidated damages clause, or simply as a provision that entitled the employer to withhold pay for a period of time not worked during a notice period.

The instant case should not operate as authority that in every similar case there would necessarily be seen to be a clause which operated as a genuine pre-estimate of damage (paras 33–34, 46–47).

Repayment for recruitment costs, etc

If an employer is put to expensive recruitment costs such as recruitment fees, advertisements and assessment centres, etc. it may be possible to recoup those costs if the employee does not start in employment at all or leaves within a short period of time.

Any recoupment clause must be reasonable and a genuine pre-estimate of loss otherwise it will be deemed to be a penalty clause and will be unenforceable.

In *Cleeve Link Ltd v. E Bryla* [2014] IRLR 86, the EAT overturned an Employment Tribunal decision that a 'hiring fee', to be deducted by the employer from the employee's wages if she did not start or left after a short period of time, was unenforceable as it was a penalty clause. The EAT held there had been no unlawful deduction from wages pursuant to ss.13–27 of the Employment Rights Act 1996.

The clause in this contract read:

If the employee's employment is terminated as a result of the employee's misconduct or at the employee's own request within six months of their date of commencement, the employer reserves the right to recoup these costs in full from the employee. This will normally be by deduction from the employees' [sic] final pay or any other monies due to the employee.

A subsequent paragraph stated that the repayment would be on a sliding scale, and after six months in employment the repayment costs would reduce by one sixth for each month of completed employment so that by one year's service there would no longer be any liability to repay these costs.

The claimant's employment ended before six months. The respondent in this case deducted the full repayment from her final salary. The claimant was paid nothing when she left.

The EAT held that the correct time to address the enforceability of this clause was **not** at the time the contract was entered into but at the time of the alleged breach by the employer.

The EAT substituted its decision that this deduction was a genuine pre-estimate of loss and lawful both at common law and under ERA 1996.

Precedent 5S shows (i) clauses allowing for deductions from wages and (ii) a typical loan form.

5.13 Repayments for training expenses, overpayments and advance payments

Some employers offer to fund expensive external education and training courses in order to develop the skills of employees. It is common to require the employee to commit to remaining in the employment of the employer for a minimum period after the training has concluded and to repay on a sliding scale the fees and expenses paid by the employer. It is important to estimate the repayment on a sliding scale otherwise the repayment clause could be regarded as a penalty clause and not as being a genuine pre-estimate of loss and in such a case, this would be regarded as an unenforceable debt.

Similar repayment clauses are drafted where relocation expenses have been paid to new staff or existing staff.

Furthermore, there could be an issue over a repayment clause for advance commission in that such a clause could be regarded as being a contract for the provision of credit and therefore subject to the Consumer Credit Act 1974, s.8. However, in *McMillan Williams* v. *Range* [2004] 1 WLR 1858 the Court of Appeal held that such a repayment clause was not a contract for the provision of credit because the time to judge such a clause was the time at which it was made.

In this case the assistant solicitor's contract of employment provided for payment of advance commission but contained a clawback clause where there was a shortfall between actual payment and commission earned. The clause on 'Pay' was clause 9 (which read para.3):

(a) you will be paid commission of 33 per cent of all profit costs paid on bills delivered by you or on which a proportion of the profit costs is allocated to you. In anticipation of the commission you will receive you will be paid a monthly advance on your commission equivalent to £22,000 per annum. The amount of the monthly advance may be varied by mutual agreement.

(b) the first calculation of commission payable to you will be after you have been employed two years (unless your employment is terminated earlier in which case the provisions set out at (d) below apply). The difference between the commission payable to you and the total advance paid will be calculated ('the calculation') and any excess of commission payable over the total advance paid will be paid to you as bonus. Any shortfall is payable by you. After the first two year period the calculation will be carried out at the end of each six month period. At the discretion of the partners any shortfall may be carried over to the following six month period.

(c) any excess or shortfall arising from the calculation is interest free until it exceeds £10,000. Thereafter the whole sum will attract interest at five per cent over Bank of Ireland base rate and will be paid either by you or to you at the end of each month that the excess or shortfall exceeds £10,000.

(d) on the termination of your employment, howsoever occasioned, a final calculation will be carried out. No payment will be made for unbilled work in progress or profit costs that are unpaid. Any excess or shortfall on the final calculation will be paid by you or to you within twenty-eight days and you will accept that as full and final payment under this contract.

At the time of this agreement (between an assistant solicitor and her firm) it was not known whether there would be a shortfall of salary against commission or a surplus when the calculation came to be made at the end of two years or earlier upon termination of employment. Unless there was a debt, there could be no credit and therefore this arrangement was to be regarded as merely postponing any obligation to pay until such time as the future possible indebtedness had crystallised. The contract was therefore not one for provision of regulated credit under the 1974 Act.

Finally, where an employer, through one of its managers, represents to an employee that they will not lose pay protection (in this case when the employee agreed to reduce their hours from 40 to 30), despite this clearly being set out in writing in the contract which the employee signed as having been read and understood and accepted, this oral representation will override the written term.

Managers must be especially careful **not** to interpret or give assurances on matters such as pay, pay protection, bonus payments, etc. because their interpretations may be relied upon despite there being clear and unambiguous written terms to the contrary.

A case in point is *Royal Mail Group Ltd* v. *Aldous* UKEAT/0593/12/BA. Here the employer unsuccessfully appealed against a finding made by the Employment Tribunal, that withdrawing the weekly pay protection amounted to unlawful deductions from wages, despite the fact that the employer had sent an unambiguous letter to the claimant explaining to him about the loss of pay protection payments.

The claimant had signed a document and had received a lump sum payment in consideration for agreeing to the reduced hours and loss of pay protection.

The contract stated that:

> Except as varied by this letter, all terms and conditions of your employment will remain the same. Note however that in voluntarily agreeing to vary your contract of employment through the buy down hours agreement, you are agreeing to adopt the standard terms and conditions for your grade at your reduced contractual hours. This means, for example, that any reserved or personal rights and entitlements, including pay protection measures, cease from the effective date of the buy down. For the avoidance of doubt this does not however include payment of the 'ex-PHG' supplement (if applicable).

At the time the claimant was also paid a weekly pay protection payment and he had asked his line manager before signing the document whether or not the weekly pay protection would also be lost. The claimant's case was that his manager had not explained that this weekly pay protection would also be withdrawn. The letter was, however, crystal clear and unambiguous – it stated that all pay protection payments would be withdrawn.

The EAT relied on *MCI Worldcom International Inc v. Primus Telecommunications Inc* [2004] EWCA Civ 957.

The EAT held that the Employment Judge was entitled to decide in favour of the claimant – that he had had the position misrepresented by his manager and that his entitlement to this weekly pay protection was not lost.

Covert recordings

Whilst we cover this in another chapter, managers should be aware that it is becoming more and more common for employees, sometimes covertly, to use their smartphones to record conversations. Those recordings are admissible in evidence in court and Employment Tribunals.

Some employers may wish to include an express term and express provision prohibiting the covert recording of conversations or meetings and labelling this conduct gross misconduct.

A typical clause regarding repayment is set out at **Precedent 5T**.

5.14 Relocation expenses

Employers may wish to offer a relocation package either at recruitment or during an individual's employment. If the following conditions are met and the expenses paid to the employee do not exceed £8,000, they are deemed a 'qualifying cost' and do not have to be reported to HMRC (as they are exempt under the Income Taxes (Earnings and Pensions) Act 2003).

In order to qualify for the tax exemptions in ss.271 and 272 of the Income Tax (Earnings and Pensions) Act 2003:

- the relocation must occur as the employee takes up employment, has alteration in their duties or the place where they perform their duties changes;
- any change of residence has to be made wholly or mainly to allow the employee to reside 'within a reasonable daily travelling distance' from the new work location (there is no definition of this);
- the existing residence must not be within a reasonable travelling distance.

Employees may receive up to £8,000 relocation expenses as a non-taxable benefit as long as the following three conditions are met:

(a) the expenses are reasonably provided in connection with a change of an employee's residence (s.272(1)(a));
(b) they are provided on or before the limitation day, i.e. the last day of the tax year after the one in which the employee started employment or after the change of their duties with the caveat that the Revenue may extend that period if it is 'reasonable to do so having regard to all the

circumstances', e.g. the employee has desperately been trying to sell their old house but has been unable to do so; and

(c) the employee is only reimbursed for the purchase of abortive purchase expenses; expenses to take away unsaleable goods; removal costs; travelling and subsistence while looking for a new house, e.g. rent and replacement of domestic goods in the new home (s.272(1)(c)).

Bridging loans

For information on whether a bridging loan counts as a 'qualifying' cost, when an employer provides such a benefit, please see: **www.gov.uk/expenses-and-benefits-relocation/whats-exempt**.

The rules include the fact that the employee (or members of their family) must sell their old home and buy a new one and the loan must be expressly to bridge the gap between buying the new house and selling their old house.

This loan may only be used to buy the new house or to pay off any mortgage payments or loans on their old house.

Finally, the loan cannot exceed the market value of the old house valued at the time of the purchase of the new house.

Further information on income tax and National Insurance contributions on relocation packages is available from HMRC: *HMRC 480(2017) – Expenses and Benefits – A Tax Guide* (amended December 2016).

A typical policy on relocation can be found at **Precedent 5W**.

5.15 Policy for world or sporting events

The year 2012 saw the Olympic Games being held in London and in Rio in 2016. Major sporting events and world events sometimes provide issues and difficulties for employers with employees wishing to watch these events, staying up all night to watch them or travelling to these sporting events and missing work.

A typical policy is reproduced at **Precedent 5X**.

PRECEDENT 5A: Salary terms

1. Your rate of pay is £ . . . per annum and as subsequently amended in writing.

2. Your salary is paid [monthly in arrears on the last day of each calendar month] [on *specify day* of each month or nearest working day of the month in which salary is due although payment is for the full calendar month].

3. Salary is deemed to accrue from day to day and is paid in 12 equal monthly amounts irrespective of the length of the month.

4. If you join or leave part-way through a month, your salary will be calculated as a proportion of annual salary (i.e. the number of days that you were employed as a proportion of 365).

5. You receive a monthly itemised pay statement, which sets out your gross salary, statutory and other deductions and the net sum paid. Salaries are credited by direct credit transfer into a bank account nominated by you.

6. **Collective agreement:** Your pay and other terms and conditions are those negotiated from time to time between the Company and the [*name*] trade union. A Collective Agreement exists for your bargaining unit and whether or not you are a member of the union, your pay and terms and conditions are determined by any agreement reached with the union. Any changes in wage rates agreed with the union will be notified to you within 4 weeks of any such change.

7. **Allowances:** In your grade you are entitled to a uniform and clothing allowance of £... per annum. This does not count as pensionable pay.

PRECEDENT 5B: Salary terms: senior director

1. The Remuneration Package set out in paragraph [*specify*] below ('Remuneration Package A') shall apply to the Executive's employment as Managing Director on his appointment and shall continue to apply provided that successful closure of the First Financing Round for a total amount of at least [US$1.5 million] has been effected by [*date*].

2. If the condition set out in paragraph 1 is not satisfied but the Company nevertheless resolves to continue the Executive's appointment as Managing Director and does not exercise its power to terminate in [*specify clause*], then the remuneration package set out in paragraph [*specify*] ('Remuneration Package B') shall apply to the Executive's appointment.

3. The Company shall pay to the Executive a total remuneration package of £... per annum. Such package shall consist of a basic salary which shall accrue day-to-day and be payable by equal monthly instalments in arrears and such of the Benefits as the Executive shall elect provided that in such circumstances the basic salary shall be reduced by the cost to the Company of providing such Benefits. The basic salary shall be deemed to include any fees receivable by the Executive as a Director of the Company or any Associated Company, or of any other Company or unincorporated body in which he holds office as nominee or representative of the Company or any Associated Company.

PRECEDENT 5C: Review of salaries

1. Salaries are reviewed annually in [*month*] at the discretion of the Company.

2. Please note there is no contractual entitlement to any increase in your salary but any salary increase usually takes effect from [1 April] and will be notified to you in writing.

For area managers:

1. Please note that your salary is linked to the size and profitability of your Sales Area/Sales Territory. If you move to another Sales Territory to manage, this could lead to a decrease in your annual gross salary if the territory to which you move commands a smaller area and a lower profitability and income generation.

2. Your salary will not be decreased when you move to any smaller Sales Territory until the normal salary review date of [1 April] in any year.

PRECEDENT 5D: Guaranteed bonus

1. We are prepared to offer you a guaranteed bonus of £... in your first year of employment conditional upon satisfactory performance of your duties up to and including [date]. Part of this cash sum will be paid by way of share options and you will be advised of the exact details of the bonus that will be paid in cash on or before [date].

2. In the event that the Company determines that your performance is not satisfactory or determines that your conduct or performance amounts to gross misconduct/gross incompetence/gross dereliction of duty and is worthy of summary dismissal, you will not be eligible for any of the guaranteed bonus should your dismissal take effect prior to [date].

Pay secrecy

3. The payment of your salary and any bonus is conditional upon you keeping your bonus number and any discussions about your bonus now and in the future strictly confidential. For the avoidance of any doubt you are not permitted to disclose at any time what bonus if any you receive or anything that is said to you about any bonus that you might receive. This is subject always to your duty of disclosure if ordered by a Court of competent jurisdiction or any regulatory body.

No detrimental action will be taken against you if you disclose your salary or bonus number to another employee who believes they may have been discriminated against for any unlawful reasons under the Equality Act 2010.

PRECEDENT 5E: Discretionary bonus

We operate a bonus scheme which is implemented at the entire discretion of the Bank. There is no contractual entitlement to any such bonuses and the Scheme may cease and be withdrawn or varied at the entire discretion of the Bank at any time. Any bonus, if awarded, in any year, may be determined by a number of factors which may vary from year to year. Those factors remain confidential to the Incentive Compensation Committee which determines these matters. We assure all staff who may receive a discretionary bonus that any decision (if any decision is made) is based on rational, non-discriminatory and objective factors. A bonus payment, if one becomes payable, may be paid at a time to be announced by the Bank. Conditions for any payment include, but are not limited to, the recipient not being the subject of a disciplinary or performance investigation or warning or under notice of termination howsoever given, on the bonus payment date. If you are not employed on bonus payment date or are under notice of termination whomsoever has given notice, you will not be entitled to be considered for any bonus for that bonus year.

PRECEDENT 5F(i): Clauses relating to conditional bonus

1. You may receive a bonus from the Company as determined by the Company from time to time. This is referred to in your Offer Letter.

2. A bonus is a discretionary payment which is made to reward individual performance and which reflects the overall level of profitability of the Company. The Company has the discretion to decide on the size and date of payment of the bonus. You will not be eligible for payment of any bonus, if you are no longer employed by the Company or if you are working out a period of notice (whether given by you or the Company) on the date that bonus payments are made.

OR

You are entitled to participate in the Company's discretionary bonus scheme applicable from time to time for senior managers. Details of the current scheme are set out in the Bonus Policy, which appears in the Staff Handbook. The Company reserves the right, in its absolute discretion, to vary the terms and/or the amount of bonus payable under the Bonus Policy which is in force from time to time. There is a cap in any event of no more than [...] per cent of your base salary.

PRECEDENT 5F(ii): Repayable bonus

1.1. In consideration for the Executive entering into this Agreement and abiding by its terms in particular given the undertakings set out in clause [...] the Company agrees to provide to [the Executive] the signing bonus described in the Schedule ('the Signing Bonus') [an amount of £X] together and at the same time as [the Executive's] first salary payment.

In the event that before expiry of the Initial Period, any of the following occurs:

(a) [the Executive] serves written notice of termination of his employment or otherwise terminates his employment (other than by reason of death);
(b) [the Executive's] employment is terminated by [the Company] in circumstances falling within clause [X] hereof; or
(c) [the Executive's] employment terminates pursuant to statute or operation of law (which includes any objection under the Transfer of Undertakings (Protection of Employment) Regulations 1981),

then [the Executive] shall be obligated to repay to the Company an amount calculated on the basis below within seven (7) days of the termination of his employment.

[The Executive] acknowledges and agrees that [the Company] may set off against or deduct any amounts owing to [the Executive] under this Agreement amounts of Signing Bonus falling to be repaid pursuant to the aforegoing:

- (a) x c (b)
  Where:
  a = the number of working days remaining until the expiry of the Initial Period from the last day of [the Executive's] employment
  b = 1,300 days [i.e. five years of 260 working days]
  c = the Signing Bonus

Notwithstanding the provisions of clause [...], if [the Executive] at any time ... is convicted of a serious crime or any criminal offence involving dishonesty or fraud or is guilty of any other misconduct bringing [the Executive] or [the Company] or any member of the Group into disrepute (such issue to be determined in the reasonable opinion of the Board) or is guilty of any wilful breach, gross misconduct or negligence or continued neglect of the provisions of this Agreement; [the Company] may by written notice given to [the Executive] terminate the Appointment ... for any reason specified in clause [...], without any period of notice and without payment and allowances (other than remuneration and benefits accrued up to the date of termination).

For the avoidance of any doubt the amount to be repaid will equate to the gross payment of the bonus paid to the Executive. It will be for the Executive to seek to reclaim any tax paid and repayable by HMRC.

PRECEDENT 5G: Shares and options

1. In addition to his annual salary, the Executive shall be entitled to an equity participation of 11.5 per cent on the terms set out below.

Shares

2. The Executive will be entitled to receive 1.5 per cent of the share capital of the Company as at the day immediately preceding the Current Capital Increase in exchange for a US$ ... cash contribution paid to the Company by the Executive, provided that such sum is received by the Company before the closure of the First Financing Round.

Options

3. The Executive will be entitled to options to acquire 10 per cent of the share of capital of the Company as at the date immediately preceding the Current Capital Increase at a strike price per share calculated by reference to a Company valuation of US$ ... (i.e. at a [70 per cent] discount to the First Round Pre-money Value of US$ ...) such options to vest and be exercisable as follows:

(a) Seven per cent to be vested over a three-year period (1/3 each year);
(b) One per cent to be vested upon successful completion of the first year objectives as stated in the Business Plan;
(c) Two per cent to be vested upon successful completion of the second year objectives as stated in the Business Plan.

PRECEDENT 5H: Share dealings

The Executive shall comply where relevant with every rule of law, every regulation of any recognised stock exchange on which the Company's or any Associated Company's shares are quoted and every regulation of the Company from time to time in force in relation to dealings in shares, debentures or other securities of the Company or any Associated Company and unpublished price sensitive information affecting the shares, debentures or other securities of any other Company provided always that in relation to overseas dealing the Executive shall also comply with all laws of the state and all regulations of the stock exchange, market or dealing system in which such dealings take place.

PRECEDENT 5I: Change of control

1. If a Change of Control of the Company takes place before [date] and as a result of the Change of Control the Company resolves to terminate the Executive's appointment the Executive shall be granted an option to acquire [five per cent] of the Company's share capital as at the date immediately prior to the Current Capital Increase at a strike price per share calculated by reference to a [70 per cent] discount to the valuation of the Company as at the date of Change of Control, but shall not in those circumstances be entitled to receive any shares or share options under [specify clause].

2. In the event that there is a Change of Control of the Company after [date] or the Company does an Initial Public Offering, all of the Executive's options to acquire shares shall vest and become exercisable instantaneously.

3. If the Company shall undergo any process of reconstruction or amalgamation (including an administrative reorganisation) whether or not involving the liquidation of the Company the Company will use its reasonable endeavours to ensure that the Executive shall be offered employment by the successor or proposed successor to the Company or any other Associated Company on the terms *mutatis mutandis* set out in this Agreement (other than the identity of the employer). If the Executive shall have failed to accept any such offer within one month, then the Company may terminate this Agreement forthwith. In such event the Executive shall have no claim for compensation

against the Company in respect of such termination save as provided under the provisions of the Employment Rights Act 1996.

PRECEDENT 5J: Car or car allowance

You are employed as the Chair's chauffeur and as such are required to have a clean, full UK driving licence. You are required to operate to the highest standards of driving, being a safe and careful driver with excellent knowledge of the UK roads and being proficient in navigation, etc.

You are required to bring the original of both parts of your photocard driving licence with you to the interview and on your first day where a photocopy will be made and retained on your file.

If you have driving offences or charges brought against you during your employment (even in your personal capacity) you are required to inform your line manager immediately.

OR

As part of your job you will be provided with a Company car as driving to customers and potential customers is an essential condition of your employment. You must hold and continue to hold a current full UK driving licence. If you lose your licence, i.e. you are banned from driving, then this will be regarded as a material breach of your employment and the Company reserves the right to dismiss you summarily for gross misconduct. You are required to report any driving offences to your line manager.

Conditions for driving

It is important that new Company car drivers or those driving their own car on Company business complete the following Driver's Questionnaire. If there are any questions that you cannot answer or are unsure of, please ask.

Driver's questionnaire

PERSONAL DETAILS	
Name	
Date of birth	
About your job	
Job title	
Company	
About your vehicle	
Make	
Model	
Body type (please indicate the body type of the vehicle)	
THE MAIN QUESTIONNAIRE	
How long have you held your licence? (years)	

0–3	
4–6	
7–10	
11–20	
21–30	
31–40	
41+ (please specify)	
Is your vehicle a:	
Company vehicle	
car allowance	
private vehicle	
What is your total mileage?	
0–510	
511–2,000	
2,001–5,000	
5,001–10,000	
10,001–20,000	
20,001–30,000	
30,001+ (please specify)	
What do you use the vehicle for? (Please tick all appropriate)	
Sales visits	
Deliveries	
Service visits	
Trips to meetings	
Training/conferences	
Other (specify)	
How many miles do you commute on a daily basis to your normal place of work? Please state if you work from your home and go out on visits, etc.	
0–10	
11–20	
21–30	
31–50	
51–70	
70+ (please specify)	
How many business miles do you do each year?	
0–500	
501–2,000	
2,001–5,000	
5,001–10,000	
10,001–20,000	

20,001–30,000	
30,001+ (please specify)	
Do you ever carry anything for the business?	
No	
Yes (please specify)	
Do you have a mobile phone that you use for business or in the course of business?	
No	
Yes (Business provided)	
Yes (Private)	
Do you have a hands free kit or Bluetooth in the car?	
No	
Yes	
Will you use the mobile whilst driving?	
No	
Yes (please indicate the length of time you normally spend on a mobile in a typical hour)	
Have you ever experienced any of the following whilst driving for business?	
Tiredness/drowsiness	Yes/No
Head nodding/jerking	Yes/No
Falling asleep at the wheel	Yes/No
What is the longest business trip you have driven in the last 12 months?	
0–100 miles	
101–200	
201–300	
300+ (please specify)	
Do you ever have to drive abroad for business?	
No	
Yes (please list the countries)	
What are your ACTUAL weekly hours? Noted from a weekly hours' sheet which I confirm I have accurately completed	
20–30	
31–40	
41–48	

49–60 (please confirm that you have opted out of the 48-hour Working Time Regulations 1998)	
60+ (please confirm that you have opted out of the 48-hour Working Time Regulations 1998)	
What is the longest working day that you have done in the last 12 months (in hours)?	
8–10	
11–13	
14–16	
17–19	
19+ (please tell us why)	
What is the longest working week you have done in the last 12 months (in hours)?	
20–30	
31–40	
41–48	
48+ (please specify)	
Have you had a road traffic accident or incident in the last 3 years?	
No	
Yes (please specify)	
Do you have any endorsements on your licence currently?	
No	
Yes (please specify how many points you currently have and when they will expire)	
Do you have any medical conditions that may affect your ability to drive or that are reportable to the DVLA?	
Yes (please specify)	
No	
Do you have any other employment paid or unpaid?	
No	
Yes (please specify)	
Signature	
Date of signing	

> I understand that I have a continuing duty to notify my line manager and HR if any circumstances change, e.g. I receive further points on my licence, I am charged with a motor offence which could lead to disqualification from driving or if there are any new or recurring medical conditions/symptoms which could affect my ability or safety or that of others, to drive.

PRECEDENT 5K: Car and company vehicle

Example 1

(A) Driving licence and authority to drive company vehicles

1. You must be in possession of a full UK current driving licence and have the written permission of a Director to drive one of our Company vehicles.

2. Your driving licence must be produced for review by a Director prior to driving any of our vehicles. A copy will be retained on your personnel file and renewed annually.

3. If at any time your licence is endorsed, i.e. you have points or you are charged with a driving offence which could lead to disqualification or you have been convicted and you have been disqualified from driving, we must be informed immediately.

4. It is your responsibility to see that the car is not used by anyone other than authorised employees. Special written permission must be obtained from a Director for the vehicle to be used by any other person.

5. You will be insured under the Company's insurance policy.

(B) Fixtures, fittings and modifications

1. No fixtures such as aerials, roof racks, towing apparatus, stickers, may be attached to the vehicle without prior written permission. When handing the vehicle back to us such attachments must remain unless adequate rectification work is carried out professionally to restore the vehicle to its former condition.

2. No change or alterations may be made to the manufacturer's mechanical or structural specification for the vehicle.

3. If you fail to adequately clean the vehicle, you may be subject to the cost of the Valet deducted from your wage.

(C) Warranty

All warranty work must be reported to us prior to it being carried out.

(D) Cleaning and maintenance

1. As the vehicle has been allocated to you, it is your responsibility to keep it in a clean and tidy fashion at all times and to ensure that the vehicle is regularly serviced in accordance with the requirements laid down by the manufacturer, and as specified in the maintenance book of the particular model of vehicle.

2. Any other maintenance or repair work or replacement of parts, including tyres, must be approved in advance by us.

(E) Fuel, etc.

1. In addition to keeping the vehicle regularly serviced, it is your responsibility to see that the oil and water levels, battery and brake fluid and tyre pressures are maintained and that the tread of all tyres conforms to the minimum legal requirements.

2. We will only reimburse you for fuel and oil used on our business. Claims must be submitted on a monthly basis, signed by yourself and accompanied by detailed mileage logs and receipted bills (in the case of oil).

(F) Fines

We shall not under any circumstances accept responsibility for parking or other fines incurred by you. The cost of these fines if not paid may be deducted from salary/pay.

(G) Congestion charge (London area only)

This should be paid directly and claimed for as part of your monthly expenses. The Company will only pay for those charges within initial time limits. Where a time limit is exceeded and an additional/higher charge is raised, this will not, under any circumstances, be the responsibility of the Company.

(H) Damage or injury

1. If you are involved in an accident which causes damage to property or another vehicle, or injury to any person or animal, you are required to give your name and address, the name and address of the vehicle owner, the registration number of the vehicle and the name of the insurance company to any person having reasonable grounds for requiring such information. IT IS IMPORTANT THAT YOU GIVE NO FURTHER INFORMATION. If for some reason it is not possible to give this information at the time of the accident, the matter must be reported to the office and where necessary the police as soon as possible, but WITHIN TWENTY-FOUR HOURS OF THE OCCURRENCE.

2. In addition, in the case of an incident involving injury to another person or to notifiable animals, you are responsible for notifying the police of the occurrence and you must produce your insurance certificate to a police officer attending the accident, or to any other person having reasonable grounds for seeing it. The accident must be reported to a police station or to a police officer WITHIN TWENTY-FOUR HOURS. If you are not then able to produce the certificate you must in any event produce it in person within five days after the accident to such police station as you may specify at the time of first reporting the accident.

3. For security reasons, insurance certificates are kept by us. However, a copy of the certificate of insurance is provided with each vehicle and this will be renewed annually. You should make sure that it is with the vehicle at all times. Replacement copies can be obtained from us if necessary.

(I) Loss

1. In the case of theft of the vehicle, we and the police must be informed immediately. Full details of the contents of the vehicle must also be given. If any contents are stolen from the vehicle, we and the police should be notified immediately.

2. Please note that only Company property is insured by us and you should make your own arrangements to cover personal effects.

3. The vehicle should be kept locked when not in use and the contents should be stored out of sight, preferably in the boot. If a vehicle is stolen we are required to prove to the insurance company that there has been no negligence and, therefore, must hold you responsible in the event of such negligence.

(J) *Accident procedure*

1. It is a condition of the insurance policy that the insurers are notified of all accidents, even if apparently of no consequence. You must, therefore, as soon as possible after the accident obtain an accident report form from us which must be completed and returned to us within 24 hours. All the information required on the form must be completed. You should note that whenever possible the following particulars should appear in the form:

(a) the name and address of the other driver and the name and address of his/her insurers;
(b) the names and addresses of all passengers in both our vehicle and the other vehicle;
(c) names and addresses of all witnesses. It will be of considerable assistance if statements can be obtained from all witnesses at the time of the accident;
(d) particulars of the police attending, i.e. name, number and division.

2. A detailed sketch must be provided showing the relative position of the vehicle before and after the accident, together with details of the roads in the vicinity, e.g. whether they are major or minor roads and as many relevant measurements as possible.

3. If our vehicle is not in a roadworthy condition, i.e. not safe to drive, you are responsible for making adequate arrangements for the vehicle to be towed to a garage, and the name and address of the garage where the vehicle may be inspected must be stated on the claim form.

4. An estimate of the repairs required to be carried out, showing details and cost of both labour and materials, must be obtained and sent to us as soon as possible.

5. Under no circumstances may repairs be put in hand until the insurance company has given its agreement. We will notify you when this has been done.

6. You should not under any circumstances express any opinion one way or the other on the degree of responsibility for the accident. Only exchange particulars mentioned in point 1 above and nothing more.

(K) *Road fund licence*

The road fund licence for the vehicle will be renewed automatically when due, but in the event that you do not receive the new licence by the expiry date, we should be notified immediately.

(L) *Travel overseas*

1. Our vehicles may not be taken out of the country without written permission from a Director.

2. Our insurance policy covers the use of the vehicle in Great Britain. Before travelling with the vehicle anywhere else you must obtain our permission and, at least seven days beforehand, give us a list of the countries to be visited and the relevant dates. A letter of authorisation will be issued which must accompany the vehicle and a Green Card may be necessary. On return to the UK, these should be returned to us for cancellation.

3. Unless the journey is on approved business, the cost of any Green Card will be charged to you and must be paid for before the journey starts.

(M) Permitted use

Subject to the restrictions already stipulated, our vehicles may only be used for social, domestic and pleasure purposes, and for our business, excluding the carriage of passengers for hire or reward. Our vehicles may not be used for any type of motoring sport, including racing, rallying or pace making, whether on the public highway or on private land. Private mileage must be shown and declared.

(N) Personal liability for damage to vehicles

1. Where any damage to one of our vehicles is due to your negligence or lack of care, we reserve the right to insist on your rectifying the damage at your own expense or paying the excess part of any claim on the insurers.

2. Repeated instances may result in the use of the vehicle being withdrawn and disciplinary action being taken.

(O) Use of alcohol, illicit substances or medication (prescribed or OTC)

1. It is strictly forbidden for you to be under the influence of alcohol or any illicit substances when you are in charge of a Company or personal motor vehicle whilst driving on business. This means we operate similar rules to the Civil Aviation Authority (CAA) for airline pilots, and 24 hours between bottle and throttle no more than eight units of alcohol should be consumed, and eight hours between bottle and throttle no alcohol should be consumed. This is because the effects of the alcohol in the bloodstream remain. Any breach of this rule will be regarded as gross misconduct for which summary dismissal is a possible penalty.

2. If you are found to be drunk or under the influence or in fact over the legal limit for drink/driving, i.e. 40 mg per 100 ml of blood whilst in possession of a Company or private vehicle during the course of your employment, i.e. when on duty and working for the Company, then this will be regarded as gross misconduct for which summary dismissal is a possible penalty.

3. It is also strictly forbidden to have any alcohol in the car or on your person during the course of your employment or to drink alcohol at any time during the course of your employment, e.g. during a lunch or other break from work.

4. In the event that these rules are breached it will be regarded as gross misconduct for which summary dismissal is a possible penalty.

5. The use or possession of or dealing in illicit substances is strictly forbidden whether in a motor vehicle or during breaks during the course of employment and any breach of this rule will be regarded as gross misconduct for which summary dismissal is a possible penalty.

6. Furthermore you may be prescribed medication by your doctor or buy medicines or medication over the counter (OTC), which affect your safety when driving. We ask you to be responsible and vigilant and if there are any known side effects of such medications, you must report this to a Director immediately bringing the medication with you and a decision will be made whether you are fit to drive or not.

(P) Mobile phones, Blackberries or other handheld devices

1. As you know the use of handheld mobile telephones/Blackberries in motor cars has been banned since 1 December 2003. You are strictly forbidden from using any

handheld devices in the car and if you wish to use a mobile telephone then you must use a Bluetooth device with an earpiece or stop the car in a safe place and then use your mobile.

2. Any breach of this rule will be regarded as gross misconduct for which summary dismissal is a possible penalty.

Example 2

Company car

1. Subject to your holding a current driving licence for motor vehicles valid in the UK, you will be supplied with a car of a make, model and specification determined by reference to our Company Car Policy from time to time in force.

2. The Directors have absolute discretion in deciding whether or not to provide you with a vehicle but will not withhold a vehicle without discussing the reasons with you. The Company Car Policy provides full details of the rules relating to the use of company cars and the main rules are given below.

3. If you are required as part of your employment to drive vehicles on company business you may be dismissed if you do not remain a holder of a current valid driving licence in respect of the vehicles of the category you are likely to be driving whilst employed. You must produce your licence for us to inspect whenever you are required to do so. You are required to notify your line manager and HR immediately, in writing, of any impending prosecutions for driving offences and to advise them of the result of such prosecutions. Failure to advise us of impending prosecutions and/or the outcome is regarded as misconduct under our disciplinary procedure and in particular your failure to advise us of any disqualification (in writing) is regarded as gross misconduct. The consequences could be very serious because you and the Company would be committing a criminal offence, your insurance would be invalid and both your safety and that of any road users could be imperilled.

4. It may sometimes be necessary to make your company car available for other employees to use and if this happens we will endeavour to give you a substitute. You may also be asked to allow another employee to drive your company car if you are ill and someone is acting in your place on a temporary basis.

5. Where the Company provides you with a vehicle, we shall pay for all motor taxes, insurance and normal running costs including fuel, oil, maintenance, repairs, car park charges, the car wash, etc. and you may pay for the fuel and other costs for reasonable private use.

6. You will be required to pay all parking, road traffic incident and other fines or costs associated with any breach of the Road Traffic Acts/byelaws or private parking rules. The Company reserves the right to pay any such fines and then deduct the amount from your salary.

7. You and your spouse or partner are insured to drive the company car as long as you both hold current valid driving licences. If you wish any other drivers to be added they must have a full car driving licence, have a driving record acceptable to the Company and our insurers and be over 25 years of age. Before allowing them to drive the company car you must obtain the written permission of a Director using the correct authorisation form.

8. When you are driving any vehicle you are expected to drive in a sensible, responsible, safe and considerate manner at all times. We reserve the right to take

disciplinary action against you if you drive negligently, carelessly or discourteously. Road rage or rudeness to other road users or to the police or other third parties is totally unacceptable and will not be tolerated.

9. Under no circumstances is any driver permitted to use a handheld mobile telephone whilst driving the vehicle (whether a company or private vehicle) unless the car is parked safely and the engine has been switched off. Drivers of company cars who are required to use a mobile telephone in the performance of their job will be provided with a hands-free kit/Bluetooth and this must be used at all times when driving unless the conditions above prevail.

10. Non-compliance with the above conditions can result in disciplinary action being taken against you.

11. You will remain responsible for ensuring that the car remains in a clean and tidy condition inside and out and is properly maintained at all times. If you own a dog or other animals and you carry them in a company car you must ensure that you place protective covers over the seats and if possible secure the animals in the boot or back of the car. In such cases you must be vigilant at all times to ensure that the car is clean and tidy.

12. It is strictly forbidden to leave any items out on display when you leave the car (whether your own car or a company car). Any valuables must always be taken out of the car when you leave the car and this would include any laptops or other company equipment, company papers, etc. You may be responsible for reimbursing the Company for any losses occasioned through breach of this rule.

13. You must at all times conform with the rules and regulations relating to company cars which from time to time may be issued. If any insurance relating to any car is voided due to your action or inaction, then you will be required to indemnify the Company against all losses and expenses resulting from your use of the vehicle. You must familiarise yourself with the terms of the Company insurance.

Maternity leave

14. During any period of ordinary maternity leave the Executive shall be entitled to retain and use the car on the same basis as above. During any period of additional maternity leave, the Company may at its discretion require the return of the car in order that the temporary maternity replacement has the use of the car for business purposes.

Example 3

1. Company vehicles

1.1 You will be provided with a fully expensed company vehicle in which to conduct your duties. This vehicle may also be used for reasonable social, domestic and pleasure mileage if you decide to take this option. Please note the vehicle plus provision of private fuel are taxable benefits.

1.2 It is your responsibility to ensure that the vehicle assigned to you is regularly serviced and maintained in accordance with the manufacturer's specification.

1.3 All servicing and repairs (other than replacement tyres) must be carried out by a franchised dealer, and must be authorised by the Technical Manager prior to the work commencing. Separate arrangements are in place for the replacement of tyres; refer to the Technical Manager for instructions.

1.4 You are responsible for checking and maintaining the following items on a regular basis:

- all vital fluids;
- tyre pressures;
- condition of tyres with regard to depth of tread, visible damage, i.e. cuts, bulges, etc;
- all lights are functioning correctly;
- ensuring that the vehicle is in a roadworthy condition.

1.5 You are responsible for ensuring that the vehicle is clean and tidy, inside and out, at all times.

1.6 A monthly vehicle inspection sheet has to be completed and returned to the Technical Services Department on the first working day of each month.

1.7 To enable the vehicle fleet to be effectively managed it may become necessary to move vehicles from person to person; you will be instructed on such movements by the Technical Manager.

2. **General equipment and spare parts**

You are responsible for the care and safekeeping of all equipment and spare parts assigned to you. The cost of repairing or replacement of lost or damaged equipment due to your neglect or lack of care will be your responsibility.

3. **Mobile phone/pager**

3.1 You will be provided with a mobile phone and pager.

3.2 You will be able to use the mobile phone for both business and private use. The Company will provide you with free private usage up to the value of £... per month. Any charges incurred over and above this amount will be deducted from your salary on a monthly basis.

3.3 The cost of repairing or replacement of lost or damaged equipment due to your neglect or lack of care will be your responsibility.

4. **Laptop**

4.1 You will be provided with a company laptop which you may need to use either in the vehicle or at home. We will carry out a risk assessment in order to ensure that you use this correctly and safely.

4.2 You will be and will remain solely responsible for the security of this laptop. You must lock it away out of sight when you leave your vehicle for any time at all and you must bring it into your home at night or at the end of your shift. You will be responsible for reimbursing the cost price of a replacement laptop unless the Company is satisfied that its loss was not due to your fault.

5. **Congestion charge**

5.1 All staff who are required to enter the charging area on a regular basis, i.e. the congestion charging area in London, please register with Human Resources. The Company will then pay any congestion charges due on each day that you enter the Congestion Charge Zone. You must of course report each day that you enter the Zone. All other staff are required to pay the charges and claim them on their expense forms. However, if you do not pay the charges and are fined, you are responsible for the fine. This has been put in writing and made as an amendment to the Car Policy and your contract so any deductions will be lawful.

5.2 The taxation of congestion charging has now been ruled upon.

If congestion charges are not exempt, we have to report them to HM Revenue and Customs (HMRC) and we may have to deduct and pay tax and National Insurance on them. The value of the benefit to use is the amount you pay in congestion charges.

Some congestion charges are covered by exemptions (which have replaced dispensations). This means we will not have to include them in your end-of-year reports.

If you use your own vehicle to travel on business

You must report the cost on form P11D. We do not have to deduct or pay any National Insurance or tax.

If we pay congestion charges directly for your private travel

We must:

- report the cost on form P11D;
- deduct and pay Class 1 National Insurance (but not PAYE tax) through payroll.

If we reimburse congestion charges for your private travel

This counts as earnings, so we must:

- add the value of the benefit to your other earnings;
- deduct and pay Class 1 National Insurance and PAYE tax through payroll.

CHECKLIST FOR HEALTHY AND SAFE DRIVING: COMPANY CAR USERS AND EMPLOYERS

Drivers should:

- Try to ensure they are well rested, and feeling fit and healthy (and not taking medication which contra-indicates using machinery), before starting long journeys.
- Plan the journey to include regular rest breaks (at least 15 minutes at least every two hours).
- If necessary, plan an overnight stop.
- Avoid setting out on a long drive after having worked a full day.
- Avoid driving into the period when they would normally be falling asleep.
- Avoid driving in the small hours (between 2 am and 6 am).
- Be extra careful when driving between 2 pm and 4 pm (especially after having eaten a meal).
- If feeling sleepy during a journey, stop somewhere safe, take drinks containing caffeine and take a short nap.

Employers

As part of our health and safety policies and practices, we adopt and implement the principles of managing occupational road risk, with particular reference to reducing the risk of employees being involved in a sleep-related driving accident.

We manage the safety of our employees who drive by:

- Considering and implementing the most suitable system of risk assessment and re-assessment for the road safety needs of the company and its employees.
- Choosing the right vehicle and the safest specification for the needs of the job.
- Ensuring that work practices, journey schedules, appointments and routes enable drivers to stay within the law.
- Providing sensible guidelines about driving and for the use of the vehicles for all employees who may drive for the company.

PRECEDENT 5L: Pension terms

1. Pension

1.1 You are entitled to become a member of the [*give details*] ('the Company Pension Scheme') subject always to the terms of the Company Pension Scheme Trust Deed and Rules in force from time to time.

1.2 A contracting-out certificate under the Pensions Schemes Act 1993 is [not] in force in respect of your employment.

1.3 The Company reserves the right to amend the terms of the Company Pension Scheme or to withdraw it completely at its sole discretion.

1.4 You will be eligible to become a member of the Company Pension Scheme if:

(a) you are a permanent employee of the Company;
(b) you are aged between [*specify*];
(c) you have completed at least [*specify*] year[s] of service with the Company.

1.5 The Company Pension Scheme Rules are available from the Human Resources Department.

2. Additional voluntary contributions (AVCs)

[If you wish, you may make additional voluntary contributions (AVCs) to a Scheme organised by the Company to increase the amount of pension you will receive at retirement. If you require further information please contact the Human Resources Department.]

OR

[You are not eligible for membership of any pension scheme as there is no scheme applicable to your employment.]

OR

[The Company shall in addition to your basic salary contribute to a personal pension scheme (approved by Her Majesty's Revenue and Customs) of your choice the sum of £... per annum.]

3. Life assurance

In addition, the Company will fund a Life Assurance policy, providing cover at the rate of 4 times your basic annual salary. This cover will be in force immediately on commencement of employment.

PRECEDENT 5M: Private medical insurance

1. The Company will make the necessary contributions for the Executive, [his/her spouse] [and dependent children] in the Company's Group private medical insurance cover. The Scheme is currently with [*give details*]. However, the Company reserves the right to terminate this cover and either take out cover with another private medical insurance provider or reduce the cover offered by [*name*]. Any new provider's scheme may not give equivalent or comparative cover as the current cover. The Company also reserves the right to withdraw the benefit at any time for reasons of cost. If this were to occur the Executive would be given at least one month's notice in order to obtain individual cover at [his/her] own expense.

2. Please note that since this is an insured scheme, the benefits to which you may become entitled are strictly governed by the insurance policy in force at the relevant

time. The Company does not warrant or offer to reimburse or pay for any medical costs incurred by the Executive where the Provider refuses payment or reimbursement of any fees or charges.

PRECEDENT 5N: Deputising conditions

1. Management determines who is competent to take on deputising duties and responsibilities.

2. The rate of pay and all other terms and conditions will be those that would have been paid if the deputy had been promoted to that grade.

3. The deputising period will be counted from the first day that the employee attends or is on call to perform the duties of the absent employee or the vacant post to the last day before the absent employee returns to work or the vacant post is filled.

4. Where the deputising period is scheduled to last longer than six months or lasts longer than six months, then this will be reviewed by senior management to determine:

(a) whether the individual is operating effectively in the temporary role;
(b) whether the deputising period should be extended;
(c) what alternative arrangements could be made;
(d) whether the deputy should be 'made up' into the substantive role.

5. When the individual reverts to their normal role, their pay will be at the level that it was immediately before deputising but including any pay increase which may have taken place during the period of deputising.

PRECEDENT 5O: Shoe and stocking allowance

Due to the nature of your job you are entitled to an annual shoe and stocking allowance of £[. . .]. gross. You should purchase some sturdy work shoes and socks or tights and submit an expenses form in order to obtain reimbursement of these costs.

PRECEDENT 5P: Expenses clause

1. Expenses claims

Expenses may be claimed in the following circumstances. From time to time you may receive amendments to this Policy by way of memoranda. Details of the latest Policy can be obtained from the Human Resources Department.

2. Travelling expenses

Travelling expenses will be paid to staff who travel on Company business to other locations, whether within or outside the UK on the following basis:

(a) standard rail fare or first class rail where the journey is over two hours;
(b) motor mileage allowance as determined from time to time;
(c) standard air travel will be permitted on Company business where the prior consent of a Director has been obtained;
(d) day subsistence may be paid according to the rules in force from time to time;
(e) meals and drinks in strict adherence to the expenses policy.

3. Overnight subsistence

Other claims for overnight expenses will only be made where they are unavoidable and prior permission must be obtained from your line manager. This allowance includes a set amount, to be determined in advance, for your evening meal, bed and breakfast.

PRECEDENT 5Q: Expenses policy

1. Any expenses incurred on Company business should be reclaimed on the Expense Form available from the Finance Department. This should be completed, attaching supporting original documentation, and signed by your Head of Department. You are encouraged to take an economical view on expenses generally and avoid, for instance, the use of taxi transportation across London during peak times.

Expenditure approval procedures

2. The following procedures set out approval requirements prior to committing the Company to any expense and how the system should operate.

3. Before ordering goods or service, or asking Central Services staff to order goods or service on the division's behalf, an Expenditure Approval Form (EAF) must be completed under the following rules.

(a) The provisions of the authorisation procedures must also be met (e.g. for expenditure above £10,000).
(b) The approval requirements do not apply to travel costs where the Group Travel Policy applies, nor to the permanent recruitment of staff where separate procedures apply, although recruitment fees will require an EAF before the job offer stage.
(c) The Facilities Manager and IT staff should not order hardware, software or other assets on behalf of any division or Central Services without having received an EAF if one is required.
(d) The Finance Department will not issue a cheque or pay an invoice unless an EAF is attached if one is required.
(e) Where expenditure is staggered (e.g. temporary staff or legal fees) an estimate of the aggregate cost should be made.
(f) For recurring expenditure (e.g. cleaning, information feeds) a list should be produced by the divisional financial controllers/support department representatives and approved by the divisional heads detailing the suppliers, description of service and a price tolerance (e.g. no more than £1,500 per month for service X from supplier Y). This will act as a 'once and for all' approval until suppliers or prices materially change. The Finance Department will have a list of approved recurring expenditures that do not require an EAF for each invoice.
(g) Non-discretionary/indirect expenses (e.g. location maps) that are allocated to divisions but ordered by Central Services will require an EAF in accordance with the Central Services limits and divisional authorisation will not be required. Central Services will inform divisional heads of material expenditure at Executive Committee meetings.
(h) Specific divisional approval limits/signatories are [*give details*].
(i) Expenses must be submitted no later than three (3) months after the month in which they were incurred. Failure to submit expenses within this period will lead to a refusal to consider or to pay those expenses unless there are exceptional circumstances, e.g. serious illness leading to hospitalisation.
(j) In the event that a company credit card is provided for use in paying for business expenses this must ONLY be used to pay for business expenses that have been authorised in advance. Any misuse of the company credit card may lead to disciplinary action being taken which could in a serious case be summary dismissal for gross misconduct (where fraud or criminal activity/conduct is believed to have taken place or where there has been deliberate misuse of the credit card).

PRECEDENT 5R: Travel expenses policy

Travel policy

1. Where travel is an element of your role, a degree of flexibility is assumed and you should, therefore, be prepared to travel in the UK and overseas on company business. You should, therefore, ensure that you maintain a valid driving licence/passport.

2. The Company policy on travel is aimed at ensuring trouble-free business travel within acceptable cost parameters, requiring minimal administration and with appropriate financial controls. This policy, which is available to all staff, clearly outlines the procedures for booking travel and should be referred to before any travel is undertaken or costs incurred.

3. This policy is intended to cover all non-chargeable travel expenditure undertaken by the group. It does not include alternative arrangements made between employees and a client, at the client's cost. Where the client is meeting the costs you should advise the Head of Compliance of all the arrangements including the reasons for the client meeting the costs, to ensure that there is no conflict with the Regulatory Bodies. If, in the view of the Head of Compliance, there is a potential infringement of the rules laid down by the Regulatory Body then the decision on the arrangement will be referred to the Chief Executive. However, you should try to adhere to the policy in order to avoid potential conflict or dissension from the client.

4. Travel arrangements should always be as cost effective as possible dependent on the particular circumstances of the trip. All travel and accommodation requirements must be arranged through [the PA to the Group Finance and Operations Director].

Air travel

5. All travel of up to two hours per journey should be in the cheapest available class. Discounts to the basic fare should be obtained whenever possible, particularly where the dates of travel have a high level of certainty. All air travel and specific exceptions to this policy must be approved in advance.

Train

6. All train travel should be standard class unless you are accompanying clients.

Car

7. The appropriate mileage rates for company and private vehicles can be found in the Company Car Scheme Rules. An employee allocated a company car and visiting other UK offices should use the car in preference to train or air travel.

Taxi/tube

8. In London, tubes, which are often faster, should be used whenever possible.

Hotels

9. Suitable hotel accommodation should be close to the place of business, be comfortable, secure and provide adequate facilities to work. Hotel costs should be 3 star or equivalent.

Expense claim forms

10. Before submitting expense claim forms to Central Finance, all forms should be authorised by your line manager.

PRECEDENT 5S: (1) Deductions clause and (2) loan form

(1) Deductions

The Company shall be entitled at any time during your employment, or in any event on termination, to deduct from your remuneration or your expenses any monies due from you to the Company. Such deductions may include, but are not limited to:

1.1   An overpayment of, or advancement on, wages, bonus, commission or expenses.

1.2   Annual leave taken as at the date of the termination of your employment which is in excess of your accrued entitlement.

1.3   Any loans, including season ticket loans.

1.4   When you leave the Company, the balance of any training funding given.

1.5   The market value of any unreturned Company property.

2.   **Deductions from salary**

The Company reserves the right to make deductions from your salary where any mistake has been made in paying you (whether this is normal salary, sick pay, maternity pay, bonus, commission, overtime, etc.), i.e. where an overpayment has been made or where a loan has been made and repayment becomes due.

We will always identify and notify you of any error in payment and will advise you of the amount overpaid and will endeavour to agree with you a repayment schedule if you cannot repay the entire overpayment in one amount. We will only reserve the right to deduct a reasonable sum each month from your salary.

Any loan repayment schedule will also be set out and you will be consulted on the schedule and we will endeavour to obtain your agreement to this schedule. However, we reserve the right to deduct a reasonable sum each month until the loan has been repaid.

(2) Loan form

[*Date*]

[2 copies]

LOAN AGREEMENT TO DEDUCT FROM WAGES/SALARY

1.   Mr/Ms [*name*] accepts that the sum of £ . . . has been made to [him/her] by way of a loan from [*name of employer*].

2.   Mr/Ms [*name*] agrees to repay all outstanding monies [*state amount outstanding*] in relation to this loan either by permitting [*employer*] to deduct the monies in [*number*] equal instalments from [his/her] salary each month or by making a direct payment by way of cheque or cash each month/on a regular basis.

3.   Mr/Ms [*name*] hereby authorises [*employer*] to deduct the amount of [*state amount per month*] from [his/her] salary for the following [*number*] months.

4.   Mr/Ms [*name*] understands that if [s/he] fails to make any or all such payments on the agreed date(s) and [s/he] leaves [his/her] employment for whatever reason, [*employer*] has the authority to deduct the balance from final salary/any outstanding expenses owing/outstanding holiday pay due, etc.

5.   If there are insufficient funds in final salary or other termination payments or expenses due and/or no repayments have been made direct to [*employer*] within 12

weeks of the termination date or agreement reached as to repayment, it is understood that legal proceedings may be brought to recover all monies due.

Signed.............................. Date ....

[employee]

Signed .... Date ....

[employer]

PRECEDENT 5T: Repayment clause due to negligence, carelessness, etc.

1. Where any losses are sustained in relation to the property or monies of the Company, client, customer, visitor or other employee, during the course of your employment caused through your carelessness, negligence, recklessness or through breach of the Company's rules or any dishonesty on your part, the Company reserves the right to require you to repay a part of or the total amount of the said losses, either by deduction from salary or by any other method acceptable to the Company. The Company may also require you to repay any damages, expenses or any other monies paid or payable by the Company to any third party for any act or omission for which the Company may be deemed vicariously liable on your behalf.

2. A typical example may be where a member of staff offers a client a discounted ticket (e.g. for air travel or a cruise) where there is no prior authorisation or permission and as a result the Company has to make up the difference to the airline or travel operator. In such a case you will be required to repay that element of the monies. As you all know, there are very strict rules about when discounts can be offered and by whom.

3. Another example may be where the client has handed over cash or a cheque to you and you fail to follow company procedures and those monies are lost. You will be held accountable for those losses and you will be required to repay those monies.

4. This clause will also apply in cases of overpayment of any remuneration or any other payments (statutory, discretionary, etc.) made by mistake or through any misrepresentation or otherwise.

5. The Company also reserves the right to withhold payment or deduct from salary a day's pay for each day of unauthorised absence. Any decision concerning this matter will be made by your immediate superior who will notify Personnel and Payroll.

PRECEDENT 5U: Loan agreement for training expenses

Loan Agreement made on [date]

Between

(1) [Name of employer] ('the Company'); and
(2) [Name and address of employee] ('the Employee')

1. The Company hereby agrees to make an award of a bursary to the Employee in order to assist him to undertake and successfully complete a four-year, 'thin sandwich', B ENG Degree in Science and Technology at [specify] University. The said course commences on [date].

2. The Company agrees to make an initial payment for the first year in the sum of £ ... thereafter to be reviewed. There will be no commitment to make any further payments after completion of the first year unless the Company is satisfied with the diligence and progress

made by the Employee. However, should the Employee, in the opinion of the Company have achieved a successful first year at the University and passed all necessary examinations, assessments, etc. at the required standard, the Company will make further payments to the Employee as deemed appropriate by the Company.

3. During the periods of study, whilst absent from the Company, the Employee's contract of employment and all terms and conditions of employment will be suspended. However, his absence from work for all statutory purposes will be regarded as maintaining continuity of employment, i.e. will not break his continuity of employment but will not count for any purpose other than accruing service for statutory purposes. Upon periods of return to work for placements, any particular term or condition of employment that may apply will be spelt out in writing, otherwise only the agreed remuneration will be paid during these periods of work. These periods of service will count as accruing both contractual and statutory service.

4. The Employee agrees to work hard and diligently and to maintain the name and reputation of the Company whilst at [specify] University. He agrees if so requested to provide copies of work completed during the course and to make available to the Company at no cost any research or papers written by him which may be relevant or helpful to the business of the Company. He also agrees to release the copyright in any such documents to the Company if requested and to apply for patents in the event of any invention that is required to be duly patented. His rights are guaranteed under the Patents Act 1977, section 40.

5. The Employee agrees that it is fair and reasonable that he returns to the service of the Company at the end of his successful completion of the said four-year course and remains in service (other than if he is dismissed by the Company) for a continuous period of two years thereafter.

6. The Employee agrees that in the event of his voluntarily resigning from the service of the Company, he will repay the whole or a proportion of the bursary paid to him on the following basis:

Length of service remaining	Proportion of bursary to be repaid
24 months, i.e. does not return	100 %
23–18 months	75 %
18–12 months	50 %
12–6 months	25 %
6 months	25 %
5 months	20 %
4 months	15 %
3 months	10 %
2 months	5 %
1 month	2.5%

Signed .... Date ....

[employee]

Signed .... Date ....

[employer]

PRECEDENT 5V: Degree funding

The Company will fund the cost of your degree subject to the normal funding rules as detailed in the Learning and Development Policy. Please note that should you leave our employment within a 24-month period from the date of qualification you will be required to reimburse the Company the proportionate cost of the degree course in accordance with the scale of reimbursement as set out in the said policy above.

In addition to funding the degree course the Company will contribute £1,000 towards the cost of purchasing your compulsory course books/degree related material. This funding is subject to the normal funding and reimbursement rules as detailed in the Learning and Development Policy and as specified in [clause XX] above.

PRECEDENT 5W: Relocation policy

1. Overview

This policy forms part of the Company's recruitment and retention strategy. It is intended to support the needs of the business to attract and appoint individuals because of their expertise in their particular professional field.

2. Scope

The Company, subject to the conditions outlined in the Procedure for Relocation Expenses will provide financial assistance to newly appointed staff who are required to relocate to take up employment at the Company and where their existing home is not within reasonable daily travelling distance of their new place of work.

3. Principles

3.1 New employees will not normally be eligible for relocation assistance if another member of their household is claiming relocation expenses from this Company.

3.2 Payments for relocation expenses are treated as part of a new employee's earnings for income tax and national insurance contributions (NICs) purposes. However, the first £8,000 is exempt from income tax and NICs as long as the following conditions are met:

(a) they had to move home to take up the job;
(b) their existing home is not within reasonable daily travelling distance of the new workplace;
(c) the home they move to is within reasonable daily travelling distance of the new workplace.

3.3 Should the employee voluntarily leave the Company within 24 months of commencing employment with the Company, they will be required to repay a proportion of the reimbursed expenses. This amount will decrease by 1/24 for every month of service completed.

4. Size of payment

In normal circumstances, relocation expenses will be reimbursed up to 10 per cent of the new employee's starting salary. If they are relocating from outside the UK they will be entitled to claim up to 20 per cent of their starting salary. The starting salary is defined as gross salary [excluding London Allowance].

5. Office equipment

The removal of office equipment and work-related items to the Company does not constitute domestic removal. Where applicable, reimbursements of these costs are at the discretion of the employee's line manager.

6. Reporting

Regular reports on trends in the payment of relocation expenses will be provided to the Company's Audit and Compliance Committee.

7. Roles and responsibilities

- Senior Area Managers: authorise relocation expense claims.
- Senior Managers, Heads of Departments: make proposals for payment of relocation expenses to individuals; make proposals to advertise relocation expenses for hard-to-fill positions.
- Senior Human Resources Advisers: provide professional Human Resources advice; administer the payment of relocation expenses; provide regular reports on trends in the payment of relocation expenses.

8. Procedures

The following procedures form part of the policy and provide guidelines for the implementation of the policy:

Procedure for the reimbursement of relocation expenses

(a) *Introduction*

The information contained in this document is intended to explain clearly the details of the Company's relocation scheme. If you have any queries regarding the scheme please contact the Senior Human Resources Adviser dealing with the appointment, who will be pleased to clarify any issues for you.

(b) *Qualifying criteria*

To qualify the employee must meet the following criteria:

- The expected duration of their employment with the Company should be at least two years.
- Moved home to take up the appointment with the Company.
- The move must have significantly reduced their travel to work time.
- Any claim should normally be made within 12 months of taking up the appointment. This may be extended to 18 months if the employee is able to provide evidence of delays beyond their control.
- Relocation formed part of the formal offer of appointment when the employee was offered the role at the Company.

(c) *Scope of payment*

Reimbursement will be in respect of the following expenditure:

- removal of furniture and effects, including insurance;
- storage of personal effects;
- legal expenses in connection with the buying and selling of property;
- travel and accommodation expenses incurred during preliminary visits to the area to view prospective property;
- for removal from overseas, one economy class or equivalent air fare for the employee and their immediate family.

The tax implications of international relocation are complex and individual guidance on the tax consequences should be sought.

(d) *Administrative process*

- Two reasonable and competitive price quotations should be obtained; the Company will reimburse costs based on the best value for money.

- Request for payment should be submitted to the Senior Human Resources Adviser dealing with the appointment, using the Relocation Expenses form. Any claims for expenses will only be payable on production of original receipts or invoices proving that the expenditure has been incurred.
- Receipts and evidence that the employee has moved to take up their appointment should be submitted with the Relocation Expenses form. The form should be signed by your Head of Department.
- Please contact the Human Resources Adviser dealing with the appointment for further advice on making a claim.

PRECEDENT 5X: Olympic Games and other events

The next Olympic Games in 2020 is being held in Tokyo from 24 July to 9 August 2020.

Staffing requirements

All requests for time off will be individually considered in light of our business needs. All staff will be required to be flexible to accommodate our business needs during this time. This may mean starting work early and/or staying late and in such a case overtime may be paid (please see our overtime policy).

You will be given as much advance notice as possible if this is to occur.

Requests for annual leave during the games

- All requests for annual leave must be submitted in writing on the holiday request form and be authorised by end of January 2020. All requests will be considered on a 'first come first served' basis and no commitment or promises will be made that any individual will be given the time off. If you have already obtained tickets then please ensure that your request for annual leave is in NOW.
- Staff may be required to take compulsory annual leave of up to 10 days during this period, depending upon any shutdowns or reduction in services and should keep accrued holiday available accordingly.
- Staff will be required to be flexible with hours dependent on requests for changes in working time from clients/customers, etc.

Other sporting events

We have the annual tennis tournament at Wimbledon every summer, rugby and cricket fixtures and football matches.

If you live in any area of the country where these fixtures occur, you will need to take special care about the time it takes to travel to and from work, etc.

Travel

- Extra time should be allowed for travel as peak times will inevitably result in delays and staff must make plans for the duration of these events to arrive on time, or early, to work.
- Staff should be informed of travel information on affected routes and travel to and from work to avoid peak times where possible.

- In some areas roads may be shut during certain times during these events. Staff should make themselves aware of any road diversions and make plans accordingly.

Lateness/sickness/absence

- Lateness during this period will be subject to the normal reporting/notification procedures and staff will be subject to disciplinary warnings if they arrive late or fail to arrive at work at all due to travel disruption.
- Any absence during these events will be subject to normal reporting and medical evidence rules. All efforts will be made to accommodate requests for annual leave but any unapproved or unauthorised absences will be dealt with through the disciplinary procedure

Alcohol and drugs

There is a genuine concern that binge drinking increases during major sporting events.

- Should there be any reason to suspect that lateness or absence is due to alcohol or other substance abuse, this will be investigated and may result in being sent home for health or safety reasons and may result in disciplinary action.
- Staff are reminded of their legal obligations regarding drink driving and of the Company rules that anyone driving a company vehicle or their own vehicle on Company business are strictly prohibited from drinking ANY alcohol for a few hours before coming on duty and during the entire course of their working day. It is regarded as gross misconduct to have anything other than a minimal amount of alcohol present in the blood.

Your safety and security

- When travelling on the Tube, please be aware that pickpockets will be taking advantage of the increase in visitor numbers. Be extra vigilant with handbags, briefcases and laptops.
- When travelling late at night, where possible avoid travelling alone and keep away from any groups of sports fans who appear to be under the influence of alcohol or are rowdy or abusive.

Bullying and harassment

- We want everyone to enjoy these sporting events and understand that everyone will be supporting different teams and events, and emotions can run high.
- Whilst banter and discussion of the events is to be expected, there will be a policy of zero tolerance regarding any discriminatory or inappropriate remarks concerning any member of or participant in an event (including racist or xenophobic remarks) and any incidents of this sort should be reported to line managers.
- Everyone is reminded of the bullying and harassment and communications policies. Bullying and harassment has no place within our Company in whatever form it takes, e.g. whether face to face or through any form of communication network or media – Twitter, Facebook, email, etc.

Watching of sporting events during working hours

- Everyone should be aware that standards of work, performance and attention to our clients, etc. must be maintained and the viewing of sporting events on mobile phones/PCs, etc. is not allowed during working hours UNLESS you have been given special permission by your line manager, which will be noted.

OR

- We may at certain times arrange for large TV screens to be placed in our Boardrooms, etc. and you may be given permission where the business permits to take breaks during the day to watch specific events but this must be booked in writing with your line manager who will give you a permission slip and will record your name and the date and time in a diary which will remain at reception.

We are committed to assisting everyone to enjoy these events whilst maintaining our service standards and staff wellbeing.

6

Absence and sick pay

> I reckon being ill is one of the great pleasures of life, provided one is not too ill and is not obliged to work until one is better. (Samuel Butler, *The Way of All Flesh*, Penguin Classics)

6.1 Absence

Since the Statement of Fitness for Work (Fit Note) replaced the MED 3 medical statement (Sick Note) in April 2010 (see **6.4** below), GPs have been encouraged to get their patients back to work earlier than they might have done or to encourage their patients not to take sick leave but instead to restrict their duties or reduce their hours of work temporarily to assist their recovery. Evidence from various studies shows that work can act as an important part of a rehabilitation process.

It is important for employers to set out in writing in their policy what they regard as authorised absence for which statutory sick pay or normal (Occupational Sick) pay will be paid. Any other absence will normally be considered as unauthorised, for which no payment is normally made. The wording for a typical definition would be as follows:

Authorised absence is defined as:
(a) genuine sickness and this has been notified to the company according to the absence reporting rules;
(b) leave for which prior permission has been granted (in writing where appropriate) by the immediate manager;
(c) absence for genuine reasons outside the employee's control which are acceptable to the company, e.g. being unable to travel to work because of an unexpected snow storm.

Requirement to report to work

Precedents 6A and **6B** set out some rules where staff are unable to come to work or where there are difficulties coming to work because of rail or other transport difficulties/strikes or bad weather or acts of God that prevent or hinder staff from coming to work.

Some employers have rules concerning the requirement to report for work during an emergency such as a transport strike or bad weather, or unexpected major acts of God (such as in April 2010 where volcanic ash above Europe disrupted air travel for over a week, delaying many people due to return to the UK after a trip abroad).

These policies cover:

(a) what staff are expected to do in an emergency such as travel difficulties or bad weather;
(b) rules applying during prolonged disruption of travel; and
(c) what staff must do when they cannot get to the office/place of work.

6.2 Time-keeping

It is important to set out the normal start time and the time when the employee is required to be in the office/practice/factory, etc.

It is also essential to define what you mean by being 'late', e.g. presenting yourself ready for work at any time after your official start time.

In some cases the individual has to wash, change into uniform or get to a work station to be ready for work at the start time of the shift. In such a case, it is essential therefore to explain to employees what is the latest time that they are required actually to arrive at work in order to be ready for work.

For example, a dental nurse, nurse or care assistant must be dressed and ready in the practice or on the ward at the start of their shift, otherwise those finishing their shift would have to remain on duty until that person comes to work or someone else can be found. So they need to be in their changing room or in their uniform at the practice or on the ward before the start time of their shift. Similarly, operatives on a continuous shift are required to be ready for their shift no later than the official start time otherwise they are deemed to be late. Dental nurses and hygienists in private practices are specifically required to be ready for the patient, with their instruments ready, etc. before the patient arrives!

Precedent 6C is an example of a term in the contract of a dental nurse in a private dental practice.

Disciplinary action and definition

It is important to spell out what is the employer's definition of 'late' and when disciplinary action will be taken. Typical wording for a definition would be as follows:

> Lateness is defined as arriving at work/arriving at your work station at any time after your official start time.
>
> If you are late more than twice in a three-month period without reasonable excuse, you may receive an official oral warning. This will last on your record for six months and any lateness during the currency of this warning or any other breach of company rules or performance issues will render you liable for the next stage of the disciplinary procedure.

6.3 Sick pay

It is particularly important to explain the circumstances under which occupational sick pay (and statutory sick pay (SSP)) will be paid. Typical wording would be as follows:

> Sick pay is paid where the illness or injury prevents you, the employee, from carrying out any duties that it is reasonable to require you to undertake under your contract. Please note that the Company reserves the right to ask you to undertake any duties that it is reasonable to expect you to do at any time during a period of sickness absence under our 'Light Duties Policy'. Unreasonable refusal to comply with such an instruction could render you liable to the cessation of sick pay and disciplinary action. Please note that not all the duties express and implied are suspended during sickness absence. You may be given reasonable and/or lawful instructions during any period of sick leave.

Such a definition means that employees will not receive sick pay for being ill or injured. They will only be paid where their illness or injury prevents them from carrying out any task that it is reasonable to ask them to do.

GPs' Fit Notes make provision for the GP to sign an employee as fit for work with modified duties during a period of rehabilitation to full fitness.

Not all the duties under the contract are suspended when an employee is ill or injured, only those duties that the illness or injury prevents the employee from doing. In *Marshall* v. *Alexander Sloan & Co. Ltd* [1981] IRLR 264, when an employee was asked to remove all the company goods from her car when she was off sick and she refused, her subsequent dismissal was held to be fair. The EAT held (p.264):

> The Industrial Tribunal had not erred in law in holding that the appellant's dismissal for failing to carry out an order to remove merchandise from her car was reasonable in the circumstances, notwithstanding that she was off work ill at the time the order was given. There was no error in the Industrial Tribunal's decision that the appellant had unjustifiably refused to carry out a reasonable and proper instruction.
>
> The argument that all the appellant's obligations under the contract were suspended because she was off work ill so that her employers had no contractual authority to issue the order could not be accepted. Though a term has to be implied into a contract limiting the employee's obligation to perform *all* the terms of his contract when he is sick, such a term should be no wider than is necessary to give the contract business effect. Business commonsense requires only that when an employee is off sick, he is relieved of the obligation to perform such services as the sickness from which he is suffering prevents him from carrying out, not that all the employee's obligations are suspended.
>
> In the present case, the Industrial Tribunal had found as a fact that the appellant could have complied with her employers' order and removed the stock from the car herself or got someone else to do so for her. Her sickness was not of a kind which prevented her from carrying out her obligation not to leave merchandise in the car. Therefore, she could be lawfully ordered to remove it.

Definition of 'incapable of work' for SSP

The definition of 'sickness' for the payment of SSP can be found in reg.2 of the Statutory Sick Pay (General) Regulations 1982, SI 1982/894.

Persons deemed incapable of work

(1) A person who is not incapable of work which he can reasonably be expected to do under a particular contract of service may be deemed to be incapable of work of such a kind by reason of some specific disease or bodily or mental disablement for any day on which either –

    (a) (i) he is under medical care in respect of a disease or disablement as aforesaid,
          (ii) it is stated by a registered medical practitioner that for precautionary or convalescent reasons consequential on such disease or disablement he should abstain from work, or from work of such a kind, and
          (iii) he does not work under that contract of service, or

    (b) he is –
          (i) excluded or abstains from work, or from work of such a kind, pursuant to a request or notice in writing lawfully made under an enactment; or
          (ii) otherwise prevented from working pursuant to an enactment,

by reason of his being a carrier, or having been in contact with a case, of a relevant disease.

The key words are that the employee is 'incapable of work', i.e. that it is the personal sickness of the individual and not the sickness or death of someone else. Not all illnesses or injuries will prevent the employee from doing some duties that they can reasonably be expected to do under their contract.

Accordingly, absence because of the illness or death of a relative counts as compassionate or bereavement leave not sick leave. Depending upon the relationship of the deceased and the employee and whether the employee has genuine depression or anxiety, the employer can decide whether or not the employee is incapable of work for SSP purposes (see page 55 of the HMRC *Employer Helpbook for Statutory Sick Pay* E14 (2013), now withdrawn and replaced by less comprehensive guidance). It is therefore perfectly reasonable to mirror this rule for occupational sick pay purposes as well: occupational sick pay may also be paid 'only in circumstances when the employee him/herself is incapable because of their own illness or injury from carrying out any duties that it is reasonable to expect them to undertake'.

It is also possible that an employee with two different contracts could be regarded as unfit for one but fit for the other. An example would be a man with a bad back whose day job is lifting heavy crates but who is a bingo caller at night – he could be regarded as fit for one job but not the other.

However, if an individual has two contracts for two different types of work with the same employer or employers trading in association, e.g. a teacher at a sixth form college who has a contract teaching PE in the day and maths at night school in the evenings, and these earnings are aggregated for NICs purposes, that person must be incapable of work under all contracts before becoming entitled to SSP.

6.4 Medical evidence and Fit Notes

Whilst Fit Notes are 'strong evidence of incapacity' they may not be conclusive evidence of incapacity for work when 'there is evidence to the contrary' (pages 12 and 19 of the HMRC *Employer Helpbook for Statutory Sick Pay* E14 (2013)).

The previous position in relation to MED 3 medical statements was confirmed in *Hutchinson* v. *Enfield Rolling Mills Ltd* [1981] IRLR 318. Mr Hutchinson was certified off sick by his doctor with 'sciatica' for a seven-day period. However, he was seen by one of the company's directors taking part in a union demonstration in Brighton. He was dismissed on the grounds that his presence in Brighton 'was not consistent with a person who was reputedly suffering from sciatica. In other words, if you were fit enough to travel to Brighton to take part in a demonstration, you were fit enough to report for work'.

The EAT held that (p.318):

> It cannot be said that it is not reasonable for employers to go behind a sick note. Employers are concerned to see that their employees are working when fit to do so; and if they are doing things away from their business which suggest that they are fit to work, then that is a matter which concerns them.

The Fit Note is in any event provided 'For SSP purposes only'. GPs issuing Fit Notes have no interest in the employers' sick pay scheme as the relationship is with their patients not the employers.

The changes mean that the GP can:

- advise when the employee may be fit for work with some support;
- suggest common ways to help the employee return to work;
- give information on how the employee's medical condition will affect what the employee can do at work.

As for the previous Sick Note, the Fit Note will not be issued until after the seventh calendar day of sickness.

When GPs sign a Fit Note they will advise their patients on one of two options. Either they are 'not fit for work' or they 'may be fit for work'.

'Not fit for work'

The GP will choose the 'not fit for work' option when the GP believes that the patient's health condition will prevent the patient from working at all for a stated period of time.

'May be fit for work'

The GP will choose the 'may be fit for work' option when the GP believes that the patient may be able to return to work while recovering, with some help from the employer.

The GP may include some comments to help the employer understand how the patient is affected by their condition. If appropriate, the GP can also suggest one or more common ways to help the employee return to work.

This could include a phased return to work (where the patient may benefit from a gradual increase in work duties or working hours, for example after an operation or after injury); altered hours (allowing the flexibility to start or leave later, for example if the patient would struggle travelling in the 'rush hour'); amended duties (to take into account the medical condition, for example removing heavy lifting if the patient has had a back injury); and changes to the workplace (to take into account the medical condition, for example allowing the patient to work on the ground floor if they have problems going up and down stairs).

If it is possible for the patient to return to work, then the employer will agree how this will happen, what support the patient will receive and for how long, and how their pay may be affected if the patient returns to work on different hours or duties. There is no requirement to pay at the normal rate of pay for normal working hours if the employee is returning on reduced hours or on reduced duties.

If the employee does not agree with the employer on when and how they will return to work, the employee and/or the GP are encouraged to talk to the employer to help the employer understand. Taking out a grievance would be a last resort.

Guidance to employers on a Statement of Fitness for Work can be found at: **www.gov.uk/government/publications/fit-note-guidance-for-employers-and-line-managers**.

Employers may accept certificates from other health practitioners such as osteopaths, chiropractors, acupuncturists, physiotherapists. These certificates should be viewed on their merits. The key is that the employer is satisfied that the employee is unfit to work.

6.5 Medical examinations

Before 8 September 2015, GPs alone could refer but since then employers may refer an employee for a voluntary occupational health assessment (normally by telephone) after four weeks' sickness absence under the government 'Fit for Work' scheme. For a guide to this scheme please see **http://fitforwork.org/government-guidance/**.

It is sensible to include a clause in the contract requiring the employee to agree to consent to a medical examination and disclosure of a medical report at any time during the course of the employment, with a company-appointed doctor at the company's expense, or with the government 'Fit for Work' scheme.

Whilst of course this is a persuasive measure in any particular instance (employees are reminded that they had agreed to this clause at the outset of their employment), employees must give their explicit informed consent on any particular occasion that such an examination and report is required. This normally occurs during or at the end of a spell of sickness absence, to advise the employer on functional capacity and functional limitation of the individual.

It is important that the consent form includes both consent to the medical examination and consent to disclosure of a medical report, as the only occasion where it is implied that consent is given to disclosure of the report to the employer is in relation to litigation where the employer has sought a medical report for the purposes of the trial (see Pill LJ in *Kapadia v. London Borough of Lambeth* [2000] IRLR 669).

A 'medical report' for the purposes of the Access to Medical Reports Act (AMRA) 1988 means 'medical report' prepared by a medical practitioner who is or has been responsible for the 'clinical care' of the individual. '..."Care" includes examination, investigation or diagnosis for the purposes of, or in connection with, any form of medical treatment' (s.2). 'Medical treatment' includes counselling (*Kapadia v. London Borough of Lambeth* above) and if an OHP has seen the employee for any purpose relating to occupational health, e.g. the giving of advice or counselling, then AMRA 1988 will apply to any subsequent report.

However, in the 2009 guidance on 'Confidentiality' from the General Medical Council (GMC) (GMC/CON/0909), para.34(d) and the supplementary guidance, 'Disclosing Information for Insurance, Employment and Similar Purposes', doctors are advised to offer to show a copy of any medical report to the individual first before sending it to the employer and to send a copy of any report to the individual at the same time as sending it to the employer.

Employees who refuse to go for a medical examination or to meet their employers

Where the employee, without good cause, refuses to co-operate with the employer, then this may be regarded as a fundamental breach of the implied term of trust and confidence warranting summary dismissal. As the Court of Appeal held in *Briscoe v. Lubrizol Ltd* [2002] IRLR 607, the employee's summary dismissal was a direct result of his failure, without explanation or excuse, to attend a meeting to discuss his position, and his failure thereafter to reply to the employers' requests to contact them. A majority of the Court of Appeal regarded this as a repudiatory breach and rejected the view that the employers were under a duty to warn the employee that if he did not make contact with them he might be dismissed. 'Duties of trust and confidence', Lord Justice Ward held, 'are mutual'. In this case, the employers were entitled to treat the employee's behaviour as gross misconduct undermining the trust and confidence term.

A term in the contract may assist: see **Precedent 6E**.

Normally the OHP or company-appointed doctor will need to see the relevant GP records before examining the employee. In such a case a consent form (see **Precedent 6F**) needs to be completed by the employee. If the employee refuses consent without any acceptable explanation, then an employer would be within its rights to refuse to continue paying any sick pay including SSP on the grounds that this 'refusal to provide consent is sufficient grounds for (the employer) to doubt that the incapacity is genuine and stop paying SSP' ('SSP Employer Guide', **www.gov.uk/employers-sick-pay/notice-and-fit-notes**).

Referring employees to a psychiatrist

Employers should note that there may be some difficulty in referring an employee to see a psychiatrist unless there is clear evidence of a mental or psychological disorder or illness, e.g. a mental illness appears on the Fit Note (medical certificate). It appears that both individuals and the courts still take the view that being referred to see a psychiatrist is something of a stigma and if the employer refers an employee without reasonable grounds, the employer may be breaching the implied term of mutual trust and confidence.

In *Bliss v. South East Thames Regional Health Authority* [1985] IRLR 308, the Court of Appeal held (p.309):

> There is no general power in an employer to require employees to undergo psychiatric examination. In the present case, there was no other relevant specific power in the plaintiff's contract or under the scheme of the National Health Service. Although it was common ground that it was an implied term of the plaintiff's contract that the defendants were entitled to require him to undergo a medical examination if they had reasonable ground for believing that he might be suffering from physical or mental disability which might cause harm to patients or adversely affect the quality of their treatment, the defendants had this power only against the background of a circular which set up a procedure for dealing with reports of incapacity on the part of hospital medical staff and provided for an enquiry by a committee called the Three Wise Men. As the conclusion of the report by the Three Wise Men in the present case merely showed a severe degree of breakdown of personal relationships and found that there was no mental or pathological illness, the defendants had no right to require the plaintiff to submit to a psychiatric examination. ...
>
> It would be difficult in this particular area of employment law to think of anything more calculated or likely to destroy the relationship of confidence and trust which ought to exist between employer and employee than, without reasonable cause, to require a consultant surgeon to undergo a psychiatric examination, and to suspend him from the hospital on his refusing to do so.

6.6   Need to inform doctor of the purpose of examination and report

It is crucial to inform both the individual and the doctor what is the purpose of the examination and the report. In *Whitbread plc v. Mills* [1988] IRLR 501, the employee thought that her employer had sent her to the company-appointed doctor for a second opinion on her back. In fact, it was to determine whether she would be fit to return to work in the near future. This ambiguity was held to be one of the unfair procedural defects in the employer's procedure.

The information that any company-appointed doctor needs to know is:

1. Job description with description of duties, e.g. night work, heavy lifting, standing, etc.
2. Length of time absent from work, with copies of self-certificates and Fit Notes.
3. Reasons for requesting the report, e.g. early retirement on health grounds;

continuation of sick pay; planning the work in the department; planning for alternative duties or modification to duties for the employee.

Employers are then entitled to non-clinical information in these categories:

(a) when the employee is expected to return to work;
(b) whether the employee will have a residual disability;
(c) whether that disability will be temporary or permanent;
(d) whether the employee will be able to render regular and efficient service upon return to work;
(e) what duties the doctor recommends that the patient does not do and for how long;
(f) whether the employee will continue to take any medication or undergo any outpatient treatment (only medically qualified personnel should ask what medication or treatment is still being taken in order to advise management on appropriate duties and working time, etc.).

Note: If the employer does not want to receive the answer 'light duties' to question (e), then it must be asked in the negative rather than 'What duties do you recommend that your patient undertakes?' Employers should not forget to offer a fee for the report!

6.7 Instructions to doctors

Instructions to doctors must contain relevant information, e.g. the sick pay scheme and early retirement rules of the pension scheme, if the doctor is to understand their instructions properly.

Instructions to an OHP such as 'Perhaps you would be good enough to indicate whether you feel that Mr X's health is such that he should be retired on grounds of permanent ill health' are too brief to be helpful (*East Lindsay District Council* v. *Daubney* [1977] IRLR 181).

It is vital that instructions to doctors remain neutral, particularly in case the matter goes to a tribunal or the county court or High Court. No doctor should be instructed in terms such as: 'Thank you for seeing this awful Scotsman. He is normally incoherent because he is drunk. If he is coherent he is lying. Now I know why Hadrian built the wall.'

In the case of *De Keyser Ltd* v. *Wilson* [2001] IRLR 324, an employment consultant who was acting as the employers' representative sent a letter of instructions to their expert medical witness. The letter of instruction made it clear that they questioned both the extent of the employee's illness and its cause. The letter included details of her private life which the employers believed had caused or contributed to her stress and asked the expert to carry out a critical examination of her GP's finding that her illness was entirely attributable to her employers' alleged actions.

It read:

> The Respondent finds the Applicant particularly easy to disbelieve, and the opinion of Dr Donk [of] the Applicant's alleged stress-related illness is wholly refuted. The

> Respondent is aware of several factors and events in the Applicant's private life which were present prior to her resignation on the 18th April 2000. Specifically, the stress-inducing factors in the Applicant's life were...

The letter to Dr Moran included the HR representative's view of the events leading to Miss Wilson's resignation:

> The Respondent's position is that all of the Applicant's allegations are cynical and vexatious in the extreme. However as a hypothesis the Respondent considers that in comparison to the Applicant's personal life the alleged actions of the Area Manager were trivial and incapable of inducing a stress-related illness of a magnitude to prevent the Applicant from working for over 8 months at the time of writing. We would like you to conduct a comprehensive medical assessment of the Applicant and to make a critical examination of Dr Donk's finding that the Applicant's alleged stress-related illness is attributable entirely to her former employer's alleged actions. At the time of writing the Applicant has decided not to call Dr Donk to give evidence that can be cross-examined and has decided to withdraw his letter of the medical opinion from her evidence.
>
> We have no doubt at all that the Applicant will simply deny any causal link between the factors in her private life and her alleged illness. We also believe that the Applicant could exaggerate the effect of her alleged illness. We will be grateful if you would provide us with a comprehensive medical report following your assessment of the Applicant. The copy of the report should be provided to the Applicant at the same time. Your full expenses will be met by the Respondent. We will also be grateful if you will express an opinion as to whether or not the alleged actions of the employer would have been capable of inducing a stress-related illness in a person with normal resilience.

The Employment Tribunal held that:

> We cannot stress enough to you that we find the tone and content of this letter to be reprehensible, wholly inappropriate and prejudicial to the Applicant's rights to have an impartial medical examination. We consider that the manner in which this gentleman has sought to influence this medical practitioner makes it entirely inappropriate for Miss Wilson to attend before Dr Moran.
>
> With the greatest of respect, we consider all of the above named [which were features of the letter of instruction to which objection was taken] to be highly prejudicial to the Applicant and do not consider how the Applicant can possibly attend before this practitioner. In the alternative we will consider that, if the Respondent wishes to have the Applicant examined, the Respondent and the Applicant should each submit the name of a consultant, a fee quotation and a CV. The Tribunal should then determine who should be instructed. Alternatively, and at the very least, there should be a joint letter of instruction in the terms attached to this correspondence.

Whilst overturning the Employment Tribunal's decision to strike out the respondents' notice of appearance (now called Grounds of Resistance), the EAT held that the tribunal had it well within its power that there should be no examination of the applicant by the doctor to whom the offensive instruction had been given and no offensive instruction of some other doctor.

Obiter, the EAT gave the following guidance for when instructing medical experts:

1. Careful thought needs to be given before any party embarks upon instructions for expert evidence. It by no means follows that because a

party wishes such evidence to be admitted that it will be. A prudent party will first explore with the Employment Tribunal at a directions hearing or in correspondence whether, in principle, expert evidence is likely to be acceptable.
2. Save where one side or the other has already committed itself to the use of its own expert (which is to be avoided in the absence of special circumstances), the joint instruction of a single expert is the preferred course.
3. If a joint expert is to be instructed, the terms which the parties need to agree include the incidence of that expert's fees and expenses. Nothing precludes the parties agreeing that they will abide by such view as the tribunal shall later indicate as to that incidence (though the tribunal will not be obliged to give any such indication) but the tribunal has for the time being no power as to costs beyond the general provisions of r.12 of the Employment Tribunals Rules of Procedure.
4. If the means available to one side or another are such that in its view it cannot agree to share or to risk any exposure to the expert's fees or expenses, or if, irrespective of its means, a party refuses to pay or share such costs, the other party or parties can reasonably be expected to prefer to require their own expert but even in such a case, the weight to be attached to that expert's evidence (a matter entirely for the tribunal to judge) may be found to have been increased if the terms of their instruction shall have been submitted to the other side, if not for agreement then for comment, ahead of their being finalised for sending to the expert.
5. If a joint expert is to be used, tribunals, lest parties dally, may fix a period within which the parties are to seek to agree the identity of the expert and the terms of a joint letter of instruction and the tribunal may fix a date by which the joint expert's report is to be made available.
6. Any letter of instruction should specify in as much detail as can be given any particular questions the expert is to be invited to answer and all more general subjects which they are to be asked to address.
7. Such instructions are as far as possible to avoid partisanship. Tendentiousness, too, is to be avoided. In so far as the expert is asked to make assumptions of fact, they are to be spelled out. It will, of course, be important not to beg the very questions to be raised. It will be wise if the letter emphasises that in preparing their evidence the expert's principal and overriding duty is to the tribunal rather than to any party.
8. Where a joint expert is to be used, the tribunal may specify that if the expert's identity or instructions have not been agreed between the parties by a specified date, the matter is to be restored to the tribunal, which may then assist the parties to settle that identity and those instructions.
9. In relation to the issues to which an expert is or is not to address themselves (whether or not they are a joint expert) the tribunal may give formal directions as it does generally in relation to the issues to be dealt with at the main hearing.

10. Where there is no joint expert the tribunal should, in the absence of appropriate agreement between the parties, specify a timetable for disclosure or exchange of experts' reports and, where there are two or more experts, for meetings (see below).
11. Any timetable may provide for the raising of supplementary questions with the expert or experts (whether there is a joint expert or not) and for the disclosure or exchange of the answers in good time before the hearing.
12. In the event of separate experts being instructed, the tribunal should encourage arrangements for them to meet on a 'without prejudice' basis with a view to their seeking to resolve any conflict between them and, where possible, to their producing and disclosing a schedule of agreed issues and of points of dispute between them.
13. If a party fails, without good reason, to follow these guidelines and if in consequence another party or parties suffer delay or are put to expense which a due performance of the guidelines would have been likely to avoid, then the tribunal may wish to consider whether, on that party's part, there has been unreasonable conduct within the meaning of r.12(1), as to costs.

6.8 Where the employer receives an incomprehensible medical report

Employers are not supposed to guess at what the doctor means if the terms of the report are ambiguous. They are supposed to write back to the consultant asking for 'amplification and clarification' (*WM Computer Services Ltd* v. *Passmore* (1988) EAT 721/86). In this case the company doctor had reported rather pessimistically on the probable results of Mr Passmore returning to work under any great strain. He did not recommend that Mr Passmore should not return to work. His report was ambiguous. The company took the pessimistic view of their company doctor's report and decided that Mr Passmore was not fit to return to work and dismissed him. The EAT held:

> The company had construed their doctor's report unreasonably, a report written without knowledge of the company's intent to terminate. The company offered no evidence that they had sought clarification or amplification before deciding to dismiss, and had relied on medical advice when dismissing without personally consulting P. This lack of consultation showed that the company had forgotten that dismissal and its procedure was an employment (not a medical) matter.

6.9 Home visits

Mindful of the Human Rights Act 1998 and Article 8 of the European Convention on Human Rights, the right to respect for privacy, family life and correspondence, it could be regarded as a breach of this right and certainly 'unreasonable' behaviour for an employer to turn up announced to make a home visit when an employee is sick.

The correct procedure is to have a standard protocol concerning the reasons for home visits, when they are made, i.e. how far into the sickness absence they are made, and the protocol for making arrangements to make the visit. At least in that way, concerns of victimisation or harassment can be allayed. It will, of course, be important to respect medical advice (particularly in cases of mental illness) not to make a visit or even contact the employee for a period of time because this could cause further distress and harm to the patient, e.g. if the patient has had suicidal ideation.

An employer should not do what one of the author's clients did (not advised by her): turn up at the door with a policeman and an axe. (Just in case the employee had fallen down the stairs and was unconscious, you understand!)

Sending correspondence to employees off sick

Ensuring that correspondence arrives safely is always a quandary. First class letters never seem to arrive unless a cheque is enclosed. On the one hand, sending a courier who is asked to obtain a signature is intrusive and may upset the sick employee. On the other hand, just finding an envelope pushed through the letterbox can be intimidating, and how many recorded delivery letters are refused at the door and returned to the Post Office? Common sense in these cases must prevail. One possibility might be to ask the individual or their union representative their preferred method for delivery of correspondence.

6.10 Occupational health advice

Employers are required to consult with the member of staff once an OHP has reported their assessment of that individual. The 2009 GMC Guidance on Confidentiality, para.34(d), requires all doctors offer to show or send a copy of their report to the individual before sending the report to the employer/insurance company, etc.

A model letter sharing the news that the OHP has declared the individual fit for work in a less stressful capacity is given at **Precedent 6J**.

6.11 Conflicting medical opinions

There are sometimes cases where the GP continues to sign the employee not fit for work but the OHP or company-appointed doctor disagrees and finds that there are all or some of the employee's duties that they are fit to carry out. In such a case, the employer is entitled to rely upon the opinion of the OHP or company-appointed specialist. This is particularly the case where the issue concerns a disability under the Equality Act 2010 and an expert risk assessment is required before medical advice can be given.

In *Jones* v. *Post Office* [2001] IRLR 384, a delivery van driver with insulin-controlled diabetes was recommended by the OHP to undertake only a maximum of two hours' driving duties per day. It was reasonable to rely upon this expert advice following a careful risk assessment.

In *Surrey Police* v. *Marshall* [2002] IRLR 843, it was held to be perfectly reasonable for the respondents to rely (after the event) upon the advice of an expert psychiatrist who advised that the police service would be taking too great a risk in offering the applicant a very senior and critical job as fingerprint recognition officer when she had bipolar affective disorder and was not taking the normal medication for her condition, lithium.

In *Nawaz* v. *Ford Motor Co. Ltd* [1987] IRLR 163, the EAT held that as long as the company doctor's report was reasonable it was reasonable for the employer to rely upon his advice rather than that of the GP who continued to sign Mr Nawaz as unfit for work.

In *Singh-Deu* v. *Chloride Metals Ltd* [1976] IRLR 56, the consultant psychiatrist recommended that his patient return to work following a diagnosis of paranoid schizophrenia. This was in a chemical factory where the employee 'had to keep his wits about him at all times'. When the psychiatrist was asked to confirm that the symptoms of paranoid schizophrenia would not return, this assurance was not given. The respondents decided to take the advice of their company doctor and refused to allow the employee back to work.

An occasion where the employer may be wise to seek a third opinion is where the company-appointed doctor has not examined the employee but has relied solely on reading the file, or where the report is 'woolly and indeterminate', or where the expert advice from the employee's consultant would add to the informed decision as to whether dismissal was an appropriate step for the employer to take (*British Gas* v. *Breeze*, EAT 503/87).

6.12 Dangers of not seeking a medical opinion

It is now an essential element of the procedure for dealing with either acute or long-term/chronic ill health cases to obtain an up-to-date medical report either from a specialist or from an OHP who has expertise in the particular illness or injury involved. Both in terms of following a fair procedure in dismissing in a long-term or acute ill health case or in defending a claim under the Equality Act 2010, obtaining expert medical advice is essential before making any decisions to terminate that employee's employment (*Holmes* v. *Whittington & Porter Ltd* (unreported)).

In *Crampton* v. *Decorum Motors* [1975] IRLR 168 the managing director received a medical certificate stating 'angina pectoris'. He looked it up in a medical dictionary and decided it was a serious illness and that it would be in Mr Crampton's best interests that his contract of employment should be terminated. The Employment Tribunal said that this was a hasty decision. The company should have invited the employee to submit to a further medical examination by a specialist, or at least the company should have discussed Mr Crampton's condition with his GP.

Similarly, if an individual claims to have a disability under the Equality Act 2010, then it will be equally important for them to adduce both written and oral evidence from a specialist rather than to rely upon a GP's Fit Notes or a report (see *Morgan v. Staffordshire University* [2002] IRLR 190, which relates to similar provisions in the Disability Discrimination Act 1995 and a GP's Sick Notes).

6.13 How long is it reasonable for an illness or injury to last?

Whilst each case must be looked at on its merits, the former Inland Revenue Manual for Employers on SSP (A30) sets out a helpful table giving some guidance as to how long a particular illness or injury could be expected to last. It is set out below. However, upon examination and depending on the severity of the illness or injury, these times could be shorter than the Manual suggests.

The now defunct HMRC *Employer Helpbook for Statutory Sick Pay* E14 (2013) included 'Control periods, common illnesses and abbreviations' (page 62).

Control periods for common illness (in weeks)

Addiction (drugs or alcohol)	10
Anaemia (other than in pregnancy)	4
Anorexia	10
Arthritis (unspecified)	10
Back and spinal disorders (PID, sciatica, spondylitis)	10
Concussion	4
Debility, cardiac, nervous, post-op, post-partum	10
other	4
Fainting	4
Fractures of lower limbs	10
Fractures of upper limbs	10
Gastro-enteritis, gastritis, D&V	4
Giddiness	4
Haemorrhage	4
Headache, migraine	4
Hernia (strangulated)	10
Inflammation and swelling	4
Insomnia	10
Investigation	10
Joint disorders (other than arthritis and rheumatism)	10
Kidney and bladder disorders, cystitis, UTI	4
Menstrual disorders, menorrhagia, D&C	10
Mouth and throat disorders	4
NAD	immediate

Nervous illnesses	10
NYD	4
Obesity	immediate
Observation	4
Post-natal conditions	10
Respiratory illness	
asthma	10
colds, coryza, URTI, influenza	4
Bronchitis	4
Skin conditions, dermatitis, eczema	10
Sprains, strains and bruises	4
Tachycardia	10
Ulcers (perforated)	10
peptic, gastric, duodenal	4
varicose	10
corneal	4
Wounds, cuts, lacerations, abrasions, burns, blisters, splinters, FB	4

Common abbreviations used on Fit Notes

CAT	coronary artery thrombosis
CHD	coronary heart disease
COAD	chronic obstructive airways disease
CVA	cerebrovascular accident
D&C	dilation and curettage
DS	disseminated (multiple) sclerosis
DU	duodenal ulcer
D&V	diarrhoea and vomiting
FB	foreign body
GU	gastric ulcer
IDK(J)	internal derangement of the knee (joint)
IHD	ischaemic heart disease
LIH	left inguinal hernia
MI	myocardial infarction
MS	multiple sclerosis
NAD	no abnormality detected
NYD	not yet diagnosed
OA	osteoarthritis
PID	prolapsed intervertebral disc
PUO	pyrexia of unknown origin

RIH	right inguinal hernia
URTI	upper respiratory tract infection
UTI	urinary tract infection
VVs	varicose veins

Other entries on Fit Notes that might be encountered are TATT (tired all the time); ergophobia (morbid fear of work); neurasthenia (nerves); debility (feebleness of mind).

6.14 Stress

Whilst 'stress' is not a medical diagnosis it is commonly written by doctors following a visit by an employee who is failing to cope either with work, work colleagues or matters of a personal nature, or a combination of these. Typical clinical symptoms are depression and/or anxiety. Whilst both of these conditions are classified as mental illnesses in the International Classification of Diseases (ICD) 10 'Diagnostic and Management Guidelines for Mental Disorders' and in the Diseases and Statistical Manual (DSM) IV, courts and tribunals require a differential diagnosis and expert psychiatric evidence in order to support the claimant's/applicant's claim that they have a recognisable mental illness or disorder.

For example, there are 17 sub-categories of depression classified in the ICD 10.

In *J* v. *DLA Piper* UKEAT/0263/09/RN the EAT considered the distinction between stress and mental illness capable of being a disability.

Para. 56 of the *DLA Piper* judgment holds:

> Unhappiness with a decision or a colleague, or a tendency to nurse grievances or a refusal to compromise are not of themselves mental impairments.

So, GPs who write 'stress' on Fit Notes do no more than cite their patient's unhappiness.

In *Herry* v. *Dudley* MBC UKEAT/0100/16/LA, the EAT (which referred to the case above) held that long-term stress does not amount to a disability unless the claimant can show by medical evidence that they have a mental impairment as well.

The claimant had alleged he had two disabilities: dyslexia and stress. He made more than 90 allegations of race and disability discrimination.

He had repeatedly been advised that his claims had no reasonable prospect of success and ignored repeated costs warnings.

Citing the dicta in the *J* v. *DLA Piper* case the Employment Tribunal dismissed the claimant's case, holding that he had failed to establish a mental impairment or to show substantial impact, presenting little or no evidence that his stress had any impact on normal day-to-day activities.

Conducting litigation and giving evidence at tribunal are not normal day-to-day activities because they do not affect participation in professional life. His appeal to the EAT was dismissed.

In *Morgan v. Staffordshire University* [2002] IRLR 190, the EAT held that terms such as 'stress', 'depression' and 'anxiety' on their own would not normally be sufficient to establish a mental illness (p.190):

> as the WHO ICD does not use such terms without qualification and there is no general acceptance of such loose terms, it is not the case that some loose description such as 'anxiety', 'stress' or 'depression' of itself will suffice unless there is credible and informed evidence that in the particular circumstances so loose a description nonetheless identifies a clinically well-recognised illness.

The weight of a GP's opinion as against a specialist psychiatrist in such cases of depression will be less. In *J v. DLA Piper LLP* the EAT stated that whilst 'a GP is fully qualified to express an opinion on whether a patient is suffering from depression ... his or her evidence would, other things being equal, have less weight than that of a specialist' (para.52).

Recently one of the author's clients received a MED 3 specifying 'Burnt out Syndrome'. There is a syndrome called 'Burn out' described by Dr Maurice Lipsedge in *Fitness for Work: Medical Aspects* (4th edn, OUP) ch. 7, 'Psychiatric Illness'. This is described as a syndrome of emotional exhaustion, depersonalisation, reduced productivity and feelings of low achievement. There are various features of burn out. No one symptom should be taken in isolation. Possible features of burn out include:

- guilt at taking time off work;
- minimising contact with colleagues;
- excessive discussions about past mistakes;
- excessive discussion about future workload;
- becoming cross with a colleague or employee at least once per day;
- drinking alcohol before working;
- inability to concentrate on the matter in hand;
- emotional exhaustion.

The employee in this case had gone off sick when his request to be paid an additional allowance for training machine operators (which was part of his normal duties) had been turned down. His GP agreed to withdraw the MED 3 when faced with the question from the author: 'I wonder what the GMC would think of your advice?'

Stress management audit

Under the duty to carry out risks assessments, a stress risk assessment may identify staff who are starting to feel symptoms caused by stress.

A typical stress management risk assessment is given at **Precedent 6K**.

'Stress' at time of disciplinary proceedings or performance review

Many employers are troubled by employees going absent having been signed off sick with 'stress' or 'work-related stress' by their GPs in the face of disciplinary proceedings or performance reviews. It may be relevant to write to the GP along the lines of **Precedent 6L**.

If the trigger for the 'stress' sickness absence is just at the time of informing the individual of disciplinary proceedings or a performance review, or comes after the dismissal of a grievance or non-payment of a salary increase or bonus (called 'sulky sick'), then the employer can make provision for this in the sick pay scheme as set out in **Precedent 6M**.

Finally on this topic, the Employment Tribunals have made it very clear that employers have no need to communicate with external lawyers who write in on behalf of an existing employee who is off sick.

In *McGivney v. Portman Mansions Management Ltd* [2009] UKEAT/0308/09 the Employment Appeal Tribunal held that:

> We also find it was not reasonable to expect the Respondent to deal with him through his solicitors, given that the law says that the employer's obligations are to manage the employee, to meet with him and to discuss the matter with him, concerning his return to work. Of course, we make every allowance for Mr McGivney's stress related illness and we have seen the letter that has been provided after the events by his GP, showing that he was suffering from anxiety and was put on medication for that and that he had symptoms of depression. However, from the Respondent's viewpoint, the Claimant was uncooperative and it was difficult for them to know what to do and how they could best manage the situation.

Chronic embitterment

'Chronic embitterment' was first coined as 'post traumatic embitterment disorder' by Dr Michael Linden in 2003 and in 2010 it was termed 'chronic embitterment' by Professor Tom Sensky. The symptoms described by Dr Linden are serious, sustained, long-term and potentially fatal.

They include persistent feelings of being let down, insulted or being a loser and of being revengeful but helpless. The employee will be off work on long-term sick leave and will probably never return to work and may be on permanent health insurance (PHI) if there is a scheme available, or be retired early on medical grounds, or sue the employer for a permanent loss of any future employment.

This condition may occur where a grievance concerning discrimination or bullying has been made and has either been dismissed in a cursory fashion or has taken months to be determined and then dismissed in a cursory fashion or has never been resolved. Reference to this is made in **Chapter 11** on grievances and harassment.

In such cases occupational health physicians, psychologists and experienced mediators need to be brought in to enable the individual to draw a line under the experience, walk away and regain their health and future employment.

(The author uses with great success the services of Dr Stuart Turner, consultant psychiatrist, The Trauma Clinic, 7 Devonshire Street, London W1W 5DY, s.turner@traumaclinic.org.uk and Dr Max Henderson, Consultant Liaison Psychiatrist, Keats House, St Thomas Street, London SE1 9RS, drmaxhenderson@gmail.com.)

6.15 Conduct during sickness absence

There are sometimes concerns that employees are seen enjoying a meal in a restaurant, playing sport, undertaking DIY jobs around the home or enjoying a holiday abroad whilst certified unfit for work. In some cases these activities may be perfectly justified but in others they may not.

It is therefore important to explain to staff what they are *not* expected to be doing during their time off sick if these activities appear to be inconsistent with the illness or injury described by the employee.

Here is a simple checklist that could be included in a sick pay procedure or policy:

1. Employees are expected to do everything possible to speed their recovery and to do nothing which could delay their return to work or aggravate their illness or injury. They are therefore responsible and trusted to conduct themselves in a sensible and honest manner.
2. Unless it is medically advised, no sick employee should be playing sports or taking part in any other hobbies or other activities such as DIY or jobs around the home, **which are inconsistent with the nature of the illness or injuries or which could aggravate the illness or injury and/or delay recovery.**
3. No employee off sick should be undertaking any other work whether paid or unpaid unless this is with the express written prior permission of the employer.
4. If the employee who is off sick wishes to take holiday, then they must notify the employer in the normal way and obtain permission. The period of holiday will be paid as holiday and not as sick leave, and that period will count towards the annual holiday entitlement. The only occasion when a holiday may still be counted as sick leave is if the doctor recommends in writing that holiday should be taken for recuperative purposes.
5. If an employee falls sick during a planned period of leave it will be counted as holiday unless the employer is notified on the first day of sickness or injury and is prepared to accept the medical evidence put forward. In such a case, holiday may be taken at another time in the holiday year.
6. Any day of sickness absence immediately before or after a public, bank or statutory holiday will not be counted as sick leave and no pay will be paid for those normal working days.
7. There are certain exclusions from occupational sick pay or from authorised sick leave (which means that the employee will need to take paid or unpaid holiday), including: time off for elective surgery such as cosmetic surgery; time off for fertility treatment; time off due to self-induced illness or injury such as sunburn; hangovers or the effects of taking illicit substances; time off for smoking-related diseases; time off for an illness or injury caused by outside employment or activities; time off for injuries

due to dangerous sports such as hang-gliding, parachuting, bungee-jumping and rugby.

It may be sensible for employers to send this to employees by way of a letter and by email as well as providing it as an update to the staff handbook.

6.16 Holidays

Some employers require their staff to take their holidays or some of their annual leave at designated times of the year, e.g. during the factory fortnight shutdown or over the Christmas/New Year break. If this is the case, i.e. the employer wishes to insist that staff take holiday at a particular time, then there must be an express requirement in the contract.

This will be important in cases where there are exceptional circumstances, such as the events of 2010 when volcanic ash disrupted air travel and delayed many employees due to return from holidays or work trips abroad, and where the employer wishes to oblige the employees concerned to take the days upon which they were unexpectedly absent as annual leave (see **Precedent 6B**). (My thanks go to Chris Bryden of 4KBW for sending me his very interesting article 'Joe vs The Volcano', NLJ, 30 April 2010 in which he reviews the law in this area.)

Under the normal rules, pursuant to the Working Time Regulations 1998, employees are required to give their employer at least twice as much notice as the amount of holiday requested. Employers must give the same amount of notice if they require a worker to take leave. Employers can also give notice that workers cannot take leave and in such a case only need to give the same number of days' notice as the leave requested.

There may also be rules governing the times when annual leave cannot be taken, e.g. during a seasonal busy period. Other rules may include the minimum or maximum leave allowed at any one time.

Where an employee wishes to take particular religious holidays, then these can normally only be taken as days of annual leave and as the dates are normally known in advance, staff should be asked to notify management of these dates well in advance.

6.17 Holidays during sick leave

Following the cases of *Stringer* v. *HM Revenue and Customs; Schultz-Hoff* v. *Deutsche Rentenversicherung Bund*, joined cases C-520/06 and C-350/06 [2009] IRLR 214, ECJ and *Pereda* v. *Madrid Movilidad SA* [2009] IRLR 959 employees who are off sick will continue to accrue holiday entitlement and can then take their holiday at another time, carrying their entitlement over for however long the national courts determine is reasonable, or if their employment is terminated, they are entitled to be paid for what has accrued but not been taken in that holiday year.

Carrying over holidays to a new holiday year when sick

In *Pereda* (above) it was held that such employees must be allowed to carry over their holiday, even if that is to a different leave year. However, the Working Time Regulations currently prohibit carrying over more than eight days of statutory holiday to another year (and then only where there is a relevant agreement). This means that the UK is in partial breach of the requirements of the Working Time Directive 93/104/EC.

In an Employment Tribunal case heard in Leeds (*Shah v. First West Yorkshire Ltd* (Case No. 1809311/2009)), it was held that the worker should have been allowed to carry over his holiday into a new holiday year, when he was off sick for three months with a broken ankle. He had already booked four weeks' holiday during the time that he was off sick. When he came back in a new holiday year he asked for this time off and was refused, being told he had lost that holiday because he was now in a new holiday year.

The Employment Tribunal held that reg.13(9) of the Working Time Regulations 1998 (which states that holiday may only be taken in the leave year in respect of which it is due) must be interpreted in line with the Directive and *Pereda*.

Employers faced with employees ringing or emailing from abroad claiming that they are ill, may seek to require stronger medical evidence rather than mere self-certification and a telephone call, as currently suffices to claim statutory sick pay.

Medical evidence from a doctor or hospital, verified if necessary by a UK doctor, may be required in future for such claims.

Carrying over holidays on sick leave

The EAT in *Plumb v. Duncan Print Group Ltd* UKEAT/2015/0071 held that sick workers do not need to provide evidence that they were unable to take holiday for it to be carried forward (citing *NHS Leeds v. Larner* [2012] EWCA Civ 1034 in the Court of Appeal) and that leave can only be carried over for 18 months from the end of the leave year.

Employees whose native country is not the UK

Where foreign workers who live and work in the UK travel abroad to visit their families and fall sick while abroad, or fall sick in the UK and choose to go home to be with their families while recovering, there may need to be special rules. Exceptionally some foreign workers may seek to extend their holiday abroad by claiming sickness whilst abroad and their inability to return to the UK or to work.

Clear rules are needed in such cases, as the employee will not be present in the UK to comply with rules such as home visits, referrals to occupational health, etc.

Provisions in the holiday and sick pay schemes need to make it clear that any abuse of the holiday/sick pay scheme will be treated under the disciplinary procedure and that an employee who goes abroad, particularly to their native country, is especially trusted to return to the UK and to work once their leave has expired. Any reasonable belief that the extended leave is an abuse of process will be dealt with seriously.

See **Precedent 6R**.

6.18 Alcohol and drugs

Some employers operate an alcohol and drugs policy under which they test job applicants and employees either for cause or on a random basis. Other employers do not carry out testing but require employees to be 100 per cent competent, alert and fit for duty. This may mean that drinking in a pub or elsewhere before coming on to shift or working in secondary employment is not permitted, e.g. doing an evening shift in a pub and then coming on to a night shift at 10 pm.

In the latter case, some employers have found it necessary to remind their staff about coming to work in a fully fit state, particularly those who work on shift and may wish to spend several hours in the pub before coming to work, or who may have a secondary job which causes them to be less rested than normal when they come to work for their primary employer.

'Bottle to the throttle' rule

In safety-critical jobs, airline companies' guidance for airline pilots could be adopted, namely:

(i) '24 hours between throttle and bottle, eight hours between bottle and throttle' – i.e. only one glass of wine or half a pint of beer can be consumed in the 24 hours before coming to work.
(ii) '12/8 hours before throttle, no alcohol permitted'. This is to ensure that a pilot is not still under the influence of alcohol.

OTC and prescribed medication

Staff who take medication, whether prescribed or over the counter (OTC), which may make them drowsy or which carries a warning not to drive or use machinery, or where there are any side effects that could affect the judgement or concentration of the employee, should be required to report this to occupational health or HR in order that their safety can be assessed, etc. and if necessary those staff are moved to a safe environment.

Model clauses are set out at **Precedent 6S**.

6.19 Light duties/alternative duties

Some employers have found it useful to have what they call a 'light duties' or 'alternative duties' policy. This requires the employee off sick to be responsible for notifying occupational health/their manager/HR when feeling better but perhaps not fully fit for work. In this way they can be given alternative duties to help them rehabilitate back to their former role.

Precedent 6T sets out a light duties policy.

6.20 Smoking

Since it became unlawful to smoke in public buildings and workplaces on 1 July 2007 (Smoke-free (Premises and Enforcement) Regulations 2006, SI 2006/3368), it is important for employers to have a 'No Smoking' policy which bans smoking in the workplace including a company vehicle. Sometimes there is reference to the requirement not to smoke during the working day in the contract. See **Precedent 6U**.

6.21 Absence through negligence of third parties

In cases where an employee is off sick through the negligence of a third party, loss of earnings can only be claimed in a personal injury claim, if the employer has not paid the employee during the absence. If sick pay is not paid but a loan is made to the employee who is required to repay that loan upon receipt of damages or a settlement, then the insurance company will make a payment for loss of earnings or the court will make an award for loss of earnings.

The employee may then be required to repay those monies to the employer.

The wording of such a clause in a sick pay scheme is critical as only actual financial losses suffered by the injured party will be awarded or paid by way of settlement.

In such cases the sick pay scheme must include a clause such as is set out at **Precedent 6V**. It would be wise to remind the employee at the start of any absence caused by an accident outside work where legal action could be taken, that in such a case sick pay is not being paid but a loan is being made that will have to be repaid when damages or a settlement is made.

6.22 Permanent health insurance or long-term disability

Those employers who offer permanent health insurance (PHI) or long-term disability (LTD) schemes should word the contract very carefully to ensure that they are not making a direct promise to pay PHI/LTD but just offer whatever the PHI/LTD provider will pay. This is because, if the insurance provider rejects the claim which would otherwise have been eligible for payment, the employer may be deemed to be liable to pay the equivalent of the PHI.

Worse still for employers, there is a line of authorities that have held that there is an implied contractual term that an employer will not terminate employment as a means of removing an employee's entitlement to benefit under such a scheme (see *Aspden v. Webbs Poultry and Meat Group (Holdings) Ltd* [1996] IRLR 521).

There are exceptions to this rule, for example where the employer has dismissed for 'good cause' or redundancy. In those cases the dismissal would not be regarded as being in breach of the implied term not to dismiss the employee and thus depriving the employee of their entitlement to benefit (*Briscoe* v. *Lubrizol Ltd* [2002] IRLR 60).

There is no implied duty to explain the financial or economic consequences of benefits under the contract. The Court of Appeal in *Crossley* v. *Faithful & Gould Holdings Ltd* [2004] EWCA Civ 293 held that there was no implied duty on an employer to inform an employee of the financial consequences on his PHI benefit of resigning from his job. Lord Justice Dyson held (para.43):

> Such an implied term would impose an unfair and unreasonable burden on employers. It is one thing to say that, if an employer assumes the responsibility for giving financial advice to his employee, he is under a duty to take reasonable care in the giving of that advice... It is quite a different matter to impose on an employer the duty to give his employee financial advice in relation to benefits accruing from his employment, or generally to safeguard the employee's economic well-being.

But the case of *Lennon* v. *Commissioner of Police of the Metropolis* [2004] IRLR 385 illustrates the case where an employer expressly assumed responsibility for advice.

A police officer in London wanted to transfer to Northern Ireland and to retain his housing allowance. His transfer arrangements were handled by a personnel executive, who assured him that the allowance would not be affected by a short break before he joined the Northern Ireland force. That advice was wrong and broke his continuity of service and his continuing right to a housing allowance.

The Court of Appeal upheld a finding that the Commissioner was liable for the resultant economic loss caused by the negligent advice on which the claimant had relied.

Precedent 6W suggests wording for a PHI clause in the contract.

6.23 Tension between dismissal and length of sick pay

The fact that a sick pay scheme sets out maximum entitlement to sick pay does not imply that dismissal will never occur before sick pay has run out. Employment Tribunals have held that it is not necessarily unfair to dismiss an employee just because sick pay has not run out (*Coulson* v. *Felixstowe Dock & Railway Co Ltd* [1975] IRLR 11).

It is also not necessarily unfair to dismiss an absent employee when their sick pay has run out. However, it is incumbent on the employer to warn the employee in advance that sick pay is running out and to enquire if the employee's return to work is reasonably imminent, before making any decision to dismiss (*Hardwick* v. *Leeds Area Health Authority* [1975] IRLR 319).

Further, just because the contract sets out maximum entitlement to sick pay, if the contract is terminated before the exhaustion of sick pay, this does not entitle the ex-employee to sue for the remainder (*Smiths Industries Aerospace & Defence Systems Ltd* v. *Brookes* [1986] IRLR 434).

Similarly, if an employee is off sick it is not a breach of contract nor necessarily unfair dismissal to select that employee for redundancy even though the employee is off sick and likely to become eligible for long-term benefit from the employer (*Hill* v. *General Accident Fire & Life Assurance Corporation plc* [1998] IRLR 641) but see brief comments on the disability provisions of the Equality Act 2010 in **6.24** and *Clark* v. *TDG Ltd t/a Novacold* [1999] IRLR 318.

There is no rule of law that requires employers to wait until the exhaustion of sick pay before taking a fair decision to dismiss – although an Employment Tribunal may require an explanation as to why a decision to dismiss was taken when sick pay had not been exhausted.

Conversely it is not necessarily fair to dismiss when sick pay does run out – all the factors set out in case law such as whether the employee will recover in the short to medium term and be able to return in some capacity; whether the employer can continue to make interim arrangements to fill the post or leave it vacant; the nature of the illness and its prognosis; the nature of the employee's duties and the employee's length of service, etc.

Similarly it is not necessarily unfair to dismiss an employee even where the employer has caused or contributed to the illness or injury. It may be perfectly fair for an employer to dismiss fairly an employee on grounds of capability when the employer's conduct has either caused or materially contributed to the employee's incapability (*McAdie* v. *Royal Bank of Scotland* [2007] IRLR 895).

Precedent 6X provides examples of clauses in a sick pay scheme.

6.24 Equality Act 2010

The Equality Act 2010 makes various forms of discrimination unlawful on the grounds of 'protected characteristics'.

In terms of disability discrimination, there is no longer the prescribed list of normal day-to-day activities set out in Sched.1 to the 1995 Act. It is up to the parties and ultimately an Employment Tribunal to determine what a day-to-day activity is and whether the disability has a substantially detrimental effect upon it.

Further, the definition of indirect discrimination has been harmonised to overcome the effect of the House of Lords' decision in *LB Lewisham* v. *Malcolm* [2008] IRLR 700. The claimant may establish indirect disability discrimination where a provision, criterion or practice (PCP) puts those who are disabled at a particular disadvantage with those who are not disabled, i.e. who do not share the claimant's particular disability.

Further, s.60 of the Equality Act 2010 requires employers not to ask job candidates any questions about their disabilities other than under certain circumstances (see **Chapter 1**, under 'Dealing with medical conditions at interview').

6.25 Time off for IVF treatment

Since treatment for infertility is not regarded as an illness, nor is it protected under the Equality Act 2010 as it is neither pregnancy nor maternity, time off for fertility treatment is not normally regarded as an occasion where sick pay would be paid.

When taking part in IVF, statistics show that women require more treatment than men, i.e. more time off, and are more likely to be disciplined as a result for absences. This could be indirect discrimination if they could prove that the employer's rule was unjustifiable.

In *London Borough of Greenwich* v. *Robinson*, EAT 745/94, the EAT determined that men also undergo fertility treatment so it cannot automatically be sex discrimination to select a woman for redundancy because her absences were as the result of IVF treatment.

The EAT held that employers are entitled to take absence levels into account including absences due to IVF treatment. This decision may now be different after the Supreme Court's decisions in two appeals that it is not necessary for a claimant to establish the reason for the particular disadvantage to which a group is put, compared to another, in an indirect discrimination claim – *Essop* v. *Home Office (UK Border Agency)* and *Naeem* v. *Secretary of State for Justice* [2017] UKSC 27.

Indirect discrimination occurs when a PCP is applied and a disadvantage is suffered, not only by the disadvantaged group, but also by the individual.

The Supreme Court has provided clarification of the law and described a number of features of indirect discrimination with lots of helpful examples.

Lady Hale explained that there are various reasons, or 'context factors', why one group may find it harder to comply with the PCP than others. They can be genetic, social or even another PCP.

The PCP does not need to put every member of the group sharing the protected characteristic at a disadvantage.

The disparate impact or disadvantage can be established on the basis of statistics.

Finally, the PCP may be able to be justified by the employer and there is no stigma or shame in doing so.

However, if a woman is dismissed on the basis of assumptions about attendance patterns or the possible consequences of the fertility treatment, i.e. it may result in pregnancy, then such a dismissal may amount to direct sex discrimination.

In *Joyce* v. *Northern Microwave Distributors Ltd* (ET/5564/93) the employer actually admitted that the claimant had been dismissed because she **would be** away from work having fertility treatment and may also become pregnant. The tribunal found that the employer's assumptions were sex stereotypical and constituted evidence of a discriminatory attitude. The Employment Tribunal held that a man would not have been treated in the same way.

Comment

Although both men and women can undergo fertility treatment, women in the main require fertility treatment more often than men and may therefore have to take more time off work and therefore may be disciplined for such absences.

So, if a woman taking time off to undergo fertility treatment is disciplined for her absences, this may amount to indirect sex discrimination, and her employer will have to justify its rules that apply disproportionately adversely to women.

However, a woman undergoing IVF treatment is clearly to be regarded as pregnant for the period following the implantation of the fertilised ova until the end of the protected period as set down in the former s.3A(3)(a)(i)–(iii) of the Sex Discrimination Act 1975 (*Sahota* v. *Home Office*, UKEAT/0342/09/LA).

Prior to implantation, less favourable treatment of a woman on the ground that she is receiving IVF treatment may constitute sex discrimination during the limited, closely defined, period set down by the ECJ in *Mayr* v. *Backerei und Konditorei Gerhard Flockner OHG* [2008] IRLR 387. The period in question is the advanced stage between the follicular puncture and the immediate transfer of the in vitro fertilised ova into the uterus. The EAT in *Sahota* (above) did not accept that there should be a wider period of protection.

Employers must now be mindful of the right of women not to be discriminated against and to be afforded the same treatment as a pregnant woman as soon as the stage has been reached where the fertilised ova is to be transferred to her uterus.

The kind of clause that employers might favour would be along the lines of that set out at **Precedent 6Z**.

6.26 Requirement to report medication

In some employments where there are safety-critical jobs, it is important that any medication that an employee is taking, whether prescribed or over the counter (OTC), is reported to a trained nurse, doctor or paramedic.

For example, the combination of anti-depressants and sleeping tablets seriously impairs concentration the following morning and an individual taking this combination of drugs must be given alternative duties if, for example, they would normally drive a tanker, control a crane or use dangerous machinery. Such a clause would read as set out in **Precedent 6AA**.

6.27 Malingering and moonlighting

There are two categories of malingerers: the lazy malingerer; and the fraudulent malingerer.

Definition

Malingering is the 'purposeful production of falsely or grossly exaggerated physical or psychological complaints with the goal of receiving a reward. These may include money, insurance settlement, drugs or the avoidance of punishment, work, jury duty, release from incarceration, the military, or some other kind of service' ('Malingering', *Psychology Today*, 29 December 2016).

Step 1: Distinguishing the fraudulent malingerer from the lazy malingerer

There is an important difference between the fraudulent malingerer and the lazy malingerer. In the former case the conduct is normally premeditated and involves dishonesty (lying and fraud). In the latter case this can be categorised as a performance issue and dealt with by seeking to motivate the employee to come to work.

Step 2: Obtain the evidence

Although *BHS* v. *Burchell* [1978] IRLR 379 (EAT) makes it clear that an employer needs 'reasonable grounds upon which to sustain his belief' and not actual proof, sometimes this is what it takes, as mere suspicion will not be enough.

You will need evidence, often covert recordings of an employee who is dishonest by claiming they are sick when they are not. This would amount or could amount to gross misconduct as it is falsification and fraud (obtaining sick pay under false pretences).

Fraud is 'wrongful or criminal deception intended to result in financial or personal gain'.

In law, under the Fraud Act 2006, s.2 defines fraud as a criminal offence:

Where the individual:

- made a false representation
- dishonestly
- knowing that the representation was or might be untrue or misleading
- with intent to make a gain for himself or another, to cause loss to another or to expose another to risk of loss.

Sometimes there is evidence from social media, e.g. from Facebook; sometimes this is a tip-off from another employee. The employer can use it in the same way as any other evidence.

In *Gill* v. *SAS Ground Services UK Ltd* ET/2705021/09 the employer used an entry on the claimant's Facebook account as evidence of misconduct. She was an actor and model in her spare time and posted entries on her Facebook pages showing these activities.

When Ms Gill went off sick on full sick pay due to surgery she was not truthful with her employer about her recovery or potential return-to-work date. Unfortunately for the claimant, her Facebook page showed her attending London Fashion Week during a week that she was signed off sick and unable to work.

During the disciplinary proceeding, Ms Gill claimed she had only attended as a guest. Her Facebook page, however, referred to her 'auditioning 300 models' and choreographing a fashion show. There was other evidence which disputed her claims that she only attended as a guest. During the hearing, other evidence emerged that she had also gone filming in India during this period of sick leave.

Her employer decided that she had committed gross misconduct and dismissed her.

The Employment Tribunal held that her employer had conducted a thorough investigation and had sufficient evidence to form a genuine and honest belief and reasonable grounds for that belief (i.e. that she was not at London Fashion Week purely as a guest – that she had been working) and that the dismissal was fair.

Clearly – just as in *Linfood Cash and Carry Ltd v. Thomson, Greenwell and Bell* [1989] IRLR 235, where the EAT held that the employer had to test the evidence very carefully, e.g. to ensure that the anonymous witnesses in that case did not bear a grudge or were making up their stories – here evidence from social media must be tested to ensure it is accurate and that the dates are correct, and so on.

There is also an argument about whether the use of someone's personal Facebook pages breaches their Article 8 rights.

Everyone has the right to respect for their private and family life, their home and their correspondence.

(Derogation: 'There shall be no interference by a public authority with the exercise of this right except such as is in accordance with the law and is necessary in a democratic society in the interests of national security, public safety or the economic well-being of the country, for the prevention of disorder or crime, for the protection of health or morals, or for the protection of the rights and freedoms of others'.)

Interference with the right to respect for privacy can be objectively justified and might be permissible in these circumstances, for example, if the employer has reasonable grounds to believe that the employee is fraudulently claiming sick pay. This is provided for in the derogation to Article 8.

So, for example, it is very important to reserve the right to monitor work email accounts.

In the case of *Bărbulescu v. Romania* (Application No. 61496/08) the European Court of Human Rights (ECtHR) held that employers need to make sure they act in a proportionate way, balancing an individual's right to privacy and the employer's business interests and considering if there is a less intrusive way of achieving the employer's aim.

Employers should remember that to justify dismissal for gross misconduct they normally need to show dishonesty and pre-meditation on the part of the employee.

Precedent 6AB deals with the fraudulent malingerer.

Precedent 6AC covers 'moonlighting' – a euphemism for working for someone else or for oneself whilst claiming sick pay or 'external business interests'.

Using private detectives and covert surveillance

Please note that when using private detectives or covert surveillance, rigorous terms of reference must be agreed and those conducting any covert surveillance must not enter the individual's home by trickery nor monitor their activities on their premises as this is a breach of Article 8 of the European Convention on Human Rights – a breach of the right to respect for privacy (*Jones* v. *University of Warwick* [2003] 3 All ER 760 (see **Chapter 13** on email and the internet)).

The Information Commissioner's Code of Practice, Part 3 'Monitoring at Work' recommends that in normal cases employees should be informed in advance if they are to be covertly videoed or recorded in the workplace.

The Code recommends that: 'Unless covert monitoring is justified, ensure that workers are informed of the extent and nature of any monitoring that is taking place and the reasons for it.'

Employers should consider including a statement in their disciplinary and sick pay policies as follows:

> In rare cases we may suspect fraud or dishonest conduct on the part of an employee. For example, they may have gone off sick but are actually taking a holiday, have threatened to or have made a claim for personal injuries for an alleged injury at work, are working for themselves or for another employer or are just shirking. In such cases where fraud is suspected the Company reserves the right to instruct private detectives to carry out covert surveillance which may mean following the individual when they leave home and recording by video or audio. Such evidence will also be shown to the individual before disciplinary proceedings are started. This evidence may be disclosed to our insurers and/or to the police and it may be used in any legal proceedings. We give clear instructions to such staff about not intruding into an individual's home and not tricking their way into a home and covertly recording their activities in their home. All covert surveillance will take place in public places.

It is, however, perfectly legitimate to use private detectives to video individuals who are claiming sickness or an injury conducting their normal life or working for themselves or others. See **Precedent 6AD**.

Instructions to private detectives

It is important to ensure that any private detectives contracted to undertake surveillance work do so in an ethical and lawful way. This means advising them as to what they can and cannot do.

The Association of British Insurers (ABI) has issued *Guidelines on the Instruction and Use of Private Investigators* (September 2014). It contains useful information on page 12 on the format and content of instructions that should be given.

Following the Leveson Inquiry (2013), the Home Secretary announced proposals to introduce the regulation of private investigators, with effect from May 2015 (made under the Private Security Industry Act 2001). This requires private investigators to obtain a licence, which will only be granted by the

Security Industry Authority (SIA) when an applicant has successfully completed due diligence checks, training and achieved a government-recognised qualification.

Operating as an unlicensed private investigator or supplying unlicensed private investigators is a criminal offence punishable by a fine of up to £5,000 or up to six months in prison. It is a criminal offence for a private investigator to operate without a licence. See **Precedent 6AE**.

Disciplinary offence

It should be made clear that any fraudulent claim for sick pay, making any false or fraudulent claims, dishonesty or deceit or lying, disobeying a lawful or reasonable instruction not to take leave, falsifying any company forms such as a self-certificate, etc. are by themselves regarded as offences of gross misconduct which could lead severally or jointly to summary dismissal (see **Chapter 8** on conduct and **Chapter 9** on disciplinary matters).

6.28 Dealing with short-term absences

Tribunals have laid down clear guidelines as to how to deal with (genuine) cases of intermittent, short-term, persistent absentees who have no underlying medical condition but are absent from work 'too much'.

The initial step is an interview of concern with the line manager and the individual with details of the number of days taken off sick, the length of the spells of absence and the reasons given by the individual/doctor, together with a calendar showing the sick days inked in red and a review of the pattern and number of days taken, asking the individual why they are not at work 'enough'.

Once the review of the sickness absence has been conducted and the individual asked the reason for the high absence level (done with 'sympathy, understanding and compassion' per Wood J in *Lynock* v. *Cereal Packaging Ltd* [1988] IRLR 510), the employee must then be 'advised' that their absence record is too high and that they are required to reduce the levels of absence. To what level and over what period of time and the length of time that the 'warning' will last should also be made clear.

Wood J advised that the word 'caution' and not 'warning' could be used, as the word 'warning' has the connotation of misconduct and this is not a misconduct issue.

If the employee consistently fails to achieve the required level of attendance and warnings are administered as per the procedure, then the employer is entitled to say 'enough is enough' and terminate their employment for 'some other substantial reason' (*International Sports Co. Ltd* v. *Thomson* [1980] IRLR 340 and *Rolls Royce Ltd* v. *Walpole* [1980] IRLR 343).

In order to distinguish absence issues from cases of misconduct, some clients of the author now send 'well done' letters, once a warning has lapsed and there has been excellent attendance following the warning. (Other clients take the

ABSENCE AND SICK PAY 253

opposite approach and send 'well done' letters to those who have taken no time off during the year!)

Precedent 6AF contains a supervisor's briefing paper and **Precedent 6AG** has model letters.

PRECEDENT 6A: Requirement to report for work (full policy)

1. Introduction

This section sets out arrangements, which may be applied at the Company's discretion in emergencies, in particular when there is a disruption of public transport or adverse weather.

2. Requirement to report for duty

2.1 All staff

During an emergency all staff are required:

(a) to make every effort to report for duty at the normal place of work unless instructed otherwise. Except where adverse weather prevents attendance, staff who are physically fit are expected to walk up to three miles each way if necessary and if safe to do so. At the discretion of the Company, staff may not be required to walk as far if they are infirm or where the journey on foot is exceptionally difficult or where it would be dangerous to be outside, e.g. in inclement weather;

(b) to carry out whatever work the Company considers necessary, which may involve duties not normally undertaken. Brief training will be given to allow staff to undertake their duties and full consideration will be given to any necessary health and safety arrangements which may be required.

During a prolonged disruption of transport, arrangements may be made for staff to report to another site if there is one within reach of their home.

Staff who are unable by any means to report for duty in person must report the fact by telephone in accordance with local instructions.

2.2 Essential staff

Staff will be informed if they have been designated as essential in connection with work that cannot be postponed. If such staff are unable to make their own arrangements for alternative transport to work, they may in certain cases be accommodated at or near the Company (see paragraph 6.2) or conveyed to and from the Company by official transport.

3. Hours of work

In order to make best use of resources or to relieve pressure on public transport, staff may be required to alter their normal hours of attendance; for example, times of arrival/departure may be altered, duties may be rearranged or part-time staff required to attend full-time on alternate days. Employees' domestic responsibilities and family commitments will be taken into account.

4. Annual leave

The Company may at its discretion impose a ban on annual leave during or immediately prior to an emergency but otherwise annual leave may be taken in the usual way subject to the needs of the work. Employees who take leave away from home during or immediately prior to an emergency or when there is a likelihood of one occurring will be expected to make every effort to report for duty at their normal place of work if there is still an emergency at the end of their leave. Employees unable to report in person must telephone the Company in accordance with local instructions and may, at the Company's discretion, be regarded as covered by paragraph 5.1.

5. Pay

5.1 Basic pay

If the Company is satisfied that a member of staff has taken all reasonable steps to report for duty and that no other work can be found for him or her, it may at its discretion approve absence from duty and continue to pay salary or wages in full. A similar concession may be extended to staff who are allowed to attend for less than a full day. These arrangements will not be sanctioned for more than a week or two and are liable to be modified at any time.

5.2 Overtime pay

Overtime is only paid in respect of hours worked in excess of conditioned hours except that staff allowed to attend for less than their full day under the terms of paragraph 5.1 above may be allowed the appropriate credit of normal conditioned hours for the day.

When the Company alters working hours in accordance with paragraph 3 and long and short days are worked, or some similar arrangement applied, overtime will be paid only if the total hours worked during the emergency exceed the total contractual hours for the period.

6. Reimbursement of extra expenditure

6.1 Extra expenditure

Claims for extra expenditure incurred during a transport emergency may be considered at Company discretion as detailed below.

6.2 Accommodation and food costs

Subject to prior agreement by local management, staff designated as essential but who are unable to travel between home and workplace during a transport emergency, may be accommodated nearer their workplace at the Company's expense. Subsistence Allowance will not be paid but the cost of bed, breakfast and an evening meal will be reimbursed. Any additional travelling expenses will also be reimbursed (see paragraph 6.3). The Company may require staff to sleep at the workplace overnight but will do so only when it is necessary and unavoidable.

6.3 Travel costs

Staff may, at the Company's discretion, be reimbursed for reasonable additional travelling expenses incurred because of a transport emergency, provided:

(a) that no unnecessary or avoidable expense has been incurred;
(b) that, unless there are exceptional circumstances, more than four miles have been travelled each way.

Passenger supplement may be claimed in respect of any official passengers who are not normally carried, provided the conditions in this paragraph have been met.

PRECEDENT 6B: Severe weather and other unforeseen circumstances policy

[*Date*]

We have experienced rare occurrences when for example in 2010 all the European airports were shut for over a week, due to ash from a volcano which was erupting in Iceland filling the airspace and making it unsafe for aircraft to fly. These were termed 'Acts of God' which are not covered by any insurance policies.

Whilst it is the responsibility of individuals to make every effort to attend work, even in exceptionally severe weather, the Company recognises that there may be circumstances such as those described above where this can prove impossible and where individuals are prevented from returning home as they had planned.

In, for example, extreme weather conditions or where there are transport strikes, it may be impossible for employees to actually get to work or if they do, they may need to leave early.

Where staff are stranded in their holiday destinations or not able to return from business trips due to the disruption to air travel caused by the volcanic ash, the Company acknowledges that some staff may not have been covered by insurance and may therefore have incurred additional expense in trying to return home. The policy below caters for these occasions.

This policy provides a framework under which absence from work due to exceptionally severe weather or other unforeseen circumstances such as a strike on public transport can be managed fairly, equitably and consistently.

Introduction

This policy forms a framework for the management of absence from work due to exceptionally severe weather conditions or other serious difficulties getting to work or working (if a peripatetic worker) such as strikes on public transport – 'Exceptional circumstances'. Any difficulties not covered by this policy should be referred to Human Resources and your line manager.

It is the responsibility of individuals to make every effort to attend for work even in exceptionally severe weather/where there is a strike on public transport. If walking to work or accepting a lift from someone else is an option, you are expected to do so (unless your health and safety would be at risk).

However, it is recognised that a journey to work may be impossible, inadvisable or may cause concern to staff.

The Company aims for fairness and consistency of treatment in such circumstances. However, this can be difficult to achieve with the number and location of workplaces, individual travelling arrangements and the operational demands and priorities which need to be taken into account.

For staff based at Head Office, authorisation to pay someone who does not attend work in the exceptional circumstances outlined above must be given by the Head of the Department or Human Resources Director.

At local offices authorisation must be given by a Director or Area/Regional Director.

Exceptional circumstances: Acts of God

Where staff are left stranded abroad with no transport, e.g. due to all air travel being suspended, and with no alternative means of returning home, e.g. by car, coach, train or ferry, the Company will be as sympathetic as possible, offering unpaid leave for the additional time off, allowing further annual paid leave to be taken or paid leave to be borrowed from the following year, or allowing time lost to be made up when the member of staff returns to work.

The options will be discussed with the individual upon their return to work.

The Company expects such members of staff to remain in contact with their line manager throughout this difficult time.

Aims

This policy aims to clarify arrangements for dealing with absences from work due to exceptionally severe weather conditions or inability to get to work for other exceptional reasons, such as strikes on public transport.

The Company aims, within the needs to continue to provide a service, to treat individuals fairly, equitably and consistently when their ability to attend or stay at work is affected by severe weather conditions.

Application

Those posts deemed 'non-essential' may be treated in a different way from those in Essential Posts such as care workers, security, maintenance and technicians, etc.

Policy details

Closure of buildings

Where it is deemed appropriate a decision may be made to close a workplace when weather conditions are exceptionally severe or expected to worsen. Any action taken will be influenced by relevant weather warnings issued, having regard to the safety and welfare of staff.

Difficulty in travelling to work

Where individuals make every reasonable effort to get to work but are unable to do so due to severe weather conditions and/or because of transport difficulties they should contact their line manager as soon as possible to advise of the situation.

They may apply for annual leave, flexi-time and/or time off in lieu owing rather than face adverse conditions or difficulties. Such requests should be sympathetically considered within the context of the needs of the business/service and having regard to the severity of the weather conditions and the impact on the work of other staff or contractors.

Those unable to travel to work, advised not to travel or prevented from attending work because of domestic problems such as dealing with burst pipes, storm damage, etc. will be expected to take annual leave, flexi-time and/or time off in lieu owing. In very exceptional circumstances line managers may consider allowing annual leave to be brought forward from the following year's entitlement.

Those prevented from attending work due to childcare commitments arising out of school closure will be expected to apply for Time Off for Dependants or to take annual leave, flexi-time and/or time off in lieu owing.

Where an individual does not expect to be able to attend their normal workplace due to its closure or inaccessibility, they should make contact with their line manager to report that they are available for work and to seek advice on what action to take.

If it is possible to report for work at another, perhaps more accessible, workplace, then the individual is expected to notify their line manager and to attend their nearest workplace or a workplace that is accessible to them, with their line manager's consent.

Those not able to work because of closure of the workplace and where there is no alternative place of work, will be paid normally but asked to make up some or all of the time by way of additional hours (for no additional pay) at a mutually acceptable time.

In the event that an employee is unable to travel to work or to an alternative, more accessible, workplace, consideration may be given by a Director or HR Director to permitting that employee temporarily to work from home.

Late arrival

Where an individual arrives within two hours of their usual starting time and it is accepted that all reasonable efforts were made to arrive at the usual time but the weather or other factors have delayed the employee, full pay for that day/those days will be authorised. If there is more than a two-hour delay then part payment for the hours actually worked may be paid.

Where an individual arrives significantly later than their usual starting time as a direct result of severe weather conditions then they may be asked to take that day off and go home and take it as leave, flexi-time and/or time off in lieu owing.

Going home earlier than usual

Line managers may also use their discretion in allowing individuals the opportunity to leave their workplace early where individuals have personal concerns about their travelling arrangements, particularly when weather conditions are severe or expected to worsen.

This may be particularly relevant where individuals live in outlying areas, have some distance to travel, may expect a difficult journey, where they are reliant on shared travel arrangements or are collecting children who may be leaving early from school, etc.

In such circumstances individuals will be required to take annual leave, flexi-time and/or time off in lieu owing.

Each case will be reviewed on its own individual merits; authorisation in one instance will not automatically imply authority for other cases. However, every attempt will be made to ensure fairness and consistency in all decisions. All decisions will be made in light of the needs of the service/business.

Appreciation of those able to attend work

Managers and Directors should ensure that appreciation is expressed to all staff who are able to attend work, cover colleagues and keep services/business running. Appreciation should also be shown to those staff who attempted to attend but were unable to do so.

Recording of absence

Line managers and individuals must ensure that any absence outlined above is adequately and clearly recorded in the most appropriate manner.

PRECEDENT 6C: Time-keeping for a private dental practice

1. Days upon which you are required to work

Monday, Tuesday, Wednesday, Thursday, Friday.

2. Hours of work

2.1 The Practice sees its first patient at 8.30 am unless an earlier time is agreed in a particular case. The last patient is normally seen at 5 pm.

2.2 You must, in normal circumstances, be ready to start work at 8.30 am, and your normal finish time is 5.30 pm. This means that you must arrive at the Practice at least 10 minutes before the first patient at 8.30 am. You must have scrubbed up and be in your uniform and have all the instruments ready for use before 8.30 am. It is particularly important that a patient is not kept waiting because you are not ready.

2.3 Please note that the first patient is seen at 8.30 am. and all of the team must be available and ready to give service to that patient at that time. You may be required to stay past 5.30 pm if the Practice needs you to stay.

2.4 If you are having particular difficulty travelling to work on a particular day it is essential that you ring the Practice either on the emergency number or on the mobile telephone of the partner in the Practice to let us know that you will be late. If you have an unreliable bus or train which regularly comes late or is cancelled or you seem to get caught in regular traffic jams, you will be asked to try to catch an earlier more reliable train or bus or leave home earlier in order not to get caught in rush hour traffic.

2.5 Being punctual is of the essence in this employment and lateness cannot be tolerated even for genuine reasons.

2.6 No overtime is paid for working any extra time on a normal working day but see clause [*specify*] for other conditions relating to overtime.

PRECEDENT 6D: Fit Note

1. The Company requires the completion of a self-certificate covering the first seven days of any sickness absence. This must be completed with your supervisor at your return to work interview and the reasons given by you must satisfy your supervisor before sick pay and your absence can be authorised. Should your pay have already been paid into your bank account and should the decision be made not to authorise sick pay, you agree that an appropriate deduction may be made from the following months' wages/salary.

2. If you are absent for longer than seven days, then you must submit a Statement of Fitness from your GP (Fit Note) or other similar medical evidence that satisfies the Company. Whilst a Fit Note normally satisfies the Company as to your unfitness for work, it is not conclusive evidence and your sickness absence may be challenged despite the production of medical evidence if there are reasonable grounds to believe that you were fit enough to attend work.

PRECEDENT 6E: Clause relating to medical examination

1. You agree to undergo, at any time during your employment and at the Company's expense, a medical examination by a doctor of the Company's choice and to the disclosure of a medical report following such examination to either our Occupational

Health Physician or to Head of Human Resources. You also agree to be referred by the Company to the government's Occupational Health team under its Fit for Work Scheme.

In either case no clinical or medically confidential/sensitive information will be disclosed. The Occupational Health Physician will not disclose any confidential or clinical information to management without your express informed consent. In any event you will be offered the opportunity of reading the report before it is sent to our Occupational Health Physician or to the Company or to be sent a copy at the same time. We ask for only functional capacity and functional limitations and what, if any, reasonable adjustments may be needed to assist your return to work.

2. During any period of long-term sick leave ('long-term' being defined as four calendar weeks or more) you agree to attend any reasonable meetings with line management and/or Human Resources and/or Occupational Health and/or any other person legitimately nominated by the Company in order to discuss non-medical matters relating to your sickness absence and any return to work. You understand that any unreasonable refusal to co-operate in this regard, without good cause, refusal to or failure to correspond or communicate with management could lead to your summary dismissal. Only where an expert medical practitioner certifies that any such communication would seriously harm or worsen your mental condition, would management deem it reasonable for you not to communicate or meet (most commonly such cases involve patients with suicidal ideation).

PRECEDENT 6F: Consent form for the disclosure of medical information

Full Name:
Address:

Date of Birth:	Employee Number:
Name of GP:	Name of Consultant:
Address:	Address:
Tel:	Tel:
Fax:	Fax:

To enable [*name of employer*] to understand the nature of your current illness, when you are likely to return to work and what reasonable adjustments may be needed (if any) it is necessary to obtain information/a report regarding your medical condition from your General Practitioner and/or your consultant/a consultant of our choice [*specify*]. [Our consultant will need to have copies of all your relevant GP health records before they see you.] This information is required in order to plan the work in your department, plan your return to work and to consider the continuation of occupational sick pay.

We therefore seek your informed consent to allow your GP to send to our consultant copies of all your relevant medical records and for you to undergo an examination for these purposes by your GP/your consultant/our consultant and for your informed consent to the disclosure of a medical report following that examination either to our Occupational Health Physician or to the Human Resources Director. In the latter case, no medically confidential information will be disclosed and if the report is sent to our Occupational Health Physician, we will only receive non-medical, non-clinical information about your condition and your fitness for work, etc.

Before applying for this information, we wish to advise you of your rights under the Access to Medical Reports Act 1988. The main points are as follows:

1. You can withhold your consent to any report being disclosed to us.
2. You can see the report before it is sent, or during the six months after that.
3. You can ask the doctor to amend any part of the report that you consider to be incorrect or misleading. If the doctor is not in agreement, you may append your comments.
4. The doctor can withhold from you the report, or part of it, if they think you would be harmed by seeing it.

For more detailed information relating to your rights under the Access to Medical Reports Act 1988 please refer to the Guidance Notes.

Access to Medical Reports Act 1988: Guidance Notes

1. Under the terms of the Access to Medical Reports Act 1988 you have the right to withhold your consent for [employer] to apply to your family doctor or hospital specialist for medical information. If you give your consent you have the right to see information about your medical condition before it is supplied to the Company's Human Resources Department.

2. You will have 21 days from the date of this letter, notifying you that a report has been requested, in which to ask your family doctor or hospital specialist to let you see the report. Your family doctor or hospital specialist will tell you if you cannot see any part of the report for professional medical reasons. If you are given access to the report your family doctor or hospital specialist will not send it to the Human Resources Department until you give your consent.

3. If you regard any information in the report as incorrect or misleading you can ask, in writing, for it to be amended. (Please note: if your family doctor or medical specialist does not accept that the information is incorrect or misleading, they are not required to make any amendment, but in these cases your family doctor or hospital specialist will invite you to prepare a written statement on the disputed information which will be attached to the medical report when it is sent to the Company.)

4. Subject to the provisions of the Act, you have the right to see the report for up to 6 months after it has been sent to the Company by requesting this in writing from your doctor.

5. If your family doctor or hospital specialist gives you a copy of the medical report at your request they may charge you a reasonable fee to cover the cost of supplying it. The Company will not be liable for this fee.

Declaration:

I have been informed of and understand my rights under the Access to Medical Reports Act 1988.

I hereby give my consent to my GP sending copies of all my relevant health records to [name] for the purposes of their examination of me.

I hereby GIVE/DO NOT GIVE* consent to my General Practitioner/Hospital Consultant providing a report giving medical information about me to the Company's Human Resources Department.

I DO/DO NOT* wish to have access to this report before it is provided.

*Delete as appropriate

Signed .... Date ....

[employee]

Full name .... Date of birth ....

PRECEDENT 6G: BMA model letter for long-term or acute sickness absence

[*Name of employee's GP/consultant/company-appointed consultant*]

[*Address*]

[*Date*]

Dear Dr [*name*]

RE: [*name, address, date of birth of employee*]

In order for us to plan the work in the department in which [*employee*] works, to administer sick pay and assess the likelihood of a return to work in the near future and his/her recovery, it would be helpful to have a report on the above-named employee who is a patient of yours.

We have included his/her signed consent form and we undertake to you that all his/her rights under the Access to Medical Reports Act 1988 have been explained in a leaflet which we sent to him/her with the consent form.

You will see that he/she has indicated that he/she wishes to receive a copy of your report before/after you have sent a copy to us.

His/her work as [*give details*] has the following major features:

- Management responsibility for [*give details*]
- Seated/standing/mobile
- Light/medium/heavy effort required
- Day/shift/night work
- Clerical/secretarial duties
- PSV/medium/private driver
- Other

The attendance record for the past year is summarised as:

- Last year, total days' attendance...
- This month...
- Previous months...

I have your patient's permission to enquire:

1. What is the likely date of return to work?
2. Will there be any disability at that date?
3. How long is it likely to last? Will it be temporary or permanent?
4. Is he/she likely to be able to render regular and efficient service in the future?
5. Is/are there any specific recommendation(s) you wish to make which would help us to find him/her alternative employment if that is necessary and if there is an opportunity for redeployment (e.g. no climbing up ladders, no driving, etc.)?
6. Do you recommend that your patient continues with any medication or treatment when he/she returns to work? If so, could you indicate whether this would affect his/her ability to undertake his/her duties or necessitate any time off work (and if so how much)?

I would be grateful for an early reply and enclose a stamped addressed envelope.

Please attach your account for your report which we will be pleased to settle with you at the BMA recommended rate.[1]

Yours sincerely

[*Note:*

1. It is the policy of some NHS Trust Hospitals to charge a far higher fee than the BMA recommended rate plus the cost of the Legal Department to check the report before sending it out. This can be in excess of £300.]

PRECEDENT 6H: Letter of instruction to consultant

[*Name of consultant*]

[*Address*]

[*Date*]

Dear [*name*]

RE: Your patient [*name, address and date of birth of employee*]

We are pleased to instruct you as our Joint Expert in the above matter. The above-named person has brought claims of unfair constructive dismissal and disability discrimination against her former employers [*name*] Ltd and others.

She is Ms Smith, The High Street, Surbiton, KT1 1AB

DOB: 18.06.69

Both parties have agreed upon a Joint Expert to assess this person and to write a Report for the purposes of this litigation.

We would be very grateful if you would make the earliest possible appointment to examine her and to write a Report covering the questions below.

Please would you also let both writers know what date(s) you could attend the Employment Tribunal, listed from 8 to 11 March 20XX, as you may be needed to attend the Watford Employment Tribunal as an expert witness.

We attach the following documents for your information. Ms Smith has given her written consent for her relevant GP records to be sent to you in advance of your examination:

- The ET1 Claim form
- The ET3 Response
- Guidance on the disability provisions in the Equality Act 2010
- The Claimant's written consent to be examined by you and for you to write a Report to be sent to both writers of this letter and to be disclosed in the course of these proceedings.

The questions that we would ask you to answer are set out below. The period over which the alleged disability discrimination is said to have occurred is between 2 and 22 February 20XX, so you should answer these questions with reference to that period of time (referred to below as 'the relevant time').

Did the Claimant, at the relevant time, have one or more impairments, either physical and/or mental impairment(s)?

If so, please identify any such impairment – giving the ICD reference.

When was/were the impairment(s) first diagnosed?

Please briefly describe the usual symptoms of the diagnosed condition.

Over the relevant period, what effect did the impairment actually have, or what effect would it have had, if the Claimant was not taking medication or having other treatment, on the Claimant's ability to carry out the normal day-to-day activities, e.g:

- Mobility
- Manual dexterity
- Physical co-ordination
- Continence
- Ability to lift, carry or otherwise move everyday objects
- Speech, hearing or eyesight
- Memory or ability to concentrate, learn or understand
- Perception of the risk of danger

There are of course other day-to-day activities that you may wish to list and consider.

Please focus on what the Claimant was unable to do or could only do with difficulty as a result of the impairment, not what she was still able to do. It may be helpful to consider the 'Equality Act 2010: Guidance on matters to be taken into account when determining questions relating to the definition of disability', Office for Disability Issues, 2011 (attached).

At the relevant time (i.e. between 2 and 22 February 20XX), had the effect of the impairment lasted 12 months, and if not, was it at that time likely to last 12 months or more, or for the rest of the Claimant's life?

To what extent are you relying upon what you were told by the Claimant? If so, is that consistent with your clinical findings?

If you are not relying on what the Claimant has told you please explain the basis for your opinions.

If the impairment had in the past but had, by the relevant time (2–22 February 20XX) ceased to have a substantial (in the sense of more than minor or trivial) adverse effect on the Claimant's ability to carry out normal day-to-day activities was that effect, at the relevant time, likely to recur (i.e. 'it could well happen' and not that it was probable that it would)? Please state whether your answer is based on your examination of the Claimant, the general progress of such an impairment or statistical likelihood. (Your Report should clearly state whether this prognosis is not to be disclosed to the Claimant.)

If the Claimant has a progressive condition which at the moment has some effect on her ability to carry out normal day-to-day activities but that effect is not yet substantial in the sense of being more than minor or trivial, is the condition likely to have such adverse effect in the future? Please state whether your answer is based on your examination of the Claimant, the general progress of such an impairment or statistical likelihood. (Your Report should clearly state whether this prognosis is not to be disclosed to the Claimant.)

Is the Claimant:

(i) capable of performing work for which she was formerly employed;
(ii) incapable of performing the work for which she was formerly employed at all; unless adjustments were made and if so what;
(iii) incapable of any further work of the kind that she was formerly performing for the Respondent?

In your view, should it be found that the Respondent's alleged actions in:

(a) failing to refer the Claimant's request for a phased return to work to the HR department; and/or

(b) (on 13 February 20XX) informing the Claimant that, on her return to work, her working hours could only be reduced by 30 minutes per day over a period of two weeks, occurred and amounted to disability discrimination,

did those actions contribute in any way to any psychiatric injury or illness suffered by the Claimant? If so, please specify the relevant psychiatric injury or illness and state to what extent the Respondent's actions contributed to/exacerbated that injury or illness.

We should be grateful if you would set out in the Report your relevant qualifications and experience and CV, etc. as required under the Experts' protocol under the CPR.

Please would you indicate when you could examine Ms Smith and by what date you could provide your Report.

The Directions are that a Report is to be produced by 30 October 20XX; any additional questions to be put to you by 7 November and your answers to be given by 21 November 20XX.

We confirm that the parties will share the costs of the examination and Report.

Please note that we would ask that your Report be provided pursuant to the CPR Expert Witness Practice Direction Part 35.

We look forward to hearing from you soonest as to possible dates for you to attend upon the claimant's home.

Yours sincerely

....

X for the Respondent

Yours sincerely

....

Y Solicitors for the Claimant

ENCS:

- ET1
- ET3
- 'Equality Act 2010: Guidance on matters to be taken into account in determining questions relating to the definition of disability' – Office for Disability Issues, 2011
- Medical consent and consent to disclosure of medical records

PRECEDENT 6I: Expert witness's declaration

(We thank Dr Maurice Lipsedge [MPhil FRCP FRCPsych FFOM (Hon) Emeritus Consultant Psychiatrist, South London and Maudsley NHS Trust] and acknowledge his permission to reprint the following declaration that he makes when writing an expert report.)

Declaration

1. I understand that my overriding duty is to the court, both in preparing reports and giving oral evidence.

2. I have set out in my report what I understand from those instructing me to be the questions in respect of which my opinions as an expert are required.

3. I have done my best, in preparing this report, to be accurate and complete. I have mentioned all matters which I regard as relevant to the opinions I have expressed. All of the matters on which I have expressed an opinion lie within my field of expertise.

4. I have drawn to the attention of the court all matters, of which I am aware, which might adversely affect my opinion.

5. Wherever I have no personal knowledge, I have indicated the source of factual information.

6. I have not included anything in this report which has been suggested to me by anyone, including the lawyers instructing me, without forming my own independent view of the matter.

7. Where, in my view, there is a range of reasonable opinion, I have indicated the extent of that range in my report.

8. At the time of signing the report I consider it to be complete and accurate. I will notify those instructing me if, for any reason, I subsequently consider that the report requires any correction or qualification.

9. I understand that this report will be the evidence that I will give under oath, subject to any correction or qualification I may make before swearing to its veracity.

10. I have attached to this report a summary of my instructions.

I believe that the facts I have stated in this report are true and that the opinions I have expressed are correct.

PRECEDENT 6J: Occupational health advice letter

[*Name*]

[*Address*]

[*Date*]

Dear [*name*]

RE: Occupational health advice for [*Name, address and date of birth of individual*]

We are very pleased that you are now fit enough to return to work.

As you know yesterday we discussed what reasonable adjustments ought to be made to your job in light of your current and previous psychological or psychiatric condition.

It was the advice of Occupational Health that we inform your line manager of some of the clinical details so that your manager could be on board with our suggestions of:

• a reduced workload for at least three and possibly six months;
• reduced hours;
• no shift work;
• reduced standards of performance.

We invite you to agree to a reduced workload, etc. upon your return to work.

We have explained to you whilst you may be feeling better, you need a transition back to work and that you may need to slow down and work at a reduced pace with a less strenuous workload in the foreseeable future. You have recognised that your work situation was the 'straw that broke the camel's back' and caused your nervous breakdown and your 5.5 months off work.

We urge you to agree to our course of action and allow us to have our round table discussion with your line manager, Occupational Health, you and your representative and Human Resources.

If you are adamant that this will not happen we may have no alternative but to terminate your employment as we cannot allow you to return to work to expose yourself to further risk of injury – which could be devastating and long lasting.

We have suggested that you might like to consider the role of Deputy Head of Department rather than returning to your original role as Head of Department.

Please consider these options and please sign two copies of this letter accordingly after having discussed the contents of this letter with both your GP and your representative.

I await your response within the next seven days in the s.a.e provided.

Yours sincerely

....

I, [name], am now well and fit and have been signed fit for work by my GP/Occupational Health subject to restrictions and a reduction in responsibilities. I understand that I have been offered the opportunity to return to lighter duties including a lower workload and reduced hours. I have also been advised that I should take a less stressful role – that of Deputy Head of Department.

I have decided to take this advice. I am fully aware of the work situation that precipitated my current/previous mental illness and being fully aware of the risks of this condition and the possibility of recurrence, I understand that I must seek the immediate advice of HR and Occupational Health if I start to feel any similar symptoms of not being able to cope/anxiety, etc.

I have discussed this matter and this letter with my GP and my representative.

Signed .... Date ....

Print full name ....

PRECEDENT 6K: Stress management: risk assessment

Type of work under review:

Description of stress factors	Risk rating (high, medium or low)	
	With controls	Without controls

Possible control measures

Are there training needs? Yes/No

Are there equipment needs? Yes/No

Assessment undertaken by:

Date:

Reviewed by:

Date:

Measure taken in action plan:

Monitoring to be undertaken:

Actions recommended for next cycle:

PRECEDENT 6L: Letter to GP relating to 'stress'

Dear Dr

RE: Your patient [*Name, address and date of birth of individual*]

You have recently signed off work [*name of employee*] diagnosing 'work stress' and have given [*name*] a Fit Note for one month which states 'work-related stress'.

This is highly concerning to us as [*name*]'s first day off sick followed a meeting with me when I informed [*name*] we had performance concerns and would be discussing a performance improvement plan with them.

[*Name*] became very upset and angry upon hearing this, burst into tears and ran out of the meeting, slamming the door behind them. We know that [*name*] has had domestic and personal worries leading to marital breakdown but they were at work throughout all that turmoil.

We therefore need answers to the following questions before we can authorise this current absence and pay [*name of employee*] any sick pay. We would be grateful therefore for your early response:

1. How was the diagnosis of 'work stress' made other than by asking your patient?
2. Into what ICD-10 classification does this diagnosis fall?
3. For how long did you see your patient before you made your diagnosis?
4. What treatment or medication have you prescribed for your patient (given that, as you have signed your patient off work for one month, the condition must be serious)?
5. Have you made a referral for your patient to see a consultant psychiatrist or for counselling?
6. Has your patient had any current, ongoing issues of a psychological or psychiatric nature? If so, when did this start?

Yours sincerely

HR Director

PRECEDENT 6M: Clause relating to stress before or during disciplinary hearings or triggered by an event at work

1. In the event that an employee fails to attend for work the day after or shortly after any of the situations outlined below or under similar circumstances and is signed off work with any description such as 'stress', 'work-related stress', 'depression and/or anxiety', then company sick pay may be suspended until management is entirely satisfied that the absence is not a response to being called to a disciplinary or performance review or to disappointment at or a concern that has arisen at work or a grievance remaining unsatisfied:

(a) the employee is working normally and has an issue of concern, a meeting or conversation that does not go the way they would have wished;

(b) the employee is either suspended from work pending or during an investigation or is made aware or informed that the Company may be or is investigating a disciplinary offence or issue of poor performance.

2. Any Fit Note or medical document containing diagnoses such as 'stress', 'anxiety' or 'depression' or any other similarly worded diagnoses, will not normally be accepted as a reason for refusing to attend any investigatory meeting or performance review or disciplinary hearing.

3. Unless or until the Company receives unequivocal medical evidence from an expert psychiatrist who confirms a diagnosis of mental illness and that there is a previous history prior to any of the material dates referred to above, no sick pay will be paid other than SSP for the duration of that absence and consideration may be given to disciplinary sanctions for the taking of such absence.

4. Management fully understands and appreciates that all employees will feel stressed at being informed of possible disciplinary or performance issues or in cases where a grievance or concern is not satisfied, but it is entirely unacceptable to 'hide' behind a medical certificate offering 'stress' or a stress-related condition as the reason for absence. The Company appreciates that all these matters can cause stress but does not accept that they justify going off sick and claiming sick pay.

5. If the employee indicates or alleges that they are not well enough to attend any disciplinary or performance hearing and sends in a Fit Note or GP's letter 'certifying' that this is the case, this will not be acceptable evidence to the Company. The only acceptable evidence would be from a consultant psychiatrist whose report confirms that the employee is too ill (with the diagnosis) to understand what would be said to them at any hearing and is too ill to give instructions to any representative to act on their behalf or to respond in any such internal hearing.

PRECEDENT 6N: Conduct during sickness absence

Letter to all staff regarding clarification of the sick pay scheme and sickness absence procedure

[Date]

Dear

RE: Conduct during sickness absence

The Company operates its sickness absence and sick pay scheme on the basis of trust and co-operation of its staff. For the vast majority of cases it works well. However, from time to time cases are brought to light which have caused the Company grave concern as it appears that there may be serious abuse of the sickness absence and sick pay schemes.

In order to remind you, clarify and help you understand what is expected of you when or if you are off work, sick, and to understand what might raise doubts or queries in the mind of your manager/Personnel Director concerning certain events and activities taking place during periods of sickness absence, the Company has drawn up some guidelines to all members of staff.

These guidelines form part of the Company's sick pay and absence authorisation procedure and form part of your terms and conditions of employment. It is therefore essential that you read and fully understand the following guidelines since failure to follow the guidelines as set out below may lead to the non-payment of or the cessation of sick pay or recoupment from your future salary, etc. of any sick pay already paid in the circumstances described below.

Conduct during sickness absence

1. Authorisation for absence due to your own personal, genuine illness or injury is only made when that illness or injury prevents you from doing the work which you are employed to do. Paid sick leave cannot be granted for the illness of another member of the family or in cases where you need some time off for personal reasons. In these cases you are expected to ask for permission in advance, so that alternative cover may be arranged. Compassionate leave in such circumstances may be unpaid or may be taken out of paid annual leave.

2. In all cases of absence due to sickness or injury which necessitates taking time off work, it is expected that you will do your utmost to make a speedy return to fitness and to work. In this regard, you are expected to act sensibly and honestly during the time that you are off work to do nothing which is likely to aggravate your illness or injury or delay your recovery.

3. The Company therefore expects you to follow the rules below which are examples only. This is not an exhaustive list. You are:

(a) Not expected to participate in any sports, hobbies or social or any other activities, or attend and participate in religious or other meetings, where these activities could aggravate the illness or injury or delay recovery. The exception to this rule would be where your doctor has prescribed exercise for you or where you have been granted prior written permission by your manager to attend a meeting during your sick leave. We expect you to be sensible. A gentle stroll to the local pub for a drink near the end of any period of sickness absence is acceptable. Going to the pub during the day or for the major part of the evening or most days/evenings will cause the Company to investigate the matter under the terms of its disciplinary procedure.

(b) Not permitted to undertake any other employment whether paid or unpaid. If you declare yourself incapacitated from work in relation to your employment with the Company, it is deemed to be gross misconduct to undertake any other duties whilst off sick. Clearly the Company is your primary employer and if you are fit for any work activity at all, the Company expects you to report to work so that suitable work can be arranged should you not be fully fit for your normal duties.

(c) Not expected to engage in any work around the home or for a friend/third party in terms of home improvements, working on a car, etc. The Company expects you to seek to get better and recover from your illness or injury and will regard any such activity as gross misconduct warranting summary dismissal in an appropriate case.

(d) Not permitted to engage in any activity which is inconsistent with the nature of your alleged illness or injuries or which could exacerbate or aggravate any illness or injury (e.g. walking around town carrying heavy bags of shopping while suffering from an alleged injury).

(e) Where a depressive illness, anxiety, nerves or stress is concerned, the Company will not pay any sick pay or authorise any form of sickness absence and reserves the right to deduct from future salary any sick pay already paid, in circumstances where you are or have been involved in social activities such as singing in a band, competing in competitions, running another business or helping someone else to run their business, which in the Company's opinion is inconsistent with your symptoms or how ill you say you feel, etc.

(f) Not normally permitted to take holiday whether pre-booked or ad hoc during any period of sick leave, except where this is authorised in writing by your doctor as convalescent or recuperative leave (e.g. after an operation) or where you have requested taking holiday and have complied with the holiday leave rules and permission has been granted.

4. If you wish to become involved in any of the above activities or any other activity while on sick leave, then you must clear this first in advance with the HR Director or your line manager. They will then decide whether to grant you permission and whether sick pay should continue.

5. This list is not exhaustive but merely contains examples of the kind of activities which the Company draws to your attention.

6. Finally I would like to thank you for your co-operation in making sure that our rules and sick pay scheme work well so that those who are genuinely in need of time off with pay receive just that.

7. The substance of this letter is incorporated into the Company's sick pay scheme.

Yours sincerely

Managing Director/HR Director

PRECEDENT 6O: Exceptions to occupational sick pay

Any sickness absence for the following reasons will not attract occupational sick pay:

(a) absence due to fertility treatment or time off receiving or recovering from such treatment (this may be granted as unpaid or taken as annual leave);
(b) absence due to elective surgery, e.g. cosmetic surgery or a sterilisation operation;
(c) absence due to injuries resulting from participation in dangerous sports, e.g. hang-gliding, bungee-jumping, parachuting, rugby, boxing, etc;
(d) absence occasioned by working for another employer or on your own behalf outside your employment;
(e) absence due to self-inflicted illness or injury, e.g. sunburn, hangover, tobacco-related illnesses, drug abuse, etc;
(f) absence due to the death or illness of a relative or friend or dependant other than a close relative;
(g) absence due to the illness or death of an animal or domestic pet;
(h) absence due to participating in a sports activity or watching sport;
(i) absence due to attendance at religious*, social/family or trade union functions.

* This may be covered under 'other leave arrangements'.

PRECEDENT 6P: Holiday clauses

Requirement to take annual leave

Management reserves the right to require you to take all or part of your annual leave at times that it designates during the holiday year, e.g. during the factory holiday fortnight shutdown; over the Christmas and New Year period when the offices are shut; during any period of notice.

Periods when leave cannot be taken

Similarly during our very busy period [*state months*] staff are not permitted to take their annual leave.

Permission

Leave is allocated on a 'first come first served basis' so it is advisable to send your proposed holiday dates to your line manager for authorisation as soon as possible. Only when you have signed authority, i.e. a signed holiday leave form, should you book your holiday.

Minimum periods of leave

Management may require you to take a minimum of [X] weeks at one time [*note that this is a common provision in banks where a Bank of England investigation can take up to two or three weeks*].

Maximum periods of leave

You are not allowed to take any more than [X] weeks at any one time. In exceptional cases up to [X] weeks' leave can be taken but only with the express advance written permission of a Director or head of Department.

Employees whose families live abroad

In cases where employees ask for extended leave of absence or take annual leave to visit their families who live abroad, e.g. in Eastern Europe or the Indian subcontinent, the employee must abide strictly to the leave arrangements and return to the UK and to work on the due date.

We would look very carefully where an employee fails to return to work after taking such leave and who asserts sickness as the reason for their failure to return. Our rules in such cases can be found in our Sickness Absence Policy.

Religious holidays

We respect all our staff and their religious beliefs. We appreciate that within different religions there are special Fast, Festival and Holy Days.

If you wish to take a particular religious holiday as a day off work, this must be sought as a day of annual leave. Since these dates are known well in advance we ask that you give your line manager written notification of such dates at the start of each religious year so that we can plan for your absences (e.g. the Feast of Eid, Yom Kippur, etc.).

PRECEDENT 6Q: Sickness during holidays and public holidays

If an employee is unable to come to work on the day before or after a holiday whether a Bank, Public or statutory holiday or pre-planned annual leave, then a medical certificate from his/her GP in Great Britain will be required from day one that confirms the nature of the illness or injury and that it prevents the employee from working and that the employee is not fit to travel (unless the holiday is recommended for rehabilitation purposes only).

Any employee who is too unfit to come to work immediately preceding or following a holiday will be regarded as too ill to travel to a holiday destination and unless their doctor or our Occupational Health specialists confirm that travelling to the holiday and taking the holiday is part of the recuperation process, the employee is required to cancel the holiday and book it at another time of the year.

If an employee falls sick during a holiday then medical evidence that satisfies the Company will have to be submitted and this will normally not be a private doctor's letter or report but a hospital doctor's report.

In any case where the employee delays his/her return to the UK because of illness on holiday, evidence of the original travel arrangements and evidence as to why the employee is too ill to return to the UK will have to be submitted and this evidence will have to satisfy the Company before sick pay is paid or the leave is authorised.

Holiday may only be taken in the leave year in respect of which it is due save where you have been prevented by illness from taking a period of holiday leave. This can be carried over for a maximum of the next 18 months only. In such a case, you will be given the opportunity of taking that holiday in the following leave year, and for a further six months.

PRECEDENT 6R: Sickness and holidays in home country abroad

Where an employee falls ill in this country, the Company will not in normal cases give permission for that employee to return to his/her home country or any other country outside the UK, for treatment, etc. Every employee is covered by the NHS which provides excellent treatment for anyone who is ill.

When in the past employees have gone back to their native country during any period of illness, they have not been able to engage in our Occupational Health procedures and the Company then loses all meaningful contact with the employee.

It will be regarded in future as a serious conduct issue for employees who fall sick for any reason to leave the UK to go home to their native country, save where for example, the illness may be terminal and they wish to be with their family. In those circumstances the Company will of course take a lenient view about those travel arrangements.

For the avoidance of any doubt where there has been suspected abuse of the sickness policy in the past, e.g. an employee has had repeated (more than one) absence before or during a holiday which has led to that employee/those employees remaining in their home country on extended leave, any future sickness notified during a holiday will not be authorised until the employee/employees return to the UK and provide acceptable medical evidence of their inability to return on the due date and an acceptable explanation, i.e. one which satisfies the Company.

If any such illness occurs abroad it is a requirement that: (a) the doctor in that country will notify the employee's GP in this country; (b) if the employee has had any form of treatment and evidence of that treatment including any medication, evidence of this will need to be provided upon their return; and (c) evidence of the original travel arrangements/booking showing the original return date will need to be produced.

It is regarded as gross misconduct, for which the final stage of the disciplinary procedure will be commenced, to:

(a) go on holiday abroad with the intention of not returning on the due date of return or not returning without good cause on the due date of return;
(b) take 'sick leave' either before or during a holiday abroad, for alleged or actual medical treatment in that foreign country when permission to do so has either not been sought or has been refused;
(c) claim sick pay during or after a holiday leave period when not genuinely ill or injured.

PRECEDENT 6S: Terms relating to fitness for work

Fitness for work

1. Because of the nature of our business and the need, for safety reasons, for you to [start your shift fully competent and alert] [present yourself for work at the helipad] in a fully sober state, you will be required to conduct yourself sensibly before the start of your shift. This may mean that you will need to abstain from any alcoholic beverages/ prescribed drugs several hours before your normal starting time since otherwise there may still be alcohol present in your blood and this may affect your ability to perform your duties or may potentially endanger yourself or others.

2. Anyone who presents themselves for work in a condition determined by their manager as unfit for any reason which may include being under the influence of alcohol or drugs (whether prescribed or not) may be suspended from duty with or without pay depending on the circumstances.

3. In normal cases, if this occurs on a single occasion, your manager will warn you either informally or formally about your condition but may decide to pay you your normal pay. On any further occasion, management reserves the right to suspend your pay and request that you return home. [Your shop steward will be requested to attend any meeting when any such problem arises.]

[4. The rules we adopt as you work in a safety-critical job:

- 24 hours between 'bottle and throttle' – maximum eight units of alcohol;
- 12 hours between 'bottle and throttle' – no alcohol.]

5. If you are taking any medication (whether prescribed or OTC) which warns that it might make you drowsy or that you should not drive or use machinery, then please report this immediately to Occupational Health who will advise your line manager accordingly.

Additional or part-time work

6. Your primary employment is with this Company. As such you are expected to be fully fit, competent, alert, healthy and in a safe condition for work at all times and especially at the start of your shift. Whilst there is no restriction on what work or employment you choose to take, you are required to:

(a) notify HR and your line manager if you are doing any other employment outside work whether this is on a self-employed or employed basis, paid or unpaid;
(b) notify HR and your line manager of the nature of the work and the number of hours and days each week upon which you do this work;
(c) notify HR and your line manager if you are considering taking up any such outside employment/work.

7. As you know, the Working Time Regulations provide that our employees only work a maximum of 48 hours in a seven-day period referenced over 17, 26 or 52 weeks in any year. This means total working hours and not just the hours that you work with us.

Regulation 9 requires us to keep records of all the hours that our employees work and not just the hours worked at this Company.

8. If we believe that your additional duties are preventing you from safely or effectively performing your duties with us, we shall discuss this first on an informal basis [with your shop steward/works convenor present]. We shall ask you to reconsider this matter and to reduce your additional hours outside work or stop your additional work altogether.

9. If you choose not to reduce or cease your external employment, then the Company will decide whether it is safe to allow you to continue working for us or whether we would be in breach of the Working Time Regulations 1998 which require us to limit your total working week to 48 hours.

10. The evidence upon which the Working Time Directive was based was on health and safety. It is believed that working long hours can be dangerous to an individual's health and safety and to that of others. We are therefore asking you to be responsible for informing us of your outside work activities so that we can perform our legal responsibilities properly and upon reliable information provided by you.

PRECEDENT 6T: Light duties policy

1. Placing employees on the Restricted/Alternative Duties Register

European Directives relating to health, safety and employment state that 'apart from relieving suffering and prolonging life, the objective of most medical treatment is to return the person to work'. Also, under the Equality Act 2010, it is our duty to make reasonable adjustments for anyone with a disability.

2. Main aim of placing employees on the Restricted/Alternative Duties Register

This is to allow those who have overcome injury and disease and wish to work, to carry out reasonable duties suitable for them.

3. Company policy for employee off work due to injury/illness

3.1 The Restricted/Alternative Duties Register is maintained by Occupational Health. It is updated on a weekly basis and a copy of the register is sent to Human Resources on a monthly basis.

3.2 The Occupational Health Team, in conjunction with Human Resources, must ensure that supervisors and managers throughout the Company are aware of the presence of this Register and how it is managed.

3.3 Any employee who is absent due to an injury or major illness must be assessed by the Occupational Health Nurse or Physician prior to returning to work.

3.4 This assessment should determine a possible return to work date, fitness to return, and any restrictions to the current job role (either long or short-term).

3.5 Where there is any doubt as to the employee's fitness, or a lack of knowledge on treatment received or ongoing from a third party (GP, Hospital Consultant or other member of the multidisciplinary team) then the OH professional will take informed written consent from the employee to obtain a report from the specified Specialist.

3.6 The individual may state that he/she may wish to see the report before it is supplied.

3.7 The employee is supplied with a copy of the Access to Medical Reports Act 1988 (Appendix [X]).

3.8   Once the report is received the OH professional will discuss the content with the employee.

3.9   The OH professional will contact the employee's manager/supervisor to discuss the proposed return and any restrictions that the employee may have, short or long term (this can be discussed without informing the manager/supervisor of the exact diagnosis, unless written consent has been given by the employee).

3.10   The OH professional will carry out a workplace risk assessment, prior to the employee's return, if there is uncertainty about the functions of the particular job or any risks to that individual.

3.11   A return to work date is set in conjunction with the OH professional, employee, supervisor/manager (and other member of the multidisciplinary team if appropriate). The HR department is informed and kept updated by the OH professional.

3.12   The manager/supervisor will arrange for the employee to be shown the alternative or restricted job role. The manager/supervisor, OH professional and employee will have agreed a review date.

3.13   The employee is then placed on the Restricted/Alternative Duties Register with the review date set. The employee is also advised to return to Occupational Health if any problems arise.

3.14   Each time the employee is reassessed a new date for assessment is given until such time as the employee can return to 'normal' duties.

3.15   If the employee is unable to return to 'normal' duties then the employee, the OH professional, manager/supervisor, the individual and HR professional will meet and discuss the possibility of remaining on the alternative job or of finding suitable redeployment. This is referred to as a 'Round Table Discussion'.

3.16   If for any reason the employee is unable to cope with any form of work, after the above procedure has been followed, then it is a management and not medical decision as to whether or not to terminate employment or offer early retirement. The OH professional's role is to provide and interpret the medical information which managers/HR will need so that they can make decisions about the employee's position.

3.17   It is the duty and responsibility of every employee off sick to keep the Occupational Health Physician/Nurse and HR fully up to date with their progress, treatment, medical reports, etc. It is also the duty of every employee off sick to alert the Occupational Health Physician/Nurse when the employee believes that there might be any chance of returning to work on light duties. Failure to report such progress and to inform HR and/or OH of any improvement in their condition, will render this Policy unworkable and may lead to a suspicion of malingering or worse.

3.18   It is therefore in everyone's interests to keep in regular contact and for the employee off sick to be as honest and open about their condition as possible.

PRECEDENT 6U: No smoking policy

It is a requirement of this Company that no one smokes any tobacco products anywhere in their workplace whether this is an office or factory or company vehicle. Anyone who breaches this policy will be subject to disciplinary action which could lead to dismissal – even for a first offence. If you experience any problems not being able to smoke other than outside the building in your lunch and tea breaks, please let either Human Resources or your line manager or Occupational Health know and we can arrange for help to quit smoking.

PRECEDENT 6V: Absence through negligence of third party

1. If you are absent through injuries caused by the actionable negligence, nuisance or breach of statutory duty of a third party in respect of which damages are recoverable, you must inform your manager immediately. Any payment that may be made for all or part of any such absence (other than SSP) shall be by way of a loan which must be repaid in full. If damages are settled on a proportionate basis, the Company will require full details. The amount of any repayment required in those circumstances will be determined by the Company but will not exceed the actual damages recovered or the part thereof identified as loss of earnings.

2. In circumstances where no claim is made or where no claim can be made, you may, at management's discretion, be paid sick pay.

PRECEDENT 6W: Permanent health insurance/long-term disability scheme

1. The Company operates a generous sick pay scheme for those who are genuinely ill or injured and their illness or injury prevents them from doing any work which it is reasonable for them to perform.

2. The Company also operates a Permanent Health Insurance (PHI) or Long Term Disability (LTD) Scheme to enable salary continuation in cases where sickness or injury lasts for longer than six months and where you (the employee) meet the requirements of the Scheme and are deemed eligible by the insurance provider.

3. Please note that this is an insured benefit and is therefore only payable where the insurer accepts you on to the Scheme. There is no express or implied promise or commitment by the Company that if you are declined entry to the PHI/LTD Scheme and your appeal fails, the Company will make any payments to you. This benefit is offered to you only on the basis of the terms of the insurer which may vary from time to time.

4. Please also note that the fact that there is a salary continuation scheme (PHI/LTD) for those whose sickness or injury continues beyond the payment of occupational sick pay in no way implies that the Company will not in any suitable case decide that the employee's contract of employment should be terminated at any earlier date. In other words there is no guarantee or promise that employment will never be terminated either before or during the payment of PHI/LTD.

5. Termination of employment would only be done in cases where the Director of Human Resources has been involved in any such decision and only after prior consultation with you. There may be serious medical, financial or sound business reasons where the decision to terminate your employment may have to be taken. For example, in any case where the employee's absence was causing serious commercial/business difficulties, a permanent or temporary replacement had to be engaged but for headcount reasons, the Company was not permitted to do so where you were still technically 'in post'/'employed'.

6. In such a case, early retirement on ill health grounds would also be considered but no guarantee would or could be made that in the particular circumstances, the employee would be eligible, e.g. his/her age, the prognosis of the illness or injury, ability to obtain new outside employment, etc.

7. The Company assures every employee that in each case where PHI/LTD would be considered, the proper exercise of its discretion will continue to be adopted.

PRECEDENT 6X: Sick pay and termination of employment

1. We aim to provide sick pay to those with either short term illness or injury or those who need longer off work to recover. We are sensitive and sympathetic to those with genuine illness or injury that prevents them from carrying out their duties and will do everything we can to alleviate financial hardship and assist a return to work on a graduated basis if required or on any other reasonable basis.

2. However, we reserve the right in any case to seek expert medical opinion at any stage during an employee's sick leave, to ascertain the nature and severity of the condition and to seek a prognosis, etc. If the prognosis is pessimistic for a return to work in any capacity and the role requires a permanent member of staff with the skills required for that post, we may take a decision before sick pay has been exhausted and we may take a decision after consultation with the individual concerned and any other medical personnel, to terminate the contract of employment – after all other options have been explored.

3. If an employee refuses to return to work after our medical expert(s) deem that the employee can return in some capacity, then we may hold a disciplinary hearing and take a view about whether such conduct constitutes a flagrant and unreasonable refusal to obey a lawful and/or reasonable instruction. In such a case, dismissal may be an outcome, with or without notice or payment in lieu of notice.

OR

1. The sick pay scheme sets out maximum entitlement to sick pay during any period of sickness absence if you satisfy all the rules of the scheme.

2. However, please be aware that by setting out these payments, this does not guarantee that consideration of the termination of employment will not occur prior to the exhaustion of sick pay should the particular circumstances of the case warrant such action. Nor does the setting of maximum benefits under our scheme imply in any way that this is an absolute entitlement as long as you remain sick nor that after your employment has ended, you would be entitled under your contract to recover any outstanding sums.

3. If anyone off sick whether on paid or unpaid sick leave is being considered for the termination of their employment, a fair procedure will be followed including our duties under the disability provisions of the Equality Act 2010 if applicable, including assessing an up-to-date medical report, consulting with the individual and considering all other possibilities other than dismissal, including modifications to the original duties, redeployment, rehabilitation and early retirement on grounds of ill health. Dismissal on ill health grounds will be the last option considered.

PRECEDENT 6Y: Disability

1. We collect data including sickness absence data about employees who are both able-bodied and disabled and this data includes information collected at recruitment, during employment and at the termination stage in order to monitor our treatment of staff with disabilities and to ensure that we make full use of the skills and qualities that people with disabilities can bring into the workplace and to ensure that we understand and do not devalue staff with disabilities. Any time off for a disability-related issue will not be used for any discriminatory or adverse purposes. We pride ourselves on valuing diversity and treating everyone with dignity and respect, irrespective of gender, race, religion, nationality or ethnic origin, sexual orientation or disability.

2. The extension of sick pay will be considered in every case. In particular where reasonable adjustments need to be made to allow anyone with a disability to return to the workplace after sickness absence, every effort will be made to accommodate that individual's needs.

PRECEDENT 6Z: Clause relating to IVF treatment

1. It is acknowledged that IVF treatment is becoming more available on the NHS and that private treatment is becoming more popular and more successful. It is also acknowledged that the majority of infertility problems require women to undergo tests and treatment. This treatment requires days off work each month and can cause unpleasant side effects for the woman as well as psychological trauma for both the male and female partners.

2. We have to be mindful that the business requires employees who can provide regular and efficient employment. However, we are willing to listen sympathetically to any employee who is undergoing IVF treatment (or similar) and who will require days off each month and who may not give 100 per cent to their job during this difficult period. We may treat this time off as paid sick leave or another form of paid leave and we will look sympathetically at requests for reduced hours or duties if required for health or safety reasons during this critical time.

3. Depending upon length of service and performance and disciplinary record and the record of time off taken in the past, Human Resources will consider each case on its merits to decide whether time off with or without pay will be required. In such a case management would reserve the right to review the arrangement at regular intervals.

PRECEDENT 6AA: Clause relating to requirement to report medication

Due to the nature of our business and your job being safety critical, you are required to report to the Occupational Health Nurse/Medic any medication whether prescribed or over the counter that you are taking. You need to report to the Nurse/Medic, bringing the bottle or packet of medicines with you. It is particularly important that you retain and show to the Nurse/Medic any safety instructions inside the bottle or packet.

You should advise the Nurse/Medic of the job that you do and he/she will then advise your line manager and HR whether any adjustments need to be made to your job. You will suffer no loss of pay or any detriment if this occurs.

Please note that this is a very important instruction as your life and the lives of others could be placed in grave danger if you continue operating in your role when the medication contra-indicates this.

We thank you for your co-operation and assure you that no details of the medication or the medical condition for which you take this medication will be disclosed without your informed, written consent and in most cases this will not be necessary.

PRECEDENT 6AB: Management procedure for malingerers

1. Asking for leave and it is declined

Employees who ask for annual leave or a day or few days' leave and it is declined may still feel that they are entitled to take it or may have already booked the holiday and therefore decide to take it anyway. The following procedure is suggested:

1.1 Manager to call the employee in to the office the afternoon before the first day of the leave requested.

1.2 Remind employee of the refused leave application and produce the form with the refusal marked, dated and signed.

1.3 Ask the employee to confirm that they have understood that the leave has been refused, why it has been refused and to confirm that he/she will be at work on the relevant day.

1.4 Explain how the Company views absence in breach of an express instruction not to take the leave, i.e. that it is regarded as gross misconduct. Explain why it is gross misconduct.

1.5 Confirm that, in the unlikely event they are unfit for work, the manager will require medical evidence which is acceptable to him/her and self-certificates may not suffice.

1.6 Confirm the conversation in writing, date and sign it and give employee a copy.

2. Employee fails to attend work

2.1 If the employee fails to attend work on a day that they should be at work, ring their telephone number and note down the number of times the telephone rings, the times of the day the number is tried and confirm with the operator there is no fault on the line.

2.2 Keep careful dated notes of this procedure.

2.3 If the employee telephones the manager, return the call immediately.

2.4 If an answerphone is on, leave an urgent message that the manager requires a conversation with the employee as soon as they feel fit enough to speak.

2.5 State on the answerphone that the manager is so concerned at the employee's non-appearance at work, that the manager intends to visit the employee at home and can the employee confirm when it would be convenient.

2.6 Visit and search for the individual. Make a note if the house is locked up. Visit a neighbour and explain that the individual has not been seen at work and enquire if the neighbour knows where the employee is.

2.7 Leave a note that you called (you will have written one in advance and have taken a copy). This note will state that you called, that there was no one in and that you require an immediate telephone call to explain where the employee is and why they are not at work.

2.8 You may also require an immediate medical examination during (or after) the absence by the OHP.

2.9 You are entitled to treat going on holiday whilst claiming sickness as gross misconduct as this is regarded as fraud (making a fraudulent claim on sick pay); breach of mutual trust and confidence (lying on the self-certificate); flagrant breach of an express instruction not to take holiday.

2.10 You are entitled to look behind a medical certificate if you have evidence of conduct inconsistent with the illness or injuries.

2.11 A full disciplinary hearing should follow with all the evidence presented and the employee asked for an explanation.

2.12 The decision whether or not to take disciplinary action, and if so what, should be taken.

2.13 An opportunity to appeal should be given.

PRECEDENT 6AC: External business activities or interests and 'moonlighting'

The Company recognises that from time to time employees may want to take up other employment in their spare time whether paid or unpaid and/or pursue outside business interests in their spare time, whilst still remaining in our employment. Although the Company has no wish to unreasonably restrict your external activities, we must protect our own interests and those of all our employees. To this end, the Company's policy is that employees will not be permitted to undertake any outside business activities whether paid or unpaid or take on any other work outside working hours where the Company considers that this is in conflict with our interests.

In any event employees must have obtained the prior written authorisation of a Director which will not be unreasonably withheld.

PROCEDURE

1. If you propose taking up any other external employment or post outside working hours or pursuing separate business interests, you must request an interview with your Head of the Department or a Director and HR to establish the likely impact of these activities on the Company.

2. You will be asked to provide full details of the proposed work and specific consideration should be given to the following areas.

(a) Working hours: are you proposing to conduct this work entirely outside your contractual hours of work, or is there likely to be some overlap?
(b) Competition: are you intending to work in competition with the Company, either in your own right or for a competing organisation? If so, is there a real risk of a conflict of interest and/or confidential information being used to the Company's detriment?
(c) Health, safety and welfare: are you proposing to carry out work which is inherently hazardous and where the risk of injury is high (should you become injured or fall sick as a result of other work, company sick pay entitlement will be affected) and is the extra work likely to cause undue fatigue, stress, etc. which will affect job performance with the Company?

3. If, after investigation, a Director considers that the proposed activities are incompatible with your express or implied obligations to the Company, permission will be refused. This should be notified to you in writing detailing the reasons for refusal. If you are dissatisfied with the decision you may place a grievance through the company's grievance procedure.

Where your proposed work does not significantly affect your employment with the Company, permission will normally be given in writing. This will include a reminder to you of your obligations to the Company that should your external activities subsequently have an effect on your employment, permission may be withdrawn. Additionally, any material changes to the circumstances of your outside interests must be brought to the attention of the Company immediately.

Where anyone is found to be 'Moonlighting', i.e. working for themselves or for someone else whether paid or unpaid either in breach of this Policy or when off sick, an immediate investigation will be carried out. This may be before the individual concerned is notified of our concerns. In some cases this may be obtaining video footage or sound recording or interviews which will then form the basis of a disciplinary hearing for gross misconduct for which summary dismissal is one possible outcome.

The Company reserves the right to monitor and read or listen to emails, correspondence addressed to the Company address and to all telephone calls made and received. No personal or private correspondence or goods are permitted to be sent to the Company premises and the Company reserves the right to open and inspect all correspondence and goods addressed to and delivered to the office.

No personal emails should be sent or received on the Company server or your work email address. The Company reserves the right to read and intercept any personal emails sent or received on its company server.

No mobile telephones other than work mobiles may be used during the working day or working hours.

CCTV is also used and this may be hidden where the Company needs to prevent or detect crime. It will not be used or located where privacy is required, e.g. in rest rooms, lavatories, lockers rooms where you change your clothes, etc.

PRECEDENT 6AD: Note to all staff about use of private detectives

You are trusted when you go off work claiming that you are sick or injured to tell the truth, to try to get better as quickly as you can and to return to work as quickly as you can. You are also trusted when at work particularly if you work alone or from home or travel on business or visit our clients, etc.

It is not expected that you would be working either for yourself or for anybody else while working for the Company. If any malpractice or dishonest conduct is suspected, the Company reserves the right to use covert surveillance including video facilities and the use of private detectives to obtain evidence of such conduct.

Any employee caught conducting themselves in such a manner will be regarded as committing gross misconduct and will be asked to explain their conduct at a disciplinary hearing where summary dismissal could be an outcome. Any CCTV or video footage or recordings of any kind will be provided to the employee and their representative prior to any disciplinary hearing.

In cases of fraud, e.g. where an employee is claiming sick pay when not genuinely ill or injured and/or is receiving income from another unauthorised source, the Company will make every effort to recover any sick pay paid through the civil courts.

PRECEDENT 6AE: Instructions to private detectives

You will be required to undertake surveillance and to interview witnesses and write a report. This may lead to criminal or civil proceedings in which you may be required to give evidence. For each assignment you will be given separate and detailed instructions on the individual under surveillance and the requirements for that assignment.

In general you are required to:

(a) undertake the investigation according to our requirements, e.g. you may be asked to carry out surveillance on an employee who is off sick but whom we suspect may be malingering;
(b) keep whatever information we give you about the individual strictly confidential save where we give you express permission to disclose it (you will not be given any medically confidential details);
(c) maintain the security and confidentiality of the information that you gather;

(d) report the results in a timely and professional manner;
(e) be knowledgeable about and adhere to all the relevant legal requirements and provisions, e.g. under the Data Protection Act 1998; Human Rights Act 1998; PACE, etc;
(f) only obtain information in a lawful way and by lawful means, e.g. you must not intrude on the individual's privacy; you must not trick your way into their homes and secretly record or film them; you must not use long lenses to film inside their homes or when they are on their property, etc;
(g) when you interview witnesses you must be professional, courteous and sensitive respecting their right to privacy and you must ensure that you obtain only reliable and accurate information; this may mean obtaining corroborative evidence and always obtaining a witness's signature and date when taking a witness statement;
(h) if following an individual, take prompt action if sight of the suspect is lost, etc.

We follow the Association of British Insurers (ABI) *Guidelines on the Instruction and Use of Private Investigators*, September 2014.

PRECEDENT 6AF: Absence control for managers

A.   Short-term, intermittent, persistent absenteeism

1.   The problem

1.1   The casual absence levels for your Unit are now running at . . . per cent losing . . . working days respectively. The figures for this year are considerably worse than the figures for last year and are the worst among all the other organisations in the retail sector.

1.2   The Company is now firmly committed to getting those figures down to a more acceptable level and to this end we are asking each manager to become more responsible for their team and to monitor closely individual records.

1.3   We are setting a new procedure in motion which if diligently carried out by all managers should lead to a reduction in short-term, intermittent, persistent absences and a more careful monitoring of genuine chronic or long-term sickness cases.

1.4   In order to ensure consistency, the following are the procedures to follow in controlling absence. Managers will be more responsible for responding to absence for own teams and for recording their actions.

2.   Short-term absences

2.1   Short-term, persistent, intermittent absences from work are in the main all genuine. The employee may have many unrelated symptoms but no underlying medical problem. However, the number, frequency and erratic nature of these absences from work lead to the employee becoming unreliable and become commercially disruptive.

2.2   Your staff working in our retail outlets should constantly be reminded of the importance of time-keeping and regular attendance at work.

2.3   Where someone genuinely cannot perform their work because of an injury or illness or where it might affect the health and/or safety of others (e.g. where someone has an infectious or contagious disease), all managers should remind their staff of the notification and medical evidence procedure and most importantly the requirement to update their managers on a regular basis during their absence from work.

3. Trigger points when individuals may be interviewed

These could be:

(a) Four separate spells of absence in a rolling 12 months or two spells in a three-month period;
(b) 10 consecutive days of absence or more in a rolling 12 months or five days in a three-month period; or
(c) an unacceptable frequency factor as defined under the Bradford Score

whichever happens first.

4. First interview of concern

4.1 The first meeting should be with the immediate line manager when this trigger level has been reached and where the employee's record calls for it. Clearly there will be obvious cases which do not require any such interview, e.g. a 10-day spell off sick with severe influenza.

4.2 The interview of concern is an informal counselling session and is not in any sense a disciplinary interview. You are expected to handle this meeting with sympathy, understanding and compassion.

4.3 You must have the individual's absence record with you at the meeting. A simple calendar with the sick days marked in red will also be useful to identify patterns, frequency or curious coincidences in days taken off work, e.g. school holidays, bank and public holidays, annual leave, spouse's or partner's annual leave, sporting fixtures, refusal of leave, etc.

5. Documents to be produced in the first counselling session

5.1 The absence record should be set out in three columns:

(a) the number of work days of absence in the left-hand column;
(b) the number of spells in the middle column; and
(c) the reasons for the absence in the right-hand column.

5.2 You should have attached all the self-certificates and any medical certificates to the record.

5.3 You should total the first two columns. You should investigate any pattern(s): any co-incidences with football matches, hobbies and interests of the individual, work patterns or holidays of the partner or the spouse, etc.

5.4 You should go through the reasons for the absences with the individual and try to find out what is the underlying cause (if any) for the amount and frequency of the time off (do not lead the individual but invite them to volunteer what lies behind all these absences).

5.5 If you have picked out the worst record in your department, then you must tell the individual that fact – the worst thing that can happen is for them to tell you of someone with a worse record within your working group.

5.6 You should check the frequency with which the individual takes days off each year. The Bradford Frequency Factor can be measured by taking:

No. of days × (no. of spells)^2

e.g.

9 days × (3 spells)^2 = 81

6. **Reasons for non-attendance**

6.1 Several possible reasons lie behind persistent, intermittent absence and they include:

(a) an underlying medical condition which is undiagnosed;
(b) a problem with work or colleagues or supervisor;
(c) a family, personal or domestic problem;
(d) an attitude or motivational problem, i.e. mere laziness;
(e) a problem with a business or other interest outside work;
(f) a response to a refusal for time off or in response to a particular shift or evening duty.

6.2 Please be aware that some individuals may need time off work to care for sick dependants or because they are disabled themselves. Is it possible to offer carers' leave or domestic leave in appropriate cases?

6.3 You will be expected to explore with the individual what lies behind the absence. Careful, persuasive and attentive questions and answers ought to be able to give you a clue as to the reason for the non-attendance at work.

6.4 It is essential that you take notes of this meeting and record what you say and what the employee has said. You will then attach these notes to any subsequent record of a warning.

6.5 You must give the individual a copy of these notes after they have been typed up. If possible, although it is not essential, get the individual to sign at the bottom of the notes that they are a true and accurate record of the interview which took place on [*date*].

7. **Medical problem**

7.1 In order to ensure that the individual does not actually have an undiagnosed medical condition, you should do the following:

7.2 Ask 'have you been to see your doctor?'

7.3 If the answer is 'No', then you can request that he/she is examined by your Occupational Health Physician (OHP) or GP. You must ask him/her to sign a consent form giving their consent to the examination and to a report being sent to your OHP. The answers to the relevant questions will then be given to you by your OHP.

7.4 Your OHP or the GP should be sent a copy of the absence record with copies of any self-certificates or medical certificates and you should ask him/her the following question: 'Is there any serious underlying medical condition which explains all these absences from work?'

7.5 If the answer is 'Yes', then further discussions must take place with the OHP (with the written consent of the individual) to find out whether the condition can be treated and whether or not the individual is fit to attend work during treatment. The GP's medical records should have been obtained in advance by your OHP to see whether any of the symptoms have been recorded by the GP. Note that:

(a) No manager should request that a doctor sends them a medical report;
(b) Any doctor must be told the reason for asking for the report;
(c) If the condition is a disability under the Equality Act 2010, take careful advice.

8. **Other explanation for absences**

If the answer from the GP is 'No', there is no 'serious underlying medical condition', then you must explore the other reasons with the individual at a further meeting.

9. Second interview of concern

9.1 In this second interview, the employee must be counselled about his/her absence record and advised that if there is not 100 per cent attendance at work, further action including disciplinary action will have to be taken.

9.2 His/her record should be further reviewed within a reasonable interval (say after one complete shift or one or two weeks) and if the absences continue and there is no underlying medical condition, then he/she must be issued with a warning letter.

9.3 A review of the attendance record should continue at the end of each complete shift (or weekly or fortnightly) until you are satisfied. With delicate handling the absence record should improve.

10. 'Sympathetic warning' letters: 'Notifications of concern'

If a 'warning' letter or 'caution' becomes necessary, then it should be given to the individual after a formal interview with a fellow colleague present if he/she so wishes. Please be sure to tell him/her that they have a right to have a colleague present. These should be 'sympathetic warning letters' rather than disciplinary warning letters as per the normal disciplinary procedure for breach of company rules.

11. Further 'warnings'

If the absences continue and you are unable to discover whether there are particular problems in this case, you will have to issue further sympathetic written warnings, a first written warning and then a final written warning.

12. Dismissal

12.1 Should the record continue, consideration will have to be given to dismissal. Before dismissal is effected, it is essential to seek and consider suitable alternative employment.

12.2 It should be made clear to the individual at each stage and in the warning letters, the problems that are being caused in terms of loss of sales, effect upon other staff, health and safety, morale among the rest of the staff, etc. by their continued absences.

13. Employees with poor records

For employees with a history of high absence levels, who have a persistent record of poor attendance, it may be appropriate to do the following:

13.1 State in their warning letters that because of their bad attendance record in the past, should they fail to improve or sustain any improvement, they will go into the next warning stage of the procedure, i.e. if they have been issued with a first written warning and this then lapses, they will not go back to the oral warning stage but will go either back on a first written warning or straight to a final written warning despite the original first written warning having lapsed.

13.2 In the alternative, state in the 'sympathetic' warning letter that because of their poor record over ... months/years of poor attendance, their warning will last for an extended period, e.g. two years and not 12 months. It is essential that the warning letter spells out why this slightly unusual procedure is being applied and how long the warning will last.

13.3 Issuing 'well done' letters after the warning has lapsed is a positive measure.

13.4 Computerised records may allow for each self-certificate generated by the computer to be individualised and by this means the computer may be able to generate the previous 12 months' absence record by spell, duration and cause at the end of the self-certificate.

13.5 Self-certificates should be completed by the individual once they have returned to work in a return to work interview with their immediate superior.

13.6 Five copies of this self-certificate should be made, one for the employee, one for the immediate line manager, one for Personnel, one for OH and one for payroll.

13.7 At the end of the year all staff should be sent a summary of their days off due to sickness.

14. Note to management: appraisal

One way to ensure that line managers will monitor absence in this way is to write into their annual targets the responsibility to reduce absence levels in their departments/area and properly control absenteeism and sickness absence. Once a year managers can be appraised on this.

B. *Long-term or chronic sickness cases*

15. Monitoring short spells of absence is fairly easy since you can see the employee on their return to work. With long-term absence it is less easy to assess what is happening. You can ask the OHP or company-nominated doctor to examine the employee who is away on sick leave after 14/28 days of absence.

16. If you are concerned about an employee, you should arrange for someone to visit them. You should telephone (or ask the HR department to telephone) the employee concerned to make an appointment. Never make unannounced visits unless you have been unable to contact the individual and are concerned about their welfare or whereabouts. These calls and visits are first to enquire how the employee is and about their progress. You should try to ensure that the employee is receiving satisfactory medical treatment. Please ensure that all these calls and visits are recorded in writing.

17. The OHP or nurse can offer an excellent second source of information and guidance to working with the GP or hospital. Employees cannot refuse a reasonable request to be seen by the OHP. If they do, then that can be used as part of the case against the employee when/if the decision to dismiss is taken. However, with careful counselling and spelling out the consequences of not co-operating with a medical examination, the employee may be persuaded.

18. If an employee is off work for a long spell and is very ill, that person's manager should arrange to visit that person personally so that the manager can show concern as well as assess the situation first hand.

C. *Summary for long-term or chronic ill health cases*

(a) Request an up-to-date medical report.

(b) Consult the employee personally and arrange to visit. Discuss the medical report and ask the individual whether they agree as to the likely date of return. Discuss sick pay entitlements, ending of sick pay, SSP and invalidity benefits, employment of temporary cover, employment of permanent replacement, etc.

(c) Also discuss suitable alternative employment upon return or modified job duties.

(d) Be aware of the obligations under the Equality Act 2010 concerning disability discrimination.

(e) Consider the medical prognosis.

(f) Before taking the decision to dismiss, consider alternative duties, modified job duties, fewer hours, etc. with the consequent effect on pay (with the employee's written agreement to any changes) or agree to 'red circle' earnings if this is possible. Be aware that 'red circling' should not last forever.

(g) If the decision to dismiss is to be taken, ensure that the person with that authority takes the decision. Communicate that decision to the individual personally and sensitively. Allow the individual to appeal against the decision if they so wish and notify them of this option.

(h) Be prepared to consider new medical reports if they are available.

(i) The employee is only entitled to request another medical report other than from the OHP or the GP if they are consulting a specialist and the management has not received any specialist's report, the OHP report is woolly or indeterminate, the OHP has not actually examined the patient but merely reviewed the files or where the continued employment of the individual would pose a risk of health and safety to that individual or others.

PRECEDENT 6AG: Letters relating to absence

A. Short-term intermittent absence: 'well done' letter

[Name of employee]

[Address]

[Date]

Dear [name]

I am writing to thank you for the effort you have made throughout the year to attend work following your official warning on [date].

The Company is naturally extremely concerned about the level and cost of short-term, intermittent absence from work and intends to take some positive measures to deal with the problem.

It is particularly heartening to note that since your warning, your own record shows that you lost no time at all from work this year.

On behalf of management I should like to extend my sincere appreciation to you for your excellent attendance and our hope and expectation that it will continue during this year despite the warning lapsing from your record.

Yours sincerely

B. Sympathetic oral warning: notification of concern

Employee's name ....

Location/Department ....

Date of oral warning ....

Offence ....

An oral warning was given to the above-named employee in respect of his/her unacceptable absence record as set out in our absence control procedure. Details of the absence record are attached.

I saw him/her on an informal basis on [date] when I asked for any explanation of his/her absence record. We had a long session together when we discussed at length his/her absence record and the reasons for it. I told him/her that if he/she had any personal problems or difficulties he/she could tell me in confidence or go to see our Company nurse/doctor. I also referred him/her to Dr [name] on [date] and received a report (attached) which did not indicate any medical problem.

I have now advised him/her that unless his/her attendance record makes an immediate, significant and substantial improvement during the next two shifts and is sustained for the next 12 months, he/she will be given a first written warning.

I will review [employee]'s absence record on [date] and after each shift, for a period of 12 months.

If the attendance record improves and is sustained over the next 12 months, this oral warning will lapse. I have advised him/her that he/she should come to see me if he/she has any problems with which the Company can help.

Signed .... Status ....

(A record of those present at the interview and summary notes of the main points should be attached.)

C.   First sympathetic written warning: second notification of concern

Employee's name .... Date ....

Location/Department ....

Further to the disciplinary hearing which took place on [date] I confirm that you have been given a first written warning for failing to achieve/maintain a satisfactory attendance record. Over the past... (weeks/months) your absence record has been [state number of days/spells].

I have discussed your record with you on two previous occasions and have tried to find out why your record is unacceptable. You have not been able to produce any explanation which satisfies me so regretfully I have had to issue you with a first written warning.

In accordance with the disciplinary procedure/absence control procedure, if there is the required improvement in your attendance which is maintained over the following 12 months, this warning will lapse. However, should your attendance not improve or be sustained over the next 12 months or should you commit any further disciplinary offence, then you will be given a final written warning.

I trust that you will be able to attend work on a regular basis and achieve a 100 per cent attendance record. If you have any problems which make it impossible for you to attend work, I would urge you to tell me immediately so that we try to find a satisfactory solution. I have explained to you the difficulties we face when you fail to attend for your rostered shifts and the effect that this has on the business. I trust that this warning will lead to the improvement required and that no further action will be necessary.

I have also reminded you of the facility for confidential counselling should you need this.

Signed .... Status ....

(A record of those present at the interview and summary notes of the main points should be attached to the Company's copy of this letter.)

D. Final sympathetic written warning: final notification of concern

Employee's name .... Date ....

Location/Department ....

Further to the disciplinary hearing which took place on [date] I confirm that you have been given a final written warning for failing to achieve/maintain a satisfactory attendance record. Over the past ... (weeks/months) your absence record has been [state number of days/spells]. I have discussed your record with you on three previous occasions and have tried to find out why your record is unacceptable. You have consistently been unable to provide a satisfactory explanation.

In accordance with the disciplinary procedure/absence control procedure, if there is the required improvement in your attendance which is maintained over the following 12 months, this warning will lapse. However, should your attendance fail to improve or be sustained over the next 12 months or should you commit any disciplinary offence, we will have no option but to terminate your contract.

I trust that this warning will lead to the desired improvement and that no further action will be necessary. You have a right of appeal within ... working days to [specify] should you consider this warning unfair.

I have also reminded you of the facility for confidential counselling should you need this.

Signed .... Status ....

(A record of those present at the interview and summary notes of the main points should be attached to the Company's copy of this letter.)

E. Short-term intermittent absence: dismissal letter

Employee's name .... Date ....

Location/Department ....

Further to the disciplinary hearing which took place on [date] in view of your previous unacceptable attendance despite counselling and formal warnings, I hereby give you notice to terminate your employment with the Company on [date].*

* Your employment therefore ceases forthwith as at the date of this letter. You will receive a payment in lieu of any notice together with any outstanding payments due to you.

or

* You will/will not be required to work out your notice and you will/will not* be given a payment in lieu of notice.

(* Delete whichever is appropriate.)

If you consider that this decision is unfair, you may appeal against it to [specify] within ... working days. Please briefly state your grounds for appeal.

Signed .... Status ....

(A record of those present at the disciplinary interview and summary notes of the main points should be attached to the Company's copy of this letter.)

7

Maternity, paternity, adoptive and parental leave

7.1 The law

Parents have a raft of rights, from women taking maternity leave to fathers taking paternity leave and either parent having the right to take shared paid parental leave (the Shared Parental Leave Regulations 2014).

Either parent has the right to take unpaid parental leave to look after a child up to the age of 18 years and when adopting a child – Maternity and Parental Leave etc. (Amendment) Regulations 2014.

It is common following a period of maternity leave for the woman returning to work to ask for flexible working arrangements. At the end of the Precedents, at **Precedent 7H**, you will find some flexible working arrangement letters, forms and policies.

It may be a form of indirect sex discrimination or a breach of the Flexible Working Regulations 2002 as amended, to refuse to allow a woman to work on a flexible arrangement.

The ACAS Code of Practice 5, *Handling in a Reasonable Manner Requests to Work Flexibly* (June 2014), is a helpful guide to flexible working.

Maternity rights: summary

In summary, the maternity rights are:

- statutory maternity pay (SMP), statutory adoption pay and maternity allowance of 33 weeks;
- nil service requirement to qualify for 52 weeks' maternity leave;
- notice of return from maternity or adoption leave from four to eight weeks if the woman wishes to return early to work – no notice is required if the full 52 weeks' leave is taken;
- no small employer exemption from automatic unfair dismissal;
- up to 10 days' work.

If a pregnant woman or when a woman returning from maternity leave is dismissed, they have an automatic right without needing to request it to a written statement of the reasons for dismissal (s.92(4)):

(4) An employee is entitled to a written statement under this section without

having to request it and irrespective of whether she has been continuously employed for any period if she is dismissed –

(a) at any time while she is pregnant, or
(b) after childbirth in circumstances in which her [ordinary or additional maternity leave period] ends by reason of the dismissal.

7.2 Statutory maternity pay, statutory adoption pay and maternity allowance

The period for payment of statutory adoption pay is currently 39 weeks (nine months). This was increased in April 2007 from 26 weeks (six months) by a combination of the Work and Families Act 2006, s.2 and the Statutory Paternity Pay and Statutory Adoption Pay (General) and the Statutory Paternity Pay and Statutory Adoption Pay (Weekly Rates) (Amendment) Regulations 2006, reg.4.

The period for payment of SMP and maternity allowance is also 39 weeks (increased from 26 weeks by the Statutory Maternity Pay, Social Security (Maternity Allowance) and Social Security (Overlapping Benefits) (Amendment) Regulations 2006, SI 2006/2379, reg.3).

7.3 Pay and benefits during maternity leave

Pay during maternity leave

During maternity leave (both ordinary and additional maternity leave), the employee's contract of employment continues, but she is not entitled to her wages or salary. She will instead be entitled to SMP if she meets the qualifying conditions relating to the length of time since she joined the company and the level of national insurance she has paid.

Shift pay, overtime, call-out and attendance allowances all count as 'wages or salary' and can be withheld during maternity leave. The position regarding car allowances and bonuses is more complicated.

Benefits during maternity leave

During ordinary maternity leave (OML), the employer must continue all benefits. This is the case even if the employee has no contractual right to the benefit and it has been provided as a matter of discretion. Although there may be a general right to withdraw discretionary benefits from all employees, it would be an unlawful exercise of discretion to withdraw it from an employee just because she is on maternity leave.

It is considered lawful to discontinue benefits during additional maternity leave (AML) unless:

- this is out of line with past practice; or

- the benefit relates to statutory holiday entitlement, pensions, life assurance, permanent health insurance or medical cover (where the law is not clear).

Women are now entitled to their full benefits throughout both OML and AML, except in relation to pensions.

Company cars during maternity leave

The company car may be required to be returned for the whole maternity leave period if it is provided purely for business use (for example if it is a pool car kept at work to be used by a number of employees).

However, if there is any personal use the car is treated as a benefit and the woman is entitled to keep it throughout OML and during AML.

Car allowance

Car allowances have always been problematic. If they are treated as part of wages/salary then employers do not need to pay them during any part of maternity leave, but if the allowances are 'benefits' then employers must continue to pay them during OML and AML as well. The problem is that it is often unclear whether they are part of the salary.

Car allowances usually appear separately on wage slips and are not pensionable. Employees often have the choice between a company car and a car allowance. It is considered likely that car allowances should be treated as wages or salary. This means that no car allowance would be paid during any part of maternity leave.

Pension contributions during maternity leave

The rules about pension contributions come under social security legislation, which is separate from UK maternity law and does not follow the same approach.

As far as the social security rules are concerned, the distinction between OML and AML was never relevant. Instead, the rules draw a distinction between paid and unpaid maternity leave. Paid leave is any time when the employee is receiving SMP or other pay. If the employee qualifies for SMP, this will be 39 weeks unless company policy is to pay company maternity pay extending beyond this period.

In a final-salary (defined benefit) scheme, employers must treat any period of paid maternity leave as pensionable service. If the employee makes contributions to the scheme, then she can be required to keep up those contributions throughout her paid maternity leave. However, her contributions must be calculated on the basis of the actual pay she is receiving rather than her normal pensionable pay.

If she wants to make additional voluntary contributions then this may be possible under the employer's scheme rules.

In a money-purchase (defined contribution) scheme, employers must keep up their contributions to the scheme for the period of paid maternity leave. The employer contributions must be based on the employee's normal pay (i.e. the pay she would be receiving if she was at work). However, the employee's contributions must be calculated on the basis of the actual pay she is receiving rather than her normal pay.

Reduced contributions on the employee's part may, of course, reduce the amount of pension she ultimately receives, so the employee may wish to top up her contributions to their previous level. There is an argument that the employer should step in to 'top up' her contributions.

Life insurance, health insurance and medical cover on maternity leave

Employers should treat life insurance, permanent health insurance and medical cover in the same way as pension rights, and maintain them throughout any period of paid maternity leave. This is because the definition of pension scheme in the relevant UK social security legislation is very wide and covers a scheme providing protection against sickness, disability and death as well as one providing for retirement. It is unclear if this definition would cover life insurance, permanent health insurance and medical cover schemes but there is clearly a strong possibility that it might do so.

In practice, many employers make a single lump sum payment to the insurers at the beginning of the policy year to cover all employees throughout the year. In those circumstances, it is often not possible to remove cover from an employee.

In any event, permanent health insurance, life insurance and medical insurance should be maintained throughout the entire period of maternity leave.

Holiday entitlement

Employees cannot take holiday and be on maternity leave at the same time. This means that an employee cannot take holiday during her maternity leave. So she must take holiday either before she starts maternity leave, i.e. accrued to the start date of her leave, or tack it on to her entitlement accrued during her maternity leave and take it when she comes back. It is reasonable to suggest that she could carry over accrued holiday from one holiday year to the next in the same way as holidays accruing during sick leave.

Employees have no statutory right to have time off for bank holidays, but many employers provide for paid bank holidays in contracts of employment. In such cases, the employee is clearly entitled to take and be paid for any bank holidays that fall before or after her maternity leave.

The legal position is less clear on bank holidays that occur during maternity leave. Employees sometimes argue they should be paid for bank holidays falling during maternity leave and some employers do make a payment for such holidays. However, the legal position has not yet been tested in the UK courts. There is one case about the related issue of teachers' holidays which, although not about bank holidays, suggests that an argument for pay on a 'missed' bank holiday would fail. Until this issue is resolved by the courts, it is probably safe for employers to refuse requests for pay for 'missed' bank holidays.

Even if there is a practice of paying for bank holidays which fall during maternity leave, the employee is still treated as being on maternity leave, not on holiday.

As a result, the days that have been paid for do not technically count as days of holiday.

Holiday entitlement accruing during maternity leave

Holidays will accrue during the whole of the maternity leave period.

The practical difficulty is the issue of carrying forward holiday days rather than the calculation of holiday entitlement. The problem can sometimes be avoided if, once the employer is informed that the employee is pregnant, her line manager reminds her about the company's normal holiday policy.

Payment in lieu of untaken holiday could have been offered to the woman returning to work but only if she agreed. However, payment in lieu is not permitted for any of the employee's statutory minimum holiday. If both parties agree to pay for the untaken holiday during the time of the maternity leave then there would be nothing stopping the parties agreeing to this. It probably should be done by way of a settlement agreement to prevent a claim later.

See **Precedent 7A** for a maternity leave and accrual of holiday clause.

Bonus payments during maternity leave

Employees are entitled to SMP, rather than 'wages or salary' during maternity leave, providing they meet the qualifying conditions.

A bonus which falls due during maternity leave counts as 'wages or salary' and is therefore not payable.

However, if the bonus relates to a period of time before the employee started maternity leave, then she will be entitled to that payment in full even if she is on maternity leave when the payment falls due (*Lewen* v. *Denda* [2000] IRLR 67).

If the bonus relates to a period of time which includes a period of maternity leave then the woman on maternity leave is entitled to a payment on a proportionate or pro rata basis to reflect the proportion of the time when the employee was:

- working;

- on compulsory maternity leave the period immediately following the birth;
- suspended on pregnancy or maternity grounds.

It does not matter whether the bonus is contractual or discretionary.

In *Hoyland* v. *Asda Stores Ltd* [2006] IRLR 468, the appellant claimed that a pro rata deduction from her share of an annual 'discretionary' bonus was contrary to the Sex Discrimination Act 1975 because she was on maternity leave. The Court of Session rejected her argument, holding that even a discretionary bonus was regulated by her contract and therefore excluded from the unfair treatment provisions of the Sex Discrimination Act 1975.

Here Asda operated an annual bonus scheme based on profits, which was pro-rated to reflect absences of eight consecutive weeks or more during the year. Maternity leave was treated as absence for the purpose of calculating bonus payments. On the facts the EAT held that as the bonus was payable in respect of the workforce's performance as a whole, it was remuneration which was capable of lawfully not being paid during maternity leave.

This may mean that the employer has to make an assessment of the employee's performance over a shorter period of time than would normally be the case.

Performance measures such as sales targets or achievement objectives are typically set at the beginning of the year on the assumption that the employee will be at work for the whole year. Where the payment of a bonus is dependent on the employee achieving such targets/objectives, they may need to be adjusted downwards or the employee's performance may need to be judged as if she had been at work.

Where a bonus is not directly related to personal performance, the position is more complicated. In *Gus Home Shopping Ltd* v. *Green* [2001] IRLR 75, which concerned the relocation of the company from its original base in Worcester to a new site in Manchester, the employer offered a discretionary bonus to all employees who co-operated in ensuring an orderly and effective transfer and who remained in post until the relocation date. Two employees were on maternity leave throughout this time and did not receive the bonus. According to the EAT, it was sex discrimination not to provide the bonus.

This case is clearly at odds with the principle that women are not entitled to 'wages or salary' for maternity leave and it may have been wrongly decided. However, it is still binding on Employment Tribunals and so employers offering similar loyalty bonuses should pay such bonuses to women on maternity leave.

Occasionally employers make payments which are genuinely intended as gifts, such as a Christmas bonus. These should also be paid to all women on maternity leave.

For an analysis of holiday pay during unpaid sick leave, see **Chapter 6**.

A model maternity leave and pay policy is set out as **Precedent 7B**.

During maternity leave/adoption or shared maternity leave where a person on temporary cover is employed to undertake the duties of the woman/parent on maternity/adoption/shared maternity leave, it is essential to make it clear in writing that:

(a) they will be dismissed upon the return to work of the woman/parent on maternity leave/adoption leave/shared maternity leave; and
(b) the dismissal is necessary in order to give the returning employee their job back.

Section 106(1) and (2) of the Employment Rights Act 1996 provides that the reason for the dismissal will be some other substantial reason (subject to the fairness of the dismissal satisfying s.98(4)):

(1) Where this section applies to an employee he shall be regarded for the purposes of section 98(1)(b) as having been dismissed for a substantial reason of a kind such as to justify the dismissal of an employee holding the position which the employee held.
(2) This section applies to an employee where –

(a) on engaging him the employer informs him in writing that his employment will be terminated on the resumption of work by another employee who is, or will be, absent wholly or partly because of pregnancy or childbirth, [or on adoption leave][or [shared parental leave]] and
(b) the employer dismisses him in order to make it possible to give work to the other employee.

In *Victoria & Albert Museum* v. *Durrant* [2011] IRLR 290, this did not happen. Mr Durrant claimed he had been made redundant (having worked for the museum for 10 years).

Mr Durrant had been given a series of short-term fixed-term contracts from 2006 to 2008 following a spell of sickness absence. His last short-term contract had been as a replacement for a post holder who was on maternity leave.

His contract, however, did not comply with the requirements of s.106(2)(a) of the Employment Rights Act 1996.

Under the heading 'Replacements', s.106 states that the dismissal of a replacement for a maternity returner will be for 'a substantial reason of a kind such as to justify the dismissal of an employee holding the position which the employee held' as long as upon engagement the employer informs that person in writing that their employment will be terminated on the resumption of work by another employee who is, or will be, absent wholly or partly because of pregnancy or childbirth, or on adoption leave or shared parental leave, and the dismissal is in order to make it possible to give work to the other employee.

Mr Durrant was dismissed when the woman on maternity leave returned to work and there was no other role for him.

He claimed unfair dismissal and a redundancy payment. The respondent tried to argue that this was a capability dismissal.

Whilst the case was remitted by the EAT to the Employment Tribunal to determine what the real reason for dismissal was, s.106 of the Employment Rights Act 1996 was not relevant and therefore the dismissal was not fair for some other substantial reason (SOSR).

It would have been a fair SOSR had the claimant's contract complied with s.106.

A model contract for temporary cover appears at **Precedent 7C**.

Job-sharing agreements

Job-sharing means the voluntary sharing by two employees of the duties and responsibilities of one full-time post. The salary and benefits are shared on a pro rata basis according to the hours worked by each job-sharer.

Job splitting is another arrangement where two 'partners' split the work so they are solely in charge of a division of the work/clients.

The important points to note when drafting a job-sharer's agreement are these. They are to define:

(a) who is eligible to apply for job-sharing posts;
(b) the time by which an application for job-sharing must be submitted;
(c) which posts can be considered for job-sharing;
(d) the right of management to determine the suitability of the individuals for the post;
(e) whether there is a right of appeal if rejected for the job-sharing role;
(f) whether the job-sharers will be required to sign a new contract (most common) or just a variation of their existing contract;
(g) the terms relating to the loss of a job-sharing partner;
(h) the job-sharing arrangements, e.g. whether the job will be split or shared; the hours of each partner; the pattern of working, e.g. 2.5 days per week each or mornings for one and afternoons for the other, or one week on and one week off; whether there is any requirement for overlap; whether there will be a probationary period;
(i) what will happen to job-sharers if one or both are deemed unsuitable and how the substantive posts will be covered during the probationary period;
(j) the terms of the posts including pay and pay increases, hours, overtime, holiday and public holidays, special leave, sick pay, maternity leave, hospital and other appointments, training, flexi-time, car allowances, car leasing, pensions, promotion, and disciplinary and grievance procedures;
(k) what cover one job-sharer will be required to provide where the other is absent because of holidays, sickness, etc.

A model agreement appears at **Precedent 7D**.

7.4 Career breaks

Career breaks are most common following maternity (and in some cases paternity) leave where the mother or father wishes to take additional time out or where the individual wishes to undertake additional and relevant study in order to improve career prospects. In such cases, a career break may be offered.

This is normally without pay and is regarded as unpaid leave of absence. There is usually a minimum and maximum time stipulation on such an absence. A career break is properly regarded as not breaking continuity of employment. Under s.212(3)(c) of the Employment Rights Act 1996 the break in service will be regarded as absence from work 'in circumstances such that, by arrangement or custom, he is regarded as continuing in the employment of his employer for any purpose'.

This preservation of continuity will only happen as long as the contract is not terminated or if it is and both parties regard the employment as continuous.

In *Curr v. Marks & Spencer plc* [2003] IRLR 74 Mrs Curr resigned from her post when offered a career break, which she took for four years. Notwithstanding that the child break scheme contained a number of conditions and provided for regular contact between the employer and the former employee, and despite what the former thought about her position, there was not the requisite mutual recognition that her employment was continuing for any purpose during the child break.

The Court of Appeal held that in order for s.212(3)(c) to apply to preserve continuity during a week when there is no contract of employment, the ex-employee must be 'regarded' as continuing in the employment for some purpose by each of the parties.

Any career break scheme should make it clear as to whether continuity of employment is retained or is broken.

Essential elements to be set out in a career break scheme are:

(a) the purpose of a career break scheme;
(b) the minimum and maximum length of time;
(c) the fact that it is unpaid but does not break continuity and that those months/years will count for statutory/contractual purposes or whether there will be a break for pension purposes;
(d) whether there will be any cover for death in service or sickness during the career break (normally once pension contributions cease no death-in-service cover is available);
(e) how to apply;
(f) the minimum notice which must be given prior to the start date of the career break;
(g) any repayment requirements if the individual fails to return to serve a minimum period of service after the career break;
(h) the grade and the job to which the individual will return;
(i) applications for promotion during career breaks;
(j) responsibility of individual to find out whether they can claim any benefits and to check the position as to NICs;
(k) what will happen if the individual fails to return on the due date.

A model agreement can be found at **Precedent 7E**.

7.5 Paternity leave

The basic position is that additional paternity leave is for a maximum of 26 weeks and minimum of two weeks, that it must not start until at least 20 weeks after the birth or placement for adoption and must end not later than 12 months after the birth or placement for adoption, and that it may only be taken in multiples of complete weeks.

To the extent that additional paternity leave is taken during the mother's 39-week maternity pay period, it will be paid leave, paid at the same rate and in the same way as the current rate of SMP.

The original regulations came into force on 6 April 2010. On 5 April 2015, regulation 15 of the Maternity and Parental Leave etc. Regulations (MPL Regulations) 1999, which set out the age limits for children in respect of whom parental leave may be taken, was amended by the Maternity and Parental Leave etc. (Amendment) Regulations 2014, SI 2014/3221. It provides that entitlement to parental leave can be taken up until a child's 18th birthday.

Under these regulations fathers are entitled to up to six months' additional paternity leave provided the mother has returned to work, thus giving parents the option of dividing a period of paid leave entitlement between them.

Parents will be required to 'self-certify' by providing details of their eligibility to their employer. Employers and HMRC will both be able to carry out further checks of entitlement if necessary.

A paternity leave policy is shown at **Precedent 7F**.

7.6 Shared parental leave

The more exciting (in theory at least) development was the introduction of shared parental leave, introduced on 5 April 2015. The Children and Families Act 2014 introduced a new system of 'shared parental leave' for eligible employees and agency workers.

Despite the similar terminology, the two concepts are unrelated, and 'shared parental leave' has no impact on the existing unpaid parental leave provisions. Rather, the new statutory shared parental leave scheme effectively allows parents to share the statutory maternity leave and pay that is otherwise available only to mothers (and adoptive parents to share the adoption leave and pay otherwise only available to the primary adopter). For further information, please see *Practical Law* which has an excellent discussion on this subject, under the heading 'Practice Note – Shared Parental Leave' at **uk.practicallaw.thomsonreuters.com**.

There is a Shared Parental Leave Policy at **Precedent 7G**.

7.7 Nanny's contract

Finally, for those parents who need to employ a nanny, a nanny's contract can be found at **Precedent 3L**, drafted and used by the author!

PRECEDENT 7A: Maternity leave and accrual of holiday

During your entire period of maternity leave, your holiday entitlement will continue to accrue. Even where your maternity leave ends in a new 'holiday year', your holiday entitlement will carry over from the earlier holiday year in which your maternity leave started into the following 'holiday year' in which it ended.

You will be permitted to take this holiday once you have returned to work for one month subject to the permission of your line manager as per the normal rules on notification of holiday, etc.

In no case other than if you elect not to return to work at the end of your maternity leave will you be paid in lieu of your untaken and accrued holiday unless you and the Company agree to this arrangement.

If in any doubt about these rules, please ask your Human Resources Officer.

PRECEDENT 7B: Maternity leave and pay policy

Introduction

It is the policy of the Company to ensure that as far as possible our employees are able to combine their career and family responsibilities. We recognise that parenthood brings additional responsibilities. We value the contributions of our female staff and every effort is made to encourage women to return to work from maternity leave. The purpose of this policy is to bring together a number of initiatives to assist women to combine their careers with motherhood.

There is a right for your Partner to share your maternity leave under our Shared Parental Leave Scheme; please see our Policy for further details [**Precedent 7G** in this Chapter].

Provision

Maternity Leave Period: Ordinary Maternity Leave

All female employees are entitled to a maximum of 26 weeks' Ordinary Maternity Leave (OML) and 26 weeks' Additional Maternity Leave (AML). For 39 weeks of this 52-week period, employees are also entitled to receive Statutory Maternity Pay (SMP) or Maternity Allowance (MA), if not entitled to SMP. Both are detailed in this policy.

Maternity leave should normally commence no earlier than 11 weeks before the Expected Week of Childbirth (EWC), and must extend to at least two weeks after the birth.

Rights during OML period

The employee will continue to benefit from all of the rights conferred by her Terms and Conditions of Employment except for the right to remuneration. The whole period of absence for OML counts for seniority and pension purposes.

[Prior to commencement of Maternity Leave the employee will be informed of the arrangements for covering her work and for remaining in contact whilst she is on leave. As far as possible, such arrangements will be finalised in consultation with the employee herself. If she has staff reporting to her, she will be involved in all decisions relating to the temporary reporting arrangements to cover her Maternity Leave.]

[In addition staff on Maternity Leave will usually remain on circulation lists for internal memoranda and other documents and will be included in invitations to work-related social events as though they were still at work. Where the employee has executive/ managerial/supervisory responsibilities we will try to ensure that she is given the opportunity for consultation about such decisions taken in her absence.]

[As far as reasonably possible, we will seek to defer key decisions until the employee's return from Maternity Leave or at least until a reasonable period after the birth of her child.]

Right to return to work following OML

The employee will be entitled to return to the job in which she was employed before her absence on terms and conditions not less favourable than those which would have applied if she had not been absent.

The employee does not have to give notice of her return unless she wishes to return early, in which case she must give eight (8) weeks' notice to her line manager and Personnel Manager. If the employee fails to give the requisite notice, we reserve the right to postpone her return so as to obtain a maximum of eight (8) weeks' notice.

Additional Maternity Leave

The employee is also entitled to Additional Maternity Leave (AML). AML is the right to return up to 26 weeks after the end of OML.

The employee's contract of employment continues to subsist throughout the period of AML, although the rights and duties of both parties are much reduced. The employee retains the right to notice, right to redundancy pay, access to disciplinary and grievance procedures and the employer's implied obligation of trust and confidence.

The employee remains bound by the implied obligation of good faith and any express terms about termination, disclosure of confidential information, acceptance of gifts and her participation in any business.

Right to return to work after AML

The employee is entitled to return after AML to the same job or, if it is not reasonably practicable, to a job which is both suitable for her and appropriate for her to do in the circumstances. The terms and conditions of such employment will be the same as or superior to those of her previous position.

The employee is required to give no notice of her intention to return if she returns at the end of the 26-week period of AML but must give 8 weeks' notice of an intention to return early. This notice must be given in writing. If the employee fails to give the requisite notice, we reserve the right to postpone her return so as to obtain a maximum of 8 weeks' notice.

Work and contact during Maternity Leave

The employee may keep in reasonable contact with us during her Maternity Leave without bringing her Maternity Leave to an end or losing her SMP.

The employee is entitled to work during her Maternity Leave on a 'keeping-in-touch' (KIT) day without bringing her Maternity Leave to an end or losing her SMP. The employee may take up to a total of 10 KIT days during her Maternity Leave.

The employee is not obliged to take any KIT days and the decision to do so remains at the employee's discretion. No detrimental action shall be taken against the employee if no KIT days are taken.

Work undertaken on a KIT day may include training or other events and is not limited to the normal job performed by the employee. If the employee wishes to work on a KIT day this must be agreed with us. Before working on a KIT day the amount of pay that the employee will receive for working on that day must be agreed, as must the weekly pay for a week during which the employee works on a KIT day. Payment cannot be lower than the weekly rate of SMP to which the employee is entitled.

The total Maternity Leave period will be unaffected whether the employee works on a KIT day or not.

Statutory Maternity Pay

An employee will be entitled to SMP if she fulfils the following criteria:

- she has taken her Maternity Leave;
- she has given 28 days' notice of her Maternity Leave (unless with good reason);
- she has provided medical evidence with a form (MATB1);
- she has been employed continuously for 26 weeks up to and including her qualifying week; and
- she has had average weekly earnings above the Lower Earnings Limit in the relevant period.

Eligible employees will be entitled to SMP for a period of 39 weeks at the following rate:

- for the first 6 weeks, at the rate of 90 per cent of normal weekly earnings; and
- for the remaining 33 weeks, either 90 per cent of normal weekly earnings or the current statutory maternity rate, whichever of these is lower.

Employees who are not eligible for SMP will be given a form SMP1. Employees should take this form to a Jobcentre Plus to claim MA. MA is paid for 39 weeks at the rate of 90 per cent of normal weekly earnings or a flat rate of the current statutory maternity rate per week, whichever of these is lower.

Meetings with HR

First meeting

As soon as practicable after notifying the company of her pregnancy, we will arrange for a meeting between the employee and the Operations/Area Manager. This will be an informal interview, the purpose of which will be to ensure that:

- She has been informed of and understands her rights regarding OML and AML, and particularly the need to give appropriate notice.
- She understands the potential opportunities for flexible working.
- She is aware of her entitlements to pay for OML and AML.
- She is given an opportunity to discuss any health and safety concerns.
- She will be provided with the company's 'New and Expectant Mother Workplace Risk Assessment' Form.

Further meetings

Before the employee is due to return to work, she will be invited for an informal meeting with her line manager in order to provide an opportunity for discussion of any material points concerning her return to work. These include:

- Updating her on developments at work.
- Considering whether any retraining needs have arisen either because of staleness or new technical or other developments. It is our aim to ensure that an employee's Maternity Leave does not put her at a disadvantage in relation to skills or other training needs.

- Providing her with the opportunity of indicating whether she wishes to be considered for flexible working.
- Considering whether she would like to avail herself of the opportunity for taking a career break.

The interview will also provide an opportunity to discuss and explain any necessary and unavoidable changes to the employee's work.

Following Maternity Leave

The opportunities for flexible working will depend on the needs of the business but we recognise that many women will be interested in reducing their working hours for a while after their return from Maternity Leave. We will make every effort to accommodate requests for part-time working and other forms of flexible work arrangements, provided that the employee's duties can still be effectively carried out on such a basis.

Where the demands of the post require full-time cover, for example because of its managerial content or because of a heavy workload, then it may still be possible for two suitably matched and qualified people to carry out the duties on a job-share basis. We will review all requests for flexible working in accordance with statutory guidance and requirements and consider whether arrangements can be made to accommodate them.

Employees who change to working on a part-time or job-share basis will be offered appropriately adjusted contracts of employment containing their new terms and conditions. Their continuity of employment and all related rights will be preserved.

Where a job-share arrangement which is acceptable to the job-sharers' line manager cannot immediately be identified, the employee will nevertheless be encouraged to return to work full-time and will be offered a job-share in a suitable post as soon as one becomes available.

This policy has been approved and authorised by:

[*name*]

Designated Officer

PRECEDENT 7C: Maternity/adoption/shared maternity leave cover

[*Date*]

[*Name and address*]

Dear [*name*]

RE: Short-Term Contract – Maternity leave/adoption leave/shared maternity leave Cover

I am very pleased to confirm my offer of employment on a short-term appointment to act as maternity cover whilst our current [*insert job title*] is on maternity/adoption/shared maternity leave, as [*insert job title*] in our Company. You will be employed on a short-term fixed term contract as set out below.

I set out below the terms and conditions upon which you will be employed.

We discussed at the interview the fact that you are being employed as a maternity/adoption/shared maternity leave cover and that the employee concerned may return at any time up to one year from the start of their leave. This date is flexible and therefore we will give you as much advance notice as possible of our member of staff's return date and in any event we will give you at least four weeks' written notice of termination and we would ask the same from you if you choose to leave us during this maternity/adoption/shared maternity leave period – we sincerely hope that this does not happen. The termination and non-renewal of your short, fixed term contract will be because of the need to give work to our member of staff when they return to work.

If the member of staff on leave decides not to return to work at all, then you will have the opportunity to apply for the permanent position in line with our equal opportunities policy. If they request to come back on a job-share or on the basis of working flexible hours/days, then we can consider offering you the opportunity to job-share or to work with them on a flexible working arrangement, should you be willing to consider such an arrangement.

Terms and conditions of employment

1. Start date [specify].

2. Job title and place of work [specify].

3. Main duties [brief description].

I confirm that this role is a maternity/adoption/shared maternity leave cover and may end by the giving of a minimum of four weeks' written notice by either party unless any other arrangement is agreed and save in any case of gross misconduct where we reserve the right to dismiss summarily, i.e. with notice or pay in lieu of notice. Where notice is served by either party, we reserve the right either to ask you to serve your notice at home on garden leave or to make a payment in lieu of notice (basic salary only) and bring forward the Termination Date.

4. Salary [specify].

5. Hours of work.

[Including normal office hours, whether overtime is required and whether it is paid or unpaid; whether weekend or Bank Holiday working may be required; whether punctuality and timekeeping is of the essence, i.e. any late arrival or not being ready to start work at the normal start time is regarded as unacceptable behaviour for which a warning may be given.]

6. Dress, appearance and manner to clients whether face to face or on the telephone.

[Need for smart business dress, helpfulness, courtesy at all times, answering the telephone promptly and before four/five rings, etc.]

7. Confidentiality.

During the course of your employment you may have access to, gain knowledge of or be entrusted with confidential information concerning individual members of staff, clients or potential clients or matters relating to the Company's business or the business or personal details of one or more of the Directors or any other employees. This information may include matters of a highly sensitive and/or personal nature. You should understand that you have access to this information in the course of and because of your employment as a [job title] of the Company.

Informing anyone either within or outside the Company of any matters relating to the Company's business (e.g. who has come into reception, who has made an appointment to see a Director, etc.) would be regarded as a serious breach of confidentiality and as such could lead to your summary dismissal.

By your signing below, you agree that you will not at any time, whether during or after your employment with the Company, disclose to any unauthorised person within or outside the Company, or make use of such confidential information. This duty includes keeping strictly confidential the names and other details relating to individuals making and keeping appointments, etc.

8. Holidays including Bank Holidays and religious holidays.

You will be entitled to [28 days'] annual leave including Bank, Public and Statutory Holidays, pro-rated for the length of service that you have in this and any following Holiday year. You must follow the rules for taking Holidays as set out in our Staff Manual.

9. Notice to terminate.

You are entitled to receive and to give a minimum of four weeks' written notice at any time during the currency of your employment with us. The Company reserves the right to make a payment in lieu of notice (basic salary only) or to ask you to serve out your notice on garden leave. In cases of gross misconduct we reserve the right to dismiss you without any pay in lieu of notice or notice, i.e. summarily.

Since this is a contract for maternity/adoption/shared maternity leave cover there are several possibilities for our member of staff to return to work after the baby is born or adopted:

(a) they can take 52 weeks from the start of their leave and then return to their full-time role – in such a case if notice has not been given at any earlier date, we will give you a minimum of four weeks' advance written notice or make you a payment in lieu of notice or ask you to serve out your notice on garden leave away from the office;

(b) they may request to return on a job-share or flexible working arrangement – in such case, if in the entire discretion of the Company this is workable, then we will offer you first the job-share partner role or a suitable flexible working arrangement to fit with the other working arrangement.

10. Pension [*give details*].

11. Grievance.

If you are dissatisfied with any decision taken against you, then you are requested to draw this to my attention as soon as possible so that the matter can be resolved.

12. Disciplinary rules and procedure.

The Company has disciplinary rules and standards of performance and conduct which it expects you to meet at all times. Any material or serious breach may lead to your summary dismissal. In the first year of your employment we reserve the right not to follow the formal disciplinary stages of formal warnings (in less serious cases) or in the case of gross misconduct, a disciplinary hearing and right of appeal. In any case of proposed dismissal for conduct or capability/performance/absence or health reasons, the Company reserves the right to inform you in a face-to-face meeting of its decision and to terminate your employment forthwith and to make you a payment in lieu of notice. There would be no right of appeal.

13. Sickness absence.

Notification if you are ill and cannot come to work:

- Self-certificate for first seven days;
- Fit Note from GP thereafter;
- Payment of SSP/full pay (at our entire discretion).

14. Equal opportunities.

The Company follows fair procedures and is committed to equal opportunities and respecting people no matter what race, religion, sex, sexual orientation, disability, age, etc.

[Insert any other terms and conditions such as use of Company facilities such as email and internet, telephone for personal use, etc.]

I trust that you will be happy here and I thank you for your commitment to work for us during this period of cover.

Please sign below that you have read, understand and accept the terms and conditions as set out below.

Yours sincerely

I, [name], have read and understand and accept the terms and conditions as set out above and I accept that this is a temporary position acting as a maternity/adoption/shared maternity leave cover.

Signed .... Date ....

[name of employee]

PRECEDENT 7D: Job-share contract

We recognise that some employees may, from time to time, experience difficulty in combining their responsibilities at work with those at home. This policy has been adopted in order to assist those with caring commitments to combine such responsibilities with those at work. We will only agree to job-sharing where it is reasonable and practicable to do so and where operational needs will not be adversely affected.

Definition

Job-share occurs where two people voluntarily share the responsibilities of one full-time position on an hourly, daily or weekly basis, with the salary and leave entitlement shared pro rata. Each job-sharer works under a normal contract of employment and is subject to the provisions of current employment legislation. Job-sharing is quite different from part-time work where the employee is individually responsible for the work. Job-sharers share all of the responsibilities of the post which they hold jointly.

Aims and objectives of the job-share scheme:

- to widen our recruitment pool in order to overcome potential skill shortages;
- to create employment prospects for those who might not otherwise have the opportunity to utilise their skills and experience;
- to retain valuable skills or employees;
- to accommodate those who would wish to work shorter hours because of personal commitments.

Terms and conditions

Contracts

Each partner to a job-share will have an individual contract of employment. The post-holder's job title will be that given to the established post with the endorsement 'job-share'.

Pay

This will be pro rata to the normal salary grade for the number of hours worked.

Hours of work

These will be individually stated for each partner to the job-share. Total hours will not exceed those of the post. There are a variety of ways in which the working week can be split for job-sharers. Ideally, each job-sharer should work exactly half time. The number of hours working and the arrangement is best determined by discussion between the job-sharers and the manager/supervisor or Head of Department.

Other examples of the way the working week may be split are:

- half days, i.e. mornings/afternoons;
- half weeks, i.e. Monday–Wednesday am/Wednesday pm–Friday;
- alternate weeks of two days and three days.

The exact agreed working arrangements will be detailed in the terms and conditions of the sharers. The job-share should include a facility for the sharers to meet together regularly to discuss the work for which they are jointly responsible.

Annual leave

Standard leave entitlement will apply pro rata to the number of hours worked.

Public, statutory holidays, etc.

Public, statutory holidays will only be paid to the job-sharer who would normally work on that day (those days).

If the public, statutory holiday falls on a day of the week when the job-sharer does not normally work, then the job-sharer will not be entitled to any pay or day off in lieu for any such holiday.

Sick pay

Job-sharers will have the normal provisions of the sickness payment schemes applied to them pro rata to the number of hours worked. Normal self-certification or a requirement for a doctor's Fit Note medical certificate will apply according to the number of calendar days' sickness involved after the seventh day.

Pensions

Pension arrangements may be affected if an employee changes to or from a job-share arrangement and staff should contact the Pensions Section in the Human Resources Directorate.

Maternity benefits

Employees who are job-sharers will, where appropriate, be entitled to the normal maternity benefits on a pro rata basis, in accordance with the terms of the scheme.

Training

Job-sharers will be treated as full-time employees in respect of the provision of training. Where day release applies, time off will be granted on a pro rata basis.

Promotion

Job-sharers may apply for advertised posts on equal terms with full-time employees when the vacant post is available for job-sharing. Job-sharers who wish to apply for posts on a full-time basis will have their applications considered in the usual way.

Application procedure

Any existing member of staff who wishes to apply for job-share should in the first instance discuss the matter with their immediate supervisor/manager. The application should then be put in writing to the Head of Department who will then, having consulted the appropriate HR representative, determine whether the post is suitable for job-sharing.

The Head of Department will, in consultation with the appropriate Human Resources Adviser, ensure that when it is agreed that the post is suitable for job-sharing any arrangement related to hours of work will take into account both the needs of the individual and the Department's requirements.

If the Head of Department rejects the application, full discussion will take place and full reasons for the decision will be given. The employee will have access to the normal grievance procedure.

Applications from employees whilst on maternity leave should be forwarded to the Head of Department as soon as reasonably practicable and not later than eight weeks before the expected date of return, to ensure that the Head of Department has sufficient time to consider the matter and if necessary make the appropriate arrangements.

When a job-share has been agreed, the remaining half of the post will be advertised and the normal recruitment procedure will apply.

Until such time as a job-share partner is recruited the existing employee will continue to work full-time subject to the department's needs.

Arrangements to apply when half of the job-share becomes vacant

In the event of one job-sharer leaving the shared post for any reason the remaining sharer shall be offered the post on a full-time basis.

If the remaining sharer does not wish to take the post it will be advertised in the normal way as a job-share.

If after advertising twice the post remains unfilled the remaining job-sharer will be asked to reconsider undertaking the work on a full-time basis as their circumstances may have changed in the intervening period.

If the remaining sharer does not wish to accept the full-time post all reasonable and practicable steps will be taken to redeploy the job-sharer to an alternative comparable post and the vacant job-share posts will be advertised as one full-time post.

Monitoring

The policy will be kept under review to ensure that it effectively meets both the Company's needs and those of the staff. The Company will make changes to this policy from time to time as appropriate.

PRECEDENT 7E: Career breaks

1. Principles

The purpose of a career break is to enable members of staff:

(a) to manage their personal/domestic affairs without detriment to their careers;
(b) to undertake activities beneficial to their perceived career development; and
(c) in exceptional circumstances, to undertake further study for which study leave would be inappropriate.

All applications will be considered on their merits; the managerial interests of the Department/School will be an important determining factor.

A career break involves unpaid leave of absence for a period of not less than one year and not more than three years with return to work at a grade equivalent to that at the time of the commencement of the break; since leave of absence is involved there shall be no break in continuity of employment.

A fixed-term appointment will normally be made to the post in which the career break is occurring.

2. **Applications**

Members of staff are expected to keep their Head of Department/School informed at all stages, and in particular, they should approach the Head of Department initially, to indicate that an application for a career break will be submitted to the Department of Human Resources. Eligibility will normally be confined to those who have been in the University's employment for at least two years on the date on which the career break would be implemented.

Applications giving at least six months' notice (unless circumstances make it impossible) should be made to the Department of Human Resources and should state the purpose of the career break and the period of time for which it is being sought. A member of the Department of Human Resources shall consult with the Head of Department/School and agree whether or not to grant the request.

The date on which the career break begins will be determined by the Head of Department/School having regard to the circumstances of the application and, subject to the University's other conditions, the likely time lapse in appointing a temporary replacement.

Employees on a career break should provide the Department of Human Resources with a forwarding address, and they will be responsible for keeping the information up to date.

3. **Continuity of service**

Periods of service before and after a career break will be treated as continuous for conditions of service purposes. There will be a break in superannuable service unless the member of staff maintains their contributions (in which case the University's contributions will also be paid).

Members of the Pension Scheme will be required to pay superannuation contributions for the first 30 days of the career break. Thereafter payments will cease. On return to work the member of staff has 30 days to decide if they wish to pay contributions for the period of absence (up to 36 months). If they decide to do so, the University will pay its contributions.

Once payments cease, staff will not be entitled to enhanced service for death or ill health. They are therefore advised to make their own arrangements for life cover for the period of the career break.

Where the member of staff fails to complete three months' service after a career break of one year; six months' after a break of one to two years; and nine months after two to three years, they will be required to repay the University's contributions to the superannuation scheme.

4. **Return to work**

The member of staff will normally return to the particular post that they occupied prior to the career break.

MATERNITY, PATERNITY, ADOPTIVE AND PARENTAL LEAVE 311

Employees who take career breaks of more than one year's duration must contact the Department of Human Resources at the end of each 12-month period to confirm their intention to return to their employment.

Employees who are unable to resume duty on the due date because of illness will be required to produce supporting medical documentation.

5. Promotion

Employees will be free to apply for promotion during career breaks. However, they would have to accept the promotion at the time of offer and take up duties when required.

6. Social Security arrangements

It is the responsibility of individual employees taking a career break to contact the Department of Health and Social Services through the local Social Security Office, to determine whether they are entitled to any benefits and to check the position with regard to national insurance contributions.

7. General

The University will provide details, to the address provided by the member of staff, of any matters which would be the subject of internal communication, such as promotion procedures, appointments to posts internally advertised, and such other matters affecting terms and conditions of employment. The member of staff will normally be expected to attend the University on at least four days per annum to receive information and training or to meet such other development needs as the management may deem necessary. Reasonable notice will be given. An employee who does not comply with the terms of the career break scheme will be dismissed.

APPENDIX A

Example

The undernoted calculation for holiday entitlement applies to all full-time, term-time working and assumes a schedule of 30 working weeks and 12 statutory and other holidays in the year.

The following salary/leave entitlements apply:

(a) Holiday entitlement:
 $7/365 \times 30/1 \times 37/1 = 21$
(b) Half the holiday entitlement to be taken as pay.

PRECEDENT 7F: Paternity and adoptive paternity pay and leave policy

1. Introduction

The aim of this document is to set out the Company's policy for Paternity Leave (Ordinary Paternity Leave and Additional Paternity Leave) and Statutory Paternity Pay (SPP) and Additional Statutory Paternity Pay (ASPP) in order to ensure consistency of approach in line with employment legislation and our commitment to good employment practice.

If you wish to exercise your paternity leave and pay entitlements, you must notify the Human Resources Department and your Manager in or by the 15th week before the qualifying week or the Expected Week of Childbirth (EWC). You must also complete a

SC3 Statutory Paternity Pay/Paternity Leave Form, which is available from the Human Resources Department.

2. **Eligibility**

In order to qualify for Ordinary and Additional Paternity Leave you must:

- have worked continuously for the Company for 26 weeks ending with the week immediately before the 14th week before the EWC, or in the case of adoption, the week the child is matched for adoption (the qualifying week);
- be continuously employed by the Company from the qualifying week up until the birth of the baby;
- have responsibility for the upbringing of the child and leave must be taken for the purpose of caring for the child;
- be the biological father of the child, or the mother's spouse, civil partner or partner. In the case of adoption you must be the adopter or the adopter's spouse, civil partner or partner.

Please note that employees who are eligible for Ordinary Paternity Leave will automatically qualify for Additional Paternity Leave.

The Company may ask you to provide a self-certificate as evidence that you meet the above conditions (as detailed in point 6).

3. **Ordinary Paternity Leave and Additional Paternity Leave**

Ordinary Paternity Leave

You will be entitled to choose to take either one or two consecutive weeks' paternity leave (not odd days). You can choose to start your leave:

- from the date of your child's birth (whether this is earlier or later than expected); or
- from a chosen numbers of days or weeks after the date of your child's birth (whether this is earlier or later than expected); or
- from a chosen date.

Leave can start on any day of the week (but not before the baby is born) following your child's birth, but must be completed:

- within 56 days of the actual date of birth of your child, or
- if your child is born early, within the period from the actual date of birth up to 56 days after the EWC.

In the case of adoption, you can choose to start your leave:

- from the date of the child's placement (whether this is earlier or later than expected); or
- from a chosen numbers of days or weeks after the date of the child's placement (whether this is earlier or later than expected).

Leave can start on any day of the week on or following the child's placement, but must be completed within 56 days of the child's placement.

Additional Paternity Leave

With effect from 6 April 2010, in line with the Additional Paternity Leave Regulations 2010, if employees are expecting a baby, or are matched for adoption, on or after 3 April 2011, eligible employees will be able to take up to 26 weeks' Additional Paternity Leave (APL), in addition to the current two weeks' leave (Ordinary Paternity Leave).

Employees will only be able to start Additional Paternity Leave (APL):

- 20 or more weeks after the child's birth or placement for adoption;
- once their partner has returned to work from statutory maternity leave (SML) or statutory adoption leave (SAL) and/or ended their entitlement to Statutory Maternity or Adoption Pay, or Maternity Allowance.

APL cannot be taken after, and must have ended by, the end of the 52nd week after the child's birth or placement for adoption.

4. **Statutory Paternity Pay and Additional Paternity Pay**

Statutory Paternity Pay

During paternity leave, you will benefit from Statutory Paternity Pay (SPP) from the Company. This will be paid for either one or two consecutive weeks, depending upon which option you have chosen. SPP is £[X] a week or 90 per cent of your average weekly earnings if you earn less than £[X] a week.

If your average weekly earnings are below the lower earnings limit for National Insurance purposes you will not qualify for SPP. However, you may be able to get Income Support whilst on paternity leave. Additional financial support may be available through Housing Benefit, Council Tax Benefit, Tax Credits or a Sure Start Maternity Grant. Further information should be obtained from your local Jobcentre Plus office or Social Security Office.

Additional Statutory Paternity Pay

In line with the Additional Statutory Paternity Pay (General) Regulations 2010, in order to qualify for Additional Statutory Paternity Pay (ASPP), the employee must have earnings on average at least equal to the lower earnings limit during the eight weeks ending with the 15th week before the baby is due (or the eight weeks ending with the week of matching for adoption). Additional Paternity Leave will be paid at the same rate as Statutory Maternity Pay, or 90 per cent of your average earnings, whichever is lower.

The employee will only receive ASPP during the time their partner would have been receiving Statutory Maternity or Adoption Pay, or Maternity Allowance.

5. **Notice of Intention to Take Paternity Leave and Paternity Pay**

You are required to inform your Line Manager of your intention to take paternity leave/pay by the 15th week before your baby is expected, unless this is not reasonably practicable. You will need to advise us:

- The week your baby is due.
- Whether you wish to take one or two weeks' consecutive leave.
- When you want your leave to start.
- Whether you wish to take Ordinary Paternity Leave and/or Additional Paternity Leave.

If you wish to take Additional Paternity Leave and Pay you will also need to provide the following eight weeks prior to the APL:

- Notice of when you wish the leave to start.
- A declaration stating that you are taking the leave to care for the child.
- A declaration from the mother or other adoptive parent stating certain information (e.g. that she is pregnant or adopting a child; the EWC (if she is pregnant); the date she intends to start maternity leave or adoptive leave, etc.).

You will be required to advise when you expect the ASPP period to begin and end.

In the case of adoption, you will be required to inform your Line Manager of your intention to take paternity leave within seven days of being notified by your adoption agency that you have been matched with a child, unless this is not reasonably practicable. You will need to advise us:

- The date by which you have been notified you have been matched with a child.
- When the child is expected to be placed.
- Whether you wish to take one or two weeks' consecutive leave.
- When you want your leave to start.

In both Additional Ordinary Paternity Leave and Additional Paternity Leave, and adoptive paternity leave, you will be able to change your mind about the date on which you want your leave to start, providing that you give your Line Manager at least 28 days' notice (unless this is not reasonably practicable).

Please note it is imperative that these timescales are followed as they allow HR Administration to adjust your salary accordingly.

6. Self-certificate

You will need to provide your Line Manager with a completed self-certificate (Form SC3 or SC4 – in the case of adoptive paternity leave) as evidence of your entitlement to SPP. This can be obtained from the Human Resources Department. By providing this certificate you will be able to satisfy both the notice and evidence conditions for paternity pay.

Contractual Benefits

You will continue to benefit from your normal terms and conditions of employment, except for terms relating to salary throughout paternity leave (albeit that SPP is usually paid).

7. Returning to Work after Paternity Leave

You are entitled to return to the same job following paternity leave.

If you require any further information in relation to this policy please contact the Human Resources Department.

PRECEDENT 7G: Shared Parental Leave Policy

[The University of York's Shared Parental Leave (ShPL) Policy, reproduced here with its kind permission. See **www.york.ac.uk/admin/hr/resources/policy/shared-parental-leave/#tab1**.]

To take Shared Parental Leave (ShPL), the mother must notify her employer that she is curtailing her maternity leave and pay. The parents can then share the remaining leave and pay between them. Each can apply for up to three periods of leave during the first year of the baby's life.

Each parent applies to their own employer for each period of leave. You must first declare your entitlement and intention to take leave before confirming that intention with a final notice to take leave.

To make your application you must use the forms provided and submit your final notification at least eight weeks before you intend to take leave.

You can provide notice of a curtailment of maternity leave (if applicable), intention to take ShPL and final notification of a block of leave simultaneously, if necessary.

Leave

Periods of leave can be continuous (i.e. an uninterrupted period of leave) or discontinuous (a mixture of work and leave – for example, you might take 10 weeks' leave over a 20 week period, working only every other week).

You are entitled to take continuous periods of leave as long as you meet the notification requirements but you need the agreement of the University to take discontinuous leave. Early notification and discussion is recommended wherever possible.

The compulsory period of Maternity Leave remains in place and therefore as a minimum the mother is required to take two weeks' Maternity Leave beginning on the day the baby is born. However, the remaining 50 weeks may be shared by the mother, father, partner or adopter (as appropriate).

Shared Parental Leave should not be confused with Parental Leave which is unaffected by Shared Parental Leave. Parental Leave is the entitlement to up to 18 weeks' unpaid leave.

Pay

Statutory Shared Parental Pay (SShPP) is available for eligible parents to share between them while on ShPL.

The number of weeks' SShPP available to the parents will depend on how much Statutory Maternity Pay (SMP) or Maternity Allowance (MA) the mother has received when her maternity leave or pay ends.

A total of 39 weeks' SMP or MA is available to the mother. As there is a compulsory maternity leave period of two weeks, a mother who ends her maternity leave at the earliest opportunity could share up to 37 weeks' SShPP with her partner.

SShPP is paid at the rate of £[X] a week or 90 per cent of your average weekly earnings, whichever is lower. This is the same as SMP except that during the first six weeks SMP is paid at 90 per cent of whatever the mother earns (with no maximum).

If both parents work at the University, they may be eligible for Occupational Shared Parental Pay. This offers the same enhancements as Occupational Maternity Pay, with the first 18 weeks being paid at the mother's usual rate of pay.

PRECEDENT 7H: Flexible working requests

Flexible working application form

1. Personal details	
Name:	Staff payroll number:
Manager:	
National insurance number:	

Note to the employee:
You can use this form to make an application to work flexibly under the right provided in law to help eligible employees care for their children. Before completing this form, you should first read the **Flexible Working Policy** (available from HR) and check that you are eligible to make a request. You should note that under the right it may take up to 14 weeks to consider a request before it can be implemented and possibly longer where difficulties arise. You should therefore ensure that you submit your application to the appropriate person well in advance of the date you wish the request to take effect. It will help us to consider your request if you provide as much information as you can about your desired working pattern. It is important that you complete all the questions as otherwise your application may not be valid. When completing sections 3 and 4, think about what effect your change in working pattern will have both on the work that you do and on your colleagues. Once you have completed the form, you should immediately forward it to the HR Manager (you might want to keep a copy for your own records). We will then have 28 days after the day your application is received in which to arrange a meeting with you to discuss your request. If the request is granted, this will be a permanent change to your terms and conditions unless otherwise agreed.

2a. Describe your current working pattern (days/hours/times worked):

2b. Describe the working pattern you would like to work in future (days/hours/times worked):

(you may continue on a separate sheet if necessary)

2c. I would like this working pattern to commence from:

[*date*]

I would like to apply to work a flexible working pattern that is different to my current working pattern under my right provided in law. I confirm I meet each of the eligibility criteria as follows:
- I have responsibility for the upbringing of either a child under six or a disabled child under 18.
- I am:
  – the mother, father, adopter, guardian or foster parent of the child; or
  – married to or the partner of the child's mother, father, adopter, guardian or foster parent
- I am making this request to help me care for the child.
- I am making this request no later than two weeks before the child's sixth birthday or 18th birthday where disabled.
- I have worked continuously as an employee of the company for the last 26 weeks.
- I have not made a request to work flexibly under this right during the past 12 months.

(If you do not meet all of the eligibility criteria then you do not qualify to make a request to work flexibly in law.
This does not mean that your request may not be considered, but you will have to explore this separately with your Line Manager.)

3. Impact of the new working pattern

I think this change in my working pattern will affect my employer and colleagues as follows:

4. Accommodating the new working pattern
I think the effect on my employer and colleagues can be dealt with as follows:
Name:
Date:
NOW PASS THIS APPLICATION TO YOUR LINE MANAGER.

Flexible working application acceptance form

Note to the employer
You must write to your employee within 14 days following the meeting with your decision. This form can be completed by the employer when accepting an application to work flexibly. If you cannot accommodate the requested working pattern you may still wish to explore alternatives to find a working pattern suitable to you both. Please note that the Flexible Working Application Rejection Form should be used if the employee's working pattern cannot be changed, and no other suitable alternatives can be found.

Dear:		Staff number:	
Following receipt of your application and our recent meeting on:		Date:	
I have considered your request for a new flexible working pattern.			
	I am pleased to confirm that I am able to accommodate your application.		
	I am unable to accommodate your original request. However, I am able to offer the alternative pattern which we have discussed and you agree would be suitable to you.		
Your new working pattern will be as follows:			
Your new working arrangements will begin from:		Date:	

Note to the employee
Please note that the change in your working pattern will be a permanent change to your terms and conditions of employment and you have no right to revert to your previous working pattern.

If you have any questions on the information provided on this form please contact me to discuss them as soon as possible.

Name:		Date:	

NOW RETURN THIS FORM TO YOUR EMPLOYEE

Refusal letter

[Date]

Dear

RE: Flexible working application

Following our meeting on [date] I am writing to inform you that your flexible working request unfortunately cannot be accommodated on the following ground(s):

(i) There will be a detrimental effect on our ability to meet customer demands.
(ii) We are unable to reorganise the work among existing staff.
(iii) There will be a detrimental impact on the quality of service/research that we are required to carry out.
(iv) We would be unable to recruit/have been unable to recruit additional staff to cover the additional days/hours.
(v) It would be inappropriate due to planned structural changes.

[*Set out any other options for flexible working that were discussed, e.g. three days asked for and four days offered, or all mornings only asked to work and other arrangements offered, etc.*]

You may appeal this within 14 days of receiving this letter. In addition, you have a right to be accompanied to the appeal meeting by another employee or a trade union representative. If you wish to discuss your return to work any further, email or call me.

Yours sincerely

HR or Line manager

8

Rules and standards of conduct

8.1 Introduction

In all organisations and professions the highest standards of probity and integrity are essential. In the finance sector special rules apply, such as non-dealing rules and a prohibition on gambling, taking part in betting syndicates such as National Lottery syndicates, being overdrawn, or accepting or giving gifts in the financial sector, and prohibitions on inducements or bribes to or from third parties in many public sector organisations.

8.2 The Anti-Slavery provisions

The Modern Slavery Act 2015 requires employers with a global turnover of £36 million to produce a statement setting out the steps they have taken to ensure there is no modern slavery in their own business and their supply chains.

The Home Office Guide *Transparency in Supply Chains etc. A Practical Guide* (2015) states that:

> 1.4 ... If an organisation has taken no steps to do this, their statement should say so. The measure is designed to create a level playing field between those businesses, whose turnover is over a certain threshold, which act responsibly and those that need to change their policies and practices. However, the Government wants to encourage businesses to do more, not just because they are legally obliged to, but also because they recognise it is the right thing to do.
> 1.5 One key purpose of this measure is to prevent modern slavery in organisations and their supply chains. A means to achieve this is to increase transparency by ensuring the public, consumers, employees and investors know what steps an organisation is taking to tackle modern slavery. Those organisations already taking action can quickly and simply articulate the work already underway and planned. Organisations will need to build on what they are doing year on year. Their first statements may show how they are starting to act on the issue and their planned actions to investigate or collaborate with others to effect change.

Personnel Today has written an excellent guide to writing a modern Slavery Statement (21 February 2017) – see www.personneltoday.com/hr/writing-a-modern-slavery-statement-guide-for-employers.

It sets out separate headings for a policy, to include:

1. A company's commitment to tackling modern slavery;
2. An explanation of the corporate structure worldwide;

3. Naming a Board member responsible for anti-slavery measures and the implementation and monitoring of the policy;
4. Any link to any other policies such as Diversity and Equal Opportunity policies;
5. Making clear the penalties for suppliers and how 'due diligence' is done and maintained.

A policy can be found at **Precedent 8A**.

8.3 The Bribery Act 2010

The Bribery Act came into force in June 2010 for individuals and in October 2010 in respect of companies, if employees offer or receive bribes. The company can be prosecuted for failing to prevent bribery.

An individual and a company can be prosecuted.

It is an offence to offer, promise or give a bribe in the public or private sectors, to request, agree to receive, or accept a bribe in the public or private sectors, to bribe a foreign public official in order to obtain or retain business and for a commercial organisation to fail to prevent bribery.

Even if the conduct in question takes place abroad, it will constitute an offence if the person performing it is a British national, is ordinarily resident in the UK, is a body incorporated in the UK or is a Scottish partnership.

The Bribery Act is similar in many respects to the US Foreign Corrupt Practices Act of 1977 but is generally considered broader and more robust than the US law.

Useful 'Guidance about procedures which relevant commercial organisations can put into place to prevent persons associated with them from bribing (section 9 of the Bribery Act 2010)' from the Ministry of Justice was published in 2011. It can be found at: **www.gov.uk/government/uploads/system/uploads/attachment_data/file/181762/bribery-act-2010-guidance.pdf**.

An anti-corruption and bribery policy can be found at **Precedent 8C**.

8.4 Codes of conduct

Many employers require their employees to follow standards of conduct at the highest level. Some employers have their own codes of business ethics and personal conduct. Organisations in the financial services industry (now governed by the Financial Conduct Authority (FCA) and the Prudential Regulation Authority (PRA)) and the Association of the British Pharmaceutical Industry (ABPI) have their own handbooks and rules of conduct.

Typically there will be rules about probity and standards of propriety and integrity, conduct towards clients and members of the public, conflict of interest, accepting gifts or offering or receiving bribes, reporting the misconduct of others, etc. In the financial sector there are rules about personal account dealing and outside directorships and share ownership.

In the housing sector the National Housing Federation published its Code of Conduct in October 2012 (updated May 2017), which sets out its standards and guidance to help organisations 'achieve the highest standards of conduct'.

For those advising local authorities, the Nolan Committee's Seven Principles of Public Life are essential and should be incorporated into any code of conduct:

1. *Selflessness:* holders of public office should take decisions solely in terms of the public interest. They should not do so in order to gain financial or other material benefits for themselves, their family, or their friends.
2. *Integrity:* holders of public office should not place themselves under any financial or other obligation to outside individuals or organisations that might influence them in the performance of their official duties.
3. *Objectivity:* in carrying out public business, including making public appointments, awarding contracts, or recommending individuals for rewards and benefits, holders of public office should make choices on merit.
4. *Accountability:* holders of public office are accountable for their decisions and actions to the public and must submit themselves to whatever scrutiny is appropriate to their office.
5. *Openness:* holders of public office should be as open as possible about all the decisions and actions that they take. They should give reasons for their decisions and restrict information only when the wider public interest clearly demands.
6. *Honesty:* holders of public office have a duty to declare any private interests relating to their public duties and to take steps to resolve any conflicts arising in a way that protects the public interest.
7. *Leadership:* holders of public office should promote and support these principles by leadership and example.

Employees of employers such as museums and art galleries, where members of the public are invited or pay to come in, are also often trained in dealing with difficult customers and in dealing with emergency situations. Curators and others with specialist knowledge are often required to give any fees earned from outside lecturing but done in the employer's time to the employer.

The policy set out at **Precedent 8D** is a comprehensive code of conduct with rules on:

(a) general conduct;
(b) gifts and hospitality;
(c) reporting suspicious incidents;
(d) fees from outside bodies;
(e) giving free services;
(f) giving lectures and writing articles and books, etc;
(g) consultancies;
(h) common responsibilities;
(i) duty to report suspicions of wrongdoing;

(j) confidentiality;
(k) copying documents;
(l) conflict of interests;
(m) talking to the press, etc;
(n) use of company facilities such as telephone, mail, etc;
(o) inviting personal visitors on site;
(p) children on company premises;
(q) political activities.

8.5 Rules for the staff of doctors and dentists in private practice/repute clauses

There are other staff, such as those who work in private medical or dental practices, where high standards of dress, appearance and conduct are essential. It would not be appropriate for a medical secretary to read the notes of a patient, particularly in front of the patient, and say 'Oh, how awful' or a dental nurse to peer into the mouth of a patient and say, 'Oh dear, what a mess'! See **Precedent 8E**.

8.6 Bringing the employer into disrepute ('repute clauses')

Some employers, who are either high profile or who give a very high standard of service, may wish to state expressly in the contract the importance attached to the reputation of the employer and the importance of not bringing the employer into disrepute.

This clause in a contract was held to be enforceable (see *Mr Hamilton Edwin Bland* v. *Mr David Sparkes* [1999] EWCA Civ J1207-35, *The Times*, 17 December 1999, CA):

> Notwithstanding the provision of clause 3.2.1 the Company may terminate this Agreement without notice or pay in lieu in the event of any of the following: ... 3.2.2.3. If the Executive shall be convicted of any criminal offence (which expression for the avoidance of doubt and without limitation includes any offence involving violence, dishonesty or immoral conduct but shall again for the avoidance of doubt and without limitation exclude any minor motoring offence or offence under the Companies Act 1985 with regard to filing of documents or returns) or otherwise be guilty of conduct tending to bring the Company into disrepute or himself into serious disrepute.

In Mr Bland's case, he was a well-known swimmer who had been associated with his employer for many years and had then become a consultant to them giving them advice on how to build and equip swimming pools. He had (unknown to his employer) taken secret bribes and commissions, which, his employers successfully argued, had brought both himself and his employer into disrepute. This clause was upheld even though the offences took place prior to the entering into of the agreement.

8.7 Other disciplinary rules

There is always an uneasy tension between giving a long list of examples of gross misconduct offences and merely highlighting those which are particularly important for that employer. In the former case, there is a danger that the tribunal might say that if the particular offence committed does not fall within such a long list of offences, the employer could not have considered that offence to amount to gross misconduct, otherwise it would have been listed.

Gross misconduct does not include by implication offences of serious or gross incompetence or gross dereliction of duty. Misconduct offences and particularly gross misconduct offences are normally characterised by premeditation and dishonesty. It is therefore important specifically to include very serious performance issues in any list of examples of gross misconduct.

Here are some examples of gross misconduct:

1. Any act of dishonesty, theft of the employer's property, other employees' or visitors' property or that belonging to a client or potential client, contractor or any person who may have any business dealings with the employer.
2. Any serious act which breaks the mutual trust and confidence between employee and employer or which brings or is likely to bring the employer into disrepute.
3. Any fraudulent act committed against the employer or a client (current or potential) or otherwise.
4. Accepting or offering improper bribes or gifts, whether for personal gain or not, except where this is in line with the employer's policy of accepting gifts or otherwise from outside third parties.
5. Fraudulent or reckless misrepresentation, e.g. holding oneself out to be the authorised agent for the employer except in the normal course of business and where so authorised to do, in order to obtain some pecuniary advantage or otherwise.
6. Disclosing or misusing any confidential information relating to the employer or clients (potential, current or past) to any outside third party except where so authorised to do.
7. Making any statements or otherwise for publication either in written form or for television or radio purporting to act on behalf of the employer unless so authorised to do.
8. Working for a competitor, direct or indirect, without permission whilst still employed by the employer.
9. Falsification of or unauthorised removal of the employer's records, forms or property, e.g. falsifying the application form, self-certification forms, leave forms, etc. other than in any case of genuine mistake.
10. Wilful damage to the employer's property.
11. Any actions which endanger one's own or other people's safety at work.
12. Assault or threatening physical assault, intimidatory behaviour or language, flagrant insubordination or rudeness to a member of staff or member of the public or any other third party.

13. Wilful, flagrant or persistent refusal to obey lawful or reasonable instructions.
14. Gross negligence, incompetence or gross dereliction of duty.
15. Any serious act of discrimination or harassment on the grounds of sex, marital status, pregnancy, sexual orientation, transsexualism, race, ethnic origin, colour or nationality, religion or holding no religious beliefs, disability or disfigurement or for a reason relating to a medical condition or for any other reason; this will include bullying, 'sending someone to Coventry', deliberately ganging up on someone, excluding them, etc.
16. Being under the influence of alcohol or illicit drugs whilst at work; coming to work under the influence of alcohol or illicit drugs; drinking on duty except when permitted to do so.
17. Unauthorised possession or use or misuse of the employer's property or property belonging to any other third party.
18. Aggravated general misconduct offences, i.e. a flagrant commission of a general misconduct offence which has serious consequences for the employer or other staff.
19. A criminal conviction (unconnected with employment) which renders the employee unsuitable for continued employment with the employer or unacceptable to other staff.
20. Gross indecency or grossly offensive behaviour or language.
21. Breach of any of the employer's compliance rules and regulations, e.g. breach of the personal account dealing rules, insider dealing, holding outside directorships without informing the employer, gambling or taking part in any betting syndicates including the National Lottery (without permission) during the course of employment.
22. Breach of the expenses and/or hospitality rules.
23. Breach of the external business interests rules.
24. Falsifying medical or scientific data.
25. Breach of the rules concerning inventions, patents or intellectual property rights properly belonging to the employer.
26. Falsifying qualifications or previous employment history or medical details or giving inaccurate or misleading information at recruitment or during employment.
27. Making false claims such as claims of personal injury or false sick pay claims.
28. Failing to report health and safety issues, incidents or near misses, defects in vehicles or machinery, etc.

8.8 Christmas/office parties, business lunches and dinners

In 1990, the author wrote an article for the now defunct journal *Occupational Health* about the legal hazards of Christmas parties, and so began an annual round of articles by many other authors ever since. For a few years Christmas and office parties went out of fashion but it appears they are now back on the agenda.

Mr Wie-Men Ho of Eversheds wrote an excellent article, 'Managing office Christmas parties' (4 December 2014), available on Eversheds' website: www.eversheds.com/global/en/what/articles/index.page?ArticleID=en/Food/Managing_office_christmas_parties.

Another excellent article can be found in *Personnel Today*: 'Christmas in the workplace: 10 common employer queries' (Ashok Kanani, 13 December 2016). See **www.personneltoday.com/hr/christmas-in-the-workplace-10-common-employer-queries**.

This article is reproduced at **Precedent 8T**.

It is wise to ask a senior member of staff (possibly in the HR department) to remain sober or at least keep alcohol intake to a minimum in order to supervise the party and be ready to take emergency action if necessary. It is also wise to remind staff that joke presents, such as a chocolate penis given to a woman at Christmas, could be an act of sexual harassment and could lead to a successful claim against the perpetrator and the employer!

Section 40 of the Equality Act 2010 making an employer vicariously liable for the discriminatory acts of a third party was repealed by the Enterprise and Regulatory Reform Act 2013, on 1 October 2013.

The individual third party will have to be pursued in law either under the common law or under another statutory provision. The employer of the person subjected to the harassment will not be liable for third party harassment.

This takes us back to the bad old days before *Burton and Rhule* v. *De Vere Hotels Ltd* [1996] IRLR 596, commonly known as the 'Bernard Manning' case.

The Sex Discrimination Act 1975 did not define or include the concept of harassment. This had been left to the case law to define. De Vere Hotels was found liable for the harassment of two of its staff who became the subject of the comedian's racist and sexist jokes during his performance, despite the fact that he was not an employee of the hotel group. De Vere Hotels was held liable for failing to take steps to prevent the discrimination complained of from taking place.

Since 1 October 2013 employers are no longer vicariously liable under the Equality Act 2010 for sexual harassment committed by third parties.

Another question is whether an employer is vicariously liable for the harassment or assaults by its *employees* at or after a Christmas party or company function.

The answer is 'Yes' if this occurs during the party but 'No' if it occurs after the party has finished and some employees stay up after drinking or socialising.

In *Bellman* v. *Northampton Recruitment* [2016] EWHC 3104 (QB) a claim was brought in the High Court against the defendant company by an employee who was left brain damaged after an altercation with a director of the company following a Christmas party. The claimant sought damages for personal injuries on the basis that the employer was vicariously liable for the actions of the assailant. The High Court dismissed the claim.

The party had been held at a golf club but afterwards a number of employees and a director had gone back to the Hilton Hotel, had carried on drinking and, during the course of the early hours, the director and claimant had 'words'; the director hit the claimant, who fell to the ground and suffered permanent brain damage as a result.

The High Court held that:

70. Firstly, the assault was committed after and not during an organised work social event. I accept that there was an expectation or obligation that employees would attend the Christmas party, unless there was a good excuse. Whilst not a contractual obligation, and refusal or failure to attend would not be a disciplinary matter, I think that in such a small enterprise it would have attracted adverse comment. In this regard I regard it as far more closely connected or incidental to their employment than ancillary activities such as playing for an employee based sports team.
71. However, the organised event at the Golf Club had ended and as a result the expectation or obligation on any employee to participate had ended. In effect a line could be drawn under the evening's event and not surprisingly some employees went home. There was not only a temporal but a substantive difference between the Christmas party at the Golf Club and the drinks at the Hilton Hotel. What followed on after the party was what Mr O'Sullivan Q.C. accurately described as an 'impromptu drink'.
72. In my judgment the spontaneous post event drink at the hotel, *a fortiori* the gathering that consisted of the remaining members of the group (which included partners) who were, remarkably, still drinking at 3.00 am (four people staying at the hotel having gone to bed) cannot be seen as a seamless extension of the Christmas party as Mr Sanderson suggests. In substance what remained were hotel guests, some being employees of the Defendant some not, having a very late drink with some visitors.
73. Secondly, there must be a limit to the effect of a discussion being about work-related issues. Upon return to the hotel for a significant period of time the conversation was about social topics and not about work. Only after that and as the group narrowed did the conversation turn to work matters. [...]
80. Standing back and considering matters broadly, what was taking place at 3.00 am at the hotel was a drunken discussion that arose after a personal choice to have yet further alcohol long after a works event had ended. Given the time and place, when the conversation was, as it was for a significant time, on social or sporting topics, no objective observer would have seen any connection at all with the jobs of those employees of the Defendant present. That it then veered into a discussion about work cannot provide a sufficient connection to support a finding of vicarious liability against the company that employed them. It was, or without any doubt became, an entirely independent, voluntary, and discreet early hours drinking session of a very different nature to the Christmas party and unconnected with the Defendant's business. To use a hackneyed expression akin to 'a frolic' of their own.
81. In my judgment there was insufficient connection between the position in which Mr Major was employed and the assault to make it right for the Defendant to be held liable under the principle of social justice.

Precedent 8F contains rules about drinking at Christmas/office parties, company functions or business lunches or dinners.

8.9 Lecturing, writing and appearing on TV, etc.

Some staff are invited to give lectures to outside bodies, write articles in outside journals and appear on TV and radio because of their special skills or expertise. It is important to have rules governing taking time off, intellectual copyright, obtaining permission, whether the members of staff must style themselves as representing the employer or must not do so, what the fee arrangement is, and the expressing of personal opinions (see clause 7 of **Precedent 8D** for one example).

8.10 Alcohol and drugs

Some organisations have rules concerning:

(a) bringing alcohol, or any glass bottles, or any food and drink on to company premises;
(b) coming to work under the influence of alcohol or drugs (prescribed, OTC and illicit substances);
(c) drinking alcohol on duty or during meal breaks;
(d) drunkenness at work whether causing physical violence to others or damaging property.

Since the possession, use and dealing of illicit substances are criminal offences, employers tend to treat these matters as gross misconduct with the normal penalty of summary dismissal.

Gross drunkenness or breaching health and safety rules which either damages or could damage the integrity of the product (e.g. food or sterile products) are also normally treated as gross misconduct. If there is any dispute about whether someone has been drinking, then some organisations offer to breathalyse the individual and in other cases offer to take urine samples to test for illicit substances.

Employers which adopt alcohol and/or drug testing policies must have a clearly defined policy which is communicated regularly to all employees and if dismissal is the sanction for testing positive, say, for illicit drugs, then the employer must be able to justify why in the circumstances dismissal is a reasonable response to a positive drug test.

In a case concerning drug testing, *Racal Services (Communications) Ltd* v. *Flockhart*, Appeal No. EAT/701/00, the company had a very strict drug testing policy which stated that anyone testing positive for drugs would be summarily dismissed. The respondent in this appeal had been dismissed following a blood test that revealed she had been using cannabis. She took that test because she wished to resume (after a period of absence followed by clerical work) her previous job, which was safety critical because it involved working by railway tracks.

She argued that: (i) the blanket imposition of the employer's drugs policy had been too draconian in the circumstances; (ii) her boyfriend had probably spiked her food; and (iii) her employer should have allowed her to move from the job instead of dismissing her outright. The Employment Tribunal held that the employer's policy was draconian and unfair. Although the tribunal found that the case was finely balanced, it was held that the dismissal itself was unfair although there was 30 per cent contributory fault on the employee's part.

The EAT held that the Employment Tribunal's approach to the appellant's drugs policy was contrary to the guidance given subsequently by the Court of

Appeal in *Post Office* v. *Foley* [2000] IRLR 827. The Employment Tribunal had not asked the question whether the decision made by this employer was one that any reasonable employer might make. However, the tribunal had answered the correct question when it found that the dismissal might have been fair but that in the circumstances the dismissal was unfair.

In another case that same year, *South West Trains Ltd* v. *Ireland*, EAT/873/01 (unreported), the EAT held that the dismissal of the applicant, a train guard in a safety-critical job, who had tested positive for cannabis and benzodiazepines, was fair as this fell within the band of reasonable responses.

Precedent 8G is a model alcohol and drug testing policy.

8.11 Gambling or taking part in betting syndicates at work

Whilst it might seem unnecessary to implement rules about gambling at work, there have been cases where disputes and fights have occurred between staff where members of staff have organised 'unofficial' gambling dens and someone reneges on the bet or refuses to pay out the winnings. Further, with the introduction of online gambling sites, it may be appropriate to warn staff that it is not permissible to access such sites at work: see **Precedent 8I**. Such rules could include a prohibition on engaging in any betting syndicates including participating in any National Lottery syndicates and the like.

8.12 Children on company premises

Some organisations where there are warehouses or areas where dangerous machinery is operated, or where guns and armaments are kept, have drafted rules about children visiting their premises. This is based on health and safety grounds. However, it is unfair and inappropriate to provide that children can be left in reception as receptionists have their own contractual duties and are not nannies or child carers. There are, of course, issues of insurance if an unauthorised visitor or child is injured. **Precedent 8J** is a model set of rules.

8.13 Money collections

In order that money collected for good causes is not left unattended or in unlocked drawers or lockers and then stolen, it may be appropriate to have strict rules about the collection of money. In any event, collections for charities should be made only by authorised collectors. **Precedent 8K** is a model clause.

8.14 Insider dealing, compliance rules and taking secret profits, etc.

In the financial sector, regulated by the Financial Conduct Authority (FCA) and Prudential Regulation Authority (PRA), investment banks have detailed rules about personal account dealing, declaration of outside directorships and insider dealing. There is also an implied duty of fidelity, and this includes the duty of employees not to take secret profits or commissions, the remedy for which could be an action for an account of profits.

In *Attorney-General* v. *Blake* [2001] IRLR 36, the House of Lords held that an employer may be entitled to an account of profits in exceptional cases (p.37):

> When, exceptionally, a just response to a breach of contract so requires, the court should be able to grant the discretionary remedy of requiring a defendant to account to the plaintiff for the benefits he has received from his breach of contract. In the same way as a plaintiff's interest in performance of a contract may render it just and equitable for the court to make an order for specific performance or grant an injunction, so the plaintiff's interest in performance may make it just and equitable that the defendant should retain no benefit from his breach of contract...
>
> No fixed rules can be prescribed. The court will have regard to all the circumstances, including the subject matter of the contract, the purpose of the contractual provision which has been breached, the circumstances in which the breach occurred, the consequences of the breach and the circumstances in which relief is being sought. A useful general guide, although not exhaustive, is whether the plaintiff had a legitimate interest in preventing the defendant's profit-making activity and, hence, in depriving him of his profit.

In *PMC Holdings Ltd* v. *Smith* [2002] All ER (D) 186 judgment was given in favour of the employer who had sued for an account of profits or damages for breach of a fiduciary duty in respect of senior employees who had interests in another company, with which they had negotiated and placed orders and approved sales and purchases, resulting in significant consultancy fees being paid to them. Mr Smith had not declared his interest in this company and was also under a fiduciary duty as a senior employee.

Conflict of interest

Some employers, particularly those with charitable status, often outlaw working in competition with the employer. The author is aware of a case in one such organisation where it was discovered that a senior employee was doing just this, for significantly large fees, while allegedly off sick. In the contract of employment it was an express term that the employee 'had to devote the whole of his working time to the service of the employer' and it was 'not permitted to engage in any activity at any time where there might be a conflict of interest with the employer. In any such case [the employee] is required to discuss the matter in advance with his line manager and HR Director. Failure to disclose any such interest would be regarded as gross misconduct for which summary dismissal might be an outcome'.

Under the Code of Conduct section in the Staff Handbook of the same charitable organisation, in a section headed 'Conflict of interest', examples of conflicts of interest were given:

- involvement for profit or not and whether personal or via a close relative or associate or friend with any property company, building company, finance

company, estate agency or other company whose work is connected with any activity of the organisation;
• involvement with the activities of another charitable body with the same or similar activities as the organisation whether paid or unpaid.

Precedent 8L is a model policy concerning compliance rules.

8.15 Personal searches

It is common in factory and warehouse environments to search staff when they are entering and leaving the premises – both body searches and searches of their property such as bags and cars. In addition employers sometimes wish to search lockers in order to detect theft or drug taking. This must be done in a reasonable manner, for cause and in a sensitive manner, e.g. in a private setting where others cannot see the search in progress, with the search carried out by a member of the same sex and a witness present for the individual.

It would be unlawful and potentially constructive dismissal, as well as a breach of Article 8 of the European Convention on Human Rights (the right to respect for privacy, etc.) as regards public sector bodies, to undertake any form of searches without an express right to do so and without conducting such a search in a reasonable manner. There is no implied right for an employer to undertake a personal search or search of an employee's bags or car. This could only be done with the employee's consent.

Precedent 8M is a model right to search clause. Such clauses usually additionally include the following:

> If you refuse to permit the search to take place your refusal will normally be treated as gross misconduct and action will be taken against you within the Company's disciplinary procedure.

8.16 Dress and appearance

Rules on dress and appearance have become a political issue and one where the anti-discrimination case law has begun to develop. Issues of dress and appearance have been raised in the context of sex discrimination, discrimination on grounds of sexual orientation and homosexuality, and racial discrimination. There have also been issues over staff wearing sensational badges and sporting facial and body piercing and tattoos.

The author once represented an Irish canteen worker who was recruited without a clear description of the uniform that she would be required to wear. On her first day, she discovered that she was required to wear a green uniform. She was superstitious and refused to wear the uniform on the grounds that green was an unlucky colour.

Recent cases have concerned the wearing of crosses and the hijab and burqa. The CJEU heard four conjoined appeals (*Eweida* v. *United Kingdom* [2013] ECHR 37) involving Christians; two cases involved claimants seeking the right to wear a cross at work and not to be discriminated against because of their religious beliefs. The claims were for indirect discrimination.

The European Court held that wearing a cross was 'a legitimate manifestation of the Christian faith' and that wearing a cross is protected by the European Convention on Human Rights (the right to freedom of religion).

In both cases, the court found in favour of the claimants that the employers had interfered with the employees' rights to display their Christian faith.

The court then had to decide whether the prohibition on wearing any manifestation of religion could be justified. Ms Eweida, who worked in a non-customer-facing job, won her case. Ms Chaplin lost.

The CJEU held that the right to manifest one's religion was always subject to exceptions, such as the banning of long hair or facial hair on health and safety grounds (contrary to the Sikh religion).

British Airways would not allow Ms Eweida to wear her cross as it was in breach of its uniform policy. The airline stated that it wished to uphold a corporate image and this included a ban on wearing any jewellery other than watches and wedding bands (not just crosses).

The European Court did not find that a compelling justification.

In contrast, Ms Chaplin was not allowed to wear her cross for reasons of health and safety. She worked at the Royal Devon and Exeter NHS Trust where all jewellery was banned for anyone in contact with patients or working on the wards (male doctors are not permitted to wear ties as they may be a source of infection). This was for health and safety reasons and therefore could be justified.

The European Court held that in Ms Chaplin's case the banning of all jewellery and the other dress rules were a proportionate means of protecting health and safety and therefore there was no unlawful discrimination.

Headscarves, burqas and niqabs

Other cases have involved the right of women to wear a headscarf, burqa or the niqab.

In the case of *Achbita* v. *G4S* (C-157/15), Advocate General Kokott gave her opinion that dismissal of an employee for wearing a headscarf in contravention of company policy was not directly discriminatory and, if indirectly discriminatory, could be justified by the employer's policy of 'neutrality'.

The previous week, Advocate General Sharpston had given a completely opposite opinion in the case of *Bougnaoui* v. *Micropole Univers* (C-188/15). She held that the dismissal of an employee for wearing a headscarf at work was directly discriminatory and could not be defended on the basis of company policy or the employee's customer-facing role.

The CJEU will make final decisions on both these cases later this year.

Until these decisions have been promulgated employers must scrutinise their dress and appearance rules, particularly if they insist on a very strict uniform policy banning other forms of dress, e.g. headscarves, jewellery or facial or long hair, as these rules adversely affect certain religious groups.

Long hair and appearance rules

There have also been cases as to whether it is a discriminatory rule to forbid male staff to wear long hair, or long hair in a pony-tail. A man who was dismissed because he refused to cut off his pony-tail was held not to have been discriminated against on grounds of sex, even though the employers would not have dismissed a woman with exactly the same hair length. In making this decision in *Smith* v. *Safeway plc* [1996] IRLR 456, the Court of Appeal laid down the principle that a dress and appearance code which applies a standard of what is 'conventional' applies an 'even-handed' approach between men and women, and not one which is discriminatory, even if its content is different for men and women.

At the other extreme, some employers might want their female staff to look 'sexy'. In some casinos, female croupiers are required to wear bright red lipstick and have brightly painted red nails. The male croupiers have other dress and appearance requirements. There could be issues of sex discrimination if by asking their female staff to be seductive and alluring to male customers, this might indicate to customers that female staff were giving them 'the come on', making them vulnerable to sexual harassment from those male customers. However, in an old Employment Tribunal case *Murphy* v. *Stakis Leisure Ltd*, ET Case Nos S/0534/89 & S/0590/89, rules requiring female employees at a casino to wear nail varnish were held not to amount to a detriment but, even if they did, the tribunal would have regarded them as *de minimis*. In other words, the tribunal held that even if it had found the difference in treatment to be discriminatory, it would have found the requirement to wear nail varnish too minor to constitute a detriment. It is doubtful whether the same decision would be reached today.

There has recently been debate in Parliament about legislating for tighter rules to outlaw discriminatory dress and appearance rules in the workplace.

Transgender discrimination

Other considerations for dress and appearance rules will now include transsexuals who wish to dress as the opposite sex whilst going through the gender transfer procedure and homosexual people who wish to make public declarations of their sexuality without discrimination (see the decision in *P* v. *S and Cornwall County Council* [1996] IRLR 347 and the former Employment Equality (Sexual Orientation) Regulations 2003, SI 2003/1661, the provisions of which are now included in the Equality Act 2010).

It is unlawful to require transvestites not to cross-dress at work (because of the possible damage to the image or reputation of the employer or discomfort of other staff).

However, there is nothing in general to stop anyone dressing in clothes traditionally worn by members of the opposite sex, e.g. women can dress in trousers, men in kilts, etc.

In 1996, the EAT rejected an appeal from a male employee claiming he had been unlawfully discriminated against because of his sex after he had been threatened with disciplinary proceedings for wearing at work what was conventionally regarded as female wear (*Kara v. London Borough of Hackney*, EAT 325/95). Here the EAT held that the claimant, a male transvestite, was not discriminated against when his employer prohibited him from wearing women's clothing to work.

Both male and female employees were required to attend for work 'appropriately dressed'. There was no less favourable treatment as women were not allowed to attend work dressed as men.

Had Mr Kara been a transsexual or undergoing gender reassignment and the case had come to be considered now, then the tribunal would need also to consider whether he was subjected to less favourable treatment under the transgender provisions of the Equality Act 2010.

Problems can arise if, for instance, a male-to-female transsexual wishes to adopt a company's female uniform, or in relation to changing facilities in working environments where uniforms are not worn home. Transvestism is, however, outside the scope of the Equality Act 2010. Therefore a biological male who is not transsexual but is a transvestite – as was Mr Kara – and wishes to wear a skirt to work is likely to be subject to the same rules as in *Schmidt v. Austicks Bookshops Ltd* [1977] IRLR 360, i.e. the employer is entitled to set the standards of dress and appearance as long as they are not patently discriminatory, i.e. affect only one sex or are abundantly unreasonable.

Employers will need to review their dress and appearance codes to reflect modern image and dress conventions across the sexes applicable in 2017. If a dress code has not been reviewed for many years, it is now the time to do so, in order that on the whole it does not treat one sex less favourably than the other in light of modern dress conventions for the sexes. Line management also needs to be very clear what the rules are in order to bring an even-handed approach to the enforcement of these rules.

Here are some examples of dress and appearance rules for different religious groups:

(a) Khalsa Sikhs are required to wear five religious symbols, one of which is uncut hair which means a beard for men and hair covered by a turban.
(b) A code of modesty laid down in the Qur'an requires a Muslim woman to cover her whole body excluding the face, resulting in the wearing of trousers, a hijab, which is a scarf covering the top of the head and, if the woman prefers, a veil (a burqa), which covers the whole face except the eyes.
(c) The tilaka or bindi is a vermilion mark applied on the forehead as a visible sign of a person belonging to the Hindu religion.
(d) Rastafarians wear their hair in the form of long 'dreadlocks' which represent the Lion of Judah;
(e) Religious Jewish men wear a 'kippah'.

To avoid indirect discrimination, employers need to assess how dress codes could be adapted to allow employees to wear the required items/adornments. There may be times when religious dress may conflict with health and safety requirements and therefore objective justification may have to be established as there is no other option.

To avoid any allegations of unlawful discrimination, employers need to apply an even-handed and sensitive approach to the issue of any dress code which they seek to implement and to be flexible by trying to accommodate individual needs to dress in a specific way, e.g. for religious purposes, unless there is objective justification for insisting on a certain requirement.

Dress and appearance policies can be found at **Precedent 8N**.

8.17 Moonlighting

If any competing or commercially damaging 'external business interests' take place without the express written consent of the primary employer then it is colloquially called 'moonlighting'. Such activity is a breach of either an express prohibition or of the implied duty of fidelity and loyalty and can be grounds for summary dismissal. A policy forbidding moonlighting can be found in Chapter 6 at **Precedent 6AC**.

8.18 Consensual relationships at work

Restricting or banning relationships at work may be difficult but may be essential, e.g. staff working in Human Resources have access to highly confidential information which could be compromised if they had an intimate relationship with a colleague.

In some cases reporting lines are changed if a consensual relationship exists, and a duty to report such a relationship is imposed. Clearly any policy must not sexually discriminate against one member of the pair, e.g. that it is always the female employee who is moved.

In addition, it is considered unprofessional and in some cases illegal for those in positions of trust to have a relationship, e.g. teacher and pupil, lecturer and student, social worker and client, doctor and patient. Whilst keeping in mind the right to respect for privacy and family life, etc. in Article 8 of the European Convention on Human Rights, there has to be some protection not only for the pupil, student, client and patient but also for the teacher, etc. who may be accused of sexual harassment where the relationship comes to an end non-consensually. A policy for prohibiting relationships between students and academic staff can be found at **Precedent 8P**.

For teachers, supervisors, partners in law firms with trainees and barristers with pupils, sports coaches, etc. it is unwise to embark on any kind of romantic or sexual relationship when there is the teacher-pupil relationship even where the pupil is over the age of consent, i.e. 16 years of age or over.

It can lead to complaints or claims of favouritism, sexual harassment or worse. For the medical profession, it is against the GMC Code of Conduct for a doctor to engage in any relationship with a patient (called Gross Professional Misconduct) or to treat a close member of the family or a person with whom they are having a relationship.

In the GMC's *Good Medical Practice* (2013), para.53 states:

> You must not use your professional position to pursue a sexual or improper emotional relationship with a patient or someone close to them.

The GMC guidance warns that:

> Serious or persistent failure to follow this guidance will put your registration at risk.

So, there are mandatory rules which if broken can lead to serious penalties including suspension or erasure from the Register, such as para.53.

In contrast, there are guidance rules such as:

> Wherever possible, you should avoid providing medical care to anyone with whom you have a close personal relationship.

The GMC's guidance, *Maintaining a Professional Boundary Between You and Your Patient* (2013), states:

Doctor-patient partnership

3. Trust is the foundation of the doctor-patient partnership. Patients should be able to trust that their doctor will behave professionally towards them during consultations and not see them as a potential sexual partner.

Current patients

4. You must not pursue a sexual or improper emotional relationship with a current patient.
5. If a patient pursues a sexual or improper emotional relationship with you, you should treat them politely and considerately and try to re-establish a professional boundary. If trust has broken down and you find it necessary to end the professional relationship, you must follow the guidance in *Ending Your Professional Relationship With a Patient*.
6. You must not use your professional relationship with a patient to pursue a relationship with someone close to them. For example, you must not use home visits to pursue a relationship with a member of a patient's family.
7. You must not end a professional relationship with a patient solely to pursue a personal relationship with them.

Former patients

8. Personal relationships with former patients may also be inappropriate depending on factors such as:
    a. the length of time since the professional relationship ended (see paragraphs 9–10)
    b. the nature of the previous professional relationship
    c. whether the patient was particularly vulnerable at the time of the professional relationship, and whether they are still vulnerable (see paragraphs 11–13)
    d. whether you will be caring for other members of the patient's family.

You must consider these issues carefully before pursuing a personal relationship with a former patient.

Timing

9. It is not possible to specify a length of time after which it would be acceptable to begin a relationship with a former patient. However, the more recently a professional relationship with a patient ended, the less likely it is that beginning a personal relationship with that patient would be appropriate.
10. The duration of the professional relationship may also be relevant. For example, a relationship with a former patient you treated over a number of years is more likely to be inappropriate than a relationship with a patient with whom you had a single consultation.

Vulnerability of the patient

11. Some patients may be more vulnerable than others and the more vulnerable someone is, the more likely it is that having a relationship with them would be an abuse of power and your position as a doctor.
12. Pursuing a relationship with a former patient is more likely to be (or be seen to be) an abuse of your position if you are a psychiatrist or a paediatrician.
13. Whatever your specialty, you must not pursue a personal relationship with a former patient who is still vulnerable. If the former patient was vulnerable at the time that you treated them, but is no longer vulnerable, you should be satisfied that:

    - the patient's decisions and actions are not influenced by the previous relationship between you
    - you are not (and could not be seen to be) abusing your professional position.

Social media

14. You must consider the potential risks involved in using social media and the impact that inappropriate use could have on your patients' trust in you and society's trust in the medical profession. Social media can blur the boundaries between a doctor's personal and professional lives and may change the nature of the relationship between a doctor and a patient. You must follow our guidance on the use of social media.

Help and advice

15. If you are not sure whether you are (or could be seen to be) abusing your professional position, you should seek advice about your situation from an impartial colleague, your defence body or your medical association.

8.19 Harassment

Rules against harassment at work are now common. Complaints procedures for harassment are dealt with in **Chapter 9**. Here we set out some disciplinary rules and some examples of what is meant by harassment.

The European Commission definition is found in Commission Recommendation 92/131/EEC of 27 November 1991 on the protection of the dignity of women and men at work:

> conduct of a sexual nature, or other conduct based on sex affecting the dignity of women and men at work, including conduct of superiors and colleagues, is unacceptable if:

(a) such conduct is unwanted, unreasonable and offensive to the recipient;
(b) a person's rejection of, or submission to, such conduct on the part of employers or workers (including superiors or colleagues) is used explicitly or implicitly as a basis for a decision which affects that person's access to vocational training, access to employment, continued employment, promotion, salary or any other employment decisions; and/or
(c) such conduct creates an intimidating, hostile or humiliating work environment for the recipient

and that such conduct may, in certain circumstances, be contrary to the principle of equal treatment within the meaning of Articles 3, 4 and 5 of Directive 76/207/EEC.

The broad definition of direct disability discrimination in s.13 of the Equality Act 2010 includes discrimination by association, i.e. that the person discriminated against is caring for a disabled person, is outlawed (see *Coleman* v. *Attridge Law* [2008] IRLR 722).

The following definition should be added to employers' equal opportunities or anti-harassment policies:

> Sexual and racial harassment and harassment on the grounds of disability are all forms of unlawful sex, racial and disability discrimination and as a consequence unlawful behaviour. It is also improper and inappropriate behaviour which lowers morale and interferes with the effectiveness of people at work.

A harassment policy can be found at **Precedent 8Q**.

8.20 Duty to report the misconduct of others

There is no implied duty, save for directors under their fiduciary duties, to report wrongdoing. Directors have a fiduciary duty to do so even where by doing so they implicate themselves (*Sybron Corporation* v. *Rochem Ltd* [1983] IRLR 253 and *Item Software (UK) Ltd* v. *Fassih* [2004] IRLR 928). The EAT emphasised in *Ladbroke Racing Ltd* v. *King*, EAT/202/88 that the employer must make 'crystal clear' any rules requiring employees to report the misconduct of others, i.e. there must be clear written rules in the contract, setting out the sanction if an employee fails to do so.

In the financial services sector and other closely regulated industries such as the pharmaceutical industry, employers commonly require employees to report suspected misconduct and co-operate in any internal or external investigation and legal proceedings.

The Bar Standards Board (BSB) published its latest rules on this subject on 6 January 2014: 'Reporting Serious Misconduct of Others'.

The Law Society's rules (Rule 2.8) state that:

> a lawyer who has reasonable grounds to suspect that another lawyer has been guilty of misconduct must make a confidential report to the Law Society at the earliest opportunity.

That rule is subject to the law of privilege, but not the lawyer's obligation of confidence.

All misconduct must be reported. Some breaches that are patently misconduct are fraud, forgery or any dishonest conduct.

A typical reporting misconduct clause is shown at **Precedent 8R**.

8.21 Requirement to work at weekends

There are occasions where even though there is an express clause in the contract setting out a requirement to work at weekends or overtime or on bank or public holidays, the staff either collectively or individually refuse to do so.

Precedent 8S shows how the author dealt with one such case.

8.22 Stealing company intellectual property

There are occasions when employers discover employees have stolen intellectual property only after those employees have left. Even company stationery, i.e. headed notepaper, can be regarded as a serious matter especially if it is to be used for unlawful purposes, e.g. to give another employee or ex-employee a reference for a job.

That other ex-employee if they used such a reference to obtain a new job would be regarded as having committed theft under s.16 of the Theft Act 1968, 'obtaining a pecuniary advantage by deception'.

Of course, stealing client lists, etc. is a serious breach of express and implied terms of the contract that persist after the employment has ended.

This is the kind of letter that could be sent if such activity has occurred.

Letter regarding stolen property (including intellectual property)

[Name]
[Address]
[Date]

Dear [name]

RE: Your possession of Company information and intellectual property
I am writing to you concerning a very serious matter which the Company, your former employer, regards very seriously.

I am writing to you in relation to your ongoing obligations to the Company, in particular your duty to keep strictly confidential and not to misuse or to disclose to any unauthorised third party any company confidential information and intellectual property.

It has come to our attention that in the period leading up to you leaving our employment on 5 May 2017, i.e. at some time between 8 March 2017 and your leaving date, you downloaded company information including supplier contacts list, example contract templates and company headed paper to a memory stick and removed this information from company premises. This is not only a breach of your express terms but a flagrant and premeditated breach of your duty of fidelity and good faith.

Your contract of employment dated 17 September 2013 and signed by you on 21 September 2013 contains two clauses in respect of your obligations to protect company information and not disclose or use this information for your own benefit or that of a third person. Clause 23 sets out your obligations in relation to Confidentiality and Clause 25 details the Company's expected requirements in relation to Intellectual Property.

The information which you now have in your possession is the Company's intellectual property and is commercially sensitive, i.e. the suppliers contact list and contractual templates were created and used in the fulfilment of your role on behalf of the Company and remains our property. We regard these categories of documents as our trade secrets.

Further, we understand you have downloaded company headed paper with the intention of providing this to an ex-colleague for the purpose of them providing a character reference to future employers.

The Company has no objection to you as an ex-colleague providing a character reference as long as this is not written on company headed notepaper and it is made crystal clear that this is a personal character reference only.

However, it is an act of dishonesty and the criminal acts of misrepresentation and forgery for an ex-employee to represent themselves as a current employee of the Company. The obtaining of a job based on a false reference is considered by the Courts to be theft under s.16 of the Theft Act 1968, i.e. obtaining a pecuniary advantage by deception.

It may be fraud by false representation contrary to the Fraud Act 2006. It may also be a material falsehood. This involves the commission of, or the attempt to commit, a criminal offence in relation to an application for employment or an application to provide personal services. The material falsehood should be one that would affect any decision to offer a post to an applicant, or for an existing staff member or service provider to remain in their post or move to a new post.

For the avoidance of any doubt you are strictly forbidden to use our company headed paper for any purpose whatsoever including but not limited to using it to give an employment reference for any colleague or ex-colleague.

You must return all the company headed notepaper that you have and give us a written undertaking you have not kept any copies and will not use the notepaper for any purposes whatsoever.

You are required to return to us all company information and intellectual property irrespective of the format in which it is held, and irretrievably delete any information that you may have downloaded to your personal computer or other electronic device and provide an undertaking that this has been completed by 5 pm on 26 May 2017 by way of signing the enclosed declaration.

Should you have any questions on any of the above please do not hesitate in contacting me.

Yours sincerely
HR Director

Undertakings given by X to Y Co Ltd

I, X, hereby give the following undertakings as follows;

1. I confirm to **Y Co Ltd** and all of the companies in its group of companies (the 'Company') that I have carried out a search of all my files both electronic and hard copy and of all my personal email accounts and have permanently deleted any Company data and intellectual property including material as defined in Clause 23 of my contract of employment dated 17 September 2013 (the 'Contract') and have returned hard copies to the Company's representative Z.
2. I shall not either alone or jointly with any other person or company, use for my own purposes or disclose to any person, firm or company any of the Company's information or intellectual property.
3. I confirm I have not forwarded any company information of any kind relating to the Company to any third party.
4. I confirm that I have returned all the headed company notepaper taken by me and I have not kept any copies of the said notepaper nor will I use it or a replica of it for any purpose whatsoever now or in the future.
5. I acknowledge that in the event that I breach my ongoing obligations to the Company or the undertakings above in any way that the Company is entitled to pursue all legal action and seek injunctive and other relief including damages and costs in respect of all breaches arising before and after the date of these undertakings.

Signed: [signature]

Name: [print name]
Dated: [date]

PRECEDENT 8A: Anti-slavery policy statement

This statement is made pursuant to s.54 of the Modern Slavery Act 2015 and sets out the steps that we have taken and are continuing to take to ensure that modern slavery or human trafficking is not taking place within our business or supply chain.

Modern slavery encompasses slavery, servitude, human trafficking and forced labour. We have a zero tolerance approach to any form of modern slavery. We are committed to acting ethically and with integrity and transparency in all business dealings and to putting effective systems and controls in place to safeguard against any form of modern slavery taking place within the business or our supply chain.

Our business

[Insert brief description of business and where it operates. Include sector, any international operations, and number of suppliers.]

Our high risk areas

[Insert brief description of the areas of the business that you consider to be high risk, how you have identified these, and any additional steps that you are taking to mitigate the risk in these areas.]

Our policies

We operate a number of internal policies to ensure that we are conducting business in an ethical and transparent manner. These include:

[Insert here brief description of relevant policies, for example:

1. Anti-slavery policy. This policy sets out the organisation's stance on modern slavery and explains how employees can identify any instances of this and where they can go for help.
2. Recruitment policy. We operate a robust recruitment policy, including conducting eligibility to work in the UK checks for all employees to safeguard against human trafficking or individuals being forced to work against their will.
3. Whistleblowing policy. We operate a whistleblowing policy so that all employees know that they can raise concerns about how colleagues are being treated, or practices within our business or supply chain, without fear of reprisals.
4. Code of business conduct. This code explains the manner in which we behave as an organisation and how we expect our employees and suppliers to act.]

Our suppliers

We operate a supplier policy and maintain a preferred supplier list. We conduct due diligence on all suppliers before allowing them to become a preferred supplier. This due diligence includes an online search to ensure that particular organisation has never been convicted of offences relating to modern slavery [and on-site audits which include a review of working conditions]. Our anti-slavery policy forms part of our contract with all suppliers and they are required to confirm that no part of their business operations contradicts this policy.

In addition to the above, as part of our contract with suppliers, we require that they confirm to us that:

[Insert here any relevant contract clauses, for example:

1. They have taken steps to eradicate modern slavery within their business.
2. They hold their own suppliers to account over modern slavery.
3. (For UK based suppliers) They pay their employees at least the National Minimum Wage/National Living Wage (as appropriate).
4. (For international suppliers) They pay their employees any prevailing minimum wage applicable within their country of operations.
5. We may terminate the contract at any time should any instances of modern slavery come to light.]

Training

We regularly conduct training for our procurement/buying teams so that they understand the signs of modern slavery and what to do if they suspect that it is taking place within our supply chain.

Our performance indicators

We will know the effectiveness of the steps that we are taking to ensure that slavery and/or human trafficking is not taking place within our business or supply chain if:

[Insert here any relevant performance indicators, for example:

- No reports are received from employees, the public, or law enforcement agencies to indicate that modern slavery practices have been identified.]

Approval for this statement

This statement was approved by the Board of Directors on [*date*]

Name (Director)

Signature

Date

PRECEDENT 8B: Hospitality and gifts policy

Introduction

The Company recognises that trust and confidence in the propriety of its activities is essential to its continuing success and growth. In order to foster the trust and confidence that clients, suppliers, workers and the community in general have in the Company, it is important that the Company, its employees and agents behave, and are seen to behave, appropriately and honestly at all times.

This Hospitality and Gifts Policy aims to:

- Protect the reputation of the Company;
- Protect employees from accusations of impropriety;
- Ensure that all clients and suppliers are dealt with on an equal basis;
- Avoid any potential conflicts between employees' private interests and professional duties;
- Instil a strong anti-corruption culture in the Company and put in place a gift and hospitality monitoring process to further ensure compliance with the Bribery Act 2010.

Employees are advised that, notwithstanding anything contained herein, where there is any doubt over the permissibility or propriety of accepting a gift or hospitality offer they should decline that offer. Nothing should be accepted which would bring the Company into disrepute.

This policy applies to the Company and to any associated persons as defined by the Bribery Act 2010.

Receiving gifts

Save for gifts of low value and which are mere tokens (such as industry related food and wine samples, promotional pens, calendars and stationery), excluding money, employees of the Company are not permitted to accept any substantial gifts from customers, suppliers or other third parties involved with the Company.

The Company recognises that there may be exceptional instances when refusing a gift will cause significant offence or embarrassment. In such instances the gift may be accepted and subsequently donated to a charity or used at Christmas raffles for charities of the Company's choice.

Where practicable any employee minded to accept a gift should first seek approval from their line manager. If it is not practicable to gain prior approval, the accepting employee should inform a Board Director as soon as possible after receiving the gift.

An accurate record must be kept of all gift offers made to the Company or to employees of the Company by third parties, and must be recorded in the Hospitality log. The records will be monitored by the Finance Director. Any employee who is offered a gift, which is not merely a token, should record as soon as is reasonably practicable:

- a description of the gift offered;
- an estimation of the value of the gift offered;
- whether it was rejected or accepted;
- if accepted, why it was accepted;
- whether prior approval was obtained and, if so, from whom;
- to whom it is donated.

Hospitality

For the purposes of this policy and for the sake of clarity, the following are not normally considered 'Corporate Hospitality' and will not require any approval prior to acceptance:

- normal working lunches or refreshments provided during a business visit;
- hospitality extended to employees attending a Company approved seminar, conference or other external event, provided that such hospitality is extended to all who are in attendance;
- hospitality received at Food and Beverage events which promote the industry and understanding of competition within the industry;
- free seminars, talks or workshops, provided that they are free to all in attendance and are not provided solely for employees of the Company.

All employees are required to obtain approval before accepting any form of Corporate Hospitality which is offered to them.

Approval must be sought from their line manager or, where the value of the Corporate Hospitality is likely to be significant (e.g. Royal Ascot, prestigious sporting events) from the Managing Director.

An accurate record must be kept of all Corporate Hospitality offered to the Company or to employees of the Company by an entry on the Whereabouts and Hospitality log. Any employee offered any form of Corporate Hospitality must record, as soon as is reasonably practicable:

- a description of the hospitality offered;
  'Corporate Hospitality', for the purposes of this policy, is any form of accommodation, entertainment or other hospitality provided for an employee of the Company by a third party and which is extended to the employee solely or significantly due to their position as a representative of the Company.
- an estimation of the likely value of the hospitality;
- whether it was rejected or accepted;
- if accepted, why it was accepted; and
- from whom prior approval was obtained.

Hospitality and Gifts Records

The Finance Director (FD) shall be responsible for ensuring that a proper record of hospitality and gifts received is maintained.

All offers and receipts of gifts and hospitality must be recorded by the recipients at Head Office on the [insert appropriate record-keeping log here], available on the Company's intranet, to include all of the information specified in this policy. The log will be reviewed at the Board Meeting monthly. Any hospitality and gift expenses over £100 will require prior approval from a Board Director via an email confirming the request and cc'd to the FD for recording.

It is anticipated that instances may arise where a gift accepted by the Company or one of its employees has not been donated by the time that the relevant entry is made on the Register. In such cases the Register must be updated within ten (10) working days of the date on which the donation was made.

Breach of this Policy

Compliance with this policy is essential to the protection of the Company's reputation and that of its employees. Any employee or associated person who is found to have acted in contravention of this policy or its principles may be subject to disciplinary action, including summary dismissal where the breach amounts to gross misconduct.

Any employee or any associated person (as defined by section 8 of the Bribery Act 2010) found giving or receiving bribes or bribing a foreign official will face criminal charges under the provisions of the Bribery Act 2010. Anyone found guilty of bribery will be responsible for bearing any related remedial costs such as losses, court fees or expenses.

PRECEDENT 8C: Anti-corruption, bribery and fraud policy

1. Policy statement

It is our policy to conduct all of our business in an honest and ethical manner. We take a zero-tolerance approach to bribery and corruption and are committed to acting professionally, fairly and with integrity in all our business dealings and relationships wherever we operate and implementing and enforcing effective systems to counter bribery.

We will uphold all laws relevant to countering bribery and corruption in all the jurisdictions in which we operate. However, we continue to abide by the laws of the UK, including the Bribery Act 2010, in respect of our conduct both at home and abroad.

The purpose of this policy is to:

1. set out our responsibilities, and of those working for us, in observing and upholding our position on bribery and corruption; and
2. provide information and guidance to those working for us on how to recognise and deal with bribery and corruption issues.

Bribery and corruption are punishable for individuals by up to ten years' imprisonment and if we are found to have taken part in corruption we could face an unlimited fine, be excluded from tendering for public contracts and face damage to our reputation. We therefore take our legal responsibilities very seriously.

In this policy, third party means any individual or organisation you come into contact with during the course of your work for us, and includes actual and potential clients, customers, suppliers, distributors, business contacts, agents, advisers, and government and public bodies, including their advisers, representatives and officials, politicians and political parties.

2. Who is covered by the policy?

This policy applies to all individuals working at all levels, including partners, consultants, employees (whether permanent, fixed-term or temporary), contractors, trainees, seconded staff, homeworkers, casual workers and agency staff, volunteers, or any other person associated with us, wherever located (collectively referred to as 'workers' in this policy).

3. What is bribery?

A bribe is an inducement or reward offered, promised or provided in order to gain any commercial, contractual, regulatory or personal advantage.

Examples

OFFERING A BRIBE

You offer a potential client tickets to a major sporting event such as Wimbledon or a Test Match but only if they agree to place a contract with us.

This would be an offence as you are making the offer to gain a commercial and contractual advantage. We may also be found to have committed an offence because the offer has been made to obtain business for us. It may also be an offence for the potential client to accept your offer.

RECEIVING A BRIBE

A supplier offers to supply you and your partner with a fantastic modern new Italian kitchen, but makes it clear that in return they expect you to use your influence in our organisation to ensure we continue to do business with them. It is an offence for the supplier to offer you a bribe.

It would be an offence for you to accept that offer as you would be doing so to gain a personal advantage.

4. Gifts and hospitality

This policy does not prohibit normal and appropriate hospitality (given and received) to or from third parties.

The giving or receipt of gifts is not prohibited, if the following requirements are met:

- it is not made with the intention of influencing a third party to obtain or retain business or a business advantage, or to reward the provision or retention of business or a business advantage, or in explicit or implicit exchange for favours or benefits;
- it complies with local law;
- it is given in our name, not in your name;
- it does not include cash or a cash equivalent (such as gift certificates or vouchers);
- it is appropriate in the circumstances. For example, in the UK it is customary for small gifts to be given at Christmas time;

- taking into account the reason for the gift, it is of an appropriate type and value and given at an appropriate time;
- it is given openly, not secretly; and
- gifts should not be offered to, or accepted from, government officials or representatives, or politicians or political parties, without the prior approval of the Compliance Manager.

The test to be applied is whether in all the circumstances the gift or hospitality is reasonable and justifiable. The intention behind the gift should always be considered.

Clients will, on occasion, express appreciation with a gift of flowers, chocolate or wine. This policy does not prohibit the receipt of such gifts provided that you are satisfied that they are proportionate and reasonable in the circumstances. Any concern should be discussed with the Compliance Manager. Gifts of a value in excess of £100 must always be disclosed to the Compliance Manager.

Gifts from suppliers should always be disclosed to the Compliance Manager.

5. What is not acceptable?

It is not acceptable for you (or someone on your behalf) to:

- give, promise to give, or offer, a payment, gift or hospitality to a government official, agent or representative to 'facilitate' or expedite a routine procedure;
- accept a payment from a third party that you know or suspect is offered with the expectation or hope that it could be a business advantage for them;
- accept a gift or hospitality from a third party if you know or suspect that it is offered or provided with an expectation that a business advantage will be provided by us in return;
- threaten or retaliate against another worker who has refused to commit a bribery offence or who has raised concerns under this policy;
- offer legal services to a client or instructing officer on a personal basis (e.g. residential conveyancing or preparation of a Will) at a reduced rate or at no cost (pro bono) with the expectation that it will obtain a business advantage; or
- engage in any activity that might lead to a breach of this policy.

6. Facilitation payments and kickbacks

We do not make, and will not accept, facilitation payments or 'kickbacks' of any kind. Facilitation payments are typically small, unofficial payments made to secure or expedite a routine government action by a government official.

If you are asked to make a payment on our behalf, you should always be mindful of what the payment is for and whether the amount requested is proportionate to the goods or services provided. You should always ask for a receipt which details the reason for the payment. If you have any suspicions, concerns or queries regarding a payment, you should raise these with the Compliance Manager.

Kickbacks are typically payments made in return for a business favour or advantage. All workers must avoid any activity that might lead to, or suggest, that a facilitation payment or kickback will be made or accepted by us.

7. Donations

We do not make contributions to political parties. We only make charitable donations that are legal and ethical under local laws and practices. No donation must be offered or made without the prior approval of the Compliance Manager.

8. *Your responsibilities*

(a) You must ensure that you read, understand and comply with this policy.

(b) The prevention, detection and reporting of bribery and other forms of corruption are the responsibility of all those working for us or under our control. All workers are required to avoid activity that might lead to, or suggest a breach of this policy.

(c) You must notify the Compliance Manager as soon as possible if you believe or suspect that a conflict with this policy has occurred, or may occur in the future, for example if a client or potential client offers you something to gain a business advantage with us, or indicates to you that a gift or payment is required to secure their business. Further 'red flags' that may indicate bribery or corruption are set out in the X Manual.

(d) Any employee who breaches this policy will face disciplinary action, which could result in summary dismissal for gross misconduct. We reserve the right to terminate our contractual relationship with other workers if they breach this policy.

9. *Record-keeping*

(a) We must keep financial records and have appropriate internal controls in place which will evidence the business reason for making payments to third parties.

(b) You must declare and keep a written record of all hospitality or gifts accepted or offered, which will be subject to managerial review.

(c) You must ensure all expenses claims relating to hospitality, gifts or expenses incurred to third parties are submitted in accordance with our expenses policy and specifically record the reason for the expenditure.

(d) All accounts, invoices, memoranda and other documents and records relating to dealings with third parties, such as clients, suppliers and business contacts, should be prepared and maintained with strict accuracy and completeness. No accounts must be kept 'off-book' to facilitate or conceal improper payments.

10. *How to raise a concern*

You are encouraged to raise concerns about any issue or suspicion of malpractice at the earliest possible stage. If you are unsure whether a particular act constitutes bribery or corruption, or if you have any other queries, these should be raised with the Compliance Manager.

11. *What to do if you are a victim of bribery or corruption*

It is important that you tell the Compliance Manager as soon as possible if you are offered a bribe by a third party, are asked to make one, suspect that this may happen in the future, or believe that you are a victim of another form of unlawful activity.

12. *Protection*

Workers who refuse to accept or offer a bribe, or those who raise concerns or report another person's wrongdoing, are sometimes worried about possible repercussions. We aim to encourage openness and will support anyone who raises genuine concerns in good faith under this policy, even if they turn out to be mistaken.

We are committed to ensuring no one suffers any detrimental treatment as a result of refusing to take part in bribery or corruption, or because of reporting in good faith their suspicion that an actual or potential bribery or other corruption offence has taken place, or may take place in the future. Detrimental treatment includes dismissal, disciplinary action, threats or other unfavourable treatment connected with raising a concern. If you believe that you have suffered any such treatment, you should inform the Compliance Manager immediately. If the matter is not remedied, and you are an employee, you should raise it formally using our Grievance Procedure, which can be found on the intranet.

13. Training and communication

(a) Training on this policy forms part of the induction process for all new workers. All existing workers will receive regular, relevant training on how to implement and adhere to this policy.

(b) Our zero-tolerance approach to bribery and corruption must be communicated to all suppliers, contractors and business partners at the outset of our business relationship with them and as appropriate thereafter.

14. Who is responsible for the policy?

(a) The Board of Directors has overall responsibility for ensuring this policy complies with our legal and ethical obligations, and that all those under our control comply with it.

(b) The Compliance Manager has primary and day-to-day responsibility for implementing this policy and for monitoring its use and effectiveness and dealing with any queries on its interpretation. Management at all levels are responsible for ensuring those reporting to them are made aware of and understand this policy and are given adequate and regular training on it.

15. Monitoring and review

The Compliance Manager will monitor the effectiveness and review the implementation of this policy, regularly considering its suitability, adequacy and effectiveness. Any improvements identified will be made as soon as possible. Internal control systems and procedures will be subject to regular audits to provide assurance that they are effective in countering bribery and corruption.

All workers are responsible for the success of this policy and should ensure they use it to disclose any suspected danger or wrongdoing.

Workers are invited to comment on this policy and suggest ways in which it might be improved. Comments, suggestions and queries should be addressed to the Compliance Manager.

This policy does not form part of any employee's Contract of Employment and it may be amended at any time.

PRECEDENT 8D: Code of conduct and common responsibilities

All members of staff are part of a team which shares the responsibility of furthering the interests of [the Museum]. This burden is lightened by everyone paying close attention to the expected code of behaviour so as to avoid bringing [the Museum] into disrepute.

1. General principles

1.1 Conduct of individuals

The conduct of individuals should not foster conflict or the suspicion of conflict between their official duty and their private interest.

1.2 Actions of individual employees

The actions of employees in an official capacity should not give the impression to any member of the public, to any organisation with which they deal, or to their colleagues that they have been or may have been influenced to show favour or disfavour to any person or organisation by the giving or the absence of any gift or consideration. If there is any doubt as to the propriety of accepting or giving a gift, do neither.

2. Gifts and hospitality

2.1 Criminal Justice Act (CJA) 1988 and Bribery Act (BA) 2010

It is an offence under CJA 1988 or BA 2010 for [Museum] employees in their official capacity to corruptly accept any gift or consideration as an inducement or reward, or to do or refrain from doing anything, or to show favour or disfavour to any person.

Under CJA 1988 or BA 2010 any money or gift or consideration (which includes hospitality received by a [Museum] employee from a person or organisation seeking to obtain a contract) will be deemed by the courts to have been received corruptly unless proved to the contrary by the accused.

2.2 Reporting suspicious incidents

An offer of a bribe or commission or an irregular suggestion made to a member of staff by a contractor or his agent, by a member of the public or by any Crown Servant, must be reported to the [Museum Secretary] at once.

3. Gifts

Gifts should not be retained or accepted by employees unless of a trivial, seasonal nature, or unless refusal would cause offence. Gifts should, in general, be surrendered to the [Museum Secretary] and all cases must be reported to the [Museum Secretary].

4. Hospitality

All offers of hospitality are to be treated openly. The [Museum Secretary] keeps a Hospitality Book in which offers of hospitality are recorded by the employees to whom they are made, recording the source of the offer, its scope and nature. However, [the Museum's] offers of hospitality to potential donors or other persons interested in the welfare and progress of the [Museum] are not subject to these constraints.

5. Fees

Any fee paid to any employee in connection with [Museum] duties is to be paid into [Museum] funds through the secretariat. This is without prejudice to the rights of the employee carrying out private engagements for which he is entitled to earn and receive private fees, provided those engagements have no bearing whatsoever on his work as a [Museum] employee.

6. Dealers and auction rooms

[Museum] staff must take care to avoid dealers obtaining pro bono services, such as valuations, from [the Museum], although if such services are provided on an interchangeable basis, [the Museum] may permit such exchange of information. All opinions or research services provided should be recorded in the Services Book kept by the secretariat showing the name of the individual making the request, the company name, the date of the request, the employee who dealt with it, and the type and scope of the enquiry.

7. Publications, lectures and interviews

7.1 [Museum] publications

Any proposed [Museum] publication should be agreed to by the Director in advance of such work being undertaken. Preparation of the work should take place during normal working hours, with any overtime being agreed in advance with the appropriate Assistant Director. The copyright of the publication belongs to [the Museum] and no fee will be paid to the author(s).

7.2 [Non-Museum] publications

If the Director refuses to sponsor the publication on behalf of [the Museum], the employee may offer it to a commercial publisher but must not use [Museum] time in the preparation of the work. Payment is then a private matter between the employee and the publisher. If any [Museum] time is involved, payment to the individual concerned will be at the discretion of the Director who, in any event, reserves the right to approve text where [the Museum's] name is to be used in connection with the publication. The writer must take responsibility for all copyright clearance and permission must be sought for the use of or reference to any [Museum] photograph or other artifact. The [Museum] reserves the right to charge the employee at a rate to be agreed for photographic processing and reproduction fees.

7.3 Lectures and interviews

Fees for lectures or interviews given during working hours must be paid into [Museum] funds. Fees for lectures or interviews given outside working hours accrue directly to the employee. Where work of this nature is undertaken, albeit outside working hours, permission must be sought from the Director if the subject of the lecture or interview concerns [Museum] material.

If the subject of the lecture or interview is not related in any way to the [Museum], the Director merely requires the courtesy of being informed that the lecture or interview is to take place. The [Museum] takes a serious view of failure to so inform and may consider disciplinary action against employees who fail to give the appropriate information.

8. Consultancies

No consultancy may be taken up by any member of staff in any capacity whatsoever without prior authorisation by the Director.

9. Common responsibilities

In addition to the requirements to avoid any risk of implication in corruption, and to respect [the Museum's] interest in dissemination of knowledge, your job includes the following commitment from you.

It is expected that you will:

(a) perform the job to a high level of competence in accordance with the requirements of [the Museum] as set out in your job description, or as directed by your supervisor or as set out in any other official document;
(b) maintain a high standard of efficiency and quality in all aspects of your work;
(c) safeguard and uphold the high reputation and integrity of [the Museum];
(d) maintain good relations at all times with the public and colleagues;
(e) protect confidential information about or in the possession of [the Museum];

(f) observe conscientiously your terms and conditions of employment;
(g) carry out any reasonable instructions as requested by your supervisor or any other member of staff;
(h) keep informed of new developments in your field;
(i) observe all health and safety rules and policies as set out by [the Museum] or as required by law;
(j) keep all physical assets belonging to [the Museum], whether or not part of the collections, in good repair;
(k) protect the collections, cash, stock and equipment free from fire, damage, theft or misuse;
(l) maintain the highest standards of dress, personal appearance and hygiene at all times;
(m) maintain the highest standards of conduct and behaviour out of work where you are in the public domain and where such actions could bring [the Museum] into disrepute.

10. Additional duties: duty to report wrongdoing or suspected wrongdoing

Everyone who works for [the Museum] is expected to act diligently and with utmost honesty and integrity at all times. Should any matters of concern come to your attention, e.g. should you overhear or suspect other staff or suppliers, contractors, clients, etc. discussing matters which you know or suspect to be dishonest or a breach of [the Museum's] rules, you must report this immediately to your supervisor or an Assistant Director.

It is your duty to report any such acts of misconduct, dishonesty, breach of [Museum] rules or breach of any other relevant rules or codes of conduct, committed, contemplated or discussed by any other member of staff or any other third party.

[The Museum] will treat what you say in confidence as far as this is practicable but you may be required to give evidence about such matters either to an internal enquiry or to a court of law.

Should the circumstances require it, you may be granted anonymity from the alleged offender(s).

It is seen as a dereliction of your duty to do nothing about such matters which come to your attention. Please note that 'dereliction of duty' is an offence under [the Museum's] disciplinary procedure.

11. Confidential information

11.1 Under the Official Secrets Act 1989

All members of staff are required to sign the Official Secrets Act 1989 as a term of their contracts of employment.

11.2 Ethical duty to keep confidentiality

All [Museum] staff are expected, whether during employment or after it has terminated, to maintain confidentiality and not to disclose to any unauthorised person or misuse any confidential information relating to the operation of [the Museum's] business, unless expressly authorised in writing by the Director.

Confidential information in this context includes (but is not limited to) any details about [the Museum's] client or dealer or donor base, accounts and finances, employees, actual, potential or past, the financial status of [the Museum], its future plans and all details concerning [the Museum collections], all matters relating to security and all details relating to information on any of [the Museum's] databases.

12. Copying or making abstracts, etc.

No member of staff is permitted to make any copy, abstract, summary or précis of the whole or part of any document belonging to [the Museum] except where expressly authorised so to do or in the proper performance of their duties. Serious disciplinary action may be taken against anyone who is found to have done this for any improper or unlawful purpose(s) or otherwise.

13. Conflict of interests

Because of the nature of [the Museum] and the position of trust in which some staff are placed, it is essential that every member of staff's business dealings are above reproach. For this reason, [the Museum] has set the rules concerning hospitality and gifts.

14. Outside communications

You must not make contact with or communicate with any member of the press or media, or anyone so connected, on behalf of [the Museum], unless you have obtained the prior written permission of the Director.

No member of staff is permitted to publish any letters, articles or otherwise purporting to represent [the Museum] (other than in your personal capacity) unless you have obtained prior permission in writing from the Director.

Failure to comply with these rules may, if the circumstances warrant it, be regarded as gross misconduct for which you may be liable to summary dismissal.

15. Use of [Museum] property, private mail, private telephone calls

15.1 Correspondence

No private correspondence of any kind should be addressed to any member of staff at your place of work.

Your supervisor or Assistant Director reserves the right to open all letters and packages delivered to their premises except where these have been addressed 'Private and Confidential' and the Assistant Director in charge of your department has been told in advance.

15.2 Use of property belonging to [the Museum]

It is strictly forbidden for any member of staff to use any property belonging to [the Museum] (e.g. photocopier, computers, stationery, etc.) for their own private use or for any use other than for [the Museum's] legitimate business. Disciplinary action may be taken against anyone found doing so.

15.3 Use of telephones for private calls

It is not expected that members of staff will make telephone calls of a personal nature other than in an emergency whilst at work. Abuse of the telephone in this manner is a disciplinary matter.

Anyone wishing to make any private calls must obtain the prior permission of the [Museum Secretary] and will be required to pay for the call(s).

15.4 Personal visitors

Staff are not allowed to receive personal visitors on [the Museum's] premises during working hours other than in lunch breaks or at the beginning or end of the working day. Adequate arrangements must be made for children during the school holidays and at the end of the school day.

Should any member of staff find themselves with any domestic problems in this respect, they should speak to their supervisor and every effort will be made to find a satisfactory solution.

16. Political activities

Because of the sensitive nature of the exhibits and the business of [the Museum] in general, it is not deemed appropriate that any member of staff takes an active part in the political activities of any political party, pressure group, campaigning group, etc.

Any member of staff who wishes to take any part, whether at local or national level, with any outside body, party, campaign, etc. is required to seek the written permission of the Director which will not be unreasonably refused.

Any failure to honour this undertaking may lead to disciplinary action or even summary dismissal.

PRECEDENT 8E: Conduct for professional practices

(This precedent is reproduced by the kind permission of Dr Michael Wise's private dental practice in Wimpole Street.)

The Practice will instruct you either in person or in writing from time to time in its normal working procedures and you will be expected to follow these instructions carefully, particularly with regard to maintaining confidentiality; the handling of materials, instruments and equipment; appearance, presentation and dealing with patients. Failure to carry out any of these duties satisfactorily could render you liable to disciplinary action or in severe cases, summary dismissal.

Below we highlight some of the more important rules of the Practice:

1. Please note that there is no smoking in the practice.
2. Please greet all patients with a smile regardless of how you are feeling.
3. If you are doing something in the presence of a patient and something does not go according to plan, don't make comments such as 'Oh dear . . .' because what you have done may be very minor but a nervous patient may misinterpret your comments.
4. Never mention one patient's name in front of another.
5. If you need to give me a message about a patient in the presence of another patient, write it on a piece of paper.
6. Try and move around the practice in a quiet and calm manner, no door or drawer banging.
7. Always remember that the patient comes first.
8. Everyone must be neat, tidy and well groomed at all times.
9. We are on first name terms among the members of the team and with most patients. For guidance on the latter please speak to either [*name*] or myself.
10. All details of a patient's condition, medical history and treatment are strictly confidential and must be confined to the practice as must financial details of the practice and details of management.
11. The telephone should be answered by the third ring. If the practice manager has not answered it then you are the next person to respond, answering by the fourth ring.

PRECEDENT 8F: Rules for company functions/parties/dinners and lunches

1. No Christmas parties, lunches or dinners are to be held anywhere where offence could be taken by a member of staff on the grounds of sexual lewdness or racist

behaviour. For example, it is unacceptable to visit a strip club, lap dancing club or bar or nightclub during such office functions where sexist or racist conduct or language is known to take place. It is equally unacceptable to go to any clubs where drugs are known to be taken or where drugs are easily accessible. A police raid on the club or you being caught with drugs in your possession, with you ending up in the cells and a prosecution in the New Year, is not what we would envisage as a great ending to our celebrations!

2. No alcohol can be consumed on Company premises during working hours save in the staff restaurant at meal times or on the occasion of entertaining business clients where so authorised to do subject to the rules set out below.

3. Drinks cabinets in senior management offices must be kept securely locked at all times and only used for specific business entertaining.

4. Where you are authorised to entertain business clients, we would expect you to drink sensibly and moderately. Normally one alcoholic drink would be regarded as sufficient; soft drinks are always available. We do not expect you to drink spirits at such times but you may offer spirits if appropriate.

[If you should drink any alcohol during your lunch hour off the Company premises, you must limit yourself to a small amount, say one pint of beer, one glass of wine, one single spirit. The Company does not encourage you to drink alcohol during your breaks.]

OR

[It is against Company Policy and the disciplinary rules to drink any alcohol during any meal breaks whether these are paid or unpaid. You may drink soft drinks only.]

It is particularly important that you observe these sensible/no drink rules since those of you who drive a Company car must be in a fit and competent state to drive. In this regard the Company does not accept the limit set for the purpose of the Road Traffic Act of 80 micrograms of alcohol per 100 mm of blood. We regard nil alcohol levels as appropriate.

5. Anyone who is deemed by their supervisor as unfit for work because they are under the influence of alcohol will be suspended from work immediately and sent home (normally driven by a colleague or sent home in a taxi). Once the employee is fit for work, they will be counselled about this behaviour and if appropriate reminded of the disciplinary action which may follow if there is any repetition. Anyone who admits to alcohol dependency problems will be referred to Occupational Health for advice, counselling and referral for treatment (where appropriate).

6. **Rules for Christmas parties**

6.1 Discipline

We will expect the same standards of behaviour at the Christmas party as we expect at work. Any rowdiness, abusive or inappropriate conduct or language, drunkenness or drug-taking will be dealt with under the disciplinary procedure and any perpetrator will be required to leave the party and go home. We also expect you to advise your guest/spouse/partner whom you will be bringing with you on the rules and behaviour expected.

6.2 Violence or fighting

Any intimidatory behaviour or menacing behaviour or actual violence of any kind will be regarded as gross misconduct. If you see a nasty situation arising either try to diffuse it there and then or call for assistance immediately.

6.3 Alcohol abuse

It is strictly forbidden to 'lace' anyone's drinks or mix the drinks or to place any drug in someone's drink. This is regarded as gross misconduct and could also result in a police prosecution.

6.4 Drug-taking

It is strictly forbidden to come to the party with any illicit substances or to use them or distribute them. Anyone found doing any of these activities will be escorted off the premises and will be subject to gross misconduct charges. The police may also intervene.

6.5 Horseplay

It may seem funny to play practical jokes or engage in horseplay BUT IT IS NOT! [Last year a female member of staff was locked in the ladies lavatory. She suffers from mild claustrophobia and was greatly distressed.]

6.6 Sexual activity or harassment

Any form of sexual activity whether consensual or not is strictly forbidden at the Christmas party. Please do not get carried away.

6.7 Texting offensive messages

It is entirely inappropriate for anyone to send lewd or offensive text messages. Please turn off your mobile phones and enjoy the party.

6.8 Organising your own department party

Remember that there are certain places that are not permitted for Christmas parties including casinos, sex clubs, strip clubs, lap dancing clubs, etc.

6.9 Unauthorised absence

We try to hold the Christmas party on a Friday evening so that staff have the weekend to get over the fun. If for any reason the party precedes a work day you are expected to attend work punctually the next day unless you have been given permission to take that day as a day of annual leave.

PRECEDENT 8G: Drinking, drugs and driving policy

(This precedent is reproduced with the kind permission of Arun Sharma Healthcare plc.)

1. Medicines at the wheel

If you have a bad cold or a bout of flu and you are taking a cough or cold remedy, think twice before you pick up your car keys because it is quite possible that the remedy you are taking to help your symptoms could impair your driving ability. And it is not just cough and cold remedies that can cause danger: other over-the-counter and prescription medicines can also affect your reactions.

2. What's in the bottle?

The risks of drinking alcohol and driving are well known, but many people don't realise that there could be danger lurking in their medicine bottle. Modern medicines are very safe and effective when they are taken correctly, but some do have side effects. Some can have a sedative effect and make you drowsy, while others can act as a stimulant. Either way, these side effects may affect your judgement – and driving ability. Everybody reacts differently to medicines, so you won't know how a medicine will affect you until after you have taken it.

3. What's on the label?

3.1 All medicines are supplied with a patient information leaflet or with important information printed on the medicine label. This will tell you how and when to take the medicine and whether there are any side effects that could alter your normal levels of concentration and co-ordination.

3.2 Part of your pharmacist's job is to make sure that you have all the information you need to get the best result from your medicine with the minimum of risk, so if there is anything you are unsure about please ask – your pharmacist will be happy to explain anything you don't understand.

4. Adding alcohol

Alcohol can make the side effects of certain medicines worse, so always check with your pharmacist that it is safe to drink alcohol with any medicine that you buy, or are prescribed. It is also worth knowing that some medicines can stay in your bloodstream for several hours after they have been taken, so if your medicine carries a warning to avoid alcohol, don't assume you will be safe to have a drink if you just wait a couple of hours after you have taken a dose.

5. The drug-driving danger list

Our list gives details of some common prescription and over-the-counter medicines which cause drowsiness as a side effect, but there are other medicines that also have side effects that you should be aware of if you are driving. So always read the patient information leaflet or label carefully, and ask your pharmacist for advice.

Medicine	Side effect
Cough and cold remedies	Some day or night-time remedies may have a sedative effect.
Sleeping tablets	These remain in the body for several hours and will probably affect driving the morning after they have been taken.
Tranquillisers/anti-depressants and anti-epilepsy medicines	These can make you unusually drowsy and can affect driving the same day or the day after they have been taken.
Antihistamines/allergy treatments and travel sickness pills	These may make you drowsy and if so, you shouldn't drive for several hours after taking them. They can also impair your vision and make you more susceptible to 'dazzle'.
Painkillers	Some can make you feel tired and less alert and others act as a stimulant, which can all affect your driving.

PRECEDENT 8H: Alcohol and drug control policy

Introduction

Alcohol dependency and drug dependency have become growing problems affecting all occupations. The consequences of alcohol or drug dependency can be disastrous for the individual, their families and in certain circumstances members of the general public. The Company, by the very nature of its business, is concerned and recognises its responsibility in this area.

This Company is committed to ensuring the highest safety standards in all its operations and to this end has introduced the following Policy. The Policy contains guidelines for those suffering from alcohol or drug dependency, rules about alcohol and the taking of drugs whilst at work or when attending work and rules concerning the testing of individuals for the presence of alcohol and drugs. All staff are expected to follow the rules and procedures set down in this Policy.

The Company has initiated an Employee Assistance Programme and a Rehabilitation Programme to help any member of staff with any personal or medical problem. This may include alcohol or drug dependency problems and it is the Company's intention to help any employee who recognises that they have a problem.

Definition

This Policy will apply to any employee whose drink or drugs dependency, in the opinion of the Company, interferes with their work, their performance or ability to do their work or relationships at work.

Alcohol dependence is most commonly recognised by erratic attendance at work, poor time-keeping, long lunch hours, erratic performance at work and sometimes a breakdown in relationships with other colleagues. This Policy does not cover social drinking within working time where permitted or outside working time or drinking within the guidelines set down in this Policy nor does it cover the taking of drugs properly prescribed by a registered medical practitioner.

Drug dependence often exhibits itself in impaired work performance, behaviour or appearance. Where there is any suspicion of drugs, the employee will be counselled on a confidential basis in the first instance by their supervisor or manager, to establish whether there is a health problem requiring the employee to take medication which might adversely affect their work performance.

Outline of the policy

1. Statement of policy

1.1 Alcoholism is regarded primarily as a health problem and those affected will need treatment and assistance. The Company will do all that it can to ensure that any employee suffering from alcoholism is identified, counselled and encouraged to follow a prescribed form of treatment.

1.2 For the purposes of the Company's Policy, 'alcoholism' is defined as:

'The habitual and uncontrollable drinking of intoxicating liquor by an employee, whereby an employee's ability to perform their duties is impaired or their attendance at work is affected or they endanger, or are deemed to be a danger to, the safety of themselves or others.'

1.3 For the purposes of the Company's Policy, 'drug dependence' is defined as:

'The habitual taking of drugs by an employee other than drugs prescribed as medication by a registered medical practitioner, whereby the employee's ability to perform their duties is impaired, or their attendance at work is affected or they endanger, or are deemed to be a danger to, the safety of themselves or others.'

1.4 In the context of this Policy statement the term 'drug abuse' is defined as the sale, or medically unauthorised use or possession of any controlled substance (dangerous drug) which means narcotic drug (including cannabis), hallucinogenic drug, or depressant or stimulant drug as defined in law.

1.5 Employees who are recognised to have an alcohol or drug dependency problem will be encouraged to seek help and treatment voluntarily through the Employee Assistance Programme and in some cases by reference to the Occupational Health Department.

1.6 No employee will be accused of using drugs or being dependent upon alcohol but it will be emphasised in all interviews that a failure to acknowledge any problem will normally result in disciplinary action being taken in respect of the conduct or performance at work.

1.7 Any employee caught selling or distributing controlled substances on or outside Company premises shall be deemed to have breached the terms and conditions of their employment on grounds of gross misconduct thus rendering themselves liable to summary dismissal.

1.8 In serious cases of alcohol or drug dependency employees undergoing treatment away from work are considered to be on sick leave and entitled to the Company's normal sickness benefits although payments to them will be reviewed at such times as their progress is reviewed.

1.9 Every effort will be made to ensure that the employee will be able to return to the same job that they held prior to treatment, unless the resumption of the same job would lead to a serious risk of undermining a satisfactory recovery.

1.10 Should the employee not be able to return to the same job every effort will be made to offer an alternative job of equal status. Where this is not possible the employee will be invited to consider alternative vacancies within the Company which are considered appropriate for their medical condition.

1.11 Employees who decline to accept referral for diagnosis and treatment or who discontinue a course of treatment before its satisfactory completion will be warned that should their performance at work or conduct at work fall below the standard required or continue to fall below the standard required, they will be subject to the normal disciplinary procedures. This will mean that unless an immediate and sustained improvement is made in overall performance, appropriate disciplinary action will be taken.

1.12 Following a return to work after or during treatment, should work performance or conduct again suffer as a result of alcoholism or alcohol misuse or drug abuse, each case will be considered on its merits and if appropriate a further opportunity to accept and co-operate with treatment may be provided or disciplinary action may be instigated.

1.13 This Policy is not concerned with social drinking and is limited to those instances of alcoholism which affect work performance, conduct at work or the safety of the individual or others.

1.14 This Policy does not apply to those who indulge in random, excessive bouts of drunkenness or behave in any manner contrary to the rules of the Company or standards set by the Company from time to time. Such behaviour will be dealt with under the normal disciplinary rules and procedures.

1.15 The confidential nature of any alcohol or drug dependency problem is recognised by the Company and for that reason confidentiality will be strictly preserved. Only where the individual concerned has consented to disclosure to another named person will any disclosure be made other than in a rare case where the health and safety of that individual or others are in paramount danger. In such a case only a senior person with a 'need to know' will be told and they will be told only what they 'need to know'. In such a case, that senior person will guarantee absolute confidentiality.

Rehabilitation and assistance programme

The Company intends to treat anyone suffering from alcohol or drug dependency in the same way as any employee suffering from any other serious health condition. The aim of any treatment is that the employee will ultimately be able to return to full-time employment at an acceptable level of performance and with no recurrence of the original or related problems.

The Company intends to give every support and assistance for those who have an alcohol or drug dependency problem to get treatment. In some cases the treatment recommended may entail some absence from work. In other cases, continued attendance at work will be possible. The following rules will apply.

2. Written agreement

2.1 In the case of an employee who is able to continue at work during their treatment programme, the employee will be expected to agree to written guidelines concerning attendance at work, performance at work, general standards of conduct at work and any rules deemed appropriate concerning abstinence from alcohol or drugs.

2.2 In any case where the employee has time off work for treatment and rehabilitation recommended by the appropriate medical staff, a written agreement will be completed before resumption of work setting down the agreed standards of performance, attendance, conduct and other rules whilst at work. This agreement will be worked out between the employee concerned and their supervisor/manager with advice from the Company Medical Advisers and Employee Relations.

2.3 Any failure to comply with this agreement may render the employee liable to the normal disciplinary procedures.

3. Successful completion of the programme

The Company expects that any employee who is recognised as having an alcohol or drug dependency problem will agree to undertake the appropriate course of treatment and will complete the course of treatment. Any failure to attend for treatment or any failure to complete the course of recommended treatment will render the employee liable to the normal disciplinary procedures.

4. Commission of disciplinary offences

4.1 Even though an employee is the subject of this Policy of treatment and rehabilitation, every employee is reminded of their continuing obligations to abide by the terms of their contract and the Company Rules, Procedures and Policies which may be amended from time to time.

4.2 Alcohol or drug dependency is not recognised as a reason for the commission of any disciplinary offence or breach of Company Rules or Standards. Employees should be aware that they will still be subject to the normal disciplinary procedures in any such case.

5. Referral

There are three forms of referral within this Policy:

(a) self-referral;
(b) voluntary referral;
(c) mandatory referral.

5.1 *Self-referral*

In the case of self-referral, an employee may recognise that they have an alcohol or drug dependency problem and they may refer themselves to their own doctor, the confidential counsellors working within the Employee Assistance Programme or to some other treatment facility. If the employee's problems resolve and the Company has no reason to be further concerned about the employee's health, work performance or conduct, the Company will take the matter no further.

However, should the employee's performance or conduct at work cause concern, the employee will be counselled and encouraged to seek help via the voluntary referral programme.

5.2 *Voluntary referral*

More commonly an employee will be counselled by their supervisor that their work performance or some other aspect of their conduct at work is unsatisfactory. Every opportunity will be given for an explanation and the employee will be encouraged to accept help should there be an underlying problem such as alcohol or drug dependency or family or personal problems.

Should the employee admit that they have a problem, they will be asked to refer themselves to the Company Medical Adviser. Such referrals will be in the strictest of confidence. The Company Medical Adviser will then discuss any problems with the individual, identify the underlying cause and refer to a specialist organisation or body for the treatment of the particular problem concerned.

The individual will be asked for their consent for certain details to be disclosed to their own medical practitioner but this will only be done with the employee's informed consent.

No details will be disclosed to any member of management without the employee's informed, written consent and in most cases this will not be required. The Company Medical Adviser will only confirm that there is a medical problem and that it is being treated. They will further advise management whether or not paid time off work is required and if not whether certain allowances should be made in relation to work performance and capacity in the interim.

5.3 *Mandatory referral*

Should an employee's work performance or conduct at work be a cause for concern and should the employee's supervisor or manager consider that there may be certain underlying problems concerning alcohol or drug abuse, the employee may be required to attend for a medical examination or assessment with the Company Medical Adviser where any such matters will be discussed in confidence.

The employee may be requested to give their written informed consent to a medical report or advice being sent to their supervisor or manager. Any such report would be given in the strictest confidence and no other party would be involved at this stage.

If the Company Medical Adviser recommends some form of therapy or treatment, then the employee will be offered the opportunity to accept it.

Should there be a refusal to accept there is a problem or a refusal to accept the help that has been recommended and offered, the employee should realise that they will be subject to the normal disciplinary procedures which could lead ultimately to their dismissal.

6. **Reporting requirement**

Every employee who receives help and treatment under this Policy will be required to report in confidence to the appropriate Company Medical Adviser on a regular basis as agreed between the parties. This will include but will not be limited to a requirement to show some form of documentary evidence of attendance at the treatment clinic/outside agency and the employee giving their informed consent to the Company Medical Adviser liaising with the person in the outside agency responsible for the treatment in order to receive regular reports about the progress of the treatment.

7. **Report to management**

Should the Company Medical Adviser deem it appropriate, the employee may be asked to give their written informed consent to a report being made in confidence to their supervisor/manager giving details only of progress of treatment and likely return to work (or normal work). No medical details or details of the exact nature of the condition will be given.

8. **Suspension on pay**

In some cases, particularly those working offshore, the Company Medical Adviser may recommend that until treatment has been successfully completed, in the interests of health and safety, the employee should refrain from work on pay pending a satisfactory medical assessment after the treatment has been concluded.

9. **Medical examinations**

9.1 In any case deemed necessary by the Company, the employee will be required to submit to a medical examination by the Company Medical Adviser or any Company-nominated doctor and to give their written informed consent to a medical report being sent to management. This will be in the best interests of the individual since the rehabilitation process may require a less strenuous workload or other considerations at work until a full recovery has been made.

9.2 Further medical examinations may be required throughout the employment.

10. **Future work programme**

A future work programme will be discussed and agreed between the individual employee and their supervisor following discussions with the Company Medical Adviser and Employee Relations. The employee will be required to adhere to the agreement and should there be any lapses in conduct or work performance, the normal Company procedures will apply.

11. **Repetition of alcohol or drug problem**

The Company recognises that relapses during or after the treatment of alcohol or drug abuse are a common feature. Whilst the Company will be sympathetic to anyone with such problems, it cannot condone any employee who wilfully or knowingly contributes to further alcohol or drug problems. Every case will be considered on its merits but every employee is expected to act sensibly and to contribute as far as possible to a successful recovery. In particular, every employee is expected to follow the medical advice given during or after the treatment programme.

Rules concerning alcohol and drugs whilst on duty or on company property or company business

Because of the nature of the business the Company has certain rules about the consumption of alcohol before attending work, whilst at work and when coming back from meal breaks. Any breach of the rules (which may be amended from time to time) will render any individual liable to disciplinary action which may result in summary dismissal on any one occasion if the circumstances warrant it.

12. Offshore

12.1 It is everyone's responsibility to ensure that they arrive at the heliport in a sober condition fit to fly. For this reason the Company now requires all staff, visitors and contractors who work or visit offshore to observe the following rules.

12.2 Because of the nature of our business and the need, for safety reasons, for all staff (including contractors) to start their shift fully competent and alert and present themselves at the heliport in a fully sober state, all staff and contractors will be required to conduct themselves sensibly before the start of their shift. This may mean that they will need to abstain from any alcoholic beverages several hours before the normal check-in time since there may still be alcohol present in the bloodstream and this may affect the ability to perform their contractual duties or may potentially endanger themselves or others.

12.3 Anyone who presents themselves for work in an unfit condition determined by the Air Traffic Controller in accordance with this Policy (which may include being under the influence of alcohol or drugs, whether prescribed or not) may be suspended from duty with or without pay depending on the circumstances.

12.4 Furthermore, should there be any delay in boarding the helicopter, it will be strictly forbidden for any member of staff, visitor or contractor to drink any alcohol during such time. Non-alcoholic beverages are available for all staff.

12.5 The Air Traffic Controller has absolute authority to refuse to allow any person they deem unfit through alcohol or drugs to board the helicopter and will require that person either to remain at heliport whilst other members of staff are summoned or to be escorted off the premises and accompanied home. Employee Relations will be informed of any incident and will then investigate the matter (normally within 24 hours) and take whatever action is deemed necessary.

12.6 Any member of staff who is subject to any investigation or disciplinary proceedings may bring a fellow representative to attend any meeting when any such issue arises.

12.7 It is strictly forbidden for any alcohol to be taken offshore or consumed offshore and anyone caught in possession of alcohol, or under the influence of alcohol or drinking alcohol offshore will be dealt with under the Company's disciplinary procedure for which the normal penalty is summary dismissal.

13. Onshore

13.1 Everyone is expected to conduct themselves sensibly whilst at work and this means staying in a sober and fit condition for work. As a general rule no alcohol may be brought on to Company premises or consumed on company premises except in the following circumstances:

(a) in the Company restaurants where it is available on request during lunchtime opening hours and is to be consumed in the restaurant only;
(b) at official presentations/seminars/other functions in conference rooms at onshore facilities with prior management approval and in that room only;
(c) in any office if that person is so authorised to have alcohol and if so doing on official company business;

During lunch and other meal breaks off company premises alcohol may be consumed in moderation.

13.2 Every member of staff is expected to act sensibly when drinking alcohol. Particular care must be taken in any case where a member of staff is driving. In such a case it is expected that non-alcoholic drinks will be consumed. Where staff are returning to work, the Company reminds all staff that they are expected to return in a fit and sober state.

14. Disciplinary rules

The following rules form part of the Company's Disciplinary Policy under the general heading of 'gross misconduct' for which the normal penalty is summary dismissal even for a first offence or 'general misconduct' where at least one warning will be administered before dismissal.

15. Offshore: gross misconduct

(a) Being in possession of any alcohol whilst on duty or at the heliport;
(b) Being under the influence of alcohol whilst on duty or at the heliport;
(c) Any act of drunkenness;
(d) The selling, possession of or use of any controlled substance or dangerous drug or prescribed drug not reported to Occupational Health;
(e) Gross negligence, gross dereliction of duty or gross incompetence endangering the health or safety of the employee or any other persons or the property of the Company, its employees, customers or other persons;
(f) Wilful, flagrant or persistent refusal to submit to any medical test (including blood and/or urine tests for the presence of alcohol or drugs) or medical examination requested by the Company in the course of employment;
(g) Unreasonable refusal to give consent to the results of any medical examination, assessment or evaluation or tests being disclosed to a senior member of management;
(h) Flagrant or persistent refusal to submit to a search when lawfully requested to do so.

16. Onshore

16.1 *Gross misconduct*

(a) Gross drunkenness;
(b) The selling, possession of or use of any controlled substance or dangerous drug on or outside Company premises (including attending work whilst under the influence of controlled substances, i.e. other than prescribed medication);
(c) Gross negligence, gross dereliction of duty or gross incompetence endangering the health or safety of the employee or any other persons or the property of the Company, its employees, customers or other persons;
(d) Wilful, flagrant or persistent refusal to submit to any medical test (including blood and/or urine tests for the presence of alcohol or drugs) or medical examination requested by the Company in the course of employment;
(e) Unreasonable refusal to give consent to the results of any medical examination, assessment or evaluation or tests being disclosed to a senior member of management;
(f) Flagrant or persistent refusal to submit to a search when lawfully requested to do so.

16.2 *General misconduct*

For which at least one official warning will normally be given.

(a) Coming to work under the influence of alcohol;
(b) Drinking on duty or whilst on Company business save where this is permitted;
(c) Possessing alcohol whilst on duty or on Company premises save where this is authorised;
(d) Refusing to submit to a search when lawfully requested to do so.

17. Procedure for gross misconduct

17.1 In any case where a case of gross misconduct concerning alcohol or drug abuse is suspected, the following procedure will be followed:

(a) the employee will be informed by their supervisor/manager of the allegations or suspicions;
(b) the employee will be suspended on full pay and required to go home if in a sober and fit condition. Those working offshore will be required to return home when considered in a fit state to fly;
(c) the matter will be fully investigated by an appropriate member of management. The facts will be collected and witnesses (if any) interviewed;
(d) the employee will be invited to attend a disciplinary hearing at which a fellow colleague may act as the employee's representative where the facts will be presented and the employee given an opportunity to state their case;
(e) the meeting will be adjourned so that full consideration may be given to the case and any representations made by the employee;
(f) the decision will be communicated to the employee and confirmed in writing. If the decision is summary dismissal, then the letter will spell out the effective date of dismissal;
(g) the employee will be given the right of appeal to an appropriate member of management against any decision to dismiss. The effective date of dismissal will stand but in the event of the decision being set aside, the employee will be reinstated with full back pay and rights.

17.2 At any stage the employee will be given every opportunity to admit any dependency problem in which case they will be referred to Occupational Health and any disciplinary action contemplated will be suspended.

18. Procedure for general misconduct

18.1 In the event of an act of general misconduct being committed in relation to alcohol or drugs, the matter will be investigated and a disciplinary hearing convened. The employee will be asked for any explanation and pending the outcome of that meeting, management will make a decision as to the appropriate penalty. This will normally be a formal warning. A fellow colleague may attend any such meeting to act as the employee's representative.

18.2 At any stage the employee will be given every opportunity to admit any dependency problem in which case they will be referred to Occupational Health and any disciplinary action contemplated will be suspended.

Alcohol and drug screening

Management considers the health and safety of its employees of paramount importance and is committed to ensuring that the operation of its facilities is carried out to the highest possible safety standards. Because of the serious nature of the problems connected with the misuse of alcohol, drugs and other potentially harmful substances (for example, solvents) and the impact which the use of such substances can have on work, safety and performance, management will take such steps as are deemed necessary when an employee's job performance becomes adversely affected or where there is reasonable cause to believe that the safe and productive operation of any facility is in danger as a consequence of the use of such substances.

19. Pre-employment

19.1 All candidates for employment will be required as a condition of employment to submit to alcohol and drug screening. Any such testing will follow the recognised protocol as set down by the Medical Authorities in the UK and endorsed by the Faculty of Occupational Medicine and General Medical Council.

19.2　Any job applicant will be made aware that as a condition of employment they will be required to agree to this Policy which forms part of their terms and conditions of employment. They will be required to sign their terms and conditions of employment which confirms that they have read and understood this Policy and that they will comply with its provisions.

19.3　Every job applicant will be required to complete a Consent Form for alcohol and drug testing, the results of which will be disclosed to the individual only and the results kept in the medical records. Management will not be informed of any test results, merely that the job applicant is 'fit or not fit for employment'.

19.4　It must be understood that anyone whose test results prove positive will not be offered employment with any of the Company's offshore operations neither will they be considered for any future vacancies.

19.5　The Company offers an absolute assurance that these test results will not be disclosed to any other person or body unless the individual has given their informed written consent to any such disclosure.

19.6　No offer of employment will be made to any job applicant until medical clearance has been obtained from the Occupational Health Department.

20.　Screening during employment

20.1　Medical screening and evaluation of employees for the presence of alcohol or drugs will be conducted where a senior member of management determines that there is 'reasonable cause' to believe that an alcohol or drug-related problem exists.

20.2　'Reasonable cause' will be deemed to exist in but is not limited to the following cases:

(a)　Where the employee on the job is observed to be mentally or physically impaired and as a result is deemed to be unable to perform work in a safe or productive manner where management has reason to believe that the use or abuse of alcohol or drugs may have been a contributory factor.
(b)　Where the employee is involved in any incident adversely affecting any person or property, e.g. involved in any fight, threatening behaviour or language, asleep on the job, accident to themselves, another person or where property is damaged, either on Company property or while on Company business, where management has reason to believe that the use or abuse of alcohol or drugs may have been a contributory factor.
(c)　Where the Company has reason to believe alcohol or drug abuse may be responsible for poor or deteriorating work performance, e.g. job performance is unsatisfactory and the employee is known or suspected to abuse alcohol or drugs outside working hours. Reasonable cause cannot be established on the basis of poor or deteriorating job performance alone. In such cases, however, the employee may be referred to the Company Medical Adviser for a medical assessment.
(d)　When evidence of alcohol or unauthorised drugs is detected in the workplace, e.g. these substances or the equipment associated with them (syringes, silver foil, etc.) are found on the person or on the job and can be linked to a specific employee or group of employees.

20.3　The Platform Manager in case of offshore employees and department manager in the case of employees working onshore shall have absolute authority to request that an employee undertakes alcohol or drug tests. Any such decision to request any such tests will only be made after discussion with Employee Relations.

20.4 Any employee required to submit to medical tests for the presence of alcohol or drugs will normally be suspended on normal pay until the tests have been carried out and the outcome of the results confirmed with management. Any unreasonable refusal to submit to any medical tests or examination deemed necessary under this Policy will lead to disciplinary suspension on pay pending further disciplinary action.

20.5 Before any tests are conducted, the employee will be asked to read and sign the written Consent Form which will be kept in the employee's medical record. Refusal to sign the form and submit to any such tests and/or a medical examination is regarded as a fundamental breach of contract and an act of gross misconduct for which the normal penalty is summary dismissal. The employee will be asked on at least one further occasion for their consent before any disciplinary action is taken. Before any decision to terminate the employment is taken, a full investigation into the facts of the case will be conducted and any mitigating circumstances taken into account.

20.6 Before any tests are carried out the Company Medical Adviser conducting the examination will explain the protocol to the employee. This will involve sending the samples away to an independent laboratory for testing and all positive samples will be re-tested at least once.

20.7 The test results will only be disclosed to the individual, unless the individual has given their written informed consent on the Consent Form in which case only a named senior member of management will receive any test results.

20.8 In the event of the employee refusing to give their consent to the test results being disclosed, the Company Medical Adviser will advise management accordingly. Such conduct is regarded as gross misconduct for which summary dismissal may be the appropriate penalty. The appropriate procedure as set out in the Company's disciplinary procedure and as outlined above will be followed.

20.9 The employee will be informed in any such case that unreasonable refusal to give consent to the test results being disclosed to a senior member of management may lead to their ultimate dismissal.

20.10 If the results of the tests and examination prove positive, the employee will be informed that they are regarded as unfit for work and will continue to be suspended on pay pending an evaluation of the case by management and the Company Medical Adviser.

20.11 The Company Medical Adviser will evaluate the medical circumstances of each case and recommend a course of action. If rehabilitation is recommended the employee will be required to discuss and agree in writing with their supervisor/manager the following matters:
(a) return date to work if time off work is recommended;
(b) short-term objectives/targets/standards of work;
(c) standards of time-keeping and attendance at work;
(d) standards of behaviour at work;
(e) abstinence from alcohol or drugs at all times or as agreed with the Company Medical Adviser/ person in charge of the rehabilitation;
(f) date for reviews.

20.12 If it is agreed or recommended not to offer rehabilitation or if the offer is rejected, then the Company will terminate the employment after all the appropriate procedures have been followed.

20.13 If the test results prove negative, the employee will be notified promptly and requested to return to work.

20.14 In all cases the supervisor/manager will be required to write a detailed report describing the circumstances that led to the decision to screen, their observations, what was said, whether any materials were seized and brief description and any other relevant facts. All conclusions, e.g. employee appeared to be under the influence of a substance, was not co-operative, was hostile, etc. should be supported by facts, e.g. speech was slurred, eyes did not focus, concentration wandered, employee said or did certain irrational things. Witnesses should be listed and written statements obtained.

21. Searches

In line with management's commitment to the protection of employees, its operations and the public, the Company will conduct searches to the extent deemed necessary to ensure the safe and productive operation of its facilities.

21.1 Condition of employment

It is a condition of employment that employees are required to submit to a search including a personal search and search of cars or lockers or any other personal property belonging to or accompanying an employee. Employees entering or leaving Company property, including parking areas and any heliport, may be subject to searches by a duly authorised member of personnel. Searches may be carried out where there is 'reasonable cause' as listed above.

Failure to submit to a search when requested will be regarded as breach of contract for which disciplinary action including summary dismissal may be the penalty, after all persuasion has failed. Employees will be subject to the normal disciplinary procedures as set out in the Company's Code of Conduct and above in this Policy.

21.2 Search procedure

Searches will only be carried out by a duly authorised member of management who will normally be a member of Security accompanied by a member of management. A witness will be present to act as impartial observer to ensure fair play. Searches may include lockers, vehicles, personal effects such as pockets and handbags and shall as in the case of screening be carried out in privacy and in confidence.

21.3 Seized property

Any unauthorised alcohol, drugs, controlled or illegal substances or any materials associated with the use of such substances, will be seized, labelled, dated and carefully sealed. They will be locked in a secure place by a senior member of management. It is essential that proper and strict procedures are maintained so that the evidence does not go astray or become accessible to any unauthorised individuals.

It should be noted that an occupier of premises, i.e. the Company, commits a criminal offence under the Misuse of Drugs Act 1971 (section 28) if there are controlled substances on their premises. Only certain senior members of personnel are authorised to inform the police in such a case.

It is the duty of every member of the Company to co-operate fully with the police in the event of any criminal investigation.

22. Prescribed drugs

22.1 Drugs prescribed by a registered medical practitioner or purchased over the counter are also a cause for concern because they may impair mental or physical performance in the job. Employees who have been prescribed drugs should keep them in their original container which identifies drug dosage, date of prescription and prescribing chemist or hospital. Any employee taking prescribed medication which adversely affects job performance must notify the Company Medical Adviser prior to starting work. Any restrictions on work will be discussed with the individual and their supervisor.

22.2 Anyone working offshore is required to hand over all prescribed drugs to the Air Traffic Controller at the heliport where it will be logged in. It will be handed over to the individual once the helicopter has landed on the platform.

23. Contractors, visitors, etc

23.1 The above rules relating to the abuse, use or consumption of drugs, controlled substances or alcohol apply to all contractors, sub-contractors, visitors, etc. who work on or offshore.

23.2 A copy of this Policy will be attached to the Standard Services Agreement and Service Work Order Forms.

23.3 It will be a requirement of all Agreements with contractors that all their staff working on any Company premises whether on or offshore have been tested for the presence of alcohol or drugs. Similarly, if there is 'reasonable cause' as defined above, the Company reserves the right to require an employee of a contractor working on any premises to submit to a test for alcohol or drugs. The Company reserves the right to require any such person to be removed immediately from the premises or from the work until a negative result has been confirmed.

GUIDELINES FOR SUPERVISORS

24. Checklist of physical, psychological, social and work patterns associated with alcohol abuse

24.1 If you suspect that a member of staff or employee of a contractor has an alcohol problem look for the following signs:

In appearance:

- The shakes, particularly of the hands
- Dilated pupils
- Sour breath
- Heavy unnatural perspiration
- Puffiness around the face
- Bruising, in keeping with a fall
- Untidiness, lack of hygiene

In behaviour:

- A depressed outlook
- Defiance towards authority
- A tense, suspicious demeanour
- Unpredictable actions

In personal situation:

- Lack of interests
- Marriage difficulties
- Financial problems
- Absenteeism

At work:

- Poor time-keeping

- Accidents at work
- Frequent errors
- Low productivity

24.2 Once a problem has been identified, but before you step in to provide constructive counselling, it is important that you establish the background of your suspicions. Below you will find guidelines on how best to proceed from your initial identification.

25. How to proceed from your initial identification of an alcohol problem

Before you intervene it is important that you have to hand any documentation that is relevant to the case, i.e.:

- job performance, absenteeism, lateness records;
- reports on any financial or family problems;
- any assessments detailing changes in personality, sloppiness of dress or standards of hygiene;
- any other data that may support your case.

25.1 The initial interview

Keep to the facts. Keep it brief. Outline your observations ensuring that they are all supported by the relevant documentation. Leave no doubt in the employee's mind that the problem has been identified and noted.

Your role is, however, not to threaten. You are offering help; make sure that the employee understands this and realises that during any period of recommended treatment all benefits and statutory rights laid down in the contract of employment will continue.

If for some reason they refuse to accept referral for diagnosis or treatment or discontinue the treatment before an agreed date and then continue to perform unsatisfactorily, let them know that only then will they be subject to disciplinary procedures.

Throughout the interview emphasise your role as supervisor, as a guide and as a friend. Advise the employee to go away and think fully about what has been said at the interview before making any decisions.

Lastly, arrange a follow-up meeting where their decision can be discussed and further action if necessary can be taken.

Make sure that you keep a record of all discussions held with the employee and wherever possible see to it that whatever decisions are taken are confirmed in writing.

This will take the form of a 'written agreement' noted in paragraph 2 of this Policy.

25.2 After treatment and the employee returns to work

When an employee returns to work after treatment for a drinking problem, treat them as you would anyone else who had been away off sick. Remember a drinker is not some sort of freak, so do not go out of your way to make things easier for them; simply monitor stress situations and intervene if necessary in a calm, friendly manner.

25.3 Relapses

A relapse should be handled with sympathy and firmness. A relapse is normally brief and can be seen as a catalyst to an effective recovery. Intervene if necessary but remember you cannot change a person. A person can only change themselves when and if they want to. All you can do is offer guidance and constructive advice. If a person makes a decision to return to drinking for whatever reason, let their job performance be your guide to further or final action.

25.4 Why the relapse might occur

If a relapse does occur, it is important to check on the facts to see where the problem lies and how any practical steps can be taken to alleviate it.

Would altering their tasks or job or location help? Do any family members and/or partner need to be seen?

PRECEDENT 8I: Rules on gambling

1. It may seem unnecessary to set out these rules but recently we have discovered that some staff have organised trips to the local betting shop during working time and this has resulted in unfortunate consequences.

2. The Company does not believe that it is appropriate for any member of staff to place bets during the course of their employment either on their own behalf or on behalf of any other third party – this means during working hours and during unpaid meal breaks. Anyone caught either visiting or having visited a betting shop or placing bets by telephone will be disciplined under the Disciplinary Procedure and in a case of flagrant breach of these rules or where this is an aggravated offence, it will be treated as gross misconduct for which the normal penalty will be summary dismissal.

3. Similarly, it is strictly forbidden to visit any gambling sites on the internet or to place orders for shares or stocks either by telephone or on the internet during the course of your employment. Again breach of this rule is considered to be gross misconduct for which summary dismissal is one possible outcome.

4. These rules include taking part in any syndicates at work for the National Lottery or any other similar activity.

PRECEDENT 8J: Prohibition on children and young persons on company premises

1. It may have been the practice (however against Company rules) over the years for members of staff to bring babies or young children on to Company premises and for children to visit or be brought to their parents, either at the end of the school day or during the half-term breaks or school holidays. In other cases, friends or relatives sometimes wish to come to Company premises to visit a member of staff.

2. It is not possible for this to continue as the Company is not insured in the event that any accident occurs to any such child or young person.

3. In order to ensure that every child's safety is assured, staff are reminded that it is strictly forbidden for babies, infants, children or young persons under the age of 18 to attend upon the non-public areas of the Company's premises.

4. Children over the age of 16 who wish to meet their parents or friends during the lunch hour or after working hours must remain at reception for the staff member to come down to the ground floor. No babies or children under the age of 16 may remain unaccompanied in reception for their own safety.

5. Any member of staff breaching this rule for whatever reason will be regarded as in breach of a serious health and safety rule and may be subject to disciplinary action up to and including summary dismissal. It will not be possible to obtain permission for this rule to be rescinded on any given occasion and it will not be regarded by the Company as a mitigating factor if any member of staff seeks such permission and then breaches this rule.

6. No member of staff is authorised to give permission for this rule to be breached and any member of staff purporting to give such permission will be doing so without the authority of the Company and will also be subject to serious disciplinary action.

PRECEDENT 8K: Clause relating to money collections

Money collections, other than for staff who are leaving, getting married, having a baby, who are ill or have been bereaved, are not allowed unless the prior written permission of your line manager has been obtained. In such a case you will be required to show that you have written authorisation to collect money or goods on behalf of the charity and will need to have obtained a secure place to store the goods or money.

PRECEDENT 8L: Compliance rules

A. Individual responsibilities

1. Background

Individuals carrying out certain roles within financial services firms need to be approved by the FCA. The consequences of this are as follows:

(a) if you are carrying out such a role, you will be vetted by the regulator prior to being able to work;
(b) once registered, you will be accountable to the regulator for your actions and can be disciplined for breaches of the rules applicable to you and to the Firm, and for breaches of high-level principles. (These are described below.) This can involve being fined or having your registration withdrawn, with the consequent loss of your ability to work.

2. Approved persons

2.1 Individuals holding any of the following roles (known as Controlled Functions) within any of the regulated statutory entities will need to be approved by the FCA:

(a) Management functions:

   (i) Director and Non-executive Director;
   (ii) Chief Executive;
   (iii) Apportionment and Oversight;
   (iv) Compliance Oversight;
   (v) Money Laundering Reporting;
   (vi) Finance.

   (The Chief Executive will be the person responsible for the Apportionment and Oversight of responsibilities and systems within the Firm. The Head of Compliance will be the person responsible for Compliance Oversight and Money Laundering Reporting. The Chief Financial Officer will be the person responsible for Finance.)

(b) Customer-facing functions:

   (i) Investment Adviser;
   (ii) Investment Adviser (Trainee);
   (iii) Corporate Finance Adviser;
   (iv) Customer Trading;
   (v) Investment Management.

What must I do?

2.2 If you are recruiting anybody for any of the above roles, they will need to be approved by the FCA before they can start work. See the section on Recruitment in this section of the Manual.

3. **Consequences of approval**

3.1 If you are an Approved Person you will be directly regulated by the FCA and subject to the FCA's statutory and disciplinary powers. You will be personally responsible for your own compliance with regulations applicable to individuals.

3.2 In particular, you must adhere to the Statements of Principle for Approved Persons and the related Code of Practice.

3.3 You may be personally fined by the FCA if:

- you have failed to comply with the Statements of Principle; or
- you are knowingly concerned in the Firm breaching regulatory requirements.

3.4 The FCA may also withdraw approval, with serious consequences for your ability to work in financial services.

What must I do?

3.5 You should read the Statements of Principle and Code of Practice and ensure that your behaviour is at all times consistent with them.

4. **Statements of Principle and Code of Practice for Approved Persons**

4.1 The Statements of Principle and Code of Practice directly regulate individuals. They complement the detailed rules applicable to the company. There are seven Principles. The first four apply to all approved persons. The last three are additional Principles applicable to Senior Managers, including Directors. These are discussed below.

4.2 The aim of the Code of Practice is to then establish whether your behaviour is in compliance with the Statements of Principle. It sets out descriptions of conduct which, in the FCA's opinion, do not comply with each of the Statements of Principle. The Code also sets out factors which are to be taken into account in determining whether a person's conduct complies with a particular Statement of Principle. The Code is not, however, exhaustive, so conduct which is not specifically mentioned in it may still fall foul of the Principles.

5. **Additional Principles for Directors and Senior Managers**

5.1 Principles 5–7 are applicable to Senior Managers and Directors, in addition to Principles 1–4.

5.2 The term 'Senior Manager' will include all Board Directors and those who are responsible for the management of key areas of the Firm and who report to the Board. Anybody who is responsible for directing teams or who has day-to-day responsibility for transactions may also be defined as a Senior Manager.

5.3 Your job description will state whether you are a Senior Manager and whether these additional principles apply to you.

5.4 These three Principles refer to 'the regulated business of the firm for which they are responsible'. For Senior Managers who are not Directors, this has the effect of limiting their responsibility to those areas for which they actually have specific responsibility.

5.5 For statutory directors, the overlay of company law on this has the consequence that statutory directors cannot ignore areas of the business for which they have not specifically been allocated responsibility. Statutory directors are still seen as being responsible for the running of the business as a whole. They will continue to need to exercise reasonable care in the discharge of their responsibilities as Directors.

Again, the Code of Practice gives examples of behaviour which is not consistent with the Principles.

6. Changes to an Approved Person's function

6.1 If your role changes to the extent that you are no longer carrying out the same controlled function (see above) as that for which you were originally approved, you will need to advise the FCA of your new role.

What must I do?

6.2 Advise the Compliance Department who will make the appropriate notifications to the FCA.

7. Ceasing to be an Approved Person

7.1 If you leave the Firm, you will no longer need to be registered with this Firm as an Approved Person.

What must I do?

7.2 Advise the HR and Compliance Departments. The Compliance Department will make the appropriate notifications to the FCA.

8. Changes to your personal circumstances

8.1 Should your personal circumstances change, you should notify both the HR Department and the Compliance Department. Notify the Compliance Department immediately should any event take place which has an impact on your 'Fitness and Propriety'. Such events are listed on the forms you sign for registration with the FCA and on joining the firm. They include, but are not limited to: criminal conviction, judgment against you in a civil case, bankruptcy proceedings initiated against you.

What must I do?

8.2 Remember to keep the Compliance and HR Departments informed immediately such a change in personal circumstances takes place.

B. *Inducements, bribes and gifts and entertainment*

9. Gifts

9.1 The gifts policy applies to all our dealings with all our customers and potential customers.

9.2 Neither you nor parties connected to you (i.e. spouse, children, close family) should accept or give gifts or benefits that create the appearance of improper influence. Cash gifts should not be given or accepted.

9.3 You must receive prior approval from the Compliance Department before accepting or offering a gift with a monetary value in excess of £100.

What must I do?

9.4 Never offer nor accept cash gifts. Notify the Compliance Department if you are ever offered a cash gift.

9.5   Notify the Compliance Department if you receive a gift with a monetary value in excess of £100, stating the nature of the gift, the name of the giver and the nature of your relationship. This will be recorded in the Gifts/Entertainment Register.

10.   Entertainment

10.1   Any hospitality invitations given to or received from clients should be reported to the Compliance Department unless they are in the normal course of business (i.e. occasional meals and corporate events attended for bona fide business reasons). Lunches and dinners that take place on a recurring (if infrequent) basis do not require reporting unless they become so lavish or frequent that they might be perceived to exercise an influence over the judgement of the attendee.

10.2   Attendance at corporate hospitality events, and the organising of these events by ourselves, should be disclosed to the Compliance Department, giving the names of attendees and details of the event. This will be recorded in the Gifts/Entertainment Register.

10.3   The Compliance Department should be contacted with any questions regarding this policy.

What must I do?

10.4   If you are a manager and approve the expenses of employees who report to you, consider any expenses charged in the light of this policy and ensure that the employee has, if appropriate, made the appropriate disclosures.

10.5   Notify the Compliance Department if you receive an invitation to a hospitality event which is outside the normal course of business, stating the nature of the entertainment, the name of the host and the nature of your relationship.

10.6   Disclose to the Compliance Department any corporate hospitality events you are organising, giving the names of attendees and details of the event.

11.   Foreign corrupt practices and the Bribery Act 2010

11.1   We require all staff to act with the highest level of professional and ethical standards in all aspects of the business which we conduct. We are now in the UK subject to the Bribery Act 2010. Our parent company is subject to the Foreign Corrupt Practices Act of the US Government. As such, any business that we conduct with or through government officials in the UK or other countries is covered by this Act. Our policy with respect to this Act is as follows:

11.2   Employees will not knowingly engage in illegal or unethical activity to obtain or retain business, or to gain an improper advantage in its business dealings. Bribes and kickbacks are strictly forbidden. No gift or anything of value intended to influence any business dealing in which any Group company is involved may be given to any government official of any country or any individual known to be or suspected to be a conduit to any government official. All transactions or business dealings with government entities or government officials, including entertainment expenses or gifts, must be properly recorded on the books of the relevant Group company. No payments of company funds may be made outside of the company's system of internal controls and accountability, or be inaccurately recorded by any Associate. No personal funds may be used to influence or to control the business relationships between the Firm or any affiliate of the Firm and any government entity or government official.

11.3   High standards can only be attained and maintained through your actions and conduct. You must conduct yourself in a manner that ensures compliance with these standards. Insensitivity to or disregard for the principles of the regulatory policy may be grounds for disciplinary action.

11.4 In adhering to this policy, you must abide by all local laws, acts, and regulations, and foreign laws and regulations that apply to and affect the conduct of our business affairs, whether at home or abroad. You have an obligation to understand that such laws and regulations exist and that this policy incorporates the intent of such laws and regulation.

11.5 While we will make every effort to provide you with compliance information, education and training, and to respond to your inquiries, no educational or training programme, however comprehensive, can anticipate every situation that may arise. Responsibility for compliance with these procedures, including the duty to seek guidance when in doubt, rests with you.

What must I do?

11.6 You must make an immediate report of any suspected or actual violations (whether or not based on personal knowledge) of applicable Firm policy, law or regulations relating to the Foreign Corrupt Practices Act and the Bribery Act 2010 to the Compliance Department. After you have made a report, you must update the report as new information comes into your possession. Under no circumstances shall the reporting of any such information or possible impropriety serve as a basis for any actions to be taken by the Firm against you.

11.7 Every year you must complete and sign a Personal Activities Questionnaire to the effect that you understand the terms of this policy and acknowledge your agreement to comply with it. Each certificate shall be retained in the Compliance Department.

11.8 If you violate this policy or any related law or regulation in the course of your employment, you may be subject to disciplinary sanctions. In addition, to the extent that you violated or appeared to have violated laws, foreign or domestic related to this policy, the Firm will take appropriate action to disclose such inappropriate activity to the proper authorities.

11.9 In addition to direct participation in an illegal act, you may be subject to disciplinary actions by the Firm for failure to co-operate in the oversight or compliance with the policy. Examples of actions or omissions that can subject you to disciplinary action include, but are not limited to, the following:

(a) failure to report a suspected or actual violation of law, or of the Firm's policy or the Guidelines;
(b) failure to make, or falsification of, any certification required under this policy;
(c) lack of attention or diligence on the part of supervisory personnel that directly or indirectly leads to a violation of law; or
(d) direct or indirect retaliation against an Associate who reports a violation.

C. *Personal account dealing rules*

12. Personal Account Dealing Rules

12.1 Dealing on your own account is covered by the Personal Account Dealing Rules. These are themselves based on the law on insider dealing and the FCA rules on Market Abuse. The key provisions of the legislation on insider dealing are to be found attached below.

12.2 Breach of the insider dealing laws is a criminal offence, punishable by a maximum sentence of seven years in prison and an unlimited fine.

12.3 The law requires that we take reasonable steps to ensure that:

- any personal account deal undertaken by you does not conflict with your own or the Firm's duties to customers; and
- where we give permission to you to undertake a personal account transaction, we receive prompt notification of, or are otherwise able to identify, that transaction.

12.4 Consequently, neither you, nor any person connected with you, should undertake any personal account transaction:

(a) unless you have been given permission in writing;
(b) if you have reasonable grounds for believing that it is likely to conflict with your duty to the customer;
(c) if the Firm intends to publish a written recommendation which could reasonably be expected to affect the price of the investment.

What must I do?

12.5 Be aware of the full text of our Personal Account Dealing Rules – these form part of your contract of employment.

12.6 Complete a Permission to Deal form in advance of dealing. This must be signed off by the Compliance Department in advance of your dealing.

12.7 Obtain permission in advance if you wish to hold an account or deal other than through [*give details*]. A separate permission form must be completed in these cases. It will be a requirement for the Compliance Department to be sent copy contract notes direct from your broker.

13. Approving deals

13.1 The procedure for granting approval for dealing trades is outlined as follows:

13.2 Individuals bring the permission form to the Compliance Department for approval. The Regulatory Assistant will then carry out the following checks against the following lists of stocks maintained in the Compliance Department:

(a) House Stock. If the stock appears on this list, permission should not be granted. Staff are not allowed to deal in House Stocks. This can be explained to the applicant.
(b) Research List. If the stock appears on this list, it may be inappropriate for permission to be granted. The Regulatory Assistant will discuss with the relevant analyst the following factors:

  (i) When is the next research due out? If it is intended that research coverage be commenced for the first time, no deals are to take place in that stock 10 days prior to the publication date, or for two days after issue.
  (ii) Is s/he likely to change his/her recommendation? If there has been a change in recommendation or forecast, there is to be no dealing for two days after research has been issued.
  (iii) When dealing in Research Stock, there is a 40-day hold required. Staff buying Research Stock should be reminded of this. Previous deals should be checked when staff are selling Research Stock to ensure that this period has been observed.

(c) Market Making List. If the stock appears on this list, it may not be appropriate for permission to be granted. The Regulatory Assistant should inform the Head of Trading to see whether they have any view as to the appropriateness or otherwise of the proposed trade. Applicants should be reminded of the provision in the rules to hold such stocks for a minimum period of 40 days.
(d) Watch List. If the stock appears on the Watch List, this should be brought to the attention of the Head of Compliance without alerting the applicant.

13.3 Once permission has been granted, the Regulatory Assistant will sign and date the form where indicated. Return the form to the applicant with the request that they forward a copy of the form once they have dealt.

13.4 The copy of the form will be filed immediately in the Personal Dealing File with a copy of the contract note filed alphabetically under that person's name.

13.5 The Regulatory Assistant will report any trends or any repeat occurrences to the Head of Compliance.

14. Accounts outside the firm

Staff members may in exceptional circumstances be allowed to have dealing accounts outside the Firm. Should this be the case, they must complete a form 'Dealing Accounts Outside the Firm'.

D. Insider dealing prohibitions

15. Introduction

15.1 The general principles of these rules are as follows:

(a) all your deals in either public or private companies should be approved in advance;

(b) none of your deals should put you or the Firm in a position where your own interest conflicts with either that of the Firm or that of a client;

(c) nobody should be dealing to the extent that such dealing prejudices their carrying out of their job.

15.2 These rules apply to all Group staff, irrespective of geographic location, and to all their investment activity, whether domestic or overseas.

15.3 Upon commencement of your employment, and prior to any personal account dealing, you must sign the undertaking attached below.

15.4 Compliance with the Personal Account Dealing Rules and insider dealing legislation is a condition of your employment and therefore if you breach these rules you could be liable to be dismissed without compensation.

16. The rules

16.1 Approval must be obtained from the Compliance Department prior to any personal account transactions carried out by you or any connected person (see definition). This approval must be recorded on a Personal Account Dealing Form. These forms are available [*give details*] and are to be retained by you.

16.2 Such approval may be refused. No reason may be given for such a refusal. Staff are not allowed to deal in House Stocks, i.e. those stocks where we are either adviser or broker. However, if you are a pre-existing holder of a House Stock and wish to sell, such sales are prohibited for 2 days after a material announcement.

16.3 All dealings shall be within your financial capability and should not be unduly speculative in terms of either the deal size or the frequency. No member of staff is allowed to have positions in excess of £150,000 unsettled at any time, unless prior permission has been obtained from the Head of Equities.

16.4 The Compliance Officer has the right to require a deal to be reversed where this is considered by them to be in the best interests of the Firm as a whole.

16.5 You and your connected persons must execute all personal account transactions through the Equities institutional trading desk. This rule also applies to family trusts for connected persons.

16.6 In exceptional circumstances, you may use your own stockbroker. However, this must be notified to the Compliance Department at the commencement of your employment and arrangements made for copy contract notes to be sent directly by the broker to the Compliance Department.

16.7 No short sales, options, warrants or other derivatives securities transactions will be permitted, unless specific permission has been granted by the Compliance Department.

16.8 You may deal in stocks in which the Firm either carries out research or makes a market in with the following conditions:

(a)   a 40-day hold is required;
(b)   there is to be no dealing for 2 days after research has been issued by the Department in which there is a change in recommendation or forecast, or when we are initiating coverage of a stock;
(c)   where it is intended that research coverage be commenced, no deals are to take place in that stock 10 days prior to the publication date.

The Research Stock List and Market Making Stock List are available [*give details*].

16.9 Should you receive an offer for an existing holding, or an offer to take up rights, warrants or any other benefit as a shareholder, you should seek permission in the same manner as if you were applying for these shares/benefits for the first time.

16.10 Where permission is given for a transaction, the other requirements set out in these regulations must still be complied with as well as those of Part V of the Criminal Justice Act 1993, Insider Dealing.

17.   General exemptions

The above restrictions do not extend to:

(a)   any transaction by you in an authorised unit trust, a regulated collective investment scheme or a life insurance policy (including a pension); or
(b)   any discretionary transaction entered into without consultation with you, where the discretionary account is not held with a Group company.

18.   Settlement procedures

18.1 Staff are required to pay for any purchases within 2 days of settlement. Where stock is not held in a nominee account, settlement will be [*time + 10*]. In cases where staff are engaged in selling shares, then delivery of the appropriate certificates and signed stock transfer forms must also be made to enable settlement within normal periods.

18.2 When a member of staff is making switches in their portfolio and, in consequence, purchases are balanced by sales, payment need not be made provided that the appropriate stock and stock transfer forms have been delivered within the period to fund the purchase.

18.3 However, should this result in the unsettled gross amount exceeding £150,000 prior permission must be obtained from the Head of Equities.

19.   Connected persons

19.1 Connected person means a person who is connected with an employee by reason of any domestic or business relationship (other than a relationship arising solely because s/he is a client), such that the employee can reasonably be expected:

(a) to have influence over that person's judgement as to how their property is to be invested and how they are to exercise their rights attaching to their investments; or
(b) to be consulted before any such judgement is made.

19.2 Spouses, live-in partners and children under the age of 18 would normally fall within the definition of a connected person.

19.3 If you are unsure as to whether any person is a connected person you should seek guidance from the Compliance Officer.

20. Consultation

These regulations should be followed in the 'spirit' as well as the 'letter'. If you are in any doubt about a course of action you propose to take you should not hesitate to consult the Compliance Department.

UNDERTAKING BY STAFF: PERSONAL ACCOUNT DEALING AND INSIDER DEALING

Declaration by: [name]

1. I undertake to observe the Criminal Justice Act 1993 (Part V Insider Dealing), in its present form and as it may be amended in future, and the requirements regarding personal account transactions that are set out in the foregoing notice.

2. I am aware that breaches of any aspect of this Undertaking dated [date], and any subsequent amendment or update published to all staff, may be dealt with under the Firm's disciplinary procedures. I also understand that such breaches may constitute gross misconduct and could result in dismissal and/or prosecution.

Signed   Date

[employee]

Witnessed by:

[name and address]

Signed   Date

[employer]

INSIDER DEALING: PART V OF CRIMINAL JUSTICE ACT 1993

Notice to employees

[date]

1. Under the rules of the FCA we are required to provide you with a brief summary of the insider dealing regulations.

2. The insider dealing provisions contained in Part V of the Criminal Justice Act 1993 ('the Act') are complex, and if you would like fuller details or are in any doubt whether a particular transaction would be prohibited, you should consult the Compliance Department.

3. The Act applies to all securities traded on a regulated market (which currently includes all EC Stock Exchanges, LIFFE, OMLX and NASDAQ), and to warrants and derivatives (including index options and futures) relating to these securities (even if these warrants and derivatives are only 'over the counter' or not otherwise publicly traded).

4. In broad terms, and subject to the exemptions provided by the Act, the Act makes it a criminal offence, with a maximum penalty of 7 years' imprisonment and an unlimited fine, for an individual who has non-public information to deal in price-affected securities (including warrants or derivatives relating to them) on a regulated market, or with or through a professional intermediary, or by acting themselves as a professional intermediary. Securities are 'price-affected' if the inside information, if made public, would be likely to have a significant effect on the price of the securities. This applies to all companies' securities affected by the information, whether directly or indirectly (for example, competitors of a company about to bring out a new product).

5. The Act applies whether you deal as part of your employment or on your own account. It also covers information which you obtain directly or indirectly from an insider, whether or not in the course of your employment, e.g. by social contacts.

6. If you are precluded from dealing, normally you are also prohibited from:

(a) dealing on behalf of the Firm or client (except perhaps on an unsolicited basis);
(b) procuring or encouraging another person to deal in the price-affected securities (whether or not the other person knows they are price-affected); and
(c) passing the inside information to another person other than in the proper performance of your employment.

7. It is possible for a transaction which involves insider dealing to constitute an offence otherwise than under the insider dealing provisions of the Criminal Justice Act. In particular, under section 397 of the Financial Services and Markets Act 2000 a person who 'dishonestly conceals any material facts' is guilty of an offence if they do so for the purpose of inducing, or is reckless as to whether it may induce, another person (whether or not the person from whom the facts are concealed) to buy or sell an investment, or to refrain from buying or selling an investment. This offence could well be committed by a person who conceals price-sensitive information from a counterparty to induce them to deal, if the concealment is dishonest.

PERMISSION TO DEAL FORM

To: Trading, Equities

Cc: Compliance Department

Date:

From:

Details of proposed transaction

Buy/Sell   Share   Quantity

1

2

3

Declaration

I confirm that at the date hereof I am not in possession of any unpublished price-sensitive information in relation to the securities which are the subject of this application and the proposed transaction will not to my knowledge involve me or the Firm or any of its associates in a conflict of my or its interest with the interest of any customer of the Firm or any of its associates or with my or its duty to such a customer.

Signature of applicant: Signature of Compliance Department

Name:

Date:

Time:

Note: This permission is valid only for 24 hours from the time appearing above. Where an instruction is given to deal at best or within a particular price and full details of the instruction are set out in this application form, the dealing shall be treated as having taken place at the time at which the instruction to deal was given.

E. Responsibility for others

21. Responsibility for others

21.1 We must accept responsibility for anything said, written, done or omitted in relation to these rules by any agent of ours. This includes any custodian or settlement agent whom we might appoint.

21.2 You must recognise that the delegation of responsibility to a third party does not mean that you divest yourself of regulatory responsibilities.

What must I do?

21.3 Monitor the performance of those to whom you delegate responsibility to ensure that they are adhering to the relevant rules. (This is a management responsibility and applies particularly to our relationships with custodian or settlement agents.)

F. Training competencies

22. Attaining competency

22.1 Once recruited, a new employee will need to be judged 'competent' to carry out their role. What comprises 'competency' in detail will vary from role to role, but this will be defined in the job description. However, 'competency' will include an assessment under the following headings:

- formal qualifications;
- practical experience;
- number of years performing a similar role;
- passes in the exams relevant for their role (see below).

22.2 No new recruit will start their role without having been assessed as competent, unless they are being recruited as a trainee. Their recruiting manager will need to sign off the interview note.

22.3 If the new recruit is not initially competent for their role and is being recruited into a trainee role, they must be supervised by their manager until such a time that they are competent. When they have attained competency, the manager must complete the Competency Sign-Off form and return this to HR.

What must I do?

22.4 If you are recruiting a trainee, complete both the interview note and the Competency Sign-Off form when the trainee has completed their training. If you are recruiting anyone other than a trainee, complete the interview note.

23. Exams

23.1 Some Controlled Functions require the jobholder to have passed a specific exam prior to their being judged as competent. For people in these roles, the Firm recommends the following exams: [give details]

23.2 Given the importance of passing these exams, time limits for passing them have been imposed by the Firm. These are follows: [give details]

23.3 Failure to pass the required exam within the required time frame will mean that we may no longer be able to employ the person.

23.4 The day-to-day overseeing of administrative functions in relation to investment management also requires relevant exams to have been passed. These cover [give details]. Unlike the exams above, these must be passed within [2 years] of starting the role.

What must I do?

23.5 Ensure that new recruits are enrolled for the relevant exam.

23.6 Advise HR so that they can keep a record of:
- the date the course commenced;
- the date the course was completed.

24. Maintaining competency

24.1 Once competency has been attained, it must be maintained. It is the responsibility of all staff members to keep their skills and abilities up to date. To this end the Firm requires that all members of staff undertake training every year. For Approved Persons, the requirement is to complete a minimum of [14 hours] formal training. This is to include the following: [give details].

24.2 For staff who are not Approved Persons carrying out Controlled Functions these hours are a target.

24.3 This requirement can be met through any combination of internal or external courses, seminars or briefings. Human Resources will arrange any external courses that you wish to attend.

24.4 You are responsible for maintaining your own record of training undertaken in the year. Any training that you undertake – whether external courses, conferences, seminars or briefings – whether internal or external, must be recorded on your Personal Training Log. You should mail a copy of your Personal Training Log to HR every time you update it so that HR have an up-to-date record of training carried out.

24.5 The Personal Training Log will form part of your Annual Appraisal and should be attached to the Appraisal papers.

24.6 Human Resources will on a quarterly basis review your Personal Training Log to ensure that it is up to date and that:
- you are carrying out the training that was agreed at your last appraisal;
- you are on target to achieve the required hours for the year.

24.7 They will then provide feedback and make any recommendations they think necessary.

25. Annual Appraisal

25.1 The Annual Appraisal will be a key part of assessing whether any member of staff remains competent.

25.2 The key part of the Appraisal Process is the completion by the manager of Section C of the forms. This is the Competency Assessment and it should be judged, among other things, on whether the individual has achieved the competencies as defined in their job description. The following criteria will also form a part of the Appraisal discussion:

(a) whether training has been undertaken during the year;
(b) whether the individual is abreast of relevant industry developments;
(c) whether the individual possesses the appropriate IT skills;
(d) whether the role has been carried out to the satisfaction of the manager.

25.3 Based on these, and other, criteria the individual will be assessed as competent for the forthcoming year.

25.4 The person being appraised will also be asked to reconfirm that they remain of good standing and repute.

PRECEDENT 8M: Clause relating to personal searches

1. The Company reserves the right to search you, your office or any of your property held on Company premises at any time if there are reasonable grounds to believe that you are guilty of any breach of the Company's rules and regulations or the commission of a civil or criminal offence. This will include a body search, search of your bags, clothing, locker and car.

2. Personal searches will be carried out by security, with your consent and in the presence of at least one agreed witness. The searches will be carried out by a member of the same sex, who is a trained security staff member.

3. The Company also reserves the right to invite the police to obtain a warrant to search the Company premises and/or people suspected of possession of drugs or who are suspected of having committed any other criminal offence.

Right of search policy

The Company reserves the right to make personal searches of your outer clothing and bags and vehicles (personal and company).

Any more personal search, i.e. strip search, would only be done with clear evidence of theft and will be conducted either by a trained police officer of the same sex as the individual being searched or a medically trained member of staff or independent contractor.

The right of search and any actual search does not imply any guilt on your part. We carry out random and for cause searches in order to maintain security of our property, tools and equipment and our customers' goods.

Where you are asked to be searched, the following procedure is in place:

1. Searches will only be carried out by a trained member of security.
2. The search will be conducted in a private room, properly secured and where you will be asked to empty your pockets in your outer or inner clothing and empty any bags or receptacles. There will be no physical contact from those carrying out the search.
3. You may be accompanied by a work colleague or Union representative who is available at that time.

4. You will be searched by a member of the same sex and when a witness is present who is the same sex as yourself.
5. Your vehicles – private and company – on Company premises may be searched inside and out.
6. If you refuse to agree to a search this may be a disciplinary offence.
7. Only a Director has authority to call the police where theft or any other criminal activity is suspected.
8. Where an employee is found to be in possession of illicit substances or there is evidence to suggest that a criminal offence has been committed, we reserve the right to suspend the employee on basic pay pursuant to the disciplinary procedure whilst further investigation ensues.
9. Where there is any evidence of illicit substances either on company premises, or being sold or used or stored on Company premises, a Director may authorise the calling of the police to deal with the matter as well as the taking of disciplinary action under our disciplinary procedure.

PRECEDENT 8N: Dress and appearance

Dress code (professional firm)

1. This policy allows all employees the flexibility to wear formal business attire around clients, or to wear smart/casual clothing, as appropriate. The following explains the policy, how it will be applied throughout the Firm, and some tips on what you should consider when you are dressing for work each day.

In offering this policy, the Firm is responding to the needs of our clients and employees – always remember that our clients come first. The Firm's dress policy gives you the freedom to choose your clothes based on what will make you an effective contributor, given your role, the nature of your work, and the impression you need to create with our clients. If clients prefer a more formal business setting when they visit, we need to provide that setting for them. Balancing that need is the Firm's desire to provide a comfortable business setting for our employees. First impressions count – judgements are made within the first few minutes of meeting someone!

2. The following guidelines have been created to assist you.

Guideline 1: Match your clients

Many clients do wear traditional business attire. Therefore, there will be days when you will want to wear a business suit. This is true whether you are in a client-facing role or may be welcoming a client to the office or joining a meeting, or any other employee who needs to match what a client is wearing. In fact, for many employees, traditional business attire may still be the rule rather than the exception because that is what they need to wear to be effective.

Guideline 2: Maintaining our professional environment

It is never professional and, therefore, it is not appropriate, to wear clothes that look crumpled, worn or faded. All clothing should be neat and clean. If in doubt, don't wear it!

Guideline 3: Be conservative

If a client unexpectedly drops in to see you, in a suit, and you are wearing smart casual, you might want to have a back-up. It may be appropriate to keep a jacket, tie or suit hanging in a nearby cabinet or on the back of the door, just in case you are called to a last-minute meeting in or outside the office. If you are in a role where it might happen regularly, then you will be most effective if you are dressed for any situation that might arise, including a visit from a client or request from a client for a last-minute meeting, and you will want to choose more formal traditional business wear for most business days. In other situations, you can explain to your clients our dress code and make sure you wear what the client wears the next time you meet.

Guideline 4: Do not dress inappropriately

Inappropriate clothing for men or women includes the following;

- T-shirts;
- jeans of any colour (including denim shirts, dresses, skirts or vests);
- cargo trousers, tracksuits or leggings;
- cropped trousers, Capri pants;
- shorts;
- sleeveless tops;
- boob tubes (women);
- trainers.

Dress code

1. Staff are expected to dress to a 'professional and business-like standard'. Any male member of staff not coming into contact with members of the public or our customers, etc. will not be required to wear a suit, collar and tie but will still need to look smart, i.e. not wear jeans and a T-shirt. Any female member of staff not coming into contact with members of the public or our customers, etc. will be permitted to wear trousers and a top, but not jeans and this must be smart work wear which is clean and neat-looking. Even in the summer, skimpy tops/boob tubes, strappy vests and T-shirts, shorts or mini skirts are not acceptable.

2. Where you are going to meet a member of the public or a customer or client or potential customer or client or any outside third party or where so directed by management, men must wear a smart business suit, shirt and tie and women must wear a smart business suit (skirt or trouser suit or dress) and smart shoes (e.g. no trainers or clumpy boots, etc).

3. Any member of staff in senior management grades [*specify*] will be required to wear formal business dress consisting of a smart business suit and formal business shoes.

4. No body or face piercing or tattoos that are visible are permitted. Hair must be neat and tidy. Employees are not permitted to come to work with shaved heads or with hair of an unusual colour or what is known as a 'punk' style.

5. Cleanliness both personal and in your clothes and shoes and good personal hygiene are essential. It hardly needs saying that you are expected to bathe or shower in the morning before you come to work and to use deodorant and wear clean underwear, a clean shirt or blouse, etc. You should regularly have your suits, jackets, etc. dry cleaned or laundered. In the summer, in the really hot weather, you may wish to bring a clean shirt or other clean clothes to work. We would encourage you to do so. We also encourage you to bring wash bags and deodorants, etc. to work and to leave a spare set here so you are able to freshen up during the day.

Religious dress

6. The wearing of religious jewellery and emblems, etc. is permitted, for example a simple cross on a necklace or Magen David, etc. but you should please check first with your manager to ensure that there are no health or safety issues.

7. The wearing of headscarves (including a hijab) for religious or medical reasons is permissible. The hijab covers the head and neck and leaves the face clear.

8. The niqab is a veil for the face that leaves the area around the eyes clear. However, it may be worn with a separate eye veil. It is worn with an accompanying headscarf.

9. The burqa is the most concealing of all Islamic veils. It is a one-piece veil that covers the face and body, often leaving just a mesh screen to see through.

10. Neither a burqa nor niqab are acceptable forms of dress at work where you have any client or customer contact or where there is any health or safety risk or where you may meet visitors on site. We expect staff to communicate with each other and customers and clients and visitors and the wearing of such covering would not be appropriate or acceptable.

Please ask HR and/or your manager if you have any queries on these issues.

Transvestite/transgender cross dressing

11. No cross dressing (a man coming to work in women's clothing or vice versa) is permitted where the individual is a cross dresser only.

12. However, any man or woman undergoing a transgender programme/process under medical supervision who has got to the stage of dressing and living as a woman/man, may of course dress as a woman/man and attend work in that clothing.

13. Before doing so please ensure that you speak to HR and to your line manager so that this process can be managed sensitively and appropriately.

You will be entitled to use the lavatory of your choice, either the gentleman's or ladies' lavatories or the unisex lavatory reserved for the disabled, but when this is not in use staff of either sex can use it.

Please ask HR and/or your manager if you have any queries on these issues.

PRECEDENT 80: Dress code (museum)

1. **Formal working clothes**

The [Museum] expects that all staff will maintain a standard of dress that appropriately reflects the character of the [Museum] and the work that we do. We rely on your judgement and discretion in this matter. If necessary your supervisor will advise you on the suitability of your dress and appearance. Please note that this matter will be taken seriously and as a last resort it could be taken up as a disciplinary matter.

The appearance of staff is a reflection of the standards of the [Museum]. Male office staff and curators are normally expected to be formally dressed in collar and tie, trousers and jacket. Female office staff and curators are expected to wear a smart skirt or culottes and jacket or top, or dress, or trouser suit or trousers and top. Denim jeans are not acceptable.

2. **Protective clothing**

From time to time, routine work in the [Museum] will require protective clothing to be worn. Under those circumstances, dress appropriate to the work in hand may be worn, provided a suitable dust-coat or other protective overalls are worn. Where dust or debris are likely to accumulate, gloves should be worn at all times to protect the employee and the artefacts which are likely to be handled.

3. Photographers' clothing

Photographers have a particular responsibility in matters of dress. They should always have clean, smart and formal clothing ready, as they are frequently required to appear in public at very short notice to take photographs of distinguished guests.

PRECEDENT 8P: Guidelines on professional relations between student and academic staff

1. The relationship between student and lecturer (or supervisor) is an integral part of the educational development of the student. In order that enquiry and learning can be facilitated, this relationship must be supportive and one characterised by good communication, trust and confidence.

2. This Policy is particularly designed to protect, safeguard and promote the welfare of our students and particularly those who may be vulnerable whether socially, economically, physically or emotionally and to protect them from sexual activity from those teaching and looking after their welfare. It should be recognised that students who form close friendships of this nature find themselves in relationships that are often unequal and potentially damaging.

3. The Policy also aims to protect the person in a position of trust by preventing them from entering into a relationship deliberately or accidentally. Any relationship of this nature is wholly inappropriate and will be regarded as gross misconduct for as long as the student remains a student at the College.

4. The College therefore expects good professional relationships between academic staff and students within the classroom and laboratory, in one-to-one tutorials and in social gatherings.

5. Lecturing and supervisory staff are not permitted to enter into any sexual/romantic or other potentially incompatible relationships with students because:

(a) this compromises the relationship of academic trust, or could reasonably appear to do so in the eyes of other students;
(b) it may lead to allegations of favouritism;
(c) it could lead to untrue allegations of sexual harassment if the lecturer wishes to end the relationship and the student is unwilling;
(d) it could lead to sexual harassment of the student if the student wishes to end the relationship but the lecturer does not; and
(e) it also has become a criminal offence.

6. Members of staff should be particularly aware that such an abuse of professional relationships may also lead to complaints of sexual harassment. Staff should note that it could prove exceedingly difficult to defend themselves against such complaints on grounds of mutual consent.

CRIMINAL LAW

7. The Sexual Offences (Amendment) Act 2002 makes it a criminal offence for any teacher or person in a position of trust, where young persons or vulnerable people are in their charge, to have any form of inappropriate sexual relationship.

WHAT IS PROHIBITED

8. The College regards not only a full sexual relationship but also any form of sexual activity or intimate friendship or relationship as a breach of this Policy, wholly unprofessional and potentially gross misconduct.

9. This includes but is not limited to any form of sexual activity such as kissing, fondling or a relationship of an intimate nature.

10. It also covers making unwanted and persistent telephone calls, texts, emails or other messaging to a student at home, visiting their home for social purposes or making any kind of unwanted advances such as constantly asking the student to accompany the lecturer for meals or the giving of lavish and expensive presents.

11. Clearly, where a student needs or asks for individual attention or extra help in their work, it is perfectly acceptable for staff to arrange to meet the student after College hours to give whatever support is required. It is, however, inappropriate in most cases to visit students at their home, ring them at home or see them outside College other than on legitimate College business.

HOMOSEXUAL AND HETEROSEXUAL RELATIONSHIPS

12. Whether heterosexual or homosexual, no member of staff may form an intimate relationship with a student whether that member of staff teaches that student or not.

DUTY TO REPORT MISCONDUCT OF OTHERS

13. The College will have to rely on others reporting any concerns they may have about a colleague becoming attracted to a student or to someone in their care, e.g. a tutor and his/her student.

14. If such a relationship does occur, it is the duty of any member of staff who knows or suspects that a breach of this Policy has occurred to report this immediately either to his/her Head of Department and, where appropriate, to the student's union representative(s) or to the Principal's Department.

15. In the case of a Head of Department, the Principal or Deputy Principal should be informed in the first instance. A member of staff who is in doubt about their position vis-à-vis a relationship with a student or is not sure what to do about a concern that they may have, is encouraged to discuss this with a member(s) of their union and Personnel and/or their Head of Department.

16. For a member of staff to leave unreported a known or suspected sexual/romantic or other potentially incompatible association will be regarded as serious misconduct and could leave the member of staff who knows but does not inform open to disciplinary action themselves.

17. Be in no doubt: any member of staff breaching the letter or spirit of this Policy will be subject to the most stringent investigation and disciplinary measures which include summary dismissal in the first instance. Criminal proceedings may also be taken against any lecturer or supervisor contravening this Policy.

PRECEDENT 8Q: Harassment

1. 'Harassment' means unwanted conduct of, for example, a sexual or racial nature or conduct based on sexual, racial or other forms of personal abuse which is offensive to the recipient.

2. Sexual harassment does not refer to behaviour of a socially acceptable nature. It refers to behaviour which is unsolicited, that is personally offensive and that fails to respect the rights of others and is such that it could interfere with an individual's performance and approach to work.

3. Harassment may be intentional or unintentional. The key issue is that it is unwanted by the recipient or undermines people's dignity at work. Since behaviour or language

may be acceptable to one person and unacceptable to another, objections to unintentional harassment or to behaviour or language which the harasser thought was welcome should therefore be taken seriously.

4. Harassment is not a joke to the recipient and complaints of harassment should not be assumed to be the result of touchiness or over-sensitivity.

5. Racist language which causes offence does not become permissible just because the speaker claims that nothing was meant by it. Some types of sexually related behaviour which may be acceptable to an individual outside work may cause a complaint of harassment if they occur in the workplace because they interfere with and undermine the individual's dignity and role at work.

6. Friendly or romantic behaviour which is welcome and mutual is not harassment, although it may be regarded as unprofessional and inappropriate in the workplace. Such behaviour becomes harassment if it is persisted in once it has been made clear that it is regarded as such even though the perpetrator claims to have been only flirting, joking or intending to be friendly. If s/he is in any doubt as to whether such behaviour is acceptable to the recipient, s/he should ask or desist.

7. It should be noted that sexual harassment does not necessarily have to be 'sexual' in nature in the sense of being an attempt to initiate sexual relations. It is sufficient that the conduct is 'sex-based'. Therefore any behaviour which ridicules, denigrates or abuses an employee because of his or her sex is harassment.

8. Whilst it is not possible to give an exhaustive list of every type of behaviour covered by this Policy, we list below some more common examples:

- Physical conduct of a sexual nature: any unwanted physical contact including unnecessary touching, patting, pinching or brushing up against another employee's body, placing hands on parts of the body, assault, coercing sexual intercourse.
- Verbal conduct of a sexual or racial nature: unwelcome sexual advances, propositions or pressure for sexual activity, intrusion by pestering including continued suggestions for social activity outside the workplace after it has been made clear that such suggestions are unwelcome, offensive flirtations, suggestive remarks, innuendoes or lewd comments, slander or malicious gossip, the singing of sectarian songs or songs of a derogatory and/or offensive nature.
- Non-verbal conduct of a sexual or racial nature: the display of pornographic or sexually suggestive pictures, objects or written materials including pin-ups and 'girlie' or 'Page 3' pictures, leering, whistling or making sexually suggestive gestures, organising or condoning kiss-o-grams or strip-o-grams either at work or in a public place where other work colleagues are present, graffiti, flags, bunting or emblems representing a group which are known to be against a sector of the community, e.g. the National Front.
- Sex-based or racially abusive conduct: conduct which denigrates or ridicules or is intimidatory or physically abusive to an employee because of his or her sex or race such as derogatory or degrading abuse or insults which are gender-related or of a racial nature and offensive or highly personal comments about dress or appearance or physique, hygiene, etc.

9. Harassment is not only unwanted physical contact, assault or propositions. It includes suggestive remarks or gestures, pin-ups, graffiti, offensive comments, jokes and banter based on race, religion, sex or other personal characteristics. None of this is part of a culture in which all staff and groups of staff are treated with dignity and respect.

PRECEDENT 8R: Duty to report wrongdoing

1. Due to the nature of our business it is expected that you will act with due diligence and utmost honesty at all times. Should any matters of concern come to your attention,

you must report them immediately to your supervising officer or Head of Department or a member of Human Resources.

2. The Company sees it as your duty to report any acts of misconduct, dishonesty, breach of company rules or breach of any of the rules of the relevant regulatory bodies committed, contemplated or discussed by any other member of staff or any other third party. Please note that any failure to do so on your part may be regarded as serious or gross misconduct depending on the circumstances.

3. The Company will guarantee that whatever you report will be treated with the utmost confidentiality as far as this is practicable. You are also assured that no discriminatory or retaliatory action will be taken against you in any case where you make such reports to management neither shall any adverse action of any kind be taken against you now or in the future.

4. The Company is a member of or regulated by [specify] and you are therefore required as a condition of your employment to observe and comply carefully and diligently with all the Rules as laid down by [specify] from time to time.

5. Since you act in an authorised capacity on behalf of the Company you must ensure that at all times you are fully complying with all the relevant Regulatory Body Rules. Failure to do so may result in legal action being taken against either the Company or you personally [and disqualification from trading].

6. You are required to co-operate fully with all directions and reasonable requests properly made by or on behalf of the Company or [specify]. This may include but is not limited to a requirement that you make yourself readily available for and truthfully answer all questions put to you in the course of any Inspection, Investigation, Summary Process or Proceeding of any Appeal Tribunal or any other legal proceedings.

7. Breach of the above undertakings will be a matter of serious misconduct which may entitle the Company in any case it deems fit to dismiss with or without notice or payment in lieu.

PRECEDENT 8S: Requirement to work on Saturdays

TO ALL STAFF

[Date]

RE: Requirement to work 3 pm to 11 pm on Saturdays

1. Following all our consultations and discussions, this letter informs you that as at [date four weeks hence] the Depot will remain open until 11 pm and thus you will be rostered once a month to work on Saturdays 3 pm to 11 pm.

2. I would point out that this decision has not been taken lightly. [name of client] for whom this depot is solely dedicated requires extremely high-quality service. This is why our Company has been awarded the contract to store and transport their goods. It is now absolutely essential that the Depot remains open until 11 pm on every Saturday so that we can deliver the goods on time and according to the terms of our contract with [client].

3. Your terms and conditions of employment which you signed willingly states that you understood this commitment. Your contract states: 'In entering into employment with the Company, you are, therefore, giving a commitment to change hours of work or days of duty or to work additional hours as may be necessary to ensure a service is provided'.

4. This quite clearly gives the Company the right to require you to change your hours when the business requires this.

5. In addition, it was clearly pointed out to you at your interview that you would be required to work different shift hours and it was only upon your express agreement to this important commitment that you were offered the job. Your induction also referred to the importance of your commitment to flexible working hours and shifts.

6. May I point out to you that your rota will only require you to work from 3 pm to 11 pm one Saturday in four, i.e. 12 times a year. As with any shift, if you foresee any difficulty because of an important family commitment, you are free either to arrange an exchange of shift with any of your colleagues and then to inform management; alternatively you may see your line manager in order to sort out any problems in advance. Inevitably any 'one-off' difficulties will normally be resolved well in advance.

7. We believe that we have been very reasonable in giving you sufficient notice of our intention to enforce the term of your contract as our discussions with you and your trade union representatives on this subject commenced on [date].

8. Please be advised that if you fail to honour your contractual commitment and refuse to accept your obligation to work these changed shift hours on Saturdays, we will have no option but to treat your conduct as a flagrant breach of contract and as such formally warn you through the disciplinary procedure which may eventually lead to your dismissal. We sincerely hope that it does not come to this.

9. Please will you sign both copies of the following undertaking and return one copy to your line manager before [date]. We look forward to hearing from you before this date.

10. May we also point out that if you refuse to sign the undertaking below you will be regarded by the Company as breaching your duty to co-operate with management. As you will be continuing to refuse to accept this lawful instruction, you will be counselled before being sent home without pay as such conduct will amount to a fundamental breach of contract. The Company does not and will not accept part performance of your contract of employment.

11. We look forward to receiving your signed agreement.

I hereby accept and undertake to honour the terms of my contract and freely and willingly recognise that I agreed at the outset of my employment to work flexible hours as reasonably requested by management for the proper functioning of the business and now agree to work the revised shift hours on Saturdays of 3 pm to 11 pm when rostered so to do.

Signed .... Date ....

[employee]

PRECEDENT 8T: Checklist for Christmas parties

Christmas in the workplace: 10 common employer queries

Workplace Christmas parties bring up issues of conduct and discrimination. For example, employees may misbehave, or fail to turn up the next day.

Holiday and overtime issues also commonly arise at this time. Annual leave requests can be concentrated around the same days, while overtime requirements can conflict with employees' personal plans.

1. *What should employers do to prepare for the festive season?*

Christmas 2018 for employers

Managers should familiarise themselves with their employer's policy on Christmas parties or work-related social events.

Additionally, employers should consider the option of issuing a statement to employees in advance of a Christmas party or similar work-related event.

This statement can remind employees of conduct matters, including the dangers of excess alcohol consumption, and behaviours that could be viewed as harassment.

2. *Do employers really need a policy on workplace social events?*

Yes. Employers should maintain a policy because they have a duty of care towards staff, and as a matter of good practice.

The Equality Act 2010 makes employers liable for acts of discrimination, harassment and victimisation carried out by their employees in the course of employment, unless they can show that they took reasonable steps to prevent such acts.

3. *Is an employer responsible for what happens at a Christmas party?*

It is prudent to assume that an employer will be liable. Legislation refers to the term 'in the course of employment'.

In *Chief Constable of the Lincolnshire Police* v. *Stubbs* [1999] IRLR 81, a police officer complained of sexual harassment by work colleagues in a pub outside working hours.

The Employment Appeal Tribunal held that social events away from the police station involving officers from work either immediately after work, or for an organised leaving party, fell within the remit of 'course of employment'.

4. *Can employees be disciplined for misconduct after a Christmas party?*

Yes, if the incident is sufficiently closely connected to work to have had an impact on the working situation.

In *Gimson* v. *Display By Design Ltd* (ET/1900336/2012) the employer was found to have fairly dismissed an employee for a brawl after the end of a Christmas party.

5. *What should an employer do where more than one employee is involved in the same incident?*

Where the circumstances are truly parallel, employees must generally be treated the same.

Establishing 'who is to blame', however, can be difficult where memories are blurred by alcohol and the evidence is unclear.

In *Westlake* v. *ZSL London Zoo* (ET/2201118/2015), two zoo keepers got into a fight at London Zoo's Christmas party as a result of which Ms Westlake was dismissed and the other zoo keeper, Ms Sanders, was issued with a final written warning.

Given the lack of clear evidence as to who started the fight, the Employment Tribunal found Ms Westlake's dismissal to be unfair.

The tribunal observed that the employer could have legitimately dismissed them both, or issued both with final written warnings.

6. *Can employers compel their employees to work overtime in the run-up to Christmas?*

If the contract of employment includes a clause requiring an employee to work overtime when required, then it will generally be reasonable to take disciplinary action if an employee refuses to do so.

In *Edwards v. Bramble Foods Ltd* (ET/20601556/2015), an employee of a small food company was dismissed for gross misconduct, having refused to work overtime during the company's busiest period, despite a clause in her contract requiring her to work extra hours when required.

An Employment Tribunal found the dismissal to be fair and within the 'range of reasonable responses', not least because the consequences for the employer's business of not dismissing her could have been 'disastrous'.

7. *Can an employee insist on taking holidays during the Christmas period?*

No. In the absence of an agreement to the contrary, workers must give notice equal to twice the length of the holiday that they wish to take.

The employer can then give counter notice requiring that the leave not be taken, so long as this counter notice is equivalent to the length of the holiday requested, and the worker is not prevented from taking the leave to which he or she is entitled in that holiday year.

Where an employee has accrued untaken leave and gives reasonable notice to the employer to take the leave, the employer must have valid business reasons for refusing the employee's request to take leave.

Where an employee insists on taking leave and does so without approval, the employer should approach the issue sensibly and be careful not to impose a disproportionate penalty on the employee.

In *Stott v. Next Retail Ltd* (ET/2100960/11), an employee who was dismissed for failing to attend work without permission on Christmas Eve was found to have been unfairly dismissed by an Employment Tribunal.

8. *What if an employee comes to work late or not at all the day after the Christmas party?*

An employer can make deductions from employees' pay if they turn up for work late the morning after the company Christmas party as long as the right to make deductions from wages for unauthorised absence is reserved in the employment contract.

If disciplinary action is to be taken for lateness or non-attendance after the Christmas party, employers should ensure that staff are informed that this is a possibility in the disciplinary policy.

Where an employee does not attend due to illness, the employer should follow its attendance management policy and procedures.

Offering an attendance allowance to encourage workers not to take time off sick, as the retailer Argos has reportedly done in its distribution centres, may appear attractive.

However, it carries the serious risk of an indirect disability discrimination complaint that may be difficult to justify.

9. *Can employers require employees to take annual leave during the Christmas period?*

For those businesses that close over the Christmas period, employers will need to put in place arrangements requiring workers to take annual leave at that time.

Provided that there is no agreement to the contrary, employers can allocate leave to a particular time.

An employer needs to give notice that is at least double the period of leave that the employee is required to take although, in practice, employers should build the requirement into their holiday policy.

10. *What if travel disruption delays an employee returning to work following the Christmas break?*

This can be a common issue, particularly given planned strike action on rail services over the Christmas period.

While there is no obligation to pay employees who fail to attend work due to public transport issues, many employers will want to offer flexibility and alternative options.

For example, if the role is suitable, technology may allow the employee to work from home or from another location.

Alternatively, the employer could require the employee to make up the time later or take the time as paid annual leave.

[This article was originally written for *Personnel Today* by Ashok Kanani on 11 December 2015. It was updated by Laura Merrylees on 13 December 2016. With grateful thanks for permission to reproduce this article.]

9

Disciplinary and performance procedures

9.1 Disciplinary procedures: Code and Guidance

The ACAS Code of Practice 2015 sets out recommendations about disciplinary and grievance procedures, and provides that a 25 per cent adjustment in compensation can be made for a failure by either party to follow the Code.

Accompanying the Code is a comprehensive Guide (updated in 2016) on issues such as what employers should do when employees fail to attend hearings, how to deal with a grievance raised during a disciplinary process and the right to be accompanied during a disciplinary or grievance hearing.

The Code specifically excludes redundancy dismissals and dismissals when a fixed-term contract comes to an end and is not renewed.

References to these matters can be found in the model disciplinary procedure at **Precedent 9R**, together with matters such as the right to be represented by a lawyer and recording the hearings.

9.2 Conduct issues

The basic elements of many company procedures are as follows.

First two years of employment

Some employers exclude the operation of their disciplinary procedure for the first two years of employment (one year, 11 months and three weeks) and reserve the right to exclude the warning stages and in some cases the hearing and appeal stage. See **Precedent 9A**.

Contractual or not?

If the procedure forms part of the contract, then even without two years' service a failure to follow the disciplinary procedure may give rise to a breach of contract claim. Some employers opt therefore to keep the disciplinary and grievance procedures (but not the rules) non-contractual.

Preamble

A general preamble normally concerns the purposes of the procedure: to set down standards of behaviour and to help employees to reach and maintain standards of conduct and performance and to stop them repeating the misconduct which could lead to dismissal.

9.3 Interviews of concern/alternative less serious procedure

Some employers also hold 'interviews of concern' or 'meetings without coffee' that are outside the disciplinary procedure but which are designed to advise and counsel employees where there are initial performance or conduct concerns. This meeting does not form any part of the disciplinary procedure but can remain on file as a record.

Other employers have decided to adopt alternative procedures to the formal disciplinary procedure in appropriate cases. These normally aim at resolving relatively minor performance and conduct issues by negotiation and agreement. If an employer goes down this route then it will not be held to be fair to change the rules or to introduce another rule or an additional sanction that had not been discussed beforehand and agreed with the individual.

If employers use the more informal procedure it is normally regarded as unfair to use the same facts to proceed to the formal disciplinary procedure and treat what had previously been regarded as less serious as sufficient to dismiss for gross misconduct (so held the Court of Appeal in *Sarkar* v. *West London Mental Health NHS Trust* [2010] IRLR 508).

In this case a Fair Blame Policy (FBP) was being trialled by the Trust in question. The FBP was part of the disciplinary policy and could apply sanctions up to the level of a first written warning. It also contained provision for the issue to be dealt with under the formal policy if it became apparent, during or after a preliminary investigation, that the alleged misconduct was more serious than originally envisaged.

In this case, Dr Sarkar, a psychiatrist working at Broadmoor, against whom allegations of bullying and harassing behaviour had been made, was taken through the FBP after he had acted inappropriately on two further occasions following his agreement to cease clinical work and move to a different workplace.

The Trust decided that the FBP would apply and, at a final meeting, the action agreed included a formal written warning, continued consultation with the occupational health department and the claimant's relocation within the Trust to a different directorate. However, at the end of that meeting, the Trust's medical director announced that she would report the claimant to the General Medical Council. This had never previously been discussed and was unacceptable to the claimant so he withdrew from the FBP and was placed under the normal disciplinary procedure instead. The outcome was his summary dismissal for repeated incidents of unacceptable behaviour and bullying and harassment, which the Trust concluded amounted to gross misconduct.

The Court of Appeal held that the Employment Tribunal was correct in finding the dismissal unfair.

In its view, the tribunal had clearly been entitled to consider that it was inconsistent of the Trust to first agree with Dr Sarkar the use of the FBP, indicating that it regarded the allegations of misconduct to be relatively minor and not warranting dismissal, and then to dismiss him for gross misconduct based on the same matters. This was a factor which it was proper for the tribunal to consider when applying the 'range of reasonable responses' test.

Furthermore, the Court of Appeal held that the tribunal had been entitled to accept the evidence of the chair of the dismissing panel that these incidents were 'relatively minor' and that the late introduction of the condition that the claimant be reported to the General Medical Council was the reason why the FBP terminated.

9.4 Suspension

The ACAS Code of Practice 2015 (para.8) and the Guide, pages 17 and 18, recognise that employers may need to suspend an employee during an investigation for a short period, which should be kept under review.

It is essential to conduct a preliminary check of the facts before making any decision to suspend an employee.

In *Aziz* v. *Crown Prosecution Service* [2007] ICR 153 (CA), Ms Aziz successfully claimed racial discrimination when she was suspended before the employer had even made a cursory investigation or had even *prima facie* evidence of her wrongdoing.

In the *Aziz* case the Court of Appeal held that:

> In my view it is important (both under the code and as a requirement of fairness and good employment practice) that disciplinary proceedings should not be initiated unless the suspicion of misconduct is based on reasonable grounds.
>
> This was plainly a case in which such preliminary enquiries were necessary. The only information available to Mr Cowgill and Mrs Ashton was a hearsay report that offensive words had been spoken and that a racial disturbance had taken place. It was plainly incumbent on either Mr Cowgill or Mrs Ashton to make preliminary enquiries to ascertain what offensive words had allegedly been spoken to whom and whether a disturbance had in fact taken place, apparently as a result. It must have been easy enough to find out whether there had been a disturbance.
>
> In fact there had not. A wholly hearsay and unparticularised account emanating from unnamed complainants and alleging unspecified offensive words allegedly giving rise to a disturbance (the time and place of which are not known) could not be said to give rise to a reasonable suspicion of gross misconduct.
>
> That is particularly so when the allegedly offensive words were said to relate to sensitive political issues, to have been uttered by a Muslim woman at a time (shortly after 11th September 2001) and in a place (Bradford) of high racial tension.
>
> I share the view of the Employment Tribunal that such an allegation cried out for preliminary enquiries to be made. They were required as a matter of fairness and reasonableness, good employment practice and also by the CPS disciplinary code.

The ACAS Code 2015 and Guide expressly state that suspension is a neutral act and that it does not imply guilt and is not a form of discipline.

However, it has been disputed by Sedley LJ in *Mezey* v. *South West London and St George's Mental Health NHS Trust* [2007] EWCA Civ 106 whether suspension is a 'neutral act' where the individual is a professional person (in this case a consultant psychiatrist) – whilst not disputing that it can be done.

He stated that he disagreed with the proposition that suspension is (paras.11–12):

> 'a neutral act preserving the employment relationship' ... at least in relation to the employment of a qualified professional in a function which is as much a vocation as a job. Suspension changes the status quo from work to no work, and it inevitably casts a shadow over the employee's competence. Of course this does not mean that it cannot be done, but it is not a neutral act.

Even without an express power to suspend, employers have an implied right to suspend on 'reasonable grounds' (*McClory* v. *The Post Office* [1993] IRLR 159).

Suspension would be regarded as reasonable where the employer has a genuine fear that evidence has been or may be tampered with, that the investigation may be compromised, that a witness may be pressurised into falsifying their evidence or refusing to give evidence or that personal safety of individuals or the security of property may be placed at risk. In other cases it may be appropriate to suspend the employees who were on shift or present when a fatal accident has occurred either to safeguard those employees' mental health, to protect them from making another serious mistake or to protect the integrity of the investigation.

Employers must be careful about when they decide to suspend staff during a disciplinary investigation despite having this express power to do so. Employers are advised to have a meeting with senior management recording the reasons for the need to suspend.

In *Gogay* v. *Hertfordshire County Council* [2000] IRLR 703, the disciplinary charges were wrongly described, there was no *prima facie* evidence of the allegation and the suspension went on for many months. The health of Mrs Gogay was badly damaged because of this lengthy and unnecessary suspension and she succeeded in her claim for damages for personal injuries as a result.

It is essential to prepare a statement and to inform telephonists, reception staff, etc. as to why the individual is not at work or answering work calls.

An 'out of office' email message should be switched on with a neutral message and a neutral message should be communicated to staff and clients, etc.

For the suspended employee, they should receive a letter informing them of the following:

- the anticipated length of suspension;
- their rights and obligations during suspension;
- an explanation not to report to work or to contact staff or clients or represent themselves as acting for the company;
- a point of contact for the suspended employee;
- that suspension is not an indication of guilt or a disciplinary sanction.

Purpose of and pay during suspension

It is important for the contract to spell out what level of pay will be made during any period of suspension. In *McClory* v. *The Post Office* (see above) the High Court confirmed that even where there is a contractual entitlement to overtime, etc. the employer was entitled to pay basic salary only during the period of suspension despite the fact that the employees would have worked and earned overtime but for the suspension. Here the employer reserved the following right: 'in the event of misconduct or where there is a need for enquiries to be made into alleged misconduct you may be suspended from your employment either with or without pay'.

The standard wording is as set out in **Precedent 9B**.

The suspension letter should spell out the reasons for the suspension, the timetable and the conditions for the suspension, e.g. prohibiting the individual from attending work; from contacting witnesses save through HR; whether the individual will be asked to co-operate in the investigation, etc.

See **Precedent 9C** for such a letter.

9.5 Confidentiality

It is important to ensure that the individual who is the subject of the investigation understands and commits to their duty of confidentiality during the disciplinary process.

Precedent 9D is a model letter/undertaking that all participants in disciplinary and grievance procedures should be asked to sign.

Allegations of breach of confidentiality

It is not uncommon for suspended employees to become very upset and allege that their employer has been less than discreet in keeping the details of the disciplinary issues confidential. See **Precedent 9E** for a response to such an allegation.

9.6 Investigations

The need to conduct a thorough investigation into any alleged misconduct is critical, as the third limb of the *BHS* v. *Burchell* test (see *BHS* v. *Burchell* [1978] IRLR 379 (EAT)) provides that the employer 'must have carried out as much investigation into the matter as was reasonable in all the circumstances of the case'.

The person conducting the investigation should not be the same person who makes the disciplinary decision. The latter cannot be 'prosecutor, judge and jury' (*Slater* v. *Leicestershire Health Authority* [1989] IRLR 16 and *Sartor* v. *P&O European Ferries* [1992] IRLR 271; see also ACAS Code of Practice 2015, paragraph 6).

The disciplinary investigation usually consists of the following:

1. Taking statements from any eyewitnesses or contemporaneous witnesses as soon as possible so memories do not fade.
2. Taking an initial statement from the individual suspected of the offence, making it clear that no negative inference will be drawn if the individual declines the invitation to attend an investigation interview. Whilst there is no statutory right to have a representative present, it may be good practice to allow a representative to be present to ensure fair play.
3. In all cases the person(s) conducting the investigation should be experienced. They should ask open questions and keep careful notes of the questions and answers and should ask supplementary questions as they arise. They should try to test the answers with additional questions and should listen.
4. In some cases it may be advisable to record the interview and have the transcript typed. In other cases it may be sensible to ask the individual to write, in their own words, what they saw and heard and then sign and date the statement. If you are a lawyer acting on behalf of an employer, beware of being asked by your client to take the witness's statement, i.e. to write it for the witness and then ask them to sign it. In *Alex Lawrie Factors Ltd* v. *Morgan, Morgan and Turner, The Times*, 18 August 1999, CA, the court warned about 'the grave danger of lawyers putting their sophisticated legal arguments into a witness' mouth in affidavit evidence, to which the witness would not be able to speak if cross-examined'.
5. When the investigation is complete, a summary report containing the evidence and attaching documentation, etc. should be compiled but it should be noted that it is not the duty of the investigator to make recommendations about the case or the outcome. That task can only be done by the person(s) conducting the disciplinary hearing and assessing the credibility of the witnesses for themselves. The investigator's report should sum up the evidence and produce the complete witness statements as appendices.
6. If witnesses are too frightened to be identified to the alleged perpetrator and are too frightened to attend the disciplinary hearing, then the person(s) conducting the hearing should hear their evidence face to face, in the absence of the alleged perpetrator, so that their credibility can be assessed. Since it will often be one person's word against another's, it will be very important for the person making the decision in the case to be able to determine the credibility of the witnesses as well as that of the alleged offender.

Employers should always send to the employee concerned all the relevant documents, including the policies it is alleged have been breached, the specific 'charges' and all supporting documentation, well in advance of the hearing.

Collecting witness evidence

Normally the following process is followed for the collection of evidence for a serious offence constituting gross misconduct.

1. *The order of collecting evidence.* The order in which you collect evidence is important, although how you investigate and collect evidence will depend on the individual circumstances of your case.
2. *The stages of collecting evidence* are:
    (a) *Obtaining evidence from witnesses of fact.* If you are investigating an incident, you should identify and obtain evidence from the 'witnesses of fact' (i.e. those able to give factual information about what actually occurred, usual work systems and relevant employment issues, etc.). This will normally be done by taking a statement.
    (b) *Identifying the causes of the incident/the facts of the issues.* Once you have obtained evidence from the witnesses of fact, you should then seek to identify the underlying causes of the suspected breach(es) by seeking further information. This may involve taking statements from people who hold more senior positions in the organisation under investigation who may not have witnessed the incident. You should avoid seeking information from people who you suspect may have committed an offence as an individual under the Health and Safety at Work etc. Act 1974 and/or regulations. The contents of written documents, assessments, procedures, policies, etc. may help to inform you as to who may, or may not, be at fault.
    (c) *Speaking to the alleged offender.* The final stage of the investigation will usually be to speak to those people suspected of having committed an offence.
3. Where a person is asked questions about their suspected involvement in a criminal offence, the questioning should always be in the form of a formal interview under caution. This will include interviewing a nominated representative of a company where the company is suspected of committing an offence.
4. It will usually be appropriate to conduct an interview under caution at the end of your investigation, although there may be rare cases where the interview should be conducted at an earlier stage.
5. You should not forget that, at any stage in your investigation, you may need to go back to witnesses you interviewed earlier and put to them documents or comments that you have received subsequently.
6. *Using interview information.* Information obtained in the course of an interview under caution (i.e. following the rules of the Police and Criminal Evidence Act 1984 (PACE)) is only admissible as evidence against the interviewee in the case of an individual, or the company in the case where a representative of the company is interviewed.
7. Therefore, if a person whom you interviewed under caution ceases to be under suspicion and you wish to rely on that person's evidence, you will

need to go back and obtain the information in an admissible form, i.e. a statement under the Criminal Justice Act 1967, s.9.
8. Alternatively, you may draft a statement from the content of the interview under caution and then ask the individual to sign the statement.
9. In either case you should make it clear to witnesses that they can, under these circumstances, add to their statements if they wish – they are not restricted to what they said when interviewed under caution.

Checklist for investigations

In cases of complaints of sex or race discrimination or harassment or investigations into misconduct, the following checklist is useful.

1. The person investigating should be experienced in undertaking investigations.
2. Keep an open mind and go into the investigation without any pre-judgements.
3. Decide on a strategy and plan the investigation, e.g. how much time will it take, how many days will it last, who will assist, who will be interviewed, who will be interviewed first and last, will it be recorded or will notes be taken and witness statements drawn up.
4. Go through the complaints/grievances and number them and prioritise the most important ones and then check with the complainant that they are happy with your priority.
5. Ask the complainant in writing to assist you by telling you who you should interview and what documents you should look at.
6. Everyone, including the complainant, should sign a confidentiality agreement (see below).
7. Interview the complainant first and take very careful and detailed notes. Then draft a statement which must be signed and dated as accurate and truthful by the complainant, or allow the complainant to write everything down and sign and date it.
8. Time and date each interview.
9. Take verbatim notes.
10. Prepare some standard questions in advance and write them down and ask them of all witnesses.
11. Ask open questions.
12. Ask if interviewees have anything that they would wish to add.
13. Be aware of body language, etc.
14. Check the HR files of the complainant, alleged wrongdoer and witnesses.
15. Check references and CVs and application forms, job descriptions, etc.
16. Do not make any assumptions or put words into the witnesses' mouths.
17. Get witnesses to sign and date their statements.
18. Ascertain whether witnesses are happy to attend on their own for this interview or whether they want someone to attend with them.
19. The alleged harasser or person against whom the complaint has been

made should be the last person interviewed, and should be told/shown exactly what has been said against and about them.
20. Review the witness statements with someone to assist and bounce off ideas.
21. Weigh the evidence and then draft a 'pros' and 'cons' list – for and against the grievance/complaint and why in your opinion some people can be believed and others not.
22. Draft your report and ask someone to review your description of the facts of the grievance, your evaluation of the evidence and your conclusion.
23. Ask the complainant for their views on your draft report.
24. Then make the decision and interview both parties on a confidential basis to disclose the result/outcome and give both a confidential copy of your report.
25. It is important that the person who has interviewed and assessed the credibility of witnesses makes the decision, as there is often a conflict of evidence of fact.

Interviewing witnesses on a non-identifiable basis; misconduct cases

If witnesses are afraid to be identified (e.g. in cases where physical reprisal is likely) then take the following steps (according to *Linfood Cash and Carry Ltd* v. *Thomson Greenwell & Bell* [1989] IRLR 235):

1. Written statements should be taken with full details and names. Later on it may be important to erase names, etc.
2. Statements must include:
   (a) date, time and place of each observation or incident;
   (b) the opportunity and ability to observe clearly and accurately;
   (c) the circumstantial evidence such as knowledge of a system or arrangement or the reason for the presence of the informer and why certain small details are memorable;
   (d) whether the informant has suffered at the hands of the accused or has any other reason to fabricate, whether from personal grudge or any other reason.
3. Further investigations can then take place to see whether or not to rely on the informant's evidence and to seek corroboration (which is clearly advisable).
4. Tactful inquiries should be made into the character and background of the informant or any other information which may tend to add or detract from the value of the information.
5. If the employer is satisfied that the informant has a genuine fear then a decision will have to be made as to whether or not to continue with the disciplinary proceedings.
6. At each stage of the procedure, a member of management should

interview the informant and satisfy themselves what weight ought to be given to that person's evidence.
7. The written statement of the informant – if necessary with omissions to avoid identification – should be made available to the employee and their representative.
8. If the employee or their representative raise any particular and relevant issues which should be put to the informant, then management should adjourn and make further inquiries.
9. Full and careful notes of the disciplinary hearing should be taken.
10. Although not peculiar to cases where informants have precipitated the initiation of an investigation, if evidence from an investigating officer is to be taken at the hearing it should where possible be in written form.

Investigating grievances and disciplinary cases

ACAS has published a useful guide on 'Conducting Workplace Investigations', October 2015. It should be essential reading for anyone conducting a grievance or disciplinary investigation.

For example, when drafting a grievance investigation report it is essential to summarise the facts and then to make findings of fact, draw inferences of discrimination from the primary facts where appropriate, and draw conclusions from omissions or contradictions in the evidence. In most cases there will not be a 'silver bullet' as employment judge Joanna Wade has put it. Therefore inferences of discrimination may be drawn from either actual or hypothetical comparators as to how they have or would have been treated (where there are no material differences between the circumstances – s.23 of the Equality Act 2010).

9.7 Whistleblowing

It is common for employers to have 'whistleblowing policies' so that staff and third parties have a separate and confidential procedure to draw to the employer's attention suspicions of malpractice, breach of regulatory or health and safety rules, etc.

Precedent 11G is an example of such a policy.

9.8 Investigating dishonesty

In cases of suspected dishonesty it is common for the employer to carry out covert investigations before making the suspicions known to the staff who may be concerned. It is quite common for employees to be suspended from work (on pay) whilst an investigation into dishonesty is undertaken.

Precedent 9G is a checklist for such cases.

Right to be accompanied

Section 10 of the Employment Relations Act 1999 allows for 'a worker' to be accompanied to a 'disciplinary or grievance hearing' by a 'single companion' who may either be a fellow worker or a trade union representative. A disciplinary hearing is defined as a hearing which could result in:

(a) the administration of a formal warning;
(b) the taking of some other action; or
(c) the confirmation of a warning issued or some other action taken.

'Worker' is defined in s.13 of the Employment Relations Act 1999 and includes anyone who performs work personally for someone else, but is not genuinely self-employed, as well as agency workers and home workers, workers in Parliament and Crown employees other than members of the armed forces. There are no exclusions for part-time or casual workers, those on short-term contracts, or for individuals who work overseas (subject to any jurisdictional rules).

The ACAS Code of Practice 2015 makes it clear that the companion can be anyone of the employee's choice falling into the categories set out in s.10.

In *Toal* v. *GB Oils Ltd* UKEAT/0569/12/LA the EAT ruled that:

> 14. The companion is to be chosen by the worker, not by the employer, but the companion must come from within one of the three categories of individuals identified in subsection 3. That is to say, (1) he must be employed by a trade union (in other words a paid official), or (2) an unpaid official who is certified by the union or (3) a fellow worker.

The only discretion that an employer has to 'veto' the companion is with regard to the identity or class of companion, e.g. a member of HR or the Legal Department would be conflicted or the employee's own line manager or a relative who works at the Company.

The EAT held that:

> It is possible to conceive of circumstances in which an employer might wish to interfere with the exercise of that right without proper reason in a manner that would put the worker at a disadvantage. Consequently, Parliament has, in our view, legislated for the choice to be that of the worker, subject only to the safeguards set out in subsection 3 as to the identity or the class of person who might be available to be a companion.

9.9 Legal representation

Following the cases of *Kulkarni* v. *Milton Keynes Hospital NHS Trust* [2009] IRLR 829, CA and *R (on the application of G)* v. *X School Governors & Y City Council (Interested Party)* [2010] IRLR 222, CA, it has been held that Article 6 of the European Convention on Human Rights gives individuals the right to legal representation in internal disciplinary proceedings where the decision in the internal disciplinary proceedings is likely to have 'a substantial influence or effect' on the claimant's civil right to practise their profession – in the *Kulkarni* case that of a doctor and in the latter case that of a teacher.

Some employers choose to reserve the right to have a lawyer present at gross misconduct and grievance hearings particularly where harassment or discrimination has been alleged. In such cases it is important for an employer to include such a provision in its disciplinary procedure with the corresponding right for the employee to bring a lawyer if they so wish. The same rules for lawyers apply as for ordinary representatives.

In other cases, e.g. where the worker is young and inexperienced and they have asked for a parent to attend a disciplinary hearing with them, employers may consider such a request sympathetically.

Additional wording has been added to the model disciplinary procedure at **Precedent 9R**.

9.10 Ordinary right to be accompanied

The general right to be accompanied applies where a worker is invited to a 'disciplinary hearing' and for these purposes a 'disciplinary hearing' is one which could result in a formal warning, the taking of some other action, or the confirmation of a warning issued or some other action taken (Employment Relations Act 1999, s.13(4)).

The 2015 ACAS Code of Practice, paragraph 17, confirms that the representative may address the hearing to put and sum up the employee's case, respond on behalf of the employee to any views expressed at the meeting and confer with the employee during the hearing.

The representative does not have the right to answer questions on the employee's behalf, address the hearing if the employee does not wish the representative to do so, or prevent the employer from explaining its case.

9.11 Distinction between 'formal' and 'informal' warnings

The tribunals have made a clear distinction between hearings which result in informal warnings (i.e. do not form part of the employee's disciplinary record) and a warning, whatever it might be called, which does. In the latter case the worker has a right to be accompanied by a representative. Paragraph 13 of the 2015 Code of Practice sets out three different types of meetings where a representative should be permitted, i.e. where the disciplinary meeting could result in:

- a formal warning being issued; or
- the taking of some other disciplinary action; or
- the confirmation of a warning or some other disciplinary action (appeal hearings).

The distinction between an 'informal' and a 'formal' warning is that an informal warning merely indicates that formal disciplinary action will be taken in the future. A disciplinary warning becomes a 'formal warning' in terms of the Employment Relations Act 1999, s.13(4)(a) if it forms part of the employee's disciplinary record.

Similarly there is no right to be represented at an investigatory meeting because this will not result in disciplinary action. However, an employer may allow the individual to be represented nonetheless.

9.12 Other representative allowed?

It may be necessary to spell out that outside persons such as family members or solicitors may or may not be allowed to attend disciplinary hearings and if they are permitted, the circumstances in which this may be allowed is as a concession by management and not as any right.

This may be appropriate where a serious, potentially criminal, charge is in issue, the member of staff is particularly senior and would find some difficulty in finding someone to attend with them, or is very junior and young and therefore wants a family member present.

Suitable wording might be:

> In special or exceptional cases, e.g. where serious dishonesty or fraud or manslaughter or murder has been alleged, or where criminal charges may follow, or where the employee is very young and inexperienced, management may at its entire discretion allow a family member, friend or solicitor to attend the hearing. The same rules will apply to them as to any other representative, i.e. they will be permitted to ask questions but not answer them, sum up, etc.

Dealing with lawyers during employment

The Employment Tribunals have made it very clear. Employers have no need to communicate with external lawyers who write in on behalf of an existing employee.

In *McGivney v. Portman Mansions Management Ltd* [2009] UKEAT/0308/09 the EAT held that:

> We also find it was not reasonable to expect the Respondent to deal with him through his solicitors, given that the law says that the employer's obligations are to manage the employee, to meet with him and to discuss the matter with him.

9.13 Performance as well as conduct issues: cumulative procedure

Some employers combine both conduct and performance in one disciplinary procedure. If this is the case then this must be made very clear. It must also be clear that warnings are cumulative and that the next stage of the procedure may be instigated where an offence of an entirely different nature occurs.

In *Auguste Noel Ltd v. Curtis* [1990] IRLR 326, Mr Noel was dismissed for damaging company property (a performance issue) whilst two outstanding warnings were on his record for unacceptable absence and failure to complete company documentation. The EAT held that the employers were entitled to take into account two final warnings for completely different offences. See **Precedent 9H**.

Escalating the stages

Employers may wish to escalate the warning stages from a first written warning to dismissal and skip one or two stages depending upon the seriousness of the offence. For example, if an employee spends a lot of time talking to colleagues and talking on the telephone, the employee may be guilty of 'disrupting the work of others' which may warrant a warning. Contrast this with an employee who calls everyone away from their work, outside the building during working hours to incite them to take industrial action (where the employee is not an accredited shop steward). The latter is a much more serious offence and deserves a much tougher penalty, even for a first offence.

Paragraph 20 of the ACAS Code 2015 confirms that:

> If an employee's first misconduct or unsatisfactory performance is sufficiently serious, it may be appropriate to move directly to a final written warning. This might occur where the employee's actions have had, or are liable to have, a serious or harmful impact on the organisation.

Suitable wording might be as follows:

> Management reserves the right to initiate the procedure at any stage that it deems appropriate, e.g. if an offence of general misconduct is so flagrant or serious in its consequences, the employee may face summary dismissal, i.e. be taken to the final stage of the procedure in the first instance.

9.14 Warnings

Warnings should be distinguished in terms of oral, first written and final written warnings and it is recommended by the ACAS Code that time limits are placed on warnings so that a 'sword of Damocles' is not left hanging over the individual forever.

The time limits on warnings will be determined by the employer. Common time limits are six months for an oral warning and 12 months for a written warning, with the proviso that the warning may be extended if some improvement has been made but this improvement is not sufficient.

It is important for an employer to use the correct wording for the 'lapsing' of a disciplinary warning. The wording should be 'disregarded for disciplinary purposes save for the circumstances described below' or 'lapse for the purposes of progressing the stages of the disciplinary procedure'.

In some employers' disciplinary procedures, warnings are 'destroyed' or 'expunged' after the period of the warning. This means that previous disciplinary warnings cannot be used legitimately for any purpose.

However, spent or lapsed warnings can be used in certain circumstances, e.g. to determine an appropriate penalty in a later case.

An EAT case, *Stratford* v. *Auto Trail VR Ltd* UKEAT/0116/16, has endorsed this. Here the EAT held that it was fair to dismiss the employee for gross misconduct despite this penalty having been decided by reference to a history of expired warnings and future expectations. The EAT held that the claimant had been fairly dismissed.

Employers must go through a two-stage approach. First, they must determine whether on the balance of probabilities the employee committed the offence. If yes, then the second stage is to determine an appropriate penalty and in doing so the full history of the employee may be taken into account, including expired warnings and the benefit, if any, of giving the employee another chance. The EAT reviewed the decisions of the Inner House of the Court of Session in *Diosynth Ltd* v. *Thomson* and of the Court of Appeal in *Airbus Ltd* v. *Webb*.

These cases are authority for it being impermissible to have regard to a spent warning so as to elevate an offence from one which would not have attracted dismissal into one which does, but that once an employer finds an employee guilty of an offence of gross misconduct, the employee's disciplinary history (including expired warnings) can be taken into account when determining sanction.

In the *Stratford* case, the EAT upheld the tribunal's decision that the employer had behaved permissibly. Even if the previous warning has expired, the entire history of the employee – i.e. whether they have had an exemplary and disciplinary-free history or whether they have had a chequered history of previous warnings – fits with the words in s.98(4) of the Employment Rights Act 1996, i.e. whether the employer has acted reasonably 'in all the circumstances of the case'.

So, previous or lapsed warnings can be used for the following purposes as long as this is clearly spelt out in the procedure:

(a) in order to establish whether the employee has had an exemplary record in future cases of misconduct or gross misconduct;
(b) where the same or a similar offence has been committed in the past and the fact of the earlier warning will go towards the credibility of the employee's explanation on the future occasion and will help to determine an appropriate penalty;
(c) in redundancy selection criteria, the fact of previous disciplinary warnings may be used as one of the objective criteria for selection for redundancy.

Final written warning lapses and further issues come to light

If a final written warning has expired on a particular date, this will not be affected by the fact that the individual has not been notified that the warning has lapsed, as the date of lapse will be on the face of the warning letter itself.

However, it sometimes happens that other matters then come to the attention of the HR or line manager after the warning has lapsed but which took place before the warning lapsed. For example, a caretaker may have been disciplined for performance issues and have been given a final written warning. After the warning has lapsed it may come to light that there are still performance issues with the caretaker's work, such as work not having been carried out as requested, buildings left unlocked or a telephone log showing private calls on the company telephone to a mobile number.

It would be too late to dismiss the employee as the next stage under the final written warning, because that warning has lapsed. However, the employer could either give the employee another final written warning because they have not improved, or on this occasion go straight to dismissal with pay in lieu of notice on the grounds that they cannot be trusted any longer.

9.15 Extending the lifetime of a warning

There may be occasions when an employer may not wish to dismiss but may wish to give a more powerful penalty than a 12-month warning. One way to do this is to give an extended final warning or a final written warning which lasts forever, on the basis that the employer could have dismissed for the offence but wishes for a particular reason to give the employee a second chance. As long as this is clearly spelt out in the warning letter and the employee understands why this is being done, then it should be a reasonable penalty and one that could be defended if, following another instance of the same offence, the employer went straight to dismissal as the penalty.

A typical final written warning of this nature is set out at **Precedent 9K**.

9.16 Not fair to hold a hearing

There may be circumstances where it is unfair for an employer to hold any kind of a hearing whether for capability or conduct and in rare cases employees may seek injunctive relief to restrain their employer from holding any such disciplinary hearings. The drafting of the capability/disciplinary procedure must be sufficiently robust and wide to allow for invoking the procedure where there is a *prima facie* case of incompetence/error of judgement which in the circumstances should not have happened, carelessness, dereliction of duty, etc.

Any procedure which expresses a high threshold before invoking the procedure may not be helpful to an employer – as in the case below.

In *Mezey v. South West London & St George's Mental Health NHS Trust* [2010] IRLR 512, the Court of Appeal upheld an earlier injunction, restraining the hospital authorities from holding a hearing under the national disciplinary and capability procedure.

The capability procedure states that the procedure only applies where 'there has been a clear failure by an individual to deliver an adequate standard of management through lack of knowledge, ability or consistently poor performance'.

The investigation found that whilst the conduct of Dr Gillian Mezey, a well-known and respected psychiatrist, who had allowed a patient to go on unsupervised release during which he absconded and killed a stranger was inappropriate, it did not amount to serious professional incompetence. In order to invoke the procedure Dr Mezey must be shown to have lacked knowledge or ability or to have rendered consistently poor performance so as to have demonstrated her capability to practise was in question.

Given the findings of the investigatory panel, the threshold for invoking the capability procedure was not crossed. It was therefore a breach of contract to seek to invoke it and the Trust's actions were restrained by way of an injunction.

9.17 'Undertaking to behave'

In some cases it is not enough merely to warn the employee, as the warning is no guarantee that the individual will not repeat the conduct that gave rise to the warning.

In cases such as refusing to obey an instruction, breaching a particular rule or calling or taking part in unofficial industrial action, it is important for the individual to sign what some employers call an 'undertaking to behave'. The author was involved in a case of a local authority gardener who, after 24 years' service, refused to work in the rain. After much persuasion, counselling and three warnings, he faced dismissal. However, it was discovered (finally) that he was unhappy with his new and much younger supervisor because the gardener believed he was rude. The gardener agreed to sign an undertaking to behave in the future, which effectively saved his job.

Such an undertaking is set out at **Precedent 9M**.

9.18 Warnings and discipline where staff are abroad

Where staff are assigned abroad but retained under a UK contract and either work for an entirely different employer or for a joint venture, specific arrangements must be made in the event that disciplinary action has to be taken.

Some employers manage these situations in the following way:

1. The contract specifies that the UK disciplinary procedure will apply but local rules and regulations will also apply and these will be notified to the individual upon assignment (e.g. a no alcohol rule in Muslim countries).
2. The UK employer then delegates authority to the host employer to take disciplinary measures including suspension without pay and a first written warning.
3. If it is proposed to administer a final written warning, then prior consultation must take place and confirmation that it is appropriate must be given by the UK employer.

4. The right to be accompanied by a fellow worker applies to those workers abroad whose home base is in the UK. It is therefore important that the person to whom delegated authority has been given in the host country ensures that the worker is aware of these rights. A failure to do so could render the hearing unfair (see appeals at **9.21** below).

5. In any case where dismissal is contemplated, e.g. a case where a senior lawyer is found to have downloaded obscene materials from the internet and distributed them to colleagues, the individual will be flown back to the host country where the matter will be investigated and any appropriate disciplinary action taken.

9.19 Recording the hearing

It is advisable to include in the disciplinary and grievance procedure that the employer reserves the right to record a disciplinary hearing (and appeals and grievance hearings) so that an accurate record of the questions and answers and comments made is taken. In many Employment Tribunal hearings the parties spend an inordinate amount of time disputing what was said by each other. A recording with a transcript thereafter avoids this unnecessary argument. Either a double-headed professional tape recorder with sufficient microphones to allow for everyone in the room to be heard and recorded, or a modern digital voice recorder, which produces recordings that can be stored electronically, are recommended. A copy of one complete set of the recordings should be handed to the employee or their representative at the end of the hearing or the recording can be sent by email. Advance notice should be given of this procedure. See **Precedent 9N**.

Secret or covert recording

Covert recordings taken by an employee are admissible in Employment Tribunal proceedings albeit the Employment Tribunals have referred to them as 'distasteful'. The Employment Tribunal will require the claimant to provide transcripts. The Employment Tribunal will not sit through and listen to hours of recordings.

In *Punjab National Bank* v. *Gosain* UKEAT/0003/14/SM, Ms Gosain covertly recorded her grievance hearing in November 2012 and a disciplinary hearing in January 2013, both the hearings themselves and during the adjournments when she left the room. This was without the knowledge or consent of the respondent.

These records were disclosed in July 2013. The respondent objected to these recordings being admissible, but at a pre-hearing review the Tribunal Judge found that they were admissible. He held that:

> The fact that the recordings were made covertly was not, of itself, a ground for ruling them inadmissible…

That case considered the authorities of *Amwell View School Governors v. Dogherty* [2007] ICR 125, *Vaughan v. London Borough of Lewisham* [2013] UKEAT/0534/12 and *Williamson v. Chief Constable of Greater Manchester Police* UKEAT/0346/09, 9 March 2010.

In the case of *Dogherty* the claimant had made covert recordings of both the appeal hearing and the private deliberation session of the Council members who thought they were discussing the appeal, and their thoughts about it, in private. That part of the recording, i.e. the recording of the private deliberations, was held to be inadmissible on the basis that the members should be entitled to deliberate in private and speak freely among each other, and if they could be secretly recorded and for that recording to be admitted in future legal proceedings, they would be inhibited from so doing. In the case of *Vaughan* the employee sought to rely on covert recordings but refused to provide them prior to a pre-hearing review.

The EAT held that:

> the practice of making secret recordings in this way is, to put it no higher, very distasteful; but employees such as the Claimant will no doubt say that it is a necessary step in order to expose injustice. Perhaps they are sometimes right, but the Council has already made it clear that it will rely on the Claimant's conduct in making these covert recordings as illustrative of the way in which her conduct had destroyed any relationship of trust and confidence between her and it.
>
> ... The law is now established that covert recordings are not inadmissible simply because the way in which they were taken may be regarded as discreditable.

In *Gosain* the Court of Appeal held that *Dogherty* did not lay down any firm guidelines; rather, it made it clear that a balancing exercise had to be carried out.

It may be sensible for employers who do not record hearings and do not want their staff to record hearings to make this an express prohibition in the contract and staff handbook and to add the activity of covertly-recording hearings, meetings and conversations as potential gross misconduct.

Precedent 90 is a letter that could go out to all employees explaining about the consequences of secret recording. Employees have been known to make recordings of telephone calls as well as face-to-face discussions and meetings, so everyone should be very careful as to what they say.

9.20 If the employee refuses to attend or cannot attend the hearing

There may be good or less good reasons why an employee cannot attend a disciplinary or grievance hearing. Genuine illness, unexpected domestic crisis, unavailability of transport, and unavailability of the chosen representative are all reasonable reasons for seeking a postponement of a hearing.

It is questionable whether being signed off with 'stress' is a reasonable reason for postponement. A Fit Note recommends that the employee refrain from work because of an illness. It does not certify unfitness to attend a meeting (see below). In such a case it is essential to get an occupational health assessment as to the employee's fitness to attend a hearing.

The ACAS Code of Practice 2015 advises at para.25: 'Where an employee is persistently unable or unwilling to attend a disciplinary meeting without good cause the employer should make a decision on the evidence available.'

In the event that the employee has 'good cause' not to be able to attend, the employee should be asked to notify the employer as soon as possible and to give the reason for the non-attendance, preferably in advance of the meeting. The employer should then offer to reconvene the meeting. The author recommends that where transport difficulties are the problem, the employer should offer either to arrange transport by taxi or to ensure that someone collects the employee and returns them home.

However, if there are no good reasons for non-attendance, the employer should either inform the employee that the hearing will take place as originally scheduled and advise the employee of the consequences of their absence or inform the employee that a second hearing will take place and that any decisions will be taken in their absence if they continue to refuse to attend in person.

If the employee produces a Fit Note from a GP advising the employee to refrain from work because of 'stress', the employer has the right to offer options other than a face-to-face meeting or to ask the occupational health department for a report on whether the employee would be fit enough to attend the hearing. The employer has the right to ask for evidence as to whether this 'stress' was triggered by the fact of the disciplinary issues and to ask that the employee do one of six things:

(a) provide further medical evidence that the mental illness is so serious that the employee cannot attend a meeting as they would be unable to understand questions or give instructions to their representative;
(b) attend in person at the hearing either on the original date or on a reconvened date, either at the original venue or at another venue;
(c) send written representations for management to consider at the hearing;
(d) send their representative to speak on their behalf;
(e) send their representative to read a prepared submission from them and to speak on their behalf;
(f) be available on the telephone for a telephone conference.

There has been interesting guidance on when Employment Tribunals should adjourn tribunal hearings, and with suitable modifications this advice is equally applicable to internal disciplinary hearings. The approach in *Andreou* v. *Lord Chancellor's Department* [2002] IRLR 728 was that where a person is certified on medical grounds as 'not fit to attend work', that does not automatically mean that the individual is 'not fit to attend a tribunal hearing'. Hale LJ added in that case that where a person seeks an adjournment on the basis of 'stress' or 'anxiety', they should expect to produce details of the symptoms, causes and severity of their condition, i.e. that they are so confused that they are unable to understand the questions or give answers or give instructions to their representatives.

In *Teinaz* v. *London Borough of Wandsworth* [2002] IRLR 721, the Court of Appeal held that an adjournment must be granted if not to do so amounts to a denial of justice. Peter Gibson LJ set out the general principle (para.21):

> A litigant whose presence is needed for the fair trial of a case, but who is unable to be present through no fault of his own, will usually have to be granted an adjournment, however inconvenient it may be to the tribunal or court and to the other parties. That litigant's right to a fair trial under Article 6 of the European Convention on Human Rights demands nothing less. But the tribunal or court is entitled to be satisfied that the inability of the litigant to be present is genuine, and the onus is on the applicant for an adjournment to prove the need for such an adjournment.

If there is evidence that a litigant has been advised by a qualified person not to attend the hearing on medical grounds, and the employer has doubts whether the evidence is genuine or sufficient, the employer is entitled to ask that further evidence should be promptly provided.

9.21 Appeals

Problems may sometimes be experienced at appeal hearings because the employer is unclear what the appeal is intended to be. Most appeals are held to 'review' the original decision on the basis that the punishment is too harsh, e.g. because of a lack of consistency with other allegedly parallel cases or because new evidence has come to light which was not available at the hearing and is relevant.

The only occasion where it is legitimate for an employee to insist upon a complete rehearing of the case is where a *prima facie* case is made out of bias, prejudice or an unfair hearing: *Calvin* v. *Carr* [1980] AC 574, PC; *Whitbread plc* v. *Mills* [1988] IRLR 501 and *Dennis Wise* v. *Leicester City Football Club* [2004] All ER (D) 134.

The three grounds for appeal are therefore:

(a) unfair, biased or prejudiced hearing (e.g. the hearing attended by the author where the personnel officer said to the employee as she walked into the hearing 'I am so sorry that you are going to get the sack for this'!): this is the occasion for a complete rehearing;
(b) too harsh a penalty, e.g. through lack of consistency in similar cases; and
(c) new evidence that was not available at the time of the hearing and is relevant.

The effect of an appeal

If the appeals procedure is worded correctly then if the appeal is successful and the employee is reinstated or re-engaged, the notice of dismissal is automatically withdrawn.

In *Roberts* v. *West Coast Trains Ltd* [2004] IRLR 788 the disciplinary procedure stated that:

16.1 ... If charged with any disciplinary offence you will be given a hearing at which you can state your case. You may be suspended from work during investigations prior to the hearing [that happened in this case]. After the hearing, if the charge is proved, InterCity West Coast Limited may –

- dismiss you without notice; or
- suspend you from work for a defined period; and/or
- reduce you in grade; and/or
- transfer you to another post or location (which may reduce you in grade); and/or
- suspend or limit your travel facilities.

The EAT held that the terms of Mr Roberts' employment contract permitted West Coast Trains to impose such a sanction in place of the earlier decision to dismiss. Thus when his appeal was successful, his notice of dismissal was automatically revoked.

If an internal appeal is successful and it overturns the dismissal, then the employee's contract is brought back to life and they are automatically re-instated.

If an employee fails to appeal or withdraws their appeal or makes an application to an Employment Tribunal before the appeal has been determined, then it is likely the dismissal has ended the employment relationship.

9.22 Admissions of guilt

Some employers state in their policy for disciplinary procedures that employees who admit guilt at the start of an investigation will be given some credit for their admission, although it is rightly pointed out that this cannot of itself absolve the employee nor would it necessarily result in a lesser penalty than dismissal. However, if it was only through the employee's admissions that the misconduct came to light, this should be a major factor in determining an appropriate penalty and it should reduce the likelihood of any potential summary dismissal accordingly (*Ladbroke Racing Ltd* v. *Arnott* [1983] IRLR 154, Court of Session).

Admissions made without the correct caution or made under threat or with an inducement are inadmissible in criminal proceedings under the Police and Criminal Evidence Act 1984 and therefore the employee should not be concerned at admitting matters in a disciplinary hearing. Any such admissions would not be admissible in any criminal trial. See **Precedent 9P**.

9.23 Resigning before a gross misconduct hearing

Some employees decide to resign rather than be dismissed. If an employee resigns in such circumstances, it is not open to an employer to refuse to accept the resignation. However, the employer can in theory continue with the disciplinary hearing, invite the ex-employee to attend and then write a determination that had the employee not chosen to resign the employee would have been dismissed for gross misconduct.

This may then be reflected in any employment reference (*Bartholomew* v. *London Borough of Hackney* [1999] IRLR 246).

9.24 Raising a grievance during a disciplinary process

In some cases employees raise a grievance during a disciplinary process which impacts upon the outcome or upon the integrity of one of the managers involved. Employees should not invoke the grievance procedure as a means of interrupting any disciplinary process. If a genuine grievance is raised which throws doubt on the credibility of the disciplinary issues or could threaten the integrity of the procedure, management should consider whether in any case it is appropriate to suspend the disciplinary procedure for a short period in order for the grievance to be considered.

It may also be considered appropriate for another manager to deal with the disciplinary case to ensure that both matters are dealt with impartially. The advice in the ACAS Code of Practice 2015 at para.46 is:

> Where an employee raises a grievance during a disciplinary process the disciplinary process may be temporarily suspended in order to deal with the grievance. Where the grievance and disciplinary cases are related it may be appropriate to deal with both issues concurrently.

No status quo or standstill clause

It is essential in such cases that the disciplinary procedure contains no status quo or standstill clauses that would require the employer to adjourn any disciplinary proceedings until the outcome of the grievance and the appeal from the grievance decision.

In *Samuel Smith Ltd* v. *Marshall*, UKEAT/0488/09 the EAT held that as there was no 'standstill' or 'status quo' clause requiring the employer to adjourn the disciplinary hearing until after the grievance appeal and since the employee had refused to agree six dates offered for the disciplinary hearing, the Employment Tribunal had erred in law in holding that any reasonable employer would have adjourned the disciplinary hearing until the outcome of the grievance appeal.

In this case the grievance had already been heard by the time of the disciplinary hearing and this, said the EAT, made the employer's case stronger.

The EAT held that it was (para.44):

> perverse to find that a reasonable employer would have been bound to have adjourned the disciplinary hearing for the reasons already submitted; there was no contractual right to a standstill, no reference in the ACAS code [2004], the adjournment of the disciplinary hearing and failure on the part of the Claimants to agree to some six dates between 20 March and 14 April ...

The 2015 ACAS Code differs from the earlier Code, in that para.46 of the 2015 Code refers to the option of suspending the disciplinary process until after the outcome of the grievance or, where they are linked, to hearing them both concurrently.

The latter may prove unworkable where it would be unfair for the same person to determine the grievance and grievance appeal and disciplinary hearing and any appeal from the disciplinary decision.

The 2015 ACAS Guide records that when an employee raises a grievance during the meeting it may sometimes be appropriate to consider stopping the meeting and suspending the disciplinary procedure – for example when:

- the grievance relates to a conflict of interest that the manager holding the disciplinary meeting is alleged to have;
- bias is alleged in the conduct of the disciplinary meeting;
- senior management has been selective in the evidence supplied to the manager holding the meeting;
- there is possible discrimination.

Other common issues raised by employees are that they have not been supplied with all the relevant documents or they have not been shown witness statements being relied upon by management. This latter complaint is easily remedied by supplying the employee with all the relevant paperwork.

The ACAS Guide suggests that it would not be appropriate to suspend the meeting where the employee makes an invalid point, for example if the employee mistakenly claims to have the right to be legally represented or that a collectively agreed and applicable procedure does not apply to the employee because the employee is not a union member.

Outstanding appeal from earlier

Where there is an outstanding appeal against a final written warning and a further misconduct matter arises, employers should complete the appeal against the earlier warning before addressing the later misconduct issue (*Tower Hamlets Health Authority v. Anthony* [1988] IRLR 331).

In such a case the employer should postpone the final stage of the disciplinary procedure (the dismissal hearing for another offence) until the appeal against the issuing of a final written warning has been properly dealt with.

9.25 Criminal convictions or charges

The ACAS Code of Practice 2015, para.31 provides that:

> an employer may consider dismissing an employee who has been charged with a criminal offence and who has been convicted of a criminal offence after careful consideration has been given to what effect the charge or conviction has on the employee's suitability to do their job and their relationship with their employer, work colleagues and customers.

9.26 Performance

The Introduction to the ACAS Code of Practice 2015 recognises that disciplinary matters can also include performance or capability issues but that some employers prefer to address performance issues under a separate capability procedure. If this is the case then similar rules of fairness will be necessary albeit that some of the principles and procedures may need to be adapted (see below).

The rationale for dealing with performance concerns under a separate procedure is that they are conceptually different from misconduct (misconduct normally implies premeditation and often dishonesty). These separate procedures are called by different names such as improved performance review (IPR), performance improvement plan (PIP), etc.

As in the case of misconduct, where the employee immediately goes off sick triggered by an improved performance review, an employer may reserve the right to suspend the warning for performance until the employee returns to work on the basis that the warning is to allow the employee to improve performance and when the employee is away from work there is no opportunity to do so.

A typical IPR or PIP is shown at **Precedent 9Q**.

9.27 Termination checklist

Employers should draw up termination checklists to ensure all the leaving details are in order. The following is a checklist for terminating an employee's employment.

1. Ensure the termination date is certain and known by both parties and spelt out in writing.
2. Ensure all leaving documents and P45 are sent out at the appropriate time.
3. Ensure that all the following documents are consistent:
    (a) letter of dismissal/resignation;
    (b) reference (when sent);
    (c) answers to job seeker's allowance forms;
    (d) ET3 response;
    (e) letter stating reason for dismissal under s.95 of the Employment Rights Act 1996.
4. If the dismissed employee is an authorised signatory on the company bank account ensure that the accounts department, bank, etc. are informed promptly.
5. Credit cards: take any company credit cards back from the employer and inform the credit card issuing company, etc. and ensure that there are no outstanding bills.
6. Ensure that any cash float and expenses in advance, etc. given to the employee are returned and that all expenses claims have been dealt with.
7. Ensure that any passwords for security entry and computers are changed. Ensure that remote access has been stopped.

8. Ensure that all company property has been returned including car, PC, documents, USB flash drives, keys, door entry cards, files, etc.
9. If any loans are outstanding ensure that a clause in the contract entitles the company to deduct the full amount outstanding from final salary.
10. If a season ticket has been bought for the employee by the company, ensure that it has been cashed in and any refund returned to the company.
11. Any petrol card should be returned and the account closed.
12. Ensure that the company car insurers are notified that the employee is no longer employed and no longer insured to drive a company vehicle.
13. Advise all relevant authorities that the employee has left employment, e.g. the FCA or any other regulatory body, HMRC, etc.
14. Ensure that confidential information is not released by the employee by reminding the employee of the continuing obligation of confidentiality.
15. If a director, check whether the director has resigned from all directorships with no claims for fees, etc.
16. Ensure a forwarding address is obtained which can be used if the company needs to contact the ex-employee or if personal mail is delivered to the office.

9.28 Duty of disclosure

Employers are under an obligation to search for all relevant documents and to disclose them. These documents can be formal records, telephone attendance notes, diary entries, emails, etc.

A document is relevant if it assists in proving or disproving any part of either the employer's case or the claimant's case. Documents that are unhelpful must also be disclosed. Disclosure is not an exercise in cherry picking.

The allegations in most cases may be fairly broad. To get an idea of what will be relevant, the employer should read carefully the ET1 and ET3 (Response). They will contain various allegations, references to documents, meetings, etc.

Some likely sources of documents are: personnel files, files that managers keep in their personal filing cabinets, desk drawers, briefcases, notebooks, desk diaries, personal diaries, electronic diaries, policies, etc. on the company intranet, etc.

A search for emails relevant to any allegations made by the employee must also be made. Choose appropriate search terms such as the name of the employee, 'disciplinary hearing', etc.

It is of crucial importance that this task is done thoroughly. It is a substantial burden in terms of time, but if it is incomplete an Employment Tribunal will have good reason to doubt the credibility of the employer, and if all relevant documents are not disclosed, it might be the basis for an adverse inference against the employer.

When retrieved, the documents should be sorted into chronological order and a list compiled of the title of the documents and their dates, e.g. 'Letter from [HR manager] to [claimant], [date]'.

9.29   Sex in the office

The ACAS Code of Practice 2015 recommends at paragraph 24 that disciplinary rules should give examples of acts which the employer regards as acts of gross misconduct.

You may not think that you would need to warn employees if they engage in sexual encounters with co-workers in the office but it may be wise to point this out. It is certainly fair to dismiss (after following a fair procedure) for such misconduct even if this takes place out of office hours.

In the case of *GM Packaging (UK) Ltd* v. *Haslem* UKEAT/0259/13/LA the EAT held the dismissal of an employee (a senior manager) was fair when he was seen having sex with another, more junior female employee on company property, even though this was taking place out of office hours.

The managing director of a very small packaging firm, who had witnessed this, seconded two external HR consultants to investigate the matter. They recommended to the managing director after their investigation to dismiss and so the managing director dismissed the more senior manager.

The EAT held:

- The crucial factor was the managing director's reason for dismissing Mr Haslem, rather than the HR consultants' recommendations for dismissal.
- The Employment Tribunal recognised that it was understandable that consultants had been hired to deal with such matters and that they had advised the managing director to dismiss the employee and asked permission to implement that decision. The decision had, therefore, been taken by the consultants.
- The 'principal reason' requirement in s.98(1) of the Employment Rights Act 1996 requires that employers establish the principal reason for dismissal.
- The EAT overturned the Employment Tribunal's finding that it was not within the band of reasonable responses for an employer to dismiss an employee for gross misconduct on the basis of sexual activity between consenting adults in the workplace but out of hours.
- In this case the Employment Tribunal had clearly substituted its own views for that of the employer, rather than considering whether the decision had been within the band of reasonable responses that any reasonable employer could have adopted.

The EAT found that staff engaging in consensual sex in the workplace even out of office hours can justify summary dismissal.

9.30   Prohibition on discussing salary or bonus

Some employers, particularly those in the City, wish their staff to keep their salary and bonus details confidential. This is mainly so that women, who in the main are paid less and receive lower bonuses, cannot easily find out what their male counterparts are being paid.

But employers beware. If the disclosure is sought or made for the purpose of enabling the person who makes it, or the person to whom it is made, to find out whether or to what extent there is, in relation to the work in question, a connection between pay and having (or not having) a particular protected characteristic, i.e. an equal pay or sex discrimination claim, such a clause preventing the disclosure is unenforceable (s.77 of the Equality Act 2010). Any retaliatory action against the person seeking or making the disclosure will be unlawful victimisation under s.27 of the Equality Act 2010.

Section 77 of the Equality Act 2010 makes such clauses unenforceable as any such clause:

(1) ... [that] purports to prevent or restrict the person (P) from disclosing or seeking to disclose information about the terms of P's work is unenforceable against P in so far as P makes or seeks to make a relevant pay disclosure.

(2) A term of a person's work that purports to prevent or restrict the person (P) from seeking disclosure of information from a colleague about the terms of the colleague's work is unenforceable against P in so far as P seeks a relevant pay disclosure from the colleague; and 'colleague' includes a former colleague in relation to the work in question.

The protected acts for which victimisation is unlawful are:

(a) seeking a disclosure that would be a relevant pay disclosure;
(b) making or seeking to make a relevant pay disclosure;
(c) receiving information disclosed in a relevant pay disclosure.

Clause about non-disclosure of salary or bonus

The kind of wording that an employer may consider would be:

> We treat everyone's personal data confidentially and personal salary and bonus numbers fall into this category. It is therefore strictly forbidden to disclose or discuss your salary, salary increase, bonus, share option allocation or incentive payments or any other part of our remuneration package with any other employee or third party without the express permission of a Managing Director.
>
> **Exception**
>
> There is one exception where this prohibition does not apply and that is if a colleague's salary details are being requested for the purposes of an equal pay or other discrimination complaint either internal or before an Employment Tribunal. In such a case disclosure is permitted and no retaliation or criticism or victimisation of any kind will occur.

PRECEDENT 9A: Clauses excluding disciplinary procedure

Please note that during the first one year, 11 months and three weeks of your employment the Company reserves the right to terminate your employment without recourse to the warning stages of the disciplinary procedure or to the hearing or appeal stages. Your employment may be terminated with notice or pay in lieu except in cases of gross misconduct where no notice or pay in lieu becomes due.

In other words, during this period you are subject to all of the rules and regulations of the Company but the disciplinary **procedure** (e.g. of investigations, warnings and hearings and appeals do not apply to you).

OR

During the first two years of employment you will be entitled to one official warning only where your conduct or performance falls below the standard required of you. In any case where dismissal is contemplated you will be given a chance to state your case before any final decision is taken. You will also be afforded the right of appeal.

PRECEDENT 9B: Suspension

1. During any period of suspension you will be paid your basic salary only with no shift premium or overtime payment or other allowances.

2. Please note that suspension at this time is a neutral act and does not imply any guilt on your part or any pre-judgement on the part of the Company.

3. We hope to keep the suspension as brief as possible but inevitably this investigation may take weeks rather than days. We will keep you regularly updated as to the progress of the investigation.

4. During your suspension you should keep yourself available to assist in the investigation if called upon to do so. You may be asked to provide a statement to assist the investigation. At such a meeting you will be permitted to be accompanied by your union representative or a fellow worker despite the fact that this meeting is not a disciplinary hearing.

5. It is strictly forbidden for you to undertake any other paid or unpaid employment during this time.

6. It is also forbidden to enter any of the Company's premises or contact any member of staff without first obtaining the written permission of the HR Director.

7. Any contact by you with other witnesses or any complainant will be seen as an attempt to destroy the integrity of the investigation or to harass or threaten, so please do not attempt to do so. If you wish to interview anyone, please contact a member of HR directly or through your representative in the first instance.

8. Please note also that any documents which you may wish to consult should be requested via the HR Department and they will be sent to you where deemed appropriate.

9. We understand that this is a stressful time for you and will endeavour to assist you as far as possible.

PRECEDENT 9C: Letter reminding suspended employee of obligations

[Name of employee]

[Address]

[Date]

Dear [name]

RE: Conditions relating to your suspension

You are currently under suspension pending our investigation into allegations of [give details].

We are aiming to conclude this investigation within the next two weeks. If it continues past this date we will notify you as soon as possible.

It is recognised that during this period of suspension you may become anxious and concerned. We refer you to our Employee Assistance Programme and Employee Counselling Service and recommend that you make a self-referral.

We have discussed with you the terms of your suspension but for the avoidance of doubt, we confirm them again:

1. You should remain away from work but available at home, i.e. you should not go away from your normal residence, unless you seek permission first in writing from me and you should remain available to be contacted by mobile telephone.

2. You should not contact anyone at work other than your representative or me.

3. You should ask your representative to contact anyone from work whom you would like to ask questions or give evidence for you at your hearing. This instruction is very important as the integrity of this investigation could be seriously damaged if witnesses from whom we are taking evidence feel pressurised or scared because of contact from you, and therefore become unwilling to give evidence.

4. You will be invited with your representative to attend an interview as part of our investigations. You are free to decline to do so and no negative inference will be drawn if you do so. However, credit will be given to you for co-operating at this stage if you are able to help us with the investigation. You and/or your representative will be able to question witnesses at your hearing either directly at the hearing or during an adjournment by your representative if the witnesses are unwilling to face you directly in the hearing.

5. You will understand the seriousness of any attempt by you or your representative to contact witnesses who are preparing statements for the hearing for us.

6. Of course, if you wish to ask the same witnesses to make a statement on your behalf, this will be arranged with that person's consent.

7. Would your representative please inform me as soon as possible whether you intend to call any person to give information on your behalf and if so their names and where they work.

8. We will then arrange for your representative to see them either alone or with someone whom they wish to attend, in order to give a statement for you.

For the avoidance of doubt, any attempt on your part to disobey the above instructions will be regarded very seriously and could amount to gross misconduct on its own and/or would be taken into account in respect of the original charges.

If you have any questions about any of the arrangements during your suspension please do not hesitate to telephone me on my direct line [*give details*].

We understand what a difficult and stressful time this must be for you and appreciate your co-operation.

Yours sincerely

PRECEDENT 9D: Undertaking of confidentiality clause

I, [*name*] understand that an investigation is being conducted into complaint(s) against me of [*details*].

I am being given copies of all the witness statements taken during this investigation and I understand that it is critical that I keep them strictly confidential because it could discredit the investigation and affect the evidence or the willingness of the witnesses to continue with this matter.

I agree to keep the fact of these witness statements, their contents and the identity of those making the statements strictly confidential save for disclosure to my legal representative, union representative or lay colleague who will accompany me to any hearing.

I also agree not to discuss the contents of these statements with any of the witnesses or anyone else save as identified above and will not attempt in any way to contact or ask anyone else to contact or to influence any of the potential witnesses. I also undertake that I will do nothing that could act to their detriment [*if a teacher*, affect their marks or appraisals, etc.]. I agree not to take any retaliatory action of any kind against any of the [students,] complainants or other witnesses.

I understand that if I breach this undertaking, I will be subject to serious disciplinary action which could lead to my summary dismissal.

Signed ……………………………… Date …………………

[*employee*]

PRECEDENT 9E: Letter responding to allegation of breach of confidentiality

[*Name of employee*]

[*Address*]

[*Date*]

Dear [*name*]

RE: Alleged breach of confidentiality

I was very sorry and concerned to read your email of today's date. The Company's investigation has only necessitated taking a statement from one member of staff that being [*name*]. In accordance with our usual procedure she has signed a confidentiality clause and has given her assurance orally that she has not discussed this matter with anyone other than [*specify*] and myself. I cannot therefore comment or be held liable, if this matter has developed into gossip or found its way on to the Company 'grapevine'. I can assure you that I am most concerned at the discussion that you allegedly had with the ex-member of staff.

Unfortunately we are not able to investigate this matter further without specific names as to whom you suspect has breached confidentiality. To call staff in, to ask questions regarding this matter which they may know nothing about at present, would in itself be a breach of implied trust and could lead to innocently disseminating details of your disciplinary case to staff who currently are unaware of anything going on.

If you have the name of any member of staff about whom you have any evidence that they have breached confidentiality then please be assured that we will pursue this further. Please disclose any names as soon as possible. It would not, however, be appropriate for us to call in all staff as this would disseminate the fact of this disciplinary investigation.

Yours sincerely

PRECEDENT 9F: Complaints handling policy

1. Introduction

1.1 The purpose of this document is to ensure that we deal effectively with any complaint or allegation made about the conduct or behaviour of a member of staff. Allegations or complaints may arise from a variety of sources: tenants, residents, staff members, relatives of residents, members of the public or through the Whistleblowing Policy.

1.2 However allegations/complaints are brought to our attention we will deal with them fairly, effectively and speedily. A fair and thorough investigation is the cornerstone of a good disciplinary process. It is at this stage of the process that employers make most mistakes; an inadequate investigation may lead to a dismissal being ruled as unfair by an Employment Tribunal.

1.3 This can happen even when, on the face of it, the employee has behaved inappropriately. Upon receipt of an allegation or complaint the Divisional Director will decide which policy or procedure should be followed. The following procedure will be used if the complaint or allegation relates to the conduct or behaviour of a member of staff. The Divisional Director will liaise with the HR Director who will implement the procedure.

2. PR Department/Chief Executive

It may be necessary to inform the PR Department when we receive an allegation or a complaint. There are areas of the Trust's work in which the press is particularly interested, for example, serious failure to maintain a property resulting in injury or illness; failure to service gas appliances in our properties; or failure to maintain a safe level of care in one of our care homes. The HR Director will inform the PR Department and the Chief Executive about any serious allegation or complaint relating to a member of staff.

3. The whistleblowing policy

If the complaint has come about through the whistleblowing policy the policy must be followed and, if required, anonymity provided for those raising the complaint. An investigation if necessary will be concluded in the usual way. A copy of the whistleblowing policy is found in the Staff Handbook or can be obtained directly from the HR Department.

4. The complaints policy

If the complaint has come through the complaints policy, the policy must be followed. Tenants and residents can make a complaint about the services we provide; this may include a complaint or allegation about the performance or conduct of a member of staff. A copy of the Complaints Procedure is available directly from the Corporate Strategy Department.

5. The aim of the investigation

5.1 The aim of the investigation should be to establish the facts without delay. It is vital that utmost confidentiality is maintained at all times. Investigations should be carried out as discreetly and sensitively as possible.

5.2 It should be emphasised to the employee being investigated that the investigation is an objective and non-judgemental inquiry into the facts of the case, and the purpose is not to build a case against the employee but to search for evidence which supports or rebuts any allegations. It is essential that evidence is gathered quickly.

5.3 This may necessitate interviewing employees or others involved at their homes or calling employees in when not on duty. The employee being investigated may well be suspended from duty; suspension allows for any reasonable request from Management to attend an interview. The Manager undertaking the investigation may make special arrangements to meet the employee at the trade union office or at the employee's home.

6. The investigator

6.1 It is a well-established principle of employment law that the person undertaking the investigation should be someone other than the person who will hear the disciplinary case.

6.2 Therefore once an incident occurs the Line Manager for the employee concerned and Director for the Region/Division where the incident has occurred will not be involved or discuss the investigation with anyone connected with it. The Line Manager or Director will be hearing matters presented at a Disciplinary Hearing and therefore must not be involved in the investigation.

6.3 It is good practice for the investigation to be carried out by a person who has no involvement with the day-to-day running of the area being investigated, e.g. a Manager from another department with an understanding of the nature of the work.

6.4 This ensures objectivity and is less likely to damage working relationships. The HR Director/Manager will nominate the Manager to investigate, brief the Manager and arrange for an HR Officer to be attached to the case to arrange and attend all meetings and take notes.

6.5 When carrying out the investigation, it helps if the investigator has someone to make arrangements and take notes. This allows the investigator to concentrate on establishing a rapport and setting the interviewee at ease.

6.6 At the end of each interview the HR Officer can read both the questions and answers to reach agreement with the interviewee, the notes can be signed and a copy provided for the interviewee. Alternatively the notes agreed at the time can be typed up later and sent to the interviewee for signing.

7. Representation

7.1 It is good practice to offer to those being interviewed the opportunity to be accompanied by either a trade union representative or a colleague of their choice who must be an employee of the Association or a lawyer of their choice.

7.2 Sometimes we find that employees do not want to be accompanied or do not belong to a trade union. At the outset of the interview the investigator should be clear in their mind that the employee is happy to continue without representation and it should be confirmed that the lack of representation is not a problem of timing or availability of the employee's union representative or colleague.

8. Notice of the allegation

8.1 A decision may be taken to suspend an employee about whom we have received a complaint. Suspension does not imply guilt nor is it disciplinary action in itself. Suspension may be required to enable the investigation to go ahead unhindered, to protect the employee, or to enable a fair investigation to be carried out.

8.2 Sometimes suspension is necessary to prevent a recurrence of the incident, or to protect residents or colleagues. The employee should be advised as soon as possible that a complaint has been made and that an investigation will take place. Arrangements will be made by HR to ensure the employee is kept up to date with the course of the investigation.

9. Arranging the investigatory interview

9.1 The HR Officer attached to the investigation will arrange the interviews. In all cases the employee and witnesses will be given advance notice of an impending interview. The employee will be told that they may be accompanied if they wish.

9.2 The interviews will be arranged as soon as possible after the allegation/complaint is received so advance notice may, of necessity, be short. The closer to the incident the more likely it is that memories will be fresh. The HR Officer may liaise with the Chair of our recognised unions to ensure that representation can be arranged. Special arrangements may be necessary to allow extra time off for union representatives to support their members.

10. The interview

10.1 The interview should be carried out away from the normal place of work if possible. Refreshments will be provided. The investigator will explain the purpose of the interview and the need for confidentiality. A written record of the meeting should be made. Where possible a signed statement should be prepared by each individual. If witnesses are unwilling to provide a statement a record of the interview should be signed by the witness.

10.2 The individual being interviewed should be advised that a further interview may be necessary if the investigator needs to clarify a particular point or corroborate an account from another source.

10.3 Good questioning technique is essential. Avoid leading questions, such as: 'I understand that you saw the cleaner, Mary, take the phone cards from the drawer'.

10.4 Also avoid multiple questions. They do not allow the interviewee time to think and as a result you may miss information, for example: 'Were you at work on the 2nd? Did you go out to lunch? What can you see from your desk?'

10.5 Instead use open questions which invite information such as: 'Can you tell me what you saw on the 2nd?'

10.6 Closed questions are useful to establish fact: use closed questions to clarify information, to control the conversation and to confirm facts. For example: 'Did you see Mary that day?'

10.7 Ask questions that are designed to elicit information and are not clearly being asked in order to prove whatever has been alleged took place. So for example ask the individual to describe exactly where they were, what they were doing, how it was they saw or heard anything, what the alleged offender was wearing and what others were wearing, where they were standing, etc.

10.8 Take photographs of the scene and make diagrams and measure how far away the persons were from the eyewitnesses.

10.9 It must be remembered that the interviewee will be nervous, particularly if suspended, and witnesses may also feel very anxious: the investigator should try to put them at their ease.

10.10 This ensures that both interviewees and interviewers agree the evidence given. This also allows the witness the opportunity to add anything they may have forgotten to mention.

10.11 Never put words into the mouths of the witnesses nor attempt to summarise what they have told you, the investigator.

10.12 The individual will be given the opportunity to write a statement if they are willing to do so, and this will be signed and kept as part of the investigation. At the end of the interview the HR Officer will arrange for the notes to be typed and sent to the interviewee for agreement.

11. Information to be examined by the investigator

11.1 As part of the investigation the investigator should examine documents such as the Staff Handbook, Work Schedules, Duty Rotas, Operational Polices/Procedures, Disciplinary Rules and Procedures.

11.2 Where the disciplinary matters relate to a failure to adhere to rules and standards, the investigator should check when and how the employee was made aware of them, for instance during induction, formal or informal or in written material such as the Staff Handbook, Notices, Bulletins, Policies or Procedures.

11.3 The investigator should check how common knowledge about matters to be relied upon is. For example, if the complaint relates to lifting a resident inappropriately or a serious failure to follow Standing Orders during the development process, the investigator must check how reasonable it is to expect the employee to know the correct method of working. Have they been trained? Do they have access to and an understanding of the documents? The HR Officer attached to the case will provide evidence of training sessions attended or written information provided for employees.

12. Following the investigating interview

12.1 Having interviewed the relevant witnesses, the investigator should decide whether anyone else needs to be interviewed in the light of the information received so far. The investigator should also decide whether individuals need to be interviewed again. This would be necessary where witnesses' accounts differ, or to corroborate information obtained after the initial interview.

12.2 The investigator will then prepare a written report which will be received by the HR Director/Manager and the Manager responsible for the area under investigation.

12.3 The report should not recommend any specific action but should include the schedule of people interviewed showing dates and times, copies of notes and witness statements, and a factual account of the investigation. An example of a witness statement and an investigation report are set out in Appendix 1 and 2 respectively.

12.4 The Manager concerned together with the HR Director/Manager will decide the appropriateness or otherwise of proceeding to a disciplinary hearing.

12.5 Following the outcome of the investigation, the Manager and HR Director/Manager will consider how witnesses or complainants should be informed of the outcome. There is a need to balance the obligation to maintain confidentiality, particularly in relation to the Whistleblowing Policy, with the need for employees to know that matters have been dealt with effectively. If an employee is accused and subsequently cleared, it is important that all employees who know of the accusation also know that the person was cleared.

13. The Human Resources Department: special arrangements

Should a complaint arise against a member of the HR, Training or Facilities Department, a Director from another Division/Region would be nominated to undertake the role performed by the HR Department in the investigatory process.

14. The investigator's role at disciplinary hearing

The investigator will present the case to the Manager or Director. If it is thought that matters may amount to gross misconduct the case will always be heard by a Director.

The Manager of the area concerned will always attend to answer any questions on normal practice, etc. HR will always attend to clarify any points on employment law or Company practice.

15. **Documentation**

All documentation relating to an investigation will be kept in the HR Department and not in other offices. At the end of an investigation all relating documentation will be collated and kept in the HR Department.

APPENDIX 1   EXAMPLE OF A WITNESS STATEMENT

Witness statement by [*name of witness*]

I am employed by [*Company*] as a Contract Cleaner. I work in the [*specify*] Office.

On [*date*] I was cleaning the interview room off the Reception area, it must have been just before 5 pm. I work from 5 pm to 8 pm but I was early for work last Friday as my neighbour gave me a lift, I'd say it was about 10 minutes to 5. I heard raised voices in the Reception. I stopped what I was doing and peered round the door, and I had a good view of Reception.

In Reception I saw [*name of employee*], arguing with a lady I assumed to be a tenant, she was upset about being evicted, I think. She had two small kids with her, she looked upset.

The lady said to [*employee*] 'You've got to do something'. [*employee*] said 'You are too late, can't you read? We close at 4.45, now get out.' The lady said, 'What's your name?' Her voice was shaky. [*employee*] said 'It's none of your bloody business – get out.' The lady left, she was upset and crying and dragged the kids out of the door. [*employee*] slammed it, then as he turned to go he saw me. He looked surprised and then, I was amazed, he raised his fist to me and said, 'You keep your mouth shut if you know what's good for you.'

I told my Supervisor what I saw the next day.

This statement was written by me and is in my own words. It is accurate and true to the best of my knowledge and belief.

Signed .... Date ....

[*witness*]

APPENDIX 2   EXAMPLE OF AN INVESTIGATION REPORT

Investigation report by [*name of manager*]

On [*date*] I was advised by [*name*], Area Manager of the [*specify*] Office that she had received a complaint from a tenant [*name of complainant*]. The complaint was that a Housing Officer, [*name of employee*], was rude and unhelpful towards [*complainant*] on [*date*]. Following [*name*]'s discussion with the HR Director the investigatory procedure had been implemented and I was the nominated investigator. [*name of HR officer*] had been allocated to the investigation. [*HR officer*] contacted [*complainant*] and explained that we would like to interview her about the complaint she had made earlier in the day. We said that we would be quite happy for her to have a friend or relative with her if she wishes. We also offered to pay for childminding if it would be helpful. [*complainant*] accepted the offer of childminding but was quite happy to see us alone.

[HR officer] and I visited [complainant] by arrangement at her home at [date]. The [complainant], explained that she had visited the [specify] Office as she had just returned home from visiting her sick mother to find a Notice of Seeking Possession Order. She said she didn't really understand it and panicked, thinking that she may be evicted on to the street. She immediately went to [specify] Office, but she didn't know that they closed early on Fridays and got there just as a woman was locking the door. She said she pleaded to be let in to see her Housing Officer. [complainant]'s Housing Officer was not on duty on Friday so the woman who let her in said she would find the Duty Housing Officer. The woman came back and told her to wait, then the woman left and locked the door behind her.

It was then that a man appeared; he had his coat on. It must have been about 10 to 5. He looked angry. [complainant] showed him the Notice of Seeking Possession. He just gestured with his hands and said, 'So what, you should pay your rent, it's your fault.' [complainant] then asked him to check. [complainant] was receiving Housing Benefit so she couldn't understand how this had happened. He then started shouting and said he'd had enough dealing with time wasters and he was going, and he told her to get out.

[complainant] asked him for his name and he swore at her and said 'Can't you read? We close at 4.45.' He wouldn't give his name and said it was 'none of her bloody business'. [complainant] had no alternative, as he opened the door she left with her children. She was in tears all the way to the bus stop. So were the children. She phoned the Area Manager, [name]. She was very kind. The Notice of Seeking Possession was sent because of a mix up in Housing Benefit. I asked [complainant] if she could describe the Housing Officer, and she said he was of medium height, with dark receding hair, he wore glasses without frames and spoke with a Northern accent. I asked [complainant] if she would confirm the complaint in writing; she said she was happy to do so. As [complainant] was writing down her statement she remembered that the Housing Officer got into a green Volkswagen Beetle and drove past her as he left. The witness statement from [complainant] is attached, as are the full notes of our meeting.

The description matched that of [employee]. I was also able to confirm that he drives a green Volkswagen Beetle car. I checked the duty rota and [employee] was on duty that day and would have been leaving the building at around that time. I also reminded myself of the Trust's Disciplinary Procedure where to be abusive to a tenant could be construed as gross misconduct. [HR officer] made arrangements for me to see [employee] with his union representative on [date].

I was made aware on [date] that the incident complained of by [complainant] was witnessed by a cleaner. The cleaner had reported the incident to her Contract Supervisor on [date] during the evening shift. [HR officer] contacted the cleaner at home and she agreed to meet with us on [date]; she was clear that she did not want to be accompanied.

We met with [employee] and his representative at [time] on [date]. [employee] confirmed that he had spoken to the tenant but had explained that everything was locked up but he would get back to her first thing on Monday. He denied that he had been abusive in any way. I checked that [employee] and his representative were aware of the Disciplinary Procedure. They both acknowledged that they were and both had a copy of the Handbook. [employee] provided a statement, a copy of which is attached, as are notes of the meeting.

We interviewed the cleaner on [date]. The cleaner confirmed that she heard [employee] swear and be abusive towards the tenant such that the tenant left in tears. [witness] also stated that [employee] had threatened her not to tell anyone what she saw. [witness]'s statement is attached, as are the full notes of our meeting.

PRECEDENT 9G: Investigating dishonesty

1. **Theft of Company property**

   - Has the employee been authorised to remove the property? Is there any stock missing?
   - Should such authorisation have been given?
   - Are there any witnesses who saw the employee taking the goods? Does anybody know anything about it (hearsay)?
   - Is it common practice for such property to be removed from the company's premises?

2. **Fiddling expenses**

   - Is there any documentary evidence?
   - Have past records been checked for other evidence?
   - Was it a genuine mistake or an intention to defraud?
   - Is it in breach of Company procedures?
   - What is the Company procedure and does the employee know about it?
   - Has it been informally sanctioned in the past?

3. **Till offences**

   - How recently did the alleged offence take place? Can the employee be expected to remember the incident?
   - Have any test purchases corroborated the evidence?
   - Has a recent stock check thrown up any discrepancies?
   - Has the Company till procedure been followed?

4. **Important issues**

   - Accurate documentary evidence.
   - Catching the employee red-handed.
   - Considering two different versions of the events.
   - Circumstantial evidence concerning character of the accused, etc.
   - Further corroboration where there is conflicting evidence.

5. **Dishonesty outside work: charged or convicted of criminal offences outside work**

   - Make sure of the facts. Call the employee to an interview to confirm the facts (or call their solicitor if they are in custody on remand).
   - Find out and assess the implications: likelihood of bail; length of sentence; serious offence; how long will the employee be absent if imprisoned, etc.
   - Assess the work implications: trust and confidence; have they entered a guilty plea; would their retention affect the employer's credibility with clients, customers, etc; does the job or specific rules require appointment without criminal conviction?
   - What steps can be taken to make continued employment possible?
   - What has the employee said in mitigation?

PRECEDENT 9H: Combined procedure

In order that everyone understands the application of the disciplinary procedure, you should note that issues of misconduct and poor performance come within the scope of this procedure. Whilst it is accepted that in general, misconduct normally implies dishonest behaviour which is often premeditated, poor performance is not normally the 'fault' of the individual and neither is it normally planned in advance. However, the warning stages of the procedure will escalate whether the same, similar or different misconduct offence is committed during the lifetime of a warning or where an issue of poor performance arises.

PRECEDENT 9I: Lapsed warnings

Previous warnings which have lapsed will normally be disregarded where further offences or work problems occur. However, they will be taken into account:

(a) where the same or similar offence is committed at any time in the future in order to assess the credibility of the evidence submitted by the employee (including any statement that the employee did not know that such conduct amounted to a disciplinary issue or in the context of 'similar fact' evidence) and in order to determine an appropriate penalty;

(b) where the same employee has committed an offence of misconduct or gross misconduct after the warning has lapsed, the previous warning will be taken into account in order to determine an appropriate penalty, e.g. someone who has an exemplary record and has committed a one-off offence may be given a second chance even in a case of gross misconduct or where they are on a final written warning;

(c) where a redundancy selection exercise is being carried out and the history of disciplinary warnings may be used as one of the selection criteria.

PRECEDENT 9J: Dismissal letter following a lapsed final warning

[name of employee]

[address]

[date]

Dear [name]

RE: Dismissal with pay in lieu of notice

As you will be aware, your last final written warning for serious performance and incompetency issues expired on [expiry date].

However, it has come to light since [expiry date] (Management was unaware of these matters at the time), that [you have failed on several occasions to lock up the building or put on the burglar alarm; you failed to set up the Council Chamber for [give details] and our telephone logs reveal that you have been making private calls to a mobile number during your working hours, this latter offence being a clear breach of our telephone facilities policy.]

You were unable to give any convincing explanation for any of these matters and apart from saying you were 'Sorry', could not give any satisfactory response. [Even your union representative could not put forward a convincing case on your behalf.]

It is with regret that I have decided that we can no longer trust you [in your role as caretaker], given that you have only just completed one year under a final written warning and now these other matters have come to light. It is clear that the final warning did not have the desired effect.

There are no other vacant suitable posts for you and we cannot trust you to work on your own any longer.

I have therefore decided that you will be dismissed as at today's date and will be given 12 weeks' pay in lieu of notice.

You have a right of appeal and if you wish to do so you should send your written appeal setting out the grounds to [specify] no later than five working days from the date of this letter.

Yours sincerely

PRECEDENT 9K: Final written warning

[name of employee]

[address]

[job title]

[date]

Dear [name]

RE: Final written warning

I heard your disciplinary case this afternoon concerning [the sending by you of a letter to [name] concerning 'Cuts in Commission Rates' purporting that your letter had been written by our Accounts Department. I note that you wrongly dated this letter [date] and signed it 'Head of Accounts' (with an illegible signature). You are of course a senior travel consultant and have nothing to do with Accounts.]

I regard your conduct as being of the most serious nature, given that [you sent this letter without any authority from the Company and more seriously you misrepresented that this letter sent by you had come from our Accounts Department and you signed it 'Head of Accounts'] your conduct amounts to [forgery].

I wish to make it absolutely clear that in doing what you have done, [i.e. sending a letter of this nature without my authority and forging this letter, misrepresenting the author of that letter,] I regard your conduct as gross misconduct and in normal circumstances I would dismiss you without notice or pay in lieu.

However, this is an exceptional case, [given your exemplary track record with us of 24 years, the reasons you gave for doing it, the fact that your mother is seriously ill and you say that 'you were not yourself' and your genuine signs of contrition and remorse]. I believe that you are genuinely very sorry for what you did and I am prepared to give you one more chance, but only one. I would not do this for any other member of staff.

As a result I intend this letter to be a final written warning, which will remain live on your file for the remainder of your employment with us. Any further act of any nature which is dishonest, deceitful or which brings or is likely to bring the Company into disrepute or any further breach of Company rules or the standards of probity and integrity expected of someone of your seniority and status within the Company will be dealt with by summary dismissal.

Please note that I will need you to sign both copies of this letter and keep one copy and return the other to me, to be signed in my presence. This will ensure that both you and I know that you fully understand the procedure [for sending out letters of any nature and that you fully understand that you have no authority to send out any letters of any kind to clients, potential clients, suppliers or potential suppliers or any other third party other than details of travel. If you wish to send out a letter or information of any other kind then you must seek and obtain my prior written permission or in my absence the prior written permission of another Director of this Company.]

Let me repeat so that you are absolutely clear, any repetition of the conduct that gave rise to this final warning or any conduct of any nature that is regarded as unacceptable or a breach of Company rules or policy will result in your summary dismissal.

I trust that you have learnt from this episode and that I will have no further cause for concern.

I am deeply saddened that you have let me down and let yourself down and trust that you will never do this kind of thing again.

Yours sincerely

I, [employee], accept this final written warning will remain on my record for ever. I understand and accept the instruction [that I have no authority to send out any letters of any kind to clients, potential clients, suppliers or potential suppliers or any other third party other than details of travel. If I wish to send out a letter or information of any other kind then I must seek and obtain [name]'s prior written permission or in [name]'s absence, the prior written permission of another Director of this Company.]

I understand what will happen to my employment if the Company has any further cause for concern.

Signed .... Date ....

[employee]

Precedent 9L: Consolidated disciplinary warning letters

MODEL LETTER 1 – Investigatory Meeting

[Name]

[Address]

[Date]

Private and Confidential

Dear

RE: Investigatory meeting

Further to our recent discussion with [name], I am writing to inform you that you are required to attend a formal investigatory meeting to discuss the allegations of:

[Insert allegations]

The meeting will be held in [office] at [location] on [date] at [time]. You may be accompanied at this meeting by a trade union representative or work colleague.

We will have a note-taker at this hearing and it will be recorded in order to have an accurate recording of what is said. You may also record the meeting if you wish and we will send to you a copy of our recording and any transcript thereafter.

Depending on the outcome, a decision will be taken as to whether formal disciplinary action will be taken under our Disciplinary Procedure.

Please confirm with me by [date] that you will attend.

If you choose not to attend then this will be noted but no negative or adverse inference will be drawn from your decision not to attend. Your attendance will assist the investigation.

Yours sincerely

[name]
Investigating officer

MODEL LETTER 2 – Notification of Suspension

[Name]

[Address]

[Date]

Private and Confidential

Dear

RE: Suspension from work

Further to our recent discussion, I confirm that in view of the incident(s) which has/have come to light [give reasons], you are suspended from work, with immediate effect.

The suspension is not a disciplinary measure and therefore you have no right of appeal against this decision.

You will be on full pay pending investigations into the alleged incident(s) outlined above. This is a neutral act and does not imply guilt on your part. It is being done so that the investigation will not be adversely impeded or affected.

Whilst I cannot confirm at this stage when the investigation will be completed, I can assure you that I am aware of how difficult this situation must be for you and that the investigation will take place without delay. I will update you after seven days.

I consider that by the nature of your employment, your continued presence at work may be prejudicial to the investigation. You may not enter any Company premises while suspended or communicate directly with anyone at work save for me, or any client or customer of the Company. Please direct any queries that you may have through me.

If, at any point, you wish to speak to me personally about your situation or the procedure, then please do not hesitate to contact me.

Yours sincerely

[name]
HR Director

Copies: trade union rep/work colleague

MODEL LETTER 3 – Notification of Hearing

[*Name*]

[*Address*]

[*Date*]

Private and Confidential

Dear

RE: Disciplinary hearing – potential gross misconduct

Further to our recent discussions, I now write to inform you that you are required to attend a Disciplinary Hearing pursuant to our Disciplinary Procedure. The meeting will consider the allegation that:

[*Details of reason for disciplinary hearing*]

The Hearing will be held at the final stage of the Procedure (see below), i.e. gross misconduct is being considered. A copy of the Disciplinary Procedure is enclosed for your information.

The meeting will be with me and [*name*] and will be held in [*place*] on [*date*] at [*time*]. Specifically, the meeting will consider your conduct relating to [*details of disciplinary issues*].

You are entitled to receive copies of the documents which will be considered at the hearing. I attach, for your information, copies of the following documents:

[*List of documents*]

If there is any documentation that you would like to submit to me for consideration, will you please let me have this by [*date*] so that I can circulate copies.

You have a right to be represented at the meeting by your trade union representative or a work colleague. You may, if you wish, call witnesses to support your case and if this is your intention, please let me know in advance of the meeting so that arrangements can be made to accommodate them. Please let me know who will accompany you as we will need to know for security reasons.

In view of the seriousness of the incident(s) which have been investigated, I have to inform you that the outcome of the hearing may lead to a decision that your actions constitute gross misconduct and therefore could lead to your summary dismissal.

Yours sincerely

[*name*]
Investigating officer

ENCS: please specify documents enclosed

Copy to: Director of Human Resources

MODEL LETTER 4 – Notification of Outcome: First Written Warning

[*Name*]

[*Address*]

[*Date*]

Private and Confidential

Dear

RE: First written warning

I refer to your hearing with [name], Investigating Officer and me on [date] in the presence of [HR officer] and your representative [name, trade union] **or** despite being advised of your right to representation you chose not to exercise it **or** you chose not to attend. The meeting was arranged under our Disciplinary Procedure.

At this meeting reference was made to [details of disciplinary issues]. Having fully considered the points at issue, it was decided [outcome of meeting].

This first written warning will remain on your personnel file for a period of 12 months, after which time it will lapse for the purposes of instigating the next stage of the procedure.

I must also warn you that should there be any concerns of any kind concerning your conduct or performance during this 12-month period, this may result in further disciplinary action including a final written warning or dismissal depending upon the seriousness of these fresh matters. I certainly hope that this will not occur and that the next 12 months will be free from conduct or performance issues.

If you wish to appeal against this decision you may do so to me within 10 calendar days of the date of this letter. You should state the grounds of your appeal, i.e. a) prejudicial or biased hearing – giving details; b) new evidence has come to light; c) too harsh a penalty.

You will be offered the opportunity of being heard in person. At this time you may be represented, if you so wish, by a trade union representative or a fellow worker.

Yours sincerely

[name]
Disciplining manager

Copy: Human Resources, trade union rep

MODEL LETTER 5 – *Notification of Outcome: Final Written Warning*

[Name]

[Address]

[Date]

Private and Confidential

Dear

RE: Final written warning

I refer to your hearing with the Investigating Officer [name] and me on [date] with [anyone else present] and your representative [name, trade union] **or** despite being advised of your right to representation you chose not to exercise it. The meeting was held under our Disciplinary Procedure.

At this meeting reference was made to [details of disciplinary issues]. During the meeting, it was also recorded that an improvement in your conduct/performance would be expected in the following areas: [detail]

Having fully considered these new/further matters, I have decided to issue a **final written warning** in respect of your conduct/performance/attitude. This warning will remain on your personnel file for a period of 12 months, after which time it will lapse for the purpose of initiating the next stage of the procedure. If there are any further issues concerning your conduct or performance, this may lead to further disciplinary action which may result in your dismissal.

If you wish to appeal against this decision you may do so in writing to me at the above address within 10 calendar days of the receipt of this letter stating briefly the grounds of your appeal. You will be offered the opportunity of being heard in person represented, if you so wish, by your trade union representative or a work colleague.

Yours sincerely

[name]
Disciplining manager

Copy: Human Resources, trade union rep

MODEL LETTER 6 – *Notification of Outcome: Dismissal*

[Name]

[Address]

[Date]

Private and Confidential

Dear

RE: Decision to dismiss

I refer to your hearing with me on [date] with [names of others present] and [either] your representative [name, trade union] **or** despite being advised of your right to representation you chose not to exercise it. The meeting was held under our Disciplinary Procedure.

At the hearing, reference was made to [details of disciplinary issues].

In view of the circumstances [and (if appropriate) in view of the fact that you had already received a previous warning/final warning], I have decided that you should be dismissed from your post of [job title].

I did not find your explanations or mitigation convincing or persuasive [state briefly what the individual said].

I have considered other penalties such as an extended final written warning, demotion, transfer to another role, bar on promotion, etc. but in view of your attitude and explanation and the gravity of the matters in issue I have dismissed all other options and believe that the only appropriate penalty in this particular case is dismissal [state summary or with notice or PILON]. Your Termination Date is [date].

[*If already on a live final warning:*

You are already on a live final warning. In these circumstances and in the alternative I am dismissing you for (serious) misconduct which warrants the next stage of our disciplinary procedure, which is dismissal (with or without notice or pay in lieu of notice).]

If you wish to appeal against this decision you may do so in writing to me at the above address within 10 calendar days of the receipt of this letter stating the grounds of your appeal. You will be offered the opportunity of being heard in person accompanied, if you so wish, by your trade union representative or a person of your own choosing.

You will receive any outstanding salary, payments and expenses due to you following your last day of employment together with your P45.

In these circumstances we will decline to give you a reference in line with our policy of not providing references to anyone dismissed for misconduct or performance issues **or** [We will only provide your employment dates, job title and reason for leaving in any future reference].

Yours sincerely

[name]
Disciplining manager

Copy: Human Resources, trade union rep

MODEL LETTER 7 – Appeal

[Name]

[Address]

[Date]

Private and Confidential

Dear

RE: Your appeal

Further to the disciplinary hearing held on [date] and to my letter dated [date] informing you of my decision, I understand from your letter dated [date] that you now wish to appeal against the decision to [refer to the outcome of the initial hearing].

In accordance with our Disciplinary Procedure I would advise you that I have arranged a meeting to consider your appeal. A copy of the disciplinary procedure is attached for your information. The meeting will be with [state] and will be at [place] on [date]. The meeting will consider [detail here the grounds for appeal].

Under our Disciplinary Procedure you are entitled to receive copies of the documents relating to the case that will be considered at the Appeal. I attach for your information, copies of the following documents:

(a) [List and send all of the information as previously sent out for the initial hearing.]
(b) [List and send any information submitted by the individual either before the initial hearing or at the hearing.]

If there is any further information relating to this case that you would like to submit to the governors for their consideration, will you please arrange for this to be sent to me as soon as possible and by [date] at the latest so that I can circulate copies to the Appeals Manager in plenty of time for their consideration before the meeting.

You have the right to be represented at this meeting by your trade union representative or a work colleague and you may if you wish call witnesses to support your case. Please let me know if you are intending to do this so that arrangements to accommodate your witnesses can be made.

Please confirm with me that you are able to attend this meeting on the date and times given. I have enclosed an additional copy of this letter and accompanying details for you to give to your trade union representative/work colleague.

Yours sincerely

[name]
Human Resources Manager

MODEL LETTER 8 – Notification of Outcome of Appeal

[Name]

[Address]

[Date]

Private and Confidential

Dear

RE: Outcome of appeal

I refer to your appeal hearing on [date].

My decision is not to uphold your appeal and confirm that [details of the disciplinary outcome].

My reasons are [give short reasons].

You will no doubt be disappointed at this decision and I am sorry that your career has ended in this way. I wish you all the best for the future.

Yours sincerely

[name]
Appeals manager

Copy: Human Resources, trade union rep

PRECEDENT 9M: Undertaking to behave

To [managing director]

[Date]

Following the disciplinary hearing held on [date], I hereby warrant and undertake the following matters:

1. I accept that I have in the past refused to co-operate with [name of manager] and others when asked to undertake routine, reasonable and legitimate requests and that, on several occasions I have refused to speak to [manager] or attend meetings when requested to do so. I have also refused to carry out tasks when asked to do so which has seriously affected [manager] and the running of the business.

2. I have apologised for all these matters and give an undertaking to [*manager*], being a duly authorised officer of the Company, that I will stop this negative and obstructive behaviour immediately and that I will from now on co-operate fully both in spirit as well as to the letter with [*manager*] and any other third parties conducting business with the Company. I further give an undertaking that I will respond to any reasonable and legitimate requests in a friendly and cheerful manner and that I will work in a constructive way in the future.

3. I understand that, in return for the undertakings given in (1) and (2) above, my employment has not been terminated. I accept that a Final Written Warning will be placed on my record recording the facts raised in my disciplinary hearing and I understand that this Warning will not lapse until a minimum of three years from the date of issue. If during that time there is any repetition of incidents that led to the disciplinary hearing, or any matters concerning my conduct or competence, I understand that the Company has the right to terminate my employment.

Signed .... Date ....

[*employee*]

PRECEDENT 9N: Recording the hearing

1. In order that an accurate account of the hearing can be taken, we intend to record the hearing using a double-headed recorder and to give you, immediately after the hearing has ended, a copy of all the recordings. We will then arrange for the recordings to be transcribed and you will be sent a copy as soon as it is ready.

2. Only if you have compelling objections will we reconsider this matter.

3. At the request of either party we can always switch off the recording if one party wishes to say something 'off the record'.

4. You may also record the hearing and you should ensure that you bring any recording equipment with you.

5. Any secret or covert recording of any meeting by an employee is regarded as unacceptable conduct. We would hope that if you wish to record any other form of meeting, you would say so upfront and we would not unreasonably withhold our consent.

PRECEDENT 9O: Letter regarding secret recording

[*Date*]

Dear [*name*]

RE: Recording disciplinary and grievance hearings

There have been occasions in the recent past when employees have secretly recorded grievance or disciplinary and appeal hearings or other meetings or telephone calls.

This has led to management being taken by surprise having talked openly and candidly unaware that the hearing or meeting or telephone call was being recorded.

In other cases the transcript and not the original tape has been produced for the Employment Tribunal hearing by the ex-employee and it has not accurately reflected what was said.

In order to regularise these matters and to ensure that the parties are on a level playing field and that there is a verbatim record of what was said, we will be recording every disciplinary hearing and appeal and grievance hearing. This will be done on a digital recorder which will then be transcribed and sent to the individual concerned as soon as possible thereafter. The recording can also be sent by email if requested.

It is often very important to repeat what was said at these hearings and in order to save the debate and dispute that follows when the meeting is not recorded, this is the procedure that will be followed in the future.

Finally, in one case the ex-employee felt it appropriate to play the secret recording that he had made to his former colleagues and outside third parties. This is of course a serious breach of confidentiality and a gross abuse of trust.

We hardly believe it is necessary to remind all staff that any such recordings whether overt or covert contain highly confidential material and must never be disclosed to any other third party. If necessary we would be prepared to seek an injunction restraining anyone from using that recording in the future and an Order to deliver up all such recordings.

I trust that you will see that recording such meetings will benefit everyone as everyone will then have a word-for-word record of what was said.

Yours sincerely

Managing Director

PRECEDENT 9P: Admissions of guilt

1. In any case where the employee admits what they have done, apologises and shows a real and genuine desire to improve their conduct or is convincing that this was a one-off incident and they have learnt from their mistake, immediately management discovers the offence and informs the individual, such admission and subsequent conduct will be taken into account in determining an appropriate penalty.

2. No such admission will be accepted unless it is made with the full knowledge and approval of the relevant union representative. If such admission is made, it will not be accepted on the basis of a 'plea bargain', i.e. a deal whereby if the employee admits the offence, management will necessarily treat them less severely.

3. Such admission must be made without any duress placed on the individual or inducement made to that individual. Any statement made by the individual will always be made in the presence of their union official.

4. The mere fact of an admission will not of itself be sufficient to reduce any potentially serious penalty. It would be highly significant and relevant, however, if by the employee owning up, the misconduct came to light.

5. Management will take into account the fact that any investigations into the matter and the disciplinary hearing have therefore been shortened.

6. If dismissal is deemed to be an appropriate sanction it might be effected with pay in lieu of notice and a reference may be given which stated that this was a one-off piece of conduct in an otherwise exemplary career and the employee made good in part by owning up and assisting management in its investigation.

PRECEDENT 9Q: Improved performance review (IPR) or performance improvement procedure (PIP)

1. Status of this procedure

1.1 This procedure runs in parallel with, i.e. concurrently with, and is not integrated into the Company's Disciplinary Procedure which is concerned primarily with misconduct issues. Management recognises that poor or unsatisfactory performance carries with it no fault in the normal case, as distinct from misconduct which often carries with it an element of dishonesty and premeditation, i.e. fault. As such, management is prepared to treat poor performance problems separately and distinct from the misconduct Disciplinary Procedure.

1.2 Thus an employee could be subject to two oral warnings in parallel, one issued for misconduct and one issued for poor performance. The time limits on those warnings may however be different (see below).

1.3 Please note that if a warning is given and at any time during the course of a warning for a work performance issue, the time for which the warning will run will be suspended for the period of the employee's sickness absence. This is on the grounds that the warning is to give the employee the opportunity to improve over a given period, say three months, and there will have been no such opportunity for improvement during a period of sick leave.

2. Purpose and scope

The capability procedure is separate and distinct from the Company's Performance Appraisal, Disciplinary and Grievance Procedures. This procedure will apply in the event that an employee's performance fails to meet the standards required as a result of inadequate skill-set or aptitude. The overall aim of this procedure is to identify and address areas of concern at an early stage in order to ensure that Company standards are achieved and maintained and that employees receive the opportunity and support required to improve.

3. General principles

In the event of poor performance, the following principles will apply:

3.1 There will be an initial counselling session where the cause of the poor performance will be investigated and established, for example it could be lack of skills, training, support staff, tools. The manager carrying out this initial counselling will give factual examples of the matters under review:

(a) the employee will be asked for their explanation and the explanation checked;
(b) where job descriptions are prepared, they should accurately convey the main purpose and scope of each job and tasks involved;
(c) where the reason is lack of the required skills, the employee, where practicable, should be assisted through training and be given reasonable time to reach the required standard of performance. If it is a question of lack of support staff or facilities, attention should be paid to this and assistance provided if appropriate.

3.2 The employee will be made aware of areas of under-performance and given a full opportunity to discuss underlying issues.

3.3 Additional training and support will be provided where it is felt that this may address the issues identified.

3.4 A reasonable amount of time, reflecting the circumstances of each case, will be allowed for improvement to be demonstrated.

3.5 If felt appropriate as a course of action, assistance will be provided in identifying any suitable alternative working arrangements or internal positions for which the employee may be eligible to apply.

3.6 An employee has the right to be accompanied by a work colleague or a trade union representative from Stage 2 of the procedure. In the event that the chosen representative is unavailable for a specified date, it will be postponed for a maximum of five working days.

3.7 An employee has the right of appeal against dismissal resulting from poor performance.

3.8 In some circumstances, the Company may consider that the employee's unsatisfactory performance amounts to, or has become, a matter of misconduct. In these circumstances, the Disciplinary Procedure may be initiated at a stage that the Company considers appropriate.

4. Procedure

Stage 1

Should an employee's level of performance give cause for concern in respect of skill or aptitude, the line manager should discuss this fully with the employee and explore:

(a) why the performance is under par or unsatisfactory and then check the employee's explanation;
(b) methods of improving the situation at an early stage, for example through the provision of guidance, direction, training or support.

An indication should be given and noted that this represents Stage 1 of this procedure.

Stage 2

Where unsatisfactory performance persists, relevant capability objectives will be discussed and set for a specific period. This period will be appropriate to the circumstances but will not normally be less than one month. During this period, progress against the objectives will be regularly monitored and discussed. If felt appropriate by either side, discussions about identifying different working arrangements or suitable alternative roles for which the employee may be eligible to apply may take place. At the end of the review period, a meeting will be held to discuss and assess the employee's progress against the objectives.

Stage 3

If the employee's performance remains unsatisfactory after Stage 2, a further formal interview will be arranged at which the circumstances of the problem and ways to improve performance will be discussed. If, as a result of the discussion, the line manager is satisfied that further action is required to improve performance, the necessary standards will be set out along with timescales for improvement. Again, the review period will be appropriate to the circumstances but will not normally be less than one month, and progress during the review period will be regularly monitored and discussed. At the end of the review period, a full report will be prepared and a meeting will be held to discuss and assess the employee's progress against the objectives.

5. Capability objectives

Capability objectives are set in order to clarify the standards of performance required. These objectives may require demonstration of a particular skill, or the ability to deliver a particular outcome or target. In all cases the objectives should be realistic and capable of being measured within set timescales. They should allow the employee to clearly understand the areas in which improvement is required, the priorities (if any) to be applied, the action needed to achieve improvement and the date by which improvement must be demonstrated.

6. **Potential outcomes**

6.1 Subject to the outcome at Stage 3, it will be confirmed that one of the following will apply:

(a) that the period of capability objectives will cease as substantive progress has been made against all of the original objectives set. The employee will be sent a letter confirming this, a copy of which will be placed on their personnel file;
(b) that although the employee has failed to meet the overall requirements in relation to the stated objectives, a further opportunity will be given to achieve Company standards during a period of extended capability objectives. The period of extension will be confirmed in writing and regular reports and discussions will continue throughout this period;
(c) that the employee has failed either to attain or show substantive progress towards reaching these objectives. In this instance, subject to there being no suitable alternative role, the Company reserves the right to terminate employment. This decision may only be taken by a manager at [*specify*] level or above after consultation with an HR Adviser.

6.2 Owing to the nature of capability, a proper account will be taken of the particular circumstances surrounding an individual's case.

7. **Appeals**

If dismissal is confirmed, the employee has the right of appeal against the decision.

An employee who wishes to appeal against dismissal must do so within seven working days of being informed of that decision. The employee should state clearly in writing the full grounds on which the appeal is based, e.g:

(a) where they consider that they have been dismissed unjustly;
(b) where they contend that a matter of fact has been omitted or not properly taken into account.

8. **Appeal procedure**

8.1 The appeal should be made to the line manager of the person who instigated the dismissal.

8.2 Where practicable the appeal will be heard within 10 working days.

Please note that if an employee appeals and the dismissal decision is commuted/revoked, then their notice of dismissal is automatically revoked and they will be reinstated or re-engaged with or without a lesser penalty.

8.3 If an appeal against dismissal is successful and the employee continues in the Company's employment, they may be reinstated or re-engaged or have another lesser penalty than dismissal. If reinstated then continuous service will be unaffected and they will be recompensed for any loss of pay.

8.4 If a decision to dismiss is confirmed, then the date of termination of employment shall be as originally stated in the employee's letter of dismissal.

8.5 In most circumstances the decision will be communicated to the employee within five working days of the hearing.

9. Probationary employees

9.1 Please note that in cases of employees during their probationary service, i.e. during the first [six] months of employment, only one official warning under this procedure will be given. If performance fails to meet the required standards after this official warning, then the employee will be liable to dismissal with due notice or payment in lieu. There will be no right of appeal against any such decision to dismiss in such circumstances.

9.2 Any official warning deemed necessary will not be given until at least [six] weeks' service has been completed.

10. Internal promotions

Where the employee is promoted, the consequences of 'failing to make the grade' should be explained. In some cases the employee will be promoted on the basis of a probationary period with the condition that the Company has the right to transfer or downgrade should the employee fail to satisfy their immediate manager that they are competent in the promoted post. In other cases, the 'promoted' member of staff will remain on the same grade and salary for the duration of the probationary period and will receive an 'acting up' allowance during such time. If the probationary period is not confirmed, the employee will not transfer to the higher grade.

PRECEDENT 9R: Disciplinary and dismissal procedures

We hope and expect that all employees will enjoy their work and will observe the rules and standards which the Company has set. However, in the event of an employee failing to follow the Company rules of conduct, the Company will implement the procedure outlined below.

This procedure is designed to ensure fair and consistent treatment of all employees where disciplinary or dismissal action applies. We will ensure that any disciplinary matters are dealt with promptly and consistently.

Where it is alleged that an employee has committed a disciplinary offence, this may be dealt with at an informal interview of concern or at Stage 1 or at any other stage of the procedure that the Company deems appropriate.

Disciplinary procedure: informal – interview of concern

In some cases before formal disciplinary action is taken, the Company may carry out some informal action such as counselling or holding 'an interview of concern'.

These will be of an informal nature between the Manager/Supervisor/Team Manager and employee to identify and explore problems or situations that have arisen. The objective is to encourage and help the employee to understand their conduct and improve, to determine alternative measures to overcome problems if appropriate or to resolve the problem without resorting to any formal procedures.

Records of interviews of concern will be placed on the employee's personnel file and can be referred to in any later proceedings.

Where it is not possible to overcome issues informally through an interview of concern or if the issue is sufficiently serious to warrant further action, then it will be referred to an appropriate Line Manager to consider the formal disciplinary process. Where a decision is taken to initiate the formal procedure, the interview of concern will be deemed to be part of the investigation process.

Disciplinary procedure: formal

The Company reserves the right to enter the formal procedure at any stage, depending upon the seriousness of the offence.

The following points will be observed when conducting any disciplinary hearing:

- The employee will be informed in writing prior to any hearing of the nature of the complaint/alleged offence or wrongdoing against them.
- The notification will also give details of the time and venue for the hearing.
- A reasonable investigation will be carried out in order to establish the facts of the case.
- The employee will be provided, where appropriate, with written copies of evidence and relevant witness statements in advance of the hearing.
- Hearings will take place in private and sufficient notice given in advance to enable both parties to have adequate time to prepare.
- The employee will be advised of their right to be accompanied by a work colleague or trade union representative (a representative does not have to belong to a trade union which is recognised by the Company), acting as a witness to the proceedings. (For employees under 18 a parent or guardian may accompany them.)
- In very serious cases or cases where the employee has been or will be reported to their professional body/Regulatory Body or to the police and there is a possibility they may not be permitted to continue working in their profession, e.g. doctors, nurses, teachers, etc. or that they might be imprisoned, they will be permitted to be represented/accompanied by a lawyer of their choice and at their expense. The Company reserves the right at such a hearing or at any other time to have their own lawyer present. In all cases where this happens, the employee will be given the right to be accompanied by a lawyer of their choice.
- The employee's immediate Manager/Line Manager will normally be present unless they have been involved at the investigation stage, in which case a suitable alternative Line Manager will hold the meeting, and where possible, a member of the Human Resources Team will also be present to act in the capacity of the Human Resources Representative. If a Human Resources member cannot be present, a suitable impartial Manager will act as their substitute; however, this will only happen with the prior written agreement of the Human Resources Director/Human Resources Business Partner. The Company also reserves the right in any serious case to have a lawyer present and in such a case the employee will also be granted the right to bring a lawyer or another suitable third party to the hearing. All parties will be required to sign a confidentiality agreement in respect of the contents of the hearing.
- At the hearing the Manager/Line Manager will inform the employee of the basis of the issue/complaint and give them an opportunity to state their case before any decision is made.
- Management reserves the right to record any disciplinary or performance hearing in order to have an accurate and verbatim record. The employee may also record the hearing. Management will give the employee a copy of the recording as soon as possible after the hearing.
- The hearing will always be adjourned before any decisions are reached by management. The length of adjournment will depend upon the circumstances of the hearing.
- The warning will make it quite clear what breach has occurred and what must and must not be done in the future and this will be recorded on the employee's file and treated as confidential.
- The employee will be made aware of their right to appeal and the appeals procedure.

- Where appropriate and in exceptional circumstances, the option of counselling or welfare action will be considered.
- Confidentiality will be respected at all times. However, it is recognised that relevant parties and witnesses will need to be consulted subject to the issue below.
- In the case of complaints such as discrimination, harassment or bullying, management reserves the right to disclose to the victim what the disciplinary outcome is but they will be required to keep some information strictly confidential.
- If requested by the employee, copies of notes (if any) taken during the disciplinary meeting will be provided as soon as possible.
- In any case where a grievance is raised during the disciplinary process, management will determine whether to suspend the disciplinary procedure until the grievance is resolved or to hear the grievance at the same hearing as the disciplinary offence.
- In any case where the employee does not attend the disciplinary hearing or provides medical evidence that they are not well enough to attend, the hearing will be postponed at least on one occasion and reconvened no earlier than seven days from the original date. Any further requests for postponements will be considered but it may be decided to hold the hearing giving the employee the following options:
    (a) to attend by telephone;
    (b) to send a representative;
    (c) to send in written representations;
    (d) to combine (b) and (c);
    (e) to attend at a different location or neutral location.

Lapsed warnings

Please note that lapsed warnings for a future offence which is the same or similar can be taken into account in the following circumstances:

- in order to establish whether the employee has had an exemplary record in future cases of misconduct or gross misconduct;
- where the same or a similar offence has been committed in the past where the fact of the earlier warning will go towards the credibility of the employee's explanation on the future occasion and will assist in determining an appropriate penalty, e.g. if the employee has previously been warned about claiming for private mileage when they alleged they had not been told that only business mileage can be claimed and they are found making claims for private mileage on a future occasion outside the time limit of that earlier warning;
- in redundancy selection criteria the fact of previous disciplinary warnings may be used as one of the objective criteria for selection for redundancy.

Drugs and alcohol offences

Someone with a drugs or alcohol addiction is normally considered ill and as such every opportunity will be given to them through the Company's drugs and alcohol policy to be treated for their addiction and to have a period of adjustment when back at work.

However, refusal to be tested for drugs/illicit substances or alcohol when there is a suspicion of alcohol or drug abuse or a simple case of drunkenness or coming to work or being at work under the influence of alcohol or illicit substances or drinking at work or taking illicit substances at work, etc. are all deemed to be serious or gross misconduct which will normally be dealt with under either Stage 3 or Stage 4 of this procedure.

Stages of the disciplinary procedure

Investigation

An investigation will be undertaken in every case of misconduct and witnesses may be interviewed and documentary evidence gathered. During this time the individual may be suspended (see below).

The individual concerned will be invited to attend an investigation meeting and invited to make a statement and answer questions. If the employee declines to do so no negative inference will be drawn.

An independent person will carry out the investigation and this person will not be involved in any decision-making.

Witness statements and other evidence will normally be sent to the employee in advance of any disciplinary hearing.

In rare cases we may suspect fraud or dishonest conduct on the part of an employee, for example where an individual has gone off sick but is actually taking a holiday, is working for themselves, has threatened to or has made a claim for personal injuries for an alleged injury at work, or is just shirking. In such cases where fraud is suspected the Company reserves the right to instruct private detectives to carry out covert surveillance, which may mean following the individual when they leave home and recording these activities by video and/or audio. Such evidence will be shown to the individual before disciplinary proceedings are started for an explanation to be given. This surveillance evidence may be disclosed to our insurers and/or to the police and it may be used in any legal proceedings. We give clear instructions to such staff about not intruding into an individual's home, e.g. not tricking their way into a home and covertly recording the individual's activities in their home. All covert surveillance will take place in public places.

Stage 1 Oral Warning

A Stage 1 Oral Warning will be issued by the Line Manager/Supervisor/Team Manager in conjunction with the Human Resources Department and will normally be disregarded for disciplinary purposes after six months from the date of issue. The warning and duration of the warning will be confirmed in writing to the employee.

Stage 2 First Written Warning

Should the employee repeat the misconduct or commit another offence within the currency of the warning the Manager/Supervisor/Team Manager may move to this next stage of the disciplinary procedure.

A Stage 2 First Written Warning will be recorded but will be disregarded for disciplinary purposes after 12 months from the date of issue. The warning will be confirmed in writing to the employee. The warning will give details of the conduct complained about and the consequences of repetition. It will also warn that a Stage 3 Final Written Warning may be issued if there is any recurrence of the conduct or if another misconduct offence is committed within the required period and will advise of the right to appeal.

Stage 3 Final Written Warning

A Stage 3 Final Written Warning will be issued in the following circumstances:

- if a further breach of Company procedures, standards, conduct has taken place or a commission of another misconduct offence has taken place; or
- if there is misconduct that is serious enough to warrant a Stage 3 Final Written Warning rather than dismissal.

The Stage 3 Final Written Warning will be recorded but will be disregarded for disciplinary purposes after a 12-month period from the date of issue. The Stage 3 Final Written Warning will give details of the complaint and will warn that dismissal, or some other action short of dismissal, may result if there is any recurrence of the misconduct or the commission of another misconduct offence, within a stated period. It will also advise of the right to appeal.

Any subsequent act may result in a Stage 4 Dismissal.

The Company reserves the right where the circumstances warrant it and where dismissal could have been an option, to give an extended final written warning and/or demotion for specified period, a bar on promotion or training, no pay increase, transfer to a different department or location, etc. in place of dismissal.

Stage 4 Dismissal

Dismissal will be determined by an appropriate impartial, authorised Senior Manager/Director in conjunction with the Human Resources Department. Dismissal may take place if:

- there has been a recurrence of the offence or the commission of a new offence during the currency of a warning; or
- the misconduct is sufficiently serious that it warrants dismissal for a first offence (see gross misconduct below).

If dismissal takes place, Human Resources will issue a written statement to the employee, which will contain:

- a statement of the case found against the employee and the reasons for dismissal;
- the date on which the employment contract will end;
- the appropriate details of payment in lieu of notice;
- details of the right to appeal.

Suspension

Suspension of an employee will occur where it is deemed inappropriate for the employee to continue working or remain upon Company premises or if it is reasonably believed that the disciplinary process could be compromised. Employees will be advised of the reason for suspension. The suspension is not considered a disciplinary act or sanction.

Suspension may take place while investigations are carried out where for example relationships have broken down, in gross misconduct cases or where there are risks to an employee's or the Company's property or responsibilities to other parties or where an employer has reasonable grounds for concern that evidence has been or might be tampered with, destroyed or witnesses pressurised before the meeting.

Suspension with pay will not be unnecessarily protracted. It is not an assumption of guilt and is not considered a disciplinary sanction.

During suspension, we will carry out appropriate investigations before inviting the employee to attend first an investigation hearing and then a disciplinary hearing.

Whilst the employee is suspended, all terms and conditions of employment will remain unchanged and basic pay (excluding any bonus/performance payments) will be paid.

The Company retains the right to retrieve Company cars when necessary. However, if this occurs a suitable alternative vehicle will be supplied unless the issue concerns alcohol or drug abuse when the car will be removed for health and safety reasons.

Gross misconduct/summary dismissal

Summary dismissal means that the employee's contract of employment is terminated with immediate effect and without contractual notice or payment in lieu of notice. Summary dismissal may be an appropriate penalty in cases of gross misconduct.

If gross misconduct is alleged against you, the Company may suspend you from work in line with the process above. This is a neutral act and does not signify or imply any guilt on your part or finding of guilt on the part of the Company.

If, following an investigation and after a full disciplinary meeting, the Company is satisfied that there has been an act of gross misconduct, the outcome will normally be summary dismissal without notice or payment in lieu of notice.

Where the outcome for a gross misconduct offence is termination of employment but the Company believes there are sufficient mitigating factors, the Company may make a payment equivalent to all or part of an employee's contractual notice period. This payment is solely at the Company's discretion.

No employee will be dismissed without the Company carrying out any investigation or requesting attendance at a disciplinary meeting.

The following are examples of gross misconduct. The list is non-exhaustive.

- Theft, any form of dishonesty, fraud, deliberate falsification of records, etc.
- Acts of violence or intimidation either by conduct or language or inciting others to do so.
- Impairment on duty through alcohol or substance abuse or drinking on duty or taking illicit substances on duty or being found in possession of alcohol or illicit substances or dealing in illicit substances whilst on duty.
- Driving a company vehicle whilst under the influence of alcohol or substance abuse.
- Wilful damage to Company property/equipment or that of any third party.
- Inappropriate language or conduct to customers/clients/colleagues/managers/ directors.
- Physical or sexual assault or threatening physical assault or verbal abuse.
- Any serious breaches of data protection or confidentiality rules.
- Any act which brings or is likely to bring the Company into potential or actual disrepute.
- Engaging in sexual or libidinous behaviour (including downloading and/or watching porn or child porn) in the workplace whether in or out of office hours; attending strip clubs or lap dancing clubs or other unsuitable premises, where members of the public may recognise you and where this is incompatible with your role in the organisation or our organisation.
- Claiming expenses for items specifically excluded from our expenses policy, e.g. visits to strip clubs and lap dancing clubs, gambling houses or casinos, etc.
- Gross negligence/gross dereliction of duty which could cause or actually causes loss, damage or injury to the Company or to a third party.
- Serious act of insubordination.
- Refusal to obey a lawful or reasonable instruction.
- Misuse of the Company's computer, telephone or other communications systems.
- Serious breach of the media policy.
- Serious breach of the company health & safety policy.

- Serious breach of the email, internet and communications policies.
- Getting into serious and significant debt.
- Unauthorised disclosure of your (or anyone else's) remuneration package save in the context of an equal pay or sex discrimination complaint about unequal pay.

Appeals procedure

Employees have the right to appeal against any disciplinary action and they will be advised of this at every stage of the formal disciplinary procedure.

The grounds for appeal are that:

(a) the oral or written warning or penalty is unfair, i.e. too harsh or not warranted at all;
(b) new evidence has come to light that was not or could not have been available at the original hearing; or
(c) the procedure followed was unfair, biased or prejudiced.

In all cases of appeals against a warning or decision to dismiss, the appeal should be made in writing within five working days of receipt of the decision, to the Senior Manager (as advised in your letter of dismissal/disciplinary action via the Human Resources Department). In exceptional circumstances it may be necessary for a Manager of a similar or senior grade to determine an appeal.

You will be informed in writing of the date and time of any appeal hearing and you will be entitled to bring a work colleague or a full-time trade union representative (a representative does not have to belong to a trade union which is recognised by the Company), acting as a witness to the proceedings. (For employees under 18 a parent or guardian may accompany them or in cases detailed above, a lawyer.) The appropriate Manager will consider the appeal, investigate and consult the parties and will normally give a decision, confirmed in writing, within 10 working days (via the Human Resources Department). Such decisions are final.

In cases of gross misconduct resulting in summary dismissal, the appeal should be made in writing via the Human Resources Department. Wherever possible, the appeal will be chaired by a member of the Executive Board (with the exception of the HR Director).

All appeals will be treated confidentially and should be heard without unreasonable delay (normally within 10 working days of receiving the appeal). Nothing in the procedure shall remove an employee's statutory rights. The Manager's decision will be final and this will be the end of the internal process.

Grievances raised during the disciplinary procedure

Sometimes employees who are the subject of disciplinary proceedings raise a grievance during the course of the proceedings. If it is a serious allegation of discrimination or victimisation against their manager and there are *prima facie* grounds for this allegation, then we will hear the grievance raised before the disciplinary hearing takes place and determine the grievance first. However, there may be cases where we deem it appropriate to hear the grievance at the same time as the disciplinary hearing – hearing the grievance first and then going on to the disciplinary issues.

Human Resources Department

[*Date*]

10

Redundancy

10.1 Redundancy dismissals

Redundancy is one of the potentially fair reasons for dismissal pursuant to s.98(2)(c) of the Employment Rights Act 1996.

Definition of redundancy

The definition of 'redundancy' in s.139 of the Employment Rights Act 1996 is whether the requirement for employees doing that particular kind of work has ceased or diminished or is expected to cease or diminish in the place where they are so employed.

Points to note

Whether the work has increased or not is not the issue. The issue is whether the demand for employees doing that particular work has ceased or diminished. In *Safeway Stores Ltd* v. *Burrell* [1997] IRLR 200 the EAT observed:

> From time to time the mistake is made of focusing on a diminution in the work to be done, not the employees who do it.

In *Aylward* v. *Glamorgan Holiday Home Ltd* UKEAT/0167/02 (unreported), the EAT stated:

> It is necessary to look at the overall requirement for employees to do work of a particular kind, not at the amount of work to be done[.]

Furthermore, even if the employees have been replaced by contractors or agency staff or independent consultants or even robots, then those employees will still have been dismissed for redundancy, because the need for 'employees' has ceased or diminished.

Finally, whether the employer's profits are increasing is irrelevant. The balance sheet is irrelevant in a redundancy case.

TNS UK Ltd v. *Swainston* [2014] UKEAT 0603/12 (unreported) is a case where the EAT held that cost may drive the need for redundancy but nevertheless the dismissal is still attributable to redundancy.

Even where there is still a need for the same amount of work to be done, albeit that it can be done by fewer employees, there is still a redundancy.

Particular kind of work

The question often for Employment Tribunals is whether the words 'particular kind of work' mean the work specified in the contract or the work that the employee is actually doing at the time of the redundancy.

The 'particular kind' of work is not restricted to what work is required to be performed under the contract. Harvey (in *Harvey on Industrial Relations and Employment Law*) points out that the House of Lords in *Murray* v. *Foyle Meats Ltd* [1999] IRLR 562 'rejected the heresy that the expression "work of a particular kind" in section 139 meant the work for which the employee was contractually employed; that is, the work as defined by the contract of employment'.

In *Murray* the House of Lords confirmed that employees will be dismissed for reason of redundancy if the employer no longer needs employees doing a particular kind of work, whether or not the contract specifies that particular work. Here meat plant operatives normally working in the slaughter hall were found by the Northern Ireland courts to have been dismissed on grounds of redundancy when the employer decided that it needed fewer employees in the slaughter hall, notwithstanding that all those made redundant could be required to work in any part of the factory.

Two questions of fact need to be determined in order to ascertain whether there is a redundancy.

The first is whether one or other of various states of economic affairs exists. In this case, the relevant one is whether the requirements of the business for employees to carry out work of a particular kind have diminished.

The second question is whether the dismissal is attributable, wholly or mainly, to that state of affairs. This is a question of causation.

The decision in *Murray* means that a dismissal must now be regarded as by reason of redundancy wherever it is 'attributable' to redundancy. This appears to resolve any doubts about 'bumping' redundancies, i.e. selecting someone for redundancy whose job has not diminished or ceased to make room for someone whose job has diminished or ceased. Redundancies by reason of bumping (see below) are covered by the statutory definition of redundancy, provided the necessary causal connection can be established.

The House of Lords' decision in *Murray* allows attention to shift from whether a technical definition is satisfied to the substantive questions of whether it was fair to select an employee to be made redundant and whether the redundancy dismissal was carried out in a fair manner.

10.2 Procedure

The foreword to the ACAS Code of Practice 2015 makes it clear that the recommendations contained in the Code do not apply in the case of redundancy dismissals. This means, at least in theory, there is no need to hold a 'hearing' or an appeal. However, many employers hold a termination meeting and an appeal hearing in redundancy dismissal cases.

A redundancy dismissal can be unfair for one of three reasons:

(a) failure to consult at all or not in a meaningful way;
(b) unfair selection;
(c) failure to consider suitable alternative employment.

The dicta in *Williams* v. *Compair Maxam Ltd* [1982] IRLR 83 is still good law.

1. The employer will seek to give as much warning as possible of impending redundancies so as to enable the union and employees who may be affected to take early steps to inform themselves of the relevant facts, consider possible alternative solutions and, if necessary, find alternative employment in the undertaking or elsewhere.
2. The employer will consult the union as to the best means by which the desired management result can be achieved fairly and with as little hardship to the employees as possible. In particular, the employer will seek to agree with the union the criteria to be applied in selecting the employees to be made redundant. When a selection has been made, the employer will consider with the union whether the selection has been made in accordance with those criteria.
3. Whether or not an agreement as to the criteria to be adopted has been agreed with the union, the employer will seek to establish criteria for selection which so far as possible do not depend solely upon the opinion of the person making the selection but can be objectively checked against such things as attendance record, efficiency at the job, experience or length of service.
4. The employer will seek to ensure that the selection is made fairly in accordance with these criteria and will consider any representations the union may make as to such selection.
5. The employer will seek to see whether instead of dismissing an employee, they could be offered alternative employment.

10.3 Bumping

'Bumping' occurs where an employee whose job is redundant 'bumps' another employee out of their job so that the employee who was 'bumped' is the one who is actually made redundant. This sometimes happens when a more senior employee is prepared to take a more junior role to avoid redundancy.

In *North* v. *Lionel Leventhal Ltd* UKEAT/0265/04/MAA the claimant was a senior editor and was made redundant in a cost-cutting exercise. The only alternative role that he could have been offered was a more junior one. It was assumed by the employer that as the employee had not raised the possibility of a junior role he would not consider it. The employer failed to offer this junior role and the employee argued that he had been unfairly dismissed. The original tribunal held the employer had acted unfairly by failing to give proper consideration to this alternative employment. The employer appealed, but the EAT upheld the decision of the tribunal. It added that there is no absolute rule that an employee must initiate discussions about a more junior role and employers may not necessarily rely on such a failure as being a defence to an allegation of unfair dismissal.

The EAT did not hold that there was a duty on employers to consider bumping in every case. Instead, the EAT held that whether it was reasonable for the employer to consider bumping would depend on a number of factors, namely:

- whether there is a vacancy for the junior role;
- how different the two jobs are;
- the difference in remuneration between the two jobs;
- the relative length of service of the two employees;
- the qualifications of the employee in danger of redundancy;
- other factors which may apply in a particular case.

However, in *Byrne* v. *Arvin Meritor LVS (UK) Ltd* EAT/239/02/MAA the EAT had held in 2003 that a tribunal had correctly concluded that a dismissal was not unfair because the employer had failed to consider dismissing a long-serving junior employee in order to retain a more highly experienced senior employee. The EAT held that the obligation on an employer to act reasonably is not one which imposes absolute obligations, and certainly no absolute obligation to 'bump' or even consider it. The issue is what a reasonable employer would do in the circumstances and in particular, by way of consideration by the tribunal, whether what the employer did do was within the reasonable band of responses open to a reasonable employer.

There are conflicting decisions on 'bumping'. It will be for each tribunal to decide, on the facts in issue, whether a lack of consideration of 'bumping' is unreasonable and therefore an unfair dismissal. The factors as listed in the *North* case above will influence a tribunal's decision, as will if the employer has previously engaged in the practice of 'bumping'.

Employers should consider whether 'bumping' would be appropriate in every potential redundancy situation when looking at the issue of suitable alternative employment.

A paper trail should be kept to demonstrate that bumping was considered, even if the employer concludes that it was not appropriate in the circumstances. 'Bumping' is not appropriate in every case and in some cases it would even be inappropriate to 'bump' as an employer must be fair to both employees concerned. There must be compelling reasons for making employee A redundant and giving employee B their job and employers should remember that if employee A is made redundant they could claim unfair dismissal. A fair consultation procedure must be followed in both cases.

It seems that a tribunal will want to see that the employer at least considered 'bumping' as a possibility and that the employer did not just dismiss the possibility out of hand because it assumed that the employee would not take a more junior role.

Does the need to reduce a full-time post to part-time or increase the hours from part-time to full-time constitute redundancy?

Unfortunately, there are two conflicting decisions on whether a reduction or increase in hours from full-time to part-time or vice versa constitutes a redundancy.

In *Mr Ron Packman T/A Packman Lucas Associates* v. *Ms P Fauchon* UKEAT/0017/12/LA the EAT upheld the Employment Tribunal's decision that the claimant had been dismissed for redundancy when she refused to work on reduced hours when a software programme was introduced that reduced the number of hours for which she was needed.

Harvey on Industrial Relations and Employment Law (para.E911) argued that:

> ... a reduction in hours does not per se give rise to a claim for a redundancy payment, because a reduction in hours does not as such constitute a dismissal. If, however, the reduction of hours is achieved by way of dismissal, actual, constructive or otherwise, then the dismissal is by reason of redundancy, if and in so far as the reduction in hours demonstrates that overall the business now requires less work from its workforce.

The Employment Tribunal found that Ms Fauchon was entitled to a redundancy payment, holding the textbook *Harvey* as a higher authority than the unreported EAT decision in *Aylward* (see above).

On appeal, the EAT came to the same decision, concluding that there can be a redundancy dismissal following a downturn in work and subsequent reduction in hours in which that work is carried out, where the work done by the workforce is reduced but the headcount remains the same.

One approach is to address some cases of potential redundancy in the alternative as one of a reorganisation and after following a proper consultation on the proposed variation, etc. if fewer than 50 per cent of the staff object, their dismissal may be fair for 'some other substantial reason'.

10.4 Redundancy checklist

Here is a checklist for employers embarking on a redundancy exercise:

1. Preliminaries

- Consider ways of avoiding redundancies such as flexible working or job-share arrangements. Other options include seconding staff to charities or clients, encouraging employees to take career breaks/sabbaticals, reducing overtime, salary sacrifice arrangements, a hiring freeze, a pay freeze/

- deferral, reducing/cutting bonuses and/or pension payments, reducing the use of agency workers, and seeking agreement to reduce hours of work.
- In a difficult job market, many people would rather keep their job under a different arrangement than be unemployed. The above strategies can also mean that when the market picks up, it is easier, cheaper and quicker for companies to react.
- Asking staff to volunteer for redundancy is also a possible solution but, as most employers will want to retain a balanced workforce, they should make it clear that they retain a veto on any such application. More experienced, longer-serving staff will tend to volunteer because they are more likely to get enhanced redundancy payments or pension arrangements. Employers must make it clear that the needs of the business are paramount and that they need to retain essential skills – and therefore they can reject applications for voluntary redundancy where appropriate. Wording such as the following will suffice:

  > We reserve the right not to accept all or any applications for voluntary redundancy, particularly if we consider that it is in the best interests of the company to retain certain staff.

- If headcount reduction is unavoidable, take legal and other advice before starting on a redundancy exercise.

2. Ensure that it is a genuine redundancy

- Dismissal by reason of redundancy is one of the potentially fair reasons for dismissal – but it is essential that there is a genuine redundancy situation to start with.
- Ensure that the role or jobs are 'redundant' within the statutory definition. There is a genuine redundancy situation where:
    - the employer ceases to carry out the work for which that employee was employed (i.e. business closure);
    - the employer ceases to carry out the work for which the particular employee was employed at the place where the employee worked (i.e. workplace closure);
    - the employer needs fewer people to carry out the kind of work for which the employee was employed (i.e. reduced requirement for employees);
    - the employer needs fewer people to carry out work of the kind for which the employee was employed at the place where they worked (i.e. reduced requirement for employees at the employee's workplace).
- For example, if a replacement is to be recruited to work in the same or very similar role in the same establishment, then that role is not redundant because the work of that particular kind has not ceased or diminished – even if it is given a different job title!

- The employer's reasons will need to fall within the statutory definition of redundancy in order to be a potentially fair reason.

3. Establish how many proposed dismissals

- If there is a proposal to dismiss as redundant 20 or more employees at one establishment, within a period of 90 days, the collective consultation obligations are triggered: see point 6 below.
- Staff who apply and are accepted for voluntary redundancy should be included when calculating the number of proposed dismissals.
- If there are fewer than 20 proposed dismissals, an individual consultation process should be followed: see point 7 below.

4. Maternity and redundancy

- Take particular care if within the pool at risk of redundancy there are women on maternity leave – if their roles are dismissed as 'redundant' and they are dismissed because they are on maternity leave, then those dismissals may well be both automatically unfair and unlawful (sex discrimination).
- If redundancies occur during a woman's maternity leave she is entitled to ignore any dismissal notice and has the right to be offered, in preference to others, any suitable available vacancy. This means that if a woman is not due to return for several weeks or months, a temporary worker may need to be recruited until she returns in order to keep the alternative position available for her. Regulation 10 of the MPL Regulations requires this otherwise it is an automatic unfair dismissal.
- Do not forget to involve potentially redundant women on maternity leave in all discussions and consultations on their potential redundancy and when considering alternative roles.
- Employers should be flexible when consulting with staff on maternity leave, e.g. by holding individual meetings with them at home or on the telephone.

5. Selection criteria and process

- Ensure that the selection of staff, if there is more than one role at risk of being terminated, is done on a fair and objective basis.
- Criteria such as 'being a good team player' or 'popular with clients' are too subjective as they are often based simply on the personal views of line managers. Criteria based on the skills and knowledge required to carry out the job are more likely to be assessed objectively.
- Provided sensible precautions are taken, subjective criteria can be incorporated, e.g. the quality of the individual's relationship with customers. Tribunals are tolerant of some subjectivity, as long as decisions are substantiated by evidence sourced from robust performance management

systems, or based on the views of at least two managers who are familiar with the employee's work.
- Avoid any criteria that are potentially discriminatory on the grounds of sex, race, disability and age. For example, when applying an attendance criterion, ensure that this does not discriminate indirectly against women who have taken maternity leave or staff who are/have been absent because of a disability.
- The selection procedure should place everyone in the same or similar role being considered for redundancy into a selection matrix. Factors or criteria can be chosen and given marks, which, say, add up to 100.
- A timeframe should be chosen – say over the last 12 or 24 months.
- For scoring to be as fair as possible, it is best if two people score the individuals separately without conferring with the other scorer and then take the average score for each person (there will then be evidence of impartiality if an employee makes a claim for unfair dismissal).
- Using factual material such as absence records, appraisals, meeting notes, emails and sales records, marks should be awarded and those marks should then be checked by another manager. An option to consider (for larger employers) is anonymising the matrix using a key in substitution for the names of people being selected for redundancy, and then those selected should individually be consulted (see below). The employee can be given a copy of the matrix with a ring round the letter or number that corresponds with the employee's name.
- Before the selection criteria are actually applied, the individual consultation process (see point 7 below) should be started. Even where a collective consultation process is followed (see point 6 below), a failure to carry out an individual consultation can lead to a dismissal being unfair. The individual process can start following discussion of the selection criteria in the collective process, but all people at risk of redundancy should have the chance to give their input before the selection criteria are applied.
- During the consultation period regular emails and notices of internal vacancies should be given and an email sent from the Human Resources department to all Heads of Departments setting out the skill-sets of those at risk of redundancy and asking the Heads of Department to notify Human Resources immediately of any actual or future vacancies in their departments. Keep these emails as evidence of seeking alternative employment.
- There is no fixed period for consultation but a fair consultation period is likely to take between two and four weeks. In practice it could be shorter or longer than that, depending on the business, the number of staff involved, how the scoring works, etc.
- Do not forget that while an employee needs two years' continuous employment to qualify for the right not to be unfairly dismissed and a statutory redundancy payment, there are many reasons which will make selection for redundancy automatically unfair (and hence no qualifying

service is required). These include such things as selecting someone for a health and safety reason; a reason connected with pregnancy, maternity or parental leave; a reason relating to rights under the Working Time Regulations, or any other of the protected grounds.

6. *Collective consultation*

- Remember that the definition of redundancy for consultation purposes is different from the definition of redundancy for dismissal purposes. For consultation purposes 'redundancy' means any dismissal for a reason (or reasons) not related to the individual concerned. This is a wider definition which encompasses reorganisations which do not result in an overall reduction in numbers (e.g. because new staff are also recruited), and employees who are dismissed and re-engaged to effect a change in terms and conditions.
- If 20 or more staff are at risk of redundancy, then collective consultation needs to take place with union or work representatives at least 30 days before the first dismissal is due to take effect, i.e. when notice is due to expire not when notice is given.
- If 100 or more are at risk at any one establishment, then consultation must take place at least 90 days before the first dismissal is due to take effect, i.e. when notice is due to expire not when notice is given.
- Before consultations can start, the following information must be given in writing:
    - the reasons for the proposals for redundancy;
    - the numbers and descriptions of employees whom it is proposed to dismiss as redundant;
    - the total number of employees of any such description employed at the establishment in question;
    - the way in which employees will be selected for redundancy;
    - how the dismissals are to be carried out (including any procedure that has been agreed, e.g. contractual procedures), plus the period over which the dismissals are to take effect;
    - the proposed way in which any redundancy payments in excess of the statutory minimum are to be calculated.
- Remember the following on collective consultation:
    - Consultation must cover ways of avoiding the dismissals, reducing the number of staff to be dismissed and mitigating the consequences of the dismissals.
    - Employers must consult about the business reasons for redundancies as part of the obligation to consult about the ways in which redundancies can be avoided.
    - Consultation must start 'in good time', i.e. as soon as there is a proposal to dismiss and certainly before the giving of notice of redundancy. Ideally, consultation should begin when proposals are

at a formative stage. Tribunals are tightening up on this and an employer runs big risks if decisions are taken on dismissal prior to consultation.
- Consultation must be undertaken 'with a view to reaching agreement' which implies some form of negotiation – but this does not mean that employers have actually to reach an agreement with the appropriate representatives.
- Check to see whether there are any additional obligations under the Information and Consultation of Employees Regulations 2004, SI 2004/3426 which now affect employers with 50 or more staff.
- Failure to comply with the rules may lead to a protective award of up to 90 days' pay for each affected employee. This is a punitive measure and the presumption is that it will be 90 days' pay (even if the minimum period of consultation is 30 days).

- Where collective consultation requirements are triggered, employers must notify the Secretary of State (on form HR1). Most, but not all, of the information which must be disclosed for consultation purposes is also required on form HR1. Failure to notify the Secretary of State is a criminal offence.

7. Individual consultation

- Individual consultation is essential in relation to those provisionally selected for redundancy. This is to allow the individual a chance to give their comments on the selection as well as for both parties to consider what alternative employment is available (see point 8 below).
- Such consultation must take place before any notice of termination is served.
- Ideally before individual consultation meetings, the employer should set out in writing that the employee is at risk of dismissal and why, together with an invitation to attend a meeting.
- For the dismissal to be procedurally fair, the employer must then hold a meeting with the employee.
- Individual consultation should take place over two or three meetings, depending on whether a selection process is required. The matters to be discussed in the first individual meeting should include explaining the reasons for the proposed redundancies, considering ways of avoiding redundancies, the proposed selection criteria and who will carry out the process. A further consultation meeting should then be held once the selection criteria have been applied to discuss the results, consider any alternative roles (see point 8 below) and possibly to discuss the terms that will be applied if the redundancy is confirmed. The redundancy should not be confirmed at this meeting, however. Further consultation should be arranged as necessary before dismissal is confirmed.

- Only after consultation has been concluded should the employer give notice of termination. The notice must be in writing and should include a right of appeal.
- If the employee exercises their right of appeal, then an appeal hearing must be arranged. The employee should be informed after the meeting (preferably in writing) of the outcome of the appeal. (The right of appeal, whilst outside the scope of the ACAS Code of Practice on disciplinary and grievance procedures 2015, is recommended in the ACAS guide on handling small-scale redundancies (**www.acas.org.uk/index.aspx?articleid=4547**). See also its guidance for handling large-scale redundancies (**www.acas.org.uk/media/pdf/4/t/Handling-large-scale-collective-redundancies-advisory-booklet.pdf**).

    There is no statutory right for an employee to be accompanied at redundancy meetings.

    The ACAS Code of Practice on disciplinary and grievance procedures does not apply to meetings relating to redundancy dismissals. However, a tribunal hearing an unfair redundancy dismissal claim will look at whether or not the employer operated a fair procedure in carrying out the dismissal. It is therefore good practice for employers to offer employees the right to be accompanied at consultation and dismissal and appeal meetings under the redundancy procedure.

8. *Alternative employment and trial periods*

- Before dismissing an employee as redundant, the employer should satisfy itself that there is no alternative employment available.
- If a suitable alternative post is available, and the employer does not offer this post to the employee selected for redundancy, the resulting dismissal may well be unfair.
- Employers should ensure that vacancies are brought to the employee's attention and that information is provided about the financial prospects of any alternative job.
- If an employee is interested in taking up alternative employment, the terms should be put in writing.
- The offer must state how the employment differs from the former job and must take effect within four weeks of the former job ending, with a statutory trial period of four weeks. A longer trial period may be offered in writing if it is for the purposes of retraining.
- If at the end of the trial period the employee or employer decide that the alternative employment is not suitable, the employee will still be entitled to a statutory redundancy payment.
- Whether or not the job is suitable depends on a number of factors including the job status, the pay level, the location where the employee is to work, the working environment and the hours of work.
- If the employer believes that the alternative job is clearly suitable and the employee unreasonably refuses to accept it, the employee will not be

entitled to a statutory redundancy payment. Employers should however tread carefully where this is an issue because whether or not an employee's refusal to take up an alternative job is reasonable is a subjective one for the employee and the way in which the employee has been treated during the whole redundancy process will be a relevant consideration.
- An employee who is to be dismissed for redundancy, and has two years' service, is legally entitled to a reasonable amount of paid time off work to look for a new job.

9. Statutory redundancy pay

- An employee who is dismissed for redundancy must be given proper notice of termination (or an appropriate payment in lieu of notice).
- Provided the employee has two years' continuous employment, the employee will be entitled to a statutory redundancy payment which is based on age, salary and length of service.
- For each year of completed employment up to the age of 21, the employee receives half a week's pay; for each year of completed employment between the ages of 22 and 40, one week's pay; and for each year of completed employment after the age of 41, one and a half week's pay.
- The maximum amount of a week's pay which can be taken into account in calculating statutory redundancy pay is [£X] as at April [year].
- In general, statutory redundancy pay is calculated in the same way as the basic award component of unfair dismissal compensation. Redundancy pay is set off against unfair dismissal basic award if any dismissal is subsequently found to be unfair (so as a general rule they cancel each other out).
- A redundant employee must be given a written statement showing how the employee's redundancy pay has been calculated, and failure to do so is a criminal offence.

10. Contractual/enhanced redundancy pay

- Employees may have an expectation of an enhanced redundancy payment under a company policy.
- For such an enhanced payment not to infringe the rules on age discrimination, it must mirror the statutory redundancy scheme with regard to age bands and multipliers, and all payments must be calculated in the same way.
- A permitted enhancement is one or more of the following:
    - not applying the cap on a week's pay (e.g. calculating it using the employee's actual weekly pay) or using a higher cap;
    - multiplying the number of weeks' pay for each year of service by a

factor (e.g. applying a scheme of 1–2–3 weeks' pay for each year of service under the statutory age bandings, instead of the statutory ½–1–1½);
- multiplying the total amount produced by the statutory calculation or by these variations by a factor (e.g. twice the amount of statutory redundancy pay).

- If an employer has a redundancy scheme that pays more than statutory redundancy, it should first look at whether the age bands and criteria used mirror those of the statutory scheme. If they do, the scheme will probably be lawful. If the criteria do not mirror the statutory scheme, and benefits are different for employees of different ages, it discriminates on grounds of age and the employer should then consider whether that discrimination can be objectively justified.
- First consider the aims of the scheme, and whether they are legitimate. It is useful to keep a paper trail of the aims of the scheme, as failing to do so will make it more difficult to prove at a later stage that an aim was in fact an aim. Case law shows that it is not permissible to rely on an aim that was not considered at the time the scheme was implemented. Case law shows that the following are likely to be legitimate aims:

    - rewarding loyalty;
    - cushioning the impact for older employees;
    - encouraging employee turnover by preventing blockages in the progression of junior employees;
    - avoiding a windfall to some employees; and
    - reducing the likelihood of industrial action.

- The next stage is to consider whether the details of the scheme itself are reasonably necessary to achieve those aims. A practical way to do this would be to produce a series of worked out examples to demonstrate how the financial pot has been distributed, and to document how the decision to treat certain age groups differently was reached to achieve the stated purpose.
- It may also be worth consulting the employees as a group: although this would not on its own make an unlawful act lawful, the fact that a provision has been agreed with staff collectively could be a relevant consideration when a tribunal considers proportionality.
- Enhanced redundancy payments may attract the £30,000 tax-free exemption, but only if they are not a contractual entitlement and/or the employee does not have an expectation of receiving it.
- Such a termination payment should be made after the termination date – and only under the terms of a settlement agreement. Care must also be taken not to obtain an agreement under a settlement agreement too far in advance of the termination date, otherwise HMRC may deem the agreement to be a contract during employment and not a genuine termination agreement, in which case the entire payment would be subject to deduction of tax.

In such a case it is possible to serve a settlement agreement with a reaffirmation certificate on or shortly before the effective date of termination.

Reaffirmation certificate

> I hereby confirm that, having taken legal advice, as at the date hereof, there are no matters or circumstances which do or might give rise to any claims by me in connection with my employment by [*name*] plc (the 'Company') or the termination of my employment with the Company which have arisen since the date of the Agreement set out above. I further confirm that the warranties given by me in the Agreement remain true and correct as at the date of this Certificate. I acknowledge that it is a condition of this Agreement that I give this Reaffirmation, upon which the Company will rely.
>
> Signed ....
>
> Dated ....

11. Rehiring redundant employees

- Rehiring redundant staff can be a cost-effective option but there are employment law implications to consider, the chief of which are the rules on continuous employment.
- If a formerly redundant employee is rehired and can establish continuity of employment, the employer will be exposed to claims relating to the previous period of employment. Remember that certain types of claim (e.g. discrimination) do not require any period of continuous employment.
- Generally, continuous employment ends with dismissal. Continuity is broken and length of service goes back to nil.
- As long as there is a break of at least one week between the two periods of employment, continuity will be broken.
- There are exceptions to this, chiefly where the break in employment can be described as a 'temporary cessation of work'. This is more likely to happen where a pattern is evident of this happening previously.
- Another exception is where the ex-employee is rehired and required to repay any redundancy payment.

10.5 Failure to consider suitable alternative employment

There is very little case law on what is considered 'suitable alternative employment', but it will mean substantially similar or the same. The general rule is that in order to act fairly in a redundancy situation an employer is obliged to look for alternative work and satisfy itself that alternative work is not available before dismissing for redundancy. Even where there is no other work to do, a failure to try to find alternative employment may make an otherwise fair dismissal for redundancy unfair.

The courts have been more relaxed about this in recent years and have held that the duty on the employer is only to take 'reasonable steps', not to take every conceivable step possible to find the employee alternative employment (*Quinton Hazell Ltd* v. *Earl* [1976] IRLR 296).

It may not however be reasonable to expect a potentially redundant employee to compete with other candidates where the employment appears to be suitable (*Ralph Martindale & Co Ltd* v. *Harris* [2008] UKEAT/166/07).

Whether alternative employment is deemed 'suitable' is looked at objectively by the Employment Tribunals – e.g. is this a declining industry where there is little job security? Is there a similar level of job satisfaction and similar terms and conditions? – but whether it was reasonably or unreasonably refused is looked at subjectively – i.e. from the point of view of the individual and their circumstances, e.g. is the new location disruptive of that person's family life, etc.

Duty to give priority to woman on maternity leave if there is a suitable available vacancy

Failure to appoint a woman on maternity leave to a suitable vacant role if her role is redundant will result in an automatic unfair dismissal. It will not necessarily be direct discrimination on the grounds of pregnancy or maternity (s.18 of the Equality Act 2010) if, for example, the successful candidate is far better qualified, etc.

The Regulation duty only arises if the redundancy occurs whilst the woman is on maternity leave and not at any time before.

Regulation 10 of the MPL Regulations 1999 (set out below) makes it clear that the statutory obligation to offer suitable alternative employment only arises once the employee has commenced maternity leave, rather than prior to it commencing, when a woman is simply pregnant.

10.6 Redundancy during maternity leave

Regulation 10 of the MPL Regulations 1999 states:

(1) This regulation applies where, during an employee's ordinary or additional maternity leave period, it is not practicable by reason of redundancy or her employer to continue to employ her under her existing contract of employment.

(2) Where there is a suitable available vacancy, the employee is entitled to be offered (before the end of her employment under her existing contract) alternative employment with her employer or his successor, or an associated employer, under a new contract of employment which complies with paragraph (3) (and takes effect immediately on the ending of her employment under the previous contract).

In *Sefton Borough Council* v. *Wainwright* UKEAT/0168/14/LA, the EAT clarified:

(a) An employer should apply Regulation 10 to a woman on maternity leave once it becomes clear that she is at risk of redundancy (i.e. notice of dismissal does not actually have to have been given).

(b) There is no authority to suggest that an employer may adopt a flexible approach to the issue of timing in so far as the start of maternity leave is concerned.

(c) Regulation 10 does not apply prior to the commencement of maternity leave since that would go against the explicit wording of the Regulation itself. However, once on maternity leave, the preferential treatment afforded by the Regulation would apply if a redundancy situation still existed.

(d) Finally, it is not necessarily direct discrimination under s.18 of the Equality Act 2010 (discrimination on grounds of pregnancy or maternity) not to appoint the woman to the vacancy if, for example, the successful candidate is better qualified.

Here the Employment Tribunal had not asked the 'reason why' question.

10.7 Warning and consultation

In *Williams v. Compair Maxam Ltd* [1982] IRLR 83 the EAT held:

> The employer will seek to give as much warning as possible of impending redundancies so as to enable the union and employees who may be affected to take early steps to inform themselves of the relevant facts, consider possible alternative solutions and, if necessary, find alternative employment in the undertaking or elsewhere.

Collective consultation must take place where there are 20 or more employees proposed to be dismissed as 'redundant' within a 90-day period at one establishment. The statutory requirement to consult is in good time and at least 30 days before the first dismissal is due to take effect (s.188 of Trade Union and Labour Relations (Consolidation) Act 1992 – TULRCA). 'Due to take effect' means the date at which the dismissal takes effect and not the date that notice is given.

Where there are 100 or more employees proposed to be made redundant in a 90-day period at one establishment the duty to consult is at least 45 days before the first dismissal is due to take effect.

There are useful non-statutory guides from ACAS on 'Handling Large-Scale Redundancies' and 'Handling Small-Scale Redundancies' on this subject.

The definition of 'redundancy' for the purpose of redundancy consultation is far wider than under s.139 of the Employment Rights Act 1996. Section 195(1) of TULRCA defines dismissal due to redundancy as 'dismissal for a reason not related to the individual concerned or for a number of reasons all of which are not so related'.

At least one, if not two, consultation meetings with a potentially redundant employee should be held.

In *Pinewood Repro Ltd t/a County Print v. Page* [2010] UKEAT 0028_10_1310 the EAT held that fair consultation during redundancy also involves giving an employee an explanation for why they have been marked down in a scoring exercise.

An example of a script for a consultation meeting can be found at **Precedent 10A**.

10.8 Selection criteria

Selection criteria must be objective, transparent and validated and the scores must be based on objective or documentary evidence and not on a subjective view of a manager.

It is not for the Employment Tribunals to scrutinise the marking in redundancy selections in the absence of an obvious mistake or absence of good faith – *Dabson* v. *David Cover & Sons Ltd* UKEAT//0374/10/SM.

On the subject of disclosure of other selection forms who were not dismissed as redundant, the courts have held that those in the same selection group as the claimant should be disclosed so that a comparison can be made, particularly if the complaints are of unfavourable treatment.

Stuart Smith LJ in *British Aerospace plc* v. *Green* [1995] ICR 1006 said:

> Expense and delay are themselves often due to excessive and unnecessary documentation. In considering applications for discovery, courts and tribunals should be vigilant to see that the rules relating to discovery of documents are not abused. Only those documents which are relevant and necessary for fairly disposing of the action or matter or for saving costs should be disclosed. Industrial Tribunals are intended to be a cheap, quick and effective means of resolving disputes within their jurisdiction. This purpose will be frustrated unless these restrictions on discovery are borne in mind.

The Court of Appeal also made it clear that whilst comparison of the scores of those not selected for redundancy with those who were is fair and relevant, it is not for the tribunals to embark on a re-scoring exercise.

> The Tribunal is not entitled to embark upon a re-assessment exercise. I would endorse the observations of the Employment Appeal Tribunal in *Eaton Ltd* v. *King* [1995] IRLR 75 that it is sufficient for the employer to show that he set up a good system of selection and that it was fairly administered, and that ordinarily there is no need for the employer to justify all the assessments on which the selection for redundancy was based.

The main considerations for employers when considering and completing a selection exercise for redundancy are (in accordance with *Williams* v. *Compair Maxam Ltd* [1982] IRLR 83) as follows:

1. The employer will consult the union as to the best means by which the desired management result can be achieved fairly and with as little hardship to the employees as possible. In particular, the employer will seek to agree with the union the criteria to be applied in selecting the employees to be made redundant. When a selection has been made, the employer will consider with the union whether the selection has been made in accordance with those criteria.
2. Whether or not an agreement as to the criteria to be adopted has been agreed with the union, the employer will seek to establish criteria for selection which so far as possible do not depend solely upon the opinion of the person making

the selection but can be objectively checked against such things as attendance record, efficiency at the job, experience, or length of service.
3. The employer will seek to ensure that the selection is made fairly in accordance with these criteria and will consider any representations the union may make as to such selection.
4. The employer will seek to see whether instead of dismissing an employee he could offer him alternative employment.

Recent cases have highlighted the need for an employer to devise objective redundancy selection criteria and apply them fairly, and explored the controls on managerial prerogative.

They consider the application of the 'band of reasonable responses' test in determining whether an employer behaved reasonably in dismissing an employee for redundancy.

They review the case law on the extent to which Employment Tribunals will scrutinise selection processes, including the importance of avoiding a re-scoring exercise.

There is much case law on redundancy selection criteria, but most of it concerns selecting from a pool those employees who will be retained to continue to do their existing work.

In *Wrexham Golf Club* v. *Ingham* UKEAT/0190/12/RN the Employment Appeal Tribunal held that a tribunal must not interfere with an employer's decision in this regard unless the employer acts outside the 'range of reasonable responses'.

It is not for the tribunal to decide whether it would have thought it fairer to act in another way. The question is whether the dismissal lay within the range of conduct which a reasonable employer could have adopted – *Williams* v. *Compair Maxam Ltd*:

• the reasonable response test applies to the selection of the pool from which the redundancies are to be drawn – *Hendy Banks City Print Ltd* v. *Fairbrother*;
• there is no legal requirement that a pool should be limited to employees doing the same or similar work. The question of how the pool should be defined is primarily a matter for the employer to determine. It would be difficult for the employee to challenge it where the employer has genuinely applied its mind to the problem – *Taymech* v. *Ryan*;
• the tribunal is entitled, if not obliged, to scrutinise carefully the reasoning of the employer to determine if it has 'genuinely applied' its mind as to who should be in the pool; and
• if the employer has genuinely applied its mind to the issue of who should be in the redundancy pool, it will be difficult, but not impossible, for an employee to challenge it.

Where the redundancy arises as a consequence of a reorganisation and there are new roles to be filled, the process is more aligned to recruitment, with the unsuccessful candidates being dismissed for redundancy.

The EAT in *Morgan* v. *Welsh Rugby Union* [2011] IRLR 376 appears to have given employers a little more discretion to decide upon who is the more suitable candidate to re-deploy where there is an internal recruitment. In such a case an employer may use its subjective knowledge of a candidate rather than merely relying on the paperwork and the interview.

In this case, the unsuccessful candidate for a new role as national coach development manager claimed that his redundancy dismissal was unfair because, unlike the successful candidate, he met the job description fully.

Dismissing an appeal against a finding that the selection was fair, HH Judge Richardson commented that in such a situation, 'the employer's decision must of necessity be forward-looking. It is likely to centre upon an assessment of the ability of the individual to perform in his new role'.

The EAT emphasised that 'an employer's assessment of which candidate will best perform in a new role is likely to involve a substantial element of judgement'.

In particular, the EAT held that the employer is not bound to adhere to the job description or person specification 'slavishly or precisely'.

In *Watkins* v. *Crouch t/a Temple Bird Solicitors* [2011] IRLR 382, the claimant was employed as a conveyancing secretary in a small high street practice. The firm had defined redundancy selection criteria, but Mrs Watkins was selected for redundancy notwithstanding that she scored higher than the firm's receptionist. The receptionist was retained because of the overall requirements of the business. She was regarded as an asset to the firm whose particular skills the firm could not do without.

An Employment Tribunal considered that the dismissal was fair but the EAT allowed an appeal and remitted the case for rehearing.

In a rather scathing analysis, Mr Justice Keith said:

> First, so subjective a criterion, namely the overall requirements of the business, might well be said not to satisfy the requirement for selection criteria to be sufficiently objective so as to eliminate, if at all possible, decisions being made on a basis which cannot withstand close scrutiny.
>
> Secondly, the requirements of the business could be said to be no more than a statement of the obvious – a statement that the objective of any redundancy exercise is to retain those employees who are best equipped to enable the company, whether a small or large one, to trade profitably in the future.
>
> Thirdly and perhaps most importantly of all, if the overall requirements of the business are to be taken into account in deciding whether members of staff should be made redundant, it could be said that that is a factor which should have been reflected in the selection criteria themselves which were to apply to all members of the workforce, and on which all members of the workforce should have been scored.

Finally, it is possible for an employer to choose a 'pool' of one, as long as the employer has directed its mind to the matter of the extent and scale of the 'pool'.

There is no rule that there must be a pool: an employer, if it has good reason for doing so, may consider a single employee for redundancy.

The Employment Tribunal is entitled, if not obliged, to consider with care and scrutinise carefully the reasoning of the employer to determine if it has 'genuinely applied' its mind to the issue of who should be in the pool for consideration for redundancy:

There is no inherent reason why there should not be a pool of one. There must be cases where it is so obvious which person should be selected for redundancy that it is reasonable for an employer not to consider other employees for redundancy at the same time.

See **Precedent 10B**.

10.9 Questions and answers

It may be helpful for employers to prepare in advance questions and answers when consulting staff for the first time.

Precedent 10C shows some model questions and answers.

10.10 Redundancy procedure

Precedent 10D is a model redundancy policy, which is not normally published in non-unionised companies.

10.11 Redundancy letters

Precedent 10E shows redundancy letters that can be used in the redundancy process. It is not for this book to distinguish a case of redundancy from a transfer of an undertaking under the Transfer of Undertakings (Protection of Employment) Regulations 2006 (TUPE). The question of whether an employee should transfer to a new service provider or be dismissed as redundant by their employer is often very complex.

PRECEDENT 10A: Script for consultation meeting

Good morning

I am holding this meeting with you because these are very difficult times. The Board has been working on some radical plans to restructure the business going forward so that we can compete effectively and grow the business. As a result I am announcing to you that we are restructuring the business model.

We are in a very difficult market and we have to look continually at ways in which we can improve our efficiency and our turnover.

Here is our business case where you will see the business rationale for the proposals on redundancy and for our new business model.

It has been decided to completely restructure the sales and marketing teams and as a result the job that you currently do here will no longer be performed within the business.

Your jobs are now at risk of redundancy.

[*State what the new structure will be, and why it will be more efficient, etc.*]

It is therefore with great regret that I am starting the consultation process with you to warn you that your job is now 'under the microscope'.

The purpose of our meeting you today is to warn you of this possibility and to begin the process of consultation with you which will be carried out over the next four weeks.

You will have the opportunity to apply for the new roles and I will ensure that you are given the person spec and job descriptions for these new roles.

We have [have not] done a scoring exercise as your role is one of several at risk of redundancy [is a one-off so there was no pool for redundancy, only your role has been placed at risk].

Here are your scores with explanations for the scores in the final column and you will see the scores of the re-marker who reviewed your scores.

I am happy for you to take this away and meet me again if you have any questions about your scores.

We will have a further meeting to let you know our final decision in four weeks' time. In the meantime I am happy to meet again to consider any alternative proposals you may have to avoid any redundancy.

At that meeting you will have the right to be accompanied by a fellow colleague or trade union representative.

We really value you and all that you have done for the business, and it grieves us all that we have to refocus the business and lose your roles.

We know that this must come as a dreadful shock to you.

[We would not expect you to come to work during these following four weeks as we can imagine how dispirited this would make you, so we are placing you on 'Garden Leave' for the next four weeks and you will be paid in full during this time.] OR [We hope you will work enthusiastically for the next four weeks and you may have reasonable time off to look for alternative employment. Please agree this with [name].]

Do you have any questions for us?

I will send you a letter confirming what I have said at this meeting and please ring or email me if I can help you in any way during the next four weeks.

PRECEDENT 10B: Model selection criteria

The current selection criteria are attached as Appendix 2 and the proposed criteria are contained in Appendix 1 [*these should be customised to each redundancy exercise*]. The main changes are as follows:

Criterion	Change
Customer orientation	Rename client/customer focus
Skills and abilities	Rename work performance
Flexibility	Rename versatility and adaptability
Presentation	Remove
Quality of work	Add
Qualifications	Add – but only where they are relevant to the type of work and future needs of business
Length of service	Add – but only to be used where two individuals' scores are within one or two points of each other

Two managers must assess all the individuals who may be selected for redundancy. Each individual will be scored against each criterion using the following marking:

Below acceptable	(0)
Minimum acceptable	(3)
Fully meets required standards	(7)
Exceeds required standards	(10)

The managers must provide a rationale for their marking, and must attach relevant evidence, e.g. appraisal forms, attendance records, disciplinary records, notes of meetings, etc.

The scores will be totalled and if they are within a few points of each other, length of service may be taken into account to reach the final decision.

The rationale which justifies the individual scores must be verified by the Director and Head of HR.

The other steps in the selection process, including consultation with employees and union/employee representatives, and the right to appeal, remain unchanged.

Selection decisions

Selection decisions will not be made (directly or indirectly) on the basis of gender, race, colour or ethnic origin, sexual orientation, religion, disability, age, marital status or trade union activities.

The Service Director/manager in consultation with the Head of HR will determine the group of employees from which those who are to be made redundant will be drawn (i.e. the pool for selection).

Initial selection of employees to be made redundant will be made by the relevant Director having considered evidence and written reports of relevant managers.

The Head of HR will consider the initial selection in the corporate context. There will be consultation with the union/employee representatives on the final number of redundancies in accordance with s.188 of the Trade Union and Labour Relations (Consolidation) Act 1992 as amended.

NOTE: Even though the criteria may satisfy the test of objectivity, the selection will still be unfair if these criteria are carelessly or mistakenly applied.

Appeals against selection

Appeals against final selection for redundancy will be heard by an Appeal Panel. Appeals must be registered with the Head of HR within seven days of receipt of the formal notice of redundancy or such period as may be agreed.

All employees have the right of appeal if they feel that the selection criteria have been unfairly applied in their case. The decision of the Appeals Panel will be final.

Appendix 1: Proposed selection criteria

For the selection criteria account may be taken of any or all of the factors as follows:

(a) *Attitude:* Has a positive attitude about the service and continually strives to improve it and has effective relationships with colleagues.
(b) *Client/customer focus:* Recognises the importance of the client/customer and is courteous at all times. Deals with customer enquiries and complaints in a helpful manner. Meets customer care standards.
(c) *Work performance:* Has the experience, skill and ability to achieve and maintain high standards of performance in the job and achieve agreed objectives and targets.
(d) *Versatility and adaptability:* Recognises the need for flexibility, is willing to adapt to change and has an ability to undertake duties other than those normally carried out.
(e) *Conduct:* Has a good record of attendance, is generally reliable and has a clean disciplinary record.
(f) *Quality of work:* Is able to achieve good quality and accurate work.
(g) *Qualifications:* Provided professional and/or occupational qualifications are relevant to the type of work or the future needs of the business they may be taken into account.
(h) *Length of service:* Where the scores are within a few points of each other the employee(s) with the shorter service will be selected for redundancy.

NOTE: Length of service on its own is not a criterion for retention; therefore 'last in, first out' will not apply.

Appendix 2: Current selection criteria

If, after having taken as many measures as practicable, the number of employees still exceeds requirements, the Company will strive to retain a workforce that is best able to provide competitive services to the required standards.

In determining which employees will be retained the following criteria shall be applied:

(a) *Attitude:* Has a positive attitude about the service and continually strives to improve it.
(b) *Customer orientation:* Recognises the importance of the customer and is courteous at all times. Deals with customer enquiries and complaints in a helpful manner.
(c) *Skills and abilities:* Has the skill and ability to achieve and maintain high standards of performance in the job.
(d) *Flexibility:* Recognises the need for flexibility and is willing to adapt to change.
(e) *Presentation:* Creates a good image of the Company in terms of personal presentation and manner.
(f) *Reliability and conduct:* Has a good record of attendance, general reliability and conduct.
(g) *Experience:* Uses experience in the job to maintain and promote high standards and to contribute to improvement.

When assessing employees on the basis of the above criteria the Company is committed to a fair, consistent, objective and non-discriminatory selection procedure.

Assessments made against the above criteria should be supported by objective evidence.

NOTE: Length of service on its own is not a criterion for retention. Therefore 'last in, first out' will not apply.

Review and selection tool for redundancy

Suggested review criteria	Person A			Person B			Person C		
	Excellent	Adequate	Poor	Excellent	Adequate	Poor	Excellent	Adequate	Poor
Product knowledge									
Technical skills									
Inter-personal skills									
Communication									
Team work									
Attitude									
Time management									
Appraisal result 2017									
Future potential									

PRECEDENT 10C: Consultation on redundancy: questions and answers

TO: ALL STAFF

FROM: [name]

[date]

RE: Consultation process questions and answers

The Board realises that employees have a lot of questions during this difficult time. General questions should be addressed to the Board via your employee representative. In the meantime, below are answers to some of the questions that have been put forward so far; these answers reflect the current position.

1. **Are all branches affected?**

Branches where the customer continues to agree to pay for a set number of staff will not be affected, nor will those branches where the efficiency rating has remained high as this shows that they have the correct level of staffing in place.

2. Are central staff affected by these changes as well as operational staff?

There is a need to reduce costs across the company and therefore central staff will also be affected.

3. Why are employee representatives being elected?

3.1 The Company is asking staff to elect employee representatives as part of its legal obligations to consult with employee representatives where it is contemplated that 20 or more employees may be affected by redundancies. The purpose of the consultation is for employees to put forward suggestions as to the best way to achieve the required cost savings.

3.2 The Company is not bound to accept those suggestions but will explain why any suggestions are rejected. The overall objective is to reach agreement, whether to the satisfaction of all parties or otherwise.

4. How long will the consultation period last?

At present the Board believes that the consultation period will be complete by [date] and changes will therefore be implemented at [date].

5. What options are available to achieve these cost savings?

The Board will discuss all possible options with the employee representatives in order to gauge the views of employees. At present the most viable options to achieve the required savings appear to be short-time working with associated pay cuts or redundancies.

6. What is short-time working?

6.1 The company needs to save 15 per cent in costs, of which approximately 62 per cent are directly payroll related. Therefore staff working fewer hours and as a result receiving less salary could achieve this.

6.2 A full-time employee who currently works 37.5 hours per week could take a reduction of 20 per cent of hours and only work 30 hours per week. If this option were taken then the salary would also drop by this percentage.

6.3 This would be implemented on a pro rata basis for part-time employees.

6.4 If short-time working were adopted so that there is still enough cover within the branch, a rota system would have to operate as to when the hours are not worked.

6.5 If a branch is currently running at high efficiency levels or if the requirement for that job is not reduced then there will be no requirement for those employees to take the option of short-time working with associated pay cuts.

7. What is the difference between pay cuts and short-time working with pay cuts?

A pay cut is where an employee is asked to work the same hours for less money; short-time working with pay cuts is where the employee works fewer hours per week and receives payment only for those hours worked at their normal hourly rate of pay.

8. Do these cost savings apply to all staff including Senior Managers and Directors?

Yes, it affects all staff including Directors. In fact the Directors agreed at [date] not to take any bonus or increase in their basic remuneration and all such increases and bonuses are being frozen until at least [date].

9. If we opt for short-time working will there still be redundancies?

The Board cannot guarantee that there will not be any redundancies. However, the more people who opt for short-time working the fewer the number of redundancies that will be needed.

10. I cannot afford to opt for short-time working. What will happen if I refuse?

All employees have the right to refuse this option and must not be pressurised into accepting it by their colleagues. However, refusal to accept short-time working may be taken into consideration when selecting employees for redundancy. This will be discussed with the employee representatives.

11. If I opt for short-time working now, when will my salary go back to the normal level?

At present the Board is unable to predict when salaries will return to the normal level, as it is currently difficult to determine when our business will improve to such an extent as to allow this.

12. If I opt for short-time working, will my pension be affected?

12.1 For members of a Group Personal Pension Plan such as [*give details*] the contributions will remain at the same level. However, if the employee wished to decide to drop them in line with any salary decrease then they will have the option to do so.

12.2 For members of the final salary scheme, the contributions are based on salary at the date of renewal and therefore they will not be affected until renewal on [*date*].

13. Will short-time working affect my holiday entitlement?

13.1 Short-time working will not reduce your annual holiday entitlement. Once you have opted for short-time working, if you wish to take holiday you only need to book holiday for those days/hours you are scheduled to work. For example, if you are only working four days a week you only need to book four days' holiday to take a week off.

13.2 If you already have holiday booked, this will be adjusted to take into account any agreed short-time working and holiday not taken will be credited back.

13.3 As per normal procedures no holiday can be carried forward to the new holiday year and holiday can only be taken with the prior approval of your manager.

14. Can I take holiday instead of short-time working so that I can still be paid?

No. Once you have agreed to short-time working you cannot take holiday on the days when you are scheduled not to work.

15. Will the Company buy out any unused holiday entitlement at the end of the year?

As per company procedures and government regulations, the Company will not buy out unused holiday entitlement.

16. What happens to my pay if I am sick whilst I am on short-time working?

16.1 Once you have opted for short-time working, you are only entitled to payment of sick pay for the days/hours you are scheduled to work. You are not entitled to payment for any days/hours that you are not scheduled to work. This includes payment of statutory sick pay. Sick forms should therefore only be completed for the days/hours you are scheduled to work.

16.2 Apart from the above, normal sickness rules and procedures will apply.

17. Will there still be salary reviews on [*date*]?

No.

18. **Will the bonus still be paid?**

18.1 Not yet determined – this is to be part of employee representative discussions. The bonus would be calculated as previously notified. However, it will be based on the efficiencies and salary paid, and as the efficiencies have been affected by [give details] the bonus will also be affected. If the salary paid drops this will also affect the calculations.

18.2 As already stated, when the bonus guidelines were published it was made clear that there is no entitlement to a bonus payment if the employee is no longer employed by the Company at the date of payment.

19. **If the bonus and pay review are forfeited will there still be redundancies and/or pay cuts?**

19.1 The forfeiting of the bonus would save some £... (less than 10 per cent of the saving required), so yes.

19.2 The cancelling of salary reviews on [date] will mean that the company will not increase its costs. It does not actually save on current costs and therefore reductions will still need to be made.

20. **What is redundancy?**

Redundancy occurs when a company ceases to require people with the particular skills of the employee or needs fewer people with those skills at that establishment.

21. **What criteria will be used for selection for redundancy?**

21.1 The first criteria for selection have to be whether there is still a need for that type or level of work at that location (these criteria are in the original announcement). Once this has been determined then if there is only one person doing that type of work at that location they will be selected. If there is more than one person doing that type of work at that location, then objective selection criteria will be applied.

21.2 The objective selection criteria will be discussed with the employee representatives, and are likely to include length of service, disciplinary records (which are still valid), number of sick days/occurrences, qualifications/exam successes, appraisal notes, etc.

22. **What is the redundancy package?**

22.1 The redundancy package is statutory redundancy, the provisions for which are set by the government and are based on age and length of continuous service. Brief outlines of the calculations involved are:

- An employee has to have at least two years' continuous service to qualify for a redundancy payment.
- Any service prior to an employee's 18th birthday is discounted and entitlement ceases once an employee reaches the age of 65.
- 2½ weeks' pay for each full year of employment with the Company during which the employee was aged 41 or over, but had not reached the age of 65.
- One week's pay for each full year of employment with the Company during which the employee was aged 22–40 inclusive.
- A ½ week's pay for each full year of employment with the Company during which the employee was aged 18–21 inclusive.
- Reckonable service is to be limited to the last 20 years before redundancy and earnings above £380.00 per week will not be taken into account. The maximum payment under the scheme is therefore £11,400.00 which would be payable where the employee has 20 years' service when aged 41 or over.

22.2 Redundancy payments are not subject to tax or national insurance.

23. **What are the notice provisions?**

23.1 Employees are entitled to the notice under their contract which is normally one month's or one week's notice for each full year of employment, whichever is the greater up to a maximum of 12 weeks' notice. This is payable at the full rate of pay.

23.2 During the notice period normal benefits also apply.

23.3 Payment of notice is subject to tax and national insurance.

24. **Is there any entitlement to holiday pay?**

24.1 Employees who are made redundant continue to accrue holiday up to the end of their notice period. An adjustment will then be made for any holiday that has not been taken or has been taken in excess of the normal entitlements.

24.2 These payments are subject to tax and national insurance.

25. **Can I elect to put myself forward for voluntary redundancy?**

25.1 If you wish to be considered for voluntary redundancy you can put your request in writing to [*specify*] in the HR Department who will raise your request with the Board.

25.2 Whilst such requests will be considered by the Company, we reserve the right to refuse such requests from employees the Company considers it is necessary to retain to ensure the long-term viability of the business.

25.3 Applicants should also be aware that volunteering for redundancy could affect payments under redundancy insurance policy and payment of social security benefits.

26. **Is there any enhanced package for voluntary redundancy?**

As this is a cost-saving exercise there is no provision for an enhanced redundancy package for employees who volunteer for redundancy.

27. **When will I know if I am selected for redundancy?**

As soon as the selection criteria have been agreed with the employee representatives and there appears to be no alternative to redundancies, then the criteria will be applied and the affected employees will be notified individually.

28. **How much notice do I have to give if I find employment elsewhere and will I be entitled to any redundancy pay if I accept?**

28.1 Normal notice provisions will apply during the consultation period and no redundancy payments are due to any employees who leave during this time.

28.2 If an employee is selected for redundancy and is given notice of this and they wish to leave during the notice period, they will not be entitled to payment of the rest of their notice period. However, they will be entitled to their redundancy payment.

29. **Who will make the overall decision on the cost-saving measures that will be implemented?**

The ultimate decision on the implementation of cost-saving measures rests with the Board of Directors.

30. **How will these changes affect people on maternity leave?**

30.1 Employees on maternity leave will be treated the same as all other employees in terms of selection for redundancy and the right to be consulted.

30.2 However, women on maternity leave are given (by statute) a preferential right to be offered any suitable available vacancy when they return to work and this means that if any vacancy occurred now, we would have to fill it temporarily and then offer it to a maternity returner prior to her returning to work.

30.3 However, employees who are on maternity leave are not working and are therefore exempt from short-time working and their maternity pay will continue as normal.

31. How will these changes affect employees due to take maternity leave?

If an employee opts for short-time working this could affect the payments made to them in the first six weeks of their maternity pay period because this is calculated on their average salary in the eight weeks prior to the qualifying week. The qualifying week is the 15th week prior to the date the baby is due.

32. If I want to take on additional work outside the company to top up my income during short-time working can I do so?

There is an exclusivity clause in your contract of employment, therefore you should discuss the option of any work outside the Company with your manager and get written permission prior to commencing work for another employer. Provided this work does not conflict with or affect your work for the Company, permission will not be unreasonably refused.

33. How will these cost savings affect training courses for staff advancement?

33.1 The Company will still train staff to improve their service, particularly in retail and business departments. As per normal procedures, all training expenses must be pre-authorised by the Training Department.

33.2 The Company will expect, where it commits to train staff, that those staff commit to refund any costs thereof if they leave voluntarily shortly after completing the training. This is to avoid unnecessary cost.

34. Is the Company still going to make a profit?

If we make the costs savings we need we will only make sufficient profit to honour our repayment commitments.

35. Will the Christmas Party/entertaining staff over Christmas go ahead?

This is budgeted to happen and a lot of arrangements and commitments have already been made in relation to this. If the consensus of any one office is that these functions should not go ahead in that particular office, then this is acceptable. However, employees should be aware that other offices might elect to go ahead with their own arrangements and that this is also acceptable.

PRECEDENT 10D: Model redundancy policy

1. Preamble

This Policy Document is strictly confidential and must not be disclosed to any other parties whether inside or outside the Company.

Circulation of this Policy is restricted to [insert names or job roles].

All the terms set down below are not contractual and do not therefore form part of any member of staff's contract of employment.

Any redundancy payments or terms provided over and above the statutory requirements are made on a discretionary basis only. This Policy or any of its terms described below may be withdrawn, modified or varied at any time at the sole discretion of the Company.

2. Aims

The aim of the Company is to avoid as far as possible compulsory redundancies and in some cases this may be achieved by asking for volunteers or natural wastage.

However, in the event that the Company at its entire discretion decides that compulsory redundancies are necessary, the ultimate objective in the exercise of this Policy is to achieve and maintain a balanced workforce. This may mean in certain cases retaining technical, managerial or staff with particular skills and/or abilities in preference to unskilled or clerical staff or retaining some younger staff with shorter service in preference to some older, longer serving staff. Any decision will be based in part on the needs of the business, commercial factors and any other business reasons.

3. Legal definition

Redundancy occurs when:

(a) the Company either ceases or intends to cease to trade altogether in the UK or ceases or intends to cease to trade in the place where the member of staff is contractually employed; OR

(b) the Company no longer has any requirement for employees to carry out work of the particular kind which they are contractually employed to do or no longer requires employees to carry out work of the particular kind which they are contractually employed to do in the place where they are employed.

PLEASE NOTE: Redundancy should not be confused with dismissal where an employee fails to meet the standards expected by the Company or their manager whether this be through failure to meet required work performance standards or misconduct.

4. Selection criteria

In order to achieve and maintain a balanced workforce, the following factors will be used (neither the same weightings nor the same criteria will be given or used in each case of redundancy, the criteria and weightings may vary depending on the sector of business affected, market forces, etc.); the following are placed in no particular order of preference:

- transferability of skills;
- promotability;
- ability to obtain, to sell and acquire new business;
- seniority;
- qualifications;
- work experience;
- efficiency at the job including proven track record;
- management potential;
- managerial and technical skills, expertise and knowledge;
- other relevant skills, e.g. interpersonal, communication, etc;
- attendance and timekeeping record;
- creative abilities;
- relationship with clients and customers;
- ability to work on own initiative/in a team;
- ability to develop ideas/projects, etc;
- past disciplinary record;
- length of service;
- ability to work with precision;
- ability to work under pressure/to meet deadlines;

- ability to adapt efficiently to new techniques, software, hardware, etc;
- ability to learn new skills effectively and quickly.

In the event that these factors are equal, then length of service may be one of the determining factors.

The factors chosen may be given scores out of 100. For example: absence record may have a score of 20; transferability of skills may have a score of 40. A score of 20 may be awarded for nil absence in the last 12 months; 15 where there have been under five days' absence, etc. Discount should be made for time off to look after dependants, etc.

A typical table would look like this:

	Criterion 1	Criterion 2	Criterion 3	Criterion 4	Score
A					
B					
C					
D					
E					

5. *Consultation and prior warning*

It is this Company's Policy to give as much advance warning as possible of impending redundancies both to all staff as a group and to those individuals whose jobs are threatened. Please note that during all such discussions, no notice of termination of employment will be issued and anyone leaving voluntarily before formal written notice of dismissal has been issued will lose all entitlement to notice pay and redundancy pay.

The member(s) of staff concerned may be advised of the following:

(a) why this action is being considered, e.g. the department is unprofitable, economic climate, fall in the value of the dollar/pound, etc;

(b) that an exercise is currently being undertaken to ascertain who should be selected for redundancy and that the outcome will be advised as soon as possible;

(c) that alternative posts are being looked for in the event that certain posts are declared redundant.

Please note that any suitable vacancy will be notified to any employee who is either to have notice of dismissal served upon them or has already been served with notice of termination. Whilst preference will be given to any such candidate, the relevant manager concerned must reserve the right to appoint the best candidate for the job. If retraining can be offered to any internal candidate who is subject to any redundancy notice, then the Company will so far as is reasonably practicable offer such retraining. SEE PARAGRAPH 6 BELOW.

It is important that this stage is carried out because a failure to consult prior to any notice of dismissal for redundancy is issued will almost certainly render any dismissal unfair in any Employment Tribunal claim for unfair dismissal. Consultation must still in the normal case take place even if this is in the period between the day when the decision to dismiss is made and the day when the employee is told of that decision.

Exception to the rule about consultation

The Tribunals have recognised only one situation where no prior consultation may be regarded as 'reasonable in the circumstances' and this is where there are extreme circumstances such as a catastrophic cashflow problem making it essential to take immediate steps to reduce the wages bill, e.g. the Bank has told you that there is no money in your account to pay next week's wages.

No consultation

Should it be decided that there can be no consultation with a particular member of staff, this must be discussed IN ADVANCE with the Head of HR. In such a case, arrangements will be made for the member of staff concerned to be told about the termination of their employment and for them to be escorted off the premises after first having returned all keys, security passes, company property, passwords, etc. A written undertaking may also be obtained from the individual confirming that all such items have been returned and giving assurances about confidential information, etc.

Proper arrangements will have to be made where necessary to change passwords on data systems and other security systems. Head of Security and HR will be in charge of such matters.

6. *Alternative employment*

The HR Department will do its utmost to obtain details of all internal vacancies within the Company and to publicise them to all those affected by redundancy. Preference will be given to all suitable internal candidates. Should any suitable alternative employment be possible, then this will be offered in writing by the HR Department before the existing contract is terminated.

A trial period of four weeks will be provided or longer for retraining purposes (and any offer letter will spell this out clearly). If at the end of the trial period the Manager of the relevant department or the employee is dissatisfied (on reasonable grounds), then they will be declared redundant from their original position. The redundancy would be on the terms originally discussed, i.e. although the employee may have worked for an extra period, this will not alter the final package. That extra period will not be taken into account in any way, i.e. for statutory or contractual purposes.

If the Company believes that the employee has unreasonably refused alternative employment, either prior to or after ceasing the trial period, then the Company may withhold all or part of the compensation for loss of office. The employee would still however be entitled to receive a payment in lieu of notice (if applicable).

7. *Reasonable paid time off to look for alternative work*

Once notice of dismissal has been issued all those under notice will be entitled to take reasonable time off with pay to look for alternative work. This must be agreed and booked in advance with the Head of Department and some documentary evidence may be required.

8. *References*

The HR Department is solely responsible for issuing references to prospective employers. The Company requires a written request. No 'open references' will be given save in special cases, such as where the employee is going to live abroad. It is at the Company's entire discretion whether or not to give a reference; however, an employee may request that the terms of any reference may be discussed and agreed with them. An agreed set of wording may be kept on file if appropriate.

Our standard reference wording gives employment dates, job title and reason for leaving only and it is only in rare cases that we will depart from this practice.

9. Statutory redundancy pay

Eligibility: no age limitation.

Calculation: the statutory redundancy payments are governed by rules depending upon age, service and pay. There is a limit on 'week's pay' (as at 2016/2017 a week's pay is capped at £479); 20 years' service and depending upon age up to 30 weeks' pay subject to the limit referred to above.

10. Compensation for loss of office

In addition to any statutory redundancy payment the following ex gratia payment(s) will be made to any employee(s) to compensate them for loss of office:

[Insert details]

11. Payment of termination monies

All termination payments including notice pay (if appropriate) and redundancy payments will be itemised in a formal letter and paid on or after the last day of employment. All appropriate deductions of tax and national insurance will be made at source.

If the contract has been terminated without any notice and payments in lieu have been made, such payments will now have to be paid from April 2018 with tax and NICs deducted. After consultation, government has decided that all payments in lieu of notice and any other post-employment payments (such as expected bonus income) that would have been treated as earnings if the employee had received them during the notice period will be taxed. This will apply even if the employee does not work out any or all of the notice period.

The first £30,000 of any ex gratia termination payment will continue to attract the tax exemption but any payments in excess of £30,000 will have to have tax and NICs deducted at source.

12. Payment for loss of other contractual benefits

(a) Contractual benefits

The loss of all contractual benefits during the notice period, i.e. those which form part of the employee's contract of employment, will be compensated for in any final termination payment.

(b) Company Car

With the agreement of a senior member of the Company's management an employee may be permitted to keep the Company Car during the period of notice. If this is permitted the Company will continue to insure the car but any servicing or repairs will be the employee's responsibility.

Staff are reminded of their duties under the Company's Car Policy to look after the car and return it in a clean and roadworthy condition. In some circumstances it may be decided to withhold part of the compensation for loss of office payment until the car is returned and its condition assessed.

Staff may be given the opportunity to purchase their Company Car at a price determined by [insert details].

[The Company reserves the right to withdraw the Company Car forthwith and make a cash allowance in lieu of the use of the car during the notice period. The car will have to be returned immediately subject to the same conditions above concerning cleanliness and roadworthiness. The Company reserves the right to adjust any cash allowance to reflect the condition of the car or the need for repairs.]

(c) Outstanding holiday entitlement

Any outstanding holiday entitlement untaken at the termination date of the employment will be paid with the final salary payments and will be subject to deduction of tax and national insurance contributions in the normal way. Please note that if you are serving all or part of your notice either at work or on garden leave you may be required to take any outstanding holiday before your termination date.

(d) Medical insurance/death in service cover

Medical insurance will cease either on the last day at work or at the end of the notice period. Death in service cover will cease on the last day of work.

13. Procedure

When the decision has been made by the authorised person(s) about who is to be made redundant and when the redundancies are to take place, the following procedure must be adopted:

- Inform and gain the approval of [insert details].
- Obtain details from the HR Department of the compensation for loss of office payments, statutory redundancy payments, early retirement figures (if applicable), etc.
- All documentation must be treated with the strictest of confidence at all times.
- It is essential that no other member of staff (other than an authorised member of HR) discusses orally or in writing any of the employee's entitlements in terms of salary, redundancy payments, pension benefits or any other matters relating to the termination of the employment.
- After obtaining the information from HR, obtain from the appropriate Senior Manager [insert details] approval and agreement prior to advising the employee.
- Agree a plan with the HR Department for communicating and administering the redundancy, e.g. timescales, whether pay in lieu of notice will be given, etc.
- If the employee has been continuously employed for two years or more, it may be advisable for the employee to see an ACAS Conciliation Officer to:
  (a) ensure that the employee is clear about their rights;
  (b) ensure that a COT 3 form is completed.
- No compensation for loss of office will normally be made by the Company until [the employee has signed a COT 3 OR a legally binding settlement has been obtained by way of the Settlement Agreement].
- The HR Department will liaise with ACAS if appropriate and will prepare suitably worded letters.

PRECEDENT 10E: Model redundancy letters

Letter 1 – Initial letter

RECORDED DELIVERY

[*Employer's letterhead*]

[*Date*]

Dear [*name*]

RE: Confirmation of our consultation meeting

This letter confirms our meeting on [*date*] in which I explained that we are now entering a consultation period as your job is at risk of redundancy.

I explained that the decision to place your role as one of the three night shift porters 'at risk of redundancy' was as a result of the current economic climate and the Residents' wish to reduce their service charge. We are reorganising the night shift porters' duties so that they will now alternate their shifts, requiring only two and not three night shift porters.

We went through a selection procedure with all three of you on the night shift, asking basic questions about your role and the building. Unfortunately you scored the lowest scores of all three.

We did not use LIFO (Last In First Out) as this would have led to an arbitrary and unfair result. Instead we asked questions that in fact you should have known in better and more accurate detail than one of your colleagues who has much less service than you.

We tried to make the questions as fair as possible in order to determine which night shift porter was to be selected for redundancy.

During the following two (2) weeks we will make every effort to look a suitable alternative position within [*building name*] and within any of the buildings that we manage.

You should come to work as normal but you are entitled to reasonable time off with pay to look for alternative work. You should notify your manager in advance if you wish to take such time off.

This letter is NOT a letter giving you notice of redundancy or termination of your employment. It is merely confirming our meeting that you are 'at risk of redundancy'.

We must emphasise that should you leave before notice of termination has been given, without your employer's prior written consent, you will not be eligible to receive any redundancy or severance payment.

We regret that the situation has arisen but as I emphasised when we met, we find ourselves in an increasingly difficult financial position with a difficult time ahead this year and we are trying to make the building as efficient and as cost effective as possible. We will of course continue to make every effort to find a suitable post for you.

Yours sincerely

. . . .

HR Manager

Letter 2 – Invitation to dismissal hearing

RECORDED DELIVERY

[*Employer's letterhead*]

[*Date*]

Dear [*Name*]

RE: Invitation to redundancy termination meeting

Further to our previous letter of [*date*] and the meeting that we had on [*date*] I very much regret that we have been unable to find any suitable alternative employment and it is therefore necessary to ask you to attend a meeting to discuss the termination of your employment on the grounds of redundancy.

We have previously explained the need for the redundancies and why your role has been deemed not necessary going forward.

You are entitled to be accompanied to the appeal hearing by a fellow worker or trade union representative of your choice.

The meeting will take place on [*date*] at [*time*] in [*location*] and the person chairing the meeting will be [*name*].

If you have any queries in the meantime please contact me.

Please also confirm the name of your representative and that you will both be attending.

I appreciate that this is a very difficult time for you.

Yours sincerely

....

HR Manager

Letter 3 – Giving notice of termination on grounds of redundancy

[*Employer's letterhead*]

RECORDED DELIVERY

[*Date*]

Dear [*Name*]

RE: Notice of termination of employment

Further to our previous letter of [*date*] and the meeting that we had on [*date*] I very much regret that the decision has had to be made to declare you redundant.

Please accept this letter as formal notice that your employment will end on [*date*/with immediate effect].

EITHER

You will be paid your full contractual pay and benefits in lieu of notice and any redundancy pay due to you.

OR

Upon termination of your employment you will receive your final salary together with a redundancy payment calculated as follows [*set out calculation*]. In addition [you will receive a payment in respect of any holiday entitlement accrued but not taken **OR** you will be asked to take any untaken holiday during your notice period].

I regret the necessity of having to send you this letter and would like to thank you personally for your loyal service during your time with us.

I wish you every success with your future employment. We will of course provide you with an employment reference should any prospective employer ask us for one. Please ask any prospective employer to direct their written request for a reference to [*insert details*].

You have a right of appeal against this decision and should you wish to appeal, you should do so in writing addressed to [*insert details*] but sent to me in the first instance, setting out your grounds and ensure that it is received by me no later than seven calendar days from receipt of this letter.

I will then pass this on to the persons hearing the appeal and will notify you of the date and the time and location of the appeal hearing. You have a right to be accompanied to the appeal hearing by a fellow worker or trade union representative of your choice.

Yours sincerely

....

Director

11

Grievances, harassment, bullying and 'whistleblowing'

11.1 Company grievance procedures

Under the Employment Rights Act 1996, s.3 an employer must either give the details of the grievance procedure to the individual in writing within the principal statement or refer the individual to a document which is readily accessible. It must be clear both how the individual makes a grievance and to whom.

This procedure is 'for the purpose of seeking redress of any grievance relating to his employment'. The (non-binding) ACAS Guidance 2009 (updated in 2016) defines a grievance as 'concerns, problems or complaints that employees raise with their employers'.

A grievance can involve:

- terms and conditions of employment;
- health and safety;
- work relations;
- bullying and harassment;
- new working practices;
- working environment;
- organisational change;
- discrimination.

It would not be a legitimate grievance if an employee placed a grievance about the Chief Executive's salary or bonus. It has to concern the individual in some direct or indirect way.

Distinguishing between appeals against disciplinary decisions and grievances

It is wise to distinguish in the grievance procedure between dissatisfaction with a disciplinary decision, for which action must be taken through the appeals procedure of the disciplinary procedure, and any other grievance.

It is also important to point out that the grievance procedure refers to the right of 'the employee' to pursue redress for their grievance and does not provide for collective grievances or for colleagues disturbed by a disciplinary decision against a colleague to pursue individual grievances about such a matter. That can be left for collective disputes procedures.

Status quo clauses

It was fashionable to include a status quo clause in both appeals procedures under the disciplinary procedure and/or in grievance procedures, whereby unions agreed not to take industrial action until the final stages of the procedure had been followed and management agreed to suspend the decision which was the subject of the appeal or grievance until the final stage had been exhausted. These status quo clauses are far less common nowadays.

Scope of the procedure

Furthermore, a grievance procedure is for 'employees' only. Checks should be made if a grievance is received that it is not from an ex-employee, contractor, visitor, disgruntled customer or client, student or volunteer.

Separate complaints procedures should exist for these categories of individuals.

11.2 Stages of the procedure

Normally individuals are encouraged to raise matters informally with their line managers and only where no satisfaction is obtained is the individual required to place the grievance in writing to the next level of management.

Similarly a grievance may still be a grievance about discrimination even though it does not refer to 'sex discrimination' or 'discrimination on the grounds of part-time working', e.g:

> I believe that I have been moved to a 'non-job' during this recent restructure because I have recently returned from maternity leave and now work on a part-time basis. I note that all my full-time colleagues and male colleagues have all been appointed in this restructure to fulfilling and equivalent or in some cases promoted posts. I am the only person to be removed from my post and given what is quite clearly an assistant Product Developer role reporting to one of my former male peers.

Advice to employees

The advice to employees is always to use the words 'formal grievance' and 'pursuant to the Company's Grievance Procedure'. It is important for the employee to spell out the nature of the grievance including the dates and details of each and every act that constitutes the grievance.

11.3   Grievance procedures

A typical grievance procedure has three stages:

1. The employee must put in writing the nature of the alleged grievance and send the written complaint to the employer. The employee must inform the employer of the basis for the complaint.
2. The employer must invite the employee to at least one hearing at a reasonable time and place, at which the alleged grievance can be discussed. The employee should take all reasonable steps to attend. After the grievance hearing, the employer must inform the employee about any decision, and offer the employee the right of appeal.
3. If the employee considers that the grievance has not been satisfactorily resolved, they should inform the employer that they wish to appeal against the employer's decision or failure to make a decision. The employer should arrange another hearing to discuss the appeal. After that hearing, the employer's final decision should be communicated to the employee.

Grievance investigations into discrimination complaints

It is essential that, where the grievance consists of discrimination concerns, the investigator:

1. has been trained in how to investigate grievances and how to investigate discrimination complaints;
2. understands how to ask open questions, probe and test responses;
3. understands and sets out the definition of discrimination;
4. understands and sets out the standard of proof, i.e. on the balance of probabilities and standard of proof (where there is no eye witness or admission, etc. for example how other men have been or would have been treated in similar situations; the CVs and interview notes of the other candidates; whether the role was ever advertised or interviewed for, etc.);
5. understands that there are rarely eye witnesses but there may be contemporaneous witnesses whom the victim may have told;
6. understands how to measure the evidence and the facts with the benchmark for establishing discriminatory conduct;
7. obtains signed and dated interview notes;
8. considers recording interviews and getting transcripts prepared;

9. considers similar fact evidence (e.g. similar conduct in the past, other past complaints of a similar nature, etc.);
10. considers the responses of the alleged perpetrator, e.g. admissions, failure to recall, remarks such as 'I would have said ....'; checks against previous emails on the subject, etc.

Mediation

ACAS recommends that the parties in dispute consider mediation, as in the example below:

> Where management believes it would be useful, you will be offered the opportunity to go to Mediation to resolve this grievance at any stage of the procedure. An external, professionally trained and accredited Mediator will be appointed to seek to resolve your complaints. This is an optional process.

11.4 Special complaints procedures for harassment or bullying

The ACAS Guidance (p.52) recognises that in sensitive cases, e.g. bullying, sexual or racial harassment, or concerns about how staff are treating an individual because of that person's gender reassignment, cross-dressing, HIV infection, etc. it is appropriate to have separate procedures for dealing with such matters.

The Guidance points out that:

> Clearly confidentiality is of prime importance when handling any such grievance, although the outcome may need to be made known if, for instance, someone is found to have bullied or harassed an individual and the result is disciplinary action. Mediation may be particularly useful in these types of cases ...

See **Precedent 11F** for a full anti-harassment policy.

It is always important for an employer to investigate any complaints of sexual harassment or bullying in a sensitive, impartial and independent manner – all the more so when the allegation is a very serious one such as rape or sexual assault.

It may be appropriate in such cases to call in someone experienced from outside, such as a QC or other senior figure, used to carrying out independent and impartial enquiries.

In *Deadman v. Bristol City Council* [2007] IRLR 888, the Court of Appeal held that although there is no freestanding, implied term that an employer investigating an allegation of harassment against an employee will act 'sensitively', there is a 'need to deal with harassment positively, quickly and sensitively'. This constitutes both part of the employer's contractual obligation not to undermine mutual trust and confidence and its duty of care towards employees.

According to Lord Justice Moore-Bick (para.17):

where an employer has published and implemented with the concurrence of employees' representatives formal procedures providing for the manner in which complaints are to be investigated, it will usually become a term of the contract of employment that those procedures will be followed unless and until withdrawn by agreement. The fact that in this case the procedures were made in the implementation of a non-contractual policy is in my view of no significance.

Mediation

ACAS recommends mediation and suggests that it could be incorporated into grievance and/or disciplinary procedures as an optional procedure (see **Chapter 15** for more details).

In *B v. A* [2010] IRLR 400, the EAT held that the local authority (B) had failed to investigate or assess the evidence, on the balance of probabilities after X (a director in another department) had reported (some six weeks later) to the chief executive (C) that A (an assistant director) had raped her. C believed her with only a cursory and wholly inadequate investigation and summarily dismissed A. The complainant did not testify at the Employment Tribunal. The tribunal found there was insufficient evidence that the rape had occurred and that C, to whom the rape had been reported and who had known X for some time, at once believed her account.

The following are some tips on drafting an anti-harassment policy.

1. Ensure that the policy is defined in terms of wide scope and extent, such as:

    All forms of bullying, intimidation, 'sending people to Coventry', deliberately teasing or ignoring the individual, deliberately leaving them out of social events such as going to lunch or having a drink in the evening, stalking, making nuisance telephone calls, misuse of email, sending hate mail, oral or physical abuse, etc.

2. Ensure that the definition of 'harassment' is clear and covers both unlawful and objectionable harassment (not just what is outlawed by statute), i.e.:

    any unwanted treatment on the grounds of: age, creed, disability, nationality, race, religion, sex, sexual orientation, political opinions, family status, health, gender or any other personal characteristic which is *unwanted by the recipient* or any conduct based on the above characteristics which affects the dignity of any individual or group of individuals at work. Harassment may be persistent or an isolated incident and may be directed towards more than one individual.

3. It is sensible to give examples of harassment or bullying (though making sure that it is clear that these are examples only) such as:

    unwanted physical contact or assault or battery; suggestive and offensive remarks, gestures, leers, pin-ups of nude or semi-nude men or women or individuals displayed for sexual effect; jokes and banter of a sexual, racist, etc. nature; displaying or sending offensive emails, organising strip-o-grams or kiss-o-grams or any activity of a similar nature which is offensive to others or causes offence, etc; sending hate mail or making offensive or nuisance telephone calls; stalking; 'ganging up on someone'; ridiculing them or trying to put them down; mimicking them or playing practical jokes.

4. It is important in the procedure to require managers and supervisors to deal effectively with (or at the very least report) any form of harassment or bullying that they believe is happening. Monitoring and enforcement of equal opportunities may be included in the manager's key responsibilities, targets, key performance objectives and standards of performance and may include how well they have undertaken this task in their annual appraisal.

5. The procedure should allow for the aggrieved party to report 'in confidence' to someone who is either in a trusted position such as human resources or occupational health or has been designated as a 'listener' or 'supporter' or 'counsellor'.

6. In relation to 'confidentiality', the recipient of the complaint must make it clear at the outset of the meeting that 'confidentiality' will be assured but there may be a need to inform certain senior managers if the conduct is so serious that management must take action in order to protect others, e.g. if there is an allegation of false imprisonment, violence or intimidation, stalking or hate mail, etc.

   This relieves the individual of the responsibility for taking the decision whether to proceed with the complaint but assures them that they will be protected from retaliation of any sort or physical reprisal. If the latter is the concern, then apart from anonymising the complaint, steps such as providing some form of security and/or bodyguards should be considered in rare cases.

7. It is particularly important that the person complaining of harassment or bullying is treated with dignity and respect and is not cross-examined or treated in a hostile fashion. Comments such as 'Well, if you wear those short skirts and flimsy blouses, you can't expect anything else, can you?' are to be avoided.

8. Once the complainant has made a full written statement, the matter must be investigated. The alleged perpetrator may be suspended during this time. If this is the case it may be appropriate at such a sensitive time to call this 'special leave' or 'annual leave' both for internal and external purposes. This ensures that the 'grapevine' does not start rumours that may harm the individual, who may be innocent of all complaints.

9. All witnesses should then be separately interviewed. It is rare for there to be eyewitnesses in harassment or bullying cases. It is more common to find 'contemporaneous' witnesses.

   Full support should be given to the complainant. If the complainant wishes to take time off from work during this time, this should of course be approved.

10. In order that gossip does not start or is limited and that witnesses have not discussed their evidence or their answers in advance or at all, each witness in turn should be required to sign a confidentiality agreement,

promising to keep the fact of the interview and its contents strictly confidential. See **Precedent 11B**.

11. The complainant and the accused may be offered the opportunity to go to mediation where an external, professionally trained and accredited mediator will be appointed to seek to resolve their complaints. This is an optional process.

Terms of suspension of alleged perpetrator

It is important to stipulate the terms upon which the suspension must be carried out. If the employer can move the alleged perpetrator or transfer that person to another location instead of suspending them, this should be carefully considered. Suspension must be wholly appropriate in the circumstances of the case even if there is an express right to suspend in the procedure or in the contract.

11.5 Making sure the decision in the grievance letter is correct

Once a grievance letter has been written and sent, the decision binds the employer. It is therefore very important to check and re-check the decision letter.

In *Hershaw v. Sheffield City Council* UKEAT/0033/14/BA the claimant alleged that their employer had made unauthorised deductions from wages contrary to s.13 of the Employment Rights Act 1996.

The employer had implemented a single status pay and grading review which was disputed by the claimant and other colleagues. They appealed, but were never informed of the outcome until after they raised a grievance complaining they had not been told.

In a letter from the HR consultant tasked with responding to it the claimant was informed that the appeal panel had decided they would be placed on Grade 5 (whereas they had previously been placed on Grade 3).

This never happened and the employer argued that the letter was a mistake and reconvened the appeal panel to determine what it had actually decided (which was a lesser increase, to Grade 4).

The EAT held that in context, the letter responded to a complaint that the employees had not been told what the decision as to their grade was. The letter told them. It was written by an HR staff member who was authorised to tell them what had been decided, even if she was not authorised to decide questions of pay herself. The issue of whether there was a common mistake was remitted to a fresh tribunal.

In determining whether someone has authority to bind an employer when sending a decision to an employee, viewed objectively, was a communication intended to set out what is being offered (or has been decided), and is it from someone held out by the employer as authorised to make that communication?

The EAT in *Hershaw* case said this:

> The employer arranged for Ms Senior Wadsworth to be the person to give that answer. The answer was thus given by someone who was held out by the employer to provide an authoritative answer to the grievance. Though not authorised to determine pay, she was authorised to communicate what others had decided. If she had not been, the Council's appointment of her to deal with the grievance would have had no purpose, since it was the outcome of the pay appeal which was centrally in issue.
>
> There may be many cases in which a communication from someone who is not a decision maker may nonetheless be treated as an authoritative record of that decision: it could hardly be said, for instance, that a letter written by the boss's secretary, on headed notepaper, recording an offer being made by him would not be capable of binding the company if accepted (subject only to something unusual in surrounding circumstances); the secretary to a committee may not be a decision maker, but plainly has authority to communicate the decision even if not to make it. The critical principle, as we see it, is whether viewed objectively a communication is intended to set out what is being offered (or has been decided), and is from someone held out by the employer as authorised to make that communication.

11.6 Personal liability, indemnifying individual respondents and conflict of interest

When named individual respondents are joined in a discrimination claim against an employer, it may be inappropriate for the same lawyers to represent all the parties as there may be a conflict of interest. If the first respondent (the company) seeks to claim its statutory defence that it 'took all reasonable steps' to prevent the employee or agent from doing either the specific act in question or anything of that description (Equality Act 2010, s.109(4)), then there will inevitably be a conflict of interest in representing the other named respondents.

Whilst in such cases it is appropriate to instruct the individual respondents to seek independent representation, the question of the company indemnifying those individuals for their legal costs and payment of any compensation awarded against them has sometimes been raised. As a matter of common sense it seems illogical to offer to indemnify the individuals for their legal costs and any awards of compensation made against them personally before the Employment Tribunal has adjudicated on the claim.

If such an indemnity were offered before the trial of the action, there would be little incentive on managers to comply with the anti-discrimination legislation or equal opportunities policies. The joining of individual respondents was commented upon in an early decision, *Read v. Tiverton District Council and Bull* [1997] IRLR 202, when the Employment Tribunal held (p.203):

> It is implicit from ss.41(1) and (2) of the Sex Discrimination Act, which state that anything done by a person in the course of his employment or as an agent for another person shall be treated as done by his employer or that other person 'as well as by him', that Parliament was there recognising that such agent should also himself be personally responsible for an act of discrimination.
>
> This construction was supported by s.42(1) which provides that a person who knowingly aids another to unlawfully discriminate shall be treated 'as himself' doing

an unlawful act and s.42(2) which provides that an employee or agent for whose act the employer is liable under s.41 shall be deemed to aid the doing of the act by the employer.

A decision to indemnify the individual respondent by the company may be against public policy and void. If this occurred the shareholders or other directors could legitimately refuse to honour such a promise in the event that the individuals were found liable by a tribunal.

Precedent 11D is for use by anyone who wishes to consider such a promise.

11.7 Monitoring recruitment and gender pay reporting

Monitoring female and ethnic minority recruitment and promotion, etc. lies at the heart of the Equality and Human Rights Commission (EHRC).

The Equality Act 2010 (Gender Pay Gap Information) Regulations 2017, SI 2017/172 require employers with 250 or more employees to publish statutory calculations every year showing how large the pay gap is between their male and female employees.

For example, according to ACAS, it may show that on average men earn 10 per cent more pay per hour than women, that men earn five per cent more in bonuses per year than women, or that the lowest paid quarter of the workforce is mostly female.

These results must be published on the employer's own website and a government site. This means that the gender pay gap will be publicly available, including to customers, employees and potential future recruits. As a result, employers should consider taking new or faster actions to reduce or eliminate their gender pay gaps.

The Regulations came into force on 6 April 2017, from which point employers will have up to 12 months to publish this information.

ACAS has published several useful guides on the subject – 'Managing Gender Pay Reporting'; 'Gender Pay Reporting: Obligations for Employers'; 'The Top Ten Myths about Gender Pay Reporting' and a 'Gender Pay Reporting Notification Template'.

See **Precedent 11E** for an example of monitoring records and the Gender Pay Reporting template.

11.8 Harassment and/or bullying

The European Commission Recommendation and Code of Practice 92/131/EEC on the Protection of the Dignity of Women and Men at Work lays down clear guidelines to employers about procedures, etc. that should be in place as regards harassment and bullying. The Equality and Human Rights Commission (EHRC) has produced helpful guidance on how to tackle and deal with harassment and bullying at work.

The key issues are:

(a) to have a sensitive and supportive procedure for complainants;

(b) to have a special complaints procedure where the individual does not have first to complain to the line manager;
(c) that the complainant has a 'supporter', colleague, friend, counsellor or 'listener' to whom they can go in confidence at any stage;
(d) that an open mind is kept at all times;
(e) as there will very rarely be eyewitnesses, that a considered approach is made to the standard of proof;
(f) that complainants are not questioned in a manner that makes them believe the employer does not believe them, or in a manner which is more akin to cross-examination;
(g) that the complainant is not asked questions about their personal or sexual life;
(h) that the complainant is not accused of inappropriate dress or conduct suggesting that they provoked the conduct complained of;
(i) an understanding of and allowance for the fact that the complainant may not have made the complaint straightaway, and that there might have been some time-lag since the events complained of, because of reluctance to raise a grievance or complaint and the fear of reprisals or dismissal;
(j) that an alleged harasser's typical responses are recognised denial, i.e. 'It was only a joke' or 'They asked for it';
(k) to allow for someone independent and senior to conduct the investigation, especially where one or other of the parties is well known to the senior management.

Criminal offence

Under the Protection from Harassment Act 1997 there is a statutory tort of intentional infliction of harm. Other criminal offences such as breach of the peace and offences under the Offences against the Person Act 1861 could be committed in such a context.

It is now prudent to include in any harassment policy reference to the Protection from Harassment Act 1997, which makes it a criminal offence to harass with an intention to inflict harm.

According to the House of Lords in *Majrowski* v. *Guy's and St Thomas's NHS Trust* [2006] UKHL 34, the Protection from Harassment Act 1997 would apply where the conduct crosses 'the boundary from the regrettable to the unacceptable' and the gravity of the misconduct must be of an order which would sustain criminal liability under s.2 of the 1997 Act.

Civil damages

The High Court heard a claim for personal injuries as a result of serious bullying and harassment in the case of *Green* v. *DB Group Services (UK) Ltd* [2006] IRLR 764. Here the claimant was the subject of a 'relentless campaign of mean and spiteful behaviour' by four women who worked in close proximity to her and in respect of behaviour by a male co-worker which was found to be 'domineering, disrespectful, dismissive, confrontatory, and designed to undermine and belittle her in the view of others'.

The High Court held that a 'reasonable and responsible employer' would have intervened as soon as it became aware of the problem. Instead, 'the managers collectively closed their eyes to what was going on, no doubt in the hope that the problem would go away', and the bank's HR department is found to be guilty of 'a culpable want of care'. The award of damages included £639,000 in respect of future losses and her legal costs.

If an employee's actions become unpleasant and unacceptable to another member of staff, the correct course of action is for the employer to undertake its own investigation and then determine an appropriate penalty.

Unfair dismissal

If an Employment Tribunal finds that the employer was 'heavy handed and prejudged' the issue, the dismissal of the alleged perpetrator is likely to be found to be unfair.

This is what happened in *Grampian Joint Police Board* v. *Sighe* EAT/951/00 (unreported, EAT, 16 March 2001) where a scenes of crime officer was dismissed after being convicted of 'lurking' near the house of a colleague with whom he had become infatuated. The EAT held that even though the conduct that led to Mr Sighe's dismissal involved a fellow officer, it did not relate to his employment and the fact of a conviction for a breach of the peace 'provided no reason to undermine the employer's trust and confidence in [the officer's] ability to carry out his tasks'. Reinstatement was ordered as there was evidence before the Employment Tribunal that Mr Sighe would not come into contact with the colleague. The Employment Tribunal had held that the band of reasonable responses stopped short of dismissal and any reasonable employer would have issued a warning to the officer.

Aggravated damages

Where an employer acts in a 'high-handed, malicious, insulting or oppressive manner committing the act of discrimination' then aggravated damages can be awarded (*Alexander* v. *The Home Office* [1988] IRLR 190), and also where the conduct of the defence of the proceedings is unreasonable (*Zaiwalla & Co* v. *Walia* [2002] IRLR 697).

In *HM Land Registry* v. *McGlue* EAT/0435/11, the EAT held that tribunals must recognise that aggravated damages are **not** punitive and are not dependent 'upon any sense of outrage by a tribunal as to the conduct which has occurred'. The EAT noted that an award for aggravated damages is appropriate where the distress caused by an act of discrimination is made worse by:

- it being done in an upsetting way, for example where it is done in a 'high-handed, malicious, insulting or oppressive way' (*Broome* v. *Cassell* [1972] AC 1027);

- motive, for example conduct based on prejudice, animosity, spite or vindictiveness; or
- subsequent conduct, for example where a case is conducted at a trial in an unnecessarily offensive manner, or a serious complaint is not taken seriously, or there has been a failure to apologise (*HM Prison Service* v. *Salmon* [2001] IRLR 425 EAT and *British Telecommunications plc* v. *Reid* [2004] IRLR 327 (CA)).

In *Commissioner of Police of the Metropolis* v. *Shaw* UKEAT/0125/11/ZT, the EAT held that the Employment Tribunal's award of aggravated damages of £20,000 fell outside the recognised range for such awards. The Employment Tribunal had made a mistake of focusing entirely on the seriousness of the conduct of the respondent rather than on the impact on the claimant. In effect, the Employment Tribunal had awarded punitive damages whereas they are to compensate the claimant for the additional distress caused.

There was also discussion on whether or not injury to feelings and aggravated damages were separate heads of loss and the danger of double counting. The award was reduced to £7,500 as the award for aggravated damages.

Dealing with infatuation

Dealing with employees who become infatuated with another member of staff can be problematic. This behaviour can be very threatening and is often conducted outside working hours, such as following the person home, 'lurking' outside their house, etc. The 'perpetrator' as well as the 'victim' may well require psychological or psychiatric treatment. It may be wise for the employer to consider other forms of assistance, such as providing additional security measures, including in some cases bodyguards, automatic lights outside and alarms, etc.

Precedent 11F is a model policy in respect of harassment or bullying.

Informing the complainant of action taken

Whilst there is no express requirement to notify the victim of harassment or bullying of the outcome in terms of what action has been taken against the harasser/bully, it is implicit that this will be done in the strictest of confidence.

The former EOC's publication 'Sexual Harassment – Managers' questions answered' (March 2006) recommended that the employer should:

> inform the complainant of his/her right to appeal if they are dissatisfied with the outcome of their grievance. The courts have, however, held that it is not for the complainant to dictate the disciplinary action that should be taken against the alleged harasser.

Vicarious liability: Christmas parties

Employers can and have been held liable for the acts and omissions of their staff at Christmas parties and other social events put on by their employer.

11.9 Whistleblowing: what it is and policies

Under the Employment Rights Act 1996, s.43A (inserted by the Public Interest Disclosure Act 1998), employees are protected from any form of discriminatory action including dismissal where they act in accordance with the Act and make 'protected disclosures'. The disclosure must relate to information concerning:

(a) a criminal offence;
(b) a breach of a legal obligation;
(c) a miscarriage of justice;
(d) a danger to the health or safety of any individual;
(e) damage to the environment; or
(f) a deliberate covering up of information tending to show any of the above.

The whistleblowing provisions were amended from 20 June 2013 by the Enterprise and Regulatory Reform Act 2013. Section 43B of the Employment Rights Act 1996 states that in order to qualify as a protected disclosure the disclosure had to be made, in the reasonable belief of the worker, 'in the public interest'.

There is no longer a good faith requirement but any disclosure made in bad faith may reduce any compensation.

There is a three-stage test now:

1. What information did the worker consider was in the public interest?
2. Do they believe their disclosure will benefit this public interest?
3. Was such a belief 'reasonable'?

Whistleblowing: Guidance for Employers and Code of Practice has been produced by the Department for Business, Energy & Industrial Strategy (formerly BIS) (March 2015). Disappointingly, there is no guidance as to what could be 'in the public interest'.

There are only four references to 'in the public interest':

1. 'acting in the public interest... means in particular that personal grievances and complaints are not usually covered by whistleblowing law'.
2. 'Workers who make a disclosure under an organisation's whistleblowing policy should believe that they are acting in the public interest. This means in particular that personal grievances and complaints are not usually covered by whistleblowing law'.
3. Clarification that any so-called 'gagging clauses' in settlement agreements do not prevent workers from making disclosures in the public interest.
4. Confirmation that any clauses in settlement agreements do not prevent workers from making disclosures in the public interest.

A decision of the Court of Appeal is awaited in the case of *Chesterton Global Ltd v. Nurmohamed* [UK EAT/U335/14]. It has been listed in June 2017.

The claimant, a senior manager, had complained about his employer allegedly manipulating the company's finances and accounts, which he believed had had a negative impact on the commission that he and other senior managers had received.

The EAT acknowledged that the intention of the 2013 amendment was to prevent a complaint about an individual's own employment constituting a qualifying protected disclosure. The fact this matter affected around 100 senior managers and shareholders raised it to a matter of public interest – or that is how the claimant has argued it. If only a particular section of the public is affected by the issue then it can still make the matter one of 'public interest'. The intention was to exclude whistleblowing claims where they are solely about an individual's terms and conditions (referred to below as 'removing the opportunistic use of the legislation for private purposes' – the *Parkins* v. *Sodexho Ltd* case).

In the Committee debate on the Bill on 3 July 2012 Mr Norman Lamb, the Parliamentary Under-Secretary of State for Business, Innovations and Skills (the promoter of the Bill) stated:

> The amendment would, in addition to the inclusion of the public interest test that we propose, disallow Public Interest Disclosure Act claims based on breaches of an individual's employment contract.
>
> In a sense, the amendment seeks to add an additional hurdle for claimants to clear on top of what the Government intend.
>
> Setting out the issue that the Government seek to address might be helpful. The original aim of the public interest disclosure legislation was to provide protection to individuals who made a disclosure in the public interest – otherwise known as blowing the whistle. The clause seeks to make that public interest clear, and the hint is in the title of the original legislation, which was designed to deal with public interest disclosure – that is what we are talking about [...]
>
> To return to my explanation of the purpose of the clause and of why the Government have designed it in such a way, the decision in the case *Parkins* v. *Sodexho Ltd* has resulted in a fundamental change in how the Public Interest Disclosure Act operates and has widened its scope beyond what was originally intended.
>
> The ruling in that case stated that there is no reason to distinguish a legal obligation that arises from a contract of employment from any other form of legal obligation. The effect is that individuals make a disclosure about a breach of their employment contract, where this is a matter of purely private rather than public interest, and then claim protection, for example, for unfair dismissal...
>
> The clause will amend part IVA of the Employment Rights Act 1996 to close the loophole that case law has created... The clause in no way takes away rights from those who seek to blow the whistle on matters of genuine public interest.
>
> [...]
>
> The clause will remove the opportunistic use of the legislation for private purposes.
>
> It is in the original spirit of the Public Interest Disclosure Act that those seeking its protection should reasonably believe that their raising an issue is in the public interest. Including a public interest test in the Bill deals with the *Parkins* v. *Sodexho Ltd* case in its entirety. Therefore there is no need to disallow claims based on an individual's contract (as suggested in the amendment).
>
> Indeed, although our aim is to prevent the opportunistic use of breaches of an individual's contract that are of a personal nature, there are also likely to be instances where a worker should be able to rely on breaches of his own contract where those engage wider public interest issues. In other words, in a worker's complaint about a breach of their contract, the breach in itself might have wider public interest implications.

In *Underwood v. Wincanton plc* UKEAT/0163/15 the employee claimed that there had been an unfair allocation of overtime. The Employment Tribunal originally rejected that this was a qualifying protected disclosure (as it related to private interest regarding working conditions).

The EAT overturned this, again noting that a disclosure may still meet the public interest test even if it is only potentially in the public interest of a sub-set or specific category of the public.

It also noted that a complaint relating to terms and conditions of employment could still be in the public interest in certain circumstances and should not automatically be assumed to be of private interest only.

Precedent 11G is an example of a whistleblowing policy.

PRECEDENT 11A: Clause defining when grievance procedure may be initiated

1. An individual who feels that they have been treated unfairly or is dissatisfied about a decision taken about them, has the right to express their grievance through the Grievance Procedure. Human Resources will advise any employee who asks about the procedures including at which stage the grievance should be heard.

2. It should be noted that the grievance procedure cannot be initiated as a means of interrupting any disciplinary process. However, if a genuine grievance is raised which throws doubt on the credibility of the disciplinary issues or could threaten the integrity of the procedure, management will consider whether in any case it is appropriate to suspend the disciplinary procedure for a short period in order for the grievance to be considered.

3. It may be considered appropriate for another manager to deal with the disciplinary case on the basis of ensuring that both matters are dealt with impartially.

PRECEDENT 11B: Undertaking of confidentiality

1. I, [name], understand that I am being asked to co-operate and answer questions in relation to a complaint of [give details] concerning [names of parties].

2. I understand that it is critical that I keep the fact of this interview, the fact that this investigation is being carried out and the contents of the interview and any details that I may learn, e.g. the questions and answers that are asked and given, strictly confidential.

3. I understand that if I breach this undertaking it would discredit and harm the integrity of the investigation and taint the evidence if others knew of the existence of this investigation and any answers given by any of the witnesses. I could also seriously prejudice the integrity and credibility of either the complainant or the subject of the complaint.

4. For these reasons I understand my duty to keep strictly confidential the fact that I have been interviewed, the fact that this investigation is being conducted, the nature of the investigation and names of the parties concerned and the content of what was discussed with me in any interview. I will not contact any other witness to discuss this matter nor will I discuss this matter with the alleged perpetrator nor the complainant nor their representatives.

5. I will co-operate fully with management in this investigation and will answer any questions truthfully and openly.

Signed .... Dated ....

[employee]

PRECEDENT 11C: Letter confirming terms of suspension

[Name of employee]

[Address]

[Date]

Dear [Name]

RE: Your suspension

1. Our investigation

We understand your natural concern and distress over your suspension and the ongoing investigation.

We can assure you that the investigation is being conducted with the utmost integrity and that nothing improper is or will be done by the Company.

We are required to conduct a thorough investigation into all the allegations that are made against you in respect of [give details].

2. No implication of guilt

There is no implication of guilt or any finding thereof during this investigation. The purpose of the investigation is to get to the truth. This will assist you if there are innocent explanations for the charges against you.

You are, however, required not to attend our offices or contact anyone during working hours nor make any attempt to contact clients, customers or suppliers.

3. Your opportunity to give your side of the story

The Company has a procedure to follow in all cases of suspected dishonest conduct. You will have a full opportunity to explain your side of the story and to rebut any evidence that management puts forward, at the hearing that has been arranged for [date].

This will be before the Finance Director. He is quite independent, has not been involved in this matter and will give you a fair hearing.

Anyone in your position naturally feels very vulnerable and stressed and this is why we are seeking to be as thorough but as expeditious as possible so that you can have the opportunity to come to the hearing and 'clear your name'.

4. Instruction that you do not contact anyone other than your representative

We need to make this very clear – you should not contact anyone personally other than your representative during this time. Your representative and only your representative should contact potential witnesses on your behalf. You can call as witnesses whomsoever you choose.

In line with the Data Protection Act 1998, we cannot give you the addresses or telephone numbers of the individuals you have requested as witnesses. We will act as post box and will promise to pass on immediately any correspondence placed in a sealed envelope delivered to the HR Director, with their name clearly marked on the outside.

5. Reason for this instruction

This instruction is for your own good because there might otherwise be an accusation that you tried to put pressure on a witness or that you threatened a witness or tried to or did put words into their mouth. Worse still, someone who has willingly given us a statement may, if contacted by you, seek to retract or withdraw their statement willingly and voluntarily given before being contacted by you.

I hope that you will see the reason and rationale for this instruction.

However, if a lawyer working on your behalf wishes to contact any witness, they should do so via the HR Department as instructed above. The instruction only relates to you not contacting anyone directly.

6. Asking questions of witnesses through the HR Director

We have already sent to you and to your representative copies of all the witness statements that we intend to use at the hearing. You have the opportunity to supply any questions for them to us and we will forward them and ask for their answers and we will then forward them to you. You will also have the opportunity to ask questions of them personally at the disciplinary hearing as they will both be attending the hearing.

7. **Your request for the** [*specify documents*]

We are forwarding to you under separate cover to be delivered by hand tonight [*specify documents*] requested by you in your latest email.

Yours sincerely

PRECEDENT 11D: Personal liability

1. Under various employment statutes, personal liability as well as corporate liability can be imposed: see, for example, the Health and Safety at Work etc. Act 1974 and the Equality Act 2010. Under the Health and Safety at Work etc. Act 1974 there is criminal liability for breaches of the Act which may render the Company or an individual liable to a fine and/or imprisonment. Other statutes and regulations impose civil liability.

2. Whilst the Company has primary responsibility for ensuring compliance with these statutes, individual employees may also be held liable where they have consented to or connived at the acts or been neglectful or have deliberately ignored or disobeyed correct instructions.

3. It would be contrary to public policy for any insurance company to offer an indemnity for any penalty imposed under any statute imposing criminal penalties, although limited insurance cover is available for legal expenses incurred in respect of certain prosecutions under the Health and Safety at Work etc. Act 1974 subject to certain conditions laid down in the Company's Insurance Policy.

4. The Company would look carefully at any case where an individual employee is prosecuted and/or sued under these statutes and a senior executive will determine whether it would be appropriate to grant any financial or any other assistance (and if so the level of any financial assistance) after the case has been heard and the individual has been found innocent.

PRECEDENT 11E: Ethnic and gender monitoring in recruitment and training

> ACAS has published some useful guidance on this topic in a series of booklets – the first being 'Managing Gender Pay Reporting' (March 2017). They can all be found at: www.acas.org.uk/index.aspx?articleid=5768.

1. Introduction

Each year at this time we report to the Governing Board on our performance in relation to equal opportunities in recruitment and training. We have at the Governing Board's request included information relating to age and length of service.

2. Present practice

2.1 We continue to maintain a policy of equal opportunities for all, looking at all aspects of opportunity, not only ethnicity but also gender. Our aim is not to positively discriminate, but to encourage applicants from all backgrounds to apply for posts in the knowledge that their applications will be fairly and carefully considered.

2.2 Women continue to be well represented at all levels: 65 per cent of the current workforce are female. During the last year 54 per cent of all appointees were women.

2.3 In order to improve our equal opportunities performance in all aspects, we continually seek to improve our methods of recruitment and selection in line with best practice. We continue to:

(a) advertise externally all posts and issue each advert to the relevant disablement/ resettlement officer and appropriate job centre. We are also using our own intranet plus [*an external job search website*];
(b) train all those involved in interviewing in recruitment and selection skills. Untrained staff are not allowed to take part in the selection process;
(c) shortlist with agreed criteria set by the interview panel to ensure skills match between candidates and job description;
(d) ensure that interview and shortlisting panels are attended by a Human Resources professional to ensure a consistent Trustwide approach, and to maintain good practice;
(e) monitor the response to advertising and selection, training and promotion;
(f) produce monthly key indicators on the ethnicity of appointees which are discussed at Executive Group.

3. Recruitment: an overview

3.1 During the last 12 months there has been a decrease in the number of jobs advertised and an increase in successful appointments. We have been particularly careful to outline the essential selection criteria in all recruitment advertisements, thereby allowing prospective candidates to eliminate themselves prior to application if they do not meet the criteria.

	2011/12	2012/13	2013/14	2014/15	2015/16	2016/17
Posts advertised	111	164	151	201	205	160
Applicants	2,107	2,317	2,753	2,945	1,685	1,372

	2011/12	2012/13	2013/14	2014/15	2015/16	2016/17
Average applicants per post	19	14	18	15	8	9

3.2 The Company continues to enjoy a strong position in [our sector] which makes us attractive to prospective employees. We receive many applications from those already employed by [our competitors] because of our good terms and conditions of employment and recognition of the Company as an expanding dynamic organisation.

4. Results: recruitment (BAME/gender)

4.1 Our detailed figures (available for inspection if needed) show the five categories of staff monitored. This year's results show continued success in recruiting people from black, Asian and minority ethnic (BAME) groups at a professional and technical level. In this group 42 per cent of appointees were from a BAME background, details shown below:

Professional and technical appointments grades 5 and 6

No. of posts	Ethnic group	Male	Female
1	Asian	1	0
6	African	3	3
7	Black British	2	5
30	European	16	14
2	Irish	1	1
6	Combi/other	2	4

4.2 Recruitment to Management posts has this year totalled 11 posts; of these, three appointees were from a minority ethnic background.

4.3 During 2016/17, appointments from BAME groups were as follows:

Group	% of BAME appointees
Directors	No appointments made in this group
Assistant Directors/Managers	30%
Supervisory grades 7 and 8	35%
Technical/Professional grades 5 and 6	42%
Secretarial/Clerical grades 1–4	24%
Wardens/Caretakers	37%
All appointees	33%

4.4 Proportion of posts by minority ethnic/gender.

Category	Minority ethnic						No. of posts recruited		Gender Appts (15/16) 16/17	
	Applicants		Interviews		Appointees						
	15/16	16/17	15/16	16/17	15/16	16/17	15/16	16/17	M	F
Sec/Clerical grades 1–4	41%	43%	20%	38%	24%	24%	30	31	(9) 6	(21) 25
Tech/Prof grades 5 and 6	63%	50%	34%	50%	66%	39%	24	52	(14) 27	(10) 25
Supervisory grades 7 and 8	62%	39%	35%	37%	50%	35%	26	31	(11) 22	(15) 9
Assistant Director/ Managers	48%	45%	35%	44%	40%	30%	5	11	(3) 5	(2) 6
Wardens/ Caretakers	25%	24%	7%	21%	16%	37%	6	8	(1) 6	(5) 2
All vacancies	58%	43%	49%	41%	54%	33%	91	133	(38) 66	(53) 67

4.5 Number of staff promoted internally (01.04.16 to 31.03.17). These figures are included in the table above.

	No. of internal promotions	% of minority ethnic appointees	Gender of appointees	
Graded staff	40	40% (16 posts)	females	23
			males	17
Managers	6	50% (3 posts)	females	3
			males	3
All promotions	46	41% (19 posts)	females	26
			males	20

4.6 Current workforce 16/17 by ethnicity and gender.

Ethnicity	Gender
62% European	65% female
29% BAME	35% male
9% did not disclose	

5. **Results: training (minority ethnic/gender)**

5.1 *Ethnicity*

The Training Department has continued to monitor course attendance by ethnicity. The management training courses are well recognised in our industry sector.

5.2 Gender

We continue to monitor course attendance by gender. This take up of training courses is in line with the gender breakdown in the workforce.

6. Conclusions

The ethnic breakdown of applicants has shown little change in the categories examined over the last three years.

7. Disciplinary action

7.1 We continue to monitor ethnicity and gender of staff involved in disciplinary action.

7.2 Between 1 April 2016 and 31 March 2017 there were a total of six disciplinary cases within the Trust involving three white European staff and three staff from the ethnic minorities (of whom five were male and one was female).

7.3 Two members of staff failed their probationary period, both from white European background.

PRECEDENT 11F: Model harassment/bullying policy

Harassment: statement

1. In pursuance of the Company's policy of equal opportunities for all employees, it is clear that conduct involving the harassment of any member of staff for any reason is unacceptable. The Company will conform with all the Equality and Human Rights Commission and European Union Codes of Practice and Recommendations such as the Protection of the Dignity of Women and Men at Work 1991 and the EC Code of Practice and Guidance to Employers on Sexual Harassment. The Company recognises the problems that harassment can cause at work.

2. This statement and policy includes all forms of bullying, intimidation, 'sending people to Coventry', deliberately teasing or ignoring the individual, deliberately leaving them out of social events such as going to lunch or having a drink in the evening, stalking, making nuisance telephone calls, conducting a campaign of rudeness and unfriendliness, misuse of email, e.g. with offensive attachments, sending hate mail, verbal or physical abuse, etc.

3. Specific reference to this issue will be made on every induction training course for new starters and the Company will from time to time undertake to remind all staff of both the policy and their individual responsibilities.

4. The Company aims to ensure that such unacceptable behaviour does not take place and will communicate this Statement and the accompanying policy to all members of staff. The Company defines harassment as any conduct related to age, creed, disability, nationality, race, religion, sex, sexual orientation, political opinions, family status, health, gender or any other personal characteristic which is *unwanted by the recipient* or any conduct based on the above characteristics which affects the dignity of any individual or group of individuals at work. Harassment may be persistent or an isolated incident and may be directed towards more than one individual.

5. Sexual and racial harassment and harassment on the grounds of disability are all forms of unlawful sex, racial and disability discrimination and as a consequence unlawful behaviour. It is also improper and inappropriate behaviour which lowers morale and interferes with the effectiveness of people at work.

6. It is the policy of the Company to make every effort to provide a working environment free from all forms of harassment and intimidation. The Company is committed to equality of opportunity in reality and in which every individual can seek, obtain and continue employment without unfair discrimination. In line with its philosophy, the Company expects all members of staff to be treated with respect.

7. Harassment is not only unwanted physical contact, assault or propositions. It includes suggestive remarks or gestures, pin-ups, graffiti, offensive comments, jokes and banter based on race, religion, sex or other personal characteristics. None of this is part of a culture in which all staff and groups of staff are treated with dignity and respect.

8. Harassment is not acceptable under any circumstances. Every effort will be made to deal with alleged harassment on an informal basis in the first instance where appropriate by explaining its effect on the alleged harasser. Nevertheless any member of staff regardless of grade or position found responsible for inciting, perpetrating or condoning harassment may be disciplined and can be held personally liable if the person who is harassed makes a tribunal claim.

9. Some types of harassment are classed as criminal offences which can lead to prosecution. These include offences under the Protection of Harassment Act 1997, which makes it a criminal offence under section 4 of the Act to cause a reasonable person to fear that violence will be used against them.

10. An example of this might be where a male accused of harassment telephones the woman threatening to kill or harm her and/or her children including making statements such as 'I know where you live'; 'I know where your children go to school'.

11. All members of staff are expected to comply with the policy and to ensure that such conduct does not occur. Appropriate disciplinary action including summary dismissal for serious offences will be taken against any staff member who violates this policy. All staff will undergo specialist training in order to understand what harassment is and how it is dealt with.

12. In all cases harassment concerns the behaviour by both members of staff and third parties which occurs at the workplace or in direct connection with a person's employment, e.g. at a public house in a lunch hour. Generally this excludes social events not organised by the Company and not held on Company premises; however, all members of staff are expected to behave properly outside work.

13. If any such behaviour as described in the policy occurs in relation to another member of staff at a social function directly after working hours or in unpaid meal breaks or on a training course or study day or where the reputation of the Company is brought into question, the Company will take firm action in relation to any such activities.

14. Any member of staff who believes herself or himself to be harassed should first ask the harasser to stop. If this is not possible or if the harassment continues following the request to stop or if the incident is considered to be serious, s/he has the right to complain and should contact his or her immediate manager, personnel manager or counsellor designated for the purpose. The matter will be dealt with quickly and in confidence.

15. Where appropriate the alleged harasser will be moved to another work area during the investigation or suspended. Where the investigation shows that the complaint is well founded, it will be the Company's primary concern in all cases to prevent a recurrence of the harassment. Where considered appropriate (bearing in mind the unacceptability of harassment within the Company), for example where the harasser persists following a request to stop, disciplinary action up to and including summary dismissal will be taken.

If it is necessary to separate the people concerned, every effort will be made to move the harasser and not the person who has been harassed unless it is the stated wish of the latter to move.

16. All managers and supervisors in charge of groups of people are responsible for dealing with any harassment or intimidation of which they become aware, whether or not it has been formally brought to their attention. Failure to do so will be regarded as a failure to fulfil all the responsibilities of their position.

17. The Company will not tolerate intimidation, victimisation or unfair discrimination against any member of staff who makes a complaint or who assists in an investigation of alleged harassment. Retaliation against a member of staff who complains of harassment can be expected to lead to disciplinary action and may be a criminal offence resulting in prosecution.

18. The Company reserves the right to seek outside assistance in conducting any investigation or disciplinary proceedings and this person may include a senior law enforcement officer or retired officer, a barrister or solicitor or any other third party with experience in conducting investigations into matters of a serious nature. In such cases the individuals concerned, both the alleged harasser and the complainant, will be permitted to have legal or other representation at all stages of the procedure.

19. The above statement is fully supported by [*specify*] trade union.

20. In particular we draw to everyone's attention that it is a criminal offence under the Public Order Act 1986 for anyone intentionally to cause a person harassment, alarm or distress and an offence under the Protection from Harassment Act 1997. The Public Order Act applies not only to racial and sexual harassment but also to harassment on the grounds of disability or sexual orientation. The essence of the offence is that a person causes harassment, alarm or distress:

(a) by using threatening, abusive or insulting words or behaviour; or
(b) by disorderly behaviour; or
(c) by displaying any writing, sign or other visible representation which is threatening, abusive or insulting.

The offence may be committed in public or private but excluding a place which is exclusively a domestic home. The need to prove intent is an important element of the offence and it will be a defence for the accused person to prove that his or her conduct was reasonable in the circumstances. It is clear from the wording in section 4A that this is meant to cover harassment in the workplace.

21. This policy also covers all forms of bullying, including but not limited to ridiculing others, 'sending them to Coventry', 'ganging up on' an individual or a group or isolating an individual or group of individuals, any deliberate or malicious act intended or designed to ridicule or 'put down' in any way; mimicking or playing practical jokes on others, etc. ACAS has produced guidance to both employers and employees on bullying and harassment at work (available online at **www.acas.org.uk**).

Preventing and dealing with harassment: Guidelines

1. Introduction

1.1 These Guidelines should be read in conjunction with the Statement on Harassment.

1.2 They replace all previous Company Guidelines on Harassment.

2. What is harassment?

2.1 'Harassment' means unwanted conduct of, for example, a sexual or racial nature or conduct based on sexual, racial or other forms of personal abuse which is offensive to the recipient.

2.2 Sexual harassment does not refer to behaviour of a socially acceptable nature. It refers to behaviour which is unsolicited, that is *personally* offensive and that fails to respect the rights of others and is such that it could interfere with an individual's performance and approach to work.

2.3 Harassment may be intentional or unintentional. The key issue is that it is unwanted by the recipient or undermines people's dignity at work. Since behaviour or language may be acceptable to one person and unacceptable to another, objections to unintentional harassment or to behaviour or language which the harasser thought was welcome should therefore be taken seriously.

2.4 Harassment is not a joke to the recipient and complaints of harassment should not be assumed to be the result of touchiness or over-sensitivity.

2.5 Racist language which causes offence does not become permissible just because the speaker claims that nothing was meant by it. Some types of sexually related behaviour which may be acceptable to an individual outside work may cause a complaint of harassment if they occur in the workplace because they interfere with and undermine the individual's dignity and role at work.

2.6 Friendly or romantic behaviour which is welcome and mutual is not harassment, although it may be regarded as unprofessional and inappropriate in the workplace. Such behaviour becomes harassment if it is persisted in once it has been made clear that it is regarded as such even though the perpetrator claims to have been only flirting, joking or intending to be friendly. If s/he is in any doubt as to whether such behaviour is acceptable to the recipient, s/he should ask or desist.

2.7 It should be noted that sexual harassment does not necessarily have to be 'sexual' in nature in the sense of being an attempt to initiate sexual relations. It is sufficient that the conduct is 'sex-based'. Therefore any behaviour which ridicules, denigrates or abuses an employee because of his or her sex is harassment.

2.8 Whilst it is not possible to give an exhaustive list of every type of behaviour covered by this policy, we list below some more common examples. The following are examples of inappropriate behaviour covered by this policy:

- Physical conduct of a sexual nature: any unwanted physical contact including unnecessary touching, patting, pinching or brushing up against another employee's body, placing hands on parts of the body, assault, coercing sexual intercourse.
- Verbal conduct of a sexual or racial nature: unwelcome sexual advances, propositions or pressure for sexual activity, intrusion by pestering including continued suggestions for social activity outside the workplace after it has been made clear that such suggestions are unwelcome, offensive flirtations, suggestive remarks, innuendoes or lewd comments, slander or malicious gossip, the singing of sectarian songs or songs of a derogatory and/or offensive nature.
- Non-verbal conduct of a sexual or racial nature: the display of pornographic or sexually suggestive pictures, objects or written materials including pin-ups and 'girlie' or 'Page 3' pictures, leering, whistling or making sexually suggestive gestures, organising or condoning kiss-o-grams or strip-o-grams either at work or in a public place where other work colleagues are present, graffiti, flags, bunting or emblems representing a group which is known to be against a sector of the community, e.g. the National Front.
- Sex-based or racially abusive conduct: conduct which denigrates or ridicules or is

intimidatory or physically abusive to an employee because of his or her sex or race such as derogatory or degrading abuse or insults which are gender-related or of a racial nature and offensive or highly personal comments about dress or appearance or physique, hygiene, etc.

3. Duty of managers and supervisors

3.1 All supervisors and managers are responsible for eliminating any sexual or racial harassment or intimidation of which they are aware. Failure to do so will be treated as a failure to fulfil all the responsibilities of their position.

3.2 No supervisor or manager shall threaten or insinuate, either explicitly or implicitly, that rejection by a member of staff of sexual advances or resistance to any racial abuse will be used as a basis for an employment decision affecting that member of staff. Such conduct shall be treated by the Company as a serious disciplinary offence by the supervisor or manager.

3.3 All managers and supervisors should fully understand the Company's harassment policy and feel confident to offer advice on the procedure when required to do so.

3.4 They should ensure that all their staff are aware of and understand this policy.

3.5 They should all be alert to physical and verbal harassment in their work area and deal with it immediately whether or not it is formally brought to their attention.

3.6 They should ensure that they are supportive to individuals who state that they have been harassed and take full account of their feelings and perception of the situation.

3.7 They should ensure that no further harassment or victimisation occurs.

3.8 They should not participate in, encourage or condone gossip relating to cases of actual or alleged harassment and take appropriate steps to prevent or stop gossip in their work area.

3.9 They should attend training sessions which may be arranged to increase their awareness of the issues involved in harassment.

3.10 They should maintain complete confidentiality relating to all aspects of cases of harassment at all times and should ensure that they do not mention or discuss the case unnecessarily with any person involved in its investigation.

3.11 However, it is important that if any serious matter is identified which could threaten the health and safety of the individual any further or that of others or where a criminal offence has been committed and disclosed, they are under a duty to report this to a senior member of Personnel, keeping so far as is possible the name of the individual anonymous. (An example could be the disclosure that the alleged harasser has made threatening telephone calls at night and has followed the complainant home or has 'stalked' the complainant out of office hours.)

3.12 In such a case the individual will be offered professional counselling and any other help such as taking a taped statement, offering time off work with pay and/or the alleged harasser to be suspended pending the outcome of the investigation.

4. Special complaints procedure

4.1 It is clearly inappropriate for the normal grievance procedure to be used for complaints of harassment particularly where it is the manager of the person against whom the complaint has been made. This special procedure has therefore been designed to deal with complaints of sexual or racial harassment.

4.2 Complaints of this nature clearly need to be handled sensitively. The procedure therefore ensures minimal stress for the complainant, timely resolution of complaints and a degree of flexibility appropriate to the individual circumstances.

4.3 At all stages of the procedure, the need to ensure confidentiality will be paramount. Information about any complaint will be given on a 'need to know' basis only and will be strictly restricted to ensure a fair hearing both to the complainant and alleged offender. Anonymity may be offered where this protects the interests of both parties involved. Every person giving evidence will be interviewed and required to agree in writing to keep the fact of the interview and the details of the interview strictly confidential and not to disclose to any other third party the content or fact of the interview.

4.4 During any investigation the person against whom the complaint has been made may be moved or suspended on pay for as long as management deems necessary. He/she will be given full details of any complaint at the appropriate time, well in advance of any investigatory or disciplinary hearing.

Please note that in any cases deemed appropriate by management, an external person who is experienced in investigations/harassment, may be called in to conduct any or all of the investigation stages.

In addition an external person such as a barrister or solicitor may be called in to adjudicate on any appeals or other stages of the grievance or disciplinary meetings.

4.5 Harassment is not acceptable under any circumstances at any of the Company's premises or locations or whilst away on business, at a Company training seminar or conference being held away from Company premises whether in work time or in the evenings or at weekends. Every effort will be made to deal with alleged harassment on an informal basis in the first instance, where this is appropriate, by explaining its effect on the harassed person(s). Nevertheless, any member of staff, regardless of grade or position, found to be responsible for inciting, perpetrating or condoning harassment may be disciplined and can be held personally liable if the person who has been harassed takes legal proceedings. Some types of harassment are classed as criminal offences and as such can lead to prosecution (see above).

Please note: where management believes it would be useful, you will be offered the opportunity to go to Mediation to resolve this grievance, at any stage of the procedure. An external, professionally trained and accredited Mediator will be appointed to seek to resolve your complaints. This is an optional process.

5. **Stages of the procedure**

5.1 Stage 1

Wherever possible the person who believes that they are the subject of sexual or racial harassment should ask the person responsible to stop the harassing behaviour. This should be done as soon as the harassment becomes apparent. If this is not possible or where the incident is too serious or where this does not stop or some employment consequences result, then a complaint under 5.2 below should be made.

Any informal action of this nature should be recorded by him or her with a note of the date and what was said by all those involved, in case this is needed as evidence should the harassment continue or subsequently recur.

5.2 Stage 2

There is no obligation on an individual to take matters further if s/he does not wish to do so. However, if the person considers the incident to be a serious one or if the harassment continues following the request to stop, s/he should then either report the alleged act to the appropriate line manager or Director; or the employee may instead approach the appropriate Personnel Manager nominated as a Counsellor in harassment cases.

5.3 Stage 3

The Counsellor's role is to provide support, counselling and assistance to the complainant during a potentially stressful period prior to a formal complaint being made to line management. At this stage the complaint is discussed in confidence between the individual and the Counsellor (subject to the qualification as stated above). The role extends to providing advice to any individual and professional counselling will be available to the alleged harasser if requested. Due to the particular nature of harassment it is often helpful for an individual who has been harassed to talk to a member of a group of similar ethnic origin and sex to him or herself who is familiar with the issues surrounding harassment.

5.4 Stage 4

If the complainant then wishes to make a formal complaint to management, he/she should both see the line manager and put the complaint(s) in writing. Obviously it will have been important to keep documentary evidence such as a diary of dates and events, etc.

The Counsellor will be available to help write down the formal complaint if requested. This procedure allows for the Counsellor to advise the individual at what level the complaint should be heard.

5.5 Stage 5

A timely investigation will be conducted into the complaint in a confidential manner. All parties will be guaranteed a fair and impartial hearing. In any serious or appropriate case either or both of the parties may be suspended without loss of pay pending the completion of the investigation.

Please see above about the right of management to authorise an external third party to conduct any or all of the investigation stages or to assist in or adjudicate on the disciplinary or grievance hearings. The person conducting the investigation will not be the same person as the person adjudicating on the 'guilt' or 'innocence' of the alleged perpetrator.

5.6 Stage 6

The complainant will be interviewed preferably by a person of the same sex and/or race. Confidentiality will be assured. A diary should be kept by the complainant of the details of the allegations and dates when they occurred. A person who has been harassed often finds it very difficult and distressing to talk about the incident(s) to a third party. S/he may be embarrassed, afraid of being disbelieved or not taken seriously, afraid of further damaging the working atmosphere or afraid of bias because the manager is of the same ethnic background or sex as the harasser. Talking and being questioned about the incident therefore often serves to add considerably to the stress already suffered as a result of the harassment itself.

An individual who has reported being harassed should not be questioned in a way which implies s/he has consciously or unconsciously invited the harassment. That is a form of harassment in itself and will add to the individual's experience of stress. Remarks implying that the harassing behaviour must have been meant as a joke, or that the harasser was only being friendly, or asking what clothes the individual was wearing at the time (in the case of sexual harassment) are similarly unacceptable.

As this investigation will be stressful to the complainant, s/he should not be placed in a position of having to repeat the same statement to different managers. A full, written and signed statement should be taken at an early stage. All interviews should be recorded, i.e. verbatim notes taken and dated.

5.7 Stage 7

If the investigation reveals that the complaint is valid, senior management will give it its prompt attention and disciplinary action will be taken to stop the harassment immediately and prevent its recurrence.

If relocation proves necessary, every effort will be made to relocate the harasser and not the complainant unless it is the stated wish of the latter. Where the investigation shows that the complaint is well founded, it is the primary aim of the Company in all cases to prevent recurrence of the harassment.

Any decision will be made on the balance of probabilities but fairness and natural justice will be applied in all cases. It will be taken into account that it is rare for there to be any witnesses and it is often difficult for an alleged perpetrator to deny a negative. Nonetheless it is also recognised that it is often impossible for a complainant to have corroboration for their complaints.

Any and all stages may be recorded so that an accurate verbatim account of all interviews and meetings can be taken.

6. Discussion with alleged harasser

The alleged harasser normally gives one of three possible responses:

6.1 Did not realise that their behaviour was unwelcome

In this case a request to stop, with if necessary an explanation of the Company's policy and that it is up to the harassed individual to say what behaviour s/he regards as unwelcome, should resolve the situation. It must be made clear that if the harasser persists in the unwelcome behaviour, s/he will face disciplinary action. The manager must in no way imply that s/he condones the harasser's behaviour or that the complainant was being over-sensitive.

In this context whether the complainant him/herself acted in a sexually aggressive manner or frequently used sexually explicit language may be relevant in determining whether comparable conduct by others was genuinely unwelcome or whether it damaged the working environment.

However, any past conduct cited by the harasser as being 'welcome' to the complainant must relate to the harasser only. If the harasser cites instances of similar behaviour by him or her being apparently welcomed by other individuals or similar behaviour by other people being apparently acceptable to the complainant, it must be made clear that it is up to each individual what behaviour is acceptable to him or her from various people. What is accepted, for example, as a friendly hug from one person may be perceived as unwelcome physical contact from another.

Furthermore, the occasional off-colour joke by the complainant does not make welcome or excuse more extreme or abusive or persistent comments by others.

If there are any doubts as to the credibility of the complainant or if there is some indication that the conduct was welcome, the complainant's case will be considerably strengthened if s/he made a contemporaneous complaint or protest.

6.2 Did not realise that their behaviour was offensive

Ensuring that every member of staff is aware of the Company policy should prevent this. The situation, if arising, should be dealt with as above with the harasser being helped to understand the point of view of the complainant and his or her right not to be the recipient of behaviour which s/he considers unacceptable and affecting his or her dignity. In both the above instances, conciliation by the manager or another third party, e.g. the Personnel Manager, can help each person to see the other's point of view and help to re-establish normal working relationships.

6.3 Denies the harassment complained of

This is more difficult to deal with as often by the very nature of much harassment, there is no eyewitness. Lack of corroborative evidence should not be fatal to a complaint but it may be decisive where such evidence should logically exist. However, if someone was working very close by at the time of the alleged incident, weight should be given to their evidence as to how the complainant looked and what s/he said at the time or shortly after the alleged incident took place. Therefore, persons with whom the complainant discussed the incident should be interviewed. It may also be advisable to ascertain from other members of staff whether they noticed changes in the complainant's behaviour at work or in the alleged harasser's treatment of him/her.

7. Key points during the investigation and subsequent hearing

7.1 All interviews will be conducted with the Personnel Department's support, although the Personnel Manager or Equal Opportunities Officer concerned will be different from the Counsellor already involved with the case.

7.2 The complainant may be accompanied by a union representative, any employee of their choice or by the Counsellor, to help them put their case.

7.3 Verbatim notes will be taken at all interviews and these will always be agreed by the interviewee. An assurance that the interview and the contents of the interview will be kept strictly confidential and will not be discussed with any other person must be obtained at the start of the interview.

7.4 Particular care and consideration will be taken when interviewing the complainant in order to minimise stress.

7.5 All individuals will be interviewed separately and it is normally appropriate for any witnesses to be interviewed before the alleged harasser to prevent the possibility of influencing the witnesses' views. A confidentiality agreement will be signed by each interviewee who will agree not to disclose anything asked or mentioned in the interview.

7.6 All witness statements will be shown to the alleged harasser before any disciplinary hearing takes place. The complainant will be asked to sign a statement of his/her complaint(s).

7.7 If the complaint is well founded then management will decide what penalty will be applied. One serious incident can constitute gross misconduct for which an employee can be summarily dismissed.

7.8 Should the investigation, in the opinion of the Company, produce a *prima facie* case of minor, serious or gross misconduct, then a formal disciplinary hearing, with safeguards for both the alleged harasser and the complainant will take place. An appeal from the decision of this hearing shall be taken through the normal disciplinary appeals procedure.

7.9 Moving and demoting the harasser may be another option once the complaint has been heard in a formal disciplinary hearing. In any case where a complaint has been found to be substantiated (on the basis of the balance of probabilities) and the harasser is moved, after a period of time has elapsed, the immediate manager should speak informally to the staff working with this individual in the new location. They will be reminded of the sexual harassment policy but no specific reference will be made to the harasser's case or punishment.

7.10 All members of staff shall also be protected from intimidation, victimisation or discrimination for filing a complaint or assisting in an investigation. Retaliating against an employee for complaining about harassment is a disciplinary offence.

7.11 In some cases it might be appropriate to call in an outside expert at any stage of this procedure. If it is decided to ask the outside expert to make any decision, then both parties will be notified and the decision will be final and binding. No further internal appeals will be allowed concerning this expert's decision.

[7.12 Whilst this special complaints procedure is progressing, it is agreed that there will be no lockout, strike, collective restrictions on output, banning of overtime, go-slow or other interference with working procedures or refusal to accept legitimate instructions. This clause applies both to individuals and to groups of workers. The Company and the union will oppose any unofficial industrial action and agree that any industrial action is contrary to the spirit of this procedure.]

7.13 The Company, where recommended by expert medical practitioners, may require the harasser and/or the complainant to undergo psychological counselling or other forms of medical treatment as deemed appropriate. Failure to agree or to complete the course or to accept any recommendations from the practitioner(s) may result in a decision to dismiss being taken.

7.14 The complainant will be offered counselling after a period of time has elapsed to ensure that no further problems have arisen and they will be offered medical help including cognitive behavioural therapy (CBT) if appropriate, organised, if he/she so wishes, through the Company or outside the Company.

7.15 Management must be aware that in rare cases untrue complaints are made of harassment for a variety of reasons. Careful consideration of all the evidence and the previous history of both parties will need to be given.

7.16 Both parties will always be informed of any outcomes and decisions as to action in the future and the complainant will always be told whether or not any punishment has been given and the nature of this penalty in the strictest confidence. Regard will be had to any previous lapsed warnings for the same or a similar offence in order to assess the credibility of the alleged harasser and in order to assess an appropriate penalty.

7.17 Where a complaint is not upheld because the evidence is regarded as inconclusive, consideration should be given to transferring or rescheduling the work of one of the employees concerned rather than requiring them to continue to work together if this is against the wishes of either party.

7.18 If the complainant and/or his or her evidence is discredited, then consideration must be given to disciplinary action in respect of the complaint made and/or counselling and medical help.

PRECEDENT 11G: Whistleblowing policy

1. Introduction

1.1 The Company's gross budget for the 2016/2017 year is approximately £28m per annum. The Company aims to ensure that this is spent properly on providing Company services for the local community.

1.2 The Company is committed to the highest possible standards of openness, probity and accountability. In line with that commitment it expects staff and others that it deals with who have serious concerns about any aspect of the Company's work to come forward and voice those concerns.

1.3 This Policy explains how you can confidentially report, without fear of recrimination, cases where suspected fraud, corruption or instances of malpractice affect the Company.

1.4 The adoption of this Confidential Reporting Policy by the Company is intended to encourage and enable any individual including staff to raise any serious concerns they have about the Company, rather than overlooking a problem or 'blowing the whistle' outside. The Policy makes it clear that you can raise concerns on a confidential basis, without fear of victimisation, subsequent discrimination or disadvantage. It is based on the Public Interest Disclosure Act 1998, which gave staff raising concerns under its rules legal protection against reprisals.

1.5 The Policy applies to all employees and those contractors engaged by the Company on [*give details*] work. It also covers suppliers and those providing services under a contract with the Company in their own premises, for example temporary accommodation for the homeless. Partners and subsidiaries are also expected to meet the expectations set out in the Policy.

2. **Aims and scope of this Policy**

2.1 This Policy aims to:

- encourage you to feel confident about raising serious concerns that are in the public interest;
- encourage you to question practice and act upon any concerns;
- provide clear channels for you to raise those concerns;
- ensure that you receive a response to concerns you raise and that you are clear about how to pursue them if you are not satisfied;
- reassure you that you will be protected from possible reprisals or victimisation if you raise a concern in good faith reasonably believing something is wrong.

3. **Safeguards**

Harassment or Victimisation

3.1 The Company is committed to good practice and high standards and wants to be supportive of staff.

3.2 The Company recognises that making the decision to report a concern can be difficult. If what you are saying is true, you should have nothing to fear because you will be doing your duty to the Company and those for whom you are providing a service.

3.3 The Company will not tolerate any harassment or victimisation (including informal pressures) of someone raising something of concern to them and will take appropriate action to protect you against this when you raise a concern in good faith.

3.4 Any investigation into allegations of potential malpractice will not influence or be influenced by any disciplinary or redundancy procedures that already affect you.

4. **Confidentiality**

4.1 All concerns raised will be treated in confidence and every effort will be made not to reveal your identity if you so wish. At the appropriate time, however, you may need to come forward as a witness.

5. **Anonymous allegations**

5.1 This Policy encourages you to put your name to your allegation whenever possible.

5.2 Concerns expressed anonymously are much less powerful but will be considered at the discretion of the Company.

5.3 In deciding whether to consider anonymous concerns the following are some of the factors which will be taken into account:

- the seriousness of the issues raised;
- the credibility of the concern; and
- the likelihood of confirming the allegation from attributable sources.

6. Untrue allegations

6.1 If you make an allegation in good faith, but it is not confirmed by the investigation, no action will be taken against you. If, however, you make an allegation frivolously, maliciously or for personal gain, disciplinary action may be taken against you in accordance with the Company's disciplinary procedures.

7. How to raise a concern

7.1 As a first step, you should normally raise concerns with your immediate Manager or their Manager. This depends, however, on the seriousness and sensitivity of the issues involved and who is suspected of the malpractice. For example, if you believe that your management is involved, you should approach the Chief Executive, HR Director, the Compliance Officer or the Chief Finance Office (CFO).

7.2 Concerns may be raised orally or in writing. If you wish to make a written report it is best to use the following format:

- the background and history of your concern (giving relevant dates);
- the reason why you are particularly concerned about the situation.

7.3 You are advised to report your concerns to one of the following Senior Officers:

- Chief Executive;
- HR Director;
- Compliance Officer;
- CFO.

7.4 It is important that you:

- make an immediate note of your concerns;
- note all relevant details, such as what has occurred, the date, time and name of any parties involved;
- report your suspicions promptly; any delay may cause the Company to suffer further financial loss.

7.5 Do not:

- ignore the matter;
- be afraid of raising your concerns; you will not suffer any recrimination;
- approach or accuse individuals directly;
- try to investigate the matter yourself;
- convey your suspicions to anyone other than those with the proper authority;
- illegally record a conversation.

8. How the company will deal with the concern

8.1 The Company will always respond to your concerns. Do not forget that testing out your concerns is not the same as either accepting or rejecting them.

8.2 If you raise a concern with your Manager which they feel is beyond the scope of their authority or of a serious nature they will refer it to one of the Officers listed in paragraph 7.3 above rather than dealing with it personally.

8.3　Where appropriate, the matters you raise may:

- be investigated by Managers, internal audit or through the disciplinary process;
- be referred to the police;
- be referred to the external auditor;
- form the subject of an independent inquiry.

8.4　In order to protect individuals and those accused of misdeeds or possible malpractice, initial enquiries will be made to decide whether an investigation is appropriate and, if so, what form it should take. The overriding principle for the Company is the protection of public interest. Concerns or allegations which fall within the scope of specific procedures (for example grievance or sexual harassment) will normally be referred for consideration under those procedures.

8.5　Some concerns may be resolved by agreed action without the need for investigation. If urgent action is required this will be taken before any investigation is conducted.

8.6　As soon as possible after a concern has been received, the Manager with whom you raise your concern will refer it to one of the senior staff members listed in paragraph 7.3 above and within 10 working days this Officer will write to you in confidence:

- acknowledging that your concern has been received;
- indicating how the Company proposes to deal with the matter;
- giving an estimate of how long it will take to provide a final response;
- telling you whether any initial enquiries have been made;
- supplying you with information on staff support mechanisms; and
- telling you whether further investigations will take place and if not, why not.

8.7　The amount of contact between the Managers/Directors considering the issues and you will depend on the nature of the matters raised, the potential difficulties involved and the clarity of the information provided. If necessary, the Company will seek further information from you.

8.8　Where any meeting is arranged, which can be away from the offices or your place of work if you so wish, you can be accompanied by a union or professional association representative or a friend.

8.9　The Company will take steps to minimise any difficulties which you may experience as a result of raising a concern. For instance, if you are required to give evidence in criminal or disciplinary proceedings the Company will arrange for you to receive independent legal advice about the procedure.

8.10　The Company accepts that you need to be assured that the matter has been properly addressed and so subject to legal constraints, will inform you of the outcome of any investigation.

9. The responsible Manager/Director

9.1　The Managers/Directors listed in paragraph 7.3 above are responsible for the operation of this Policy and for maintaining a record of concerns raised and the outcomes (but in a form which does not endanger confidentiality) and will report as necessary to the Company.

Confidential Reporting (Whistleblowing)

[*insert name*]

Email: whistleblowing@company.co.uk

Compliance Officer

Email: legalservices@company.co.uk

Chief Finance Officer

Email: internalaudit@company.co.uk

External

Public Concern At Work

This is a charity whose mission is to ensure that concerns about malpractice are properly raised and addressed in the workplace. Free advice and legal help is provided to those concerned about abuse, public danger, fraud and other serious crime in the workplace.

CAN Mezzanine
7–14 Great Dover Street
London
SE1 4YR

020 7404 6609

Fax: 020 7403 8823

Email: whistle@pcaw.co.uk

Website: **www.pcaw.co.uk**

12

Notice and notice clauses

12.1 Notice term: statutory and contractual

Under the Employment Rights Act (ERA) 1996, s.86 employees are entitled to minimum periods of notice. Within the first month of employment no notice is due under statute; one week's notice becomes due after one month's employment and up to two years' continuous service. Thereafter an additional week's notice becomes due for each complete year of service up to a maximum of 12 weeks' notice for 12 years' continuous service or more (s.86(1)(a)–(c)).

Employees with one month's service or more are required to give not less than one week's notice (s.86(2)).

No employer can agree in the contract to give less than statutory notice but an employer may provide for greater notice on either side (s.86(3)).

Any employee with at least three months' continuous service who is then given a fixed-term contract of one month or less is deemed to be entitled to minimum statutory notice (s.86(4)).

In cases of alleged gross misconduct or an alleged fundamental breach by the employee, the employer is entitled to dismiss. The employee would be entitled to resign without notice if they are able to argue fundamental breach of contract by the employer (normally a breach of the implied term of mutual trust and confidence) – (s.86(6)).

12.2 When notice is deemed to be given

Unless otherwise agreed, notice may be oral. When notice is given orally, the period of notice commences on the day upon which notice is given (*West* v. *Kneels Ltd* [1986] IRLR 430, EAT).

In cases where no notice is given and the employer notifies the employee of their summary dismissal the effective date of termination is not the date when the letter is deemed to have been delivered at the employee's house. It is the date that the employee reasonably could have read the letter of dismissal.

In *Gisda Cyf* v. *Barratt* [2010] UKSC 41, the Supreme Court held that (1) the effective date of termination (EDT) of employment for the purposes of unfair dismissals, where termination is immediate (i.e. without notice), is the date when an employee learns of their dismissal or when they have had a reasonable opportunity of reading that they have been dismissed; and (2) their behaviour may properly be considered when assessing whether they have had a 'reasonable opportunity' to discover they have been dismissed.

This was because:

> An essential part of the protection of employees is the requirement that they be informed of any possible breach of their rights. For that reason we emphatically agree with the EAT's view in *McMaster* that the doctrine of constructive knowledge has no place in the debate as to whether a dismissal has been communicated.
>
> For the short time of three months to begin to run against an employee, he or she must be informed of the event that triggers the start of that period, namely, their dismissal or, at least, he or she must have the chance to find out that that short period has begun. Again, this case exemplifies the need for this.
>
> During the three months after Ms Barratt's dismissal, she pursued an internal appeal; she learned that she was unsuccessful in that appeal; she sought advice in relation to the lodging of a complaint of unfair dismissal; and she presumably required some time to absorb and act upon that advice.
>
> Viewed in the abstract, three months might appear to be a substantial period. In reality, however, when momentous decisions have to be taken, it is not an unduly generous time.

This case has recently been followed by the majority in the Court of Appeal which has held that where the contract says nothing about when notice of termination is deemed to be given, it takes effect when the letter is actually received, not when it is deemed to have been received – *Newcastle Upon Tyne NHS Foundation Trust* v. *Haywood* [2017] EWCA Civ 153.

The employer sent three letters of notice of dismissal.

One letter was sent by recorded delivery to the claimant's home address and, as Ms Haywood was not at home, a delivery slip was left at her house.

Her father-in-law collected the recorded delivery letter from the Post Office on 26 April and left it at her home on the same day. The claimant returned home from her holiday on 27 April and confirmed that she read this letter at about 8.30 am on 27 April.

Another letter was sent by ordinary post but no specific findings were made as to when this letter was received.

The other letter was sent by email to Ms Haywood's husband's email account. Mr Haywood read the email on 27 April.

In the absence of an express term in the employment contract, if notice of termination is sent by post, the majority of the Court of Appeal held that it must be received, i.e. read by the employee, in order to be effective and it cannot be deemed to take effect on a particular date, e.g. the day after posting.

The Court did state that posting a letter giving notice of termination cannot be sufficient by itself, although posting a correctly addressed and properly stamped letter gives rise to a rebuttable presumption of receipt. The employee has the burden of proof of showing that they did not receive it, e.g. they were on holiday until a date after the receipt of that letter.

It is sensible and good practice to require either party to put notice to terminate employment in writing and to make clear what is the effective date of termination. In some cases this may mean telephoning the employee and reading the dismissal letter over the telephone and confirming the conversation in an email to the dismissed employee. It may also be appropriate to record the call (informing the employee that this is being done).

The reason this date may be critical is for the purposes of calculating two years' continuous service (ERA 1996, s.108), for ensuring that the complaint (of unfair dismissal) to the Employment Tribunal is presented within three months of the effective date of termination (s.111(2)(a)).

12.3 Withdrawing notice or not accepting notice

Once given, notice may not be withdrawn unilaterally, but may only be done by mutual consent. No party has the right to refuse to accept notice when given.

The one exception to the rule that once notice has been given it cannot be unilaterally withdrawn is where the employer has given notice of dismissal and the appeal against dismissal is successful and the employee is reinstated. In such a case the notice of dismissal is automatically revoked.

In *Roberts* v. *West Coast Trains Ltd* [2004] IRLR 788 the Court of Appeal held that:

> The effect of the decision on the internal appeal was to resurrect the Claimant's contract of employment and that was something that he had agreed to in his contract of employment. The fact was that the internal appeal had a retrospective effect so as to treat R as if he had never been dismissed. The fact that the Claimant had made a complaint to an employment tribunal before a decision was reached in the internal appeal did not affect the decision. It would have been of relevance if he had not made an internal appeal or had withdrawn his internal appeal. Once the decision to reinstate Mr Roberts had been taken there ceased to be any dismissal of which he could complain.

In Mr Roberts' case the disciplinary and appeals procedures formed part of his contract. The appeals procedure allowed the employer to revoke the original decision to dismiss and to substitute another lesser penalty. This is what this employer did.

However, some employers purport not to accept an immediate resignation or resignation giving shorter notice than is legally required. If the resignation occurs in advance of a disciplinary hearing, then the employer should consider carefully why it might want to carry on with the disciplinary hearing, continuing to extend to the ex-employee the right to attend the hearing with their representative.

This is common practice in the City where an employee may choose to resign without notice shortly before a gross misconduct hearing.

See **Precedent 12A** for examples of letters that are commonly written and a letter about no pay for no notice or short notice having been given by the employee.

12.4 When does notice expire?

If notice rather than pay in lieu is given, then the contract terminates when the notice expires, not when it is given (ERA 1996, s.97(1)(a)). That is true even if employees are told they need not 'work out' the period of notice but may go home and not return to the office ('garden leave').

However, if a payment in lieu of notice is made, the employment will terminate on the date that the employer identifies as the effective date of termination and the P45 will reflect this.

12.5 Short notice agreed or not agreed

It is open to the parties to waive notice, or to agree to short notice. If either the employer gives notice or the employee resigns by giving notice and the employee asks to shorten the notice period (normally to start a new job) then it is very important to clarify whether the employer is merely waiving its right for the employee to serve out their notice or whether the employer is demanding an equivalent waiver – for the remainder of the notice pay in lieu of the notice not worked, to be waived by the employee.

Short notice not agreed

If short notice is not agreed, in some cases employers may be able to enforce the notice period and in effect restrain the individual from going to work for a rival (*Evening Standard Co. Ltd* v. *Henderson* [1987] IRLR 64).

In this case the *Evening Standard* was very keen to prevent its 17-year-service production manager going to work for Robert Maxwell's new rival London evening newspaper, *London Daily News*. The *Evening Standard* had agreed to pay Mr Henderson for the year he would be prevented from working for the rival newspaper.

The *Evening Standard* sought a 10-month injunction, which was granted:

> the injunction must not force the defendant to work for the Plaintiffs and it must not reduce him, certainly, to a condition of starvation or to a condition of idleness, whatever that may mean on the authorities on this topic. But all that, in my judgement, is overcome by the fact that the Plaintiffs have made the offer they have. The Defendant can go back to work for them. If he elects not to go back (and it will be a matter entirely for his election: there will be nothing in the judgment which forces an election on him) he can receive his salary and full contractual benefits under his contract until such time as his notice would have expired had it been for the proper period.

Another course of action where no notice or no proper notice is given is not to pay the departing employee further pay and to argue correctly that the employee is still employed and therefore not able to go to work for another employer. This has to be done by way of obtaining an injunction preventing the employee from working for any other employer and a declaration concerning their contract.

In *Sunrise Brokers LLP* v. *Michael William Rodgers* [2014] EWHC 2633 (QB) an employee left work without giving notice, notwithstanding that his contract obliged him to give 12 months' notice. He argued that his post-termination restrictive covenants fell away and that his employer had accepted his repudiatory breach by ceasing to pay his salary. The High Court held that the employer's decision to cease paying the employee did not amount to an acceptance of his repudiatory breach.

The High Court ruled:

> Work and wages were mutual obligations that employer and employee both had to be ready and willing to perform. The fact that the non-performance of one obligation excused performance of the other did not mean that the contract of which those obligations formed part automatically ceased to exist if either was not performed.
>
> Nor was R entitled to payment of his salary irrespective of work. It followed that the Defendant remained employed by the Claimant and would so remain until October 16, 2014 (paras.58–62). [...] It was appropriate to impose an injunction requiring R to obey the terms of his contract until October 16, 2014 so that he was prevented from working for E or any other of S's competitors, and from contacting his former clients. If R chose to return to work during that notice period, S would have to pay him.

Another way of tackling this issue is to have a well-drafted clause in the contract allowing for the employer not to pay the employee for all of the notice period not worked.

In *Yizhen Li* v. *First Marine Solutions Ltd* UKEATS/0045/13/BI the President of the EAT, Mr Justice Langstaff, said that employers should be careful to ensure that such terms 'better represent the realities of the workplace' to avoid them being interpreted as penalties in future.

A penalty clause is one which is regarded as not being a genuine pre-estimate of loss; rather it is a penalty for the breach referred to in the clause.

In the *Li* case above, both parties accepted the original Employment Tribunal's interpretation of the clause as allowing the employer to deduct payments from an employee who did not work their notice.

The clause stated: 'If an employee leaves, without working the appropriate notice, the company will deduct a sum equal in value to the salary payable for the shortfall in the period of notice.'

Mr Justice Langstaff said the clause was not a penalty clause in this case but that this would not necessarily be true in every such case.

> If a tribunal has a contract such as this to construe in future, it should ask itself whether the parties, in enacting a clause such as this, really intended that, if an employee left not having worked the full amount of notice – irrespective of whether the notice was given by the company or the employee – there should be paid by the employee to the employer a sum equal to the amount of time which was not spent working during that notice period, but should have been.
>
> I recommend to tribunals who consider such a clause in future that they may wish to think carefully, in the light of the evidence before them in the particular case, whether the parties actually intended a clause such as this to operate as a penalty clause, liquidated damages clause, or simply as a provision that entitled the employer to withhold pay for the period of time not worked during notice. All will, of course,

depend upon the particular conclusions and the particular facts, contracts of employment being individual,' he said.

The clause only permitted the employer to deduct payments from wages due, not to receive or demand a payment, the judge said. Similarly, it did not oblige the employee to make that payment. This meant that the employer would have had no recourse if the employee 'simply upped sticks and left' at the end of a salary period without working notice, or if the employee was dismissed by the employer for a proper reason.

A penalty clause will not be enforceable. A repayment clause must be reasonable and account for what the parties anticipate the losses may be when the contract is terminated, i.e. looked at when the parties enter into the agreement (and not at the time of the actual losses).

> This contract, on the face of the contract itself, was for a very different type of employee. This was not just an engineer but a project engineer. She was engaged at a high salary compared to that which would apply to a driver.
>
> Engineers are not as common as are drivers, and to obtain one at short notice is always likely to be of particular difficulty. Significant expense might be incurred. When the contract as a whole is examined in the context within which it was made, to which reference must be had to decide what the parties intended at the time that they made the contract, it is plain that the fact that she was headhunted meant that the employer placed a particular value upon her services... There is nothing, on the face of it, which means that a sum of a month's salary is necessarily excessive.

12.6   Payment in lieu of notice clauses

Employers may choose to include in the contract of employment an express right to make a payment in lieu of notice (PILON) as an alternative to giving notice. This may be a right to make a payment of basic salary only. If the employer exercises this option the dismissal takes immediate effect. However, in order to determine continuous service for the purposes of unfair dismissal, the employee is permitted to add the notional one week's statutory notice (ERA 1996, s.97(2)(b)). In such circumstances there is no breach of contract when the employer elects to pay in lieu of the employee working out the notice period.

The advantages of PILON clauses are:

(a) that the employer is not in breach of contract if it elects to dismiss with immediate effect and pay in lieu;
(b) without such a clause there may be some doubt as to whether the employer would be entitled to enforce any of the post-termination clauses (see *General Billposting Ltd* v. *Atkinson* [1909] AC 118 and a modification to that rule in *Rock Refrigeration* v. *Jones* [1996] IRLR 675).

See **Precedent 12F**.

12.7   Where there is no PILON clause

Nothing prevents an employee from agreeing to accept a payment in lieu of notice despite the absence of any such right in the contact (ERA 1996, s.86(3)).

Even if the employer has no PILON clause and breaches the contract by dismissing summarily in circumstances that do not permit such dismissal without notice, the employee will not be able to claim the loss of opportunity to claim unfair dismissal had the proper notice been given. In the case of *Harper* v. *Virgin Net Ltd* [2004] IRLR 390 (CA), Ms Harper had a three-month notice period and no PILON clause in her contract. The Court of Appeal ruled that she could not claim damages in such circumstances for losing her opportunity of claiming unfair dismissal, even though had she been given proper notice of three months, she would then have had one year's continuous service and would have been able to present a claim for unfair dismissal.

12.8 No notice provision: common law/reasonable notice

It is remarkable that even today there are still cases where the employer has failed to provide any written terms so there is no term about notice.

In such a case, i.e. where there is no evidence that the parties have orally agreed a notice clause, the employee is entitled to common law notice, i.e. 'reasonable notice'.

Depending upon factors such as the status and length of service of the individual, the parties' expectations, the nature of the employment, frequency of pay intervals and what others of a similar grade and length of service have been offered, reasonable notice can range from one month to one year or in rare cases even longer.

12.9 Duty to mitigate

Particularly where long notice periods are offered, employers are entitled to argue that the employee's duty to mitigate may reduce the amount of pay in lieu of notice as such payment is regarded as damages and not a contractual debt for which no mitigation is required (*Cerberus Software Co Ltd* v. *Rowley* [2001] IRLR 160).

In the context of a notice clause of one year, the following wording (drafted by a well-known City firm) purports to reserve the right to the company to reduce any lump sum payment in lieu of notice in respect of the duty to mitigate and accelerated receipt. This author wishes to point out that there is some doubt as to the enforceability of such a clause as it could be argued it is void for uncertainty, or as a penalty clause not being a genuine pre-estimate of loss, or as in effect a 'back door' restrictive covenant:

> Notwithstanding any other provision, the Company may, at its sole discretion, by written notice elect to give you a payment of salary for any unexpired notice in connection with your employment, less any sum as it considers at its sole discretion appropriate (having regard to your obligation to mitigate your loss and subject to receipt of a lump sum payment) and such other deductions as are required by law. For the avoidance of doubt this clause will not prevent the Company from terminating your employment in breach of its terms.

12.10 Notice during absence

If notice is given during an employee's absence, e.g. sickness absence, there are idiosyncratic rules about the requirement to give payment during such notice. The Employment Rights Act 1996, s.88 provides that during periods of absence due to sickness, pregnancy or maternity, holidays or where there is no work but the employee is ready and willing to work, if the employer gives notice of termination, then the employee is entitled to be paid during that notice period.

However, under s.87(4) the protection in ERA 1996, ss.88–91 does not apply where the contractual notice is at least one week more than the statutory minimum. In *Scotts Co. (UK) Ltd* v. *Budd* [2003] IRLR 145, the EAT ruled that no payment was due during notice when Mr Budd was off sick with stress and migraines and was given notice of dismissal, because under s.88(1)(b) his contract provided for 13 weeks' notice, i.e. one week more than statutory notice.

12.11 Notice during probationary periods

It is common to see notice clauses of considerably shorter length during probationary periods (notice cannot be shorter than that provided by statute but can be longer: ERA 1996, s.86(3)). See **Precedent 12C**.

12.12 Garden leave

'Garden leave' clauses can operate during employment or during any notice term and allow the employer lawfully to require the employee to remain away from work, away from the premises and away from clients. Without an express garden leave clause, however, it has been held that in some cases it may be a breach of contract to force an employee to remain away from work on garden leave (*William Hill* v. *Tucker* [1998] IRLR 113).

Whether there is a right to work as opposed merely to the right to be paid wages will depend upon the nature of the post and the status of the post-holder; whether the post-holder exercises unique skills which are required to do that job and required to be exercised; how the remuneration is earned and how the contract defines duties, i.e. whether the contract requires the employee to work those hours necessary to carry out their duties in a full and professional manner and whether it would be inconsistent with that provision for the employee to be entitled or bound to draw remuneration without doing any available work. In Mr Tucker's case, the Court of Appeal held that without an express garden leave clause, his employers should be injuncted to restrain their unlawful suspension of Mr Tucker for the six months of his notice period.

Some employers have a policy and a term in the contract that any untaken and accrued holiday must be taken during any period of notice or garden leave. It is essential to spell out this obligation and to inform the individual in such a case how much accrued and untaken holiday they have owing to them. See **Precedent 12D**.

12.13 References

There is no legal obligation to give a reference, save under the FCA Regulations. However, where an employer gives a reference it must be true, accurate and fair; in other words the employer must 'make full and frank disclosure of all relevant matters which are believed to be true' (*Spring v. Guardian Assurance* [1994] IRLR 460, HL). In *Spring* the Court of Appeal suggested that there may be a 'social or moral duty' to give a reference (*Spring v. Guardian Assurance plc* [1993] 2 All ER 273). It stated that (p.295):

> Other employers not under the equivalent FCA Regulations are not under a legal duty to give a reference, though they are commonly thought to be under a moral or social duty to do so if a reference is requested by either the employee or the prospective employer. If, however, a former employer declines to give a reference, this may almost be as damaging to the employee as an unsatisfactory reference.

Under new FCA Regulations CP15/3 and PRA CP14/14 that came into force on 7 March 2017, applying at the moment only to banks and insurance companies but being extended to other employers in the future, the giving of references has been considerably strengthened.

It will be essential to check that a reference has really come from a legitimate source as on occasion they have been forged by another employee or ex-employee who has stolen company headed notepaper in order to do so.

A model letter, for use if this has been found to be the case, can be found in **Chapter 8**.

Bad leavers and penalties

It is common to see clauses in contracts and incentive schemes and share option schemes that penalise someone regarded as a 'bad leaver', i.e. someone who resigns or is dismissed for cause other than redundancy.

Two recent cases determined whether such clauses were penalty clauses and for different reasons both cases upheld the clauses and ruled that neither were penalty clauses.

David Collins of Dentons has written an excellent article on bad leavers and penalties – www.dentons.com/en/insights/newsletters/2016/october/20/uk-corporate-briefing/uk-corporate-briefing-autumn-2016/bad-leaver-clauses-and-the-new-rule-against-contractual-penalties.

The two cases on this point are *Richards v. IP Solutions Group Ltd* [2016] EWHC 1835 (QB) and *Re Braid Group (Holdings) Ltd* [2016] CSIH 68.

In *Richards* the High Court ruled that the leaver provisions in the Articles of Association regarding shares in the company, including the bad leaver clause, were not a penalty clause – it was rather a 'primary obligation' when being allocated the shares. The clauses in the Articles of Association included the following definitions:

'**Bad Leaver**' means:

(a) a person who ceases to be an Employee:

(i) where the person terminated his contract of employment with his employing company other than in circumstances constituting him a Good Leaver;
(ii) in circumstances where he is dismissed, or his employing company was entitled to dismiss him, for a reason justifying summary dismissal (other than where such circumstances would otherwise constitute a Good Leaver event); or
(iii) ceases to be an Employee for whatever reason and who, whether before or after he ceases to be an Employee, was or is in breach of clause 9.1 of the Investment Agreement (undertakings by the Managers); or

(b) a person who remains as an Employee but becomes entitled by reasons of illness or disablement giving rise to permanent incapacity to receive benefits under the permanent health insurance scheme of the Company or any other Group Company, and who was or is whilst an Employee in breach of clause 9.1 of the Investment Agreement (Undertakings by the Managers).

'Good Leaver' means:

(a) a person (other than a Bad Leaver) who ceases to be an Employee where such cessation occurs for one of the following reasons:
(i) that person's death; or
(ii) illness or disablement of that person giving rise to permanent incapacity to continue in employment; or
(iii) the termination of that person's employment by his employing company:
(A) in circumstances that are determined by an Employment Tribunal or Court to be or amount to wrongful dismissal (and for the avoidance of doubt, this shall exclude any finding of unfair dismissal); or
(B) for reasons of redundancy; or
(iv) that person terminating his contract of employment with his employing company in circumstances where he has reached the age of 65 and is retiring; or

(b) a person who ceases to be an Employee where the Board with Investor Consent resolves that such person is to be treated as a Good Leaver in the circumstances where such person would not, but for this provision, be a Good Leaver; or

(c) an Employee (other than a Bad Leaver) who remains an employee but becomes entitled by reason of illness or disablement giving rise to permanent incapacity to receive benefits under the permanent health insurance scheme of the Company or any other Group Company;

together with, in each case, any other person who becomes a Leaver as a consequence thereof.

'Leaver' means:

(a) any Employee who is a shareholder who ceases to be an Employee for whatever reason;
(b) any person who becomes entitled to any shares:
(i) on the death of a Shareholder (if an individual);
(ii) on the receivership, administrative receivership, administration, liquidation or other arrangement for the winding up (whether solvent or insolvent) of a shareholder (if a company); or
(iii) on the exercise of an option after ceasing to be an Employee;

(c) any Shareholder holding Shares as a nominee for any person who ceases to be an Employee;
(d) any Employee who remains an Employee but becomes entitled by reason of illness or disablement giving rise to permanent incapacity to receive benefits under the permanent health insurance scheme of the Company or any other Group Company;

These terms were agreed between the parties as a shareholder leaving the company, rather than obligations that would arise on breach of the employment contract.

Mrs Justice May held that:

> ..... the price of £1 payable for the aggregate shareholding of a person who is a 'Bad Leaver' is simply the agreed price on transfer. Moreover, even if the transfer and pricing provisions in the Articles were to be construed as secondary obligations consequent upon breach of the employment contract, I would have found, as Lord Hodge did in the *Makdessi* case, that there was nothing unconscionable in an arrangement arrived at between parties dealing at arms-length with the benefit of extensive expert advice. Had it been necessary, therefore, I would have found that the Transfer provisions relating to a 'Bad Leaver' were enforceable.

In *Braid*, in contrast, the Court agreed that the transfer provisions in the bad leaver clause were secondary obligations. Mr Gray had been found to have committed gross misconduct. The bad leaver provisions deprived him of his shares in such circumstances.

The Court held that these bad leaver provisions reflected a primary obligation to comply with a service contract and provided a mechanism for dealing with the effects of a breach of that primary obligation, i.e. to honour the terms of the contract and not commit gross misconduct.

Even if the bad leaver provisions were secondary obligations, the majority (two out of three Judges) held that they were not a penalty clause and thus unenforceable.

The two Judges ruled that it was fair that a shareholder who was found guilty of gross misconduct (he had accepted bribes) should have to give up his shareholding and only get back his original financial stake.

PRECEDENT 12A: Letter refusing to accept short notice

Letter 1

[*Name of employee*]
[*Address*]
[*Date*]

Dear [*name*]

RE: Your immediate resignation

We note that the day after receiving notification of the date of your disciplinary hearing you tendered your resignation with immediate effect.

You are in breach of contract as there are no circumstances that we believe entitle you to do this. It is our policy (and our duty under [*specify*]) to continue with this investigation and to conclude the hearing and make a determination. Of course it could be that you are found innocent of all charges. In such a case we would of course reconsider the payment in lieu of notice to you and the giving of a good reference.

We therefore continue to open our invitation to you to attend the hearing with your nominated representative on [date].

Please let us know if you will be attending and with whom.

Yours sincerely

Human Resources Director

Letter 2

[Name of employee]
[Address]
[Date]

Dear [name]

RE: Disciplinary outcome

Following the disciplinary hearing that was held in your absence, this is what we have concluded. Had you not resigned, we would have dismissed you for gross misconduct on the following grounds:

1. [Allegation 1]
2. [Allegation 2]
3. [Allegation 3]

For the reasons given above we regard your conduct as gross misconduct and any future reference given will reflect the above.

Yours sincerely

Human Resources Director

Letter 3: No pay for no or short notice

[Name of employee]
[Address]
[Date]

Dear [name]

RE: Your immediate resignation

We note that the day after receiving notification of the date of your disciplinary hearing you tendered your resignation with immediate effect.

You are in breach of contract as there are no circumstances that we believe entitle you to do this. Your contract provides in Clause X that you will agree not to be paid during any period for which you have not given proper notice.

As you were required to give us one month's notice, we will not be paying you for the month of [month].

We are sorry that you have chosen to conduct yourself in this way.

Any reference will record that you left us in breach of contract.

Yours sincerely

HR Director

PRECEDENT 12B: Letter accepting short notice

[*Name of employee*]
[*Address*]
[*Date*]

Dear [*name*]

RE: Agreement to waive your notice

You asked me to consider whether the Company would be prepared to release you from your four weeks' notice at the end of this week, thus your employment would terminate three weeks earlier than it was due to do.

You explained that you were keen to start your new job as soon as possible.

We are prepared to allow your employment to end this Friday in consideration for which you agree to release the Company from any further obligations to pay in respect of the notice not worked by you.

If you are happy with this arrangement, please sign a copy of this letter and return it to me before the close of business on [*date*].

Yours sincerely

Human Resources Director

I, [*name*], thank the Company for agreeing to release me on [*date*] from the remainder of my notice period. In consideration for this, I agree to release the Company from any continuing obligation to pay me any further monies save for any accrued holiday pay at my new effective date of termination.

Signed .... Date ....

[*employee*]

PRECEDENT 12C: Clause relating to notice during probation

During your probationary period the Company reserves the right (other than in case of gross misconduct where no notice or pay in lieu of notice is due) to terminate your employment by the giving of one week's written notice or payment in lieu without reference to any of the stages of the disciplinary procedure. You will be required to give the Company one week's notice if you choose to resign during this period.

PRECEDENT 12D: Garden leave

1. If the Company wishes to terminate your employment or if you wish to leave the employment of the Company, in either case before the expiry of the period of notice in [*specify*] and whether or not notice has been given under that provision, the Company may require you to perform duties not within your normal duties or special projects.

2. Alternatively it may, whilst continuing to provide you with your contractual benefits (except for any bonus, profit share or other benefit due or accruing under any incentive scheme), require you not to attend for work for the period of notice given under [specify] or (if notice has not been given) for a period equivalent to the notice period required to be given by you to terminate your employment.

3. During that time you will continue to be bound by all the terms of your employment including but not limited to your duty of confidentiality. You will not directly or indirectly work for any person, enter any of the Company's premises, have any contact with any customer, supplier or employee of the Group or purport to act or represent yourself as acting in your capacity as Director or employee for any purpose without the prior written consent of the Board.

4. If you are not to attend for work under this provision, the Company will be entitled to require you to take any outstanding accrued holiday due to you and in such a case unless there is more outstanding holiday leave than days during which you have served garden leave, you will not be entitled to any payment for holidays 'untaken'.

OR

In this event the Company may require you to remain at home during all or part of any such period (the 'garden leave period') performing such duties (if any) as it may reasonably specify. During the garden leave period you:

(a) shall not be entitled without prior permission from the Group Personnel Director to gain access to any premises of the Company or any subsidiary or associated company;
(b) will be requested to refrain from contact with any of the Company's clients or suppliers with whom you were previously in the habit of dealing during your employment with the Company (unless specifically requested to do so in the course of any duties which you are asked to perform);
(c) shall, save in certain cases as prescribed in the Company's Conduct Code, continue to receive the remuneration and other benefits to which you are contractually entitled; provided that the rights of the Company pursuant to this clause shall not be exercised for a period exceeding [six] months in aggregate. During the garden leave period you remain an employee of the Company bound by the terms of your employment contract (other than that to perform work for the Company unless specifically required to do so). In particular, but without limitation, you remain bound by your obligations of loyalty and good faith, of exclusive service to the Company and of confidentiality, which obligations, *inter alia*, preclude you from taking up any employment during the garden leave period.

PRECEDENT 12E: Reference policy and waiver

Company policy

1. It is Company policy to provide references on former employees where a written request has been received by a prospective employer and where it is considered appropriate. There is no legal duty to give a reference but if one is given, there are strict legal rules that apply.

2. A reference must be honest and accurate. Anything that is omitted or by innuendo gives a misleading picture is negligent mis-statement and we can be sued by a prospective employer.

3. Employers and authors of references must take great care when writing references to ensure that they are accurate and honest. In law a duty of care is owed to the

prospective employer who will often rely upon a reference to confirm a prospective employee's employment.

4. It is our policy to give factual references and not to give opinions which may be flawed or prejudicial to the individual (either too favourable or unreasonably unkind and untrue).

5. If mistakes are made then claims can be brought against both the employer and the writer of the reference for negligence (negligent mis-statement) and for other claims such as breach of contract, defamation (slander if it is spoken and libel if it is written), malicious falsehood, etc.

6. There may be cases where the Company does not wish to give any form of reference and in other cases the dates of employment only and job title will be confirmed.

7. For this reason, we set out the following instructions in respect of references:

- No person other than the HR Manager is authorised by the Company to give any references on current or former employees.
- The reference will normally be drafted by the appropriate line manager and then checked for accuracy, etc. by HR and sent out in the name of the HR Director.
- The reference contains a legal waiver drafted for us by our lawyer, which we hope will protect us if we are ever sued.
- Open references, i.e. 'TO WHOM IT MAY CONCERN' given to an employee upon leaving is NOT this Company's practice. However, in the event of a closure of a site or office, or where the employee is leaving to live and work abroad, such a reference may be provided at the discretion of the HR Director.
- If any member of staff is asked to give a 'personal' reference, then it is important to note that you must only use your home notepaper and make no reference to the fact that you work for this Company in case it could later be argued that you purported to be writing on your employer's behalf.

PLEASE TAKE CAREFUL NOTICE OF THIS INSTRUCTION AS RECENT CASE LAW SHOWS HOW EASY IT IS TO FALL FOUL OF THE LAW.

REFERENCE

This reference is given and received in the strictest of confidence and is not for any purpose other than for consideration for future employment. It is written and accepted in good faith but without any legal liability on the part of the Company or the author of this reference. It is written upon the request of the subject and accepted by the recipient on this basis.

Waiver

It is not the policy of the Company to provide any further information for references. This does not imply any comment, positive or negative about the employee or their course of employment with the Company.

In accordance with the policy of the Company this information is given in the strictest of confidence and is given by the Company and is received by you without financial or other liabilities on behalf of the Company or any of its officers.

Any use of the term Director is purely to reflect titular status. This does not imply any shareholding or legal interest in the Company on behalf of the above named employee.

Please be advised that no additional information concerning the above named employee will be given over the telephone.

PRECEDENT 12F: Clauses related to notice

1. **Pay in lieu**

On serving notice for any reason to terminate this Agreement or at any time thereafter during the currency of such notice the Company shall be entitled (but not obliged) to pay to the Executive in full and final settlement of all claims which he has or may have against the Company or any Group Company under his employment or this Agreement or otherwise, his salary and other benefits (but, for the avoidance of doubt, not including any bonus) (at the rate then payable under clause [...] hereof) for the unexpired portion of his entitlement to notice.

2. **Garden leave**

During all or part of any notice period, the Company shall be under no obligation to assign any duties to the Executive, may require the Executive to perform duties not within his normal duties or to undertake special projects, to work from home or not to attend for work or not to enter on to the premises of the Company. During any such period when the Executive is not required to work during the notice period, he will remain an employee of the Company. He will continue to receive his salary and other contractual entitlements (except any bonus, unless agreed otherwise by the Board) and be bound by all the terms of this Agreement. During such period the Company may require the Executive not, directly or indirectly, to work for any person or business, or communicate with any client of the Company or, for business purposes, any employee of the Company. Further, at any time during such period, the Company may require the Executive to resign from any and all offices held by him in the Company.

3. **Miscellaneous**

On the termination of this Agreement for whatever reason, the Executive shall at the request of the Company resign (without prejudice to any claims which the Executive may have against any Company arising out of this Agreement or the termination thereof) from all and any offices which he may hold as a Director of the Company or of any Group Company and from all other appointments or offices which he holds as nominee or representative of the Company or any Group Company and if he should fail to do so within seven days the Company is hereby irrevocably authorised to appoint some person in his name and on his behalf to sign any documents or do any things necessary or requisite to effect such resignation(s) and/or transfer(s).

4. On the termination of this Agreement for whatever reason, the Executive shall at the request of the Company immediately repay all outstanding debts or loans due to the Company.

13

Emails, the internet, social media and data protection

13.1 The issues

Considerations for employers in drafting social media and email/internet policies include cyber-bullying including putting up malicious posts and offensive tweets about colleagues and employees; posting inappropriate material on websites and on social media sites; employees criticising their employer and/or managers and/or other employees and/or clients online, etc.

Postings which are potentially libellous or not can have potential legal and commercial risks for the organisation.

The following are examples of such risks, arising from employees' use or misuse of social media. They have been taken from the 'Schools Personnel Services' website which has quoted *Personnel Today* and Croner 'Dismissals for Email and Internet Use'. (We are most grateful for permission to quote from this material.)

- Defamation, e.g. an employee making negative comments about their employer, another employee, a competitor, client or another third party.
- Breach of copyright/plagiarism, e.g. using someone else's work without proper attribution.
- Harassment and discrimination, e.g. abusive comments relating to another's sex, race or religion.
- Misconduct at work leading to unfair dismissal, e.g. making inappropriate videos posted on YouTube.
- Spending work time on personal business, i.e. cyber-skiving – overuse of social media/internet/emails for personal purposes during working hours.
- Breach of confidentiality and restrictive covenants, e.g. revealing client details or trade secrets of the employer, etc.
- Unauthorised references, e.g. unauthorised and untruthful (favourable) recommendation of employee by another employee or 'friend'.

13.2 Defamation on social media

With the growth of the internet and cyberspace, there is an ever-growing risk of hacking and stealing personal data and the misuse of company emails, posting offensive or potentially libellous posts on Facebook and the misuse of Twitter.

Comments on any social media may constitute defamation if they are untrue and malicious and ridicule the target of the publication, i.e. lower the claimant in the estimation of right-thinking members of society. Defamation is now governed by the Defamation Act 2013 (see below).

In the first libel case of its kind, involving libel on Twitter, *Talbot* v. *Elsbury* (2011) HC (CDR) LR 2012, 19(5), 220), Law Review (CTLR 142) the High Court found that the claimant had been libelled and awarded £3,000 damages and £50,000 costs.

Councillor Elsbury wrote on Twitter, about his rival, 'It's not in our nature to deride our opponents however Eddie Talbot had to be removed by the Police from a polling station'.

Mr Talbot's solicitor Nigel Jones told the court that the implication of the Twitter statement was that his client had been forcibly removed for criminal or disreputable conduct, adding that the allegation was completely untrue and defamatory.

However, this case was heard before the Defamation Act 2013 (2013 Act), which came into force on 1 January 2015. Now a claimant has to show 'serious harm' meaning 'serious financial loss' and there are new defences of 'truth' and 'honest opinion' and 'publication on matters of public interest'.

There is a new provision for website operators in s.5 of the 2013 Act. Here a website operator may have a defence to an action for defamation in respect of a statement published on its website if the operator can show that they are not the operator who posted the statement on the website.

The defence is defeated if the claimant shows that:

(a) it was not possible for the claimant to identify the person who posted the statement;
(b) the claimant gave the operator a notice of complaint in relation to the statement; and
(c) the operator failed to respond to the notice of complaint in accordance with any provision contained in regulations.

13.3 Summary of legislation concerning emails

Under the Regulation of Investigatory Powers Act (RIPA) 2000 and the Telecommunications (Lawful Business Practice) (Interception of Communications) Regulations 2000, SI 2000/2699 ('the Lawful Business Regulations') it is unlawful for an employer (or someone else with its express or implied consent) to intercept a communication in the course of its transmission by means of a private telecommunication unless:

(a) both the maker or sender and the intended recipient of the communication have consented to its interception, or the interceptor has 'reasonable grounds' for believing that they have so consented; or
(b) the interception is authorised by the Lawful Business Regulations.

Section 1(3) of RIPA 2000 provides:

> Any interception of a communication which is carried out at any place in the United Kingdom by, or with the express or implied consent of, a person having the right to control the operation or the use of a private telecommunication system shall be actionable at the suit or instance of the sender or recipient, or intended recipient, of the communication if it is without lawful authority and is either:
>
> (a) an interception of that communication in the course of its transmission by means of that private system; or
> (b) an interception of that communication in the course of its transmission, by means of a public telecommunication system, to or from apparatus comprised in that private telecommunication system.

13.4 Gateways

The Lawful Business Regulations provide exemptions or 'gateways' to enable employers to intercept communications for certain limited purposes and for the government to authorise interceptions for purposes such as the prevention and detection of crime and in the interests of national security. (My thanks to Anthony Korn of Counsel, No 5 Barristers Chambers, for first referring to the Regulations in this way.)

It is permissible for employers or someone with their implied or express consent to monitor and record the contents of a communication on their own internal system (i.e. not on someone else's property) without the consent of the sender or intended recipient, for the following purposes:

(a) to establish the existence of facts, e.g. to provide evidence of commercial transactions or other business communications in case of disputes arising (reg.3(1)(a)(i)(aa)); or
(b) to ascertain compliance with regulatory or self-regulatory practices or procedures that apply to the employer, or another person supervised by the employer in respect of those practices or procedures in the carrying on of its business (reg.3(1)(a)(i)(bb)); or
(c) to ascertain or demonstrate the standards which are or ought to be achieved by persons using the system in the course of their duties, e.g. customer call monitoring for quality control and staff training purposes (reg.3(1)(a)(i)(cc)); or
(d) to prevent or detect crime (such as fraud or corruption) (reg.3(1)(a)(iii)); or
(e) to investigate or detect the unauthorised use of that or any other telecommunication system, e.g. to check that employees are not using the internet for purposes that are prohibited by the employer's policy on internet use (reg.3(1)(a)(iv)); or

(f) to secure, or as an inherent part of, the effective operation of the system, e.g. to protect the system against viruses and hackers and to make routine interceptions for operational purposes such as backing up (reg.3(1)(a)(v)).

Authorised interceptions must take place on the employer's premises, or somewhere else under its control in relation to the telephone or email services of the employer and not during the transmission of the communication on a public network.

13.5 Duty to inform staff/third parties

Regulation 3(2)(c) provides that employers must make 'reasonable efforts' to inform everyone who may be affected if the employer intends to monitor, intercept or read emails sent or received on its server or the internet history of the employee or listen to telephone calls or record calls. Affected persons are those who send emails to or from the employer's server or who make calls to the employer and the warning must include a warning that the emails may be intercepted and read or the call is recorded or may be recorded. Employers usually do this by way of a memo or email and statement in the staff handbook, or in the contract of employment and in the footer of all emails sent out from their server, or in a recorded message on the telephone before a party is put through to anyone. See **Precedent 13A**.

13.6 Email misuse

Clear rules should be set out concerning email and internet use at work. These can range from 'no private use of the company's email or internet at all', to 'permission to use the company email server for personal use' subject to the words 'reasonable use' and save for prohibition on the unauthorised downloading of offensive emails/internet sites.

Some employers understand and recognise that employees do not separate personal and work time entirely and they may work long hours or shift hours which make it more difficult to send emails or conduct personal business in out-of-work-hours time.

Emails which may be defamatory or discriminatory can lead to legal liability for the employer for actions in libel or discrimination claims on the grounds of vicarious liability. There may also be an issue of 'cyber-skiving', i.e. wasting work time surfing the internet or writing and receiving private emails.

Some employers also have rules forbidding the transfer of company data to the employee's private email account or to any other third party email or cloud – for security and confidentiality reasons. This is common in the financial sector.

Some employers remind their staff about the rules on email and internet misuse when they log on. See **Precedent 13B** and the email disclaimer at **Precedent 13J**.

Some employers include clauses governing email and internet use in contracts of employment and in the staff handbook. See **Precedent 13C** for a clause where the employer is happy to leave the responsibility for email and internet use on a private basis to the employee.

13.7 Disciplinary action for email and internet misuse

Dismissals for flagrant breach of the email system and/or internet appear to be fair where there are clear rules forbidding such use and a thorough investigation and the 'punishment fits the crime'. Some employers grade the penalty according to the seriousness of the offence. For example, 'cyber-skiving', i.e. spending too much time using the email system for personal or inefficient usage, may carry a formal warning for a first offence, although, as in one case, the sending of nearly 4,000 emails (most of which were personal) in a six-month period, an average of 30 per working day, might constitute gross misconduct. The sending of libellous or grossly offensive emails or downloading pornography may carry the penalty of summary dismissal for a first offence because it is regarded as gross misconduct.

However, it is essential to investigate allegations of misuse of the email policy or the internet and to consider the explanation of the individual concerned.

In an Employment Tribunal case, *Buckley* v. *Waters Edge Ceramics*, Ms Buckley was awarded £19,000 compensation for unfair dismissal after she had been dismissed for gross misconduct, allegedly viewing hard core porn sites at work. The Employment Tribunal held that there was no evidence that she had been viewing these sites. Her explanation was that they had been 'pop up sites' and she had had no idea how they came on to her screen and that others had been using her computer to view porn sites.

The Employment Tribunal held that her employer had failed:

(a) to conduct a reasonable investigation and therefore the decision to dismiss her which is within the reasonable range of responses in the circumstances;
(b) to explain the consequences of misuse of work computers (or made accessible what misuse of computers at work entails and what the consequences may be);
(c) to obtain evidence that would reasonably suggest that she had been misusing her computer at work; and
(d) to consider her explanations but took the evidence at face value.

A failure to do all of this and to consider any medical evidence that could explain the employee's behaviour may render the dismissal unfair.

In *The City of Edinburgh Council* v. *Dickson* UKEATS/0038/09, the claimant was a diabetic. He was dismissed for watching pornographic material on a computer at work. His defence was that he was suffering a hypoglycaemic episode and was not responsible for his actions. His employer rejected this defence and dismissed him for gross misconduct. The claimant sued for unfair dismissal and disability discrimination.

The Employment Tribunal held that:

(a) the dismissal was unfair because the decision-taker refused to 'engage with' the defence notwithstanding material adduced in support of it; and that if the defence had been properly considered it would have been accepted; and

(b) the dismissal constituted direct disability discrimination, alternatively disability-related discrimination.

The Employment Appeal Tribunal held that the dismissal was unfair but that it did not constitute either direct disability discrimination or disability-related discrimination. It held:

(1) The tribunal was entitled on the evidence before it to reach the conclusions that it did, and to order reinstatement.

(2) The council's conduct did not constitute either direct or disability-related discrimination.

The fact that the explanation which the council rejected related to the claimant's disability did not mean that the rejection was on the ground of that disability or of a reason related to it.

It was necessary that the disability should be (at least part of) the reason for that rejection in the sense explained in such cases as *Nagarajan* v. *London Regional Transport* [1999] IRLR 572 and *Taylor* v. *OCS Group Ltd* [2006] EWCA Civ 702, i.e. the claimant was treated in that way 'by reason that' they had a disability and that 'the disability-related reason must affect the employer's mind, whether consciously or subconsciously. Unless that reason has affected his mind, he cannot discriminate...'

In *Mason* v. *CXC Advantage Ltd* ET/2203930/2013 the claimant was found to have been fairly dismissed for sending 'saucy' emails from the employer's server.

In *Meadows* v. *East Riding of Yorkshire Council* ET/1805363/2012 the case concerned the claimant's misuse of his work internet and email. His employer dismissed him on the basis that the misconduct led to a breakdown in trust and confidence. The dismissal was upheld as fair.

A stricter approach to email and internet use is provided in **Precedent 13D(1)**.

A current social media policy can be found at **Precedent 13D(2)**.

13.8 Checklist

Below is a checklist for employers as to what can be included in disciplinary rules governing emails and internet usage. For example employers may wish to ban the personal use of company mobile telephones and mobile internet access on the company's account, because there is a potential for running up large bills in the company's name. (Also see **13.13** on use of social networking sites such as Facebook.)

1. Any disciplinary procedure should be in writing and accessible to those who are affected.
2. Rules should make it clear:
    (a) what kind of use of email and the internet is permitted;
    (b) when the use of email and the internet is permitted;
    (c) the maximum time per day that users are permitted to spend on private use of email and the internet;
    (d) what the likely sanction will be for misuse of email and the internet (it may not be advisable to have inflexible sanctions).
3. Permissible restrictions: certain matters can be absolutely prohibited:
    (a) the use of the employer's system to download pornography or any other inappropriate or offensive material;
    (b) the use of the employer's system to download racially charged material;
    (c) the writing of emails that do not comply with or conform to the employer's standards, e.g. no information which is unlawful, defamatory, lewd, obscene or otherwise inappropriate, or likely to result in any form of liability on the part of the employer, is to be stored, sent, forwarded, downloaded, printed or otherwise dealt with, whilst using the employer's systems;
    (d) the personal use of company mobile telephones and mobile internet access on the company's account.

    Employees should be encouraged and required to report (on an anonymous basis if the individual wishes) any emails that they receive or see being sent, containing inappropriate language or messages or to which are attached offensive or inappropriate images or texts.
4. When formulating the rules it may be advisable to keep the restrictions proportionate in order to ensure objectivity. This would be consistent with approaches in other fields such as the monitoring of communications.
5. Informing employees how to report abuse of the system serves a twofold function: it helps as an internal monitoring aid (discouraging, among other things, abusive emails sent internally to employees which may give rise to a complaint); and it assists in showing that the employer has acted reasonably in providing support to staff.
6. Other matters may require more care or discretion:
    (a) personal emails sent to colleagues at other organisations;
    (b) use of internet services, such as online banking, which reflects for example any existing policy regarding personal telephone use, removing direct responsibility from employers.
7. There must be clear documentary evidence that these rules and the consequences of a breach of the rules has been brought to the attention of all staff.

The full extent of email and internet litigation is probably yet to be seen. From the above a certain amount can be gleaned as to the likely approach of the tribunals. Employers should, therefore, have clear policies on the use of internet and email systems and should aim to supervise the same in the best way possible.

The use of mail-sweeping services so that offensive words are automatically omitted or so that there is some form of regulation will probably assist in removing direct responsibility from employers, leaving only vicarious responsibility, the effects of which can be mitigated by surveillance and ample punishment for the employees concerned.

13.9 Covert surveillance

Authorisation for the conduct or use of covert surveillance must not be issued unless arrangements exist that satisfy the requirements of RIPA 2000, s.29(5). Details are set out in the Regulation of Investigatory Powers (Source Records) Regulations 2000, SI 2000/2725. A Code of Practice 2002 on 'covert surveillance' was published by the Information Commissioner and came into effect on 1 August 2002 (see the Regulation of Investigatory Powers (Covert Surveillance: Code of Practice) Order 2002, SI 2002/1933) and further guidance was published on 1 February 2004. In addition, a checklist for 'small users' was published in September 2002.

In essence, the principle is that employers should ensure that employees are made expressly aware (if this is the case) that neither email nor telephone privacy is guaranteed. Some employers make available payphones for employees to use at work for making unmonitored private calls and set aside rest rooms and other private rooms where unmonitored calls may be made.

13.10 'Cyber-liability'

It should be made clear to staff that lists of business contacts, potential and actual clients, compiled during an employee's employment belong to the employer and not to the employee.

In *Pennwell Publishing (UK) Ltd* v. *Ornstein* [2007] IRLR 700, the High Court made it clear that a list of contacts which a journalist had stored in an email address list on his employer's computer was the property of his employer.

Three employees left the company to set up a rival business. Mr Junior Isles, one of the triumvirate, had drawn up a contact list, which was maintained on the company's computers. Before Mr Isles left to work for his competing business, he downloaded his contact list, known as 'Junior contact list'. The employers successfully claimed that the list was company property and not that of their former employee, even though the list contained contacts that pre-dated his employment with them and had been started when working with a previous employer. The judge held that (paras.127–31):

.... where an address list is contained on Outlook or some similar program which is part of the employer's email system and backed up by the employer or by arrangement made with the employer, the database or list of information ... will belong to the employer. I do not consider that the position will change where the database is accessed not from the employer's computer but from the employee's home computer by 'dialling up' or otherwise 'logging on' to the employer's email system by some form of remote access.

In all those circumstances, I find that such lists will be the property of the employer and may not be copied or removed in their entirety by employees for use outside their employment or after their employment comes to an end.

Because this is not likely to be appreciated by many employees, it is in my judgment highly desirable that employers should devise and publish an email policy of the kind which in this case was devised by PennWell but on my findings not adequately communicated to Mr Isles. ...

In my judgment it is reasonable to imply in the absence of any laid down guidance a term that an employee will at the end of their employment be entitled to take copies of their own personal information and, where the information is personal and confidential to them, such as details of their doctor, banker or legal adviser, to remove them from the employer's system.

The now-famous cases which settled for damages and costs, of *Godfrey* v. *Demon Internet* [2003] 3 WLR 1020, illustrates how vulnerable internet service providers (ISPs) are under the law of defamation with the caveats in s.5 of the Defamation Act 2013.

Morland J in his judgment in the first of two actions in defamation involving Demon Internet held:

1. ISPs such as Demon were to be treated as publishers for the purpose of English libel law.
2. Demon could not rely upon the s.1(1)(b) and (c) defence in the Defamation Act 1996 in the period following Dr Godfrey's complaint (1994) about the offending posting on Demon's services because Demon was 'put on notice' and was required to 'take reasonable care', and it did not do so.

13.11 Prosecutions

Rare though it may be there have been prosecutions for internet offences. In *R* v. *Maxwell-King* [2001] 2 Cr App R(S) 28 the defendant was found guilty of an offence under ss.1–2 of the Computer Misuse Act 1990. This case concerned the illegal manufacturing and supplying of set-top boxes for cable television services. However, the 1990 Act is relevant in the employment field and data protection policies should refer to this issue (see below).

13.12 Human rights

The Human Rights Act 1998, Sched.1 prescribes the conduct of 'public bodies' pursuant to the European Convention on Human Rights. The Act makes it unlawful for public authorities or any person certain of whose functions are functions of a public nature (e.g. Employment Tribunals and courts) to act in a way which is incompatible with the European Convention on Human Rights.

There are some areas of monitoring and recording telephone calls and the use of covert surveillance upon which the 1998 Act impacts directly.

Unite has produced a useful guide, 'Privacy at Work' (2013).

The cases of *Jones* v. *University of Warwick* [2003] 3 All ER 760, CA and *Halford* v. *United Kingdom* [1997] IRLR 471 both involved breaches of Article 8 of the European Convention on Human Rights. In the former case, private detectives tricked their way into Ms Jones' home masquerading as market researchers and secretly filmed her. This was held to be a blatant infringement of her 'right to respect to privacy and family life' under Article 8. In Ms Halford's case, she successfully sued her employers, the Merseyside Police Authority, for authorising her telephone in her private office to be 'tapped' during her litigation for sex discrimination. The European Court of Human Rights (ECHR) held that this was a blatant violation of Ms Halford's rights to respect for her privacy because her employers had not informed her in advance that her private telephone line in her private office at work could be monitored.

The ECHR held (p.472):

> Telephone calls made from business premises may be covered by notions of 'private life' and 'correspondence' within the meaning of Article 8. The argument of the UK Government that an employer should in principle, without the prior knowledge of the employee, be able to monitor calls made by the employee on telephones provided by the employer, could not be accepted. As no warning had been given to the applicant that calls made on the telephones in her office at Merseyside Police Headquarters would be liable to interception, she would have had a reasonable expectation of privacy for such calls. Therefore, Article 8 was applicable.

Codes of Practice

A Code of Practice on 'Covert Surveillance and Property Interference' pursuant to s.71 of the Regulation of Investigatory Powers Act 2000 has been updated by the Home Office, December 2014 (see **www.gov.uk/government/uploads/ system/uploads/attachment_data/file/384975/Covert_Surveillance_Property_ Interrefernce_web__2_.pdf**).

Part II of the 2000 Act provides for the authorisation of covert surveillance by public authorities where that surveillance is likely to result in the obtaining of private information about a person.

Surveillance, for the purpose of the 2000 Act, includes monitoring, observing or listening to persons, their movements, conversations or other activities and communications. It may be conducted with or without the assistance of a surveillance device and includes the recording of any information obtained.

Surveillance is covert if, and only if, it is carried out in a manner calculated to ensure that any persons who are subject to the surveillance are unaware that it is or may be taking place.

Specifically, covert surveillance may be authorised under the 2000 Act if it is either intrusive or directed:

- Intrusive surveillance is covert surveillance that is carried out in relation to anything taking place on residential premises or in any private vehicle (and that involves the presence of an individual on the premises or in the vehicle or is carried out by means of a surveillance device).
- Directed surveillance is covert surveillance that is not intrusive but is carried out in relation to a specific investigation or operation in such a manner as is likely to result in the obtaining of private information about any person (other than by way of an immediate response to events or circumstances such that it is not reasonably practicable to seek authorisation under the 2000 Act).

Chapter 2 of this code provides a fuller description of directed and intrusive surveillance, along with definitions of terms, exceptions and examples.

A further Code of Practice on 'Covert Human Intelligence Sources' has been published by the Home Office, December 2014.

A person is a covert human intelligence source (CHIS) if:

(a) they establish or maintain a personal or other relationship with a person for the covert purpose of facilitating the doing of anything falling within paragraph b) or c);
(b) they covertly use such a relationship to obtain information or to provide access to any information to another person; or
(c) they covertly disclose information obtained by the use of such a relationship or as a consequence of the existence of such a relationship.

A relationship is established or maintained for a covert purpose if and only if it is conducted in a manner that is calculated to ensure that one of the parties to the relationship is unaware of the purpose.

A relationship is used covertly, and information obtained is disclosed covertly, if and only if the relationship is used or the information is disclosed in a manner that is calculated to ensure that one of the parties to the relationship is unaware of the use or disclosure in question.

The 2013 Order further defines a particular type of CHIS as a 'relevant source'. This is a source holding an office, rank or position with the public authorities listed in the Order and Annex B to this Code of Practice. Enhanced authorisation arrangements are in place for this type of source as detailed in the Code.

13.13 Social networking

With the advent of Facebook, Instagram, blogs and other social networking websites, some employees have failed to be discreet, using their Facebook pages to refer to their employer in less than complimentary ways and sometimes even disclosing confidential information about a matter going on in the company and their own activities.

Employers may wish to include an addendum to their email and internet policies such as the one shown at **Precedent 13F**.

Here are 10 matters to be covered:

1. *A clear company philosophy*. Define the company's attitude toward social networking. Is it something that you consider to be a strictly personal activity, which should be generally restricted – like personal phone calls and visits from family members – to the employees' break and lunch times? Or is the company interested in encouraging employees to use social networking for business purposes and incorporate it into their working time?

    Some sites, such as MySpace and Instagram, are primarily for personal socialising.

    Some, such as LinkedIn, are purely for business. But others, such as Facebook and Twitter, can be used for both purposes.

    You may want to allow or disallow use of specific sites during work time.

2. *The definition of 'social networking'*. It is important that the policy defines what is meant by 'social networking' or 'social media', since the term means different things to different people. For example, Facebook is a social networking site; Flickr is a photo-sharing site; Indaba is a musicians' collaboration site; LiveJournal is a blogging site; and Mumsnet is an internet forum.

    You may want to name specific sites and technologies, but because new sites are always popping up, you should make it clear that the policies are not limited to the named sites.

3. *Identifying oneself as an employee of the company*. The social networking policy should also make it clear whether employees are allowed to identify themselves as representatives of the company. Most social networking sites have fields in the user profile for work experience, job title, etc. By identifying themselves as an employee of XYZ Ltd, social networkers become, to some extent, representatives of that company and everything posted has the potential to reflect on the company and its image. Unless the employee is engaging in social networking for the specific purpose of promoting the company, some organisations prohibit their employees from listing the company name on such sites. If employees are allowed to advertise their association with the company, the policy should impress upon them that they take on the responsibility for representing the company in a professional manner.

    If social networking users identify themselves as employees of the company, the policies should require that any personal blogs and other personal posts contain disclaimers that make it clear that the opinions expressed are solely those of the author and do not represent the views of the company.

4. *Recommending others*. Some social sites provide for members to write recommendations or referrals for friends/associates. If an employee does this as a representative of the company, it may give the appearance that the company endorses the individual being recommended. That could

create a liability situation if another company hires the recommended person on the basis of the recommendation. For that reason, some company policies prohibit employees from making such recommendations or referrals.

5. *Referring to clients, customers or partners.* The company's relationships with clients, customers and partners are valuable assets that can be damaged through a thoughtless comment. Even a positive reference could be picked up by a competitor and used to your company's disadvantage. The social networking policy should make it clear that employees are not to reference any clients, customers or partners without obtaining express permission to do so.

6. *Proprietary or confidential information.* Even though there may be other policies that cover the dissemination of the company's proprietary or confidential information, trade secrets, etc. the social networking policy should repeat those policies and provide specific examples as they relate to social networking sites.

   Social networking sites have varying levels of security and as public sites, all are vulnerable to security breaches. Your policy should make it clear that proprietary information is not to be discussed or referred to on such sites, even in private messages between site members who have authorised access to the information.

   Some employers spell out examples of information that is considered to be confidential and not to be published, such as the company's financial information, intellectual property, information about customers, etc.

7. *Terms of service.* Most social networking sites require that users, when they sign up, agree to abide by a terms of service (tos) document. The company policy should hold employees responsible for reading, knowing, and complying with the tos of the sites they use. It should not contain rules that require employees to violate the common tos stipulations. For example, most tos agreements prohibit users from giving false names or other false information, so the company policy should not require users to use pseudonyms when signing up for social networking sites.

8. *Copyright and other legal issues.* Policies should require employees at all times to comply with the law with regard to copyright/plagiarism. Posting of someone else's work without permission is not allowed (other than short quotes that comply with the 'fair use' exceptions). Other relevant laws include those related to libel, i.e. defamation. Defamatory statements can lead to legal action against the author of the statement – and if that is an employee, at the very least it can bring bad publicity for the company. For example, the performer Courtney Love is being sued for libel by a fashion designer for comments she made about the designer on Twitter. The suit alleges that Love posted derogatory and false comments about the designer.

9. *Cyber-skiving.* Social networking sites can be good tools for developing business relationships, but they can also waste working time. It is important to set guidelines and priorities. The policy should make it clear

that social networking activities are not to interfere with the employee's primary job responsibilities.
10. *Disciplinary action.* The policy must include consequences for breaches. The policy should spell out that breach of the policy can result in disciplinary action, up to and including summary dismissal.

13.14 Data protection

The EU General Data Protection Regulation (GDPR) is being implemented into UK legislation on 25 May 2018. It will give far greater rights to the data subject to give or withhold or withdraw their consent.

There are some interesting tensions between RIPA 2000 and the Data Protection Act 1998. This causes particular difficulty with regard to employers' rights to monitor employees' email. Employers are given statutory powers to intercept and monitor emails at work by RIPA 2000, and yet data subjects have the right to have their personal data kept secure and in some cases the employer must obtain the individual's express consent before processing it.

It is also very important to remind staff of the need for employees to keep customers' and other people's personal information safe if this is taken out of the office, e.g. on memory sticks or on laptops.

A Code of Practice on the 'Acquisition and Disclosure of Communications Data' (Home Office) was revised in March 2015 (**www.gov.uk/government/ uploads/system/uploads/attachment_data/file/426248/Acquisition_and_ Disclosure_of_Communications_Data_Code_of_Practice_March_2015.pdf**).

A Code of Practice on the 'Retention of Communications Data' was also revised in March 2015 (**www.gov.uk/government/uploads/system/uploads/ attachment_data/file/426249/Retention_of_Communications_Data_Code_of_ Practice_March_2015.pdf**).

The Code on the 'Acquisition and Disclosure of Communications Data' is intended for government departments but the guidance on monitoring telephone calls, email and internet use is relevant for all organisations.

The Code on 'Retention of Communications Data' applies to Communications Service Providers (CSPs) who have been issued with a data retention notice under the Data Retention and Investigatory Powers Act 2014 (DRIPA). Chapters 6, 7 and 8 also apply to those who retain data under the voluntary Code of Practice under the Anti-terrorism, Crime and Security Act 2001 (ATCSA).

Information Commissioner's Code of Practice

The Information Commissioner published the 'Employment Practices Code' in November 2011 (**ico.org.uk/media/for-organisations/documents/1064/the_ employment_practices_code.pdf**).

It deals with the impact of data protection laws on the employment relationship. It covers issues such as the obtaining of information about workers, the retention of records, access to records and disclosure of them.

'Relevant filing system' and 'personal data'

At the heart of the Data Protection Act (DPA) 1998 lies the data subjects' right to have access to their 'personal data'. Employers used to dread receiving such requests, and lawyers such as the author when acting for an employee would use this 'right' to obtain disclosure pre-action in order to assess the strength of the case or to assist in a grievance or appeal.

The Court of Appeal in *John Durant* v. *Financial Services Authority* [2003] EWCA Civ 1746 held that the 1998 Act:

> is not an automatic key to any information, readily accessible or not, of matters in which he may be named or involved. Nor is [it] to assist him, for example, to obtain discovery of documents that may assist him in litigation or complaints against third parties.

There is a far more limited and restrictive definition of 'personal data' in relation to 'manual records' as defined in DPA 1998, s.1.

The Information Commissioner published a guide to 'Determining What is Personal Data' (revised in 2012) – ico.org.uk/media/1554/determining-what-is-personal-data.pdf.

The Court of Appeal in *Durant* held that 'personal data' is information that affects a person's privacy, whether personal, family, business or professional. The question then is whether it is capable of having an adverse impact on that person. In determining whether the information is such that it affects the person's privacy, there are two key concepts:

1. Is the information biographical in a significant sense, that is going beyond recording the person's involvement in a matter or event which has no personal connotations?
2. Does the information have as its focus the individual rather than some other person with whom they may have been involved or some transaction or event that they may have figured or have had an interest in?

Examples of 'personal data'

These include:

- medical information;
- salary details;
- a person's tax liabilities;
- a person's bank statements;
- a person's spending preferences.

Not every piece of information retrieved from a computer search against a person's name or unique identifier is 'personal data'. Even though an individual's name may appear on a document or in an email, this does not in itself make that personal data where the name is not associated with any other personal information. If the individual is the recipient or is copied in on that email or memo, it will only be 'personal data' under DPA 1998 if there is other information about the individual within it. An example of such 'personal data' disclosed in litigation was an email calling an individual 'deaf and stupid' in relation to 'feedback' that her line manager had had concerning her bonus.

Incidental mention in minutes of meetings of a person's attendance at that meeting in their official capacity does not mean that that document is personal data.

Examples of breaches of the DPA 1998

One employer (B) telephoned a female member of staff's (C) previous employer (A) after she had lodged proceedings for sex discrimination against B, whilst still in B's employment. B's HR manager asked for and was given details by A's HR manager from C's old personnel file (she had left A over seven years earlier) about her reasons for leaving and the details of an ET1 and originating application that had been issued as a protective measure during severance discussions which took longer than three months from her effective date of termination. C had had a new male manager at A who had treated a number of his female colleagues in a discriminatory fashion and all the women chose to leave and accept severance packages. B intended to use this information in C's litigation against it. In this example, A had breached Principles 2, 3, 4 and 5 of Sched.1 to DPA 1998 and the individuals concerned may have committed a criminal offence under DPA 1998 if they were not authorised in their actions by the Data Controller.

In another example, D's HR department used the confidential bank details of a former employee, E, who was suing D for significant damages, in order to investigate whether he had another job and had, as they suspected (wrongly) obtained new and lucrative employment, thus mitigating his loss. This was achieved by D passing on the bank details to a private detective who rang the bank in question and managed after 13 attempts to infiltrate the system and gain access to these bank details. E had never even given the details of this account to his wife. His ex-employers were the only other people (other than D himself) who knew about this account. It was one into which his very sizeable salary and bonuses were paid. In this example, both the bank and D had breached the DPA 1998.

Commissioner's guidance on what is a 'relevant filing system'

According to the Information Commissioner's guide to the Data Protection Act 1998:

> Relevant filing system (referred to in paragraph (c) of the definition) is defined in the Act as:
> 'any set of information relating to individuals to the extent that, although the information is not processed by means of equipment operating automatically in response to instructions given for that purpose, the set is structured, either by reference to individuals or by reference to criteria relating to individuals, in such a way that specific information relating to a particular individual is readily accessible'.

This is not an easy definition. Our view is that it is intended to cover non-automated records that are structured in a way which allows ready access to information about individuals. As a broad rule, we consider that a relevant filing system exists where records relating to individuals (such as personnel records) are held in a sufficiently systematic, structured way as to allow ready access to specific information about those individuals. For further guidance see the FAQs about relevant filing systems.

'Accessible record' (referred to in paragraph (d) of the definition) means:

- a health record that consists of information about the physical or mental health or condition of an individual, made by or on behalf of a health professional (another term defined in the Act) in connection with the care of that individual;
- an educational record that consists of information about a pupil, which is held by a local education authority or special school (see Schedule 11 of the Act for full details); or
- an accessible public record that consists of information held by a local authority for housing or social services purposes (see Schedule 12 for full details).

Accessible records were included in the definition of 'data' because pre-existing access rights to information were not restricted to automatically processed records, or records held in non-automated systems falling within the definition of 'relevant filing systems'. So, to preserve all these pre-existing access rights, the definition of 'data' covers accessible records even if they do not fall in categories (a), (b), or (c).

The Information Commissioner advises that personal data filed in subject divisions such as 'sickness', 'absence' or 'contact details' would constitute a relevant filing system. He suggests that 'very few manual files will be covered by the provisions' of DPA 1998. Therefore 'most information about individuals held in manual form does not fall within the data protection regime'.

Other useful guides to the GDPR from the Information Commissioner's Officer include:

- 'GDPR consent draft guidance' (consultation ended March 2017) (see **ico.org.uk/media/about-the-ico/consultations/2013551/draft-gdpr-consent-guidance-for-consultation-201703.pdf**).
- 'Preparing for GDPR: 12 steps to take now' (see **ico.org.uk/media/1624219/preparing-for-the-gdpr-12-steps.pdf**).

TUPE clause in contract

When a business or part of a business is transferred under the Transfer of Undertakings (Protection of Employment) Regulations 2006, SI 2006/246 (TUPE), during the due diligence process the transferee naturally seeks data on an anonymous basis about the staff and their terms and conditions. Once the transfer is concluded, the transferee will then seek the transfer of all personnel and occupational health records.

In the case of the latter, consent is required and letters should go out to all staff in the terms of **Precedent 13G**.

The Information Commissioner's Office (ICO) issued guidance on 'Disclosure of Employee Information Under TUPE' (**ico.org.uk/media/1063/disclosure-of-employee-information-under-tupe.pdf**).

It confirms that wherever possible, the employer should release information that is anonymous or, at the very least, should remove obvious identifiers such as name. Employers should only disclose this extra information with the consent of the individuals concerned, or put in place appropriate safeguards to make sure that the information will only be used in connection with the proposed business transfer and will not be kept once it has been used for this purpose.

TUPE requires the transferee to be provided with information about their new workforce in advance of any transfer or change in service provision. Disclosures are permitted under the DPA 1998 as they are required by law. However, the parties must still comply with data protection principles when handling this information.

Information given to new employer

TUPE requires the following information to be passed on to the new employer at least 28 days before the transfer of employment:

- identity and age of employees being transferred;
- information contained in their statements of employment particulars, e.g. statement of pay, hours of work, holiday, etc;
- information about any collective agreements;
- details of any disciplinary action in the last two years;
- details of any grievance action raised by an employee in the last two years;
- details of any legal action brought against the company by an employee in the last two years.

Employment records

The guidance also provides information on whether employment records can be given to the new employer. It says a large portion of the employment record is likely to be required, and that the employee's consent is not needed to transfer this. It advises transferees to consider whether they require all the personal information in the files, and to delete or destroy unnecessary information.

Transferor's position

The transferor is permitted to keep some personal information about employees who have been transferred. This will normally be to deal with any liabilities, and the former employer should only keep it so long as is necessary, and delete or securely destroy any information they do not need to keep.

Good practice tips

The guidance also provides a list of good practice tips. These include:

- agreeing what information is to be transferred well before the transfer takes place;
- telling employees their information is being passed to the new employer;

- considering whether any personal information can be anonymised before providing it if not required under TUPE.

Blogging

A blog is basically a journal or diary that is on the internet. Some employers have rules about what and whether employees may write a blog either at work or about work.

A few employers recognise the PR potential of employee blogging. The personal style of a blog provides the kind of genuine intimacy that marketing and PR departments spend millions trying to create.

But blogging may not suit all companies, businesses or staff roles. ACAS has produced some useful guidance about good work practices and social media.

Employers need to draft a set of clearly written rules and consequences but unless they do employees may need to avoid blogging about work.

Social media advice

The ACAS advice page 'Social media in the workplace' (**www.acas.org.uk/index.aspx?articleid=3375**) states:

> The impact of social media on the workplace is increasing. Social media is the broad term for internet-based tools used on PCs, laptops, tablets and smart phones to help people make contact, keep in touch and interact.
>
> This trend can affect communications among managers, employees and job applicants, how organisations promote and control their reputation, and how colleagues treat one another. It can also distort what boundaries there are between home and work.
>
> **Key Points**
>
> - **Develop a policy**: Employers should include what is and what is not acceptable for general behaviour in the use at work of the internet, emails, smart phones and social media, such as networking websites, blogs and tweets. However, it might prove impractical to have an overly formal policy that also includes rigidly covering the use of social media in recruitment.
> - **Rules for recruitment**: While a rigid policy on using social media in recruitment could soon become obsolete, because the trend is changing and developing so quickly, it is still advisable for an employer to have at least some rules, or procedures, which managers and employees should follow.
> - **Screening job candidates**: In particular when recruiting, employers should be careful if assessing applicants by looking at their social networking pages – this can be discriminatory and unfair.
> - **Who can see your profile?** Employees should regularly check the privacy settings on their social networking pages, as they can change. Also, they should consider whether they want or need co-workers to see those profiles.
> - **Talk to your staff**: Employers should inform and consult with their employees if planning to monitor social media activity affecting the workplace.
> - **Update other policies**: For example, an organisation's policy on bullying should include references to 'cyber bullying'.

- **Be sensitive**: Employers should promote a work-life balance – the line between work and home is becoming increasingly blurred by the use of modern technology.

Smart phones, the internet, tweeting and blogging – we have accepted all of these innovations, and many more, as part of our working lives, helping us to work more flexibly, stay in touch for longer and respond to each other quicker.

Some estimates report that misuse of the internet and social media by workers costs Britain's economy billions of pounds every year and add that many employers are already grappling with issues like time theft, defamation, cyber bullying, freedom of speech and the invasion of privacy.

A policy can be found at **Precedent 13D(2)**.

PRECEDENT 13A: Email monitoring

1. The use of email is governed by legislation, and also by the Company's own rules for the proper use of computing and networking facilities.

2. Each Department operates email systems for the use and convenience of its business and they are not there for the personal use of employees.

3. This statement indicates the policy for normal operations of the Departmental email system, and describes situations in which email events are monitored and logged during those operations. Users should be aware that the Department might additionally be required to monitor specific emails in the course of criminal or disciplinary investigations.

4. It is the intention that:

(a) bona fide mails will be delivered to their intended addressee, or, where this is not possible, an appropriate non-delivery report sent to the sender;

(b) specific forms of abuse will be detected, and an appropriate report issued to the sender to indicate the reason for rejection.

5. These abuses comprise:

- unsolicited Bulk Emails (popularly known as 'spam');
- attempts to use our mail servers to relay third-party mail;
- the sending of potentially dangerous 'active attachments', as deprecated by Company email guidelines.

6. All email transactions are logged, for the purpose of investigating transmission irregularities which only come to light after a delay; these log entries may contain timestamp, originating email address and sending system; recipient email address and mail system; message id, size.

7. Messages exhibiting irregularities which are detected by the mailer will also give rise to an exception log report: exception log reports can contain the full headers of the mail. The actual content of mails is not logged.

8. Log entries are kept for approximately two months to assist in diagnosing delayed reports of problems, after which the logs are discarded.

9. Mails are also automatically scanned for the purpose of identifying abuses under the above headings.

10. Messages which fail, or which are automatically rated as abuse, are likely to be viewed by the postmasters to determine the proper disposal: the postmasters thus may inevitably become aware also of the content of the message.

11. In particular, staff should be aware that:

(a) it is particularly difficult permanently to delete emails from a computer system, especially when using a network;
(b) emails can lead to legal action against both the individual and the employer;
(c) emails can be defamatory and breach equal opportunities policies if they are libellous or offensive;
(d) emails can be quickly disseminated very widely and very quickly by the mere pressing of the 'Forward to All' button.

Implementation summary

12. This statement shows the context and policy under which the mailer operates. The technical details of the implementation may vary, within the scope of the policy set out here, according to circumstances and experience. A general description of the technical procedure will be provided by the postmasters.

13. This statement bas been authorised by the Managing Director after consultation with the Board of Directors on [date].

Summary

1. The Company should have a policy on use of electronic communications.

2. Any monitoring should be based on business requirements and be fair and legal.

3. Staff should be clearly told whether their use of email and the internet is subject to monitoring.

4. Staff should be encouraged to use modern electronic forms of communication but not to engage in 'cyber-skiving' or unauthorised downloading or the sending of inappropriate emails, etc.

5. The policy should clearly specify who has authority to make decisions about allowing staff to make personal use of communication systems.

'E-risk'

The Company should ensure that there is:

(a) a clear definition of the extent and nature of internet usage and a detailed analysis of the scope and nature of potential claims relating to internet and e-risks;
(b) a close evaluation (supported by legal advice where appropriate) of the extent to which existing insurance cover will respond to potential e-risks within standard commercial policy wordings.
(c) an evaluation of whether existing policies provide adequate indemnity limits appropriate to the scope and nature of the e-business undertaken by insurers;
(d) an investigation of the range and scope of cyber-liability or bespoke coverage options offered by a growing number of insurers against specifically defined e-risks.

PRECEDENT 13B: Log on banner

REMEMBER!

1. The misuse of the email and internet across the Group is regarded as a serious breach of the Company's Data Protection Policy and Equal Opportunities Policy. The

Group takes all misuse of its property and data protection and its equal opportunities policies very seriously and abuse of the system will result in serious disciplinary action including summary dismissal.

2. In particular, the accessing, downloading, distribution and viewing of illegal games, pornographic and/or other offensive material from the internet or the sending, viewing or distributing of offensive emails, whether in the form of pictures or words, is regarded as gross misconduct and could lead to summary dismissal.

3. Files including emails sent and received will be periodically reviewed by the Company, without warning, for non-business material and disciplinary action will be taken against anyone who breaches these Rules.

SO PLEASE DON'T DO IT!

PRECEDENT 13C: Clause relating to email and internet monitoring

1. The Company recognises that employees may wish to use the office telephone, email and/or internet for their own personal use. As long as this privilege is not abused and everyone acts responsibly in this regard and as long as no inappropriate, adult, pornographic, gambling or other sites on the internet are accessed or downloaded, this will be permitted.

2. It is strictly forbidden for any member of staff to transfer any electronic data to any outside email account save for legitimate business purposes and under no circumstances can any company data be transferred to a private email account for any reason. This would be regarded as gross misconduct for which summary dismissal is one possible outcome.

3. Private telephone calls will be permitted as long as they are not for an excessive amount of time, e.g. over four or five minutes in duration and as long as they are local calls. Any long-distance calls (i.e. outside the UK) must not be made unless prior permission has been granted and an agreement reached over who will bear the cost.

4. Employees should note that the Company reserves the right to monitor and/or record all telephone calls to and from the office, all emails (whether marked Private or Personal) and the internet (checking the server) at any time for the purposes of ensuring that the Company rules are being complied with and for legitimate business purposes.

5. Please note that any misuse of any of the Company's facilities, e.g. telephone, IT or mail, will lead to disciplinary action being taken.

6. The Company reserves the right to use covert surveillance in cases where any suspected dishonesty may have taken place either in relation to the activities of employee(s) or third parties or in cases where there may be a suspected breach of contract, e.g. breach of a restrictive covenant or breach of confidential information, such as would be likely to damage the business or reputation of the Company.

PRECEDENT 13D(1): Internet and email policy

1. Introduction

1.1 [Access to the internet and email system will be available to you for business use only OR private or personal use of the email system must be restricted to no more than one or two messages a day.] This prohibition on personal emails includes sending messages to other employees within the Company and to suppliers, other third parties having any business connection with the Company as well as to outside friends, family and other third parties. It is expected that staff will only send personal emails in cases of necessity, e.g. in order to confirm a booking or order for goods. All other personal or private emails should be confined to the employee's home PC (see below for further rules).

1.2 It is also strictly forbidden for a member of staff to transfer any company data to a private email account whether this belongs to them, a family member, friend or third party.

1.3 Any lists of information belonging to the Company including but not limited to names and/or addresses of contacts, clients, former or potential clients, suppliers, agents, contractors, etc. must not be accessed, uploaded or downloaded or accessed remotely from home. Those lists whether compiled by an employee in their work or spare time or whether started at another employment and updated with us, remain the property of the Company and must not be copied or taken away or used for any personal purposes or for the use of any other third party.

1.4 Use of the Company's email facilities will be monitored and disciplinary action may be taken if the facilities are abused or put to unsuitable use.

2. Internet policy

2.1 The prime use of the Company internet facility is for information and research relating to the Company's business. Access to certain sites may be withdrawn and/or banned. User activity is monitored and logged. Copies of these logs are given to Compliance/Head of your Department/HR at regular intervals.

2.2 The downloading of any program or wallpaper from the internet is strictly prohibited unless explicitly instructed to do so by the IT Department. For example this would include all shareware and freeware, particularly screen savers and desktop background patterns or wallpapers. Even if another user indicates they have IT approval, it is your personal responsibility to ensure you are complying with Company policy.

2.3 The deliberate downloading or transmission of pornographic, offensive, sexist, racist, defamatory or other material of a similar nature is a serious offence and will result in dismissal.

2.4 All downloaded attachments, for example Word documents that may contain Word macros, must be virus scanned before opening.

2.5 If you are in any doubt regarding checking for viruses, contact the IT Helpdesk.

3. Email policy

3.1 The guidelines and warnings listed below are of critical importance.

3.2 You are reminded that email is subject to the same Company policies as any other form of correspondence and should be used for business purposes only. We will allow very limited use of the email facility for personal use, e.g. where it is necessary for a member of staff to confirm a booking or order for goods. Employees are not allowed to use the email system to send messages to colleagues, send jokes or forward jokes to colleagues nor to send private or personal emails to friends or family whether they live locally or abroad. This is not only an abuse of the Company facilities and expenses but is an abuse of working time. Even during rest breaks and meal breaks, staff are expected to take refreshments and fresh air or relaxation and are not permitted to remain at their desks using the Company facilities for their own personal purposes.

3.3 Beware what you say in email messages. Improper statements can give rise to personal or Company liability. Also be careful about forwarding messages.

3.4 Assume that email messages may be read by others.

3.5 Messages that are abusive, sexist, racist or defamatory are never appropriate and must not be sent or forwarded to any other person whether within or outside the Company. It is a disciplinary offence to do so, regarded as gross misconduct for which summary dismissal is the normal penalty.

3.6 Always remember that email messages, however confidential or damaging, may have to be disclosed in court proceedings or in investigations by competition authorities/ regulatory bodies if relevant to the issues. Remember that even if you have deleted an email message, a copy may still exist on backup media or in other storage areas.

3.7 If you should receive an email which you believe is offensive, obscene or otherwise inappropriate, then you should call your line manager at once to report the fact. Your line manager will advise you what to do.

3.8 Never send strictly private and confidential messages by email unless prior consent has been obtained from the addressee. Confidential emails should be sent over the internet as encrypted files.

3.9 The content of all email messages is scanned automatically and logs are given to Compliance at regular intervals.

3.10 You are required to ensure that:

- your email mailbox is checked at reasonable intervals for messages;
- any messages found there are collected;
- you must set appropriate access to your mailbox to cover both planned and unplanned absence.

3.11 Never import non-text files (e.g. executable files, Word documents) or messages on to your system without having them scanned for viruses or text bombs. If you have not been properly trained to scan for such viruses/bombs, the IT Helpdesk should be called to assist.

3.12 If you become aware of a virus warning, it should be referred to the IT Helpdesk only. Do not set about warning other internal and external bodies or individuals. If the virus warning is correct, then the IT Helpdesk will put out the usual warning email, with any specific instructions. If the warning is of the hoax type, you will be informed.

3.13 Make hard copies of emails that you need to retain for record-keeping purposes.

3.14 Always make hard copies of emails on client matters.

3.15 You must not enter into contractual commitments by email.

3.16 Do not create email congestion by sending trivial messages. It is strictly forbidden for anyone to copy/forward emails such as chain mail letters, humorous stories, etc. or large attachments.

3.17 Do not advertise by email or send messages for missing items unless genuinely urgent for business reasons. Use the intranet for the purpose.

3.18 Do not download, copy or transmit to third parties the works of others without their permission as this may infringe copyright.

3.19 Never send bank account or credit card information over the internet.

3.20 The following wording must precede the text when you send an external email:

The Company monitors and reads all emails as only business emails are permitted to be sent and received.

The Company also monitors emails for compliance reasons and to ensure that no unauthorised disclosure of confidential information is passed via the email system.

This email and any attachments are confidential. It is intended for the recipient only. If you are not the intended recipient, any use, disclosure, distribution, printing or copying of this email is unauthorised. If you have received this email in error please immediately notify the sender by replying to this email and delete the email from your computer.

The contents of any attachment to this email may contain software viruses, which could damage your own computer system. While [*name of company*] plc has taken every reasonable precaution to minimise this risk, we cannot accept liability for any damage which you sustain as a result of software viruses. You should carry out your own virus checks before opening the attachment.

4. Moves and changes

4.1 All IT purchases by any manager must be approved by the Head of IT (or in their absence by the Systems Manager) and must follow the Group policy on capital purchases.

4.2 A Change Control Form must be completed by a user or manager (and signed by their line manager) to request any move of part of the system or any change to the system (move of hardware, installation of software, change of log in, removal of a user name, etc.), which could have an impact on another part of the system. Completed forms must be returned to the Helpdesk. Note that usernames will not be removed from the system until a Change Control Form has been received requesting this to be done.

4.3 A New Starter Form must be completed to request the creation of a user account for a new member of staff or a temporary member of staff. The form must be signed by a suitable manager and returned to the Helpdesk.

5. Logging calls to the Helpdesk

5.1 All calls must be emailed to the Helpdesk using the email address [*specify*]. If you are unable to email you can phone or fax the Helpdesk provided you email your query as soon as you are able to use email again. This is to ensure that a record is kept of all calls.

5.2 The request for support must contain:

- the full details of the problem, e.g. the applications running, the text of error messages, etc., whether the problem is client/customer facing;
- details of the urgency of the problem and a reasonable date and time when the problem should be fixed.

PRECEDENT 13D(2): Social media policy

(*Based on the University of Surrey's social media policy, and produced here with its kind permission. See* www.surrey.ac.uk/currentstudents/Files/Social-Media-Policy.pdf.)

1. Introduction

Effective use of social media can bring significant and measurable benefits to the University. These include opportunities to promote the institution's success stories, develop national and international reach, improve student engagement and attract high quality staff and students.

Social media channels can spread the University's messages across the globe quickly and to a range of audiences at little or no cost and, unlike other traditional media channels, they provide instant feedback from our audiences.

Along with these benefits come the risks inherent in managing something that is dynamic and unlimited in scale.

These include the risk of reputational damage arising from misuse by staff, students or third parties, threats to the security of sensitive or confidential information, exposure to malware and a negative impact on productivity.

1.1 Purpose

This Social Media Policy aims to mitigate the risks associated with employees' use of social media. It provides all University staff with a clear articulation of the institution's expectations around the use of social media. The accompanying Social Media Toolkit encourages University of Surrey staff to use social media and gives guidance on how best to make the most of the key channels.

1.2 Scope

This policy has been produced for all University employees. A policy for University students will be provided separately.

1.3 Equality analysis

There is potential for social media channels to be used for bullying and harassment of individuals. It is therefore important that the policy is considered alongside the Dignity at Work and Study Policy.

Staff Development will include reference to this policy in induction and management training.

1.4 Definitions

According to the Chartered Institute of Public Relations (CIPR), social media are: 'Internet and mobile-based channels and tools that allow users to interact with each other and share opinions and content. It involves the building of communities or networks and encouraging participation and engagement.'

This is the recognised definition for the purpose of this document. This policy refers to three different types of social media account:

- Professional University of Surrey Account – used by representatives of the University to communicate messages from a departmental, faculty or corporate perspective; managed by a Professional Account Administrator (see 2.1.1.4).
- Professional Personal Account – used by an individual member of staff, who is identifiable as an employee of the University of Surrey through the content of their posts or their profile's biographical information.
- Private Personal Account – used by an individual primarily for non-work activity. Social networks covered by this policy include, but are not limited to, Facebook, Twitter, LinkedIn, YouTube, Instagram, Pinterest, Google+ and Tumblr.

1.5 Legislative context

- Data Protection Act 1998 and accompanying guidance in the Information Commissioner's Employment Practices Data Protection Code.
- Human Rights Act 1998.
- Regulation of Investigatory Powers Act 2000.
- Telecommunications (Lawful Business Practice) (Interception of Communications) Regulations 2000 (SI 2000/2699).
- Copyright, Designs and Patents Act 1988.

1.6 *Health & Safety Implications*

There is potential for social media channels to be used to cause emotional harm or mental distress to others. By producing this policy and its accompanying toolkit, the University hopes to minimise any distress to its staff caused by the misuse of social media.

2. Policy

2.1 *Principles*

2.1.1 *Professional use of social media*

2.1.1.1 Employees using social media in a professional capacity, either through a Professional University of Surrey account or a Professional Personal Account, should make sure that their communications do not do any of the following.

- Bring the University into disrepute. For example, by making defamatory comments about individuals, other organisations or groups, or the University; or posting images that are inappropriate, links to inappropriate content or using inappropriate language.
- Breach confidentiality. For example, revealing confidential information owned by the University relating to its activities, finances, people, or business plans, or the personal data of any individual who has not given informed consent (in writing) for their data to be published.
- Breach copyright. For example, using someone else's image or written content without their permission; failing to give acknowledgement where permission to reproduce something has been obtained.
- Do anything that may be considered discriminatory against, or bullying and harassment of, any individual. For example, making offensive or derogatory comments relating to sex, gender, race, disability, sexual orientation, religion, belief or age; using social media to bully another individual; or posting images that are discriminatory or offensive or linking to such content.
- Breach the terms of service of the social network. Each social network has different terms of use and community guidelines, which must be followed.

The University does, however, recognise Academic Freedom whereby staff shall have freedom within the law to question and test received wisdom and to put forward new ideas and controversial or unpopular opinions, without placing themselves in jeopardy of losing their jobs or privileges.

2.1.1.2 Employees using social media in a professional capacity should use the same safeguards that they would with any other form of communication about the University in the public sphere.

These safeguards may include (but are not limited to):

- ensuring that the communication has a purpose and benefit to the University;
- obtaining a manager's permission before starting a public social media campaign;
- getting an appropriate person to check the content before it is published;

- seeking advice if you are unsure of your objectives or required outcomes.

2.1.1.3 There should be a clear reason or reasons to set up a Professional University Account and processes put in place to ensure that it is monitored and updated regularly. For detailed guidance please refer to the Social Media Toolkit (which is available on Asset Bank: http://assetbank.....ac.uk).

2.1.1.4 Where a Professional University account has two or more users, one user should be assigned the Professional Account Administrator role. This person will be responsible for:
- ensuring that the account meets brand guidelines as specified in the Social Media Toolkit;
- making sure that the login details are shared only with those who have a real need to use the account;
- revoking access to the account where necessary, such as if an employee leaves the organisation;
- ensuring that all content produced for the account is in line with this policy;
- ensuring that the account is used regularly;
- reporting any incidents where the administrator feels that an employee has misused the social media account.

2.1.1.5 Employees managing a Professional University account are expected to remove any comments that fit into the categories outlined in 2.1.1.1.
Additionally, users should also remove comments that are:
- spam, or trying to sell things;
- fraudulent, deceptive or misleading;
- in violation of any law or regulation. Employees are encouraged to think carefully before removing users' comments, to ensure that users with good intentions do not feel that we are placing an unjustified restriction on their freedom of speech.

2.1.1.6 Social media users are encouraged to regularly check their accounts for messages and respond to any enquiries that they receive in a timely fashion.

2.1.1.7 Social media users who receive enquiries/approaches from media sources (newspapers, radio, TV) relating to their work at the University are encouraged to notify the University's PR & Communications Team for guidance about how to respond (as they would if they received approaches from the media via any other channel).

2.1.1.8 All employees using social media in their professional role at the University are encouraged to read the University's Social Media Toolkit – available on Asset Bank (http://assetbank......ac.uk)

2.1.2 *Personal use of social media*

2.1.2.1 The University recognises that many employees will make use of social media in a personal capacity. University employees using social media in a personal capacity should make sure that their communications do not do any of the following:
- Bring the University into disrepute.
- Breach confidentiality.
- Breach copyright.
- Breach the terms of service of the social network.
- Do anything that may be considered discriminatory against, or bullying and/or harassment of, any individual. Misuse as outlined above may be regarded as a disciplinary offence (See 2.1.1).

2.1.2.2 Employees who openly disclose that they work for the University should include on their profile a statement or disclaimer explaining that the views expressed are theirs alone and that they do not necessarily reflect the views of the University. However, if the content of a post is inappropriate, a disclaimer would not prevent disciplinary action.

2.1.2.3 To avoid confusion, the University prohibits the use of its logo(s) on social media when used for non-business reasons.

2.1.2.4 Employees are encouraged to familiarise themselves with privacy settings for each social media platform and choose a privacy level that they consider to be appropriate. For more information about privacy settings, please refer to the University's Social Media Toolkit – available on Asset Bank (http://assetbank.....ac.uk).

2.1.2.5 Employees are permitted to make reasonable and appropriate use of personal social media from the University's computers or mobile devices, provided that this usage is limited to official rest breaks.

For more information, please refer to 2.2.2 below.

2.2 *Procedures*

2.2.1 Where it is found that an employee has misused social media, it may be regarded as a disciplinary offence in accordance with the University Disciplinary Policy. Examples of misuse are outlined in 2.1.1.1 and 2.1.2.1.

2.2.2 The University reserves the right to monitor employees' internet usage in line with the IT Services Acceptable Use Policy and the University Policy for Email Use by Staff. In line with this, it may instigate an investigation into an employee's internet usage where there are suspicions that the employee has been using social media excessively for personal use when they should be working, or in a way that is in breach of the rules set out in these policies. Authorisation to instigate an investigation into an employee's internet use can only be done by either the Director of Human Resources or the Chief Information Officer, following consideration of a valid case for this from the individual's line manager.

2.2.3 The University monitors mentions of its brand name and associated terms in order to identify any risks to reputation and to gather customer feedback. Only content that is available in the public domain is subject to monitoring. Data monitored is processed anonymously for analysis purposes and is not held by the University. University employees are advised to read the privacy guidance provided in 2.1.2.4.

3. *Governance & Directory Requirements*

3.1 *Responsibility*

This policy is owned by the University's Social Media Working Group. This is currently chaired by the Director of Marketing & Communications. It will be the responsibility of the group's Chair to ensure that the policy is implemented, communicated and reviewed on an annual basis. The group will regularly review the impact of the policy and the accompanying toolkit and ensure that any subsequent issues relating to the use of social media are dealt with through the most appropriate channels.

Specific responsibilities for social media across the University are as follows.

- Reputational risk created by social media – Head of PR & Communications.
- Response to customer enquiries – Head of Market Insight & Data.
- Marketing opportunities – Head of Digital Marketing.
- Social media development – Social Media Co-ordinator.

- Internet usage monitoring infrastructure – Chief Information Officer.
- Disciplinary proceedings relating to social media – Vice-President Human Resources.

3.2   Implementation/Communication Plan

Once approved, this policy will be posted, along with the Social Media Toolkit, on to the University's website and communicated via internal communications channels including:

- Leaders' Alert, Net, Life and NetNews.
- HR will be asked to include the policy in their briefing to new staff during the induction process.
- Updates to this Policy and ongoing guidance relating to best practice in social media will be posted to the Social Media blog: blogs……ac.uk/socialmedia.

3.3   Exceptions to this Policy

In all cases where it is believed that this policy has been breached, considerable judgement will be exercised to consider the context behind the issue and the impact of the action.

However, where it is found that an employee has misused social media, it may be regarded as a disciplinary offence in accordance with the University Disciplinary Policy.

3.4   Supporting documentation

This policy should be read in conjunction with:

- the University's Social Media Toolkit;
- IT Services Acceptable Use Policy;
- University Policy for Email Use by Staff;
- Code of Practice on Freedom of Speech;
- Data Protection Policy;
- Dignity at Work and Study Policy;
- Disciplinary Policy.

PRECEDENT 13E: IT and computer equipment policy

1. This document is a summary of our Company policy on the use of company-provided computer equipment, email and voicemail systems and rules governing internet access.

2. All company-provided computer and voicemail systems and the data stored on them (including all email, files, electronic documents and voicemail messages created, sent and received) are and remain at all times the property of the Company. As such, they are not considered the private property of the employee (and any applicable privacy laws relating to such materials are excluded to the maximum extent permitted by law).

3. If you are provided with a computer to perform your duties (including portable computers) you must take all necessary steps to prevent unauthorised access to the computer and to the wider Company systems. Passwords should be used and changed regularly.

4. Employees should not use an electronic mail account assigned to another individual to either send or receive messages, except where specifically authorised to do so under delegated authority, e.g. manager–secretary working.

5. When not in use, especially out of normal working hours, at home, at work or in transit, portable computers must be securely locked away out of sight. Portable computers should always be carried as hand luggage on aircraft and kept with you at all times.

6. Sending an email or leaving a voice message is no different from providing the same message by fax or in the form of a letter. Careless terminology in emails, as with faxes and letters, can expose the Company to unwanted obligations or liabilities.

7. Email messages should be courteous, professional and businesslike. Bear in mind when composing and sending emails that the message could be repeated in a very different situation (e.g. a court of law or the front page of a newspaper) and to a different recipient (e.g. a judge)!

8. Even where passwords or other security devices are used, the confidentiality of email, copies of electronic documents or files and voicemail cannot be guaranteed. You must assume that someone may read any and all messages other than the intended or designated recipient. It is also possible that information held in electronic form may have to be disclosed to third parties in connection with litigation. This can include opposing lawyers and the police.

9. Internet emails include a disclaimer to inhibit legal action against the Company. The disclaimer is included automatically by the system.

10. Access to the internet will be made available to every user with a business need for such access. For security reasons, downloading files to or from the internet will only be available for approved users. Users who do not have a business need for the internet may use a PC in the Learning Centre outside working time.

11. To ensure that employees comply with this policy, the Company reserves the right to conduct periodic audits of email, voicemail, documents or other electronically stored information including (but not limited to) individual PCs, file servers, disks and other backup devices. This process is capable of being automated using software to scan individual accounts or entire server file systems.

12. Any personal use of Company-provided computer and voicemail systems must comply with this policy and must not interfere with normal business activities.

13. The Company takes a serious view of computer misuse and such misuse may lead to disciplinary action being taken against you under the Company's disciplinary policy. Serious offences may constitute gross misconduct and therefore be liable to summary dismissal. The following are regarded by the Company as unacceptable:

- fraud and theft of data and software;
- sabotaging the system;
- using unauthorised software;
- misuse of personal data;
- breach of Company security procedures;
- sending chain letters, off-colour jokes, abusive, offensive, pornographic or defamatory messages or pictures via electronic mail;
- accessing other users' email.

14. Offensive content would include, but would not be limited to, sexual comments or images, racial slurs, gender-specific comments, or any comments that would offend someone on the basis of their sex, age, weight, sexual orientation, religious or political beliefs, national origin or disability. The list is not exhaustive but illustrative.

15. Should you have any queries with regard to the above please contact your manager for assistance.

PRECEDENT 13F: Social networking policy

We have always had a policy of trusting our staff to act responsibly when using the internet and email server for private use.

However, recently it was discovered that some members of staff had placed inappropriate notices on Facebook about the Company which were defamatory and incited criminal acts to be committed. This is of course strictly forbidden and is viewed very seriously by the Company.

The use of the internet and email at work is primarily for business and legitimate purposes. Because we place you in a position of trust and expect you to behave responsibly, our current policy allows limited and reasonable use of the internet and email server at work for personal use.

When we say 'reasonable' and 'limited', we mean that both the activity and the time spent must be reasonable and legitimate. For example if a member of staff wishes to download information on travel, flights and holidays or information about the theatre or cinema and this is done in break times and the time spent is reasonable, then this activity would be deemed to be within the spirit of the Company's Policy.

In order to dispel any doubt about what is and is not permitted here are some examples of what is not permitted and what would be regarded as gross misconduct:

- writing any blogs and giving the Company web address or email address;
- writing anything that is defamatory, untrue, malicious, hurtful, personal or otherwise offensive about any individual or about the Company in general;
- writing anything about the Company that is either a breach of confidential information or which does or is likely to harm or lower the reputation or damage the reputation of the Company or any member of staff, director or manager or which could adversely affect the business or a client or third party with whom there is a business relationship;
- using the Company web address or email server for any Company facility for any other activity other than for work purposes, e.g. using these services for an outside interest or activity such as if an employee assisted on a helpline switchboard or internet service.

If any such activity is found to be occurring of the above nature or if an unreasonable amount of time is found to be being spent by staff either surfing the internet or downloading from the internet or writing and receiving personal emails, then the Company will have to rethink its Policy about personal use of the internet and email at work.

Breach of this policy will be regarded as misconduct or even gross misconduct for a serious breach for which disciplinary action up to and including summary dismissal may be warranted.

If anyone has any queries about the personal use of the company email or internet please ask the HR department for guidance.

PRECEDENT 13G: Letter relating to transfer of occupational health records

(I am particularly grateful to Dr Robin Cox FFOM who confirmed that the following policy was ethically sound.)

[Name of employee]
[Address]
[Date]

Dear [name]

RE: Transfer of occupational health records

As you know, your part of our business has changed hands or will be changing hands and your new employer will be [*give details*].

As a result, their Occupational Health Department will be taking over the occupational health services for you and as such we need to transfer your records to them. We are assured of their integrity and that they understand their professional obligations and responsibilities. In particular, the new organisation has similar security measures in place that guarantee absolute confidentiality of your medical records.

If you object to the transfer of your records, then please let us know by close of business [*date*]. If we do not hear from you by then your consent is implied and assumed and we will continue with our plans to transfer the files.

It has been a pleasure to look after you all these years and we wish you every success with your new employer.

Yours sincerely

PRECEDENT 13H: Clause relating to TUPE

Data protection

1. The Company and all staff are required to observe all the requirements of the Data Protection Act 1998 in relation to the processing of data, i.e. recording, holding and disclosing data relating to any employee and outside third parties who have dealings with the Company. If you are responsible for holding and/or disclosing personal data on any personal computer in your department, you must inform [*specify*] and make it your own responsibility to read and keep informed of your duties and responsibilities under the Act. In particular if you are required to process data about yourself, i.e. input or disclose data about yourself, you are trusted to provide that information accurately and not to mislead any person about the details of that data.

2. You give your express consent to the Company processing information, including sensitive personal data (as defined in the Data Protection Act 1998) including any relevant medical records (restricted to the Occupational Health Department only), details of trade union membership or ethnic origin, about you, subject to our undertaking that we will comply with our obligations under the 1998 Act.

3. You have rights of subject access under section 7 of the Data Protection Act 1998. Please read carefully the section on Data Protection in the Staff Handbook.

4. You are entitled to examine any personal data retained on you within your personnel files. In particular if there is a proposed transfer of the business or part of the business under the Transfer of Undertakings (Protection of Employment) Regulations 2006, you agree to the transfer of non-identifiable data prior to the transfer and to the transfer of all personnel and occupational health records to the transferee upon the transfer subject to adequate safeguards by the transferee about their compliance with their duties under the Data Protection Act 1998.

PRECEDENT 13I: Data protection policy 2017

1. Data protection overview

Under the Data Protection Act 1998 it is a criminal offence to give out personal information to people/agencies for whom it was not originally given and processed by the Company. The Company does not, except with the authorisation of the Chief Executive, give out personal details of any client or member of staff or donor or any other third party. We never give out home details either of staff or clients. Please pass all requests for personal information to the Chief Executive.

2. IT Code of Conduct

2.1 Purpose

The purpose of this Code of Conduct is to set out the behaviour expected of the Company's staff in their use of IT. This Code is intended to assist the Company in furthering its objectives.

Whilst the Company encourages the use of email and the internet to aid communication and improve efficiency, inappropriate use of these systems can cause serious problems which may involve legal claims against both the Company and individual members of staff.

Excessive unnecessary traffic on the network places constraint on its use for business purposes and slows the network down. The Company has therefore established this policy setting out the correct use of its computer systems and the Company's response to inappropriate use.

Use of the Company's communications systems should not bring the Company or its staff into disrepute or place them in a position of liability.

Homeworkers or anyone working from home on an ad hoc basis must abide by the Data Protection and IT Code of Practice and Rules set out at the end of the Handbook.

2.2 Organisational responsibilities

Systems will be provided to enable individuals to carry out the business of the Company.

Sanctions will be taken against those who breach this Code.

2.3 Individual responsibilities

All users of the Company's systems, including staff, will be referred to as 'individuals' for the purposes of this Code and its policies.

Individuals are required to behave in a way that will credit the Company.

Individuals are required to maintain the standards of honesty and integrity in all business dealings.

Individuals are required to behave legally.

Individuals are required to use only authorised access to systems.

Individuals are required to comply with all policies and Codes issued by the Company concerning the use of its systems.

2.4 Software

The Company will not make or condone the making of illegal copies of software.

Individuals are not permitted to download unlicensed software from the internet.

Only identified IT personnel are allowed to install software on the Company's IT systems.

Individuals will consult and seek the approval of administration during all stages in identifying, purchasing and installing all new software including freeware, abandonware and shareware.

Floppy disks and other removable media may be a source of viruses and should never be used without first having them scanned through administration.

Each successful virus scan remains valid until one of the following occurs:

- the media is removed from site;
- the media is inserted into a non-organisation computer;
- the media is inserted into a computer that contains a virus;
- a file from the internet or an email attachment is saved on the media.

3. User account policy

3.1 Purpose

Most of the information stored on the Company's IT systems relates to people. As such, this information is deemed 'sensitive' data under s.2 of the Data Protection Act 1998 and must be protected to the best of each individual's and the Company's ability.

User Accounts identify individuals as valid users of protected information and services. They also identify activities users have performed while logged in to the Company's systems, indicating moral and legal responsibility and culpability.

Access to particular areas and subsets of information are restricted to particular individuals who are identified by IT systems by their User Accounts.

3.2 Usage

Individuals must not login using another individual's User Credentials (password and/or login details).

Individuals must make every effort to ensure that their User Credentials remain private.

Individuals must not disclose or write down (including but not limited to Post-it notes, computer documents, diaries, address books and mobile phone memory) their User Credentials.

If individuals suspect that their User Credentials are known to others, they must change their password immediately and notify administration of the possible breach.

Individuals must not access any information that they knowingly should not have access to.

Individuals must always lock their workstations when they leave their desk for periods expected to be less than 15 minutes. If leaving their workstation for longer periods (including end of the day) individuals will log out completely as to allow other validated users to use the machine and for IT maintenance work to be carried out.

Individuals may be forcibly logged out of a workstation for maintenance work to be carried out if the individual's workstation has remained locked and unattended for more than 15 minutes. Individuals should note that this may result in loss of work.

Individuals must shut-down their workstations at the end of the day.

4. Personal Data Assistants (PDAs)

4.1 Purpose

The Company recognises that Personal Data Assistants (PDAs or Palmtops) are a useful tool in maintaining productivity and integrating facilities. PDAs can help individuals keep a single up-to-date calendar, check emails and even make notes during meetings.

The Company also recognises that PDAs can be a major security risk. PDAs can contain confidential and privileged information. They can contract, execute and transmit computer viruses and other malicious code. Being mobile, PDAs are easily lost or stolen.

4.2 Usage

No PDAs may be connected to the Company's equipment by any means (including but not limited to: Infrared, 802.11b, USB cables, serial leads and Cat.5 cables) without the consent of administration.

The installation of the approved connection method may only be carried out by a qualified and identified member of the Company's IT staff.

The Company's IT Department reserves the right to refuse to connect an individual's PDA for any reason.

Antivirus products must be installed and properly maintained by the individual using the PDA.

5. Email policy

5.1 Purpose

The purpose of the Company's email is to conduct Company business and therefore no personal emails should be sent or received on the Company server. All personal emails should only be sent through a personal email account.

5.2 Ownership

The Company's email equipment and messages sent via that equipment are and remain the Company's property.

Messages that are created, sent or received using the Company's email system are the property of the Company.

5.3 Usage

All the Company email communications must be handled in the same professional manner as a letter, fax, memo or other business communication.

Automatic replies to incoming emails should be activated when you are absent from the office for two days or more.

No copyrighted or proprietary information is to be distributed by individuals unless approval has been granted by the Company.

No commercial messages, individual's solicitations, messages of a religious or political nature are to be distributed using the Company's email system unless within the remit of an individual's work and expressing the official opinions of the Company.

No personal information may be distributed to external organisations or external individuals using the Company's email system without prior consent of the person in question.

No information may be distributed to external organisations or external individuals using the Company's email system if distribution would infringe on the Company's data protection policies or agreements.

The Company's email messages may not contain content that may be considered offensive or disruptive. Offensive content includes but is not limited to obscene or harassing language or images, racial, ethnic, sexual or gender-specific comments or images, or other comments or images that might offend someone on the basis of their religious or political beliefs, sexual orientation, national origin or age.

Individuals may not retrieve or read email that was intended for another individual unless authorised by the Company or by the email recipient.

Anonymous messages, bulk virus alerts and letters must not be sent, redirected or in any other way distributed externally using the Company's email system.

All external virus warning email messages received must be forwarded to the Company's IT Department only.

It is strictly forbidden to transfer any emails (or documents) relating to the Company, its business or to any other third party, from the Company email account to a personal email account, Cloud or webserver or to any other third party's email account.

5.4 Non-business emails

Incidental and occasional personal use of electronic mail is permitted. Such messages become the property of the Company and are subject to the same conditions as the Company email.

5.5 Monitoring and reading emails

The Company reserves the right to monitor, review and read any emails in its email account of any member of staff at any time. Only folders that are titled 'Confidential' will not be opened, accessed or read.

The purpose of doing this includes ensuring that if a member of staff is absent, their emails are being checked and dealt with; that the email service is being used, etc. only for legitimate Company business; that policies and procedures are being observed and not abused, e.g. that no inappropriate discriminatory, racist or sexist language is being used or inappropriate messages are being sent; that no unlawful business is being transacted; that no personal or confidential data is being misused or disclosed to any unlawful third party, etc.

6. Internet policy

6.1 Purpose

The Company provides internet access to employees to assist them in carrying out their duties. The internet may be used to look up details about suppliers, products, to access government information, educational resources and other statutory information.

It should not be used for any personal uses, e.g. to book holidays or tickets, etc.

Members of staff may only access the internet by the Company's content scanning software, firewall and router.

6.2 Usage

You must keep the use of the internet to a minimum and for legitimate Company business only.

You are required to check that any information accessed on the internet is accurate, complete and current.

You must check the validity of the information found.

You must respect the legal protections to data and software provided by copyright and licences.

You must not download text or images which contain material of a pornographic, racist or extreme political nature, or which incites violence, hatred or any illegal activity.

You must not download content from internet sites unless it is work related.

You must not download software from the internet and install it upon the Company's computer equipment unless you have been instructed to do so by the Company's IT department.

You must not use Company computers to make unauthorised entry into any other computer or network (called computer hacking).

You must not disrupt or interfere with other computers or network users, services, or equipment. Intentional disruption of the operation of computer systems and networks is a crime (called 'hacking') under the Computer Misuse Act 1990.

You must not represent yourself as another person or use aliases, etc.

You must not use internet access to transmit confidential, political, obscene, threatening, or harassing materials.

6.3 Non-business usage

Incidental and occasional personal use of the Company's internet facilities are permitted. Such access is subject to the same conditions as normal Company internet usage.

7. Data Protection

7.1 Purpose

It is the Company's policy to comply with all laws regulating computers and personal data under its Data Protection Policy. It is therefore important that you limit the Company's exposure to risk through careless practices with regard to the use or unauthorised disclosure of personal data or inappropriate or illegal use of software. The Information Commissioner has the power to impose heavy fines on data controllers (employers) whose employees breach even if accidently the rules relating to Data Protection.

7.2 Usage

Individuals must not save information relating to peoples' personal details, project-sensitive information, information marked private or confidential or any other data not already in the public domain onto floppy disk, CD-ROM or any other type of removable external storage medium without the prior written consent of the Chief Executive.

Individuals must ensure that all mobile IT equipment in their possession, containing any type of sensitive or private data is transported, used and stored securely in order to avoid loss, theft and unauthorised data access. This includes but is not limited to laptops, palmtops, phones, electronic organisers, digital audio and video equipment, etc.

If you are supplied with computer equipment you are responsible for the safety and maintenance of that equipment and the security of software and data stored either on your own system or other systems, which you can access remotely. You are only authorised to use systems and have access to information which is relevant to your work. You should neither seek information nor use systems outside of this criterion.

You are required to comply with all policy documents issued by the Company with regard to the use of computer equipment and personal data.

PRECEDENT 13J: Email footer

Unless otherwise agreed expressly in writing by a [senior manager] of [company], this communication is to be treated as confidential and the information in it may not be used or disclosed except for the purpose for which it has been sent. If you have reason to believe that you are not the intended recipient of this communication, please contact the sender immediately.

Employees are expressly required not to make any defamatory statements and not to infringe or authorise any infringement of copyright or any other legal right by email communications. Any such communication is contrary to company policy and outside the scope of the employment of the individual concerned. The company will not accept any liability in respect of such a communication, and the employee responsible will be personally liable for any damages or other liability arising.

14

Restrictive covenants and confidentiality

14.1 Status of post-termination restrictions

All restrictive covenants are initially deemed void as they are regarded as being in restraint of trade. They need to be drafted very carefully, customised to each contract and it must be 'demonstrated [that they are] necessary for the protection of the employer's legitimate business' (*Hinton & Higgs (UK) Ltd* v. *Murphy and Valentine* [1989] IRLR 519).

An employer's legitimate business interests can include 'human beings', e.g. a pool of temporary workers who register with an employment agency in certain cases. In the *Office Angels* case the Court of Appeal held that this was possible because this 'pool of temporary workers was an important source of the plaintiffs' revenue, enabling them to supply staff to clients in return for commission' (*Office Angels Ltd* v. *Rainer Thomas and O'Connor* [1991] IRLR 214).

Post-termination restrictions cannot merely seek to prevent competition after the employee has left the employer's employment. The rationale for all post-termination restrictions and particularly non-compete clauses is to protect the trade secrets and confidential information properly belonging to the employer.

They must be 'reasonable' in scope, geographical area and time. The courts will not assist an employer who has drafted a post-termination restriction too widely. Simon Brown LJ in *JA Mont Ltd* v. *Mills* [1993] IRLR 172, said (p.173):

> As a matter of policy, courts should not too urgently strive to find, within restrictive covenants *ex facie* too wide, implicit limitations such as alone would justify their imposition. Otherwise, employers would have no reason ever to impose restraints in appropriately limited terms. Thus would be perpetuated the long-recognised vice of ex-employees being left subject to apparently excessive restraints and yet quite unable, short of expensive litigation and at peril of substantial damages claims, to determine precisely what their rights may be.

In *Office Angels Ltd* v. *Rainer Thomas and O'Connor* the Court of Appeal ruled (p.214):

If a covenant between an employer and an employee designed to prevent competition by the employee after termination of the contract of employment is to be upheld as valid, it must be shown that there is some advantage or asset in the business which can properly be regarded as the employer's property and which it would be unjust to allow the employee to appropriate for his own purpose. The Court must be satisfied, however, that the restriction is no greater than is necessary for protecting the employer's legitimate interest.

In *JA Mont Ltd* v. *Mills* (above), the covenant was drafted in consideration for a severance package, which stated that 'This total payment is made on condition that [the managing director] will not join another company in the tissue industry within one year of leaving our employment'. The Court of Appeal held that there was 'no attempt whatever to formulate the covenant so as to focus upon the particular restraint necessary to guard against Mr Mills' possible misuse of confidential information, the only legitimate target for imposing any restraint on his future employment'.

Normally, if the restrictive covenant is too wide, it is ruled to be unenforceable. In *Mills*, the Court of Appeal confirmed that 'If a contract includes a covenant which is so expressed as to be too wide, it will normally be held void and of no effect'. In some cases it may be possible for the courts to 'interpret' the covenant as having a more limited application, thus satisfying the test of reasonableness. In *Mills* this was not possible because the restraint was that he would not work for a year in the tissue industry and there had been no attempt to focus on its rationale, that of protecting confidential information. Mr Mills had only ever worked in the retail sector of the paper tissue industry.

14.2 General issues

Clauses concerning restrictive covenants are negotiated at the time of the start of the employment but most only take effect once the employment is over. The critical and crucial time to consider the drafting of and need for each and every restrictive covenant is when they were agreed and not when they are being enforced.

Accordingly, when lawyers are drafting these clauses, they need to take careful instructions at the time with regard to:

(a) the interest being sought to be protected, which should be stated clearly at the start of the clause;
(b) identification of the precise information which it is said is confidential;
(c) the seniority of the employee;
(d) what 'trade secrets' the employee will have access to;
(e) whether the employee will be responsible for a territory, such as a sales representative;
(f) the scope of the employee's job duties;
(g) the number of clients/customers/suppliers with whom the employee will personally have business dealings;
(h) whether the employee will be bringing clients with them;

(i) whether the employee is under a restrictive covenant from a former employment;
(j) whether it is appropriate to include a non-solicitation and non-dealing clause;
(k) whether it is appropriate to include a non-poaching clause in respect of senior/key individuals;
(l) the length of time for which it is 'reasonable' to seek to enforce these clauses following the termination of employment.

The Court approaches the interpretation of a restrictive covenant when faced with a contractual provision that is ambiguous in its meaning in the following way. Where there is one interpretation leading to an apparent absurdity and the other to a commercially sensible solution, the Court is likely to favour the latter.

In *Prophet plc* v. *Huggett* [2014] EWCA Civ 1013, the Court of Appeal confirmed this approach.

The Court of Appeal held that the natural meaning of the words 'any products' in the context of the clause 19 proviso were those products with which Mr Huggett was involved whilst employed at Prophet Ltd (products named 'Pr2' and 'Pr3').

The Court held that, faced with a clear choice between an interpretation that gives rise to an apparent absurdity and one that achieved a commercially commonsense result, a Court will usually favour the latter.

This approach will only work where the language is ambiguous and allows for clear alternative meanings that the parties intended to achieve.

The Court held that the proviso was 'unambiguously clear' and the words 'any products' referred only to Pr2 and Pr3.

The proviso in this clause 'was a carefully drawn piece of legal prose in which the draftsman had chosen his words with deliberate and specific care'.

The Courts will not re-phrase or re-draft a clause which has a literal and clear meaning. Prophet Ltd had the chance to get it right and they did not, and now they had 'made their (Clause 19) bed and had to lie on it'.

As the meaning of the proviso was clear, there was no basis for interpreting it differently. Therefore Mr Huggett's proposed activities with his new employer, which did not include either Pr2 or Pr3, would involve no breach of clause 19, and his appeal was successful and the original injunction discharged.

14.3   Enforcing the notice period/garden leave

Section 236 of the Trade Union and Labour Relations (Consolidation) Act 1992 (TULR(C)A) provides that:

> No court shall, whether by way of –
>
> (a) an order for specific performance or specific implement of a contract of employment, or
> (b) an injunction or interdict restraining a breach or threatened breach of such a contract,

compel an employee to do any work or attend at any place for the doing of any work.

In two recent High Court cases, the Court considered whether to grant an injunction to enforce an employee's notice period. Both cases involved determining whether the employee would either have to go on working for their former employers or 'starve or be idle'.

In *Elsevier Ltd* v. *Munro* [2014] EWHC 2648 (QB), the High Court granted an injunction to prevent Mr Munro from working for a competitor during his notice period.

The Court had to determine:

1. Was Mr Munro still bound by his contract of employment, or was he constructively dismissed?
2. If Mr Munro was still bound by his contract, should its terms be enforced by any, and if so what form of, injunction?

The High Court held that there was no constructive dismissal.

The company was seeking an injunction to prevent the existing breaches of the contractual obligations in Mr Munro's contract prohibiting outside interests whilst employed by the company and the implied term that he would not assist or take up employment with a competitor during his employment with the company.

The Court held that:

> Although public policy prevented 'compulsory sterilisation' and 'potential atrophy of skills', the company had asked Mr Munro to continue working until January 2015. Mr Munro had himself chosen to stop working for the company. It therefore did not lie in his mouth to complain of 'idleness' which he had chosen in breach of his contract of employment.

He was absent through his choice and without permission.

The Courts held that it would enforce a 12-month garden leave clause where it was 'necessary to protect the employer's business interests'.

14.4 Are damages an appropriate remedy?

If an employer seeks to enforce an obligation not to work for another employer during employment it will need to show that an award of damages would not be an adequate remedy.

An injunction would not be granted merely to prevent an employee working for another employer during their notice period if the other business was not in any way a competitor.

However, an employee may be injuncted from assisting in the profitability of a rival during their employment.

In *Provident Financial Group* v. *Hayward* [1989] ICR 160 Mr Hayward was the financial director of an estate agency who left in breach of his notice provisions to go to work for a supermarket.

His former employer (the claimant) did not succeed in its attempt to obtain an injunction as the Court held that even though it was a term of his contract that Mr Hayward would not work for any other business during his garden leave, there was no reasonable prospect of serious damage to the claimant. The two employers operated entirely different businesses. Mr Hayward in any event had not taken part in selling houses for Provident and had no relevant confidential knowledge which could be of use to the other company.

The Court held that:

> [the] practice of long periods of 'garden leave' is capable of abuse. It is a weapon in the hands of employers to ensure that an ambitious and able executive will not give notice if he is going to be unable to work at all for anyone for a long period of notice.

A garden leave clause would not be enforced if the court considered that the other business for which the employee intended to work was not in any way competing with the former employer.

14.5 Types of clauses

There are a variety of clauses under the heading of 'restrictive covenants' which apply post-termination:

(a) non-compete clauses;
(b) non-solicitation and non-dealing clauses;
(c) non-poaching clauses;
(d) area covenants regarding non-competition;
(e) confidentiality clauses;
(f) 'whistleblowing' clauses;
(g) non-enticement of suppliers.

Those that will apply during employment are:

(a) prohibition on external business interests;
(b) prohibition on working for another employer or for themselves in any business which competes directly or indirectly;
(c) confidentiality, including not divulging the personal details of directors or officers or senior managers of the business;
(d) declaration of all outside business interests, directorships, etc.

14.6 Implied terms

Without even the inclusion of specific provisions, terms of 'fidelity' or 'good faith' are implied into the contract as obligations on employees, i.e. that the law gives away for free. These obligations include not acting dishonestly; not stealing confidential information; not working in competition with the employer whilst employed; not acting for their own benefit or for the benefit of any other third party without the informed consent of the employer; not taking secret profits or commissions (see *Attorney-General v. Blake* [1998] 1 All ER 833, CA).

However, save for the implied duty not to misuse or disclose trade secrets after the termination of employment, all other implied terms end upon termination of employment (*Faccenda Chicken Co. Ltd* v. *Fowler* [1986] IRLR 69).

In *Attorney-General* v. *Blake* (above), Lord Woolf, the then Master of the Rolls, stressed the importance of express restrictions required to apply after the employment has ended (p.842):

> The most important of these [implied terms] is the relationship of trust and confidence, which arises whenever one party undertakes to act in the interests of another or places himself in a position where he is obliged to act in the interests of another. The relationship between employer and employee is of this character. The core obligation of a fiduciary of this kind is the obligation of loyalty. The employer is entitled to the single-minded loyalty of his employee. The employee must act in good faith; he must not make a profit out of his trust; he must not place himself in a position where his duty and his interest may conflict; he may not act for his own benefit or the benefit of a third party without the informed consent of his employer.
>
> But these duties last only as long as the relationship which gives rise to them lasts. A former employee owes no duty of loyalty to his former employer. It is trite law that an employer who wishes to prevent his employee from damaging his legitimate commercial interests after he has left his employment must obtain contractual undertakings from his employee to this effect. He cannot achieve his object by invoking the fiduciary relationship which formerly subsisted between them. Absent a valid and enforceable contractual restraint, a former employee is free to set up in a competing business in close proximity to his former employer and deal with his former clients.

14.7 Preamble

It has been recognised that seeking to protect the legitimate business interests by way of a confidentiality restriction alone may not work because, as Lord Denning said in *Littlewoods Organisation Ltd* v. *Harris* [1978] 1 All ER 1026 (p.1033):

> experience has shown that it is not satisfactory to have simply a covenant against disclosing confidential information. The reason is because it is so difficult to draw the line between information which is confidential and information which is not; and it is very difficult to prove a breach when the information is of such a character that a servant can carry it away in his head. The difficulties are such that the only practicable solution is to take a covenant from the servant by which he is not to go to work for a rival in trade.

However, if the non-compete clause is drafted too widely, the courts will not re-draft it. If it is, on its face, unreasonable, it is likely to be declared void. In *Hinton & Higgs (UK) Ltd* v. *Murphy and Valentine* [1989] IRLR 519, the Court of Session reiterated the legal position that where there is a restrictive covenant in restraint of trade, the courts will not redraft it so as to make it reasonable. Lord Dervaird therefore suggested that employers (or their legal advisers) may attempt to get around this principle by drafting the restrictive covenant in the following terms (p.520):

The restrictions contained in clause [X] are considered reasonable by the parties, but in the event that any such restriction shall be found to be void would be valid if some part thereof were deleted or the period of application reduced such restrictions shall apply with such modifications as may be necessary to make them valid or effective.

So far as the first part of such clause is concerned, the court felt that this was probably 'an illegitimate attempt to oust the jurisdiction of the court'. So far as the second part was concerned, it contemplates that the parties will abide by the result which may be effected by the deletion of some unreasonable part of the contract, rendering the contract as a whole reasonable.

> Here, however, as it seems to me that the parties have agreed in advance that they will accept as continuing to bind them such parts of the arrangements which they have made as the Court finds by deletion only to be alterations which permit the restriction to be regarded as reasonable. On my part I do not see why the Court should refuse to perform that role ... of selecting that version of [the contract] which the parties have *inter alia* made with each other and enabling the bargain as so modified to stand. (p.520)

But would such a clause make all the restraint provisions void for uncertainty? Since the terms of the contract must be unambiguous and certain, reserving the right, at a later date, in effect to redraft the clauses in order to make them valid and enforceable may mean that a court could strike them all out as void for uncertainty.

14.8 Confidentiality clauses

In the UK, a duty of confidence is automatically implied as between an employer and its employees, even if the contract of employment is silent on this point.

There are three categories of confidential information and where there is no express confidentiality clause relating to post-termination, only the third category of confidential information can be protected from misuse or disclosure after the employee has left employment. The three categories of confidential information were held by the High Court in *Faccenda Chicken* v. *Fowler* [1984] IRLR 61 to be the following:

1. Information which is already in the public domain, because of its trivial character or its easy accessibility from public sources of information.
2. Information which an employee must treat as confidential (either because they are expressly told it is confidential, or because from its character it obviously is so) but which once learned necessarily remains in their mind and becomes part of their own skill and knowledge applied in the course of their employer's business. So long as the employment continues, they cannot otherwise use or disclose such information but when they are no longer in the same service, the law allows them to use their full skill and knowledge for their own benefit in competition with their former employer. If an employer wants to protect information of this kind, it can do so by an express clause in the contract restraining the employee from using or disclosing trade secrets during and after the end of the

employment and restraining them from competing with the employer (within reasonable limits of time and space) after the termination of the employment.
3. There are specific trade secrets so confidential that, even though they may necessarily have been learned by heart and even though the employee may have left employment, they cannot lawfully be used for anyone's benefit but the former employer's.

In *Faccenda Chicken*, the information was regarded as falling into the second category (e.g. information about the whereabouts and requirements of the former employer's customers, the prices they were paying and the routes by which they were conveniently visited).

The types of information typically deemed 'confidential' are financial, technical and commercially valuable information; business methods, prices, marketing plans, manpower and development plans; customer lists or details; computer systems and software, data, etc; specifications and drawings and information of a personal nature concerning senior managers, directors or officers of the company; pre-negotiation matters and minutes of any such discussions or meetings; discussions and notes of meetings concerning the possible sale or purchase of a business, etc.

Faccenda Chicken and other cases have confirmed that there is no implied contractual term which precludes an ex-employee from disclosing confidential information which is within their knowledge, after the employment has ended. This may relate to a former employer's solvency and its ability to carry on business, or may be the disclosure of why the employee resigned. In *Brooks* v. *Olyslager OMS (UK) Ltd* [1998] IRLR 590, the Court of Appeal confirmed that there is no implied contractual term which precluded Mr Brooks from disclosing, after his employment had ended, information relating to his former employer's solvency and its ability to carry on business and the reason for his resignation. Such information, the court held, could not be regarded as a 'trade secret' or as so confidential as to attract the protection of an implied term.

Lawyers should therefore advise their employer clients that if they wish to extend obligations of confidentiality post-employment in order to prevent former employees from disclosing detrimental information, they should do so by means of an express contractual term. See **Precedent 14A.**

14.9   What is a 'trade secret'?

A trade secret is now defined in the EU Directive 2016/943 'on the protection of undisclosed know-how and business information (trade secrets) against their unlawful acquisition, use and disclosure'.

It has to be implemented by all member states by the end of 2018. Following Brexit it will remain to be seen if the UK government adopts this Directive into UK legislation.

However, as the Directive will most likely be welcomed by the UK business community, and in many respects codifies existing English common law, it is hoped that the Directive will be adopted and implemented.

Trade secrets are the 'golden nuggets' of the employer and are protectable interests where they are properly drafted.

The Directive covers unlawful acquisition, use and disclosure of trade secrets. An EU-wide definition of 'Trade Secrets' is included in Article 2 of the Directive as follows:

> 'Trade Secret' means information which meets all of the following requirements:
>
> a) it is secret in the sense that it is not, as a body or in the precise configuration and assembly of its components, generally known among or readily accessible to persons within the circles that normally deal with the kind of information in question;
> b) it has commercial value because it is secret;
> c) it has been subject to reasonable steps under the circumstances, by the person lawfully in control of the information, to keep it secret.

'Reasonable steps' to keep matters secret

This is beautifully set out by DLA Piper on its website: **www.dlapiper.com/en/uk/insights/publications/2016/07/the-trade-secrets-directive**.

Common law

At common law a 'trade secret' ('golden nugget') is any 'confidential information which might cause real or significant damage to the interests of the company if disclosed to a competitor'. In determining whether information is a trade secret, the courts will consider (*Faccenda Chicken* v. *Fowler* [1986] IRLR 69 (p.70)):

(a) The nature of the employment. Thus employment in a capacity where 'confidential' material is habitually handled may impose a high obligation of confidentiality because the employee can be expected to realise its sensitive nature to a greater extent than if they were employed in a capacity where such material reaches them only occasionally or incidentally.

(b) The nature of the information itself. Information will only be protected if it can properly be classed as a trade secret or as material which, while not properly to be described as a trade secret, is in all the circumstances of such a highly confidential nature as to require the same protection as a trade secret *eo nomine*. Therefore, the court could not accept the suggestion by the judge below that an employer can protect, by means of a restrictive covenant, the use of confidential information which has become part of the employee's own skill and knowledge, even though it does not include either a trade secret or its equivalent. Restrictive covenant cases demonstrate that a covenant will not be upheld on the basis of the status of the information which might be disclosed by the former employee if they are not restricted, unless it can be regarded as a trade secret or the equivalent of a trade secret. It is impossible to provide a list of matters which will qualify as trade secrets or their equivalent.

Secret processes of manufacture provide obvious examples, but innumerable other pieces of information are capable of being trade secrets, though the secrecy of some information may be only short-lived. In addition, the fact that the circulation of certain information is restricted to a limited number of individuals may throw light on the status of the information and its degree of confidentiality.

(c) Whether the employer impressed on the employee the confidentiality of the information. Thus, though an employer cannot prevent the use or disclosure merely by telling the employee that certain information is confidential, the attitude of the employer towards the information provides evidence which may assist in determining whether or not the information can properly be regarded as a trade secret.

(d) Whether the relevant information can be easily isolated from other information which the employee is free to use or disclose. The separability of the information in question is not conclusive, but the fact that the alleged 'confidential' information is part of a package and that the remainder of the package is not confidential is likely to throw light on whether the information in question is really a trade secret.

Other definitions have been given by the courts. For example, in *Lansing Linde v. Kerr* [1991] IRLR 80, trade secrets were described as (p.81):

> information used in a trade or business which, if disclosed to a competitor, would be liable to cause real or significant damage to the owner of the secret. In addition, the owner must limit the dissemination of it or at least not encourage or permit widespread publication. Trade secrets can thus include not only secret formulae for the manufacture of products but also the names of customers and the goods they buy.

In the age of multinational businesses and worldwide business interests, information may be held by very senior executives which, in the hands of competitors, might cause considerable harm to the companies employing them. 'Trade secrets' has to be interpreted in the wider context of highly confidential information of a non-technical or non-scientific nature, which may come within the ambit of information the employer is entitled to have protected, albeit for a limited period.

What is clear is that taking files and lists or cards of the names of customers, clients, authors, suppliers, etc. is a breach of the implied duty of fidelity. In *Roger Bullivant Ltd v. Ellis* [1987] IRLR 491, the Court of Appeal held (p.491):

> an employee's duty of fidelity will be broken if he makes or copies a list of the employer's customers for use after his employment ends or deliberately memorises such a list, even though there is no general restriction on an ex-employee canvassing or doing business with customers of his former employer ... The principle is one of no more than fair and honourable dealing.

14.10 Misusing company facilities

Employers have the right to prohibit employees from using for their personal or private use the Company photocopying facilities, stationery, fax, telephones, etc. if they wish to do so. They may also have rules prohibiting personal correspondence coming to the office and the opening of all correspondence that is addressed to the office.

Precedent 14J is a typical clause in a staff handbook.

14.11 Not to bring materials into or take them out of work

Some employers have strict rules prohibiting tools and equipment or materials being brought on site. This is usually for health and safety reasons: for example, the equipment may breach the standards of safety adopted on site; or the materials may be hazardous to health and may be banned on site. Similarly, there may be strict rules about employees not being permitted to take any company property off the site. This may be for security reasons or health and safety reasons, or both. See **Precedent 14K**.

14.12 Non-compete clauses

The rationale for non-compete clauses is that confidentiality clauses would not go far enough to protect the employer's business interests. Making preparations to compete during employment to set up a business after an employee has left is not a breach of contract nor a dismissible offence (*Laughton and Hawley* v. *Bapp Industrial Supplies Ltd* [1986] IRLR 245). In this case, Mr Hawley and Mr Laughton knew details of the company's suppliers, customers and pricing. They wrote to 10 suppliers stating that they intended starting to trade in nuts and bolts the following January and asking for product lists, price lists and terms. A copy of that letter came into the hands of the respondent's managing director. Mr Hawley and Mr Laughton admitted that they had written the letter and that they intended to start up a nuts and bolts business. The managing director decided to dismiss them summarily. This was held to be an unfair dismissal by the EAT (p.245):

> An employee does not breach the duty of loyalty merely by indicating his intention to set up in competition with his employer in the future. Whilst it is entirely understandable that an employer should be suspicious of an employee in such circumstances, unless the employer has reasonable grounds for believing that the employee has done or is about to do some wrongful act, he is not justified in dismissing him.

It is doubtful whether this would amount to a breach of fiduciary duty of a director: see *Balston Ltd* v. *Headline Fitters Ltd* [1993] FSR 385. If setting up a rival business or going to work for a competitor is to be prohibited it must be reasonable.

14.13 Area covenants

These clauses are popular for sales and marketing staff who often have 'territories' where they gain detailed knowledge of and build up good relationships with the firm's customers. The extent of the area must be 'reasonable'. In other words, it cannot purport to stop an ex-employee working in an area of the UK or in another country where the former employer had no business interests.

In *Thomas v. Farr plc* [2007] EWCA Civ 118 the Court of Appeal upheld the area covenants in the contract of a managing director of an insurance broker. Here the contract was drafted very well (paras.11–16):

    3.1   At any time during the Restriction Period:

          3.1.1 (Except as the holder, by way of bona fide investment only, of shares or securities listed dealt in or traded on a recognised stock exchange not exceeding 3% in nominal value of the securities of that class) be engaged or concerned or interested or participate in any business which is the same as or in competition with the business or relevant part thereof anywhere in any Restricted Territory provided always that this paragraph shall not restrain the Executive from being engaged or concerned in any business concern in so far as the Executive's duties or work shall relate solely to:
                (a) geographical areas where the business concern is not in competition with the Business; or
                (b) services or activities with which the Executive was not concerned to a material extent during the 12 months prior to the Termination Date (or, if earlier, the start of any Garden Leave Period).

The 'Restriction Period' was 12 months from the date of termination of the agreement.

The 'Restricted Territory' meant:

> any geographic area in which any company in the Group conducts the Business or part thereof and for which the Executive was responsible or to which he rendered services in the 12 months preceding the Termination Date.

'The Business' meant:

> The business of providing the Specified Services or any part thereof carried on by the Company as at the termination date and during the 12 months prior thereto ... and any other business carried on by the company or any company in the group at the Termination Date to which the Executive has rendered Material Services or about which he has acquired Confidential Information or by which he has been engaged at anytime during the period of 12 months prior to the Termination Date.

'Material services' meant services to which he had devoted a substantial proportion of time in developing and promoting insurance products.

'The specified services' were defined as including property and buildings insurance and risk management and training.

See **Precedent 14M**.

14.14 Scope of clause

A non-compete clause must be specific in its scope and must not be too wide.

In *Bartholomews Agri Food v. Thornton* [2016] EWHC 648 (QB) the High Court resoundingly rejected the reasonableness of a restrictive covenant in an employment contract on various grounds.

The clause in the contract read:

> Employees shall not, for a period of six months immediately following the termination of their employment be engaged on work, supplying goods or services of a similar nature which compete with the Company to the Company's customers, with a trade competitor within the Company's trading area, (which is West and East Sussex, Kent, Hampshire, Wiltshire and Dorset) or on their own account without prior approval from the Company. In this unlikely event, the employee's full benefits will be paid during this period.

The High Court held that:

> It is to be observed at the outset that these provisions have not been well drafted. There are no definitions and, on one reading, the covenant prevents the Respondent from being able to work in the six specified counties at all, albeit that Bartholemews does not interpret the clause in that way. What then is meant by the words 'of a similar nature?'

14.15 Injunctions/damages against third parties

Employers may be very keen to recruit a senior or skilled individual from a rival. However, great care should be taken when recruiting, particularly from a competitor. The recruiting employer should be 'on notice' that it is likely that certain restrictions on employment may apply once that individual has left their current employment. The recruiting employer should at the very least ask the job candidate for a copy of the former/current employer's contract to ensure that there are no restrictive covenants which could prevent the individual from coming to work for the new employer.

Employers would be wise to require a warranty from their newly acquired employees that by taking this employment, they are not breaching any former/current employment restrictions.

The former/current employer may choose to join the new employer as a third party if there is any evidence that the new employer has induced a breach of contract or aided and abetted a breach of contract. If the new employer has had knowledge of the restrictive covenants but nonetheless has offered employment to the employee, then there is a good chance of successfully obtaining an injunction and/or suing the new employer for damages.

It will be important for a lawyer acting for the employer seeking to restrain the individual from working in competition, to write to the recruiting employer in advance of issuing proceedings with relevant terms and asking it to 'de-recruit' the employee.

Injunctive relief in cases where the contract is for the provision of personal services is highly unlikely (see *Warren v. Mendy* [1989] IRLR 210 where an injunction was refused when the boxer Nigel Benn sought to breach his existing management contract with Mr Warren and move to Mr Mendy as his manager).

It is unlikely (but not impossible) that an injunction will be granted against either the employee or the recruiting employer where damages would be an appropriate remedy. However, an injunction may be granted against the employee in order to require them to serve out a 'reasonable' garden leave clause (see *Provident Financial Group and Whitegates Estate Agency Ltd* v. *Hayward* [1989] IRLR 84).

The High Court considered non-solicitation clauses where a former client initiated contact with the ex-employee (*Baldwins (Ashby) Ltd* v. *Andrew Maidstone* [2011] EWHC B12 (Mercantile)).

Mr Maidstone accepted that a few of his former clients had followed him to Charnwoods but denied that he 'canvassed, solicited or enticed' them away.

The Court distinguished the clause in question from a 'non-dealing' clause, which is easier to police. The lack of a non-dealing clause meant that Mr Maidstone was able to undertake work for his previous clients if, in competition with Baldwins, the clients solicited him to do so without his canvassing, soliciting or enticing them. In this case the onus was on Baldwins to prove that Mr Maidstone's approach involved some 'direct and targeted' behaviour.

The Court held that Mr Maidstone had entered into a secret agreement with Charnwoods to poach back clients he had sold to Baldwins for substantial reward by way of commission payments from Charnwoods.

Telling clients they are leaving and where they are going

The Court held that Mr Maidstone's act of telling a client he was leaving and, when asked, explaining he was moving to Charnwoods, was not a breach of the non-solicitation clause.

However, when the client said he wanted to move his business to Charnwoods and Mr Maidstone actively encouraged the client to do so and informed Charnwoods of this fact, he acted in breach of the restrictive covenant. In addition, a conversation with a client during a chance meeting was found *probably* to amount to a breach, while following up this chance meeting with a formal client meeting was a *clear* breach of the non-solicitation clause.

It is always desirable to draft a non-dealing covenant as well as a non-solicitation clause in employment contracts as well as in sale agreements for businesses.

14.16 Non-solicitation/non-dealing

Non-solicitation of customers, etc

Non-solicitation clauses prevent individuals, during garden leave or after they have left their employment, from actively contacting clients, customers, brokers, contacts, suppliers, etc. with whom they have built up a good working relationship.

As long as the period of restraint is reasonable, i.e. not longer than is necessary, and the restriction applies solely to those individuals or firms with whom the employee has personally dealt over a reasonable period of time before leaving (say 12 months) excluding any clients, customers, etc. introduced by that employee upon joining, then such clauses should be enforceable.

The rationale for such a clause is that it gives the employer the opportunity to allow another member of staff to build relationships with such customers, suppliers, etc. without ex-employees using their contacts and knowledge of the customers for the advantage of their new employers or themselves.

Non-dealing

Non-dealing clauses cover the passive form of solicitation, where the customer or client learns that the employee has left the company and actively pursues that individual, contacting them in order to do business. The courts have enforced such clauses even though they affect innocent third parties who, it might be argued, should be free to do business with whomsoever they wish.

PSM International plc v. *Whitehouse and Willenhall Automation Ltd* [1992] IRLR 279 appears to be the first reported restrictive covenant case in which the Court of Appeal has approved an injunction against an ex-employee to restrain them from fulfilling a commercial contract already made with a third party, as opposed to entering into a future contract. Lloyd LJ said:

> I agree that the courts should be chary of granting an equitable remedy which would have the effect of interfering with the contractual rights of innocent third parties. But that equity has power to do so in an appropriate case, I do not doubt.

The Court of Appeal held that although the courts were wary of granting injunctions in these circumstances, they clearly had the power to do so where appropriate, e.g. where an ex-employee entered into a contract of employment with a new employer in breach of a valid restraint of trade clause. The courts had the power to interfere by way of injunction even though the new employer may be totally innocent. Here, damages were not an appropriate remedy as the ex-employee 'could not pay 15 per cent of the proceeds of the contract into court at present. The plaintiff had not suffered all the loss they were going to as there was nothing to say that [the third party] would not continue to use the [ex-employee] in the future'.

14.17 Non-poaching

Employers may be reluctant to allow key members of staff to be poached by another key employee after that person has left. A 'non-poaching' clause has limited effect. It can only apply to the poaching of 'senior' staff (*Hanover Insurance Brokers Ltd* v. *Shapiro* [1994] IRLR 82). Here, the Court of Appeal held that staff were 'not an asset of the company [such as] apples and pears or other stock in trade'.

Other cases since *Hanover* have confirmed that it is legitimate for an employer to seek 'to maintain a stable workforce'. However, the cases where this principle seems to have been endorsed are where brokers or dealers are involved and the clause relates only to senior or key personnel (*Dawnay, Day & Co Ltd* v. *De Brachonier D'Alphen* [1997] IRLR 285).

New employers need to be aware

Any new employer recruiting staff who appear to be following another employee who has recently joined from the same firm, needs to take care.

A careful examination of all these employees' previous contracts should be a first step – to ensure that there is no non-poaching clause.

The next step employers can take to keep track of potential breaches is to monitor closely firewalls, proxy and other network logs to identify unusual patterns of activity. Then the employer should identify which employees are most at risk of moving on and can focus efforts to prevent data breaches. Efforts can then be made to try to keep them on board.

If the new employee comes forward and says that it is entirely coincidental that their former colleague has applied for a role, then an employer should not take this at face value. This should include a statement from the new employee confirming that they have not in any way breached their post-termination restriction.

14.18 Breach of contract: accounting for profits

They may be exceptional cases but there will be occasions where the ex-employee may be required to repay to the employer the profits received from their breach of contract, notwithstanding that the employer has suffered no loss as a result of the breach of contract (*Attorney-General* v. *Blake* [2001] IRLR 36, HL and *Attorney-General* v. *Blake* [1998] 1 All ER 833, CA). The action will be for an account of profits.

Lord Nicholls' leading decision highlights that an account of profits will be appropriate only in 'exceptional circumstances', where the normal remedies for breach of contract are not adequate compensation for a breach of contract.

In *Blake*, the Attorney-General was held to be entitled to be paid a sum equivalent to Mr Blake's profits from his autobiography which he wrote and published in breach of a contractual undertaking that he would not divulge in book form any official information which he gained as a result of his employment in the Secret Intelligence Service. Until this case, an account of profits had only been available as a remedy in the special case where there is a breach of an equitable duty of confidence or a fiduciary duty.

14.19 Outside employment: 'whole time and attention' clauses

It is common to see an express clause either forbidding any external business interests which compete directly or indirectly with the employer's business or a requirement to report any external business interests or activities (*Hivac* v. *Park Royal Scientific Instruments* Ltd [1946] Ch 169, CA).

Employers cannot, however, prevent employees from doing things in their spare time which do not compete with their employer (*Nova Plastics Ltd* v. *Froggatt* [1982] IRLR 146).

However, there is a fine line between competing activities and employees using their special skills for others in their spare time (see *Nottingham University* v. *Fishel* [2000] IRLR 471 and *Neary* v. *Dean of Westminster* [1999] IRLR 288). In the former case, Elias J held that there was no implied term that an employee had to report outside non-competing business interests and that if the employer required such disclosure there had to be an express clause.

14.20 Representing the employer

If employees are on garden leave, the employer will usually request that they do no further work and refrain from representing themselves as working for or acting on behalf of the employer during this time.

14.21 Return of company property

It may be prudent to require the return of all company property including credit cards, keys, passes, USB flash drives, software and hardware, company cars and mobile telephones, laptops and palmtops, before the termination date and to make any severance payment dependent upon the safe return of all company property.

A typical clause is set out at **Precedent 14S**.

14.22 Whistleblowing duty to report misconduct of self as well as others

Apart from a separate policy dealing with 'whistleblowing', there are certain industries where employees are required to report the misconduct of others. Where the employees 'turn a blind eye' they could be seen as conniving in breaches of regulatory rules or aiding and abetting or being an accessory before or after the fact in a criminal offence.

Such a requirement has to be spelt out in the contract 'in bold and in capital letters' (*Ladbroke Racing Ltd* v. *King*, EAT 202/88).

Precedent 14T is a typical clause that this author has drafted into the contracts for employees in the pharmaceutical and medical research industries and the financial services industry.

Precedent 14V contains a complete set of restrictive covenants.

14.23 Inventions and patents

The law is quite straightforward in respect of employees who invent or design things in the course of their employment. As a result of the Patents Act 1977, it is essential to state expressly in the contract what an employee is required to do in order to allow the employer to hold the patent or retain the copyright in the material.

Typical clauses are set out in **Precedent 14U**.

A complete set of restrictive covenants can be found in **Precedent 14V**.

PRECEDENT 14A: Clause relating to confidential information

'Confidential Information' means all information including all financial, technical or commercially valuable information (including, but not limited to, information relating to business methods, prices, marketing, development and manpower plans, customer lists or details, equipment, materials, computer systems and software, data, processes, specifications, drawings and other documents and items) and information about personal matters or information which the Company claims is confidential or is by its nature confidential including information about any of its associated companies or any of its suppliers, agents, distributors or customers, and whether owned by the Company or by a third party, but does not include information that can be proved to be lawfully known by you prior to disclosure or in the public domain otherwise than as a result of breach of confidence or breach by you of your obligations.

PRECEDENT 14B: Confidentiality clause (senior executive)

1. The Executive warrants and represents that the Executive will be free to assign Inventions (where such Inventions constitute Company Inventions), Confidential Business Information and other intellectual property rights conceived, originated or made by the Executive during the course of this appointment to the Company pursuant hereto without any third party claims, liens, charges or encumbrances of any kind and that the Executive is free of any duties or obligations to third parties which may conflict with the terms of this Agreement.

2. The Executive shall not either during his appointment or at any time after its termination:

(a) disclose to any person or persons (except to those authorised by the Company to know or as otherwise required by law);
(b) copy or reproduce in any form or by any media or allow others access to or to copy or reproduce;
(c) use for his own purposes or for any purposes other than those of the Company;
(d) through any failure to exercise all due care and diligence cause any unauthorised disclosure of;

any Confidential Business Information which he has obtained by virtue of his appointment.

3. The obligations of confidence referred to in this clause shall not apply to any Confidential Business Information or other information which:

(a) is in the possession of and is at the free disposal of the Executive or is published or is otherwise in the public domain prior to the receipt of such Confidential Business Information or other information by the Executive;
(b) is or becomes publicly available on a non-confidential basis through no fault of the Executive;
(c) is received in good faith by the Executive from a third party who, on reasonable

enquiry by the Executive claims to have no obligations of confidence to the Company in respect of it and who imposes no obligations of confidence upon the Executive.

4. The provisions of this clause shall apply *mutatis mutandis* in relation to the Confidential Business Information of each Associated Company which the Executive may have received or obtained during his appointment and the Executive shall upon request enter into an enforceable agreement with any such Company to the like effect.

5. All notes, memoranda, records and writing made by the Executive relating to the business of the Company or any Associated Company shall be and remain the property of the Company or Associated Company to whose business they relate and shall be delivered by the Executive to the Company to which they belong forthwith upon request.

6. The Executive undertakes to do such things and sign such documents as shall be reasonably necessary to give effect to the provisions of this clause.

7. The Executive agrees that the restrictions set out above in this clause are in addition to and shall not affect all other express and implied duties of confidentiality owed by the Executive to the Company, its subsidiaries or any Associated Company and shall survive the termination or expiry (howsoever arising) of the appointment.

8. The obligations of the parties under this clause shall survive the expiry or the termination of this Agreement for whatever reason.

PRECEDENT 14C: Confidentiality clause (software)

1. In order to safeguard the legitimate interests of the Company, it is necessary to regard certain information as confidential and as trade secrets of the Company. The Company considers the following categories of information as examples of confidential and valuable trade secrets of the Company: Company databases, customer lists, business strategy, sales strategy, sales agreements, agency agreements, suppliers agreements, technical 'know-how' and investigations not within the public domain, employee records and financial records.

2. This list is intended as a guide and is not exhaustive.

3. You may not, either before or after the termination of your employment with the Company, use for your own benefit or for the benefit of any other person, firm or company or disclose any trade secrets or confidential information belonging to or relating to the business of the Company (including, but not limited to, the information referred to above) which may come to your knowledge during your employment. All notes, memoranda, or other information whatsoever relating to the business of the Company shall be and shall remain the property of the Company and shall (together with any copies) be returned to the Company on demand and in any event when you leave the service of the Company.

PRECEDENT 14D: Confidentiality agreement for temporary staff

[*name of employee*]
[*address*]
[*date*]

1. You hereby accept temporary work with [*name of company*] on the following conditions which you agree to observe both in the letter and the spirit.

2. The nature of the work that you will be asked to do as well as the information contained in our databases, document management system, etc. is highly confidential.

3. In addition, all information and documents pertaining to the matters upon which you will work are the physical and intellectual property of the Company. By signing this undertaking, you agree that at no time will you disclose any confidential information to anyone either within or outside the Company other than those authorised to have this information, whether during your term of engagement or after it has ended. You will be expected to use discretion, diplomacy and exercise sound judgement due to the nature of the work that we are asking you to undertake.

4. For the avoidance of doubt you are strictly forbidden to refer to the fact of what you will be working on or any of the details relating thereto.

We thank you for your co-operation.

I, [*name*], give my solemn undertaking that I will abide by the terms of this letter at all times even after my temporary engagement has ended.

Signed .... Date ....

[*employee*]

PRECEDENT 14E: Confidentiality clause (occupational health)

1. The Occupational Health Practitioner is employed as an impartial adviser governed at all times by his/her professional codes of ethics. The Occupational Health Practitioner fully recognises his/her duty to act in good faith and to serve the Company faithfully and loyally. He/she will however preserve his/her duty of confidentiality to any employee of the Company who may seek help or guidance.

2. The Company recognises this duty to keep confidential all information obtained in these circumstances. The Occupational Health Practitioner will only disclose such confidential information to the extent that he/she deems necessary for that particular purpose. Such disclosure will only be made following the informed consent of the employee or where such disclosure is deemed paramount by the Occupational Health Practitioner in the interests of the employee's immediate or long-term health or safety or of that of others employed in the Company.

3. No undue or unfair pressure will be exerted on any member of the Occupational Health service, by any member of management, in-house or outside solicitors or Company Insurers, for disclosure of an individual's medical details, reports, etc., whether pre-employment or during employment.

4. Access to clinical data, whether manual or computerised records, will be restricted to the Occupational Health personnel. This includes details of pre-employment medical questionnaires.

5. Where disclosure is made in the circumstances outlined above, it will be given only to a senior member of management with a direct concern for that individual and will be given on the understanding that the strictest secrecy and discretion will be observed by that senior member of management.

PRECEDENT 14F: Confidentiality agreement for non-medical staff

[name of employee]
[address]
[date]

1. During the course of your employment you may have access to, gain knowledge of or be entrusted with medical and/or personnel information concerning individual members of staff. This information may include matters of a highly sensitive and/or personal nature.

2. You should understand that access to these data, including computerised or manual records, is made available only to those members of staff who have an absolute right and need to know, that is professionally qualified medical and nursing personnel. As a direct consequence of carrying out your duties, you may at some time have or gain access to an individual's medical records or other confidential information.

3. By your signature below, you agree that you will not at any time, whether during or after your employment with the Company, disclose to any person or make use of such confidential information.

4. This duty includes keeping strictly confidential the names and other details relating to individuals making and keeping appointments within the Department.

I understand my duty of confidentiality in connection with my work in the occupational health department and agree not at any time to disclose to any person or otherwise make use of such confidential information as described above.

Signed .... Date ....

[employee]

PRECEDENT 14G: Confidentiality agreement for reception staff

[name of employee]
[address]
[date]

RE: Duty of confidentiality

1. During the course of your employment you may have access to, gain knowledge of or be entrusted with confidential information concerning individual members of staff, clients or potential clients or matters relating to the Firm's business or the business or personal details of one or more of the Partners. This information may include matters of a highly sensitive and/or personal nature.

2. You should understand that you have access to this information in the course of and because of your employment as a receptionist of the Firm.

3. Informing anyone either within or outside the Firm of any matters relating to the Firm's business (e.g. who has come into reception, who has made an appointment to see a matrimonial partner, etc.) would be regarded as a serious breach of confidentiality and as such could lead to your summary dismissal.

4. By your signing below, you agree that you will not at any time, whether during or after your employment with the Firm, disclose to any unauthorised person within or outside the Firm, or make use of such confidential information.

5. This duty includes keeping strictly confidential the names and other details relating to individuals making and keeping appointments, etc.

I understand my duty of confidentiality in connection with my work as a receptionist within the Firm and agree not at any time to disclose to any person not authorised to be informed or otherwise make use of such confidential information as described above.

Signed .... Date ....

[*employee*]

PRECEDENT 14H: Contact with, participation in or disclosure to the media

1. Prohibition on contact with media

1.1 All staff are reminded that any contact with the press or media in relation to any business of the Company or of any of its associated companies, parent company or its clients, current, past or prospective or its employees, current, past or prospective, is strictly forbidden.

1.2 If any member of staff is contacted by any member of the press or media, then this matter should be referred immediately to the Marketing Department and nothing should be said by the employee on behalf of the Company unless they are specifically authorised in advance to do so by a Director and once the statement has been cleared by the Marketing Department.

1.3 This is particularly important where litigation is pending or is ongoing.

1.4 If any member of staff wishes to become involved in any matter which will be given any publicity, e.g. a television programme or an article in a newspaper or magazine, then it is important that the member of staff does so in their personal capacity only and does not refer to or identify the Company as their employer without having first obtained the prior written permission of a Director.

1.5 For the avoidance of doubt, it is a term of every employee's contract that they are not permitted to write or engage in any outside publication of any nature whatsoever, purporting to represent or identifying the Company.

1.6 This rule applies because in some cases, whilst the individual is expressing a personal opinion, it may not be one which the Company may share or it may cause embarrassment to the business or a Director if such views were to be expressed and purported to be or were implied to reflect those of the Company.

2. Personal contact, publication, etc.

2.1 It is sometimes the case that a member of staff may have contact with the press or media for reasons totally unconnected with work.

2.2 If a member of staff wishes to publish any letters, articles or otherwise (including but not limited to being mentioned or referred to in a newspaper or magazine article or television or radio programme) it is a requirement that the appropriate line manager and/or Head of Department is notified before publication or broadcast.

2.3 This is regarded by the Company as a matter of courtesy and is also because as an individual, your name may be widely known in our business and therefore you may be readily identifiable as being a Company employee.

3. **Terms of your contract**

These rules will form part of your terms and conditions of employment and you should read them very carefully to ensure that you understand them. They come into force immediately. Please ask a member of Human Resources if you have any queries whatsoever.

4. **Disciplinary matter**

Failure to comply with the above may, if the circumstances warrant it, be regarded as gross misconduct for which the employee's employment may be terminated without notice or payment in lieu.

PRECEDENT 14I: Conflict of interest clauses

1. During this Agreement the Executive shall not (except as a representative or nominee of the Company or any Associated Company or otherwise with the prior consent in writing of the Board) be directly or indirectly engaged concerned or interested in any other business which is wholly or partly in competition with the business carried on by the Company or any Associated Company or any of the foregoing by itself or themselves or in partnership, common ownership or as a joint venture with any third party or, as regards any goods or services, is a supplier to or customer of any such Company.

2. Subject to any regulations from time to time issued by the Company which may apply to him or her, the Executive shall not receive or obtain directly or indirectly any discount, rebate, commission or other inducement in respect of any sale or purchase of any goods or services effected or other business transacted (whether or not by him or her) by or on behalf of the Company or any Associated Company and if he or she (or any firm or Company in which he or she is directly or indirectly engaged, concerned or interested) shall obtain any such discount, rebate, commission or inducement, he or she shall immediately account to the Company for the amount received by him or her or the amount received by such firm or Company.

OR

1. If any matter arises which might involve a member of staff in a situation where there could be either actual or possible conflict of interest then it is the duty of the person concerned to report the matter to his or her manager.

2. Conflict of interest arises when a member of staff has a financial or other interest or engages in any activity (paid or unpaid) which would enable him or her to secure some personal advantage as a result of his or her other employment.

3. Examples of potential conflict of interest include involvement for profit or not and whether personal or via a close relative, with any property company, building company, finance company, estate agency or any other company whose work is connected with any activity of the Company or involvement with the activities of another company in the same or similar field of activity, whether paid or unpaid.

4. Any member of staff invited to become involved in the work of another organisation should discuss the matter with his or her manager before accepting any such invitation.

5. Activities carried on outside office hours must not involve any conflict of interest – any external activity carried on during office hours is a breach of contract.

6. Anyone in the slightest doubt about something which might be regarded as conflict of interest must discuss it with their own manager or the HR Director. Failure to do so could result in disciplinary action being taken.

OR

You hereby covenant that you will not during the continuance of your employment either alone or jointly with or on behalf of others, whether directly or indirectly, engage in, carry on or be interested in or concerned in any other business, trade or professional occupation whatsoever other than that for the time being carried on by the Company or on behalf of the Company without the prior consent in writing of the Company.

PRECEDENT 14J: Clause relating to misuse of company facilities

1. **Correspondence**

1.1 No private correspondence of any kind should be addressed to any member of staff at your place of work.

1.2 Your supervisor or Head of Department reserves the right to open all letters and packages delivered to their premises except where these have been addressed 'Private and Confidential' and the Director in charge of your department has been told in advance.

2. **Use of property belonging to the Company**

It is strictly forbidden for any member of staff to use any property belonging to the Company (e.g. photocopier, computers, stationery, etc.) for their own private use or for any use other than for the Company's legitimate business. Disciplinary action may be taken against anyone found doing so.

3. **Use of telephones for private calls**

3.1 It is not expected that members of staff will make telephone calls of a personal nature other than in an emergency whilst at work. Abuse of the telephone in this manner is a disciplinary matter.

3.2 Anyone wishing to make any private calls must obtain the prior permission of the Director and will be required to pay for the call(s).

4. **Personal visitors**

4.1 Staff are not allowed to receive personal visitors on the Company's premises during working hours other than in lunch breaks or at the beginning or end of the working day. Adequate arrangements must be made for children during the school holidays and at the end of the school day.

4.2 Should any member of staff find themselves with any domestic problems in this respect, they should speak to their supervisor and every effort will be made to find a satisfactory solution.

PRECEDENT 14K: Using own tools and equipment; and borrowing company property

1. It is strictly forbidden to bring on site or for use at work any item of equipment, tools or materials or substances of any kind. We use controlled substances identified on risk assessments and there are certain substances that we as a company do not use.

2. As far as electrical and other equipment and tools are concerned, all our equipment and tools have passed our strict safety standards. Not even a personal kettle will be

allowed to be brought on site or used at work or during the course of your employment, nor are you permitted to use your own tools, other than those provided by the Company as approved for use. (For example, we have discovered that a secretary had brought in a dining room chair from home to use at her PC because she found it 'more comfortable' than the one supplied by us. This is strictly forbidden.)

3. No one is allowed to purchase materials or goods of any kind other than through the approved company procedures and ordered by an authorised person. It may seem petty but even if you require additional nuts and bolts, you must order these through the normal company procedures. You may not go shopping for any items in any local shops as they may not meet our rigorous safety standards. There is a special procedure for emergency supplies.

4. Anyone found to be in breach of such rules will be regarded as breaching the health and safety rules of the Company and will be subject to serious disciplinary action.

5. For security reasons and for your own protection, you are not permitted to take out of the premises any property belonging to the Company whether it be to borrow it overnight or otherwise. Should you wish to borrow any company equipment or property you must obtain the prior written permission of a Director of the Company and obtain the appropriate pass. Any breach of this rule is regarded as gross misconduct.

PRECEDENT 14L: Non-compete clause

You agree that during your employment and for [six] months following its termination, [less any period during which you are not required to attend for work in accordance with [specify]], you will not (except with prior written consent of the Board) directly or indirectly do or attempt to do any of the following: for [12] months undertake, carry on or be employed, engaged or interested in any capacity in those competing companies currently known as [give details] in the relevant business with which, during the relevant period, you were directly or indirectly concerned.

(a) 'Relevant business' means a business of the Company or any associated company, in which pursuant to your duties you were materially involved at any time during the relevant period.
(b) 'Relevant period' means the period of 12 months ending on the last day of your employment.

OR

You hereby covenant with the Company that you will not in competition with the Company for a period of [six] months immediately following the termination of your employment, whether on your own behalf or on behalf of any other person, firm company or organisation and whether as employee, director, principal, agent, consultant or in any other capacity be directly or indirectly employed or engaged in or perform services for any business which competes (or which once operational will so compete) with such part or parts of the Company's business with which you are personally concerned to a material extent on behalf of the Company during the final year of your employment with the Company.

PRECEDENT 14M: Area covenant

You agree that during your employment and for the periods set out below after its termination, less any period during which you are not required to attend for work in accordance with [specify], you will not (except with prior written consent of the Board) directly or indirectly do or attempt to do the following:

(a) for [12] months undertake, carry on or be employed, engaged or interested in any capacity in either any business which is competitive with or similar to a Relevant Business within the Relevant Territory or any business an objective or anticipated result of which is to compete with a Relevant Business within the Relevant Territory;
(b) 'Relevant Territory' means England, Wales, Scotland and/or Northern Ireland and any other country or state in which the Company or Associated Company or a Relevant Business is operating or is actively planning to operate at the expiry of the Relevant Period. A business of the Company or Associated Company or a Relevant Business will be operating within the Relevant Territory at the expiry of the Relevant Period if a Relevant Business has been conducted or promoted during the Relevant Period. A business will be operating within the Relevant Territory if either such business in which you are to be involved is located or to be located within the Relevant Territory or it is conducted or to be conducted wholly or partly within the Relevant Territory.

PRECEDENT 14N: Clause warranting not in breach of former restrictive covenants

The Executive warrants that by virtue of entering into this Agreement (or the other agreements or arrangements made or to be made between the Company or any Associated Company and him) he will not be in breach of any express or implied terms of any contract with or of any other obligation to any third party binding upon him.

PRECEDENT 14O: Clause relating to notification of restriction

I agree that in the event of my receiving from any person, firm or corporation an offer of employment, whether oral or in writing and whether accepted or not, either during the continuance of my employment or during the continuance in force of all or any of the restrictions set out above, I shall forthwith:

(a) provide to the person making such an offer of employment a full and accurate copy of this contract of employment including details of any variations thereof and bearing the date of its execution by the parties; and
(b) inform the Board of the identity of the offeror.

PRECEDENT 14P: Non-solicitation/non-dealing clause

You hereby covenant with the Company that you will not in competition with the Company for a period of [six] months immediately following the termination of your employment, whether on your own behalf or on behalf of any other person, firm, company or organisation and whether as employee, director, principal, agent, consultant or in any other capacity:

(a) entice, solicit or induce (or attempt or assist in so doing) away from the Company to a business which competes (or which once operational will so compete) with those parts of the Company with which you were involved to a material extent during the final year of your employment with the Company, the custom or business of any person, firm or company who during the final year of your employment was a customer of the Company and with whom during such period you had material personal contact or dealings on behalf of the Company;
(b) accept or deal with the custom or business of any person, firm or company, who during the final year of your employment was a customer of the Company and

with whom during such period you had material personal contact or dealings on behalf of the Company and in relation to such part or parts of the Company's business with which you were concerned to a material extent during the final year of your employment of a materially similar kind to those provided to such customer by the Company during the final year of your employment.

PRECEDENT 14Q: Non-poaching clause

You hereby covenant with the Company that you will not in competition with the Company for a period of [six] months immediately following the termination of your employment, whether on your own behalf or on behalf of any other person, firm, company or organisation and whether as employee, director, principal, agent, consultant or in any other capacity approach any person who, during the final year of your employment, was:

(a) a senior employee of the Company and with whom during such period you had material personal contact or dealings in the performance of your duties on behalf of the Company; or
(b) an employee of the Company who reported to you as part of your team; or
(c) an employee of the Company with whom during such period you had any material personal contact or dealings in the performance of your duties on behalf of the Company who had material personal contact or dealings on behalf of the Company with customers of such part or parts of the Company's business as you were concerned to a material extent during the final year of employment

with a view to recruiting that person to a business venture which competes, or which will, once operational compete, with such part or parts of the Company's business with which you were concerned to a material extent during the final year of your employment with the Company.

PRECEDENT 14R: Whole time and attention clause

1. You will perform all acts, duties and obligations, and comply with such rules, instructions and other directions and policies and procedures, as may from time to time relate to your employment and be required or be made by the Company. During your employment you shall:

(a) unless prevented by ill health or other unavoidable cause devote the whole of your working time, attention and abilities to carrying out your duties hereunder and will work such hours as may reasonably be required for the proper performance of your duties;
(b) well and faithfully serve the Company and its subsidiary or associated companies (as appropriate) to the best of your ability and carry out your duties in a proper and efficient manner and use your utmost endeavours to promote and maintain the interests and reputation of the Company;
(c) provide such explanations, information and assistance as to your activities relating to the business of the Company as may from time to time be required from you by the Company;
(d) refrain from doing or permitting any matter which causes any regulatory authority in the UK or elsewhere to withdraw permission or in any way prevent the Company from employing or otherwise using your services and refrain from doing or permitting any matter which is contrary to the interests of the Company.

2. Your contract is with the Company, not with your individual unit. Therefore, the impact of your work performance in the Group must always take priority over the needs

of your individual unit. Continuation of your employment will depend upon your role modelling and championing of the values and behaviours of the Company of which you are fully aware.

3. During your employment with the Company, you must not, without the Company's agreement, be involved either directly or indirectly in any other business or undertaking or any other regular work. Should you wish to accept an outside appointment or take up employment outside this employment in your spare time, you must obtain the prior written consent of the Director in charge of your Department.

PRECEDENT 14S: Clause relating to return of company property

1. [Name] hereby undertakes to account for and return on or before the Termination Date to the Company all property (including but not limited to documents and disks, his mobile telephone, credit cards, equipment, keys and passes) belonging to it or any company within the Group which is or has been in his possession or under his control. Documents and disks shall include but not be limited to correspondence, files, emails, memos, reports, minutes, plans, records, surveys, software, diagrams, computer print-outs, floppy disks, USB flash drives, manuals, customer documentation or any other medium for storing information.

2. [Name]'s obligations under this clause shall be deemed to include the return of all copies, drafts, reproductions, notes, extracts or summaries (howsoever made) of the foregoing.

3. [Name] shall, if requested by the Company, confirm in writing his compliance with his obligations under this Clause.

PRECEDENT 14T: 'Whistleblowing' clause

1. Due to the nature of our business it is expected that you will act with due diligence and utmost honesty at all times. Should any matters of concern come to your attention, you must report them immediately to your supervising officer or Head of Department or a member of HR. The Company sees it as your duty to report any acts of misconduct, dishonesty, breach of company rules or breach of any of the rules of the relevant regulatory bodies committed, contemplated or discussed by any other member of staff or any other third party. Please note that any failure to do so on your part may be regarded as serious or gross misconduct depending on the circumstances.

2. The Company will guarantee that whatever you report will be treated with the utmost confidentiality as far as this is practicable. You are also assured that no discriminatory or retaliatory action will be taken against you in any case where you make such reports to management neither shall any adverse action of any kind be taken against you now or in the future.

3. The Company is a member of [the Association of British Pharmaceutical Industries] and you are therefore required as a condition of your employment to observe and comply carefully and diligently with all the Rules as laid down by [specify] from time to time. Since you act in an authorised capacity on behalf of the Company you must ensure that at all times you are fully complying with all the relevant Regulatory Body Rules. Failure to do so may result in legal action being taken against either the Company or you personally.

4. You are required to co-operate fully with all directions and reasonable requests properly made by or on behalf of the Company or [specify]. This may include but is not

limited to a requirement that you make yourself readily available for and truthfully answer all questions put to you in the course of any inspection, investigation, summary process or proceeding of any Appeal Tribunal.

5. Breach of the above undertakings will be a matter of serious misconduct which may entitle the Company in any case it deems fit to dismiss with or without notice or payment in lieu.

PRECEDENT 14U: Inventions and patents

1. The provisions of sections 39 to 42 of the Patents Act 1977 relating to the ownership of employee inventions and the compensation of employees for certain inventions respectively are acknowledged by the Company and by you.

2. You agree that, by virtue of the nature of your duties and the responsibilities arising from them, you have a special obligation to further the interests of the Company within the meaning of section 39(1)(b) of the Patents Act.

3. Any invention, development, process, plan, design, formula, specification, programme or other matter or work whatsoever (collectively 'the inventions') made, developed or discovered by you, either alone or together with others, whilst you are employed by the Company, shall forthwith be disclosed to the Company and, subject to section 39 of the Patents Act, shall belong to and be the absolute property of the Company or such subsidiary as it may designate.

4. You shall at the request and cost of the Company (and notwithstanding the termination of your employment, howsoever arising), sign and execute all such documents and do all such acts as the Company may reasonably require:

(a) to apply for and obtain in the sole name of the Company alone (unless the Company otherwise directs) patent, registered design, or other protection of any nature whatsoever in respect of the Inventions in any country throughout the world and, when so obtained, to renew and maintain the same;
(b) to resist any objection or opposition to obtaining, and any petitions or applications for revocation of, any such patent, registered design or other protection; and
(c) to bring proceedings for infringement of any such patent, registered design or other protection.

5. The Company shall decide, in its sole discretion, whether and when to apply for patent, registered design or other protection in respect of the Inventions and reserves the right to work any of the Inventions as a secret process in which event you shall observe the obligations relating to confidential information which are outlined in clause [*specify*] of your contract of employment.

PRECEDENT 14V: Set of restrictive covenants

[*These will need to be customised for the level of the member of staff and the nature of the confidential information to which they have access.*]

Definitions

In this Agreement the following words and expressions will have the following meanings, unless the context otherwise requires:

Business Partner: any Person who has entered into a joint venture or partnership with the Company or any Group Company with whom the Executive had material dealings during the Relevant Period.

Client: any Person (i) who or which at any time during the Relevant Period was provided with goods or services by the Company or any Group Company or (ii) who or which was a Prospective Client or (iii) about whom or which the Executive has confidential information, and in each case with whom or which the Executive or any person who reported directly to him had material dealings at any time during the Relevant Period.

Company: X Limited.

Competing Business: any business in the UK which competes or is preparing to compete with any business carried on by the Company or any Group Company in which the Executive has been involved to a material extent during the Relevant Period.

Group Company: any holding company of the Company and any subsidiary of the Company or of any such holding Company each as defined by Section 736 of the Companies Act 1985.

Executive: [*name*]

Key Employee: any person who at the Termination Date or at any time during the Relevant Period is an officer or employee of or consultant to the Company or any Group Company who is at or about the level of [*insert appropriate level*] and with whom the Executive in the course of his employment has had material dealings at any time during the Relevant Period.

Person: any person, firm, limited liability partnership, company, corporation, organisation, governmental or non-governmental body or other entity.

Prospective Client: any Person to whom or which during the Relevant Period the Company or any Group Company had submitted a tender, taken part in a pitch or made a presentation or with whom or which it was otherwise negotiating for the supply of goods or services.

Relevant Period: the period of 12 months immediately preceding the Termination Date.

Restricted Services: services of a type provided by the Company or any Group Company at the Termination Date in relation to any business in which the Executive had been involved to a material extent during the Relevant Period.

Supplier: any Person who or which at any time during the Relevant Period (i) supplied goods or services (other than utilities and goods or services supplied for administrative purposes) to the Company or any Group Company or (ii) was negotiating with or had pitched to the Company or any Group Company to supply goods or services (other than utilities and goods or services supplied for administrative purposes) to the Company or any Group Company, and in each case with whom or which the Executive or any person who reported directly to him had material dealings at any time during the Relevant Period.

Termination Date: the date on which this Agreement terminates, irrespective of the cause or manner.

1. **Protection of the Company's interests**

1.1 The Executive agrees with the Company that he will not directly or indirectly:

1.1.1 For a period of six (6) months immediately following the Termination Date:

1.1.1.1 carry on or set up or be interested in a Competing Business, save that he may hold up to five per cent of any class of securities quoted or dealt in on a recognised investment exchange or 20 per cent of any class of securities not so dealt;

1.1.1.2 act as a consultant, employee or officer or in any other capacity in a Competing Business;

1.1.1.3 either on his own account or on behalf of any Competing Business:

(a) supply or facilitate the supply of Restricted Goods or Services to; or
(b) deal with

any Client;

1.1.1.4 either on his own account or on behalf of any Competing Business deal with a Supplier;

1.1.1.5 either on his own account or for any Person employ or otherwise engage or facilitate the employment or engagement of the services of any Key Employee whether or not any such Key Employee would in entering into the employment or engagement commit a breach of contract;

1.1.1.6 either on his own account or for any Person deal with any Business Partner.

1.1.2 for a period of six (6) months immediately following the Termination Date:

1.1.2.1 either on his own account or for any Person induce, solicit or entice or try to induce, solicit or entice any Key Employee to cease working for or providing their services to the Company or any relevant Group Company whether or not any such Key Employee would by entering into the proposed employment or engagement commit a breach of contract;

1.1.2.2 either on his own account or on behalf of any Competing Business directly or indirectly induce, solicit or entice or try to induce, solicit or entice any Client to cease conducting any business with the Company or any Group Company or to reduce the amount of business conducted with the Company or any Group Company or adversely to vary the terms upon which any business is conducted with the Company or any Group Company or to exclude the Company or any Group Company from new business opportunities in relation to any Restricted Goods or Services;

1.1.2.3 either on his own account or on behalf of any Competing Business directly or indirectly induce, solicit or entice or try to induce, solicit or entice any Supplier to cease conducting any business with the Company or any Group Company or to reduce the amount of business conducted with the Company or any Group Company or adversely to vary the terms upon which any business is conducted with the Company or any Group Company;

1.1.2.4 either on his own account or on behalf of any Competing Business directly or indirectly induce, solicit or entice or try to induce, solicit or entice any Business Partner to terminate its arrangements with the Company or any Group Company or to seek to vary those arrangements, irrespective of whether any such action would be in breach of the Business Partner's contractual arrangements with the Company or Group Company;

1.1.2.5 knowingly or recklessly do or say anything which is or is calculated to be prejudicial to the interests of the Company or any Group Company or its or their business or which results or may result in the discontinuance of any contract or arrangement or benefit to the Company or any Group Company.

1.1.3 at any time after the Termination Date or, if later, the date on which [if applicable] he ceases to be a director of the Company of any Group Company present himself or allow himself to be presented or held out as being in any way connected with or interested in the business of the Company or any Group Company (other than as a shareholder or consultant, if that is the case).

1.2 The Executive agrees that each of the restrictions set out in clause 1.1 constitutes entirely separate, severable and independent restrictions on him. The Executive acknowledges that he has received [or, had the opportunity to receive] independent legal advice on the terms and effect of the provisions of this Agreement, including the restrictions above.

1.3 The duration of each of the restrictions set out in clause 1.1 above will be reduced by any period during which the Company suspends the Executive from the performance of his duties pursuant to clause [Y] (garden leave).

1.4 While each of the restrictions in clause 1.1 is considered by the parties to be reasonable in all the circumstances it is agreed that if any one of more of each of the restrictions either taken by itself or themselves together, is adjudged to go beyond what is reasonable in all the circumstances for the protection of the legitimate interests of the Company or any Group Company but would be adjudged to be reasonable if any particular restriction or restrictions were deleted or if any part or parts of its or their wording were deleted, restricted or limited in a particular manner then the restrictions set out in clause 1.1 will apply with such deletions, restrictions or limitations as the case may be.

1.5 The Executive agrees that during the currency of his employment by the Company he will immediately inform the Company if he becomes aware that any director, manager, senior employee or consultant of the company has been approached by any Person wishing to employ or engage such person.

1.6 The Executive agrees that if during the currency of his employment by the Company he is approached by any Person wishing to employ or engage him, he will immediately inform the Company of any such approach.

1.7 If the Executive accepts engagement (whether as a director, consultant or in any other capacity) or employment with any third party during the period of any of the restrictions set out in clause 1.1 he will on or before such acceptance provide the third party with full details of these restrictions.

1.8 The Executive will not induce, procure, authorise or encourage any other Person to do or procure to be done anything which if done by the Executive would be a breach of any of the provisions of clause 1.1.

2. **Transfer of Undertakings**

The Executive agrees that if his employment is transferred to a Person other than the Company or any Group Company ('the new employer') pursuant to the Transfer of Undertakings (Protection of Employment) Regulations 2006 he will, if required, enter into an agreement with the new employer that will contain provisions that provide protection to the new employer similar to that provided to the Company or any Group Company in clause 1.1.

3. **Passing off**

The Executive agrees that, save in the proper performance of his duties, he will not during his employment or after the Termination Date make use of any corporate or business brand or domain name or logo or style which is identical or similar or likely to be confused or associated with any corporate or business brand or domain name of logo or style of the Company or which might suggest a connection with the same.

4. **Confidential information**

4.1 The Executive acknowledges that during the course of his employment, he will or may be privy to confidential information belonging or relating to the Company or any Group Company and to its or their Business Partners, Clients, Prospective Clients,

Suppliers and customers and that he will or may make, maintain and/or develop personal knowledge of, influence over and/or valuable contacts with such Persons. The Executive agrees that he will keep secret and shall not at any time, whether during the term of this Agreement or thereafter, for any reason whatsoever (except as necessary for the proper performance of his duties under this Agreement) disclose to any Person whatsoever or otherwise make use of for his own or another's advantage or information any confidential information or information which he may have acquired concerning the business or affairs of the Company or any of its Business Partners, Clients, Prospective Clients, Suppliers or customers, staff or any third parties.

4.2 Confidential information includes but is not limited to:

4.2.1 actual, proposed or draft corporate and marketing strategy, business development plans, tenders; pitches, sales reports and research results;

4.2.2 business methods and processes, technical information and know-how relating to the Company's business and which is not available to the public generally, including inventions, designs, programmes, techniques, database systems, formulae and ideas;

4.2.3 business contacts, lists or details of Business Partners, Clients, Prospective Clients, Suppliers or customers and details of contacts with them, their business or affairs;

4.2.4 information or details on employees and workers and their terms and conditions of employment/engagement, benefits, incentive schemes/plans, salary scales and/or current or anticipated disputes;

4.2.5 information or details of any actual, potential or threatened litigation, legal action, claim, dispute or arbitration against or with any worker/director of the Company;

4.2.6 budgets, management accounts, trading statements and other financial reports;

4.2.7 unpublished price-sensitive information;

4.2.8 any other information which any member, employee or consultant of the Company has identified (orally, in writing, or by their actions) as being secret or confidential in nature.

4.3 The Executive shall at all times comply with any relevant Company policies from time to time in force on the security of information and shall use his best endeavours to prevent any unauthorised publication or disclosure of any confidential or secret information.

4.4 The Executive agrees that he will neither store nor disseminate any of the Company's confidential information nor make, store or disseminate any copies thereof save in so far as is necessary for the proper performance of his duties under this Agreement. He further agrees that in so far as the proper performance of his said duties requires him to send any email communication containing or attaching any such confidential information, he shall (unless the Company has otherwise agreed with him in writing) only utilise his work email address for such purpose.

4.5 The restrictions in this clause 4 shall not apply to:

4.5.1 any disclosure of information which is already in the public domain otherwise than by breach of this Agreement;

4.5.2 any disclosure required by a court of law or by a governmental or regulatory body, provided that the Executive shall promptly notify the Company when any such disclosure requirement arises to enable the Company to take such action as it deems necessary, including, without limitation, to make known to the appropriate authority or court the proprietary nature of the confidential information and make any applicable claim of confidentiality with respect thereto;

4.5.3 prevent the Executive from making a protected disclosure within the meaning of Section 43A of the Employment Rights Act 1996.

5. Return of property

Upon termination of the Executive's employment for whatever reason (or, at the Company's discretion, at any earlier time) the Executive shall immediately deliver to the Company in good condition all property of the Company or any of its Business Partners, Suppliers, Clients, Prospective Clients or customers which may be in his possession or control, including without limitation all cars, keys providing access to any Company premises, credit and purchase cards, ID, IT or mobile phone equipment, correspondence, documents, specifications, reports data, papers and records in whatever medium or form (including any computer material such as disks or tapes), all confidential information or documents, any information or documents relating to the Company's intellectual property rights, together with all copies (electronic or otherwise) of any such information or documents, which the Executive has in his possession or control.

6. Termination, garden leave and suspension

6.1 Each party to this Agreement shall be entitled to terminate this Agreement by giving not less than [X months'/weeks'] written notice to the other.

6.2 The Company reserves the right to make payment to the Executive in lieu of such notice, at its absolute discretion.

6.3 Upon notice of termination having been given by either party, the Company may at its absolute discretion suspend the Executive at any time from the performance of all or any of his duties ('garden leave'). During such suspension, the Company shall be under no obligation to provide the Executive with any work or assign any duties to him. It may also require the Executive:

6.3.1 not to attend any of the Company's premises;

6.3.2 to resign with immediate effect from any offices he holds with the Company (and in such case the Executive will not be entitled to any compensation for loss of office);

6.3.3 not to speak to, contact or otherwise communicate with or engage with any director, consultant, agent, contractor or employee of the Company or any Person who, at the date of such suspension or exclusion is a Client, Prospective Client or customer of the Group unless they are members of the Executive's immediate family;

6.3.4 at any time to carry out such special projects or duties commensurate with the Executive's abilities as the Company shall in its absolute discretion determine;

6.3.5 at any time to meet with the Company's representatives in order to facilitate a handover of work and to provide assistance with ongoing business activity; and/or to take any holiday which has accrued under Clause [XXX] during any period of suspension under Clause 6.3;

6.3.6 at any time during the garden leave period as set out above to deliver up the Company's laptop, all external drives, the Company Blackberry and/or mobile telephone, all documents and all copies of documents, including but not limited to contact business cards, lists of customers/clients/members of staff (past, current or potential) and any other company equipment requested;

6.3.7 to give a written undertaking that at no time during their employment have they removed or transferred any confidential information or made copies of and retained any company information (examples of which are listed above in 6.3.6) or any confidential information or trade secrets as defined above nor have they deleted such information nor have they wiped any data from the Company laptop nor have they deleted the operating systems, etc. UNLESS they have been expressly instructed to do so in writing.

6.4 Without prejudice to Clause 6.3 above, the Company shall be entitled to suspend the Executive on full pay for so long as it may think fit.

6.5 Nothing in Clause 6.1 above shall preclude the Company from summarily terminating this Agreement without any payment in lieu in appropriate circumstances (and without prejudice to any remedy the Company may have against the Executive for breach or non-performance of the Executive's obligations and duties to the Company).

7. Screening and monitoring

7.1 During the Executive's employment, the Company may at its discretion require that the Executive undergoes screening for criminal records, sanctions list and/or credit reference checks from time to time. It is anticipated that such screening would only be undertaken if required for regulatory purposes or in order to comply with the minimum standards for the role the Executive is undertaking. The Executive agrees to submit to and fully comply with any such screening procedures.

7.2 The Executive consents to the Company monitoring his use of all the Company's resources and its communication and electronic equipment (including without limitation the telephone, fax and email systems) and information stored on the Company's equipment.

8. Obligation to show these covenants to any prospective employer

I agree that in the event of my receiving from any person, firm or corporation an offer of employment, whether oral or in writing and whether accepted or not, either during the continuance of my employment or during the continuance in force of all or any of the restrictions set out in Clauses XX–XX, I shall forthwith:

(i) provide to the person making such an offer of employment a full and accurate copy of this contract of employment including details of any variations thereof and bearing the date of its execution by the parties; and
(ii) inform the Board of the identity of the offeror.

9. General

The headings to the clauses are for convenience only and have no legal effect.

15

Settlement agreements

15.1 General rule

At common law, agreements which are in 'full and final settlement' are in the main legally binding agreements to settle the claims described in the agreement. Importantly, statutory employment protection rights cannot so easily be signed away by agreement.

Formerly known as compromise agreements, now settlement agreements (since 29 July 2013) entered into by virtue of s.203 of the Employment Rights Act 1996 and such agreements, along with COT3 agreements entered into under the auspices of ACAS, are the only legally binding forms of agreement that validly waive an employee's rights to bring legal action before an Employment Tribunal.

Any other form of agreement that purports to exclude or modify the employment protection rights of an individual is void.

ACAS published a Code of Practice 'Settlement Agreements' and non-statutory guide in July 2013.

The Enterprise and Regulatory Reform Act 2013 (ERRA), s.23, changed the name of compromise agreements to settlement agreements.

Settlement agreements are the same as compromise agreements, albeit with a new name: the same conditions need to be satisfied for them to be legally binding and they have the same effect of terminating the employment relationship whilst compromising an employees' employment rights.

A new form of settlement called a protected conversation was also added by the ERRA, amending the Employment Rights Act 1996, s.111A.

15.2 Statutory rules for settlement agreements

Settlement agreements must comply with the following conditions laid down by the Employment Rights Act 1996, s.203(3):

1. The agreement must be in writing (it is of no use orally agreeing terms at

the door of the Employment Tribunal and then seeking to enforce any oral agreements at a later date).
2. It must relate to the particular complaint or complaints or particular proceedings about which there is a dispute either in the parties' minds or within their contemplation.
3. The employee must have received independent legal advice, i.e. advice from a specified adviser who is not employed by, and has not given advice in the matter to, the employer and that advice must in particular relate to the terms of the agreement and the effect of the proposed agreement and in particular the effect on the employee's ability to pursue their rights before an Employment Tribunal.
4. The adviser must have in force a professional indemnity policy to cover the risk of giving negligent advice in respect of this agreement.
5. The agreement must identify the adviser.
6. The agreement must state that the conditions relating to compromise agreements have been satisfied.

Even if the settlement agreement does not satisfy the above conditions, it will be effective in respect of any claims it covers which could be made to the courts at common law, for example for wrongful dismissal. This was the case in *Sutherland v. Network Appliance Ltd* [2001] IRLR 12. The EAT held (p.12):

> Accordingly, where a provision in an agreement offends s.203 so far as it relates to statutory claims, there is no reason to sweep aside the whole contract. To do so would be to ignore the words 'in so far as' and to read it as if it said simply 'if'. It would have been easy for the legislature to say that if an agreement contained any offending provision, then the whole agreement would be void. By providing not for a general avoidance but only an avoidance 'in so far as', Parliament was contemplating that agreements were intended to be capable of surviving in part even though struck out as to part.

15.3 What if there is no complaint or no proceedings?

Even if the individual who is being dismissed does not have a particular complaint or has not instigated particular proceedings at the time of their dismissal, there is a provision for 'employer-led' conciliation which can lead to a valid COT3 or valid settlement agreement.

Settlement agreements are generally binding and no further claims can be made further to those that have been compromised and unless fraud has taken place or the employee has committed a material breach of the settlement agreement, the employer cannot reclaim any monies paid.

Employers must investigate thoroughly whether the employee's claims are true before signing settlement agreements with those employees. If the employer chooses to sign despite suspecting such claims are untrue, they will not be allowed to set aside agreements later – even if fresh evidence arises.

However, where fraud has been committed employers may be able to reclaim monies paid.

In *Hayward* v. *Zurich Insurance Co plc* [2016] UKSC 48 the respondent employer appealed to the Supreme Court after it had signed a settlement agreement with an employee whom it suspected was exaggerating his injuries. It disputed the compensation claimed but eventually signed a settlement agreement with him.

The employer later found out that the employee had recovered from his injuries at least a year before signing the agreement. The employee did not deny that he had dishonestly exaggerated his injuries. The employer applied to the High Court and won. Mr Hayward appealed to the Court of Appeal and won. The Supreme Court set aside the settlement agreement and the employer won.

The Supreme Court unanimously decided that where an insurer suspects fraud but has nevertheless chosen to settle a claim, it would be entitled to set aside the settlement under the tort of deceit, if it subsequently discovers proof that it was in fact fraudulent.

The Supreme Court refused to set aside that claim on the grounds that in this case:

> the lie is dishonest, but the claim is not. The immateriality of the lie to the claim makes it not just possible but appropriate to distinguish between them. I do not accept that a policy of deterrence justifies the application of the fraudulent claim rule in this situation. The law deprecates fraud in all circumstances, but the fraudulent claim rule is peculiar to contracts of insurance.

15.4 Breach of contract claims

Settlement agreements can cover breach of contract claims. In *Rock-It Cargo Ltd* v. *Green* [1997] IRLR 581, the EAT held that if a settlement agreement is entered into on termination of employment, a claim for any monetary payment under the agreement can be directly enforced in an Employment Tribunal:

> A compromise agreement as to the terms on which employment is to be brought to an end is a 'contract connected with employment' within the meaning of s.3(2) [of the Employment Tribunals Act 1996].

The Employment Tribunal's jurisdiction to hear breach of contract claims is limited to contractual claims which are either outstanding on the date of termination or which arise on termination: Industrial Tribunals Extension of Jurisdiction (England and Wales) Order 1994, SI 1994/1623, art.3, providing that proceedings may be brought before an Employment Tribunal in respect of a claim for the recovery of damages if 'the claim arises or is outstanding on the termination of the employee's employment'.

In *Miller Bros and FP Butler Ltd* v. *Johnston* [2002] IRLR 386, the EAT held that the word 'on' in the phrase 'on the termination', must be read in a 'temporal' rather than a 'causative' sense. Accordingly, the jurisdiction of an Employment Tribunal is limited to a claim which is outstanding on the date of termination of the employee's employment, or which arises on termination in a temporal sense. In this case, that meant a tribunal could not consider a claim for breach of a compromise agreement, where the agreement was not finalised until after the effective date of termination, even though the claim arose because of the termination of employment. The claimant would have to pursue their remedy in the ordinary courts. Breach of contract claims cannot be brought in an Employment Tribunal unless the employee's employment is terminated, but they cannot be brought in respect of a breach of an agreement after termination, even where negotiations were outstanding on the date of termination.

Lawyers acting for an employee must keep in mind that a valid settlement agreement relating to a breach of contract must be entered into before, rather than after, termination of the employment.

15.5 Categories of claims that can be compromised

The categories of proceedings in respect of which a settlement agreement that fulfils the above conditions is valid are spelt out in the Employment Tribunals Act 1996, s.18 and the Employment Rights Act 1996, s.203, as amended:

(a) proceedings specified in the Employment Tribunals Act 1996, s.18(1)(d), including unfair dismissal (Employment Rights 1996 Act, s.203(2)(f));

(b) proceedings for sex discrimination and equal pay under the Equality Act 2010;

(c) proceedings for racial discrimination under the Equality Act 2010;

(d) proceedings for disability discrimination;

(e) proceedings under Trade Union and Labour Relations (Consolidation) Act 1992 (see s.288(2A), as amended);

(f) proceedings under the National Minimum Wage Act 1998 (see s.49);

(g) proceedings under the Working Time Regulations 1998, SI 1998/1833 (see reg.35(2));

(h) proceedings under the Part-time Workers (Prevention of Less Favourable Treatment) Regulations 2000, SI 2000/1551 (see reg.7);

(i) proceedings under the Fixed-term Employees (Prevention of Less Favourable Treatment) Regulations 2002, SI 2002/2034 (see Sched.2, paras 2(a) and 3(17));

(j) proceedings for discrimination on grounds of age, sexual orientation, gender reassignment, or religious or other beliefs;

(k) proceedings for discrimination on grounds of pregnancy or maternity.

15.6 Settlement agreements which are *ultra vires*

Local authorities and other public bodies have powers granted by statute with respect to severance payments. Such payments will be *intra vires*. Where payments are made outside the scope of the statutory regulations, such payments are *ultra vires* and any agreement purporting to make such payments is void, thus preventing any legal action for restitution and rendering damages for breach of contract irrecoverable (*Eastbourne Borough Council* v. *Foster* [2001] EWCA Civ 1091). Here, the Court of Appeal held that the compromise agreement entered into by the local authority was void and unenforceable. Since the agreement was null and void so was the consensual termination of Mr Foster's employment and his employment continued until terminated with 'reasonable' notice.

In *Gibb v. Maidstone and Tunbridge Wells NHS Trust* [2010] EWCA Civ 678, the Court of Appeal overturned the High Court's decision to declare the award of £250,000 compensation *ultra vires*.

In this case the High Court held that the compromise agreement awarding a former NHS Trust's Chief Executive substantial compensation in addition to payment in lieu of notice upon termination of her employment had been irrationally generous. It was held to be *ultra vires* and void and her claim for money owed under the agreement failed.

Overturning the High Court's decision, the Court of Appeal held that an employer, faced with the difficulties with which this employer was faced 'in difficult and perhaps controversial circumstances with the need to terminate a long-standing employee's contract' may, when settling the terms of a severance agreement, pay regard to past service and the future likely difficulty of the employee finding new employment. Here Rose Gibb was the Chief Executive of an NHS Trust severely criticised for the outbreak of the 'super bug' *C. difficile* at the Trust's hospitals. The settlement of £75,000 pay in lieu and £175,000 compensation was restored.

In terms of entering into settlement agreements, the former Housing Corporation issued advice in 1993 that 'un-winnable' cases should be settled and in cases where junior members of staff are involved, a cost-benefit analysis could be considered. Where senior staff and large sums are involved or there are other sensitive issues, the Housing Corporation expected the associations to fight such cases, with the caveat that 'It is primarily a matter for the association's judgment'. The former Housing Corporation's advice of 17 July 2008 on Employment Tribunal cases is as follows:

1.1 Schedule 1 and Employment Tribunals

Since we amended Maintaining Standards of Probity (GPN 3) on our website in March 2003, we have had a number of queries concerning this minor change to our policy and procedures. It seems worthwhile therefore to send out this general letter to you all to explain the amendment and why we made it.

Maintaining Standards of Probity (GPN 3) replaced previous guidance on Schedule 1 and clarified existing policies and criteria for special determinations. In cases involving employment tribunals our policy was to expect an association to contest any case that it had a reasonable chance of winning. We were, however, persuaded that we should look at this again. Associations told us that to take all winnable cases to court was wasteful of time and resources and that in many situations a modest out of court settlement made good business sense.

After discussions with the National Housing Federation and Association Representatives we agreed modest changes both to policy and procedures.

1.2 Policy

We no longer expect associations to take all winnable cases to court. Instead the key is proportionality. Where the case is a straightforward one involving junior staff and small amounts, a compromise agreement may well be the most sensible way forward. Where senior staff and large sums are involved or there are other sensitive issues we would expect the association to consider pursuing the case through the courts. It is primarily a matter for the association's judgment.

1.3 Procedures

This policy modification does not affect the fact that an out-of-court settlement remains a breach of Schedule 1 and will need a special determination. To facilitate negotiations we are prepared to issue determinations in advance with an upper limit. Associations should alert their lead regulator early in the proceedings setting out the case for making a compromise settlement and indicating the maximum amount they would be prepared to pay. Applications will be considered according to our normal criteria.

The Comment under Case Study 1 on page 5 of the GPN 3 has been amended to reflect these changes.

There is now a cap on public sector exit payments at £95,000, effectively outlawing six-figure payouts. Also, a 'clawback' mechanism has come into force. Under this rule, highly paid public servants (those earning £100,000 or more) who return to the public sector within 12 months of leaving will be forced to repay their redundancy compensation. The cap on exit payments was brought into force on 1 February 2017 by virtue of the Enterprise Act 2016 (Commencement No. 2) Regulations 2017.

15.7 Consideration

A settlement agreement is a contract which involves consideration in order to compromise the employee's right to present or continue with a claim to a tribunal in respect of any matter other than the particular complaint which is the subject of the agreement.

The wording of both ACAS conciliated claims (effected under a COT3) and settlement agreements must be clear.

In the case of *Department for Work and Pensions* v. *Brindley* UKEAT/0123/16/JOJ the EAT upheld an Employment Tribunal's finding that an employee's claim for disability discrimination was not barred by the terms of a COT3 agreement settling a previous claim.

The new claim did not fall within 'all other relevant claims arising from the facts of the proceedings' that were settled under the terms of the COT3, even though the facts giving rise to the new claim occurred at around the same time as the settlement was reached and related to similar matters.

The claimant was disabled. She made her first claim (Claim 1) in relation to car parking, reasonable adjustments and a first final written warning issued on 11 April 2014 because of poor attendance.

This claim (Claim 1) was settled by a COT3 in full and final settlement of 'all other Relevant Claims arising from the facts of the Proceedings up to and including the date this Agreement [sic]'.

Mrs Brindley's second claim (Claim 2) related to a second final written warning issued on 28 November 2014. On 8 June 2015 she submitted a further

Employment Tribunal claim (Claim 2) that she had been discriminated against by being given a final written warning for her attendance on 28 November 2014.

The respondent argued that the existence of the COT3 agreement meant that the Employment Tribunal did not have jurisdiction to hear Claim 2 because Claim 2 was caught by the clause in the COT3 agreement.

The Employment Judge disagreed, concluding that a reasonable person would consider that all claims arising from the circumstances of the first claim had been settled, but that the new circumstances referred to in Claim 2 were not part of the settlement. The respondent appealed.

The EAT dismissed the appeal as the COT3 did not include 'any and all claims arising within the period up to 11 December 2014' (the date that the COT3 was signed). It also restricted the agreement to 'all claims arising from the facts of these proceedings'.

15.8 Relevant independent adviser

The meaning of the 'independent adviser' has widened under the Employment Rights (Dispute Resolution) Act 1998, Sched.1, para. 24(3), to include not only a solicitor or barrister but also:

(a) an officer, official, employee or member of an independent trade union who has been certified in writing by the trade union as competent to give advice and as authorised to do so on behalf of the trade union; or
(b) an individual who works at an advice centre (whether as an employee or a volunteer) and has been certified in writing by the centre as competent to give advice and as authorised to do so on behalf of the centre; or
(c) Fellows of the Institute of Legal Executives – ILEX (a requirement that they must be subject to supervision by a solicitor holding a practising certificate was removed on 1 October 2004 provided that they work for a solicitor's practice).

However, a representative can only enter into a binding settlement of a claim on behalf of an applicant if the actual employee holds out that a person is authorised to act on their behalf, not through a 'holding out' by a legal representative or adviser. In *Gloystarne & Co Ltd* v. *Martin* [2001] IRLR 15, Lindsay J explained (para.18):

> B does not become A's agent in dealings with C, nor does B acquire authority from A to act on A's behalf in relation to C by way only of what B says to C. If that was the case, principals could have agents completely unknown to them and over which they had no control. Rather the case is that B becomes A's agent in dealings with C by reason, in general, of what A says to C on the point or whether A conducts himself to C in some way that reflects on the possibility of B's agency.

15.9 Terms agreed

Settlement terms which have been negotiated by a 'representative' who has not been properly authorised by the applicant will not be binding on them provided that the 'representative' did not have 'ostensible authority' to bind them (*Gloystarne & Co Ltd* v. *Martin* [2001] IRLR 15).

However, once an agreement has been reached orally, with the ACAS officer, i.e. both parties have agreed to the terms, there is a binding settlement.

In *Allma Construction Ltd* v. *Bonner* UKEATS/0060/09/BI the employer appealed against the decision of an Employment Judge who had ruled that there had been no binding agreement under the auspices of ACAS.

The EAT held that all that was required of ACAS was that it had 'taken action' under s.18 of the Employment Tribunals Act 1996, and 'in some way, endeavoured to promote settlement of the claim'.

It did not matter that the wording of the COT3 agreement was negotiated at a later date.

What the ACAS officer believed as the legal status of any agreement is irrelevant.

15.10 Special terms

Gagging clauses

Some employers require 'gagging clauses' or confidentiality clauses requiring the departing employee not to disclose the facts or circumstances leading up to the negotiations and departure or the terms of the settlement (save for a partner, legal adviser or where required to do so by law).

Repayment clauses

Some employers include repayment clauses permitting repayment of some or all of the settlement monies in the event of a material breach of the settlement agreement by the employee or if they have already committed a repudiatory breach of which the employer was ignorant and for which they could have been summarily dismissed.

There must be a genuine pre-estimate of loss and not an extravagant penalty for breach of the agreement. Factors such as the following may tend to show a genuine pre-estimate of loss:

- whether the sum claimed is significantly greater than the largest loss that could have been caused by the breach;
- whether the same amount is payable in relation to any breach of contract, regardless of how serious;
- whether the clause is designed to stop one party from breaching the contract, rather than compensating the other for loss caused by a breach.

In *CMC Group plc* v. *Zhang* [2006] EWCA Civ 408, the Court of Appeal held that a clause in a commercial settlement agreement requiring the settlement sum to be repaid in the event of breach of the agreement by the recipient was a penalty clause and therefore unenforceable. The case had implications for the enforceability of similar repayment clauses in settlement agreements and employers were advised to seek repayment only of a genuine pre-estimate of loss.

In 2015 the Supreme Court handed down two important judgments concerning penalty clauses (*Cavendish Square Holding BV* v. *Talal El Makdessi* and *ParkingEye Ltd* v. *Beavis* [2015] UKSC 67).

15.11 TUPE and use of settlement agreements

Employers have often tried to get around the vexed problem of how lawfully to obtain employees' consent to change their terms and conditions following a TUPE transfer – often called 'harmonisation'. Any variation which comes about by reason of the transfer is void contrary to reg.4 even if the staff agree to the change(s) (*Wilson* v. *St Helen's Borough Council* [1998] IRLR 706 which refers to similar provisions in the 1981 regulations, reg.12).

In *Solectron Scotland Ltd* v. *Roper* [2004] IRLR 4, Elias J has assisted employers in making changes lawfully to existing contracts of employment following a TUPE transfer. The answer is to terminate the old contract, obtain the employees' agreement to waive unfair dismissal, wrongful dismissal, breach of contract, unlawful deduction of wages and redundancy payment claims and make a payment or provide some form of consideration under a compromise agreement. When those employees are issued with a new contract, it follows that there has been no variation of the former terms because there are now no longer any former terms.

A settlement agreement can be used to settle a financial claim that the employee has on termination of the contract, such as the enhanced redundancy terms the employees in *Solectron* had in their contracts which transferred under reg.5, following a TUPE transfer. The employees agreed to compromise the termination of their existing contract with the new employer and accepted consideration for this. There was no variation of that contract because it had come to an end and there was no change in the terms and conditions for the future because that contract had come to an end.

As Elias J explained (p.8):

> the effect of the compromise agreement is solely to compromise a financial claim that the employee has on the termination of his employment contract. The employer is not purporting to vary the contract but merely to compromise a dispute as to its value. Moreover, there is no change in the terms and conditions for the future by reason of the obvious fact that the contract has come to an end.

This case referred to the 1981 regulations, but the learned judge's answer is still applicable under TUPE 2006 as amended.

15.12 Specific terms

Settlement agreements should be checked to ensure the following:

1. The correct names and addresses of the parties must appear on the face of the agreement.
2. The effective date of termination and last day of work must be correctly defined. They may be different dates.
3. Provide that the employer will continue paying salary and all benefits up to and including the effective date of termination.
4. The severance or compensation for loss of office payment should be expressed to be in full and final settlement.
5. Any payment in lieu of notice (PILON) must be expressed as such and taxed at the normal tax rate for the individual whether or not there is no PILON clause in the contract of employment or staff handbook; to include reference to payment or non-payment of bonus, commission, share options, accrued but untaken holiday; pension contributions to be made during notional notice period; continuation of private medical insurance and other benefits; continuation of the use of a car or payment in lieu; return or retention of mobile telephone, computer kept at home.
6. Provide for the return of company property such as keys, passes, papers, disks, CD ROMs, PCs and knowledge of any passwords, etc.
7. Provide for repayment of season ticket or other loan or deductions from final payment.
8. Include reminder of existing restrictive covenants and confidentiality clauses.
9. Provide for any new restrictive covenants and confidentiality clauses with adequate consideration attached (which is taxed at source at 40 per cent); confidentiality to cover the fact and circumstances of leaving; the terms of the agreement (save where required to disclose by law or to spouse or advisers); and concerning personal details of directors, officers, senior managers.
10. Provide for resignation from office of director.
11. Provide for reference obligations relating to both written and oral references, with drafts attached.
12. Include non-derogation clauses (mutual).
13. Provide for warranties and undertakings from employee.
14. Provide for tax indemnity from employee to employer.
15. Include an indemnity from the employee to the employer if there is a real likelihood of a client suing the employer for the misconduct of the employee.
16. Include a repayment clause in the event that the employee breaches the agreement (see above).
17. Provide for a requirement to inform the employer if there has been an offer of new employment or there is a reasonable expectation of receiving one with details of the proposed new employer.
18. Provide for exclusions from employee waivers, e.g. with respect to personal injury claims unknown at the time of signing the agreement; accrued pension rights; any claims to enforce the terms of the settlement agreement (it is thought that any attempt to obtain a waiver from any

future and unknown personal injury claims save those relating to statutory torts may be contrary to the Unfair Contract Terms Act 1977, s.2(1) and could be void).
19. Include agreement by employee to continue to assist employer with respect to work or litigation.
20. Include agreement by employer to structure the payments in the most tax-efficient manner.
21. There should be no (or very little) time gap between the date of the agreement and the signing of the agreement otherwise HMRC could deem this to be an agreement made during employment and may not deem the payments to be 'termination payments' under s.401 of the Income Tax (Earnings and Pensions) Act 2003. If the parties do sign the settlement agreement ahead of the termination date, then a dual settlement agreement or a reaffirmation clause/letter signed on or a day before the effective date of termination will need to be signed.
22. Provide for staged payments and a requirement to repay some of the termination payment in the event of mitigation.

Taxation of pay in lieu of notice and termination payments over £30,000

The government announced that from April 2018 an employer will be required to pay NICs on any part of a termination payment that exceeds the £30,000 threshold. It is anticipated that this will be collected in 'real time', as part of the employer's standard weekly or monthly payroll returns and remittances to HM Revenue and Customs (HMRC).

In addition, all payments in lieu of notice (PILONs) will be both taxable and subject to Class 1 NICs whether they are contractual or not.

Retirement

If the individual receiving the termination payment is 'retiring' (see EIM15400 for HMRC's view of the meaning of retirement), any consideration given on or in anticipation of retirement (Income Tax (Earnings and Pension) Act (ITEPA) 2003, ss.393–399) will be subject to income tax and NICs in full as a relevant benefit.

Where the payment is compensation for genuine redundancy or loss of office, the circumstances of the termination should be documented to show this and the first £30,000 can be paid tax-free.

Payment into pension

Some employees may elect to defer part of their termination payment and have it paid into their pension. This may be deducted from the gross sum and therefore that portion of the settlement monies do not attract tax. There is a cap on this figure which attracts tax exemption.

15.13 Private medical insurance

If the employer provided private medical insurance and cannot be persuaded to continue paying for cover for the individual and their family after the termination date, then it may be possible to arrange for the individual within a short period of time thereafter to continue the cover by taking out their own personal policy and be treated as having continuous cover, i.e. not as a new entrant. This means that all pre-existing medical conditions are not treated as such and therefore will not fall outside the scope of the cover. In some cases, employers with group schemes have persuaded their provider to offer the first one/three months of cover under a personal policy free of charge.

15.14 Staged payments: duty to mitigate

Some employers seek to reduce any liability to make payments in lieu of notice by reducing these sums on the basis of the ex-employee's duty to mitigate (see **Chapter 12** on notice). Similarly, it is not unknown for the payment of a severance package to be drafted on the basis of making staged payments, subject to their cessation or reduction once new employment has been obtained.

15.15 Taxation

Here are a few tips:

1. Once the employee or ex-employee has signed the agreement, the payment is deemed to have crystallised in their hands and any ex gratia termination payment over £30,000 will be taxed and have NICs deducted at the normal tax rate for the employee and no tax-efficient scheme will be possible.
2. If the employee or ex-employee elects to ask the employer to pay part of the termination payment into their pension, this election must be done before the signing of the agreement and the amount of monies exempt from tax is capped.
3. The P45 should be sent to the employee after the effective date of termination but before any payment under the agreement is made.
4. The agreement should specify that it only becomes an open and binding agreement once the agreement has been signed by both parties.
5. Any continuation of benefits after the effective date of termination must be declared by the employer to HMRC and tax paid by the ex-employee if it becomes due.
6. Any new restrictive covenants or confidentiality clauses must have adequate consideration attached, for which the higher rate of tax must be deducted at source (Income Tax (Earnings and Pensions) Act 2003, ss.225–226).

7. Even if the employee does not have a contractual entitlement to PILON, from April 2018 HMRC will require a PILON to be taxed at source at the relevant rate.
8. Legal costs under Extra Statutory Concession A81 can be paid direct to the employee's lawyers as long as the advice given solely relates to the termination of employment; the agreement must specify that only these costs can be paid direct to the lawyer on submission of a fee note addressed to the employee but made payable by the employer.

   In cases where the dispute is settled without recourse to the courts, no charge will be imposed on payments made by the former employer:

   (a) direct to the former employee's solicitor; and
   (b) in full or partial discharge of the solicitor's bill of costs incurred by the employee only in connection with the termination of their employment; and
   (c) under a specific term in the settlement agreement providing for that payment.
9. Tax concessions on counselling, outplacement and retraining costs will only apply where the payments are made directly from the employer to the provider if the employee has two years' continuous service at the effective date of termination (Income Tax (Earnings and Pensions) Act 2003, ss.310–311).

15.16 Indemnity from employee

In any case where an employee has committed an act of gross misconduct such that it is clear that liability arises towards a third party, e.g. a client, the employer has a right to seek an indemnity from the employee within the terms of a compromise agreement: see the Court of Appeal decision in *Padden v. Arbuthnot Pensions & Investments Ltd* [2004] EWCA Civ 582. The claimant had been contacted by a stockbroker with £1.5 million in funds to be invested on behalf of a client. It was agreed that these monies would be invested in insurance bonds and other investments so as to give the client a regular income. The claimant stole the funds and used them for his own personal gain. If the claimant had invested the funds as instructed, his employer would have obtained commission of over £50,000. The employer sued him for the lost commission, won judgment and an order for 80 per cent of its costs. The claimant had entered into a compromise agreement with the client, on terms that if he returned the money to her, she would not bring proceedings against him. The employer was granted summary judgment against the claimant and a declaration that it was entitled to be indemnified by him in respect of any liability it might have incurred to the client, in respect of his misconduct. The Court of Appeal held that there was a real prospect that the client would bring proceedings against the employer.

Such an indemnity clause may read as follows:

The employee acknowledges and accepts that in respect of their actions regarding the investment of funds of [*name of client*], they have acted in breach of their fiduciary duty and as a result the employer has become or may become liable to [*client*] for damages and legal costs, interest, etc. The employee agrees to indemnify the employer against any and all claims in respect of the actions of the employee in respect of [*client*]'s investments including but not limited to [*client*]'s right to sue for damages, interest and legal costs. The employee agrees to repay any or all of the settlement monies as set out in [*specify*] and if there are insufficient funds to cover all the monies due to [*client*] from the employer, the employee agrees to pay any excess to the employer within 21 days of a written demand. This is without prejudice to any other legal rights that the employer has or may have in the future against the employee in respect of this transaction or any legal proceedings relating thereto. The employee also agrees to co-operate fully and give truthful evidence if required in any legal proceedings (civil and/or criminal) or proceedings required by the FCA or any other regulatory body.

In some cases where there is a delay between the signing of the settlement agreement and the termination date, a reaffirmation certificate will need to be signed and dated by the employee and the adviser.

Precedent 15D contains a settlement agreement with a reaffirmation clause.

15.17 'Protected conversations' and 'without prejudice' discussions

'Protected conversations' were introduced under the new s.111A of the Employment Rights Act 1996, in 2013.

They were to enable an employer to have a confidential discussion about dismissing an employee where there was as yet no dispute. This would normally be the case in instances of poor performance.

'Without prejudice' discussions can only take place where there is a legal dispute and, surprisingly for employers, a grievance is not a legal dispute (*BNP Paribas* v. *Mezzotero* [2004] IRLR 508).

Protected conversations

Protected conversations will not apply where discrimination, breach of contract or automatically unfair dismissal is claimed. Where tribunal proceedings involve a number of different claims, 'protected conversation' discussions are still protected – *Faithorn Farrell Timms plc* v. *Bailey* UKEAT/0025/16/RN.

Here the EAT ruled that when dealing with an unfair dismissal claim coupled, for example, with a discrimination claim, the Employment Tribunal must ignore the discussions in relation to the unfair dismissal claim, but not the discrimination claim – even though the same Employment Judge probably will hear both claims.

Protected conversations will lose their protections where the employer has engaged in 'improper behaviour' (s.111A(4) of the Employment Rights Act 1996).

The ACAS Code of Practice provides a non-exhaustive list of improper conduct, which includes:

- all forms of harassment, bullying and intimidation, including through the use of offensive words or aggressive behaviour;
- physical assault or the threat of physical assault and other criminal behaviour;
- all forms of victimisation;
- discrimination because of age, sex, race, disability, sexual orientation, religion or belief, transgender, pregnancy and maternity and marriage or civil partnership; and
- putting undue pressure on a party (e.g. an employer saying before any form of disciplinary process has begun that if a settlement proposal is rejected then the employee will be dismissed).

'Without prejudice' discussions

Employers must be very careful entering into 'without prejudice' discussions with employees, because if these discussions do not comply with the rules for the 'without prejudice' privilege, these discussions will not be protected from disclosure in any future legal proceedings.

A communication is considered 'without prejudice' when it is made with a bona fide intention of being a negotiating document in a dispute.

In *BNP Paribas* v. *Mezzotero*, the EAT held that the mere act of an employee raising a grievance does not by itself mean that the parties are necessarily 'in dispute' and had suggested that because a grievance might be upheld, or dismissed for reasons which the employee finds acceptable, the parties may therefore never reach the stage where they could properly be said to be 'in dispute' (see para.28).

However, the Court of Appeal in *Framlington Group* v. *Barnetson* [2007] IRLR 598 rejected the argument that for the 'without prejudice' rule to apply, there must be an express or implied threat of litigation underlying the negotiations, or some proximity in time to when the litigation began.

Lord Justice Auld held that a 'dispute' for this purpose includes a dispute where litigation has not yet commenced. He went on to say (para.34):

> However, the claim to privilege cannot, in my view, turn on purely temporal considerations. The critical feature of proximity for this purpose, it seems to me, is one of the subject matter of the dispute rather than how long before the threat, or start, of litigation it was aired in negotiations between the parties. Would they have respectively lowered their guards at that time and in the circumstances if they had not thought or hoped or contemplated that, by doing so, they could avoid the need to go to court over the very same dispute? On that approach, which I would commend, the crucial consideration would be whether in the course of negotiations the parties contemplated or might reasonably have contemplated litigation if they could not agree. Confining the operation of the rule, as the Judge did, to negotiations of a dispute in the course of, or after threat of litigation on it, or by reference to some time limit set close before litigation, does not, with respect, fully serve the public

policy interest underlying it of discouraging recourse to litigation and encouraging genuine attempts to settle whenever made.

It is difficult to reconcile the Court of Appeal's judgment with that part of the EAT's judgment in *BNP Paribas* v. *Mezzotero* which held that communications at a 'without prejudice' meeting to discuss a discrimination grievance were admissible because the grievance might have been upheld.

If there is no existing dispute between the parties, an employer cannot, for example, seek to engineer a termination of an employee's employment by mutual agreement under the guise of a 'without prejudice' discussion, and statements made in the course of such a discussion will not be privileged and will be admissible in evidence in subsequent proceedings.

Where the parties are not legally represented in 'without prejudice' discussions, there may be doubt as to whether the employee has genuinely agreed to enter into the discussions on that basis. If the employer is perceived as having taken unfair advantage of the employee, then tribunals are likely to be slow to find that there was such an agreement.

It is therefore recommended that where there is a potential dispute between the parties and an employer wishes to enter into 'without prejudice' discussions, it should:

(a) explain to the employee what 'without prejudice' means;
(b) offer the employee the opportunity to enter into such discussions with their lawyer present at the meeting;
(c) ensure that the employee has signed a letter such as the one in **Precedent 15C**.

Unambiguous impropriety

If both parties to a 'without prejudice' communication agree to waive privilege, then reference to the 'without prejudice' communication may be made.

However, in only one other case – that of unambiguous impropriety – will privilege be waived.

This has to be analogous to a blackmail threat of perjury as in the Court of Appeal case of *Savings & Investment Bank Ltd (in liquidation)* v. *Finken* [2003] EWCA Civ 1630.

Where parties in dispute agree that their correspondence will not be admissible as evidence, whether marked without prejudice or otherwise, such an agreement should only be disregarded in the most serious of circumstances, and on the clearest of evidence.

15.18 Mediation

Mediation is an ever increasingly popular method of resolving employment disputes. Judicial mediation has had some success. Mediation with trained mediators can also be highly successful. There are different styles of mediation including indicative, evaluative and judicial mediation.

Evaluative mediators give opinions – sometimes whether asked for or not. They make it clear that they have their own views on the strengths of the argument being put forward and on what the court is likely to do at trial. They also not only help the parties generate options for settlement but suggest their own and advocate them.

Indicative mediators do not say what they think the merits of the case are or how one of their fellow judges will decide the case. They identify the hurdles that each side is going to have to overcome in order to win.

Judicial mediation is a scheme offered by Employment Tribunals in specific cases (at a cost now to the parties of £600 each) that allows parties to seek a resolution to the proceedings without the need for a formal hearing. It is aimed specifically at cases involving sex, race or disability discrimination, where the claimant is still employed by the employer.

According to the Practice Note issued by the Law Society:

> A trained employment judge will act as the impartial mediator at the judicial mediation to try to help the parties to resolve their dispute. Nothing that happens or is said at the judicial mediation (including any documents prepared for the mediation) can be referred to in any subsequent tribunal hearings.

Mediation or alternative dispute resolution (ADR) is promoted in the ACAS 2009 Guide as an excellent means of resolving disputes and mediation can be drafted into disciplinary and grievance procedures as an optional stage.

ACAS recommends mediation in the following situations, in particular:

- for conflict involving colleagues of a similar job or grade, or between line managers and their staff;
- at any stage in the conflict as long as any ongoing formal procedures are put in abeyance, or where mediation is included as a stage in the procedures themselves;
- to rebuild relationships after a formal dispute has been resolved;
- to address a range of issues, including relationship breakdown, personality clashes, communication problems, bullying and harassment.

PRECEDENT 15A: Clauses relating to private medical insurance

The Company will continue your family membership of [*medical insurance scheme*] for [12 months] following your termination date at the Company's expense, subject to the Rules of the Scheme. Should you commence new employment which offers the same or comparable cover, you will surrender this benefit from the start date of your new employment. You will immediately inform [*specify*] as soon as you are offered and accept your new employment.

OR

Once your employment terminates, your private medical cover will cease. However, you may within three months of your termination date elect to take out a personal policy with our Provider and we have contacted [*give details*] who has agreed that you will be treated not as a new entrant but as having continuous cover for you and your family, thus all existing conditions will continue to be covered.

PRECEDENT 15B: Clause relating to duty to mitigate

1. The payment(s) referred to in clause [*specify*] will be made on a staged basis, in four equal three-monthly payments: the first being paid on [*date*], the second on [*date*], the third on [*date*] and the fourth on [*date*] all subject to your duty to mitigate your loss and seek new employment.

2. You will be required to report to the Managing Director each month to inform them of any interviews undertaken and any job offers made to you. Any unreasonable refusal on your part to accept a job offer will result in any or part of any further payments due ceasing.

3. Once you have received a job offer in writing, you are required to telephone in the first instance and send a copy of the offer letter in the strictest of confidence to the Managing Director and discuss whether you intend to accept the offer and any start date.

4. If you have a reasonable basis for rejecting a job offer, then further payments as set out above will continue.

5. Failure to notify the Managing Director of any job offer, acceptance of a job offer or that you have commenced new employment, will result in you being regarded as in material breach of this agreement. Any payments made during the course of any new employment where your new earnings are equivalent to or exceed the payment made by us will be recoverable as a debt under this agreement. Where the earnings in your new employment are lower than those received as at your termination date, the difference between what you received by way of a staged payment and your new earnings will be recoverable by the Company as a debt under this agreement and all future payments will cease as a result of this material breach.

PRECEDENT 15C: Without prejudice letter

(*Many thanks go to Maureen Stapley, HR Director of Allianz Global Assistance for giving me permission to use this letter.*)

[*Name and address*]

[*Date*]

Dear [*name*]

RE: Without prejudice meeting and legal representation

In order that we may hold a Without Prejudice discussion with you, please confirm the following by completing and signing one copy of this letter by [*date*].

Options

I have had the nature of the 'Without Prejudice' meeting explained and I agree ☐
to go ahead with the meeting on this basis. Without Prejudice discussions are
held between the parties to a dispute or a potential dispute to seek to settle
that dispute without either side reporting at a later date anything said during
such discussions.

Nothing that is said in Without Prejudice discussions can be repeated either to ☐
a court or tribunal or outside those discussions. However, if no agreement is
reached, such discussions and their content cannot ever be referred to in
future legal proceedings.

I agree to a meeting on a 'Without Prejudice' basis on the date specified and □
[will be/will not be] accompanied by my [solicitor/trade union representative].

I confirm that everything that is discussed at the meeting is on a 'Without □
Prejudice' basis and confirm that nothing that we discuss in this meeting can
be referred to at a later date or during tribunal proceedings and I agree to keep
everything that is discussed during the meeting strictly private and
confidential.

I agree that my [solicitor/trade union representative] may discuss this matter □
direct with you or your Legal Adviser.

Should you have any queries regarding the above, please do not hesitate in contacting me on [insert details].

Yours sincerely

I, [name], confirm that I have read and understood the declaration above and confirm that I was asked to bring a [solicitor/trade union representative] as legal representation to the above meeting. I [have chosen to bring my [solicitor/trade union representative] with me/however chose not to do so].

Signed .... Date...

PRECEDENT 15D: Model settlement agreement

PRIVATE AND CONFIDENTIAL

Without prejudice and subject to contract

Dated: [date]

(1) X PLC
and
(2) AB

Settlement agreement

THIS AGREEMENT is made on DATE

BETWEEN:-

(1) **X PLC of ADDRESS** whose registered office is [address], Company Registration No. ('the Company'); and
(2) **AB of ADDRESS** ('the Employee').

WHEREAS:

(A) The Employee's employment with the Company (unless terminated in accordance with Clause 16.5 of the Contract of Employment (in which circumstances this Agreement will not apply)) will terminate on 31 August 20[YY].
(B) Following discussions between the parties, this Agreement sets out the terms on which the Employee has agreed to compromise all of the claims the Employee has or may have against the Company, any Group Company, and/or any Associated Person, in respect of the Employee's employment and its termination.
(C) This Agreement is in full and final settlement of all claims that the Employee has

or may have against the Company, any Group Company and/or any Associated Person, unless expressly stated in this Agreement.

1. Definitions and interpretation

In this Agreement the following words and expressions shall have the following meanings save where the context otherwise requires:

'**Group**' means the Company, any holding company of the Company and any subsidiary of the Company or of any such holding company (with holding company and subsidiary having the meanings given to them by section 1159 of the Companies Act 2006) and **Group Company** shall be construed accordingly; and

'**Associated Person**' means the Company's or any Group Company's present or former officers, employees or directors.

2. Termination of employment

2.1 The Employee's employment with the Company under the terms of a service agreement dated 29 November 20.. (the '**Contract of Employment**') (unless terminated in accordance with Clause [XX] of the Contract of Employment (in which circumstances this Agreement will not apply)) will terminate on 31 August 20... (the '**Termination Date**').

2.2 The Employee will receive salary and benefits up to the Termination Date in the normal way at which date any entitlement to salary and benefits will cease, other than as provided in this Agreement.

2.3 The Employee will be reimbursed for all expenses incurred in connection with the Employee's employment up to the Termination Date, subject to receipt of satisfactory receipts and/or evidence of expenditure and the terms of the Company's expenses policy.

2.4 The Employee will not be required to attend work between 11 August 20.. and the Termination Date (the '**Garden Leave**'), but will continue to be bound by the terms and conditions of the Employee's Contract of Employment throughout the Garden Leave. During the Garden Leave, the Employee shall be contactable by the Company during normal business hours and available to attend work and for meetings and telephone conferences as required by the Company.

2.5 Upon written request from a prospective employer, in accordance with the instructions in this paragraph, the Company will supply a written reference in respect of the Employee in the terms of the draft attached at Schedule 2 to this Agreement. The Employee should inform any prospective employer that reference requests must be sent to [*address*].

3. Payments

3.1 Subject to (i) the Employee's compliance with the Employee's obligations under this Agreement; (ii) receipt of the Adviser's Certificate signed by the Adviser; and (iii) receipt by the Company of a Reaffirmation Certificate signed and dated by the Employee in accordance with Clause [XX] below, the Company shall, within 28 days of the later of the Termination Date, the date of this Agreement and receipt of a Reaffirmation Certificate signed and dated by the Employee, pay to the Employee:

   3.1.1 the sum of £............... [**figures and words**] (the '**Termination Payment**'). The Termination Payment is inclusive of any entitlement to a statutory redundancy payment;

3.1.2 a sum in respect of accrued but untaken Company holiday entitlement;
3.1.3 the sum of £....... in lieu of Pension Cash Supplement;
3.1.4 the sum of £......... in lieu of Pension contributions; and
3.1.5 the sum of £100 in respect of consideration for the obligations at Clause [XX] below.

3.2 The Termination Payment and the remainder of the payments referred to in Clause 3.1 above, will be paid subject to deduction of income tax and National Insurance contributions at the appropriate rate.

3.3 The Company will deduct from the net balance of the payments under Clause 3, before payment to the Employee, any outstanding sums in respect of the Employee's Company loan, Season Ticket Loan or overpayment of salary made to the Employee and owed by the Employee to the Company.

4. *Benefits and bonus*

4.1 Subject to (i) the Employee's compliance with the Employee's obligations under this Agreement, (ii) receipt of the Adviser's Certificate signed by the Adviser as set out in Schedule 2; and (iii) receipt by the Company of a Reaffirmation Certificate as set out in Schedule 4 signed and dated by the Employee in accordance with Clause 18 below, the Company will:

4.1.1 permit the Employee to retain and use the Employee's Staff discount on purchases made in stores until 30 April 2018, subject to the rules of the Staff Discount Scheme in force from time to time;

4.1.2 make available to the Employee career strategy and outplacement counselling and advice with .... to assist the Employee in finding new employment. The Company's liability to .... will be limited to the sum of £10,000 plus VAT and payment will be made directly to .... in accordance with the Company's standard payment terms following receipt of a properly marked VAT invoice addressed to the Company. These services can be used for the period of 12 months from the Termination Date;

4.1.3 make a discretionary lump sum payment of £............. to the Employee in full and final settlement of any entitlement to a bonus payment in respect of the 2016/2017 and 2017/18 bonus scheme years; and

4.1.4 make a discretionary payment of £[X] equivalent to 10 per cent of salary prorated for a notional nine-month period.

Except where otherwise stated, the sums payable under this Clause 4.1 will be paid to the Employee within 28 days of the Termination Date or the date of this Agreement, whichever is the later, and will be subject to deduction of tax at the appropriate rate and Employee's National Insurance Contributions.

4.2 In the event that the Employee requests the Company to pay a proportion of the payments made under this Agreement as a special contribution into the Pension Scheme ('the Scheme'), when the Employee retires and takes a Pension Commencement Lump Sum (the 'PCLS'), the Employee should be aware that HM Revenue and Customs may view this payment into the Employee's pension, or any subsequent contributions to other registered schemes, as 'recycling' sums into the Employee's pension. Accordingly, the Employee is advised to take appropriate independent advice based on the Employee's individual circumstances.

4.3 In signing this Agreement the Employee confirms that:

4.3.1 the Employee does not intend to use the Employee's PCLS directly or indirectly to increase contributions by the Employee or any of the Employee's dependants to the X Scheme or to any other registered pension arrangement; and

4.3.2 the Employee understands that if the Employee plans to do this and actually takes such action, HM Revenue and Customs may treat the PCLS as an 'unauthorised benefit' and tax it accordingly.

4.4 In the event that HM Revenue and Customs issues a penalty charge in respect of the payment of the PCLS, the Employee agrees to be responsible for the payment of such penalty, whether imposed upon the Employee or the Scheme, and, in the event that HM Revenue and Customs seeks to recover the whole or part of the penalty from the Scheme, to indemnify the Scheme fully in respect thereof. The Employee agrees to pay the Scheme the amount of any penalty within 14 days of the Scheme serving on the Employee a statement prepared by the Scheme's auditors certifying both the amount to be paid in respect of this indemnity and that the penalty falls due to be accounted for to a relevant taxing authority within 30 days of the date of the statement.

4.5 The Employee's options under the Deferred Share Bonus Plan and Performance Share Plan (the 'Share Schemes'), will be dealt with in accordance with the note sent to the Employee from the Company entitled 'Share Schemes on Leaving the Company – AB'.

4.6 With effect from the Termination Date, the Employee will have no entitlement to any bonus, or other payments or any entitlement to participate in any bonus, benefit or insurance scheme or share scheme other than as stated in this Agreement.

5. *Waiver of claims*

5.1 The Employee acknowledges that the Employee has carefully considered the facts and circumstances relating to the Employee's employment and its termination and agrees that the Employee irrevocably waives and forgoes and shall not institute or continue any claims, proceedings or complaints against the Company or any Group Company or any Associated Person before an Employment Tribunal or court arising under contract, statute, statutory instrument or European law arising out of or in connection with the Employee's employment or its termination save for the claims set out in Clause 6.1.3. In particular the Employee waives the following specific claims (the '**Specific Claims**'):

5.1.1 Any claim arising out of a contravention or alleged contravention of Part X of the Employment Rights Act 1996 (unfair dismissal);

5.1.2 Any claim arising out of a contravention or alleged contravention of the disciplinary or grievance procedures set out in the ACAS Code of Practice 1 – Disciplinary and Grievance Procedures and/or the statutory right to be accompanied at disciplinary, dismissal and grievance meetings;

5.1.3 Any claim arising out of a contravention or alleged contravention of section 135 of the Employment Rights Act 1996 (the right to a redundancy payment);

5.1.4 Any claim arising out of a contravention or an alleged contravention of a provision contained in Part II of the Employment Rights Act 1996 (Protection of Wages, including without limitation any claim for unauthorised deductions from wages and receipt of payments);

5.1.5 Any complaint under the Equality Act 2010 (including without limitation any claim for direct or indirect discrimination, harassment or victimisation on the grounds of or related to sex, marital or civil partnership status);

5.1.6 Any complaint for Equal Pay under the Equality Act 2010;

5.1.7 Any complaint for racial discrimination under the Equality Act 2010 (including without limitation any claim for direct or indirect discrimination, harassment or victimisation on the grounds of or related to colour, race, nationality and national origin);

5.1.8 Any complaint for disability discrimination under the Equality Act 2010 (including without limitation any claim for direct discrimination, disability-related discrimination, a failure to make reasonable adjustments, harassment, victimisation on the grounds of or related to disability);

5.1.9 Any claim arising out of a contravention or alleged contravention of section 92 (right to written statement of reasons for dismissal) of the Employment Rights Act 1996;

5.1.10 Any claim under the Working Time Regulations 1998 (including without limitation any claim for rest breaks, rest periods, statutory leave and holiday pay);

5.1.11 Any claim under the National Minimum Wage Act 1998;

5.1.12 Any claim for discrimination because of sexual orientation under the Equality Act 2010 (including without limitation for direct, indirect discrimination, harassment or victimisation on the grounds or nature of sexual orientation) or because of religious, religious beliefs or other beliefs under the Employment Equality (Religion or Belief) Regulations 2003 (including without limitation for direct, indirect discrimination, harassment or victimisation on the grounds or nature of religion or belief);

5.1.13 Any claim for failure to comply with obligations under the Information and Consultation of Employees Regulations 2004 and any claim under regulations 27 and 32 for failure to comply with obligations under the Trans-national Information and Consultation of Employees Regulations 1999;

5.1.14 Any claim arising out of a contravention or alleged contravention of the Occupational and Personal Pension Schemes (Consultation by Employers and Miscellaneous Amendment) Regulations 2006;

5.1.15 Any claim for age discrimination under the Equality Act 2010;

5.1.16 Any complaint under the Equality Act 2010 (including without limitation any claim for equality of terms, direct or indirect discrimination, a failure to make reasonable adjustments, harassment or victimisation or any other basis giving rise to liability because of or related to disability, age, sex, sexual orientation, gender reassignment, marital or civil partnership status, pregnancy and maternity, colour, race, religion or belief);

5.1.17 Any claim under any provision of directly applicable European Law;

5.1.18 Any claim for breach of contract;

5.1.19 Any claim for personal injury, of which the Employee is aware or ought reasonably to be aware at the date of this Agreement;

5.1.20 Any claim for detrimental treatment under Part V of the Employment Rights Act 1996 (including any detriment connected with a protected disclosure, jury service, health and safety, Sunday working, working time, flexible working, leave for family reasons);

5.1.21 Any claim under the Public Interest Disclosure Act 1998 or the relevant section of the Employment Rights Act 1996;

5.1.22 Any claim under the Maternity and Parental Leave Regulations 1999 as amended and the Shared Parental Leave Regulations 2014;

5.1.23 Any claim for statutory rights to take time off work and/or payment in respect of time off, suspension from work on maternity or medical grounds and/or payment during suspension;

5.1.24 Any claim in respect of a request to work flexibly or flexible working arrangements;

5.1.25 Any claim for less favourable treatment on the grounds of fixed-term status, under the Fixed-Term Employees (Prevention of Less Favourable Treatment) Regulations 2002;

5.1.26 Any claim for less favourable treatment on the grounds of part-time status under the Part-Time Workers Prevention of Less Favourable Treatment 2000;

5.1.27 Any claim arising out of a contravention or alleged contravention of section 188 (duty to consult on collective redundancies) or section 190 of the Trade Union and Labour Relations (Consolidation) Act 1992 (entitlement under protective award);

5.1.28 Any claim arising out of a contravention or alleged contravention of Regulation 13 (duty to inform and consult), Regulation 14 (election of employee representatives) or Regulation 15 (failure to inform and consult) of the Transfer of Undertakings (Protection of Employment) Regulations 2006;

5.1.29 Any claim for: statutory notice pay, written particulars, itemised payslips, guarantee payment under the Employment Rights Act 1996;

5.1.30 Any claim under the Protection from Harassment Act 1997;

5.1.31 Any complaint under the Human Rights Act 1998;

5.1.32 Any claim in relation to the right to be accompanied and for detriment in relation to this right under sections 11 and 12 of the Employment Relations Act 1999;

5.1.33 Any claim for failure to comply with the Data Protection Act 1998; and

5.1.34 Any claim under relevant sections of the Pensions Act 2014.

5.2 As detailed in clause 5.1.27, the Termination Payment has been paid to the Employee in full and final settlement of any entitlement to a protective award. Therefore, in the event that the Employee brings a successful claim for contravention of section 188 or section 190 of the Trade Union and Labour Relations (Consolidation) Act 1992 and is awarded a protective award by an Employment Tribunal, the Employee will refund to the Company in full from the Termination Payment, a sum equivalent to any such protective award. Such repayment will be made within 14 days of the date of the Employment Tribunal Order.

6. *Full and final settlement*

6.1 The Employee accepts the terms of this Agreement in full and final settlement:

6.1.1 of the Specific Claims; and

6.1.2 all and any other claims, or other rights of action or costs and expense whatsoever and howsoever arising whether under statute, contract, at common law or otherwise which the Employee has or may have now or in the future against the Company, any Group Company or any Associated Person arising (whether in the UK or another jurisdiction) out of or in connection with the Employee's employment by the Company or its termination, whether known or unknown to the parties, whether existing at the time of this Agreement, whether in the contemplation of the parties at the time of this Agreement and whether or not such claims fall within the jurisdiction of an Employment Tribunal;

6.1.3 but excluding any claims by the Employee to enforce this Agreement, any personal injury claims of which the Employee is not aware or could not reasonably be expected to be aware at the date of this Agreement, or any claims in relation to accrued entitlements under the Company's pension scheme. The Employee warrants that the Employee is not aware of any such claims at the date of this Agreement.

6.2 For the avoidance of doubt it is the parties' express intention when entering into this Agreement for the waiver and settlement to include a waiver of all future claims that the Employee has or may have against the Company, any Group Company or Associated Person arising out of or in connection with the Employee's employment with the Company or its termination.

6.3 Without prejudice to Clause 6.1.2 above, the Employee warrants that the Employee is not aware of any statutory claims that the Employee may have other than the Specific Claims.

7. Acknowledgement of advice

7.1 The Employee acknowledges that the Employee has taken advice from [*name*] of [*name and address of firm*] (being a 'relevant independent adviser' (as defined by Section 203(3) of the Employment Rights Act 1996 (as amended)) (the '**Adviser**') as to the terms and effect of this Agreement and in particular its effect on the Employee's ability to pursue the Employee's rights before an Employment Tribunal.

7.2 The Employee and the Company believe and agree that the Adviser is an independent adviser for the purposes of Section 147(3)(c) of the Equality Act 2010. If the Employee challenges the validity of this Agreement on the basis that the Adviser does not meet the requirements of Section 147 of the Equality Act 2010, the Employee undertakes to repay the Termination Payment immediately upon demand, to be recoverable by the Company as a debt.

7.3 The Employee warrants that the Adviser has confirmed to the Employee that at the time of the Employee taking the legal advice referred to above, the Adviser had a policy of insurance or an indemnity provided for members of a professional body covering the risk of a claim by the Employee in respect of any loss arising in consequence of such advice.

7.4 The Employee agrees and warrants that, having taken legal advice from the Adviser the Specific Claims are all the claims (whether statutory or otherwise) which the Employee has or may have against the Company, the Group and Associated Persons and the Employee confirms that the Employee has raised all relevant facts and matters pertaining to the employment, the term of employment and the termination of the Employee's employment with the Adviser and the Company and the Employee acknowledge that the Company enters into this Agreement in reliance on the warranty given by the Employee in this Clause.

7.5 The Employee warrants that the Adviser will sign the Adviser's Certificate at Schedule 3 with effect from the date of this Agreement.

8. Compliance with legislation

The conditions regulating settlement agreements under Section 203(3) of the Employment Rights Act 1996, Section 147(3)(c) and (d) of the Equality Act 2010, Section 288(2B) of the Trade Union and Labour Relations (Consolidation) Act 1992, Section 49(4) of the National Minimum Wage Act 1998, Regulation 35(3) of the Working Time Regulations 1998, Regulations 41(4) of the Transnational Information and Consultation of Employees Regulations 1999, Regulation 9 of the Part-Time Workers (Prevention of Less Favourable Treatment) Regulations 2000, Regulation 10 of the Fixed-Term Employees (Prevention of Less Favourable Treatment) Regulations 2002, Schedule 4, Part 1, Paragraph 2(2) of the Employment Equality (Sexual Orientation) Regulations 2003, Schedule 4 Part 1, Paragraph 2(2) of the Employment Equality (Religion and Belief) Regulations 2003, Regulation 40(4) of the Information and Consultation of Employees Regulations 2004, Schedule 5 Part 1, Paragraph 2(2) of the Employment Equality (Age) Regulations 2006, Regulation 18 of the Transfer of Undertakings (Protection of Employment) Regulations 2006 and Paragraph 13 of the Schedule of the

Occupational and Personal Pension Schemes (Consultation by Employers and Miscellaneous Amendment) Regulations 2006 and the Pensions Act 2014 (as such legislation has been or is amended from time to time) or any other equivalent provision in other UK legislation (the '**Employment Legislation**') have been satisfied.

9. *Tax indemnity*

The Company makes no warranty as to the taxable status of the payments made under this Agreement. In the event that the payments made and benefits provided pursuant to this Agreement if at any time assessed to income tax, PAYE and/or Employee national insurance contributions ('**Taxation**') whether in addition to such deductions as the Company may make at the time payment is made or otherwise, the Employee agrees to be responsible for the payment of such Taxation and, in the event that HM Revenue and Customs seeks to recover the whole or part of the Taxation from the Company, to indemnify the Company fully in respect thereof and in respect of any interest and penalties thereon apart from interest and penalties due as a result of unreasonable delay, default or negligence by the Company arising after any assessment by HM Revenue and Customs, in dealing with the demand. The Employee agrees to pay the Company the amount of any Taxation (together with any such interest and penalties) within 14 days of the Company serving on the Employee a statement prepared by the Company's auditors certifying both the amount to be paid in respect of this indemnity and that the Taxation falls due to be accounted for to a relevant taxing authority within 30 days of the date of the statement. The Company shall give the Employee reasonable notice of any demand for tax which may lead to liabilities on the Employee under this indemnity and shall provide the Employee with reasonable access to any documentation the Employee may reasonably require to dispute such a claim (provided that nothing in this clause shall prevent the Company from complying with its legal obligations with regard to HM Revenue and Customs or other competent body).

10. *Return of company property*

10.1 In accordance with Clause [XX] of the Employee's Contract of Employment, the Employee warrants that on or before the Termination Date the Employee will return to the Company all papers, documents and information in any form (including copies and whether written or on tape, disc or cassette or electronic format), and any other property belonging to the Company or any other Group Company in the Employee's possession, custody or power. If any property belonging to any Group Company subsequently comes into the Employee's possession, custody or power the Employee agrees to return it to the Company immediately. The Employee further undertakes that the Employee has not taken unauthorised copies of any papers or documents or information in any form.

10.2 The Employee further warrants that by the Termination Date the Employee will copy to the Company and then delete from the hard disk of any private computer used by the Employee (i.e. not being a computer in the possession of the Company, any Group Company or Associated Person) all documents and information belonging to or obtained from or prepared for the Company or any Group Company or any Associated Person or any of its or their respective customers or clients and the Employee shall inform the Company of any passwords used by the Employee which are the property of the Company or any Group Company or any Associated Person.

11. *Confidentiality*

11.1 The Employee will continue to comply with the provisions of Clause [XX] of the

Employee's Contract of Employment relating to confidential information notwithstanding the termination of the Employee's employment. These obligations are restated below.

11.2 Save insofar as such information is already in the public domain the Employee will keep secret and will not at any time (whether during the Employment or thereafter) use for the Employee's own or another's advantage, or disclose to any person, firm, company or organisation and shall use the Employee's best endeavours to prevent the publication or disclosure of any information which the Employee knows or ought reasonably to have known to be confidential, concerning the business or affairs of the Company or any Group Company or any of its or their customers. For the purposes of this Clause the following information shall, without limitation, be treated as confidential information:

- (i) information relating to the X group operational and strategic planning, including forthcoming designs and product ranges, marketing plans and opportunities, and sourcing and manufacturing arrangements;
- (ii) information relating to the X group corporate strategy, including its financing and any proposed corporate transactions; and
- (iii) information relating to the X group know-how and processes, and any other trade secrets.

The restrictions in this Clause 11 shall not apply:

- (a) to any disclosure or use authorised by the Company or required by law or by the Employee's employment by the Company;
- (b) so as to prevent the Employee from using the Employee's own personal skill in any business in which the Employee may be lawfully engaged after the Employee's employment is ended.

12. *Intellectual property*

12.1 The Employee will continue to comply with the provisions of Clause [XX] of the Employee's Contract of Employment relating to intellectual property notwithstanding the termination of the Employee's employment. These obligations are restated below.

12.2 As part of the Employee's normal duties (whether in or out of normal hours/place of work) the Employee will consider how the Company's products, processes, equipment or systems under the Employee's responsibility or with which the Employee is concerned can be improved, and to create concepts, designs (whether registrable or not) or patentable work in which copyright or other intellectual property rights can exist. The Employee will provide full details of such concepts/products/designs to the Company in confidence, and will waive in favour of the Company all rights granted to the Employee by Chapter IV of Part I of the Copyright, Designs and Patents Act 1988 for any work in which copyright or design rights or other intellectual property rights are vested in the Company, whether by this clause or otherwise. The Company will have absolute ownership and will be entitled to exclusive use of all intellectual property rights in such concepts, designs or work.

12.3 The Employee agrees to assign at any time to the Company, the copyright or other intellectual property rights of any works written, conceived, originated or made by the Employee during the Employee's employment, unless these works have been produced outside the Employee's normal working hours and are unconnected with the Employee's employment.

12.4 At any time during or after the Employee's employment, the Employee agrees to take any action or provide any information that the Company deems necessary to prove its intellectual property rights (including for the purposes of obtaining letters patent or other privileges) in any country the Company may require.

13. *Restrictions*

13.1 The Employee acknowledges that the provisions of Clause [XX] of the Employee's Contract of Employment will remain in full force and effect notwithstanding the termination of the Employee's employment. The relevant provisions are restated below.

    13.1.1 The Employee hereby covenants with the Company (for itself and as trustee and agent for each Group Company) that the Employee shall not, whether directly or indirectly, on the Employee's own behalf or on behalf of or in conjunction with any other person, firm, company or other entity:

        (a) for the period of six months (subject to Clause 13.3 below) following the Termination Date, solicit or entice away or endeavour to solicit or entice away from the Company or any Group Company any person, firm, company or other entity who is, or was, in the 12 months immediately prior to the Termination Date, a client of the Company or any Group Company with whom the Employee had business dealings during the course of the Employee's employment in that 12-month period. Nothing in this Clause 13.1.1(a) shall prohibit the seeking or doing of business not in direct or indirect competition with the business of the Company or any Group Company;

        (b) for the period of six months (subject to Clause 13.3 below) following the Termination Date, solicit or entice away or try to solicit or entice away from the Company or any Group Company any person, firm, company or other entity who is, or was, in the 12 months immediately prior to the Termination Date, a prospective client of the Company or any Group Company. For the purposes of this Clause 13.1.1(b) and Clause 13.1.1(c) the term 'prospective client' shall mean any person, firm, company or other entity which was, in the 12-month time period immediately prior to the Termination Date, being actively solicited or responded positively to canvassing by the Company or any Group Company and with which solicitation the Employee was involved during the course of the Employee's employment in that 12 months. Nothing in this Clause 13.1.1(b) shall prohibit the seeking or doing of business not in direct or indirect competition with the business of the Company or any Group Company;

        (c) for the period of six months (subject to Clause 13.3 below) following the Termination Date, have any business dealings with any person, firm, company or other entity who is, or was, in the 12 months immediately prior to the Termination Date, a client of the Company or any Group Company with whom the Employee had business dealings during the course of the Employee's employment in that 12-month period. Nothing in this Clause 13.1.1(c) shall prohibit the seeking or doing of business not in direct or indirect competition with the business of the Company or any Group Company;

        (d) for the period of six months (subject to Clause 13.3 below) following the Termination Date, have any business dealings with any person, firm, company or other entity who is, or was, in the 12 months immediately prior to the Termination Date, a prospective client of the Company or any Group Company with whom the Employee had business dealings during the course of the Employee's employment in that 12-month period;

(e) for the period of six months (subject to Clause 13.3 below) following the Termination Date, solicit or entice away or endeavour to solicit or entice away any individual person who is employed or engaged by the Company or any Group Company either (a) as a director or in a managerial, executive or technical capacity; or (b) who is in possession of confidential information belonging to the Company and/or any Group Company and with whom the Employee had business dealings during the course of the Employee's employment in the 12-month period immediately prior to the Termination Date;

(f) for the period of six months (subject to Clause 13.3 below) following the Termination Date, employ or engage, whether on an employed or self-employed basis or in any other office or capacity, any individual person who is employed or engaged by the Company or any Group Company either (a) as a director or in a managerial, executive or technical capacity or (b) who is in possession of confidential information belonging to the Company and/or any Group Company and with whom the Employee had business dealings during the course of the Employee's employment in the 12-month period immediately prior to the Termination Date; and

(g) for the period of six months (subject to Clause 13.3 below) following the Termination Date, carry on, set up, be employed, engaged or interested in a business which is a major retailer (including, but not limited to, any major online retailer) operating anywhere in the UK in competition with the business of the Company or any Group Company as at the Termination Date with which the Employee was actively involved during the 12-month period immediately prior to the Termination Date. It is agreed that in the event that any such business ceases to be in competition with the Company and/or any Group Company, then this clause will no longer apply to that business. After termination of the Employee's employment, the Employee will be able to hold shares or other capital of up to three per cent of the total issued share capital of any company, and the Employee will be able to have business dealings that are not in direct or indirect competition with the business of the Company or any Group Company.

(h) for the period of six months after the termination of the Employee's employment stop or in any way interfere or restrict the supply by a Supplier to the Company of Competitive Services or the supply of any other goods or services for a business in which the Employee was actively involved at any time during the 12 months prior to the Termination Date. Supplier is a person who was supplying or negotiating to supply goods/services to the Company or any Group Company for a business in which the Employee was actively involved and the terms of which supply or negotiation the Employee was aware. Competitive Services are goods/services that are similar to or competitive with goods/services that a Supplier was supplying or had agreed to supply or was negotiating to supply to the Company at any time during the 12 months prior to the termination of the Employee's employment).

13.2 The period during which the restrictions referred to in Clauses 13.1.1(a) to (h) inclusive shall apply following the Termination Date shall be reduced by the period of the Garden Leave.

13.3 The Employee agrees that if, during either the Employee's employment with the Company or the period of the restrictions set out in Clauses 13.1.1(a) to (h) inclusive (subject to the provisions of Clause 13.2), the Employee receives an offer of employment or engagement, the Employee will provide a copy of Clause 13 to the offeror as soon as is reasonably practicable after receiving the offer and will inform the Company of the identity of the offeror and the terms of the offer.

13.4 The Employee will, at the request and expense of the Company, enter into a separate agreement with any Group Company that the Company may require under the terms of which the Employee will agree to be bound by restrictions corresponding to those contained in Clauses 13.1.1(a) to (h) inclusive (or such as may be appropriate in the circumstances).

13.5 The Employee will not whether directly or indirectly commit any act or do any act or thing which it might reasonably be expected would damage the business, interests or reputation of the Company, any Group Company or any Associated Person.

13.6 The Employee will not whether directly or indirectly make, publish or otherwise communicate any disparaging or derogatory statements, whether in writing or otherwise, concerning the Company, any Group Company or any Associated Person.

13.7 The Employee agrees not to make any statements to the press or other media in connection with the Company, any Group Company or any Associated Person without the prior written consent of the Company.

13.8 The Company agrees to use its reasonable endeavours to ensure that any individual who is aware of the fact, terms and circumstances of this Agreement will not, at any time after the date of this Agreement, directly or indirectly make, publish, authorise or otherwise communicate any disparaging or derogatory statements whether in writing or otherwise which are intended to or which might be expected to damage or lower the business or professional reputation of the Employee.

14. Assistance with claims

In the event of a claim being brought against the Company or any Group Company or any Associated Person as a result of or otherwise connected to the period of the Employee's employment with the Company, the Employee undertakes to provide all such information, co-operation and assistance as the Company may reasonably require in the defence of that claim provided that the Company meets the Employee's reasonable expenses in respect of it.

15. Disclosure of terms

The Employee undertakes that the Employee will not at any time without the prior written consent of the Company disclose to the employees of the Company or any Group Company or to any other person the fact, terms and circumstances of this Agreement (including details regarding the negotiations leading up to this Agreement and any discussions, events, facts or circumstances leading up to the existence of this Agreement) unless required to do so by law. This provision does not preclude the Employee from disclosing the terms of this Agreement to the Employee's legal and/or other professional advisers, spouse or partner, who the Employee agrees will also be bound by the same obligations of non-disclosure.

16. *Undisclosed breaches and misconduct*

The Employee warrants that the Employee has not, at any time, committed any breach of their Contract of Employment or any serious misconduct which at the time of the breach would have entitled the Company to terminate the Employee's employment without notice. It is a strict condition of payments referred to in Clause 3.1 that this warranty is and continues to be true and accurate and that none of the circumstances outlined in Clauses [XX–XX] of the Contract of Employment are believed by the Company to have arisen.

17. *Repayment of termination payment*

If the Employee breaches any obligation contained within this Agreement, the Employee undertakes to repay such portion of the payments referred to in Clause 3.1 which corresponds to the loss, damages and costs the Company incurs as a result of such breach immediately upon demand, such portion of those payments to be recoverable by the Company as a debt.

18. *Reaffirmation certificate*

It is a further condition of this Agreement and of payment of the Termination Payment that the Employee signs and dates the Reaffirmation Certificate set out at Schedule 4 on or just prior to the Termination Date and delivers it to the Employment Team, Legal Department, [*address*].

19. *Liability*

This Agreement is made without admission of liability on the part of the Company.

20. *Law and jurisdiction*

20.1 This Agreement shall be governed by and construed in accordance with English Law.

20.2 The parties submit to the exclusive jurisdiction of the English Courts and tribunals with regard to any dispute or claim arising under this Agreement.

21. *General*

21.1 A reference to any legislative provision includes any lawful amendment or re-enactment of it.

21.2 The headings in this Agreement are for convenience only and shall not affect its interpretation.

21.3 This Agreement sets out the entire agreement and understanding between the parties and supersedes all previous agreements and arrangements (if any) both oral and in writing relating to the termination of the Employee's employment and may not be modified except by an instrument in writing signed by the duly authorised representatives of the parties.

21.4 Each Group Company and Associated Person shall be able to enforce in its or their own right the terms of this Agreement which expressly or impliedly confer any benefit on that entity or person subject to and in accordance with the Contracts (Rights of Third Parties) Act 1999. The parties also agree that they shall be entitled to rescind or vary by mutual written agreement all or any of the rights of any Group Company or Associated Person under this Agreement without the consent of the relevant Group Company or Associated Person.

22. *Binding agreement*

Notwithstanding that this Agreement is marked 'without prejudice and subject to contract', once the Agreement has been signed by both parties and the certificate is signed by the Adviser, this Agreement will cease to be 'without prejudice' and will become open and binding.

....
Signed by [*name*]   Signed by the Employee
For and on behalf of X plc   [*name*]
Dated: [*date*]   Dated: [*date*]

SCHEDULE 1 – CLAIMS

1. *Claims:*

(a) [for breach of contract or wrongful dismissal;]

(b) [for unfair dismissal, under section 111 of the Employment Rights Act 1996;]

(c) [in relation to the right to a written statement of reasons for dismissal, under section 93 of the Employment Rights Act 1996;]

(d) [for a statutory redundancy payment, under section 163 of the Employment Rights Act 1996;]

(e) [in relation to an unlawful deduction from wages or unlawful payment, under section 23 of the Employment Rights Act 1996;]

(f) [for unlawful detriment, under section 48 of the Employment Rights Act 1996 or section 56 of the Pensions Act 2008;]

(g) [in relation to written employment particulars and itemised pay statements, under section 11 of the Employment Rights Act 1996;]

(h) [in relation to guarantee payments, under section 34 of the Employment Rights Act 1996;]

(i) [in relation to suspension from work, under section 70 of the Employment Rights Act 1996;]

(j) [in relation to parental rights and flexible working, under sections 80 and 80H of the Employment Rights Act 1996;]

(k) [in relation to time off work, under sections 51, 54, 57, 57B, 60, 63 and 63C of the Employment Rights Act 1996;]

(l) [in relation to working time or holiday pay, under regulation 30 of the Working Time Regulations 1998;]

(m) [in relation to the National Minimum Wage, under sections 11, 18, 19D and 24 of the National Minimum Wage Act 1998;]

(n) [for equal pay or equality of terms under sections 120 and 127 of the Equality Act 2010 [and/or section 2 of the Equal Pay Act 1970];]

(o) [for pregnancy or maternity discrimination, direct or indirect discrimination, harassment or victimisation related to sex, marital or civil partnership status, pregnancy or maternity or gender reassignment under section 120 of the Equality Act 2010 [and/or direct or indirect discrimination, harassment or victimisation related to sex, marital or civil partnership status, gender reassignment, pregnancy or maternity under section 63 of the Sex Discrimination Act 1975];]

(p) [for direct or indirect discrimination, harassment or victimisation related to race under section 120 of the Equality Act 2010 [and/or direct or indirect discrimination, harassment or victimisation related to race, colour, race, nationality or ethnic or national origin, under section 54 of the Race Relations Act 1976];]

(q) [for direct or indirect discrimination, harassment or victimisation related to disability, discrimination arising from disability, or failure to make adjustments under section 120 of the Equality Act 2010 [and/or direct discrimination, harassment or victimisation related to disability, disability-related discrimination or failure to make adjustments under section 17A of the Disability Discrimination Act 1995];]

(r) [for direct or indirect discrimination, harassment or victimisation related to religion or belief under section 120 of the Equality Act 2010 [and/or under regulation 28 of the Employment Equality (Religion or Belief) Regulations 2003];]

(s) [for direct or indirect discrimination, harassment or victimisation related to sexual orientation, under section 120 of the Equality Act 2010 [and/or under regulation 28 of the Employment Equality (Sexual Orientation) Regulations 2003];]

(t) [for direct or indirect discrimination, harassment or victimisation related to age, under section 120 of the Equality Act 2010 [and/or under regulation 36 of the Employment Equality (Age) Regulations 2006];]

(u) [in relation to the duty to consider working beyond retirement, under paragraphs 11 and 12 of Schedule 6 to the Employment Equality (Age) Regulations 2006;]

(v) [for less favourable treatment on the grounds of part-time status, under regulation 8 of the Part-Time Workers (Prevention of Less Favourable Treatment) Regulations 2000;]

(w) [for less favourable treatment on the grounds of fixed-term status, under regulation 7 of the Fixed-Term Employees (Prevention of Less Favourable Treatment) Regulations 2002;]

(x) [under regulations 27 and 32 of the Transnational Information and Consultation etc. Regulations 1999;]

(y) [under regulations 29 and 33 of the Information and Consultation of Employees Regulations 2004;]

(z) [under regulations 45 and 51 of the Companies (Cross-Border Mergers) Regulations 2007;]

(aa) [under paragraphs 4 and 8 of the Schedule to the Occupational and Personal Pension Schemes (Consultation by Employers and Miscellaneous Amendment) Regulations 2006;]

(ab) [under sections 68A, 87, 137, 145A, 145B, 146, 168, 168A, 169, 170, 174 and 192 of the Trade Union and Labour Relations (Consolidation) Act 1992;]

(ac) [in relation to the obligations to elect appropriate representatives or any entitlement to compensation, under the Transfer of Undertakings (Protection of Employment) Regulations 2006;]

(ad) [in relation to the right to be accompanied under section 11 of the Employment Relations Act 1999;]

(ae) [in relation to refusal of employment, refusal of employment agency services and detriment under regulations 5, 6 and 9 of the Employment Relations Act 1999 (Blacklists) Regulations 2010;]

(af) [in relation to the right to request time off for study or training under section 63I of the Employment Rights Act 1996;]

(ag) [in relation to the right to equal treatment, access to collective facilities and amenities, access to employment vacancies and the right not to be subjected to a detriment under regulations 5, 12, 13 and 17(2) of the Agency Workers Regulations 2010;]

(ah) [in relation to personal injury[, whether or not the Employee is aware or ought reasonably to be aware of such claims at the date of this agreement];]

(ai) [for harassment under the Protection from Harassment Act 1997;]

(aj) [for failure to comply with obligations under the Human Rights Act 1998;]

(ak) [for failure to comply with obligations under the Data Protection Act 1998;]

(al) [arising as a consequence of the UK's membership of the European Union.]

SCHEDULE 2 – *Reference*

Private and Confidential

FAO:

[name]

[company]

[date]

Dear [name]

RE: Reference request for [name]

It is company policy to provide the following information only:

Start date:
Termination date:
Job title:

No negative inference should be drawn by the giving only of these details.

This is given and received without any legal liability on the part of the Company or the author of this reference.

Yours sincerely

[signature]

HR Director

SCHEDULE 3 – *Adviser's Certificate*

[Headed notepaper of Firm]

I, [name of solicitor and name and address of Firm] confirm that AB (the '**Employee**') has received independent legal advice from me on the terms and effect of the Settlement Agreement between the Employee and X plc (the '**Company**') (the '**Settlement Agreement**') and in particular, its effect on the Employee's ability to pursue the Employee's rights before an Employment Tribunal in accordance with the provisions of the Employment Legislation as defined in the Settlement Agreement.

I am not acting (and have not acted) in the matter for the Company or any Group Company or Associated Person (each as defined in the Settlement Agreement).

I also confirm that I am a solicitor of the Senior Courts of England and Wales, who holds a valid practising certificate and whose firm is covered by a policy of insurance or an indemnity provided for members of a professional body covering the risk of a claim in respect of any loss arising in consequence of the advice that I have given to the Employee in connection with the terms and effect of the Settlement Agreement.

SIGNED: ....

Adviser

DATED: ....

SCHEDULE 4 – *Reaffirmation Certificate*

I hereby confirm that, having taken legal advice, as at the date hereof, there are no matters or circumstances which do or might give rise to any claims by me in connection with my employment by X plc (the 'Company') or the termination of my employment with the Company which have arisen since the date of the Agreement set out above. I further confirm that the warranties given by me in the Agreement remain true and correct as at the date of this Certificate. I acknowledge that it is a condition of this Agreement that I give this Reaffirmation, upon which the Company will rely.

SIGNED: ....

Employee

DATED: ....

Index

abroad *see* overseas working; travel
absence 6.1
    absence control 6AF
    authorised absence 6.1
    BMA model letter for long-term/acute sickness absence 6G
    conduct during sickness absence 6.15, 6N
    deductions from salary 5T
    duration of sickness 6.13
    holidays during sick leave 2.6, 6.17, 6Q
    letters relating to 6AG
    managers 6AF
    negligence of third parties 6.21, 6V
    notice during 12.10
    reporting for work 6.1, 6A, 6B
    short-term absences 6.28
    unauthorised absence 5T
    withholding of payment 5T
    see also time-keeping
acceptance of offer of employment 1.3
    with signature of employee 1.1, 2.4
accidents
    travelling abroad 4T
account of profits
    breach of contract 14.18
accuracy
    requirement to work fast and accurately 4.10, 4I
admissions of guilt 9.22, 9P
adoption leave 7.1
    cover 7C
    policy 7F
adoption pay
    policy 7F
    statutory adoption pay 7.2
advance payments 5.13
advertisements 1.8
advice to staff
    duty to advise
        limited duty 1.1
        no duty to advise of consequences of terms 1.1
        specific duty 1.1
    on grievance procedures 11.2
    occupational health advice 6.10, 6J
agency workers 3.2
    security guard 3J
aggravated damages 11.8
alcohol
    company cars and 5.7
    policy on 6.18, 8.10, 8G, 8H
alternative/light duties 6.19, 6T
annualised hours 4.11, 4L
anti-slavery statement 8.2, 8A
appearance *see* dress and appearance
application forms 1.9
    care staff 1F
    retention 1.11
area covenants 14.13, 14M
asylum seekers 2.1
    policy on prevention of illegal working 2D
    see also work permits

background checks 1.5
    permission 1C
bad leavers 12.13
bank holidays 2.6
'bank' staff 3.9
banqueting staff 3.11
    job description 3I
behaviour *see* conduct
betting syndicates 8.11, 8I
blogging 13.14
bonus schemes/bonus payments 5.3
    capping 5.3
    challenging the size of the bonus 5.3
    conditional bonus 5F(i)
    discretionary bonus 1.8, 5.3, 5E
    Equality Act and 5.3
    gagging clause 5.3, 5D
    guaranteed bonus 5D
    holiday pay and 5.3

bonus schemes/bonus payments (*contd*)
    income tax issues 5.3
    maternity and 7.3
    maternity leave and 7.3
    pro rata bonuses 5.3
    profit-sharing schemes 1.8
    prohibition on discussing 9.30
    repayable bonus 5.3, 5F(ii)
    secrecy clauses 5.3, 5D
    unfair contract terms 5.3
breach of confidentiality 9.5, 9E
breach of contract
    accounting for profits 14.18
    conspiracy to commit 2.2
    restrictive covenant 14.18
    settlement agreements 15.4
bribery 8.3, 8C
    compliance rules 8L
    hospitality/gifts 8B, 8D
bridging loans 5.14
bullying
    aggravated damages 11.8
    civil damages 11.8
    confidentiality of procedures 11.4, 11B
    cyber-bullying 13.1
    informing complainant of action taken 11.8
    mediation 11.4
    policies on 11.8, 11F
    special complaints procedure 11.4
    suspension of alleged perpetrator 11.4, 11C
    see also harassment
bumping *see* redundancy
burn out syndrome 6.14
burqas 8.16
business lunches/dinners 8.8, 8F

car allowance 5.7, 5J
    maternity leave and 7.3
care staff
    application form 1F
career breaks
    maternity rights 7.4, 7E
cars *see* car allowance; company car; driving
casual workers 3.7
    appointment form 3F
    terms of engagement 3E
    weekly timesheet/payment form 3G
cell/mobile phone usage 4X, 13.8
changes to contracts 2.10, 4.1
    variation clause 4A
chauffeurs
    Working Time Regulations 4O
children
    on company premises 8.12, 8J
Christmas parties 8.8, 8F
    checklist 8T
    vicarious liability 8.8, 11.8
chronic embitterment 6.14
clauses
    bad leavers 12.13
    confidentiality *see* confidentiality clauses
    conflict of interest 14I
    consent to medical examinations 6.5, 6E
    duties in employment 4B
    email monitoring 13C
    entire agreement clause 1.4, 1.12
    excluding disciplinary procedures 9A
    expenses 5P
    fast and accurate work 4I
    gagging clause 5.3, 5D, 11.9, 15.10
    garden leave 12.12, 12D, 12F
    holidays 6P
    indemnity clauses 3D, 11.6, 11D, 15.16
    internet monitoring 13C
    liquidated damages clause 2.2
    misusing company facilities 14.10, 14J
    mobility clause 4.5, 4D
    no set working hours 4K
    non-disclosure of salary/bonus 9.30
    overtime 4J
    payment in lieu of notice 12.6, 12.7, 12.9, 12F
        duty to mitigate 12.9, 15.14, 15B
    penalty clause 2.2
    repayment clause 5.13, 5T
    repute clause 8.5, 8.6
    restrictive covenants *see* restrictive covenants
    secrecy clause 5.3, 5D
    status quo/standstill clause 9.24, 11.1
    training 4F
    variation clause 4A
    void for uncertainty 1.6, 12.9, 14.7
    whole time and attention clause 4.3, 14.19, 14R
clear desk/screen policy 4.12, 4S
close relatives
    employment of 2.12, 2K

clothing *see* dress and
    appearance
codes of conduct 8.4, 8D
collateral contracts 1.3
collections at work 8.13, 8K
commission payments 1.1, 5.5
    holiday pay and 5.5
    repayment of advance commission
        5.13
communications *see* emails;
    telephone
company car 5.7, 5J, 5K
    bad weather 5.7
    drinking and driving 5.7
    fatigue 5.7
    maternity leave and 7.3
    parking offences 5.7
complaints handling policy 9F
compliance rules 8.14, 8L
compromise agreements *see*
    settlement agreements
computers
    clear desk/screen policy 4.12, 4S
    computer operators working at
        night 4Q
    irritable desk syndrome 4.12
    IT and computer equipment
        policy 13E
    requirement to be trained/up to
        date 4.8
    Working Time Regulations 4Q
conditional bonus 5F(i)
conditional offers/pre-offers
    1.5, 1B
    background checks 1.5
    conditional on references 1E
    examination results 1.5, 2B
    medical conditions 1.5
    medical examinations 1.5
    past criminal convictions 1.5
    pre-conditions 1.5
    professional partnership 1D
    references 1.7
conduct
    disciplinary procedures and 9.2
    during sickness absence 6.15, 6N
    implied terms and 1.4
    undertaking to behave 9.17, 9M
    see also rules and standards of
        conduct
confidentiality
    allegations of breach of 9.5, 9E
    contract clauses *see* confidentiality
        clauses
    harassment/bullying 11.4, 11B

medical reports 6.5, 6E
confidentiality clauses 14.7,
    14.8, 14A
    categories of confidential
        information 14.8
    disciplinary procedures 9.5, 9D
    non-medical staff 14F
    occupational health 14E
    reception staff 14G
    senior executives 14B
    software 14C
    temporary staff 14D
    see also restrictive covenants
conflict of interest
    clauses 14I
    compliance rules 8.14
    discrimination claim 11.6
consensual relationships *see*
    relationships at work
consideration 1.3
    settlement agreements 15.7
conspiracy
    to commit breach of contract 2.2
constructive dismissal 1.8, 2.2
    implied terms and 1.4
consultants
    consultancy agreement 3C, 3K
    contract for services 3.4, 3D
    indemnity clause 3D
    specialist consultants 3.17
consultation
    redundancy *see* redundancy
continuing education 4.8
contra proferentum rule 1.1
contract for services
    checklist 3.4
    consultant/sub-contractor 3.4, 3B,
        3D
    indemnity clause 3D
corruption 8.3, 8C
    see also bribery
covenants *see* restrictive
    covenants
covert recordings 5.13, 9.19, 9O
covert surveillance
    Code of Practice 13.12
    emails 13.9
    human rights issues 13.12
    malingering/moonlighting 6.27
    private detectives 6.27, 6AD, 6AE
    telephone 13.9
    see also surveillance staff
credit checks
    authority to obtain 2G

INDEX

criminal convictions/charges 1.5, 9.25
custom
    implied terms 1.4
cyber-bullying 13.1
cyber-liability 13.10
cyber-skiving 13.1, 13.6, 13.13, 13A

damages
    against third parties 14.15
    aggravated damages 11.8
    bullying/harassment 11.8
    for libel 13.2
    liquidated damages clause 2.2
    misrepresentations 1.12
    restrictive covenants 14.4
    withdrawal of offer of employment 1.3
data protection 1.11
    blogs 13.14
    breaches 13.14
    Code of Practice 1.5, 1.7, 2.3, 13.14
    emails 13.14
    employment records 13.14
    express consent 1.5
    informed consent 1.5
    medical examinations 1.5
    occupational health records transfer 13G
    personal data 13.14
    policy 13I
    references 1.7, 2.3
    relevant filing system 13.14
    retention of data 1.11, 13.14
    sensitive data 1.11
    social media 13.14
    transfer of undertakings and 13.14, 13G, 13H
deaf people
    sign language 1.5
dealers
    Working Time Regulations 4P
deductions from wages 5.12, 5S
    failure to give notice 5.12
    repayment for recruitment costs 5.12
deep vein thrombosis (DVT) 4T, 4X
defamation
    emails 13.6
    references 2.3
    on social media 13.1, 13.2
degree funding 5V

dental nurses
    time-keeping 6.2, 6C
dental practice
    rules for staff 8.5, 8E
deputising 5.10, 5N
directors
    insider information 5.6
    salary terms 5B
    whole time and attention clause 4.3
disability
    data collection 6Y
    dealing with medical conditions at interview 1.5
    sick pay 6Y
disability discrimination 1.5, 6.24
    by association 8.19
    letter of instruction to consultant 6H
disciplinary procedures 9.1, 9R
    admissions of guilt 9.22, 9P
    alternative less serious procedure 9.3
    appeals 9.21
        effect 9.21
        grievance distinguished 11.1
    bonus, prohibition on discussing 9.30
    clauses excluding 9A
    combined procedure 9.13, 9H
    complaints handling policy 9F
    conduct issues 9.2
    confidentiality 9.5, 9D
        breach of 9.5, 9E
    criminal convictions/charges 9.25
    disclosure duty 9.28
    dishonesty 9.8, 9G
    email misuse 13.7
    evidence 9.6
    exclusion clause 9A
    final written warning 9K
    first year of employment 9.2, 9A
    fraudulent sick pay claims 6.27
    grievance raised during 9.24
    guilt, admission of 9.22, 9P
    inability to attend hearing 9.20
    internet misuse 13.7
    interviews of concern 9.3
    investigations 9.6, 9F
        of dishonesty 9.8, 9G
    lapsed warnings 9.14, 9I
    lateness 6.2
    malingering 6.27, 6AB
    not fair to hold hearing 9.16

performance issues 9.13, 9.26
    combined procedure 9.13, 9H
    improved performance review 9.26, 9Q
    performance improvement procedure 9.26, 9Q
probationary periods and 1.13
refusal to attend hearing 9.20
representation 9.8, 9.12
    dealing with lawyers 9.12
    legal representation 9.9
resignation before hearing 9.23
right to be accompanied 9.8, 9.10, 9.12
salary, prohibition on discussing 9.30
sex in the office 9.29
social networking 13.13
standstill clause 9.24
status quo clause 9.24
stress at time of 6.14, 6M
suspension *see* suspension
tape recording of hearing 9.19, 9N
    secret/covert recording 9.19, 9O
termination checklist 9.27
time-keeping and 6.2
unable to attend hearing 9.20
undertaking to behave 9.17, 9M
warnings *see* warnings
witnesses 9.6, 9F

disclosure
    disciplinary procedures 9.28
    medical information 1.5, 6F
    medical reports 6.5, 6E

discretionary bonus 1.8, 5.3, 5E

discrimination
    advertisements 1.8
    aggravated damages 11.8
    application forms 1.9
    by association 8.19
    disability discrimination 1.5, 6.24, 6H, 8.19
    dress and appearance 8.16
    employment of close relatives and 2.12
    Equality Act 2010 6.24
    ethnic monitoring 11.7, 11E
    gender monitoring 11.7, 11E
    gender pay reporting 11.7
    grievance procedures 11.3
    immigration/asylum issues 2.1, 4.9
    indirect discrimination 6.24
    monitoring recruitment 11.7, 11E
    refusal to give reference 2.3
    religious dress/symbols 8.16

    transgender discrimination 8.16

dishonesty
    investigating 9.8, 9G

dismissal
    constructive dismissal 1.4, 1.8, 2.2
    criminal convictions/charges 9.25
    dismissal letter following lapsed final warning 9J
    email misuse 13.7
    failure to reveal medical condition 1.5
    internet misuse 13.7
    length of sick pay and 6.23
    probationary periods 1.13
    procedure 9R
    redundancy *see* redundancy

disrepute *see* repute clauses

domiciliary visits
    risk assessment 4V

drafting contracts 1.1
    importance of careful drafting 1.6

dress and appearance 8.16
    dress codes 8N, 8O
    long hair 8.16
    religious dress/symbols 8.16, 8N
    shoe and stocking allowance 5O
    transgender people 8.16, 8N
    uniforms 5.10, 8.16

driving
    bad weather 5.7
    chauffeurs 4O
    drink/drugs and 5.7, 8G
    fatigue 5.7
    parking offences 5.7
    requirement to drive 4.7
    Working Time Regulations 4O
    see also car allowance; company car; travel

drugs
    policy on 6.18, 8.10, 8G, 8H

emails
    covert surveillance 13.9
    cyber-liability 13.10
    cyber-skiving 13.1, 13.6, 13A
    data protection 13.14
    defamation 13.6
    disciplinary action 13.7
    disciplinary rules checklist 13.8
    footer 13J
    interception
        data protection 13.14
        duty to inform staff/third parties 13.5
        gateways 13.4

emails (*contd*)
    interception (*contd*)
        human rights issues 13.12
        legislation 13.3
        IT/computer equipment policy 13E
        log on banner 13B
        mail sweeping services 13.8
        misuse 13.6, 13.7
        monitoring 13.4, 13.5, 13.14, 13A, 13C
        policy 13D(1)
employer
    identity of 1.1
employment agency 3.2
employment business 3.2
employment relationship
    'bank' staff 3.9
    banqueting staff 3.11
    career breaks 3.13
    casual workers 3.7
    control 1.1
    determining who is an 'employee' 3.1
    flexible working 3.13
    'gig' economy 3.15
    hospitality staff 3.11
    identity of employer 1.1
    individuals working through intermediaries 3.5
    intention of parties 1.2
    interns 3.12
    job-sharing 3.13
    maternity cover 3.13
    ministers of religion 3.6
    nanny 3.18
    part-time workers 3.13
    seasonal workers 3.8
    self-employment 3.4
    specialist consultants 3.17
    surveillance staff 3.10
    term-time working 3.13
    types of workers/contracts 3.3
    voluntary workers 3.16
    zero hours contracts 3.14
entire agreement clauses 1.4, 1.12
ethnic monitoring 11.7, 11E
evidence
    disciplinary procedures 9.6
    medical evidence 6.4
examination results
    offer subject to 1.5, 2B
expenses 5.11
    clause 5P
    policy 5Q, 5R
    relocation expenses 5.13, 5.14, 5W
    repayment clause 5.13, 5T
    travel expenses 5.11, 5P, 5R
expert witness's declaration 6I
express terms 1.4
    entire agreement clauses 1.4, 1.12
    implied terms and 1.4
expression of interest 1A

fast work
    requirement to work fast and accurately 4.10, 4I
fertility treatment
    time off for 6.25, 6Z
final examination results
    offer subject to 1.5, 2B
first year of employment
    disciplinary procedures and 9.2, 9A
Fit Note 6.1, 6.4
    attending disciplinary hearing and 9.20
    common abbreviations 6.13
    as evidence 6.4
    may be fit for work 6.4
    modified duties 6.3
    not fit for work 6.4
fitness for work
    terms relating to 6S
flexible working 3.13, 4.11
    annualised hours 4.11, 4L
    requests 7H
foreign employees
    visiting home country 6.17, 6R
    see also asylum seekers; immigrants; work permits
formation of contracts 1.2
fraud 8C
    sick pay claims 6.27

gagging clause
    bonus schemes/bonus payments 5.3, 5D
    settlement agreements 11.9, 15.10
gambling at work 8.11, 8I
garden leave 12.4, 12.12
    absence of express clause 1.4
    clauses relating to 12.12, 12D, 12F
    enforcing 14.3, 14.15
    representing the employer 14.20
gender monitoring 11.7, 11E
gender pay reporting 11.7
gifts/hospitality 8B, 8D
    compliance rules 8L
gig economy 3.15
grievance procedures 9.1, 11.1

appeal against disciplinary
    procedure and 11.1
company procedures 11.1
conflict of interest 11.6
decision in grievance letter 11.5
discrimination complaints 11.3
indemnity for legal costs 11.6, 11D
initiation of 11A
legal representation 9.9
mediation 11.3, 11.4
personal liability 11.6, 11D
raising grievance during
    disciplinary procedure 9.24
right to be accompanied 9.8
scope 11.1
stages 11.2, 11.3
see also bullying; harassment
gross misconduct 8.7
    holiday pay 2.6
    indemnity from employee 15.16
    resignation before hearing 9.23
    sex in the office 9.29
guaranteed bonus 5D
guilt
    admission of 9.22, 9P

hair 8.16
harassment 8.19, 8Q, 11.8
    aggravated damages 11.8
    anti-harassment policy 11.8, 11F
    Christmas parties 8.8, 8F
    civil damages 11.8
    confidentiality of procedures 11.4, 11B
    criminal offence 11.8
    definition 8.19, 8Q, 11.4
    infatuation 11.8
    informing complainant of action
        taken 11.8
    mediation 11.4
    racial harassment 8.19, 8Q
    sexual harassment 8.8, 8.18, 8.19, 8Q
    special complaints procedure 11.4
    suspension of alleged perpetrator
        11.4, 11C
    unfair dismissal and 11.8
    vicarious liability 8.8, 11.8
headscarves 8.16
health
    alcohol/drugs policy 6.18
    arrangements for securing health
        and safety of workers 4X
    confidentiality clause 14E

dealing with medical conditions at
    interview 1.5
deep vein thrombosis 4T, 4X
insurance *see* private health cover
long term disability schemes 6.22, 6W
medical examinations 1.5
mobile phone usage 4X
occupational health advice 6.10, 6J
occupational health records
    transfer 13G
outdoor workers 4X
peripatetic workers 4X
questionnaires 1.14, 1H
returning travellers 4T
travelling abroad 4T
see also sickness
hiring company 3.2
holiday pay
    bonus payments and 5.3
    calculation 2.6
    commission payments and 5.5
    forfeiture 2.6
    gross misconduct dismissal 2.6
    inclusions 2.6
holidays 2.6, 6.16, 6P
    bank holidays 2.6
    clauses 6P
    designated times 6.16
    entitlement 2.6
    exceptional circumstances 6.16
    field breaks 2.6
    maternity leave and 7.3, 7A
    offshore workers 2.6
    pay *see* holiday pay
    religious holidays 6.16, 6P
    sickness/sick leave and 2.6, 6.17, 6Q
        foreign employees visiting home
            country 6.17, 6R
home visits 6.9
homosexual people
    dress and appearance 8.16
hospitality staff 3.11
    job description 3I
hospitality/gifts 8B, 8D
    compliance rules 8L
hours of work 4.11
    annualised hours 4.11
    clauses void for uncertainty 1.6
    flexi-time *see* flexible working
    lunch breaks 4.11
    no set working hours 4K
    on-call time 4.11, 4M
    overtime 4.11, 4J
    Saturday working 8S

hours of work (*contd*)
    shifts 4.11
    Sunday working 4.11
    time-keeping 4.11
    travelling time 4.4, 4.11
    unmeasured time 4.11
    unsocial hours 4.11
    weekend working 4.11, 8.21, 8S
    see also Working Time Regulations
human rights
    privacy 13.12

identity of employer 1.1
illegal working 2.1
    policy on prevention 2D
immigrants
    no automatic right to work in UK 2.1
    prevention of illegal working 2D
    see also foreign employees; work permits
implied terms 1.1, 1.4
    business efficacy 1.4
    characteristic terms 1.4
    conduct after contract made 1.4
    constructive dismissal and 1.4
    custom and practice 1.4
    express terms and 1.4
    implied by statute 1.4
    legal tests 1.4
    no terms in contract 1.4
    officious bystander 1.4
    payment of wages 1.4
    provision of work 1.4
    restrictive covenants 14.6
    trust and confidence 1.4
improved performance review (IPR) 9.26, 9Q
incorporation of terms 2.7, 2H
    collective agreements 2.7
indemnity clauses
    contract for services 3D
    for legal costs 11.6, 11D
    settlement agreements 15.16
induction 2.11
infatuation 11.8
informed consent 1.5
injunctions
    non-solicitation/non-dealing clauses 14.15, 14.16
inoculations 4.13
insider dealing
    compliance rules 8.14, 8L
    share dealings 5.6, 5H

insurance
    health *see* private health cover
    life assurance 5.8
        maternity leave and 7.3
    long term disability schemes 6.22, 6W
intellectual property
    inventions 14.23, 14U
    patents 14.23, 14U
    stealing 8.22
interception of communications
    see emails
intermediaries
    individuals working through 3.5
internet
    blogging 13.14
    covert surveillance 13.9
    cyber-liability 13.10
    cyber-skiving 13.1, 13.6, 13.13, 13A
    disciplinary action 13.7
    disciplinary rules checklist 13.8
    IT/computer equipment policy 13E
    log on banner 13B
    misuse 13.6, 13.7, 13.14
    monitoring 13C
    policy 13D(1)
    prosecutions 13.11
    see also emails; social media; social networking
interns 3.12
interviews 1.10
    asking about past criminal convictions 1.5
    dealing with medical conditions 1.5
    inconsistencies in terms described 1.12
    interviews of concern 9.3
    notes 1.10, 1.11
intimidation *see* bullying; harassment
inventions 14.23, 14U
investigations
    disciplinary procedures 9.6, 9F
    of dishonesty 9.8, 9G
invitation to treat 1.5, 1A
irritable desk syndrome 4.12
IT/computer equipment policy 13E
IVF treatment
    time off for 6.25, 6Z

jet lag 4T
job description 4.1
    change to terms 4.1

clauses relating to duties 4B
defining the duties 4.3
driving requirement 4.7
hospitality/banqueting staff 3I
no confirmation of change 4.1
no express term 4.1
requirement to be trained/up to date 4.8, 4F
requirement to travel 4.4, 4C
requirement to work fast and accurately 4.10, 4I
job-sharing 3.13
contract 7D
maternity leave and 7.3

last in, first out (LIFO) 2.7
lateness 6.2
definition 6.2
disciplinary action 6.2
see also time-keeping
lavatory breaks 4U
lectures
to outside bodies 8.9, 8D
legal representation *see* representation
libel *see* defamation
life assurance 5.8
maternity leave and 7.3
light/alternative duties 6.19, 6T
limited liability partnerships
whistleblower protections 3.4
liquidated damages clause 2.2
loans to employees 5.12, 5S
agreement for training expenses 5U
bridging loans 5.14
log on banner 13B
lone workers 4.14
domiciliary visits 4V
guidance 4X
identifying 4.14
outdoor workers 4X
peripatetic workers 4.4, 4X
risk assessment 4V, 4W
working alone in buildings 4W
long term disability schemes 6.22, 6W
lunch breaks 4.11

malaria 4.13, 4T
malingering 6.27, 6AB
materials brought into/taken out of work 14.11, 14K
maternity
career breaks 7.4, 7E
rights 7.1

maternity allowance 7.2
maternity leave
benefits during 7.3
bonus payments 7.3
car allowance 7.3
company car 7.3
cover 3.13, 7C
holiday entitlement 7.3, 7A
job-sharing agreement 7.3, 7D
life insurance 7.3
medical cover 7.3
pay during 7.3
pension contributions 7.3
policy 7B
private health insurance 7.3
redundancy and 10.4, 10.5, 10.6
maternity pay
policy 7B
statutory maternity pay 7.2, 7.3
media
interviews/appearances 8.9, 8D
prohibition on contact with 14H
mediation
grievance procedures 11.3
harassment/bullying 11.4
settlement agreements 15.18
medical conditions
dealing with, at interviews 1.5
disclosure of medical information 6.5, 6F
health questionnaire 1.14, 1H
requirement to report medication 6.26, 6AA
see also medical report; sickness
medical evidence 6.4
medical examinations 6.5
conflicting medical opinions 6.11
consent clause 6.5, 6E
dangers of not seeking medical opinion 6.12
during employment 6.5, 6E
expert witness's declaration 6I
Fit for Work scheme 6.5
home visits 6.9
informing doctor of purpose of 6.6
instructions to doctors 6.7
letter of instruction to consultant 6H
prior to employment 1.5
psychiatric referral 6.5
refusal to co-operate 6.5
report *see* medical report
medical practice
rules for staff 8.5

medical report
    definition 6.5
    disclosure 6.5, 6E
    expert witness's declaration 6I
    incomprehensible to employer 6.8
    informing doctor of purpose of 6.6

medication
    requirement to report 6.26, 6AA

mental illness
    burn out syndrome 6.14
    medical questionnaires 1.14
    referral to psychiatrist 6.5
    see also stress

messengers
    Working Time Regulations 4O

ministers of religion 3.6

misconduct
    duty to report 8.20, 8R, 14.22
    see also gross misconduct

misrepresentations 1.12

misusing company facilities 14.10, 14J

mobile phone usage 4X, 13.8

mobility clause 4.5, 4D

money collections at work 8.13, 8K

monitoring recruitment 11.7, 11E

moonlighting 6.27, 6AC, 8.17

nanny's contract 3.18, 3L, 7.7

negligence
    absence through negligence of third parties 6.21, 6V
    employees travelling abroad for work 4.13
    insurance against 3.1
    repayment clause 5T

nepotism 2.12

night work
    computer operators 4Q
    Working Time Regulations 4Q

nil hour contracts 3.14

niqabs 8.16

no smoking policy 6.20, 6U

Nolan Committee
    Seven Principles of Public Life 8.4

non-compete clauses 14.12, 14L
    area covenants 14.13, 14M
    drafting 14.7
    ensuring employee is not in breach 2.8
    injunctions/damages against third parties 14.15
    rationale for 14.1, 14.12
    scope of clause 14.14

non-poaching clauses 14.17, 14Q
    ensuring employee is not in breach 2.8, 14.17
    senior staff 14.17

non-solicitation/non-dealing clauses 14.16, 14P
    breach 14.15
    ensuring employee is not in breach 2.8
    injunctions/damages against third parties 14.15, 14.16
    passive solicitation 14.16
    period of restraint 14.16
    rationale for 14.16

notice
    absence, during 12.10
    clauses related to 12F
    common law notice 12.8
    contractual notice 12.1
    enforcing notice periods 14.3
    expiration 12.4
    failure to give, deduction from final salary 5.12
    garden leave *see* garden leave
    no notice provision 12.8
    oral 12.2
    payment in lieu of notice 12.6, 12F
        duty to mitigate 12.9, 15.14
        where no clause in place 12.7
    probationary periods, during 12.11, 12C
    reasonable notice 12.8
    refusal to accept 12.3
    short notice
        agreed/not agreed 12.5
        letter accepting 12B
        letter refusing to accept 12A
    statutory notice 12.1
    term 12.1
    when deemed to be given 12.2
    withdrawal 12.3

nursing
    dental nurses 6.2, 6C
    nurse 'bank' 3.9
    requirement to be trained/up to date 4.8

occupational health
    advice 6.10, 6J
    confidentiality clause 14E
    transfer of records 13G

offer of employment 1.3

acceptance with signature of
    employee 1.1, 2.4
applicants with no automatic right
    to work in UK 2.1
conditional *see* conditional
    offers/pre-offers
confirmation of offer to
    secretary/PA 2E
making the offer 2.1
offer letters 2C
    drafting 1.6
    transfer of managing director
        from Paris to London office
        2F
principal statement 2.5, 2J
reneging on 2.2
unconditional offers
    with continuing conditions:
        examinations 2B
    with continuing obligation to
        remain registered 2A
withdrawal 1.3
office parties 8.8, 8F
    see also Christmas parties
offshore workers 4.4
    holidays 2.6
Olympic Games 5.15, 5X
on-call time 4.11, 4M
onerous terms 1.1
oral contracts 1.2
    making promises 1.12
outdoor workers
    guidance 4X
    see also lone workers
overpayments 5.13, 5T
overseas working 4.13
    disciplinary procedures 9.18
    employer negligence 4.13
    guidelines 4T
    vaccinations 4.13
    warnings 9.18
overtime 4.11
    clause relating to 4J

parental leave 7.1
    see also shared parental leave
parking offences
    company cars and 5.7
part-time workers 3.13
parties *see* Christmas parties;
    office parties
partnerships
    limited liability partnerships 3.4
    professional partnership 1D
patents 14.23, 14U

paternity leave 7.5, 7F
pay *see* salaries and wages
payment in lieu of notice 12.6,
    12F
    duty to mitigate 12.9, 15.14
    where no clause in place 12.7
penalty clause 2.2
pension schemes 5.8, 5L
    maternity leave and 7.3
**performance improvement
    procedure (PIP)** 9.26, 9Q
performance issues 9.13, 9.26
    combined procedure 9.13, 9H
    improved performance review 9.26,
        9Q
    performance improvement
        procedure 9.26, 9Q
    stress at time of performance
        review 6.14
peripatetic workers
    guidance 4X
    travelling time 4.4
    see also lone workers
permanent health insurance *see*
    private health cover
personal liability 11.6
personal searches 8.15, 8M
piercings 8.16
**pre-employment health
    questionnaire** 1.14, 1H
pre-offers *see* conditional
    offers/pre-offers
pregnancy *see* maternity
private detectives 6.27, 6AD,
    6AE
private health cover 5.9, 5M
    maternity leave and 7.3
    permanent health insurance 6.22,
        6W
    settlement agreements and 15.13,
        15A
probationary period 1.13, 1G,
    2.9, 2I
    notice during 12.11, 12C
professional practices
    standards of conduct 8.5, 8E
profit-sharing schemes 1.8
promises 1.12
    in advertisements 1.8
    of employment 1.3
protected conversations 15.1,
    15.17
psychiatrist
    referral to 6.5

racial harassment 8.19, 8Q

recruitment
    advertisements 1.8
    monitoring 11.7, 11E
    repayment for recruitment costs 5.12

redundancy 10.1
    alternative employment 10.4
        failure to consider 10.5
        trial period 10.4
    bumping 10.3
    checklist 10.4
    consultation *see* redundancy consultation
    definition 10.1
    full-time to part-time hours 10.3
    letters 10.11, 10E
    maternity leave and 10.4, 10.5, 10.6
    model redundancy policy 10D
    particular kind of work 10.1
    pay *see* redundancy pay
    procedure 10.2, 10.10, 10D
    questions and answers 10.9, 10C
    re-hiring redundant employees 10.4
    selection criteria 10.4, 10.8
        model 10B
    warning 10.7

redundancy consultation 10.4, 10.7
    collective consultation 10.4
    individual consultation 10.4
    questions and answers 10.9, 10C
    script for meeting 10A

redundancy pay
    contractual redundancy pay 10.4
    enhanced payment 10.4
    statutory redundancy pay 10.4

references 1.7, 2.3, 12.13
    authority to obtain 2G
    data protection 1.7, 2.3
    defamation 2.3
    discrimination claims 2.3
    libel 2.3
    new rules 1.7
    no legal duty to give 2.3, 12.13
    offer of employment conditional on 1E
    policy 12E
    refusal to give 2.3, 12.13
    regulatory references 1.7
    subject's right to see 2.3
    true, accurate and fair 2.3, 12.13
    waver 12E

rehabilitation of offenders 1.5

relationships at work
    consensual relationships 8.18, 8P, 9.29
    infatuation 11.8
    sex in the office 9.29
    sexual harassment 8.8, 8.18, 8.19, 8Q
    students and academic staff 8P

religion
    dress and appearance 8.16
    ministers of religion 3.6
    religious discrimination 8.16
    religious dress/symbols 8.16, 8N
    religious holidays 6.16, 6P
    Sunday working and 4.11

relocation 4.5
    bridging loans 5.14
    expenses 5.14, 5W
        repayment clause 5.13
    mobility clause 4.5, 4D
    policy 5W

remote places
    working in 4.14

reneging on offer of employment 2.2
    third party conspiracy 2.2

repayable bonus 5F(ii)

repayment clause 5.13, 5T

reporting for work 6.1, 6A, 6B

representation
    dealing with lawyers 9.12
    disciplinary procedures 9.8, 9.9, 9.12, 9.13
    settlement agreements 15.8

repute clauses 8.6
    medical/dental staff 8.5

restrictive covenants 14.1
    area covenants 14.13, 14M
    breach of contract
        account of profits following 14.18
        aiding and abetting 14.15
        inducing 14.15
    conflict of interest clauses 14I
    damages 14.4
    drafting 14.1, 14.2, 14.7
    ensuring employee is not breaching covenants 2.8
    general issues 14.2
    implied terms 14.6
    inventions 14.23, 14U
    materials brought into/taken out of work 14.11, 14K
    media, contact etc with 14H

misusing company facilities 14.10, 14J
notification of restriction 14O
outside employment 14.19
patents 14.23, 14U
preamble 14.7
reasonable scope 14.1
reporting misconduct 14.22, 14T
representing the employer 14.20
restraint of trade 14.1
return of company property 14.21, 14S
set of 14V
status of post-termination restriction 14.1
trade secrets 14.9
types of clauses 14.5
warranting not in breach of former covenant 14N
whistleblowing 14.22, 14T
whole time and attention clause 4.3, 14.19, 14R
see also confidentiality clauses; non-compete clauses; non-poaching clauses; non-solicitation/non-dealing clauses

return of company property 14.21, 14S

risk assessment
domiciliary visits 4V
lone workers 4V, 4W
stress management 6.14, 6K
working alone in buildings 4W

rules and standards of conduct 8.1
alcohol and drugs 8.10, 8G, 8H
anti-slavery statement 8.2, 8A
betting syndicates 8.11, 8I
bribery 8.3, 8C
bringing employer into disrepute 8.6
business lunches/dinners 8.8, 8F
children on company premises 8.12, 8J
Christmas parties 8.8, 8F
codes of conduct 8.4, 8D
compliance rules 8.14, 8L
conflicts of interest 8.14
consensual relationships at work 8.18, 8P
doctors'/dentists' staff 8.5
dress and appearance 8.16, 8N, 8O
duty to report misconduct 8.20, 8R, 14.22
gambling at work 8.11, 8I

harassment 8.8, 8.19, 8Q
insider dealing 8.14, 8L
lecturing/writing/TV appearances 8.9, 8D
money collections 8.13, 8K
moonlighting 8.17
office parties 8.8, 8F
other disciplinary rules 8.7
personal searches 8.15, 8M
professional practices 8.5, 8E
repute clauses 8.6
requirement to work weekends 8.21, 8S
secret profits 8.14
sexual harassment 8.8
stealing company intellectual property 8.22
students/academic staff relations 8P

salaries and wages
additional allowances 5.10
adoption pay 7.2, 7F
advance payments 5.13
basic salary terms 5.1
bonuses *see* bonus schemes/bonus payments
bridging loans 5.14
cars *see* car allowance; company car
commission payments *see* commission payments
deductions from wages 5.12, 5S
deputising 5.10, 5N
discussion of 9.30
during suspension from work 9.4
expenses *see* expenses
gagging clause 5.3, 5D
gender pay reporting 11.7
holiday pay *see* holiday pay
implied term to pay 1.4
life assurance 5.8
loans *see* loans to employees
maternity leave and 7.3
maternity pay 7.2, 7.3, 7B
non-disclosure clause 9.30
other allowances 5.10
overpayments 5.13, 5T
payment form for casual workers 3G
payment in lieu of notice *see* payment in lieu of notice
pension schemes 5.8, 5L
private health cover 5.9, 5M
prohibition on discussing salary/bonus 9.30

salaries and wages (*contd*)
    redundancy pay *see* redundancy pay
    relocation expenses 5.14
    repayment clause 5.13, 5T
    reviews 5.2, 5C
    secrecy clauses 5.3, 5D
    shares/stocks *see* share options/stock options
    shoe and stocking allowance 5O
    sick pay *see* sick pay
    terms 5A
        senior director 5B
    uniform allowance 5.10
sales staff
    commission payments 5.5
saturday working 8S
searches of employees 8.15, 8M
seasonal workers 3.8
secondary employment
    moonlighting 6.27, 6AC, 8.17
    restrictive covenants 14.19
    whole time and attention clause 4.3, 14.19, 14R
    Working Time Regulations 4R
secrecy clause 5.3, 5D
secret profits 8.14
security guards
    contract of employment 3J
    Working Time Regulations 4O
    see also surveillance staff
self-employment 3.4
    contract for services 3.4
    equity partner of law firm 3.4
    individuals working through intermediaries 3.5
senior staff
    confidentiality clause 14B
    non-poaching clauses 14.17
    Working Time Regulations 4P
services *see* contract for services
settlement agreements
    breach of contract claims 15.4
    categories of proceedings 15.5
    consideration 15.7
    duty to mitigate 15.14, 15B
    gagging clauses 11.9, 15.10
    general rule 15.1
    indemnity from employee 15.16
    independent legal adviser 15.8
    mediation 15.18
    model settlement agreement 15D
    no complaint/no proceedings 15.3
    private medical insurance 15.13, 15A
    protected conversations 15.1, 15.17
    repayment clauses 15.10
    special terms 15.10
    specific terms 15.12
    staged payments 15.14
    statutory rules 15.2
    taxation 15.15
    terms agreed 15.9
    TUPE and 15.11
    ultra vires 15.6
    unambiguous impropriety 15.17
    without prejudice discussions 15.17
    without prejudice letter 15C
sex
    in the office 9.29
sexual harassment 8.8, 8.18, 8.19, 8Q
share options/stock options 5.6, 5G
    bad leavers 12.13
    change of control 5.6, 5I
    insider information 5.6, 5H
    share dealings 5.6, 5H
shared parental leave 7.1, 7.6
    cover 7C
    policy 7G
shift work 4.11
shoe and stocking allowance 5O
shop workers
    Sunday working 4.11
short-term contract *see* casual workers
Sick Note *see* Fit Note
sick pay 6.3
    definition of 'incapable of work' 6.3
    disability 6Y
    dismissal and 6.23
    exceptions to occupational sick pay 6O
    fraudulent claim 6.27
    statutory sick pay 6.3
    termination of employment and 6X
sickness 6.1
    BMA model letter for long-term/acute sickness absence 6G
    conduct during sickness absence 6.15, 6N
    control periods for common illness 6.13

correspondence with employees off sick 6.9
disclosure of medical information/reports 1.5, 6.5, 6E, 6F
duration 6.13
expert witness's declaration 6I
Fit Note *see* Fit Note
fitness for work 6S
foreign employees visiting home country 6.17, 6R
holidays and 2.6, 6.17, 6Q, 6R
home visits 6.9
light/alternative duties 6.19, 6T
long term disability schemes 6.22, 6W
malingering 6.27, 6AB
medical evidence 6.4
medical examinations *see* medical examinations
negligence of third parties 6.21, 6V
notice during absence 12.10
pay *see* sick pay
requirement to report medication 6.26, 6AA
short-term absences 6.28
stress *see* stress
sign language 1.5
skills
computers 4.7
driving requirement 4.7
requirement to be trained/up to date 4.8
requirement to work fast and accurately 4.10, 4I
slavery
anti-slavery statement 8.2, 8A
smoking 6.20, 6U
no smoking policy 6.20, 6U
social media
ACAS advice 13.14
blogging 13.14
cyber-bullying 13.1
defamation on 13.1, 13.2
misuse 13.1, 13.14
policy 13.1, 13D(2)
see also internet
social networking 13.13
cyber-skiving 13.13
disciplinary action 13.13
policy 13.13, 13F
see also internet
Solicitors Regulation Authority (SRA)
Training Regulations 2014 1.5

speed
requirement to work fast and accurately 4.10, 4I
spent convictions 1.5
sporting events 5.15, 5X
standards of conduct *see* rules and standards of conduct
standstill/status quo clause 9.24, 11.1
start date 4.2
Statement of Fitness for Work *see* Fit Note
statement of terms of employment *see* written particulars
status quo clause 9.24, 11.1
statutory adoption pay 7.2
statutory implied terms 1.4
statutory maternity pay 7.2, 7.3
statutory redundancy pay 10.4
statutory sick pay 6.3
stealing company intellectual property 8.22
stocks *see* share options/stock options
stress 6.14
at time of disciplinary proceedings/performance review 6.14, 6M
attending disciplinary hearing and 9.20
burn out syndrome 6.14
chronic embitterment 6.14
letter to GP 6L
medical questionnaires 1.14
stress management risk assessment 6.14, 6K
students
relations with academic staff 8P
student internships 3.12
sub-contractors
contract for services 3.4, 3B, 3D
indemnity clause 3D
terms and conditions 3.4, 3B
sun exposure 4T
Sunday working 4.11, 8.21
surveillance staff
contract of employment 3.10, 3H, 3J
security guards 3J, 4O
Working Time Regulations 4O
see also covert surveillance
suspension
alleged harassment/bullying 11.4, 11C
disciplinary procedures 9.4, 9B

suspension (*contd*)
    letter confirming terms of 11C
    letter reminding suspended employee of obligations 9C
    pay during 9.4

tape recordings
    covert recordings 5.13, 9.19, 9O
    disciplinary hearings 9.19, 9N, 9O

tattoos 8.16

taxation
    bonus payments 5.3
    classes of employees 3.1
    settlement agreements 15.15

telephone
    covert surveillance 13.9
    mobile phone usage 4X, 13.8
    monitoring calls 13.5, 13.12

television
  appearances/interviews 8.9, 8D

temporary employment
    agency workers 3.2
    confidentiality agreement 14D
    deputising 5.10, 5N
    maternity cover 3.13, 7C

term-time working 3.13
    model agreement 3A

termination of employment
    bonus payments and 5.3
    checklist 9.27
    commission payments and 5.5
    resignation before gross misconduct hearing 9.23
    sick pay and 6X
    see also notice; redundancy

terms
    characteristic terms 1.4
    duty to advise employees
      limited duty 1.1
      no duty to advise of consequences of terms 1.1
      specific duty 1.1
    express terms *see* express terms
    fitness for work 6S
    implied terms *see* implied terms
    inconsistencies in terms described at interviews 1.12
    incorporation 2.7, 2H
    informing of onerous terms 1.1
    statement of terms of employment 1.2, 2.5, 2J
    unfair terms 1.1

theft
    company intellectual property 8.22

third parties
    absence through negligence of 6.21, 6V
    conspiracy 2.2
    injunctions/damages against 14.15
    liability for harassment by 11.8

tick bites 4T

time off work
    career breaks 7.4, 7E
    for fertility treatment 6.25, 6Z
    see also absence; garden leave; holidays; maternity leave; paternity leave; shared parental leave

time-keeping 6.2
    dental nurses 6.2, 6C
    lateness 6.2
    time-recording system 4.11

toilet breaks 4U

trade secrets 14.1, 14.9

traders
    Working Time Regulations 4P

training
    degree funding 5V
    requirement to be trained/up to date 4.8, 4F

training expenses
    loan agreement for 5U
    repayment of 5.13

transfer of undertakings
    data protection and 13.14, 13H
    settlement agreements and 15.11

transgender people
    dress and appearance 8.16, 8N

travel
    abroad 4.13
      employer negligence 4.13
      guidelines 4T
      vaccinations 4.13
      see also overseas working
    Acts of God 4.6, 4E, 6.16, 6B
    adverse weather 4.6, 4E, 5.7, 6.16, 6B
    driving requirement 4.7
    expenses 5.11, 5P, 5R
    mobility clause 4.5, 4D
    peripatetic workers 4.4
    requirement to travel 4.4, 4C
    returning traveller 4T
    transport strikes 4.6, 4E, 6.16, 6B
    travelling time 4.4, 4.11
    unforeseen circumstances 4.6, 4E, 6.16, 6B
    volcanic eruptions 4.6, 4E, 6.16, 6B
    working time and 4.4, 4.11

see also driving
trial period *see* probationary
  period
trust
  implied term of trust and
    confidence 1.4
  obligation of trust and confidence
    4.1
TV appearances/interviews 8.9,
  8D
ultra vires
  settlement agreements 15.6

unambiguous impropriety
  15.17
uncertainty
  clauses void for 1.6, 12.9, 14.7
undertaking to behave 9.17, 9M
unfair contract terms 1.1
  bonuses 5.3
unforeseen circumstances
  travel and 4.6, 4E, 6.16, 6B
uniforms 8.16
  allowance for 5.10
unmeasured time 4.11
unsocial hours 4.11

vaccinations 4.13
variation clause 4A
variation of contract *see* changes
  to contracts
volcanic eruptions 4.6, 4E, 6.16,
  6B
voluntary workers 3.16
  interns 3.12

wages *see* salaries and wages
warnings 9.14
  appeal 9.24
  consolidated warning letters 9L
  dismissal letter following lapsed
    final warning 9J
  extending lifetime of warning 9.15
  final written warning 9.14, 9.24, 9K
  formal warning 9.11
  informal warning 9.11
  lapsed warnings 9.14, 9I
  letters relating to absence 6AG
  staff are abroad 9.18
  time limits 9.14, 9.15
weather
  driving in bad weather 5.7
  travel and 4.6, 4E, 5.7, 6B
  unforeseen circumstances 4.6, 4E,
    6B

weekends
  requirement to work 8.21, 8S
  Saturday working 8S
  Sunday working 4.11
whistleblowing 11.9
  duty to report misconduct 14.22,
    14T
  equity partner of law firm 3.4
  policies 9.7, 9F, 11G
  protected disclosures 11.9
  restrictive covenant 14.22, 14T
whole time and attention
  clause 4.3, 14.19, 14R
withdrawal of notice 12.3
withdrawal of offer of
  employment 1.3
without prejudice discussions
  15.17
without prejudice letter 15C
witnesses
  disciplinary procedures 9.6, 9F
  expert witness's declaration 6I
work experience 3.12
work permits 4.9
  work permit contract term 4H
  work permit letter 4G
work shadowing 3.12
Working Time Regulations
  4.11
  48 hour week 4.11
    disapplication letter 4N
    opt out agreement 2.4
  business travel 4.11
  chauffeurs 4O
  computer operators working at
    night 4Q
  dealers 4P
  holidays 2.6
  limited liability partnerships 3.4
  messengers 4O
  rest period 2.6
  secondary employment 4R
  security guards 4O
  senior staff 4P
  surveillance staff 4O
  time-keeping 4.11
  traders 4P
  travelling time 4.4, 4.11
  unmeasured time 4.11
  see also hours of work
world sporting events 5.15, 5X
writing
  of articles etc 8.9, 8D
written particulars 1.2, 2.1
  failure to provide 2.5

written particulars (*contd*)
    principal statement 2.5, 2J
    start date 4.2
    Sunday working 4.11
wrongdoing
    duty to report 8.20, 8R, 14.22

young people
    on company premises 8.12, 8J

zero hours contracts 3.14